MASCULINITIES

Interdisciplinary Readings

MARK HUSSEY

Pace University

Prentice
Hall

Upper Saddle River, New Jersey 07458

Library of Congress Cataloging-in-Publication Data

Masculinities: interdisciplinary readings/[compiled by] Mark Hussey.
p. cm.
Includes bibliographical references.
ISBN 0-13-097454-4 (alk. paper)
1. Masculinity. 2. Men—Psychology. 3. Men—Socialization. 4. Men—Attitudes. I.
Hussey, Mark.

HQ1090 .M3794 2002
305.31—dc21

2002022903

AVP, Publisher: Nancy Roberts
Editorial/Production Supervision and Interior Design: Rob DeGeorge
Copyeditor: Sylvia Moore
Prepress and Manufacturing Buyer: Mary Ann Gloriande
Senior Marketing Manager: Amy Speckman
Marketing Assistant: Anne Marie Fritzky
Editorial Assistant: Lee Peterson
Cover Photo: Jose Ortega/Stock Illustration Source
Cover Art Director: Jayne Conte
Cover Design: Bruce Kenselaar

This book was set in 10/12 Baskerville by TSI Graphics, Inc.,
and was printed and bound by Hamilton Printing Company.
The cover was printed by Phoenix Color Corp.

 © 2003 by Pearson Education, Inc.
Upper Saddle River, New Jersey 07458

Printed in the United States of America

10 9 8 7 6 5 4 3 2 1

ISBN 0-13-097454-4

Pearson Education LTD., London
Pearson Education Australia PTY, Limited, Sydney
Pearson Education Singapore, Pte. Ltd
Pearson Education North Asia Ltd, Hong Kong
Pearson Education Canada, Ltd., Toronto
Pearson Educación de Mexico, S.A. de C.V.
Pearson Education—Japan, Tokyo
Pearson Education Malaysia, Pte. Ltd
Pearson Education, Upper Saddle River, New Jersey

for Xavier

Contents

At War: The Shadow of a Soldier   329

Men Changing: Visions of a Future   377

Preface

At the turn of the twentieth century, boys were often in the news. Two decades of attention to girls and women by researchers (e.g., Gilligan 1982, Pipher 1995) had catalyzed a growing recognition that similar research could benefit boys. Newspaper headlines spoke of "How Boys Lost Out to Girl Power" (Lewin 1998) and noted that "After Girls Get the Attention, Focus Shifts to Boys' Woes" (Goldberg 1998). Major U.S. publishers began to promote books on boys (Kindlon 1999, Pollack 1998, Garbarino 1999). Reviewing the academic area of gender studies devoted to men, Kenneth Clatterbaugh noted in 2000 that "In the 1980s and 1990s, a flood of writings about men and masculinity by both men and women were published. Such writings now appear in every academic field" (883). "Issues have been discussed," Clatterbaugh continued, "men and masculinity have become subjects for ongoing study, and the ideas that have been tried and presented in a variety of media are still there for individual men to draw on and pursue in their own individual accommodations of how to be a man" (892).

Stereotypical thinking about gender persists, however, in the United States and elsewhere, much of it rooted in popular notions of biology. Testosterone is often blamed for all kinds of antisocial behavior in boys, yet correlations between testosterone levels and aggression are at best dubious. A 1997 review of research concluded that there is "no evidence of an association between testosterone and aggressive behavior" (Tremblay 1997), but the ideal of tough manhood prevails and "boys will be boys" is a mantra in playgrounds and classrooms across the country. Confusingly, alongside the ideal of tough, stoic males another has taken shape, of the nurturing, sensitive "new" man. The mother of an 18-month-old male is reported as saying "It's politically incorrect to be a boy" (Rosenberg 1998). Myriam Miedzian recounts a conversation with a "sophisticated young mother of four," who told her "that while she and her friends didn't like their sons to play with guns, they still worried that if the boys didn't, if they preferred arts and crafts and dolls, perhaps they were developing homosexual tendencies" (Miedzian 108). Homophobia is one shaper of masculinities; another is racism; the cultures of everyday institutions also play their part—workplaces, classrooms, playing fields, families, religions, and organizations.

If anything is clear, it is that masculinity is up for grabs. In the aftermath of the September 11, 2001, attacks on the United States, for example, two articles in *The New York Times* offered within weeks of each other apparently contradictory reports on the state of American manhood. On the one hand, many of those who worked and died at the World Trade Center were described as belonging to "a generation of men who defy cultural stereotypes" by being deeply involved in the lives of their children (Gross). On the other hand, the iconic figure of the rescue worker was seen as heralding "the return of manly men": "After a few iffy decades in which manliness was not the most highly prized cultural attribute, men—stoic, muscle-bound, and exuding competence from every pore—are back" (Brown). Neither of these images is satisfying, and neither corresponds to the complexities of how gender is lived in the United States at the beginning of the twenty-first century.

To describe gender as socially constructed has become commonplace in the academy during the last twenty-five years. For students entering university, however, the distinction between sex and gender can still be new and startling. Although the contributions of biology to the formations of gender should not be ignored, the enormous range of what constitutes "masculine" and "feminine" across various cultures and through various histories is evidence that gender is socially constructed. In many ways, gender is an *institution* within which we are all raised and develop.

When I first proposed a course called "Men and Masculinities," a note came from the dean's office querying this odd title with its unfamiliar plural. Although the idea that masculinity is socially constructed in a wide variety of manifestations has become ordinary in several academic disciplines, "manhood" remains a complicated and confusing prospect for many young men growing up in twenty-first-century America. By talking about the "gendering" that goes on in all our lives we can, as Judith Lorber puts it, "make gender visible" (Lorber 1994), and making gender visible is a first step toward coming to critical consciousness about the masculinities that influence our lives and those of the people around us.

Ideas about gender often conform to a "natural attitude"—a kind of baseline thinking which is extremely difficult, if not impossible, to challenge because it seems so obvious to the majority of people that that's just "the way things are." Thus, men who are involved in the lives of their children are said to be "in touch with their feminine side" (Gross). Such a natural attitude to gender assumes "that there are two and only two genders; gender is invariant; genitals are the essential signs of gender; the male/female dichotomy is natural; being masculine or feminine is natural and not a matter of choice; all individuals can (and must) be classified as masculine or feminine—any deviation from such a classification [is] either a joke or a pathology" (Hawkesworth 649). This common way of thinking rests upon the notion that the subordinate status of women is universal, God-given, and immutable. Differences between men and women in general (sexual asymmetry) are offered as evidence of the rightness of this "natural" attitude: We see it a lot, so it must just be that way. This attitude is reinforced by culture, myth, law, education, and (most powerfully) by religions.

Since the inception of women's studies programs in colleges and universities in the 1960s, the study of gender has drawn on the challenges and questions raised by the second wave of the women's movement and has influenced many disciplines. Quite recently, with the increased acceptance of the idea that gender is socially constructed, women's studies programs have broadened their area of interest to take in the study of both sexes. Political scientist Mary Hawkesworth writes that "gender has become the central analytic concept in women's studies and indeed has been the focal point for the development of new interdisciplinary programs (gender studies) in colleges and universities across the United States" (650).

As women's lives in industrialized countries have changed dramatically and increasingly rapidly in every sphere during the last forty years, so inevitably have men's lives also changed. Such change has often been unwelcome because it has had the effect of making gender visible and thus threatening a status quo that works to the advantage of a significant number of men. Many men have kept their heads down during this time, hoping it would all just go away if they ignored it long enough. But it hasn't: the workplace, the family, education, healthcare, religion, politics—all have been transformed by feminism, however that phenomenon is characterized. The social world in which men live in the United States is one in which feminism exerts profound influence whether or not they agree with its tenets, and despite the fact that many of the conditions and social practices addressed by the women's movement remain unchanged. Just as race is often seen by whites as something "belonging" only to people of color, so gender has often been seen by men as an attribute solely of women. Like two sides of a sheet of paper, though, men and women share a sexual political context.

Lorber points out how pervasive gender is: "Most people find it hard to believe that gender is constantly created and re-created out of human interaction, out of social life, and is the texture and order of that social life" (13). If we reflect for a moment, it quickly becomes clear that gender is not constant: Although certain groups in a society may be strict about maintaining rigid gender boundaries (for example, sports organizations), blurring occurs in other groups within the same society. Traditional beliefs about gender have often focused on reproduction as women's chief goal in life and consign childless women to deviancy. Such beliefs also point to the superior physical strength of men (as a group) as evidence of their "natural" superiority; deviation from this norm is dismissed as just that—deviancy. As Gerda Lerner writes in *The Creation of Patriarchy,* this "common sense" kind of argument has great explanatory force, probably due to its "'scientific' trappings, based on *selected* ethnographic evidence and on the fact that it seems to account for male dominance in such a way as to relieve contemporary men of all responsibility for it" (17).

This book brings together short stories and articles from a number of disciplinary perspectives, with the aim of encouraging students and their teachers to focus attention on the meanings of masculinity in the contemporary United States. It does not aspire to "coverage" of any particular topic, but offers paradigms that might be employed in other areas for further exploration. The selections are for the most part limited to the contemporary situation in the United States, a focus for which an account of the historical dimension of the social institution of gender has had to be sacrificed. Another limitation of the book's scope is its treatment of race: Constraints of space and of economics have led me to choose readings on black masculinities alone because the specific history of the United States has given African-American men so prominent a place in its cultural narrative of gender.

Men are still very reluctant to discuss themselves *as men*. The "Men and Masculinities" course I teach, for example, has always enrolled far more women than men. Although the composition of a classroom influences the kinds of discussions that take place there, the study of men and masculinity should not be limited to male students. In our gendered world, it is important for all of us to consider how gender has inflected our lives and how it continues to define and confine us whether we be women or men.

The primary purpose of this book is to *begin* discussion in the classroom. Although the readings are organized into various sections, there are other possible combinations that might work better in individual settings. The readings also speak to one another: What is learned about masculinity on the sports field, for example, may have consequences later in the workplace; the gendering that goes on in elementary school affects future friendships; the intersections of gender and race in popular culture affect the environment for black children in school, and so on. The writers represented here also raise many questions that can be followed up in discussion and further research, as well as provide new contexts for thinking about what is studied in other courses and about what our culture offers for our everyday consumption.

ACKNOWLEDGMENTS

Many thanks to Sheila Hu at the Mortola Library, Pace University, to my colleagues Karla Jay and Ruth Johnston for their interest in and support of my work, and to the Women's & Gender Studies community at Pace. Thanks to Kelly Anderson for her corrective vision, and to all the students who have made "Men and Masculinities" such a rewarding course to teach.

I would also like to thank the following reviewers for their helpful comments: Kathryn S. Mueller, Baylor University; and Jane E. Prather, California State University, Northridge.

REFERENCES

BROWN, P.L. (2001). Heavy lifting required: The return of manly men. *The New York Times.* October 28: *Week in Review* (Sec. 5).

CLATTERBAUGH, K. (2000). Review essay. Literature of U.S. men's movements. *Signs 25*(3): 883–894.

GARBARINO, J. (1999). *Lost boys: Why our sons turn violent and how we can save them.* New York: Free Press.

GILLIGAN, CAROL. (1982). *In a different voice: Psychological theories and women's development.* Cambridge, MA: Harvard University Press.

GOLDBERG, C. (1998). After girls get the attention, focus shifts to boys' woes. *The New York Times.* April 23: A1 + A14.

GROSS, J. (2001). These fallen fathers were at-home heroes. *The New York Times.* October 1: F1 + F4.

HAWKESWORTH, M. (1997). Confounding gender. *Signs 22*(3): 649–685.

KINDLON, D., and THOMPSON, M. (1999). *Raising cain: Protecting the emotional life of boys.* New York: Ballantine.

LERNER, G. (1986). *The creation of patriarchy.* New York: Oxford University Press.

LEWIN, T. (1998). How girls lost out to boy power. *The New York Times.* December 13: 3.

LORBER, J. (1994). *Paradoxes of gender.* New Haven: Yale University Press.

MIEDZIAN, M. (1991). *Boys will be boys: Breaking the link between masculinity and violence.* New York: Doubleday.

PIPHER, M. (1995). *Reviving Ophelia: Saving the selves of adolescent girls.* New York: Ballantine.

POLLACK, W. (1998). *Real boys: Rescuing our sons from the myths of boyhood.* New York: Random House.

ROSENFELD, M. (1998). Little boys blue: Reexamining the plight of young males. *Washington Post.* March 26: A1.

TREMBLAY, R.E., et al. (1997). Male aggression, social dominance and testosterone levels at puberty: A developmental perspective. In A. Raine et al., eds., *Biosocial bases of violence.* New York: Plenum.

The Social Construction of Gender: What Makes a Man?

Sigmund Freud once said that when someone is coming toward us down the street, the first distinction we make is "male or female." We are "accustomed to make the distinction with unhesitating certainty" (Freud 146), yet masculinity and femininity, he went on, describe behaviors which are constituted by "an unknown characteristic which anatomy cannot lay hold of" (147). Despite Freud's confidence, even distinguishing the difference between male and female has proven to be not as simple as it might seem: Both the International Athletic Federation and the International Olympic Committee have discovered in the last decade that devising a foolproof scientific test to determine who is a man and who is a woman is extremely difficult (Kolata 1992).

Brown University biologist Anne Fausto-Sterling suggested in 1993 that "the two-sex system embedded in our society is not adequate to encompass the full spectrum of human sexuality" that is represented by the variety of genital formations found at birth, and she has recommended replacing it with a "five-sex system" (Fausto-Sterling 2000). Responding to her proposal, Suzanne Kessler has pointed out that "What has primacy in everyday life is the gender that is performed, regardless of the flesh's configuration under the clothes" (Fausto-Sterling 2000).

If gender is a "performance," what are the consequences for manliness, manhood, and masculinity? To begin thinking about gender as a social construction, it is helpful to distinguish among a number of terms that have become familiar in feminist scholarship. Mary Hawkesworth notes that "virtually all scholars working in the field" use some of the following distinctions (though not all in the same way):

Sex typically refers to biological difference; *sexuality* is understood to "encompass sexual practices and erotic behavior"; *sexual identity* refers to "designations such as heterosexual, homosexual/gay/lesbian/queer, bisexual, or asexual"; *gender identity* can be explained "as a psychological sense of oneself as a man or a woman"; *gender role* refers to "a set of prescriptive, culture-specific expectations about what is appropriate for men and women"; and *gender-role identity* Hawkesworth describes as "a concept devised to capture the extent to which a person approves of and participates in feelings and behaviors deemed to be appropriate to his or her culturally constituted gender" (656).

In this section, Judith Lorber gives an overview of the study of gender as a social practice, explains the varieties of schools of feminist thought, and offers categories that can be useful in reading many of the selections in this book. Kessler's article makes it clear that when it comes to determining "sex," culture can often override biology. That culture is wittily detailed in an extract from Susan Bordo's *The Male Body.* Lois Gould's famous story about a child called "X" can help us recognize in ourselves how powerful is the desire to *fix* gender as early as possible. With ideas about gender unsettled, we may become more open to the possibilities of change.

Paradoxes of Gender

Judith Lorber

INTRODUCTION

My concept of gender differs from previous conceptualizations in that I do not locate it in the individual or in interpersonal relations, although the construction and maintenance of gender are manifest in personal identities and in social interaction. Rather, I see gender as an institution that establishes patterns of expectations for individuals, orders the social processes of everyday life, is built into the major social organizations of society, such as the economy, ideology, the family, and politics, and is also an entity in and of itself.

When studies of gender started, the field was called "sex roles." The perspective of sex roles is psychological and focused on individual attitudes and attributes. Sex-role theorists argue that what children learn from their families, teachers, picture books, and school books produces masculine and feminine attitudes, motivations, and personalities that will fit children into their adult roles. Although change can take place later in life, many sex-role characteristics, such as women's parenting abilities, seem to be fixed for life. Since the liberal feminists who were promulgating the new field of sex roles believed in progress and change, the field had a built-in contradiction—where was change to take place? Reeducation and resocialization of adults? Or new, nonsexist patterns of socialization of children, which would require waiting a generation for

change to take place? If parents and teachers enacted traditional sex roles, who was to institute the new, nonsexist patterns for the new generation? And what would be the content of future, androgynous roles? The concept of roles as the connection between individuals and society is useful for exploring how the consensus and contradictions of social structure play out in interpersonal relations (Komarovsky 1992), but the roles women and men play don't explain gender as a social institution any more than the jobs people have explain the economy as a social institution.

Radical feminists like Catharine MacKinnon (1982) threw down a powerful challenge to liberal feminists, arguing that sex and gender are a worldwide system of domination of women by men through control of women's sexuality and procreative capacity. In the radical feminist view, the sex-gender system of women's oppression is deliberate, not accidental, and pervades other social institutions—the family especially, and also the mass media and religion, which produce the justification for women's subordination. Radical feminists are particularly critical of such modern social-control agencies as law and the criminal-justice system because they allow men to rape, batter, prostitute, and sexually harass women with few legal restrictions.

Marxist feminists like Heidi Hartmann (1976) and Michèle Barrett ([1980] 1988) also locate women's oppression in the structure of society. In contrast to the radical feminists' focus on sexuality, Marxist feminists focus on the gendered division of labor. They argue for the equal

Excerpted from Judith Lorber, *Paradoxes of Gender.* New Haven: Yale University Press, 1994.

importance of gender and class oppression and analyze the ways in which two parallel institutions—the economy (capitalism) and the family (patriarchy)—structure women's lives. Marxist feminists argue that work in the marketplace and work in the home are inextricably intertwined structures and that both exploit women. Recent theories claim that patriarchy, the ideological dominance of women by men, is located both in the family and in the workplace (Walby 1986, 1990).

Psychoanalytic feminists, such as Nancy Chodorow (1978), Luce Irigaray [1974] 1985), Juliet Mitchell (1975), and Gayle Rubin (1975), building on the ideas of Freud, Lacan, and Lévi-Strauss, have argued that gender is an idea of difference that emerges from family relationships, particularly mothering. In the feminist psychoanalytic perspective, gender is embedded in the unconscious and is manifest in sexuality, fantasies, language, and the incest taboo. The focus is on sexuality as a powerful cultural and ideological force that oppresses women because it is inscribed in bodies and also in the unconscious.

For radical, Marxist, and psychoanalytic feminists, *patriarchy* is a central concept, but each perspective conceptualizes it somewhat differently. For radical feminists, patriarchy is *the* central concept—the structure and process of men's misogynist domination of women through violent control of their sexuality and childbearing. For Marxist feminists, women's patriarchal domination by their husbands in the home goes hand in hand with their exploitation as workers in the capitalistic marketplace (Hartmann 1981b; Young et al. 1981). For psychoanalytic feminists, patriarchy is the symbolic rule of the father through gendered sexuality and the unconscious.

"Patriarchy" has been used so commonly by feminists of every perspective to stand for "what oppresses women" that it sometimes seems to be the theoretical equivalent of phlogiston—what causes fire to burn—before the discovery of oxygen. More than all men's individual actions, patriarchy is simultaneously the process, structure, and ideology of women's subordination. While different aspects of women's subordination are teased out and dissected, the connections among the parts are left to "patriarchy." More recently, some Marxist feminists have been developing a theory of women's subordination that connects psychological development, sexual dominance, production, procreation, child care, and ideology (Hartsock 1983; Walby 1990). They want to look at patriarchy in all aspects of society at once to see how each form of men's exploitation of women supports and reinforces the others.[1]

I have chosen not to use the term "patriarchy" as an explanatory concept because of its overuse and slippery conceptualization, but I have quoted many passages that do discuss patriarchy as "what men do that subordinates or exploits women." My focus is *gender* because this term badly needs precise definition and clearer conceptualization or it will go the way of patriarchy. Although I see patriarchy, or men's subordination and exploitation of women, as the salient feature of gender as a social institution in many societies, including late-twentieth-century postindustrial countries, gender is not synonymous with patriarchy or men's domination of women. *Gender* is a more general term encompassing all social relations that separate people into differentiated gendered statuses. I argue that inequality of the statuses of women and men was a historical development and that, as feminist research from a racial ethnic perspective has shown, there are cross-cutting racial and class statuses within each gender status that belie the universal pattern of men's domination and women's subordination implied by the concept of patriarchy.

Feminists writing from a racial ethnic perspective, such as bell hooks (1984) and Patricia Hill Collins (1989), have argued that it is incorrect to build research and feminist theory on a binary opposition of women and men when race and social class produce many categories of women and men that form hierarchical stratification systems in many societies. In that stratification system, race, class, and gender intersect to produce domination by upper-class white men *and* women and subordination of lower-class women *and* men of color.[2]

Such theorists in men's studies as R.W. Connell (1987), using a concept of hegemonic masculinity—economically successful, racially superior, and visibly heterosexual—have similarly developed the idea of a multiplicity of masculinities. In particular, they have shown how the practices of power are layered and interwoven in a society and have argued that gender dominance and its ideological justification include men's subordination and denigration of other men as well as men's exploitation of women (Carrigan, Connell, and Lee 1987).[3]

Cultural feminists—Judith Butler (1990), Donna Haraway (1989, 1991), Jane Flax (1990), and Marjorie Garber (1992), for example—also challenge the concept of gender categories as dual and oppositional. Their theories are rooted in the French feminist critique of psychoanalytic concepts of gendered sexuality and language.[4] But where the French feminists' political stance has been to valorize women's sexuality and its evocation in literature, cultural feminists claim that sexuality and gender are shifting, fluid categories. By teasing out the intertwined strands of the socially constructed body, self, desire, and symbolic representation, cultural feminists critique a feminist politics based solely on women as a subordinated status, presenting instead a more subversive view that undermines the solidity of a social order built on concepts of two sexes and two genders.[5]

The concept of gender as constructed was explored by American feminists in the 1970s, particularly Suzanne Kessler and Wendy McKenna ([1978] 1985). Building on Harold Garfinkel's (1967, 116–85) ethnomethodological analysis of how "Agnes," a transsexual, constructed a conventional womanhood, Kessler and McKenna argued that gender *and* sex are socially constructed. Their important point, that there is neither an essential sex dichotomy nor an essential gender dichotomy, was absorbed into liberal feminism. But liberal feminism emphasized only the social construction of femininity and masculinity and their translation into family and work roles. Cynthia Fuchs Epstein's *Deceptive Distinctions* (1988) is an extensive critique of the scientific premises of gender dichotomies, but it does not probe deeply enough into the way the dichotomies of sex, sexuality, and gender are built into the organization and politics of all social institutions, the interactions of everyday life, and the consciousness of self we call identity. The work on psychoanalysis and politics that the French feminists were doing in the 1970s was not translated into English until the 1980s. It is only now, in the 1990s, that a full-fledged analysis of gender as wholly constructed, symbolically loaded, and ideologically enforced is taking place in American feminism.

In this book, I have used theoretical ideas of all of these strands of feminism and drawn on research on the social aspects of gender from anthropology, history, sociology, social psychology, sociolinguistics, men's studies, and culture studies. I have tried to fit these pieces together into a coherent picture of gender as a process of social construction, a system of social stratification, and an institution that structures every aspect of our lives because of its embeddedness in the family, the workplace, and the state, as well as in sexuality, language, and culture. The intent of this book, however, is not to valorize that institution-alization but to call its naturalness and in-evitability into question. My politics is that of feminist deconstructionism, and my aim in this book is to challenge the validity, permanence, and necessity of gender. For that reason, I have not used the feminist "we," but refer to women in the third person. I agree with Judith Butler that an in-clusive, monolithic concept of "woman" denies the multiplicity, complexity, and historical and geographical location of genders (1990, 142).

PARADOXES OF GENDER

This book is called *Paradoxes of Gender* be-cause, when examined closely, much of what we take for granted about gender and its causes and effects either does not hold up or can be explained differently. For exam-ple, despite the evidence that women and men are more similar than different, the in-stitution of gender continues to create and maintain socially significant differences be-tween women and men (Hess 1990). What seems to be relevant—gender differences—is a means, not an end. The point of these differences is to justify the exploitation of an identifiable group—women. If one set of differences is successfully challenged, an-other set will take its place (Reskin 1988). As Joan Wallach Scott says, "Gender is a consti-tutive element of social relationships based on perceived differences between the sexes, and gender is a primary way of signifying re-lationships of power" (1988a, 42).

A second major paradox is the origin of gender and, especially, gender inequality. Because gender is ubiquitous in human soci-ety, the belief has been that it must be ge-netic or physiological and that gender inequality is ultimately based on procreative differences. But a close examination of fe-males' and males' relationship to procre-

ation reveals that it is females who are at an advantage, not males:

> Women's ability to bear babies in contrast to men's inability to do so, is a potential source of power unmatched in modern times by any physical advantages men have. . . . Usually, in civilized societies, varying degrees of compensations have been cre-ated for the deprived. . . . In the case of fer-tility, however, instead of repairing the disabled—that is, men—they have received compensation in the form of social cus-toms that give them power over the able—that is, over women's bodies—and fertility. (Tangri 1976, 896)

This paradox is resolved if gender is concep-tualized as a social institution often rooted in conflict over scarce resources and in so-cial relationships of power. Gender inequal-ity structures the unequal conditions of procreation, not the other way around (Rich 1977). Where women and men are different but not unequal, women's birth-giving is not a source of subordination. In-deed, for much of human history, people worshiped goddesses of fertility; statues of these goddesses can be found in every ar-chaeological museum.

Gender is a human invention, like lan-guage, kinship, religion, and technology; like them, gender organizes human social life in culturally patterned ways. Gender or-ganizes social relations in everyday life as well as in the major social structures, such as social class and the hierarchies of bureau-cratic organizations (Acker 1988, 1990). The gendered microstructure and the gendered macrostructure reproduce and reinforce each other. The social reproduction of gen-der in individuals reproduces the gendered societal structure; as individuals act out gen-der norms and expectations in face-to-face interaction, they are constructing gendered systems of dominance and power.[6] Gender has changed in the past and will change in the future, but without deliberate restructuring it will not necessarily change in the direction of greater equality between women and men.

.   .   .

WHERE ARE WE GOING?

The enormous weight of history and current institutionalized practices makes it seem as if there is no way out—no way to make significant and lasting changes in the social institution of gender. Yet changes are made every day (another paradox of gender). There is constant tension between individual and group resistance and social control, between the exceptions and the rules. Indeed, the rules of existing institutions are constantly being revised and repaired (Hilbert 1987). Human beings are both orderly and rebellious; they like knowing what to expect from others, even if they protest and challenge.

Feminists have resisted and rebelled as scholars, researchers, and activists (Chafetz and Dworkin 1986; Rowbotham 1989). The "known world" looks very different through women's eyes. As activists, feminists have promulgated reforms of existing institutional laws, rules, and norms. As researchers, feminists have made evident the built-in oppression of women in patterns of behavior that are taken for granted, particularly concerning sexuality and violence. As theorists, feminists have turned inside out the categories of production and social reproduction by demonstrating that housework and child care are unpaid *work* for the family and for society, and that paid work is so deeply gendered that there seem to be built-in sexual taboos about how women can earn money. Lesbian feminists and gay men particularly, through their open rebellions, have changed ideas of normalcy and deviance in sexual mores, living arrangements, and parenting.

But I do not think it is inevitable that gender categories will gradually blur under the weight of evidence of the similarities of women and men, or that by gradual erosion, gender will stop being the major determinant of how the work of modern society is allocated and the rewards distributed. Pendulum swings are common and social exigencies often excuse greater oppression of one group by another. It can certainly happen to women and men.[7]

In the United States during World War II, women were recruited for work in defense plants, steel mills, and other heavy industry. Day-care centers were set up in many workplaces because of the desperate need for workers. But despite women's evident ability to handle heavy physical labor and their desire to keep working and earning high wages, gender segregation of jobs persisted, and women were fired when the war ended (Milkman 1987). The day-care centers were abandoned, and the 1950s were conservative, family-oriented, and gender-segregated.[8] In Islamic countries that have become more fundamentalist, women have put on the veil over their blue jeans; more problematic, they have been stripped of all their civil rights (Kandiyoti 1991; Moghadam 1989). With the crumbling of communism and the turn to capitalist economies in Eastern Europe, women workers expect to be fired first, and liberal abortion laws are under challenge from resurgent Catholic hierarchies.[9]

Change can go the other way, too. The Persian Gulf War of 1990–91 sent 35,000 U.S. servicewomen to the frontlines, including mothers of small children, some of whom volunteered.[10] They were 6 percent of the total force of 541,425, and 10 percent of those who were killed.[11] Although the disruption of family life may lead to promulgation of protective rules once again, U.S. service-women attained widespread public recognition of their role. ("Our men and women in the Armed Services" was the slogan of the day.) Indeed, a few months after the end of the war, the U.S. House of Representatives voted to allow women to be combat pilots (*New York Times* 1991d).[12]

The paradox of women fighting and dying to protect and liberate countries that don't allow their women to vote, drive cars, or appear in public unveiled seems to have raised the consciousness of women in both cultures.[13] American servicewomen had to wear long sleeves off their bases, be accompanied into town by a man and have him pay, and use the back doors of gymnasiums and other facilities. Under orders from generals and politicians, they conformed, but grudgingly; they would have liked servicemen to give up their prerogatives in sympathy.[14] At the same time, forty-seven Saudi women were empowered enough to stage a drive-in, which resulted in eight hours of questioning by the police, harassment by the religious authorities, and loss of jobs, but also acts of support from kinsmen (*Ms. Magazine* 1991).

Because consciousness of oppression does not always lead to a push for action (Davis and Robinson 1991) and rebels are frequently publicly punished, individuals are more likely to conform than to rebel. Not surprisingly, those advantaged by the social institution of gender want to maintain the status quo, but the not-so-privileged also have an investment in a going social order that gives them some bargaining power.[15] Rebellion is hard on individual lives—it can eat up a person's livelihood, emotions, and freedom. Unless rebellion is a major group effort, supported by a substantial number of women and men, it is not likely to make a dent in an existing major institution like gender.

Real change would mean a conscious reordering of the organizing principles of social life (women take care of children, men go to work) with awareness of hidden assumptions (children have different attachments to mothers than to fathers) and latent effects (men need to suppress the feminine in themselves and can't allow women to have any authority over them). Change is unlikely to be deep-seated unless the pervasiveness of the social institution of gender and its social construction are made explicit.[16] The prime paradox of gender is that in order to dismantle the institution you must first make it very visible, which is the purpose of this book.

"NIGHT TO HIS DAY": THE SOCIAL CONSTRUCTION OF GENDER

> [Gethenians] do not see each other as men or women. This is almost impossible for our imagination to accept. What is the first question we ask about a newborn baby?
>
> —Ursula Le Guin (1969, 94)

Talking about gender for most people is the equivalent of fish talking about water. Gender is so much the routine ground of everyday activities that questioning its taken-for-granted assumptions and presuppositions is like thinking about whether the sun will come up.[17] Gender is so pervasive that in our society we assume it is bred into our genes. Most people find it hard to believe that gender is constantly created and re-created out of human interaction, out of social life, and is the texture and order of that social life. Yet gender, like culture, is a human production that depends on everyone constantly "doing gender" (West and Zimmerman 1987).

And everyone "does gender" without thinking about it. Today, on the subway, I saw a well-dressed man with a year-old child in a stroller. Yesterday, on a bus, I saw a man with a tiny baby in a carrier on his chest. Seeing men taking care of small children in public is increasingly common—at least in New York City. But both men were quite obviously stared at—and smiled at, approvingly. Everyone was doing gender—the men who were changing the role of fathers and the other passengers, who were applauding them silently. But there was more gendering going on that probably fewer people noticed. The baby was wearing a white crocheted cap and white clothes. You couldn't tell if it was a boy or a girl. The child in the stroller was wearing a dark blue T-shirt and dark print pants. As they started to leave the train, the father put a Yankee baseball cap on the child's head. Ah, a boy, I thought. Then I noticed the gleam of tiny earrings in the child's ears, and as they got off, I saw the little flowered sneakers and lace-trimmed socks. Not a boy after all. Gender done.

Gender is such a familiar part of daily life that it usually takes a deliberate disruption of our expectations of how women and men are supposed to act to pay attention to how it is produced. Gender signs and signals are so ubiquitous that we usually fail to note them—unless they are missing or ambiguous. Then we are uncomfortable until we have successfully placed the other person in a gender status; otherwise, we feel socially dislocated. In our society, in addition to man and woman, the status can be *transvestite* (a person who dresses in opposite-gender clothes) and *transsexual* (a person who has had sex-change surgery). Transvestites and transsexuals carefully construct their gender status by dressing, speaking, walking, gesturing in the ways prescribed for women or men—whichever they want to be taken for—and so does any "normal" person.

For the individual, gender construction starts with assignment to a sex category on the basis of what the genitalia look like at birth.[18] Then babies are dressed or adorned in a way that displays the category because parents don't want to be constantly asked whether their baby is a girl or a boy. A sex category becomes a gender status through naming, dress, and the use of other gender markers. Once a child's gender is evident, others treat those in one gender differently from those in the other, and the children respond to the different treatment by feeling different and behaving differently. As soon as they can talk, they start to refer to themselves as members of their gender. Sex doesn't come into play again until puberty, but by that time, sexual feelings and desires and practices have been shaped by gendered norms and expectations. Adolescent boys and girls approach and avoid each other in an elaborately scripted and gendered mating dance. Parenting is gendered, with different expectations for mothers and for fathers, and people of different genders work at different kinds of jobs. The work adults do as mothers and fathers and as low-level workers and high-level bosses, shapes women's and men's life experiences, and these experiences produce different feelings, consciousness, relationships, skills— ways of being that we call feminine or masculine.[19] All of these processes constitute the social construction of gender.

Gendered roles change—today fathers are taking care of little children, girls and boys are wearing unisex clothing and getting the same education, women and men are working at the same jobs. Although many traditional social groups are quite strict about maintaining gender differences, in other social groups they seem to be blurring. Then why the one-year-old's earrings? Why is it still so important to mark a child as a girl or a boy, to make sure she is not taken for a boy or he for a girl? What would happen if they were? They would, quite literally, have changed places in their social world.

To explain why gendering is done from birth, constantly and by everyone, we have to look not only at the way individuals experience gender but at gender as a social institution. As a social institution, gender is one of the major ways that human beings organize their lives. Human society depends on a predictable division of labor, a designated allocation of scarce goods, assigned responsibility for children and others who cannot care for themselves, common values and their systematic transmission to new members, legitimate leadership, music, art, stories, games, and other symbolic productions. One way of choosing people for the different tasks of society is on the basis of their talents, motivations, and competence—their demonstrated achievements. The other way is on the basis of gender, race, ethnicity—ascribed membership in a category of people. Although societies vary in the extent to which they use one or the other of these ways of allocating people to work and to carry out other responsibilities, every society uses gender and age grades. Every society classifies people as "girl and boy children," "girls and boys ready to be married," and "fully adult women and men," constructs similarities among them and differences between them, and assigns them to different roles and responsibilities. Personality characteristics, feelings, motivations, and ambitions flow from these different life experiences so that the members of these different groups become different kinds of people. The process of gendering and its outcome are legitimated by religion, law, science, and the society's entire set of values.

In order to understand gender as a social institution, it is important to distinguish human action from animal behavior. Animals feed themselves and their young until their young can feed themselves. Humans have to produce not only food but shelter and clothing. They also, if the group is going to continue as a social group, have to teach the children how their particular group does these tasks. In the process, humans reproduce gender, family, kinship, and a division of labor—social institutions that do not exist among animals. Primate social groups have been referred to as families, and their mating patterns as monogamy, adultery, and harems. Primate behavior has been used to prove the universality of sex differences—as built into our evolutionary inheritance (Haraway 1978a). But animals' sex differences are not at all the same as humans' gender differences; animals' bonding is not kinship; animals' mating is not ordered by marriage; and animals' dominance hierarchies are not the equivalent of human stratification systems. Animals group on sex and age, relational categories that are physiologically, not socially, different. Humans create gender and age-group categories that are socially, and not necessarily physiologically, different.[20]

For animals, physiological maturity means being able to impregnate or conceive; its markers are coming into heat (estrus) and sexual attraction. For humans, puberty means being available for marriage; it is marked by rites that demonstrate this marital eligibility. Although the onset of physiological puberty is signaled by secondary sex characteristics (menstruation, breast development, sperm ejaculation, pubic and underarm hair), the onset of social adulthood is ritualized by the coming-out party or desert walkabout or bar mitzvah or graduation from college or first successful hunt or dreaming or inheritance of property. Humans have rituals that mark the passage from childhood into puberty and puberty into full adult status, as well as for marriage, childbirth, and death; animals do not (van Gennep 1960). To the extent that infants and the dead are differentiated by whether they are male or female, there are different birth rituals for girls and boys, and different funeral rituals for men and women (Biersack 1984, 132–33). Rituals of puberty, marriage, and becoming a parent are gendered, creating a "woman," a "man," a "bride," a "groom," a "mother," a "father." Animals have no equivalents for these statuses.

Among animals, siblings mate and so do parents and children; humans have incest taboos and rules that encourage or forbid mating between members of different kin groups (Lévi-Strauss 1956, [1949] 1969). Any animal of the same species may feed another's young (or may not, depending on the species). Humans designate responsibility for particular children by kinship; humans frequently limit responsibility for children to the members of their kinship group or make them into members of their kinship group with adoption rituals.

Animals have dominance hierarchies based on size or on successful threat gestures and signals. These hierarchies are usually sexed, and in some species, moving to the top of the hierarchy physically changes the sex (Austad 1986). Humans have stratification patterns based on control of surplus food, ownership of property, legitimate demands on others' work and sexual services, enforced determinations of who marries whom, and approved use of violence. If a woman replaces a man at the top of a stratification hierarchy, her social status may be that of a man, but her sex does not change.

Mating, feeding, and nurturant behavior in animals is determined by instinct and imitative learning and ordered by physiological sex and age (Lancaster 1974). In humans, these behaviors are taught and symbolically reinforced and ordered by socially constructed gender and age grades. Social gender and age statuses sometimes ignore or override physiological sex and age completely. Male and female animals (unless they physiologically change) are not interchange-

able; infant animals cannot take the place of adult animals. Human females can become husbands and fathers, and human males can become wives and mothers, without sex-change surgery (Blackwood 1984). Human infants can reign as kings or queens.

Western society's values legitimate gendering by claiming that it all comes from physiology—female and male procreative differences. But gender and sex are not equivalent, and gender as a social construction does not flow automatically from genitalia and reproductive organs, the main physiological differences of females and males. In the construction of ascribed social statuses, physiological differences such as sex, stage of development, color of skin, and size are crude markers. They are not the source of the social statuses of gender, age grade, and race. Social statuses are carefully constructed through prescribed processes of teaching, learning, emulation, and enforcement. Whatever genes, hormones, and biological evolution contribute to human social institutions is materially as well as qualitatively transformed by social practices. Every social institution has a material base, but culture and social practices transform that base into something with qualitatively different patterns and constraints. The economy is much more than producing food and goods and distributing them to eaters and users; family and kinship are not the equivalent of having sex and procreating; morals and religions cannot be equated with the fears and ecstasies of the brain; language goes far beyond the sounds produced by tongue and larynx. No one eats "money" or "credit"; the concepts of "god" and "angels" are the subjects of theological disquisitions; not only words but objects, such as their flag, "speak" to the citizens of a country.

Similarly, gender cannot be equated with biological and physiological differences between human females and males. The building blocks of gender are *socially constructed statuses*. Western societies have only two genders, "man" and "woman." Some societies have three genders—men, women, and *berdaches* or *hijras* or *xaniths*. Berdaches, hijras, and xaniths are biological males who behave, dress, work, and are treated in most respects as social women; they are therefore not men, nor are they female women; they are, in our language, "male women."[21] There are African and American Indian societies that have a gender status called *manly hearted women*—biological females who work, marry, and parent as men; their social status is "female men" (Amadiume 1987; Blackwood 1984). They do not have to behave or dress as men to have the social responsibilities and prerogatives of husbands and fathers; what makes them men is enough wealth to buy a wife.

Modern Western societies' *transsexuals* and *transvestites* are the nearest equivalent of these crossover genders, but they are not institutionalized as third genders (Bolin 1987). Transsexuals are biological males and females who have sex-change operations to alter their genitalia. They do so in order to bring their physical anatomy in congruence with the way they want to live and with their own sense of gender identity. They do not become a third gender; they change genders. Transvestites are males who live as women and females who live as men but do not intend to have sex-change surgery. Their dress, appearance, and mannerisms fall within the range of what is expected from members of the opposite gender, so that they "pass." They also change genders, sometimes temporarily, some for most of their lives. Transvestite women have fought in wars as men soldiers as recently as the nineteenth century; some married women, and others went back to being women and married men once the war was over.[22] Some were discovered when their wounds were treated; others

not until they died. In order to work as a jazz musician, a man's occupation, Billy Tipton, a woman, lived most of her life as a man. She died recently at seventy-four, leaving a wife and three adopted sons for whom she was husband and father, and musicians with whom she had played and traveled, for whom she was "one of the boys" (*New York Times* 1989).[23] There have been many other such occurrences of women passing as men to do more prestigious or lucrative men's work (Matthaei 1982, 192–93).[24]

Genders, therefore, are not attached to a biological substratum. Gender boundaries are breachable, and individual and socially organized shifts from one gender to another call attention to "cultural, social, or aesthetic dissonances" (Garber 1992, 16). These odd or deviant or third genders show us what we ordinarily take for granted—that people have to learn to be women and men. Men who cross-dress for performances or for pleasure often learn from women's magazines how to "do femininity" convincingly (Garber 1992, 41–51). Because transvestism is direct evidence of how gender is constructed, Marjorie Garber claims it has "extraordinary power . . . to disrupt, expose, and challenge, putting in question the very notion of the 'original' and of stable identity" (1992, 16).

GENDER BENDING

It is difficult to see how gender is constructed because we take it for granted that it's all biology, or hormones, or human nature. The differences between women and men seem to be self-evident, and we think they would occur no matter what society did. But in actuality, human females and males are physiologically more similar in appearance than are the two sexes of many species of animals and are more alike than different in traits and behavior (C.F. Epstein 1988). Without the deliberate use of gendered clothing, hairstyles, jewelry, and cosmetics, women and men would look far more alike.[25] Even societies that do not cover women's breasts have gender-identifying clothing, scarification, jewelry, and hairstyles.

The ease with which many transvestite women pass as men and transvestite men as women is corroborated by the common gender misidentification in Westernized societies of people in jeans, T-shirts, and sneakers. Men with long hair may be addressed as "miss," and women with short hair are often taken for men unless they offset the potential ambiguity with deliberate gender markers (Devor 1987, 1989). Jan Morris, in *Conundrum*, an autobiographical account of events just before and just after a sex-change operation, described how easy it was to shift back and forth from being a man to being a woman when testing how it would feel to change gender status. During this time, Morris still had a penis and wore more or less unisex clothing; the context alone made the man and the woman:

> Sometimes the arena of my ambivalence was uncomfortably small. At the Travellers' Club, for example, I was obviously known as a man of sorts—women were only allowed on the premises at all during a few hours of the day, and even then were hidden away as far as possible in lesser rooms or alcoves. But I had another club, only a few hundred yards away, where I was known only as a woman, and often I went directly from one to the other, imperceptibly changing roles on the way—"Cheerio, sir," the porter would say at one club, and "Hello, madam," the porter would greet me at the other. (1975, 132)

Gender shifts are actually a common phenomenon in public roles as well. Queen Elizabeth II of England bore children, but when she went to Saudi Arabia on a state visit, she was considered an honorary man so that she could confer and dine with the men who were heads of a state that forbids unrelated men and women to have face-to-unveiled-face contact. In contemporary Egypt, lower-class women who run restaurants or shops dress in men's clothing and engage in unfeminine aggressive behavior, and middle-class educated women of professional or managerial status can take positions of authority (Rugh 1986, 131). In these situations, there is an important status change: These women are treated by the others in the situation as if they are men. From their own point of view, they are still women. From the social perspective, however, they are men.[26]

In many cultures, gender bending is prevalent in theater or dance—the Japanese kabuki are men actors who play both women and men; in Shakespeare's theater company, there were no actresses—Juliet and Lady Macbeth were played by boys. Shakespeare's comedies are full of witty comments on gender shifts. Women characters frequently masquerade as young men, and other women characters fall in love with them; the boys playing these masquerading women, meanwhile, are acting out pining for the love of men characters.[27] In *As You Like It*, when Rosalind justifies her protective crossdressing, Shakespeare also comments on manliness:

> Were it not better,
> Because that I am more than common tall,
> That I did suit me all points like a man:
> A gallant curtle-axe upon my thigh,
> A boar-spear in my hand, and in my heart
> Lie there what hidden women's fear there
>   will,
> We'll have a swashing and martial outside,
> As many other mannish cowards have
> That do outface it with their semblances.
>
> (I, i, 115–22)

Shakespeare's audience could appreciate the double subtext: Rosalind, a woman character, was a boy dressed in girl's clothing who then dressed as a boy; like bravery, masculinity and femininity can be put on and taken off with changes of costume and role (Howard 1988, 435).[28]

M Butterfly is a modern play of gender ambiguities, which David Hwang (1989) based on a real person. Shi Peipu, a male Chinese opera singer who sang women's roles, was a spy as a man and the lover as a woman of a Frenchman, Gallimard, a diplomat (Bernstein 1986). The relationship lasted twenty years, and Shi Peipu even pretended to be the mother of a child by Gallimard. "She" also pretended to be too shy to undress completely. As "Butterfly," Shi Peipu portrayed a fantasy Oriental woman who made the lover a "real man" (Kondo 1990b). In Gallimard's words, the fantasy was "of slender women in chong sams and kimonos who die for the love of unworthy foreign devils. Who are born and raised to be perfect women. Who take whatever punishment we give them, and bounce back, strengthened by love, unconditionally" (D.H. Hwang 1989, 91). When the fantasy woman betrayed him by turning out to be the more powerful "real man," Gallimard assumed the role of Butterfly and, dressed in a geisha's robes, killed himself: "because 'man' and 'woman' are oppositionally defined terms, reversals . . . are possible" (Kondo 1990b, 18).[29]

But despite the ease with which gender boundaries can be traversed in work, in social relationships, and in cultural productions, gender statuses remain. Transvestites and transsexuals do not challenge the social construction of gender. Their goal is to be feminine women and masculine men (Kondo 1973). Those who do not want to change their anatomy but do want to change their gender behavior fare less well in establishing their social identity. The women Holly Devor called "gender blenders" wore their hair short, dressed in unisex pants, shirts, and comfortable shoes, and did not wear jewelry or makeup. They described their everyday dress as women's clothing: One said, "I wore jeans all the time, but I didn't wear men's clothes" (Devor 1989, 100). Their gender identity was women, but because they refused to "do femininity," they were constantly taken for men (1987, 1989, 107–42). Devor said of them: "The most common area of complaint was with public washrooms. They repeatedly spoke of the humiliation of being challenged or ejected from women's washrooms. Similarly, they found public change rooms to be dangerous territory and the buying of undergarments to be a difficult feat to accomplish" (1987, 29). In an ultimate ironic twist, some of these women said "they would feel like transvestites if they were to wear dresses, and two women said that they had been called transvestites when they had done so" (1987, 31). They resolved the ambiguity of their gender status by identifying as women in private and passing as men in public to avoid harassment on the street, to get men's jobs, and, if they were lesbians, to make it easier to display affection publicly with their lovers (Devor 1989, 107–42). Sometimes they even used men's bathrooms. When they had gender-neutral names, like Leslie, they could avoid the bureaucratic hassles that arose when they had to present their passports or other proof of identity, but because most had names associated with women, their appearance and their cards of identity were not conventionally congruent, and their gender status was in constant jeopardy.[30] When they could, they found it easier to pass as men than to try to change the stereotyped notions of what women should look like.

Paradoxically, then, bending gender rules and passing between genders does not erode but rather preserves gender boundaries. In societies with only two genders, the gender dichotomy is not disturbed by transvestites, because others feel that a transvestite is only transitorily ambiguous—is "really a man or woman underneath." After sex-change surgery, transsexuals end up in a conventional gender status—a "man" or a "woman" with the appropriate genitals (Eichler 1989). When women dress as men for business reasons, they are indicating that in that situation, they want to be treated the way men are treated; when they dress as women, they want to be treated as women:

> By their male dress, female entrepreneurs signal their desire to suspend the expectations of accepted feminine conduct without losing respect and reputation. By wearing what is "unattractive" they signify that they are not intending to display their physical charms while engaging in public activity. Their loud, aggressive banter contrasts with the modest demeanor that attracts men. . . . Overt signalling of a suspension of the rules preserves normal conduct from eroding expectations. (Rugh 1986, 131)

FOR INDIVIDUALS, GENDER MEANS SAMENESS

Although the possible combinations of genitalia, body shapes, clothing, mannerisms, sexuality, and roles could produce infinite varieties in human beings, the social institution of gender depends on the production and maintenance of a limited number of gender statuses and of making the members of these statuses similar to each other. Individuals are born sexed but not gendered, and they have to be taught to be masculine or feminine.[31] As Simone de Beauvoir said: "One is not born, but rather becomes, a woman . . . ; it is civilization as a whole that produces this creature . . . which is described as feminine." (1952, 267).

Children learn to walk, talk, and gesture the way their social group says girls and boys should. Ray Birdwhistell, in his analysis of body motion as human communication, calls these learned gender displays *tertiary* sex characteristics and argues that they are needed to distinguish genders because humans are a weakly dimorphic species—their only sex markers are genitalia (1970, 39–46). Clothing, paradoxically, often hides the sex but displays the gender.

In early childhood, humans develop gendered personality structures and sexual orientations through their interactions with parents of the same and opposite gender. As adolescents, they conduct their sexual behavior according to gendered scripts. Schools, parents, peers, and the mass media guide young people into gendered work and family roles. As adults, they take on a gendered social status in their society's stratification system. Gender is thus both ascribed and achieved (West and Zimmerman 1987).

.   .   .

Many cultures go beyond clothing, gestures, and demeanor in gendering children. They inscribe gender directly into bodies. In traditional Chinese society, mothers bound their daughters' feet into three-inch stumps to enhance their sexual attractiveness. Jewish fathers circumcise their infant sons to show their covenant with God. Women in African societies remove the clitoris of prepubescent girls, scrape their labia, and make the lips grow together to preserve their chastity and ensure their marriageability. In Western societies, women augment their breast size with silicone and reconstruct their faces with cosmetic surgery to conform to cultural ideals of feminine beauty. Hanna Papanek (1990) notes that these practices reinforce the sense of superiority or inferiority in the adults who carry them out as well as in the children on whom they are done: The genitals of Jewish fathers and sons are physical and psychological evidence of their common dominant religious and familial status; the genitals of African mothers and daughters are physical and psychological evidence of their joint subordination.[32]

Sandra Bern (1981, 1983) argues that because gender is a powerful "schema" that orders the cognitive world, one must wage a constant, active battle for a child not to fall into typical gendered attitudes and behavior. In 1972, *Ms. Magazine* published Lois Gould's fantasy of how to raise a child free of gender-typing. The experiment calls for hiding the child's anatomy from all eyes except the parents' and treating the child as neither a girl nor a boy. The child, called X, gets to do all the things boys *and* girls do. The experiment is so successful that all the children in X's class at school want to look and behave like X. At the end of the story, the creators of the experiment are asked what will happen when X grows up. The scientists' answer is that by then it will be quite clear what X is, implying that its hormones will kick in and it will be revealed as a female or male. That ambiguous, and somewhat contradictory, ending lets Gould off the hook; neither she nor we have any idea what someone brought up totally androgynously would be like sexually or socially as an adult. The hormonal input will not create gender or sexuality but will only establish secondary sex characteristics; breasts, beards, and menstruation alone do not produce social manhood or womanhood. Indeed, it is at puberty, when sex characteristics become evident, that most societies put pubescent children through their most important rites of passage, the rituals that officially mark them as fully gendered—that is, ready to marry and become adults.

Most parents create a gendered world for their newborn by naming, birth announcements, and dress. Children's relationships with same-gendered and different-gendered caretakers structure their self-identifications and personalities. Through cognitive development, children extract and apply to their own actions the appropriate behavior for those who belong in their own gender, as well as race, religion, ethnic group, and social class, rejecting what is not appropriate. If their social categories are highly valued, they value themselves highly; if their social categories are low status, they lose self-esteem (Chodorow 1974). Many feminist parents who want to raise androgynous children soon lose their children to the pull of gendered norms (T. Gordon 1990, 87–90). My son attended a carefully nonsexist elementary school, which didn't even have girls' and boys' bathrooms. When he was seven or eight years old, I attended a class play about "squares" and "circles" and their need for each other and noticed that all the girl squares and circles wore makeup, but none of the boy squares and circles did. I asked the teacher about it after the play, and she said, "Bobby said he was not going to wear makeup, and he is a powerful child, so none of the boys would either." In a long discussion about conformity, my son confronted me with the question of who the conformists were, the boys who followed their leader or the girls who listened to the woman teacher. In actuality, they both were, because they both followed same-gender leaders and acted in gender-appropriate ways. (Actors may wear makeup, but real boys don't.)

For human beings there is no essential femaleness or maleness, femininity or masculinity, womanhood or manhood, but once gender is ascribed, the social order constructs and holds individuals to strongly gendered norms and expectations. Individuals may vary on many of the components of gender and may shift genders temporarily or permanently, but they must fit into the limited number of gender statuses their society recognizes. In the process, they re-create their society's version of women and men: "If we do gender appropriately, we simultaneously sustain, reproduce, and render legitimate the institutional arrangements. . . . If we fail to do gender appropriately, we as individuals—not the institutional arrangements—may be called to account (for our character, motives, and predispositions)" (West and Zimmerman 1987, 146).

The gendered practices of everyday life reproduce a society's view of how women and men should act (Bourdieu [1980] 1990). Gendered social arrangements are justified by religion and cultural productions and backed by law, but the most powerful means of sustaining the moral hegemony of the dominant gender ideology is that the process is made invisible; any possible alternatives are virtually unthinkable (Foucault 1972; Gramsci 1971).[33]

FOR SOCIETY, GENDER MEANS DIFFERENCE

The pervasiveness of gender as a way of structuring social life demands that gender statuses be clearly differentiated. Varied talents, sexual preferences, identities, personalities, interests, and ways of interacting fragment the individual's bodily and social experiences. Nonetheless, these are organized in Western cultures into two and only two socially and legally recognized gender statuses, "man" and "woman."[34] In the social construction of gender, it does not matter what men and women actually do; it does not even matter if they do exactly the same thing. The social institution of gender insists only that what they do is *perceived* as different.

If men and women are doing the same tasks, they are usually spatially segregated to maintain gender separation, and often the tasks are given different job titles as well, such as executive secretary and administrative assistant (Reskin 1988). If the differences between women and men begin to blur, society's "sameness taboo" goes into action (G. Rubin 1975, 178). At a rock and roll dance at West Point in 1976, the year women were admitted to the prestigious military academy for the first time, the school's administrators "were reportedly perturbed by the sight of mirror-image couples dancing in short hair and dress gray trousers," and a rule was established that women cadets could dance at these events only if they wore skirts (Barkalow and Raab 1990, 53).[35] Women recruits in the U.S. Marine Corps are required to wear makeup—at a minimum, lipstick and eye shadow—and they have to take classes in makeup, hair care, poise, and etiquette. This feminization is part of a deliberate policy of making them clearly distinguishable from men Marines. Christine Williams quotes a twenty-five-year-old woman drill instructor as saying: "A lot of the recruits who come here don't wear makeup; they're tomboyish or athletic. A lot of them have the preconceived idea that going into the military means they can still be a tomboy. They don't realize that you are a *Woman* Marine" (1989, 76–77).[36]

If gender differences were genetic, physiological, or hormonal, gender bending and gender ambiguity would occur only in hermaphrodites, who are born with chromosomes and genitalia that are not clearly female or male. Since gender differences are socially constructed, all men and all women can enact the behavior of the other, because they know the other's social script: "'Man' and 'woman' are at once empty and overflowing categories. Empty because they have no ultimate, transcendental meaning. Overflowing because even when they appear to be fixed, they still contain within them alternative, denied, or suppressed definitions." (J.W. Scott 1988a, 49). Nonetheless, though individuals may be able to shift gender statuses, the gender boundaries have to hold, or the whole gendered social order will come crashing down.

Paradoxically, it is the social importance of gender statuses and their external markers—clothing, mannerisms, and spatial segregation—that makes gender bending or gender crossing possible—or even necessary. The social viability of differentiated gender statuses produces the need or desire to shift statuses. Without gender differentiation, transvestism and transsexuality would be meaningless. You couldn't dress in the opposite gender's clothing if all clothing were unisex. There would be no need to reconstruct genitalia to match identity if interests and life-styles were not gendered. There would be no need for women to pass as men to do certain kinds of work if jobs were not typed as "women's work" and "men's work." Women would not have to dress as men in public life in order to give orders or aggressively bargain with customers.

Gender boundaries are preserved when transsexuals create congruous autobiographies of always having felt like what they are now. The transvestite's story also "recuperates social and sexual norms" (Garber 1992, 69). In the transvestite's normalized narrative, he or she "is 'compelled' by social and economic forces to disguise himself or herself in order to get a job, escape repression, or gain artistic or political 'freedom'" (Garber 1992, 70). The "true identity," when revealed, causes amazement over how easily and successfully the person passed as a member of the opposite gender, not a suspicion that gender itself is something of a put-on.

.   .   .

COMPONENTS OF GENDER

By now, it should be clear that gender is not a unitary essence but has many components as a social institution and as an individual status.[37]

As a social institution, gender is composed of:

Gender statuses, the socially recognized genders in a society and the norms and expectations for their enactment behaviorally, gesturally, linguistically, emotionally, and physically. How gender statuses are evaluated depends on historical development in any particular society.

Gendered division of labor, the assignment of productive and domestic work to members of different gender statuses. The work assigned to those of different gender statuses strengthens the society's evaluation of those statuses—the higher the status, the more prestigious and valued the work and the greater its rewards.

Gendered kinship, the family rights and responsibilities for each gender status. Kinship statuses reflect and reinforce the prestige and power differences of the different genders.

Gendered sexual scripts, the normative patterns of sexual desire and sexual behavior, as prescribed for the different gender statuses. Members of the dominant gender have more sexual prerogatives; members of a subordinate gender may be sexually exploited.

Gendered personalities, the combinations of traits patterned by gender norms of how members of different gender statuses are supposed to feel and behave. Social expectations of others in face-to-face interaction constantly bolster these norms.

Gendered social control, the formal and informal approval and reward of conforming behavior and the stigmatization, social isolation, punishment, and medical treatment of nonconforming behavior.

Gender ideology, the justification of gender statuses, particularly, their differential evaluation. The dominant ideology tends to suppress criticism by making these evaluations seem natural.

Gender imagery, the cultural representations of gender and embodiment of gender in symbolic language and artistic productions that reproduce and legitimate gender statuses. Culture is one of the main supports of the dominant gender ideology.

For an individual, gender is composed of:

Sex category to which the infant is assigned at birth based on appearance of genitalia. With prenatal testing and sex-typing, categorization is prenatal. Sex category may be changed later through surgery or reinspection of ambiguous genitalia.

Gender identity, the individual's sense of gendered self as a worker and family member.

Gendered marital and procreative status, fulfillment or nonfulfillment of allowed or disallowed mating, impregnation, childbearing, kinship roles.

Gendered sexual orientation, socially and individually patterned sexual desires, feelings, practices, and identification.

Gendered personality, internalized patterns of socially normative emotions as organized by family structure and parenting.

Gendered processes, the social practices of learning, being taught, picking up cues, enacting behavior already learned to be gender-appropriate (or inappropriate, if rebelling, testing), developing a gender identity, "doing gender" as a member of a gender status in relationships with gendered others, acting deferent or dominant.

Gender beliefs, incorporation of or resistance to gender ideology.

Gender display, presentation of self as a certain kind of gendered person through dress, cosmetics, adornments, and permanent and reversible body markers.

For an individual, all the social components are supposed to be consistent and congruent with perceived physiology. The actual combination of genes and genitalia, prenatal, adolescent, and adult hormonal input, and procreative capacity may or may not be congruous with each other and with sex-category assignment, gender identity, gendered sexual orientation and procreative status, gender display, personality, and work and family roles. At any one time, an individual's identity is a combination of the major ascribed statuses of gender, race, ethnicity, religion, and social class, and the individual's achieved statuses, such as education level, occupation or profession, marital status, parenthood, prestige, authority, and wealth. The ascribed statuses substantially limit or create opportunities for individual achievements and also diminish or enhance the luster of those achievements.

GENDER AS PROCESS, STRATIFICATION, AND STRUCTURE

As a social institution, gender is a process of creating distinguishable social statuses for the assignment of rights and responsibilities. As part of a stratification system that ranks these statuses unequally, gender is a major building block in the social structures built on these unequal statuses.

As a *process*, gender creates the social differences that define "woman" and "man." In social interaction throughout their lives, individuals learn what is expected, see what is expected, act and react in expected ways, and thus simultaneously construct and maintain the gender order: "The very injunction to be a given gender takes place through discursive routes: to be a good mother, to be a heterosexually desirable object, to be a fit worker, in sum, to signify a multiplicity of guarantees in response to a variety of different demands all at once" (J. Butler 1990, 145). Members of a social group neither make up gender as they go along nor exactly replicate in rote fashion what was done before. In almost every encounter, human beings produce gender, behaving in the ways they learned were appropriate for their gender status, or resisting or rebelling against these norms. Resistance and rebellion have altered gender norms, but so far they have rarely eroded the statuses.

Gendered patterns of interaction acquire additional layers of gendered sexuality, parenting, and work behaviors in childhood, adolescence, and adulthood. Gendered norms and expectations are enforced through informal sanctions of gender-inappropriate behavior by peers and by formal punishment or threat of punishment by those in authority should behavior deviate too far from socially imposed standards for women and men.

Everyday gendered interactions build gender into the family, the work process, and other organizations and institutions, which in turn reinforce gender expectations for individuals.[38] Because gender is a process, there is room not only for modification and variation by individuals and small groups but also for institutionalized change (J.W. Scott 1988a, 7).

As part of a *stratification* system, gender ranks men above women of the same race and class. Women and men could be different but equal. In practice, the process of creating difference depends to a great extent on differential evaluation. As Nancy Jay (1981) says: "That which is defined, separated out, isolated from all else is A and pure. Not-A is necessarily impure, a random catchall, to which nothing is external except A and the principle of order that separates it from Not-A" (45). From the individual's point of view, whichever gender is A, the other is Not-A; gender boundaries tell the individual who is like him or her, and all the rest are unlike. From society's point of view, however, one gender is usually the touchstone, the normal, the dominant, and the other is different, deviant, and subordinate. In Western society, "man" is A, "wo-man" is Not-A. (Consider what a society would be like where woman was A and man Not-A.)

The further dichotomization by race and class constructs the gradations of a heterogeneous society's stratification scheme. Thus, in the United States, white is A, African American is Not-A; middle class is A, working class is Not-A, and "African-American women occupy a position whereby the inferior half of a series of these dichotomies

converge" (P.H. Collins 1990, 70). The dominant categories are the hegemonic ideals, taken so for granted as the way things should be that white is not ordinarily thought of as a race, middle class as a class, or men as a gender. The characteristics of these categories define the Other as that which lacks the valuable qualities the dominants exhibit.

In a gender-stratified society, what men do is usually valued more highly than what women do because men do it, even when their activities are very similar or the same. In different regions of southern India, for example, harvesting rice is men's work, shared work, or women's work: "Wherever a task is done by women it is considered easy, and where it is done by [men] it is considered difficult" (Mencher 1988, 104). A gathering and hunting society's survival usually depends on the nuts, grubs, and small animals brought in by the women's foraging trips, but when the men's hunt is successful, it is the occasion for a celebration. Conversely, because they are the superior group, white men do not have to do the "dirty work," such as housework; the most inferior group does it, usually poor women of color (Palmer 1989).

Freudian psychoanalytic theory claims that boys must reject their mothers and deny the feminine in themselves in order to become men: "For boys the major goal is the achievement of personal masculine identification with their father and sense of secure masculine self, achieved through superego formation and disparagement of women" (Chodorow 1978, 165). Masculinity may be the outcome of boys' intrapsychic struggles to separate their identity from that of their mothers, but the proofs of masculinity are culturally shaped and usually ritualistic and symbolic (Gilmore 1990).

The Marxist feminist explanation for gender inequality is that by demeaning women's abilities and keeping them from learning valuable technological skills, bosses preserve them as a cheap and exploitable reserve army of labor. Unionized men who could be easily replaced by women collude in this process because it allows them to monopolize the better paid, more interesting, and more autonomous jobs: "Two factors emerge as helping men maintain their separation from women and their control of technological occupations. One is the active gendering of jobs and people. The second is the continual creation of sub-divisions in the work processes, and levels in work hierarchies, into which men can move in order to keep their distance from women" (Cockburn 1985, 13).

Societies vary in the extent of the inequality in social status of their women and men members, but where there is inequality, the status "woman" (and its attendant behavior and role allocations) is usually held in lesser esteem than the status "man." Since gender is also intertwined with a society's other constructed statuses of differential evaluation—race, religion, occupation, class, country of origin, and so on—men and women members of the favored groups command more power, more prestige, and more property than the members of the disfavored groups. Within many social groups, however, men are advantaged over women. The more economic resources, such as education and job opportunities, are available to a group, the more they tend to be monopolized by men. In poorer groups that have few resources (such as working-class African Americans in the United States), women and men are more nearly equal, and the women may even outstrip the men in education and occupational status (Almquist 1987).

As a *structure*, gender divides work in the home and in economic production, legitimates those in authority, and organizes sexuality and emotional life (Connell 1987, 91–142). As primary parents, women signifi-

cantly influence children's psychological development and emotional attachments, in the process reproducing gender. Emergent sexuality is shaped by heterosexual, homosexual, bisexual, and sadomasochistic patterns that are gendered—different for girls and boys, and for women and men—so that sexual statuses reflect gender statuses.

When gender is a major component of structured inequality, the devalued genders have less power, prestige, and economic rewards than the valued genders. In countries that discourage gender discrimination, many major roles are still gendered; women still do most of the domestic labor and child rearing, even while doing full-time paid work; women and men are segregated on the job and each does work considered "appropriate"; women's work is usually paid less than men's work. Men dominate the positions of authority and leadership in government, the military, and the law; cultural productions, religions, and sports reflect men's interests.

In societies that create the greatest gender difference, such as Saudi Arabia, women are kept out of sight behind walls or veils, have no civil rights, and often create a cultural and emotional world of their own (Bernard 1981). But even in societies with less rigid gender boundaries, women and men spend much of their time with people of their own gender because of the way work and family are organized. This spatial separation of women and men reinforces gendered differentness, identity, and ways of thinking and behaving (Coser 1986).

Gender inequality—the devaluation of "women" and the social domination of "men"—has social functions and a social history. It is not the result of sex, procreation, physiology, anatomy, hormones, or genetic predispositions. It is produced and maintained by identifiable social processes and built into the general social structure and individual identities deliberately and purposefully. The social order as we know it in Western societies is organized around racial ethnic, class, and gender inequality. I contend, therefore, that the continuing purpose of gender as a modern social institution is to construct women as a group to be the subordinates of men as a group. The life of everyone placed in the status "woman" is "night to his day—that has forever been the fantasy. Black to his white. Shut out of his system's space, she is the repressed that ensures the system's functioning" (Cixous and Clément [1975] 1986, 67).

THE PARADOX OF HUMAN NATURE

To say that sex, sexuality, and gender are all socially constructed is not to minimize their social power. These categorical imperatives govern our lives in the most profound and pervasive ways, through the social experiences and social practices of what Dorothy Smith calls the "everyday /everynight world" (1990, 31–57). The paradox of human nature is that it is *always* a manifestation of cultural meanings, social relationships, and power politics; "not biology, but culture, becomes destiny" (J. Butler 1990, 8). Gendered people emerge not from physiology or sexual orientation but from the exigencies of the social order, mostly, from the need for a reliable division of the work of food production and the social (not physical) reproduction of new members. The moral imperatives of religion and cultural representations guard the boundary lines among genders and ensure that what is demanded, what is permitted, and what is tabooed for the people in each gender is well known and followed by most (C. Davies 1982). Political power, control of scarce resources, and, if necessary, violence uphold the gendered social order in the face of resistance and rebellion. Most people, however, voluntarily go along with their society's prescriptions for those of their gender status, because the norms and expectations get built into their sense of worth and identity as a certain kind of human being, and because they believe their society's way is the natural way. These beliefs emerge from the imagery that pervades the way we think, the way we see and hear and speak, the way we fantasy, and the way we feel.

There is no core or bedrock human nature below these endlessly looping processes of the social production of sex and gender, self and other, identity and psyche, each of which is a "complex cultural construction" (J. Butler 1990, 36). *For humans, the social is the natural.* Therefore, "in its feminist senses, gender cannot mean simply the cultural appropriation of biological sexual difference. Sexual difference is itself a fundamental— and scientifically contested—construction. Both 'sex' and 'gender' are woven of multiple, asymmetrical strands of difference, charged with multifaceted dramatic narratives of domination and struggle" (Haraway 1990, 140).

NOTES

INTRODUCTION

1. The French feminist groups of the 1970s that called themselves *Psychoanalyse et Politique* were Marxists who tried to amalgamate dialectical materialism and the Freudian and Lacanian discourse on sexuality and the unconscious.

2. In addition to Hill Collins and hooks, see Chow 1987; Christian 1988; Garcia 1989; King 1988; Spelman 1988.

3. For the new scholarship in men's studies, see Brod 1987; Hearn 1987; Hearn and Morgan 1990; Kimmel 1987b; Kimmel and Messner 1992; Staples 1982.

4. For overviews, see Marks and Courtivron 1981; Mitchell and Rose 1988; Moi 1985.

5. For debates over the politics of gender as a stable or shifting category both culturally and historically, see Alcoff 1988; de Lauretis 1989; Riley 1988; J.W. Scott 1988a, 1988b.

6. Bem 1993, 133–75; Gerson and Peiss 1985; Margolis 1985; D.E. Smith 1987a, 1990; West and Zimmerman 1987.

7. Blair 1989; Jenson 1986.

8. See Riley 1983 for the British experience with war nurseries.

9. Fuszara 1991; Moghadam 1990; Rosenberg 1991; Szalai 1991; and the special issue of *Feminist Review* entitled "Shifting Territories: Feminisms and Europe," no. 39 (1991).

10. Applebome 1991; Clymer 1991; J. Gross 1990a, 1990b; Nordheimer 1991; Schmitt 1991; M.W. Segal 1986.

11. A slightly higher percentage of women were killed, .0004 to .0003 for the men. Figures are taken from the *New York Times* story looking back one year later (Applebome 1992).

12. Francke 1991; Nordheimer 1991; Quindlen 1991a, 1992; Sciolino 1990; Stiehm 1985; and U.S. General Accounting Office 1989. For a variety of feminist writings on women and war, see Cooper, Munich, and Squier 1989; Elshtain and Tobias 1990; Gioseffi 1988; and M.L. Rossiter 1986.

13. Ayres 1991; Gonzalez 1991; LeMoyne 1990a; McFadden 1991.

14. Not only were the servicemen unlikely to give up their privileges, but a year later there were published reports of twenty-three incidents of sex crimes against servicewomen, including rape (*New York Times,* 1992b).

15. Goode [1982]1993; Kandiyoti 1988; Klatch 1987.

16. Acker 1989b; Connell 1990; Stacey and Thorne 1985.

"NIGHT TO HIS DAY"

17. Gender is, in Erving Goffman's words, an aspect of *Felicity's Condition:* "any arrangement which leads us to judge an individual's . . . acts not to be a manifestation of strangeness. Behind Felicity's Condition is our sense of what it is to be sane" (1983, 27). Also see Bem 1993; Frye 1983, 17–40; Goffman 1977.

18. In cases of ambiguity in countries with modern medicine, surgery is usually performed to make the genitalia more clearly male or female.

19. See J. Butler 1990 for an analysis of how doing gender *is* gender identity.

20. Douglas 1973; MacCormack 1980; Ortner 1974; Ortner and Whitehead 1981a; Yanagisako and Collier 1987. On the social construction of childhood, see Ariès 1962; Zelizer 1985.

21. On the hijras of India, see Nanda 1990; on the xaniths of Oman, Wikan 1982, 168–86; on the American Indian berdaches, W.L. Williams 1986. Other societies that have similar institutionalized third-gender men are the Koniag of Alaska, the Tanala of Madagascar, the Mesakin of Nuba, and the Chukchee of Siberia (Wikan 1982, 170).

22. Durova 1989; Freeman and Bond 1992; Wheelwright 1989.

23. Gender segregation of work in popular music still has not changed very much, according to Groce and Cooper 1989, despite considerable androgyny in some very popular figures. See Garber 1992 on the androgyny. She discusses Tipton on pp. 67–70.

24. In the nineteenth century, not only did these women get men's wages, but they also "had male privileges and could do all manner of things other women could not: open a bank account, write checks, own property, go anywhere unaccompanied, vote in elections" (Faderman 1991, 44).

25. When unisex clothing and men wearing long hair came into vogue in the United States in the mid-1960s, beards and mustaches for men also came into style again as gender identifications.

26. For other accounts of women being treated as men in Islamic countries, as well as accounts of women and men cross-dressing in these countries, see Garber 1992, 304–52.

27. Dollimore 1986; Garber 1992, 32–40; Greenblatt 1987, 66–93; Howard 1988. For Renaissance accounts of sexual relations with women and men of ambiguous sex, see Laqueur 1990a, 134–39. For modern accounts of women passing as men that other women find sexually attractive, see Devor 1989, 136–37; Wheelwright 1989, 53–59.

28. Females who passed as men soldiers had to "do masculinity," not just dress in a uniform (Wheelwright 1989, 50–78). On the triple entendres and gender resonances of Rosalind-type characters, see Garber 1992, 71–77.

29. Also see Garber 1992, 234–66.

30. Bolin describes how many documents have to be changed by transsexuals to provide a legitimizing "paper trail" (1988, 145–47). Note that only members of the same social group know which names are women's and which men's in their culture, but many documents list "sex."

31. For an account of how a potential man-to-woman transsexual learned to be feminine, see Garfinkel 1967, 116–85, 285–88. For a gloss on this account that points out how, throughout his encounters with Agnes, Garfinkel failed to see how he himself was constructing his own masculinity, see Rogers 1992.

32. Paige and Paige (1981, 147–49) argue that circumcision ceremonies indicate a father's loyalty to his lineage elders—"visible public evidence that the head of a family unit of their lineage is willing to trust others with his and his family's most valuable political asset, his son's penis" (147). On female circumcision, see El Dareer 1982; Lightfoot-Klein 1987; van der Kwaak 1992; Walker 1992. There is a form of female circumcision that removes only the prepuce of the clitoris and is similar to male circumcision, but most forms of female circumcision are far more extensive, mutilating, and spiritually and psychologically shocking than the

usual form of male circumcision. However, among the Australian aborigines, boys' penises are slit and kept open, so that they urinate and bleed the way women do (Bettelheim 1962, 165–206).

33. The concepts of moral hegemony, the effects of everyday activities (praxis) on thought and personality, and the necessity of consciousness of these processes before political change can occur are all based on Marx's analysis of class relations.

34. Other societies recognize more than two categories, but usually no more than three or four (Jacobs and Roberts 1989).

35. Carol Barkalow's book has a photograph of eleven first-year West Pointers in a math class, who are dressed in regulation pants, shirts, and sweaters, with short haircuts. The caption challenges the reader to locate the only woman in the room.

36. The taboo on males and females looking alike reflects the U.S. military's homophobia (Bérubé 1989). If you can't tell those with a penis from those with a vagina, how are you going to determine whether their sexual interest is heterosexual or homosexual unless you watch them having sexual relations?

37. See West and Zimmerman 1987 for a similar set of gender components.

38. On the "logic of practice," or how the experience of gender is embedded in the norms of everyday interaction and the structure of formal organizations, see Acker 1990; Bourdieu [1980] 1990; Connell 1987; Smith 1987a.

The Medical Construction of Gender: Case Management of Intersexed Infants

Suzanne J. Kessler

The birth of intersexed infants, babies born with genitals that are neither clearly male nor clearly female, has been documented throughout recorded time.[1] In the late twentieth century, medical technology has advanced to allow scientists to determine chromosomal and hormonal gender, which is typically taken to be the real, natural, biological gender, usually referred to as "sex."[2] Nevertheless, physicians who handle the cases of intersexed infants consider several factors beside biological ones in determining, assigning, and announcing the gender of a particular infant. Indeed, biological factors are often preempted in their deliberations by such cultural factors as the "correct" length of the penis and capacity of the vagina.

In the literature of intersexuality, issues such as announcing a baby's gender at the time of delivery, postdelivery discussions with the parents, and consultations with patients in adolescence are considered only peripherally to the central medical issues—etiology, diagnosis, and surgical procedures.[3] Yet members of medical teams have standard practices for managing intersexuality that rely ultimately on cultural understandings of gender. The process and guidelines by which decisions about gender (re)construction are made reveal the model for the social construction of

gender generally. Moreover, in the face of apparently incontrovertible evidence—infants born with some combination of "female" and "male" reproductive and sexual features—physicians hold an incorrigible belief in and insistence upon female and male as the only "natural" options. This paradox highlights and calls into question the idea that female and male are biological givens compelling a culture of two genders.

Ideally, to undertake an extensive study of intersexed infant case management, I would like to have had direct access to particular events, for example, the deliveries of intersexed infants and the initial discussions among physicians, between physicians and parents, between parents, and among parents and family and friends of intersexed infants. The rarity with which intersexuality occurs, however, made this unfeasible.[4] Alternatively, physicians who have had considerable experience in dealing with this condition were interviewed. I do not assume that their "talk" about how they manage such cases mirrors their "talk" in the situation, but their words do reveal that they have certain assumptions about gender and that they impose those assumptions via their medical decisions on the patients they treat.

Interviews were conducted with six medical experts (three women and three men) in the field of pediatric intersexuality: one clinical geneticist, three endocrinologists (two of them pediatric specialists), one psychoendocrinologist, and one urologist. All of them have had extensive clinical experience

Signs: Journal of Women in Culture and Society (1990) vol. 16, no. 1. © 1990 by the University of Chicago. All rights reserved.

with various intersexed syndromes, and some are internationally known researchers in the field of intersexuality. They were selected on the basis of their prominence in the field and their representation of four different medical centers in New York City. Although they know one another, they do not collaborate on research and are not part of the same management team. All were interviewed in the spring of 1985, in their offices, and interviews lasted between forty-five minutes and one hour. Unless further referenced, all quotations in this article are from these interviews.

THE THEORY OF INTERSEXUALITY MANAGEMENT

The sophistication of today's medical technology has led to an extensive compilation of various intersex categories based on the various causes of malformed genitals. The "true intersexed" condition, where both ovarian and testicular tissue are present in either the same gonad or in opposite gonads, accounts for fewer than 5 percent of all cases of ambiguous genitals.[5] More commonly, the infant has either ovaries or testes, but the genitals are ambiguous. If the infant has two ovaries, the condition is referred to as female pseudohermaphroditism. If the infant has two testes, the condition is referred to as male pseudohermaphroditism. There are numerous causes of both forms of pseudohermaphroditism, and although there are life-threatening aspects to some of these conditions, having ambiguous genitals per se is not harmful to the infant's health.[6] Although most cases of ambiguous genitals do not represent true intersex, in keeping with the contemporary literature, I will refer to all such cases as intersexed.

Current attitudes toward the intersex condition are primarily influenced by three factors. First are the extraordinary advancements in surgical techniques and endocrinology in the last decade. For example, female genitals can now be constructed to be indistinguishable in appearance from normal natural ones. Some abnormally small penises can be enlarged with the exogenous application of hormones, although surgical skills are not sufficiently advanced to construct a normal-looking and functioning penis out of other tissue.[7] Second, in the contemporary United States the influence of the feminist movement has called into question the valuation of women according to strictly reproductive functions, and the presence or absence of functional gonads is no longer the only or the definitive criterion for gender assignment. Third, contemporary psychological theorists have begun to focus on "gender identity" (one's sense of oneself as belonging to the female or male category) as distinct from "gender role" (cultural expectations of one's behavior as "appropriate" for a female or male).[8] The relevance of this new gender identity theory for rethinking cases of ambiguous genitals is that gender must be assigned as early as possible in order for gender identity to develop successfully. As a result of these three factors, intersexuality is now considered a treatable condition of the genitals, one that needs to be resolved expeditiously.

According to all of the specialists interviewed, management of intersexed cases is based upon the theory of gender proposed first by John Money, J.G. Hampson, and J.L. Hampson in 1955 and developed in 1972 by Money and Anke A. Ehrhardt, which argues that gender identity is changeable until approximately eighteen months of age.[9] "To use the Pygmalion allegory, one may begin with the same clay and fashion a god or a goddess."[10] The theory rests on satisfying several conditions: the experts must insure that the parents have no doubt about whether their child is male or female; the genitals must be made to match the assigned gender as soon as possible; gender-appropriate hormones must be administered at puberty; and intersexed children must be kept informed about their situation with age-appropriate explanations. If these conditions are met, the theory proposes, the intersexed child will develop a gender identity in accordance with the gender assignment (regardless of the chromosomal gender) and will not question her or his assignment and request reassignment at a later age.

Supportive evidence for Money and Ehrhardt's theory is based on only a handful of repeatedly cited cases, but it has been accepted because of the prestige of the theoreticians and its resonance with contemporary ideas about gender, children, psychology, and medicine. Gender and children are malleable; psychology and medicine are the tools used to transform them. This theory is so strongly endorsed that it has taken on the character of gospel. "I think we [physicians] have been raised in the Money theory," one endocrinologist said. Another claimed, "We always approach the problem in a similar way and it's been dictated, to a large extent, by the work of John Money and Anke Ehrhardt because they are the only people who have published, at least in medical literature, any data, any guidelines." It is provocative that this physician immediately followed this assertion with: "And I don't know how effective it really is." Contradictory data are rarely cited in reviews of the literature, were not mentioned by any of the physicians interviewed, and have not diminished these physicians' belief in the theory's validity.[11]

The doctors interviewed concur with the argument that gender be assigned immediately, decisively, and irreversibly, and that professional opinions be presented in a clear and unambiguous way. The psychoendocrinologist said that when doctors make a statement about the infant, they should "stick to it." The urologist said, "If you make

a statement that later has to be disclaimed or discredited, you've weakened your credibility." A gender assignment made decisively, unambiguously, and irrevocably contributes, I believe, to the general impression that the infant's true, natural "sex" has been discovered, and that something that was there all along has been found. It also serves to maintain the credibility of the medical profession, reassure the parents, and reflexively substantiate Money and Ehrhardt's theory.

Also according to the theory, if operative correction is necessary, it should take place as soon as possible. If the infant is assigned the male gender, the initial stage of penis repair is usually undertaken in the first year, and further surgery is completed before the child enters school. If the infant is assigned the female gender, vulva repair (including clitoral reduction) is usually begun by three months of age. Money suggests that if reduction of phallic tissue were delayed beyond the neonatal period, the infant would have traumatic memories of having been castrated.[12] Vaginoplasty, in those females having an adequate internal structure (e.g., the vaginal canal is near its expected location), is done between the ages of one and four years. Girls who require more complicated surgical procedures might not be surgically corrected until preadolescence.[13] The complete vaginal canal is typically constructed only when the body is fully grown, following pubertal feminization with estrogen, although more recently some specialists have claimed surgical success with vaginal construction in the early childhood years.[14] Although physicians speculate about the possible trauma of an early childhood "castration" memory, there is no corresponding concern that vaginal reconstructive surgery delayed beyond the neonatal period is traumatic.

Even though gender identity theory places the critical age limit for gender reassignment between eighteen months and two years, the physicians acknowledge that diagnosis, gender assignment, and genital reconstruction cannot be delayed for as long as two years, since a clear gender assignment and correctly formed genitals will determine the kind of interactions parents will have with the child.[15] The geneticist argued that when parents "change a diaper and see genitalia that don't mean much in terms of gender assignment, I think it prolongs the negative response to the baby. . . . If you have clitoral enlargement that is so extraordinary that the parents can't distinguish between male and female, it is sometimes helpful to reduce that somewhat so that the parent views the child as female." Another physician concurred: parents "need to go home and do their job as child rearers with it very clear whether it's a boy or a girl."

DIAGNOSIS

A premature gender announcement by an obstetrician, prior to a close examination of an infant's genitals, can be problematic. Money and his colleagues claim that the primary complications in case management of intersexed infants can be traced to mishandling by medical personnel untrained in sexology.[16] According to one of the pediatric endocrinologists interviewed, obstetricians improperly educated about intersexed conditions "don't examine the babies closely enough at birth and say things just by looking, before separating legs and looking at everything, and jump to conclusions, because 99 percent of the time it's correct. . . . People get upset, physicians I mean. And they say things that are inappropriate." For example, he said that an inexperienced obstetrician might blurt out, "I think you have a boy, or no, maybe you have a girl." Other inappropriate remarks a doctor might make in postdelivery consultation with the parents include, "You have a little boy, but he'll

never function as a little boy, so you better raise him as a little girl." As a result, said the pediatric endocrinologist, "the family comes away with the idea that they have a little boy, and that's what they wanted, and that's what they're going to get." In such cases parents sometimes insist that the child be raised male despite the physician's instructions to the contrary. "People have in mind certain things they've heard, that this is a boy, and they're not likely to forget that, or they're not likely to let it go easily." The urologist agreed that the first gender attribution is critical: "Once it's been announced, you've got a big problem on your hands." "One of the worst things is to allow [the parents] to go ahead and give a name and tell everyone, and it turns out the child has to be raised in the opposite sex."[17]

Physicians feel that the mismanagement of such cases requires careful remedying. The psychoendocrinologist asserted, "When I'm involved, I spend hours with the parents to explain to them what has happened and how a mistake like that could be made, *or not really a mistake but a different decision*" (my emphasis). One pediatric endocrinologist said, "[I] try to dissuade them from previous misconceptions, and say, 'Well, I know what they meant, but the way they said it confused you. This is, I think, a better way to think about it.'" These statements reveal physicians' efforts not only to protect parents from concluding that their child is neither male nor female but also to protect other physicians' decision-making processes. Case management involves perpetuating the notion that good medical decisions are based on interpretations of the infant's real "sex" rather than on cultural understandings of gender.

"Mismanagements" are less likely to occur in communities with major medical centers, where specialists are prepared to deal with intersexuality and a medical team (perhaps drawing physicians from more than one teaching hospital) is quickly assembled. The team typically consists of the original referring doctor (obstetrician or pediatrician), a pediatric endocrinologist, a pediatric surgeon (urologist or gynecologist), and a geneticist. In addition, a psychologist, psychiatrist, or psychoendocrinologist might play a role. If an infant is born with ambiguous genitals in a small community hospital, without the relevant specialists on staff, she or he is likely to be transferred to a hospital where diagnosis and treatment are available. Intersexed infants born in poor rural areas where there is less medical intervention might never be referred for genital reconstruction. Many of these children, like those born in earlier historical periods, will grow up and live through adulthood with the condition of genital ambiguity—somehow managing.

The diagnosis of intersexed conditions includes assessing the chromosomal sex and the syndrome that produced the genital ambiguity, and may include medical procedures such as cytologic screening; chromosomal analysis; assessing serum electrolytes; hormone, gonadotropin, and steroids evaluation; digital examination; and radiographic genitography.[18] In any intersexed condition, if the infant is determined to be a genetic female (having an XX chromosome makeup), then the treatment—genital surgery to reduce the phallus size—can proceed relatively quickly, satisfying what the doctors believe are psychological and cultural demands. For example, 21-hydroxylase deficiency, a form of female pseudohermaphroditism and one of the most common conditions, can be determined by a blood test within the first few days.

If, on the other hand, the infant is determined to have at least one Y chromosome, then surgery may be considerably delayed. A decision must be made whether to test the ability of the phallic tissue to respond to

(HCG) androgen treatment, which is intended to enlarge the microphallus enough to be a penis. The endocrinologist explained, "You do HCG testing and you find out if the male can make testosterone. . . . You can get those results back probably within three weeks. . . . You're sure the male is making testosterone—but can he respond to it? It can take three months of waiting to see whether the phallus responds." If the Y-chromosome infant cannot make testosterone or cannot respond to the testosterone it makes, the phallus will not develop, and the Y-chromosome infant is not considered to be a male after all.

Should the infant's phallus respond to the local application of testosterone or a brief course of intramuscular injections of low-potency androgen, the gender assignment problem is resolved, but possibly at some later cost, since the penis will not grow again at puberty when the rest of the body develops.[19] Money's case management philosophy assumes that while it may be difficult for an adult male to have a much smaller than average penis, it is very detrimental to the morale of the young boy to have a micropenis.[20] In the former case the male's manliness might be at stake, but in the latter case his essential maleness might be. Although the psychological consequences of these experiences have not been empirically documented, Money and his colleagues suggest that it is wise to avoid the problems of both the micropenis in childhood and the still undersized penis postpuberty by reassigning many of these infants to the female gender.[21] This approach suggests that for Money and his colleagues, chromosomes are less relevant in determining gender than penis size, and that, by implication, "male" is defined not by the genetic condition of having one Y and one X chromosome or by the production of sperm but by the aesthetic condition of having an appropriately sized penis.

The tests and procedures required for diagnosis (and, consequently, for gender assignment) can take several months.[22] Although physicians are anxious not to make a premature gender assignment, their language suggests that it is difficult for them to take a completely neutral position and think and speak only of phallic tissue that belongs to an infant whose gender has not yet been determined or decided. Comments such as "seeing whether the male can respond to testosterone" imply at least a tentative male gender assignment of an XY infant. The psychoendocrinologist's explanation to parents of their infant's treatment program also illustrates this implicit male gender assignment. "Clearly this baby has an underdeveloped phallus. But if the phallus responds to this treatment, we are fairly confident that surgical techniques and hormonal techniques will help this child to look like a boy. But we want to make absolutely sure and use some hormone treatments and see whether the tissue reacts." The mere fact that this doctor refers to the genitals as an "underdeveloped" phallus rather than an overdeveloped clitoris suggests that the infant has been judged to be, at least provisionally, a male. In the case of the undersized phallus, what is ambiguous is not whether this is a penis but whether it is "good enough" to remain one. If at the end of the treatment period the phallic tissue has not responded, what had been a potential penis (referred to in the medical literature as a "clitoropenis") is now considered an enlarged clitoris (or "penoclitoris"), and reconstructive surgery is planned as for the genetic female.

The time-consuming nature of intersex diagnosis and the assumption, based on gender identity theory, that gender should be assigned as soon as possible thus present physicians with difficult dilemmas. Medical personnel are committed to discovering the etiology of the condition in order to determine the best course of treatment, which takes time. Yet they feel an urgent need to provide an immediate assignment and genitals that look and function appropriately. An immediate assignment that will need to be retracted is more problematic than a delayed assignment, since reassignment carries with it an additional set of social complications. The endocrinologist interviewed commented: "We've come very far in that we can diagnose eventually, many of the conditions. But we haven't come far enough. . . . We can't do it early enough. . . . Very frequently a decision is made before all this information is available, simply because it takes so long to make the correct diagnosis. And you cannot let a child go indefinitely, not in this society you can't. . . . There's pressure on parents [for a decision] and the parents transmit that pressure onto physicians." A pediatric endocrinologist agreed: "At times you may need to operate before a diagnosis can be made. . . . In one case parents were told to wait on the announcement while the infant was treated to see if the phallus would grow when treated with androgens. After the first month passed and there was some growth, the parents said they gave it a boy's name. They could only wait a month."

Deliberating out loud on the judiciousness of making parents wait for assignment decisions, the endocrinologist asked rhetorically, "Why do we do all these tests if in the end we're going to make the decision simply on the basis of the appearance of the genitalia?" This question suggests that the principles underlying physicians' decisions are cultural rather than biological, based on parental reaction and the medical team's perception of the infant's societal adjustment prospects given the way her/his genitals look or could be made to look. Moreover, as long as the decision rests largely on the criterion of genital appearance, and male is defined as having a "good-sized" penis, more infants will be assigned to the female gender than to the male.

THE WAITING PERIOD: DEALING WITH AMBIGUITY

During the period of ambiguity between birth and assignment, physicians not only must evaluate the infant's prospects to be a good male but also must manage parents' uncertainty about a genderless child. Physicians advise that parents postpone announcing the gender of the infant until a gender has been explicitly assigned. They believe that parents should not feel compelled to tell other people. The clinical geneticist interviewed said that physicians "basically encourage [parents] to treat [the infant] as neuter." One of the pediatric endocrinologists reported that in France parents confronted with this dilemma sometimes give the infant a neuter name, such as Claude or Jean. The psychoendocrinologist concurred: "If you have a truly borderline situation, and you want to make it dependent on the hormone treatment . . . then the parents are . . . told, 'Try not to make a decision. Refer to the baby as "baby." Don't think in terms of boy or girl.'" Yet, when asked whether this is a reasonable request to make of parents in our society, the physician answered: "I don't think so. I think parents can't do it."

New York State requires that a birth certificate be filled out within forty-eight hours of delivery, but the certificate need not be filed with the state for thirty days. The geneticist tells parents to insert "child of" instead of a name. In one case, parents filled out two birth registration forms, one for each gender, and they refused to sign either until a final gender assignment had been made.[23] One of the pediatric endocrinologists claimed, "I heard a story; I don't

know if it's true or not. There were parents of a hermaphroditic infant who told everyone they had twins, one of each gender. When the gender was determined, they said the other had died."

The geneticist explained that when directly asked by parents what to tell others about the gender of the infant, she says, "Why don't you just tell them that the baby is having problems and as soon as the problems are resolved we'll get back to you." A pediatric endocrinologist echoes this suggestion in advising parents to say, "Until the problem is solved [we] would really prefer not to discuss any of the details." According to the urologist, "If [the gender] isn't announced people may mutter about it and may grumble about it, but they haven't got anything to get their teeth into and make trouble over for the child, or the parents, or whatever." In short, parents are asked to sidestep the infant's gender rather than admit that the gender is unknown, thereby collaborating in a web of white lies, ellipses, and mystifications.[24]

Even while physicians teach the parents how to deal with others who will not find the infant's condition comprehensible or acceptable, physicians must also make the condition comprehensible and acceptable to the parents, normalizing the intersexed condition for them. In doing so they help the parents consider the infant's condition in the most positive way. There are four key aspects to this "normalizing" process.

First, physicians teach parents normal fetal development and explain that all fetuses have the potential to be male or female. One of the endocrinologists explains, "In the absence of maleness you have femaleness. . . . It's really the basic design. The other [intersex] is really a variation on a theme." This explanation presents the intersex condition as a natural phase of every fetal development. Another endocrinologist "like[s] to show picture[s] to them and explain that at a certain point in development males and females look alike and then diverge for such and such reason." The professional literature suggests that doctors use diagrams that illustrate "nature's principle of using the same anlagen to produce the external genital parts of the male and female."[25]

Second, physicians stress the normalcy of the infant in other aspects. For example, the geneticist tells parents, "The baby is healthy, but there was a problem in the way the baby was developing." The endocrinologist says the infant has "a mild defect, just like anything could be considered a birth defect, a mole or a hemangioma." This language not only eases the blow to the parents but also redirects their attention. Terms like "hermaphrodite" or "abnormal" are not used. The urologist said that he advised parents "about the generalization of sticking to the good things and not confusing people with something that is unnecessary."

Third, physicians (at least initially) imply that it is not the gender of the child that is ambiguous but the genitals. They talk about "undeveloped," "maldeveloped," or "unfinished" organs. From a number of the physicians interviewed came the following explanations: "At a point in time the development proceeded in a different way, and sometimes the development isn't complete and we may have some trouble . . . in determining what the *actual* sex is. And so we have to do a blood test to help us" (my emphasis); "The baby may be a female, which you would know after the buccal smear, but you can't prove it yet. If so, then it's a normal female with a different appearance. This can be surgically corrected"; "The gender of your child isn't apparent to us at the moment"; "While this looks like a small penis, it's actually a large clitoris. And what we're going to do is put it back in its proper

position and reduce the size of the tip of it enough so it doesn't look funny, so it looks right." Money and his colleagues report a case in which parents were advised to tell their friends that the reason their infant's gender was reannounced from male to female is that "the baby was . . . 'closed up down there' . . . when the closed skin was divided, the female organs were revealed, and the baby discovered to be, *in fact*, a girl" (emphasis mine). It was mistakenly assumed to be a male at first because "there was an excess of skin on the clitoris."[26]

The message in these examples is that the trouble lies in the doctor's ability to determine the gender, not in the baby's gender per se. The real gender will presumably be determined/proven by testing, and the "bad" genitals (which are confusing the situation for everyone) will be "repaired." The emphasis is not on the doctors creating gender but in their completing the genitals. Physicians say that they "reconstruct" the genitals rather than "construct" them. The surgeons reconstitute from remaining parts what should have been there all along. The fact that gender in an infant is "reannounced" rather than "reassigned" suggests that the first announcement was a mistake because the announcer was confused by the genitals. The gender always was what it is now seen to be.[27]

Finally, physicians tell parents that social factors are more important in gender development than biological ones, even though they are searching for biological causes. In essence, the physicians teach the parents Money and Ehrhardt's theory of gender development.[28] In doing so, they shift the emphasis from the discovery of biological factors that are a sign of the "real" gender to providing the appropriate social conditions to produce the "real" gender. What remains unsaid is the apparent contradiction in the notion that a "real" or "natural" gender can be, or needs to be, produced artificially. The physician/parent discussions make it clear to family members that gender is not a biological given (even though, of course, their own procedures for diagnosis assume that it is), and that gender is fluid. The psychoendocrinologist paraphrased an explanation to parents thus: "It will depend, ultimately, on how everybody treats your child and how your child is looking as a person. . . . I can with confidence tell them that generally gender [identity] clearly agrees with the assignment." Similarly, a pediatric endocrinologist explained: "[I] try to impress upon them that there's an enormous amount of clinical data to support the fact that if you sex-reverse an infant . . . the majority of the time the alternative gender identity is commensurate with the socialization, the way that they're raised, and how people view them, and that seems to be the most critical."

The implication of these comments is that gender identity (of all children, not just those born with ambiguous genitals) is determined primarily by social factors, that the parents and community always construct the child's gender. In the case of intersexed infants, the physicians merely provide the right genitals to go along with the socialization. Of course, at normal births, when the infant's genitals are unambiguous, the parents are not told that the child's gender is ultimately up to socialization. In those cases, doctors do treat gender as a biological given.

SOCIAL FACTORS IN DECISION MAKING

Most of the physicians interviewed claimed that personal convictions of doctors ought to play no role in the decision-making process. The psychoendocrinologist explained: "I think the most critical factors [are] what is the possibility that this child will grow up with genitals which look like that of the assigned gender and which will ultimately function according to gender . . . That's why it's so important that it's a well-established team, because [personal convictions] can't really enter into it. It has to be what is surgically and endocrinologically possible for that baby to be able to make it . . . It's really much more within medical criteria. I don't think many social factors enter into it." While this doctor eschews the importance of social factors in gender assignment, she argues forcefully that social factors are extremely important in the development of gender identity. Indeed, she implies that social factors primarily enter the picture once the infant leaves the hospital.

In fact, doctors make decisions about gender on the basis of shared cultural values that are unstated, perhaps even unconscious, and therefore considered objective rather than subjective. Money states the fundamental rule for gender assignment: "Never assign a baby to be reared, and to surgical and hormonal therapy, as a boy, unless the phallic structure, hypospadiac or otherwise, is neonatally of at least the same caliber as that of same-aged males with small-average penises."[29] Elsewhere, he and his colleagues provide specific measurements for what qualifies as a micropenis: "A penis is, by convention, designated as a micropenis when at birth its dimensions are three or more standard deviations below the mean. . . . When it is correspondingly reduced in diameter with corpora that are vestigial . . . it unquestionably qualifies as a micropenis."[30] A pediatric endocrinologist claimed that although "the [size of the] phallus is not the deciding factor . . . if the phallus is less than 2 centimeters long at birth and won't respond to androgen treatments, then it's made into a female."

These guidelines are clear, but they focus on only one physical feature, one that is distinctly imbued with cultural meaning.

This becomes especially apparent in the case of an XX infant with normal female reproductive gonads and a perfect penis. Would the size and shape of the penis, in this case, be the deciding factor in assigning the infant "male," or would the perfect penis be surgically destroyed and female genitals created? Money notes that this dilemma would be complicated by the anticipated reaction of the parents to seeing "their apparent son lose his penis."[31] Other researchers concur that parents are likely to want to raise a child with a normal-shaped penis (regardless of size) as "male," particularly if the scrotal area looks normal and if the parents have had no experience with intersexuality.[32] Elsewhere Money argues in favor of not neonatally amputating the penis of XX infants, since fetal masculinization of brain structures would predispose them "almost invariably [to] develop behaviorally as tomboys, even when reared as girls."[33] This reasoning implies, first, that tomboyish behavior in girls is bad and should be avoided; and, second, that it is preferable to remove the internal female organs, implant prosthetic testes, and regulate the "boy's" hormones for his entire life than to overlook or disregard the perfection of the penis.[34]

The ultimate proof to these physicians that they intervened appropriately and gave the intersexed infant the correct gender assignment is that the reconstructed genitals look normal and function normally once the patient reaches adulthood. The vulva, labia, and clitoris should appear ordinary to the woman and her partner(s), and the vagina should be able to receive a normal-sized penis. Similarly, the man and his partner(s) should feel that his penis (even if somewhat smaller than the norm) looks and functions in an unremarkable way. Although there is no reported data on how much emphasis the intersexed person, him- or herself, places upon genital appearance and functioning,

the physicians are absolutely clear about what they believe is important. The clinical geneticist said, "If you have . . . a seventeen-year-old young lady who has gotten hormone therapy and has breast development and pubic hair and no vaginal opening, I can't even entertain the notion that this young lady wouldn't want to have corrective surgery." The urologist summarized his criteria: "Happiness is the biggest factor. Anatomy is part of happiness." Money states, "The primary deficit [of not having a sufficient penis]—and destroyer of morale—lies in being unable to satisfy the partner."[35] Another team of clinicians reveals their phallocentrism, arguing that the most serious mistake in gender assignment is to create "an individual unable to engage in genital [heterosexual] sex."[36]

The equation of gender with genitals could only have emerged in an age when medical science can create credible-appearing and functioning genitals, and an emphasis on the good phallus above all else could only have emerged in a culture that has rigid aesthetic and performance criteria for what constitutes maleness. The formulation "good penis equals male; absence of good penis equals female" is treated in the literature and by the physicians interviewed as an objective criterion, operative in all cases. There is a striking lack of attention to the size and shape requirements of the female genitals, other than that the vagina be able to receive a penis.[37]

In the late nineteenth century when women's reproductive function was culturally designated as their essential characteristic, the presence or absence of ovaries (whether or not they were fertile) was held to be the ultimate criterion of gender assignment for hermaphrodites. The urologist interviewed recalled a case as late as the 1950s of a male child reassigned to "female" at the age of four or five because ovaries had been discovered. Nevertheless, doctors today, schooled in the etiology and treatment of the various intersex syndromes, view decisions based primarily on gonads as wrong, although, they complain, the conviction that the gonads are the ultimate criterion "still dictates the decisions of the uneducated and uninformed."[38] Presumably, the educated and informed now know that decisions based primarily on phallic size, shape, and sexual capacity are right.

While the prospect of constructing good genitals is the primary consideration in physicians' gender assignments, another extramedical factor was repeatedly cited by the six physicians interviewed—the specialty of the attending physician. Although generally intersexed infants are treated by teams of specialists, only the person who coordinates the team is actually responsible for the case. This person, acknowledged by the other physicians as having chief responsibility, acts as spokesperson to the parents. Although all of the physicians claimed that these medical teams work smoothly with few discrepancies of opinion, several of them mentioned decision-making orientations that are grounded in particular medical specializations. One endocrinologist stated, "The easiest route to take, where there is ever any question . . . is to raise the child as female. . . . In this country that is usual if the infant falls into the hands of a pediatric endocrinologist. . . . If the decision is made by the urologists, who are mostly males. . . . they're always opting, because they do the surgery, they're always feeling they can correct anything." Another endocrinologist concurred: "[Most urologists] don't think in terms of dynamic processes. They're interested in fixing pipes and lengthening pipes, and not dealing with hormonal, and certainly not psychological issues. . . . 'What can I do with what I've got.'" Urologists were defended by the clinical geneticist: "Surgeons here, now I can't speak for elsewhere, they

don't get into a situation where the child is a year old and they can't make anything." Whether or not urologists "like to make boys," as one endocrinologist claimed, the following example from a urologist who was interviewed explicitly links a cultural interpretation of masculinity to the medical treatment plan. The case involved an adolescent who had been assigned the female gender at birth but was developing some male pubertal signs and wanted to be a boy. "He was ill-equipped," said the urologist, "yet we made a very respectable male out of him. He now owns a huge construction business—those big cranes that put stuff up on the building."

POSTINFANCY CASE MANAGEMENT

After the infant's gender has been assigned, parents generally latch onto the assignment as the solution to the problem—and it is. The physician as detective has collected the evidence, as lawyer has presented the case, and as judge has rendered a verdict. Although most of the interviewees claimed that the parents are equal participants in the whole process, they gave no instances of parental participation prior to the gender assignment.[39] After the physicians assign the infant's gender, the parents are encouraged to establish the credibility of that gender publicly by, for example, giving a detailed medical explanation to a leader in their community, such as a physician or pastor, who will explain the situation to curious casual acquaintances. Money argues that "medical terminology has a special layman's magic in such a context; it is final and authoritative and closes the issue." He also recommends that eventually the mother "settle [the] argument once and for all among her women friends by allowing some of them to see the baby's reconstructed genitalia."[40] Apparently, the powerful influence of normal-looking genitals helps overcome a history of ambiguous gender.

Some of the same issues that arise in assigning gender recur some years later when, at adolescence, the child may be referred to a physician for counseling.[41] The physician then tells the adolescent many of the same things his or her parents had been told years before, with the same language. Terms like "abnormal," "disorder," "disease," and "hermaphroditism" are avoided; the condition is normalized, and the child's gender is treated as unproblematic. One clinician explains to his patients that sex organs are different in appearance for each person, not just those who are intersexed. Furthermore, he tells the girls "that while most women menstruate, not all do . . . that conception is only one of a number of ways to become a parent; [and] that today some individuals are choosing not to become parents."[42] The clinical geneticist tells a typical female patient: "You are female. Female is not determined by your genes. Lots of other things determine being a woman. And you are a woman but you won't be able to have babies."

A case reported by one of the pediatric endocrinologists involving an adolescent female with androgen insensitivity provides an intriguing insight into the postinfancy gender-management process. She was told at the age of fourteen "that her ovaries weren't normal and had been removed. That's why she needed pills to look normal. . . . I wanted to convince her of her femininity. Then I told her she could marry and have normal sexual relations . . . [her] uterus won't develop but [she] could adopt children." The urologist interviewed was asked to comment on this handling of the counseling. "It sounds like a very good solution to it. He's stating the truth, and if you don't state the truth . . . then you're in trouble later." This is a strange version of "the truth," however, since the adolescent was chromosomally XY and was born with normal testes that

produced normal quantities of androgen. There were no existing ovaries or uterus to be abnormal. Another pediatric endocrinologist, in commenting on the management of this case, hedged the issue by saying that he would have used a generic term like "the gonads." A third endocrinologist said she would say that the uterus had never formed.

Technically these physicians are lying when, for example, they explain to an adolescent XY female with an intersexed history that her "ovaries . . . had to be removed because they were unhealthy or were producing 'the wrong balance of hormones.' "[43] We can presume that these lies are told in the service of what the physicians consider a greater good—keeping individual/concrete genders as clear and uncontaminated as the notions of female and male are in the abstract. The clinician suggests that with some female patients it eventually may be possible to talk to them "about their gonads having some structures and features that are testicularlike."[44] This call for honesty might be based at least partly on the possibility of the child's discovering his or her chromosomal sex inadvertently from a buccal smear taken in a high school biology class. Today's litigious climate is possibly another encouragement.

In sum, the adolescent is typically told that certain internal organs did not form because of an endocrinological defect, not because those organs could never have developed in someone with her or his sex chromosomes. The topic of chromosomes is skirted. There are no published studies on how these adolescents experience their condition and their treatment by doctors. An endocrinologist interviewed mentioned that her adolescent patients rarely ask specifically what is wrong with them, suggesting that they are accomplices in this evasion. In spite of the "truth" having been evaded, the clinician's impression is that "their gender identities and general senses of well-being and self-esteem appear not to have suffered."[45]

CONCLUSION

Physicians conduct careful examinations of intersexed infants' genitals and perform intricate laboratory procedures. They are interpreters of the body, trained and committed to uncovering the "actual" gender obscured by ambiguous genitals. Yet they also have considerable leeway in assigning gender, and their decisions are influenced by cultural as well as medical factors. What is the relationship between the physician as discoverer and the physician as determiner of gender? Where is the relative emphasis placed in discussions with parents and adolescents and in the consciousness of physicians? It is misleading to characterize the doctors whose words are provided here as presenting themselves publicly to the parents as discoverers of the infant's real gender but privately acknowledging that the infant has no real gender other than the one being determined or constructed by the medical professionals. They are not hypocritical. It is also misleading to claim that physicians' focus shifts from discovery to determination over the course of treatment: first the doctors regard the infant's gender as an unknown but discoverable reality; then the doctors relinquish their attempts to find the real gender and treat the infant's gender as something they must construct. They are not medically incompetent or deficient. Instead, I am arguing that the peculiar balance of discovery and determination throughout treatment permits physicians to handle very problematic cases of gender in the most unproblematic of ways.

This balance relies fundamentally on a particular conception of the "natural."[46] Although the deformity of intersexed genitals would be immutable were it not for medical interference, physicians do not consider it natural. Instead they think of, and speak of, the surgical/hormonal alteration of such deformities as natural because such intervention returns the body to what it "ought to have been" if events had taken their typical course. The non-normative is converted into the normative, and the normative state is considered natural.[47] The genital ambiguity is remedied to conform to a "natural," that is, culturally indisputable, gender dichotomy. Sherry Ortner's claim that the culture/nature distinction is itself a construction—a product of culture—is relevant here. Language and imagery help create and maintain a specific view of what is natural about the two genders and, I would argue, about the very idea of gender—that it consists of two exclusive types: female and male.[48] The belief that gender consists of two exclusive types is maintained and perpetuated by the medical community in the face of incontrovertible physical evidence that this is not mandated by biology.

The lay conception of human anatomy and physiology assumes a concordance among clearly dimorphic gender markers—chromosomes, genitals, gonads, hormones—but physicians understand that concordance and dimorphism do not always exist. Their understanding of biology's complexity, however, does not inform their understanding of gender's complexity. In order for intersexuality to be managed differently than it currently is, physicians would have to take seriously Money's assertion that it is a misrepresentation of epistemology to consider any cell in the body authentically male or female.[49] If authenticity for gender resides not in a discoverable nature but in someone's proclamation, then the power to proclaim something else is available. If physicians recognized that implicit in their management of gender is the notion that finally, and always, people construct gender as well as the social systems that are grounded in gender-based concepts, the possibilities for real societal transformations would be unlimited. Unfortunately, neither in their representations to the families of the intersexed nor among themselves do the physicians interviewed for this study draw such far-reaching implications from their work. Their "understanding" that particular genders are medically (re)constructed in these cases does not lead them to see that gender is always constructed. Accepting genital ambiguity as a natural option would require that physicians also acknowledge that genital ambiguity is "corrected" not because it is threatening to the infant's life but because it is threatening to the infant's culture.

Rather than admit to their role in perpetuating gender, physicians "psychologize" the issue by talking about the parents' anxiety and humiliation in being confronted with an anomalous infant. The physicians talk as though they have no choice but to respond to the parents' pressure for a resolution of psychological discomfort, and as though they have no choice but to use medical technology in the service of a two-gender culture. Neither the psychology nor the technology is doubted, since both shield physicians from responsibility. Indeed, for the most part, neither physicians nor parents emerge from the experience of intersex case management with a greater understanding of the social construction of gender. Society's accountability, like their own, is masked by the assumption that gender is a given. Thus, cases of intersexuality, instead of illustrating nature's failure to ordain gender in these isolated "unfortunate" instances, illustrate physicians' and Western society's failure of imagination—the failure to imagine that each of these management decisions is a moment when a specific instance of biological "sex" is transformed into a culturally constructed gender.

Division of Natural Sciences
State University of New York College at Purchase

NOTES

I want to thank my student Jane Weider for skillfully conducting and transcribing the interviews for this article.

1. For historical reviews of the intersexed person in ancient Greek and Roman periods, see Leslie Fiedler, *Freaks: Myths and Images of the Second Self* (New York: Simon & Schuster, 1978); Vern Bullough, *Sexual Variance in Society and History* (New York: Wiley, 1976). For the Middle Ages and Renaissance, see Michel Foucault, *History of Sexuality* (New York: Pantheon, 1980). For the eighteenth and nineteenth centuries, see Michel Foucault, *Herculine Barbin* (New York: Pantheon, 1978); for the early twentieth century, see Havelock Ellis, *Studies in the Psychology of Sex* (New York: Random House, 1942).

2. Suzanne J. Kessler and Wendy McKenna, *Gender: An Ethnomethodological Approach* (1978; reprint, Chicago: University of Chicago Press, 1985).

3. See, e.g., M. Bolkenius, R. Daum, and E. Heinrich, "Pediatric Surgical Principles in the Management of Children with Intersex," *Progressive Pediatric Surgery* 17 (1984): 33–38; Kenneth I. Glassberg, "Gender Assignment in Newborn Male Pseudohermaphrodites," *Urologic Clinics of North America* 7 (June 1980): 409-21; and Peter A. Lee et al., "Micropenis. I. Criteria, Etiologies and Classification," *Johns Hopkins Medical Journal* 146 (1980): 156–63.

4. It is impossible to get accurate statistics on the frequency of intersexuality. Chromosomal abnormalities (like XOXX or XXXY) are registered, but those conditions do not always imply ambiguous genitals, and most cases of ambiguous genitals do not involve chromosomal abnormalities. None of the physicians interviewed for this study would venture a guess on frequency rates, but all agreed that intersexuality is rare. One physician suggested that the average obstetrician may see only two cases in twenty years. Another estimated that a specialist may see only one a year, or possibly as many as five a year.

5. Mariano Castro-Magana, Moris Angulo, and Platon J. Collipp, "Management of the Child with Ambiguous Genitalia," *Medical Aspects of Human Sexuality* 18 (April 1984): 172–88.

6. For example, infants whose intersexuality is caused by congenital adrenal hyperplasia can develop severe electrolyte disturbances unless the condition is controlled by cortisone treatments. Intersexed infants whose condition is caused by androgen insensitivity are in danger of malignant degeneration of the testes unless they are removed. For a complete catalog of clinical syndromes related to the intersexed condition, see Arye Lev-Ran, "Sex Reversal as Related to Clinical Syndromes in Human Beings," in *Handbook of Sexology II: Genetics, Hormones and Behavior,* ed. John Money and H. Musaph (New York: Elsevier, 1978),157–73.

7. Much of the surgical experimentation in this area has been accomplished by urologists who are try-

ing to create penises for female-to-male transsexuals. Although there have been some advancements in recent years in the ability to create a "reasonable-looking" penis from tissue taken elsewhere on the body, the complicated requirements of the organ (both urinary and sexual functioning) have posed surgical problems. It may be, however, that the concerns of the urologists are not identical to the concerns of the patients. While data are not yet available from the intersexed, we know that female-to-male transsexuals place greater emphasis on the "public" requirements of the penis (e.g., being able to look normal while standing at the urinal or wearing a bathing suit) than on its functional requirements (e.g., being able to carry urine or achieve an erection) (Kessler and McKenna, 128–32). As surgical techniques improve, female-to-male transsexuals (and intersexed males) might increase their demands for organs that look and function better.

8. Historically, psychology has tended to blur the distinction between the two by equating a person's acceptance of her or his genitals with gender role and ignoring gender identity. For example, Freudian theory posited that if one had a penis and accepted its reality, then masculine gender role behavior would naturally follow (Sigmund Freud, "Some Psychical Consequences of the Anatomical Distinctions between the Sexes" [1925], vol. 18 of *The Complete Psychological Works*, ed. and trans. J. Strachey [New York: Norton, 1976]).

9. Almost all of the published literature on intersexed infant case management has been written or cowritten by one researcher, John Money, professor of medical psychology and professor of pediatrics, emeritus, at the Johns Hopkins University and Hospital, where he is director of the Psychohormonal Research Unit. Even the publications that are produced independently of Money reference him and reiterate his management philosophy. Although only one of the physicians interviewed publishes with Money, all of them essentially concur with his views and give the impression of a consensus that is rarely encountered in science. The one physician who raised some questions about Money's philosophy and the gender theory on which it is based has extensive experience with intersexuality in a nonindustrialized culture where the infant is managed differently with no apparent harm to gender development. Even though psychologists fiercely argue issues of gender identity and gender role development, doctors who treat intersexed infants seem untouched by these debates. There are no renegade voices either from within the medical establishment or, thus far, from outside. Why Money has been so single-handedly influential in promoting his ideas about gender is a question worthy of a separate substantial analysis. His management philosophy is conveyed in the following sources: John Money, J.G. Hampson, and J.L. Hampson, "Hermaphroditism: Recommendations concerning Assignment of Sex, Change of Sex, and Psychologic Management," *Bulletin of the*

Johns Hopkins Hospital 97 (1955): 284–300; John Money, Reynolds Potter, and Clarice S. Stoll, "Sex Reannouncement in Hereditary Sex Deformity: Psychology and Sociology of Habilitation," *Social Science and Medicine* 3 (1969): 207–16; John Money and Anke A. Ehrhardt, *Man and Woman, Boy and Girl* (Baltimore: Johns Hopkins University Press, 1972); John Money, "Psychologic Consideration of Sex Assignment in Intersexuality," *Clinics in Plastic Surgery* 1 (April 1974): 215–22, "Psychological Counseling: Hermaphroditism," in *Endocrine and Genetic Diseases of Childhood and Adolescence*, ed. L.I. Gardner (Philadelphia: Saunders, 1975): 609–18, and "Birth Defect of the Sex Organs: Telling the Parents and the Patient," *British Journal of Sexual Medicine* 10 (March 1983): 14; John Money et al., "Micropenis, Family Mental Health, and Neonatal Management: A Report on Fourteen Patients Reared as Girls," *Journal of Preventive Psychiatry* 1, no. 1 (1981): 17–27.

10. Money and Ehrhardt, 152.

11. Contradictory data are presented in Milton Diamond, "Sexual Identity, Monozygotic Twins Reared in Discordant Sex Roles and a BBC Follow-up," *Archives of Sexual Behavior* 11, no. 2 (1982): 181–86.

12. Money, "Psychologic Consideration of Sex Assignment in Intersexuality."

13. Castro-Magana, Angulo, and Collipp (n. 5).

14. Victor Braren et al., "True Hermaphroditism: A Rational Approach to Diagnosis and Treatment," *Urology* 15 (June 1980): 569–74.

15. Studies of normal newborns have shown that from the moment of birth the parent responds to the infant based on the infant's gender. Jeffrey Rubin, F.J. Provenzano, and Z. Luria, "The Eye of the Beholder: Parents' Views on Sex of Newborns," *American Journal of Orthopsychiatry* 44, no. 4 (1974): 512–19.

16. Money et al. (n. 9 above).

17. There is evidence from other kinds of sources that once a gender attribution is made, all further information buttresses that attribution, and only the most contradictory new information will cause the original gender attribution to be questioned. See, e.g., Kessler and McKenna (n. 2).

18. Castro-Magana, Angulo, and Collipp (n. 5).

19. Money, "Psychological Consideration of Sex Assignment in Intersexuality" (n. 9 above).

20. Technically, the term "micropenis" should be reserved for an exceptionally small but well-formed structure. A small, malformed "penis" should be referred to as a "microphallus" (Lee et al. [n. 3 above]).

21. Money et al., 26. A different view is argued by another leading gender identity theorist: "When a little boy (with an imperfect penis) knows he is a male, he creates a penis that functions symbolically the same as those of boys with normal penises" (Robert J. Stoller, *Sex and Gender* [New York: Aronson, 1968], 1:49).

22. W. Ch. Hecker, "Operative Correction of Intersexual Genitals in Children," *Pediatric Surgery* 17 (1984): 21–31.

23. Elizabeth Bing and Esselyn Rudikoff, "Divergent ways of Parental Coping with Hermaphrodite Children," *Medical Aspects of Human Sexuality* (December 1970, 73–88.

24. These evasions must have many ramifications in everyday social interactions between parents and family and friends. How people "fill in" the uncertainty so that interactions remain relatively normal is an interesting issue that warrants further study. Indeed, the whole issue of parental reaction is worthy of analysis. One of the pediatric endocrinologists interviewed acknowledged that the published literature discusses intersex management only from the physicians' point of view. He asks, "How [do parents] experience what they're told; and what [do] they remember . . . and carry with them?" One published exception to this neglect of the parents' perspective is a case study comparing two couples' different coping strategies. The first couple, although initially distressed, handled the traumatic event by regarding the abnormality as an act of God. The second couple, more educated and less religious, put their faith in medical science and expressed a need to fully understand the biochemistry of the defect (ibid.).

25. Tom Mazur, "Ambiguous Genitalia: Detection and Counseling," *Pediatric Nursing* 9 (November/December 1983): 417–31; Money, "Psychologic Consideration of Sex Assignment in Intersexuality" (n. 9 above), 218.

26. Money, Potter, and Stoll (n. 9), 211.

27. The term "reassignment" is more commonly used to describe the gender changes of those who are cognizant of their earlier gender, e.g., transsexuals—people whose gender itself was a mistake.

28. Although Money and Ehrhardt's socialization theory is uncontested by the physicians who treat intersexuality and is presented to parents as a matter of fact, there is actually much debate among psychologists about the effect of prenatal hormones on brain structure and ultimately on gender role behavior and even on gender identity. The physicians interviewed agreed that the animal evidence for prenatal brain organization is compelling but that there is no evidence in humans that prenatal hormones have an inviolate or unilateral effect. If there is any effect of prenatal exposure to androgen, they believe it can easily be overcome and modified by psychosocial factors. It is this latter position that is communicated to the parents, not the controversy in the field. For an argument favoring prenatally organized gender differences in the brain, see Milton Diamond, "Human Sexual Development: Biological Foundations for Social Development," in *Human Sexuality in Four Perspectives*, ed. Frank A. Beach (Baltimore: Johns Hopkins University Press, 1976), 22–61; for a critique of that position, see Ruth

Bleier, *Science and Gender: A Critique of Biology and Its Theories on Women* (New York: Pergamon, 1984).

29. Money, "Psychological Counseling: Hermaphroditism" (n. 9 above), 610.

30. Money et al. (n. 9 above), 18.

31. John Money, "Hermaphroditism and Pseudohermaphroditism," in *Gynecologic Endocrinology*, ed. Jay J. Gold (New York: Hoeber, 1968),449–64, esp. 460.

32. Mojtaba Besheshti et al., "Gender Assignment in Male Pseudohermaphrodite Children," *Urology* (December 1983): 604–7. Of course, if the penis looked normal and the empty scrotum were overlooked, it might not be discovered until puberty that the male child was XX, with a female internal structure.

33. John Money, "Psychologic Consideration of Sex Assignment in Intersexuality" (n. 9 above), 216.

34. Weighing the probability of achieving a perfect penis against the probable trauma such procedures might involve is another social factor in decision making. According to an endocrinologist interviewed, if it seemed that an XY infant with an inadequate penis would require as many as ten genital operations over a six-year period in order to have an adequate penis, the infant would be assigned the female gender. In this case, the endocrinologist's practical and compassionate concern would override purely genital criteria.

35. Money, "Psychologic Consideration of Sex Assignment in Intersexuality," 217.

36. Castro-Magana, Angulo, and Collipp (n. 5 above), 180.

37. It is unclear how much of this bias is the result of a general, cultural devaluation of the female and how much the result of physicians' greater facility in constructing aesthetically correct and sexually functional female genitals.

38. Money, "Psychologic Consideration of Sex Assignment in Intersexuality," 215. Remnants of this anachronistic view can still be found, however, when doctors justify the removal of contradictory gonads on the grounds that they are typically sterile or at risk for malignancy (l. Dewhurst and D. B. Grant, "Intersex Problems," *Archives of Disease in Childhood* 59 [July–December 1984]: 1191–94). Presumably, if the gonads were functional and healthy their removal would provide an ethical dilemma for at least some medical professionals.

39. Although one set of authors argued that the views of the parents on the most appropriate gender for their child must be taken into account (Dewhurst and Grant, 1192), the physicians interviewed denied direct knowledge of this kind of participation. They claimed that they personally had encountered few, if any, cases of parents who insisted on their child's being assigned a particular gender. Yet each had heard about cases where a family's ethnicity or religious background bi-

ased them toward males. None of the physicians recalled whether this preference for male offspring
meant the parents wanted a male regardless of the "inadequacy" of the penis, or whether it meant that the
parents would have greater difficulty adjusting to a less-
than-perfect male than with a "normal" female.

40. Money, "Psychological Counseling: Hermaphroditism" (n. 9 above), 613.

41. As with the literature on infancy, most of the
published material on adolescents is on surgical and
hormonal management rather than on social management. See, e.g., Joel J. Roslyn, Eric W. Fonkalsrud, and
Barbara Lippe, "Intersex Disorders in Adolescents and
Adults," *American Journal of Surgery* 146 (July 1983):
138–44.

42. Mazur (n. 25 above), 421.

43. Dewhurst and Grant, 1193.

44. Mazur, 422.

45. Ibid.

46. For an extended discussion of different ways
of conceptualizing "natural," see Richard W. Smith,
"What Kind of Sex Is Natural?" in *The Frontiers of Sex Research*, ed. Vern Bullough (Buffalo: Prometheus, 1979),
103–11.

47. This supports sociologist Harold Garfinkel's
argument that we treat routine events as our due as social members and that we treat gender, like all normal
forms, as a moral imperative. It is no wonder, then,
that physicians conceptualize what they are doing as
natural and unquestionably "right" (Harold Garfinkel,
Studies in Ethnomethodology [Englewood Cliffs, N.J.:
Prentice Hall, 1967]).

48. Sherry B. Ortner, "Is Female to Male as Nature Is to Culture?" in *Woman, Culture, and Society,* ed.
Michelle Zimbalist Rosaldo and Louise Lamphere
(Stanford, Calif.: Stanford University Press, 1974),
67–87.

49. Money, "Psychological Counseling: Hermaphroditism" (n. 9 above), 618.

Does Size Matter?

Susan Bordo

The humongous penis, like the idealized female body, is a cultural fantasy. It exists in the flesh; some men—like those featured in the photos and want ads of *Playgirl*—do have very large penises. But let's put it this way: If a Martian was planning a trip to earth and was given a *Vogue* and a *Playgirl* to enlighten him on what to expect from human women and men, he'd get a very misleading impression. So does the average male reader or viewer of porn. And even if he knows, on some level (from his experience in locker rooms and the like), that the Dirk Digglers, Harry Reemses, and Jeff Strykers of the world are not the norm, that knowledge may pale beside the power of the iconography: the meanings attached to having an impressively large member. The woman in the Special K commercial is a "real" woman too (although these images are, increasingly, digitally manipulated); it's the fact that she so perfectly, precisely embodies current notions about femininity and beauty that makes her a fantasy, and an oppressive standard for the ordinary woman to aspire to.

Think, to begin with, about that adjective "impressive," which came spontaneously to my mind as I wrote the phrase "impressively large member," and all that it conveys. We wouldn't usually describe large breasts as "impressive," would we? ("Bodacious" isn't in the dictionary and I'm not sure that I know

exactly what it's supposed to mean, but it sure doesn't seem to me to suggest a body part demanding respect.) In contrast, the penis so large as to take a lover's breath away is a majestic penis, a commanding penis. From romance novels ("His strength was conspicuous beneath her hands, his muscles prominent, steel hard. He was strikingly large . . . so *very* large . . . ") to the erotic fantasies in the back pages of *Playgirl* ("I watched in curiosity and amazement as he unzipped his pants, revealing a magnificent cock . . . As his manhood sprung out at me, hard and thick, I gasped and stared . . . ") to Ally McBeal, the woman's first encounter with the male stud's member is typically one of gasping bedazzlement at his "magnificent" size. Gay male erotica has similar moments: "Lew's breath was stolen by Jeff's cock. Sure, the mountain man had seen a few in his time. Many. Some were as nicely shaped. A few were as tasty-looking. But none were as gigantic." Perusing this literature, I couldn't help but think (with a mental chuckle) about Freud's description of the origins of "penis envy"; little girls, he wrote, "notice the penis of a brother or playmate, strikingly visible and of large proportions." Sounds quite a bit like the rhetoric of erotica to me, with its fantasy of a penis so impressive it simply dazzles the onlooker, takes his or her breath away.

The bedazzlement need not be sexual, however. The warlords of the Ottoman Empire publicly posted their genital measurements for conquered tribes to admire. Appearing a "big man" to other men is an important aspect of men's preoccupation with size. I've personally heard three different variations on the following joke, most recently the garbled version told in the movie *Slingblade*: Three men are urinating off a bridge together. "River sure is cold," says the first man. "It's deep, too," says the second. "Sandy bottom," says the third. The joke is our contemporary version of the fresco at the Roman ruins at Pompeii (circa A.D. 79), which depicts a wealthy man using his enormous penis to counterbalance several bags of money on a scale. The big penis is worth its weight in gold, the winner in contests among men. One young man, who had his penis pierced to endow his "little dick with a lot of fucking attitude," suggests "the big-size thing develops in the school locker room when you're a kid. The big-dicked guys send out signals that say, 'We're better,' 'We're more masculine than you,' or 'We deserve to be here, look at the size of our dicks.'"

Penile augmentation is an increasingly booming business in this culture, and many of the men who have their penises enlarged do it for "display purposes." "I'd always been happy in an erect state," says one man, "I never had any complaints from my wife—but I had a lot of retraction when flaccid. It's not that I want to flaunt myself at the gym, but I didn't want to feel that self-conscious." Others do want to "flaunt"; according to surgeon Melvyn Rosenstein the typical phalloplasty patient "wants to get big so he can show himself off to other men, to say, 'Mine is bigger than yours,' like a buck deer displaying its antler." Most phalloplasty patients, doctors add, do not have especially small penises. "The overwhelming majority of men I do are unquestionably normal," says Rosenstein. "I had a guy in the office yesterday who was concerned that he was small. I assured him that he was normal, but he said, 'Let's go ahead and do it.'"

Like George Costanza in that "shrinkage" episode of *Seinfeld,* most phalloplasty patients are haunted by a humiliation that is likely only imagined. The cultural backdrop of their anxieties, however, is not imagined, any more than women's anxieties about the size of their breasts are of their own making. *"He's the nicest guy I ever dated. But he's just too small."* So reads the bold print of an ad from Dr. Gary Rheinschild, who specializes in penile augmentation and who in 1995 claimed to have performed more than 3,500 such operations. Rheinschild also uses phrases like "shower syndrome" and "locker room phobia" (to describe what the man I've quoted above suffers from) and hopes to make penis enlargement "as common as breast implants." But even before cosmetic surgeons began their campaigns, ads hawking miracle products for increasing penis size both exploited and exacerbated already existing male insecurities by drawing on the equation: penis size = manliness. "Dramatic Increase in Penis Size!" boast the makers of "NSP-270," marketed in the eighties:

"Boys who couldn't measure up to the Navy's proud standards of manhood . . . who would never be able to satisfy a 'woman in every port' . . . who would disgrace the uniform if they were ever allowed to wear it . . . were given massive dosages of this amazing sex nutrient . . . [and] suddenly and dramatically experienced: *Proud Erections! Dramatic New Ability in Intercourse! Supercharged Sperm That Now Can 'Do the Job!' . . . And, most amazing of all, fantastic growth in penis size!"*

Anxiety about "shrinkage" and size are not exclusively Western either. Southeast Asian men suffer from a form of male panic (some might call it hysteria) known as Koro, in which they imagine that their genitals are retracting into their bodies and will ultimately cause their death. Recent studies suggest that Koro is triggered by penile vasoconstriction (or "shrinkage") caused by cold, fright, and other states. Penile augmentations—making use of pins and inserts—are performed in many cultures. Groups ranging from the Caramoja tribe of northern Uganda to the sadhus of India have practiced the technique of tying weights to the penis in order to make it longer. The sadhus, who believe that God dwells in the penis, stretch themselves to lengths of twelve to eighteen inches. By contrast, John Bobbitt's boast to Jenny Jones that his reattached penis is "stronger and bigger than ever," with a fraction of an inch added on by the surgery that reattached it, seems pretty flaccid. (Bobbitt, as mentioned earlier, went on to have an augmentation which, he claims, added three inches in length, one inch in girth, and made his penis "like a beer can." Perhaps, at least in Bobbitt's case, Pat Califia is right about "dildo envy.")

Most of the transformations wrought by penile augmentation in this culture—usually, gains of a couple of inches at most—lack the clear, ritualistic drama of organs that have been augmented—like the sadhus'—into hyperbole. But symbolically, the change can be just as potent, a fact that surgeons exploit. "I get [my clients] to see this as an incredible change in their lives," Dr. Jamie Corvalaan explained to *Esquire* reporter John Taylor. "I tell them, 'This is going to change your self-image, change the way you walk, sit, look, do business, pursue women. You will now act like a man with a big penis.' " How does a man with a big penis act? Well, we know that he can exhibit himself with pride in the locker room. The surgeons, addressing the concerns and fantasies of men who perceive themselves as small, promote the large penis as the route to self-confidence, assertiveness, social authority. But men who are born with large penises, as I've discovered from talking to several, may experience their size as embarrassing excess rather than a cause for pride. When one of these men described his large penis to me as "a problem," my immediate reaction (thankfully, not outwardly expressed) was similar to that which I've had when very slim women complain that they just can't keep the weight on. "That's a *problem*?" But further conversation revealed that this man had indeed had problems, not only in being too large for many partners but also with an abiding sense of shame.

The fact is that human cultures have been somewhat ambivalent about very large penises. Yes, they advertise male potency, and have often functioned as symbols of reproductive fertility. But at the same time, like very large breasts, they are often viewed as gross and a sign that there is nothing much "upstairs" (the body's endowments being seen as hydraulically regulated, I guess; what accumulates at one end has been forced out the other). Long Dong Silver laughs at male proportions, turns them into so much clumsy poundage. Dong. Shlong. Alexander Portnoy aside, these are usually words of disdain, not reverence, in our culture. Also, body-part size and excessive sexuality have often been joined in our cultural imagination, and thus don't fit well with the heroic, civilized ideals that men are supposed to uphold. There are some interesting depictions of Christ with a large penis, possibly an erection. But typically, in classical Western art, the convention has been to represent the heroic body as muscular, but the actual penis as rather small. That's why my trips to the Newark Museum were so disappointing.

Ancient Greece, a highly masculinist culture but also one that placed great emphasis on male self-control in matters of sexuality, favored "small and taut" genitals. "Large sex organs," as Eva Keuls points out, "were considered coarse and ugly, and were banished to the domains of abstraction, of caricature, of satyrs, and of barbarians." In those domains, the penis was represented as often grotesquely huge, as though absorbing all the sexual excess that the "civilized"

Greek would not permit to have a place in his own self-conception. White Europeans have performed the same projection onto racist stereotypes of the overendowed black superstud,[1] stereotypes . . . that got brought right onto the floor of the United States Senate during the Clarence Thomas/Anita Hill sexual harassment hearings. Long Dong Silver is racialized pornography, of a piece with the brown dildoes that feminist writer Heather Findlay encounters in a sex-toy shop: "I turned and looked. They were not dildoes; they were *monstrosities.* Twenty-four inches and thick as my arm. 'Big Black Dick' said the wrapper . . . I looked around for some 'Big White Dick' or even 'Big Flesh Colored Dick.' No luck." Race, she concludes, "permeates American culture."

Yes, and not just American culture, but the Western psyche. Frantz Fanon, discussing the racial fantasies and dreams of his white psychiatric patients, has written: "One is no longer aware of the Negro, but only of a penis: The Negro is eclipsed. He is turned into a penis." White boys like Norman Mailer have envied this instinctual status (in *The White Negro,* he admires the Negro's "art of the primitive" and calls jazz "the music of orgasm"), and some black rappers and athletes may capitalize on it. (Jack Johnson, the first African-American world heavyweight boxing champion, wrapped his penis in gauze to emphasize its size as he paraded around the ring during his public matches.) But primitive manhood has no place under the robes of a Supreme Court Justice. There were moments when I felt deep pain for Thomas. To be on the brink of *real* respectability—perhaps the most respectable position this country can offer—and to be tailgated by Long

Dong Silver! "This dirt, this sleaze," Thomas told the committee, "is destroying what it has taken me forty-three years to build." The white senators could empathize, even identify with the pain of having charges of sexual misconduct threaten to destroy one's career. But they could not bond with the racial dimension of Thomas's predicament, only look on it with horror.

Anita Hill was the first to mention Long Dong Silver. But once he had been let loose in the Senate, Thomas knew he would be dogged by him, whatever he did, so he made a bold and cunning move. Rather than allow the equation "Negro = penis" to remain unspoken, doing unconscious damage to his hopes of confirmation, Thomas drew attention to Long Dong Silver's racial overtones, thus suggesting that Thomas *himself* was the real victim—of ugly racial stereotyping. The strategy was exploitative and outrageously misplaced. Hill was a black woman, as people seemed to forget, with little to gain by resorting to racial smears; even if she had been lying, she could easily have come up with a different, equally offensive but racially neutral image. Thomas's strategy, however, proved triumphant. The senators, going out of their way to prove to the world that *they* (unlike Fanon's patients) did *not* see the black man as penis, made him a Supreme Court justice.

NOTES

1. Robert Mapplethorpe's controversial photograph, "Man in a Polyester Suit," satirically illustrates this racist opposition between the white man's "civilization" and the black man's primitive endowments, by showing a gigantic organ spilling out from the unzipped fly of a black man in a tidy business suit, whose polyester material jokingly represents the tacky, Kmart artifice of "civilization."

X: A Fabulous Child's Story

Lois Gould

Once upon a time, a baby named X was born. This baby was named X so that nobody could tell whether it was a boy or a girl. Its parents could tell, of course, but they couldn't tell anybody else. They couldn't even tell Baby X, at first.

You see, it was all part of a very important Secret Scientific Xperiment, known officially as Project Baby X. The smartest scientists had set up this Xperiment at a cost of Xactly 23 billion dollars and 72 cents, which might seem like a lot for just one baby, even a very important Xperimental baby. But when you remember the prices of things like strained carrots and stuffed bunnies, and popcorn for the movies and booster shots for camp, let alone 28 shiny quarters from the tooth fairy, you begin to see how it adds up.

Also, long before Baby X was born, all those scientists had to be paid to work out the details of the Xperiment, and to write the *Official Instruction Manual* for Baby X's parents and, most important of all, to find the right set of parents to bring up Baby X. These parents had to be selected very carefully. Thousands of volunteers had to take thousands of tests and answer thousands of tricky questions. Almost everybody failed because, it turned out, almost everybody really wanted either a baby boy or a baby girl, and not Baby X at all. Also, almost everybody was afraid that a Baby X would be a lot more trouble than a boy or a girl. (They were probably right, the scientists admitted, but

Baby X needed parents who wouldn't *mind* the Xtra trouble.)

There were families with grandparents named Milton and Agatha, who didn't see why the baby couldn't be named Milton or Agatha instead of X, even if it *was* an X. There were families with aunts who insisted on knitting tiny dresses and uncles who insisted on sending tiny baseball mitts. Worst of all, there were families that already had other children who couldn't be trusted to keep the secret. Certainly not if they knew the secret was worth 23 billion dollars and 72 cents—and all you had to do was take one little peek at Baby X in the bathtub to know if it was a boy or a girl.

But, finally, the scientists found the Joneses, who really wanted to raise an X more than any other kind of baby—no matter how much trouble it would be. Ms. and Mr. Jones had to promise they would take equal turns caring for X, and feeding it, and singing it lullabies. And they had to promise never to hire any baby-sitters. The government scientists knew perfectly well that a baby-sitter would probably peek at X in the bathtub, too.

The day the Joneses brought their baby home, lots of friends and relatives came over to see it. None of them knew about the secret Xperiment, though. So the first thing they asked was what kind of a baby X was. When the Joneses smiled and said, "It's an X!" nobody knew what to say. They couldn't say, "Look at her cute little dimples!" And they couldn't say, "Look at his husky little biceps!" And they couldn't even say just plain "kitchy-coo." In fact, they all

First published in *Ms.* Magazine © 1972.

thought the Joneses were playing some kind of rude joke.

But, of course, the Joneses were not joking. "It's an X" was absolutely all they would say. And that made the friends and relatives very angry. The relatives all felt embarrassed about having an X in the family. "People will think there's something wrong with it!" some of them whispered. "There *is* something wrong with it!" others whispered back.

"Nonsense!" the Joneses told them all cheerfully. "What could possibly be wrong with this perfectly adorable X?"

Nobody could answer that, except Baby X, who had just finished its bottle. Baby X's answer was a loud, satisfied burp.

Clearly, nothing at all was wrong. Nevertheless, none of the relatives felt comfortable about buying a present for a Baby X. The cousins who sent the baby a tiny football helmet would not come and visit any more. And the neighbors who sent a pink-flowered romper suit pulled their shades down when the Joneses passed their house.

The *Official Instruction Manual* had warned the new parents that this would happen, so they didn't fret about it. Besides, they were too busy with Baby X and the hundreds of different Xercises for treating it properly.

Ms. and Mr. Jones had to be Xtra careful about how they played with little X. They knew that if they kept bouncing it up in the air and saying how *strong* and *active* it was, they'd be treating it more like a boy than an X. But if all they did was cuddle it and kiss it and tell it how *sweet* and *dainty* it was, they'd be treating it more like a girl than an X.

On page 1,654 of the *Official Instruction Manual,* the scientists prescribed: "plenty of bouncing and plenty of cuddling, *both.* X ought to be strong and sweet and active. Forget about *dainty* altogether."

Meanwhile, the Joneses were worrying about other problems. Toys, for instance. And clothes. On his first shopping trip, Mr.

Jones told the store clerk, "I need some clothes and toys for my new baby." The clerk smiled and said, "Well, now, is it a boy or a girl?" "It's an X," Mr. Jones said, smiling back. But the clerk got all red in the face and said huffily, "In *that* case, I'm afraid I can't help you, sir." So Mr. Jones wandered helplessly up and down the aisles trying to find what X needed. But everything in the store was piled up in sections marked "Boys" or "Girls." There were "Boys' Pajamas" and "Girls' Underwear" and "Boys' Fire Engines" and "Girls' Housekeeping Sets." Mr. Jones went home without buying anything for X. That night he and Ms. Jones consulted page 2,326 of the *Official Instruction Manual.* "Buy plenty of everything!" it said firmly.

So they bought plenty of sturdy blue pajamas in the Boys' Department and cheerful flowered underwear in the Girls' Department. And they bought all kinds of toys. A boy doll that made pee-pee and cried, "Papa." And a girl doll that talked in three languages and said, "I am the Pres-i-dent of Gen-er-al Mo-tors." They also bought a storybook about a brave princess who rescued a handsome prince from his ivory tower, and another one about a sister and brother who grew up to be a baseball star and a ballet star, and you had to guess which was which.

The head scientists of Project Baby X checked all their purchases and told them to keep up the good work. They also reminded the Joneses to see page 4,629 of the *Manual* where it said, "Never make Baby X feel *embarrassed* or *ashamed* about what it wants to play with. And if X gets dirty climbing rocks, never say 'Nice little Xes don't get dirty climbing rocks.'"

Likewise, it said, "If X falls down and cries, never say 'Brave little Xes don't cry.' Because, of course, nice little Xes *do* get dirty, and brave little Xes *do* cry. No matter how dirty X gets, or how hard it cries, don't worry. It's all part of the Xperiment."

Whenever the Joneses pushed Baby X's stroller in the park, smiling strangers would come over and coo: "Is that a boy or a girl?" The Joneses would smile back and say, "It's an X." The strangers would stop smiling then, and often snarl something nasty—as if the Joneses had snarled at *them*.

By the time X grew big enough to play with other children, the Joneses' troubles had grown bigger, too. Once a little girl grabbed X's shovel in the sandbox, and zonked X on the head with it. "Now, now, Tracy," the little girl's mother began to scold, "little girls mustn't hit little—" and she turned to ask X, "Are you a little boy or a little girl, dear?"

Mr. Jones, who was sitting near the sandbox, held his breath and crossed his fingers.

X smiled politely at the lady, even though X's head had never been zonked so hard in its life. "I'm a little X," X replied.

"You're a *what?*" the lady exclaimed angrily. "You're a little b-r-a-t, you mean!"

"But little girls mustn't hit little Xes, either!" said X, retrieving the shovel with another polite smile. "What good does hitting do, anyway?"

X's father, who was still holding his breath, finally let it out, uncrossed his fingers, and grinned back at X.

And at their next secret Project Baby X meeting, the scientists grinned, too. Baby X was doing fine.

But then it was time for X to start school. The Joneses were really worried about this, because school was even more full of rules for boys and girls, and there were no rules for Xes. The teacher would tell boys to form one line, and girls to form another line. There would be boys' games and girls' games, and boys' secrets and girls' secrets. The school library would have a list of recommended books for girls, and a different list of recommended books for boys. There would even be a bathroom marked BOYS and an-

other one marked GIRLS. Pretty soon boys and girls would hardly talk to each other. What would happen to poor little X?

The Joneses spent weeks consulting their *Instruction Manual* (there were $249\frac{1}{2}$ pages of advice under "First Day of School"), and attending urgent special conferences with the smart scientists of Project Baby X.

The scientists had to make sure that X's mother had taught X how to throw and catch a ball properly, and that X's father had been sure to teach X what to serve at a doll's tea party. X had to know how to shoot marbles and how to jump rope and, most of all, what to say when the Other Children asked whether X was a Boy or a Girl.

Finally, X was ready. The Joneses helped X button on a nice new pair of red-and-white checked overalls, and sharpened six pencils for X's nice new pencilbox, and marked X's name clearly on all the books in its nice new bookbag. X brushed its teeth and combed its hair, which just about covered its ears, and remembered to put a napkin in its lunchbox.

The Joneses had asked X's teacher if the class could line up alphabetically, instead of forming separate lines for boys and girls. And they had asked if X could use the principal's bathroom, because it wasn't marked anything except BATHROOM. X's teacher promised to take care of all those problems. But nobody could help X with the biggest problem of all—Other Children.

Nobody in X's class had ever known an X before. What would they think? How would X make friends?

You couldn't tell what X was by studying its clothes—overalls don't even button right-to-left, like girls' clothes, or left-to-right, like boys' clothes. And you couldn't guess whether X had a girl's short haircut or a boy's long haircut. And it was very hard to tell by the games X liked to play. Either X played ball very well for a girl or played house very well for a boy.

Some of the children tried to find out by asking X tricky questions, like "Who's your favorite sports star?" That was easy. X had two favorite sports stars: a girl jockey named Robyn Smith and a boy archery champion named Robin Hood. Then they asked, "What's your favorite TV program?" And that was even easier. X's favorite TV program was "Lassie," which stars a girl dog played by a boy dog.

When X said that its favorite toy was a doll, everyone decided that X must be a girl. But then X said that the doll was really a robot, and that X had computerized it, and that it was programmed to bake fudge brownies and then clean up the kitchen. After X told them that, the other children gave up guessing what X was. All they knew was they'd sure like to see X's doll.

After school, X wanted to play with the other children. "How about shooting some baskets in the gym?" X asked the girls. But all they did was make faces and giggle behind X's back.

"How about weaving some baskets in the arts and crafts room?" X asked the boys. But they all made faces and giggled behind X's back, too.

That night, Ms. and Mr. Jones asked X how things had gone at school. X told them sadly that the lessons were okay, but otherwise school was a horrible place for an X. It seemed as if the Other Children would never want an X for a friend.

Once more, the Joneses reached for the *Instruction Manual.* Under "Other Children," they found the following message: "What did you Xpect? *Other Children* have to obey all the silly boy-girl rules, because their parents taught them to. Lucky X—you don't have to stick to the rules at all! All you have to do is be yourself. P.S. We're not saying it'll be easy."

X liked being itself. But X cried a lot that night, partly because it felt afraid. So

X's father held X tight, and cuddled it, and couldn't help crying a little, too. And X's mother cheered them both up by reading an Xciting story about an enchanted prince called Sleeping Handsome, who woke up when Princess Charming kissed him.

The next morning, they all felt much better, and little X went back to school with a brave smile and a clean pair of red-and-white checked overalls.

There was a seven-letter-word spelling bee in class that day. And a seven-lap boys' relay race in the gym. And a seven-layer-cake baking contest in the girls' kitchen corner. X won the spelling bee. X also won the relay race. And X almost won the baking contest, except it forgot to light the oven. Which only proves that nobody's perfect.

One of the Other Children noticed something else, too. He said: "Winning or losing doesn't seem to count to X. X seems to have fun being good at boys' skills *and* girls' skills."

"Come to think of it," said another one of the Other Children, "maybe X is having twice as much fun as we are!"

So after school that day, the girl who beat X at the baking contest gave X a big slice of her prizewinning cake. And the boy X beat in the relay race asked X to race him home.

From then on, some really funny things began to happen. Susie, who sat next to X in class, suddenly refused to wear pink dresses to school any more. She insisted on wearing red-and-white checked overalls—just like X's. Overalls, she told her parents, were much better for climbing monkey bars.

Then Jim, the class football nut, started wheeling his little sister's doll carriage around the football field. He'd put on his entire football uniform, except for the helmet. Then he'd put the helmet *in* the carriage, lovingly tucked under an old set of shoulder pads. Then he'd start jogging around the field, pushing the carriage and singing "Rockabye Baby" to his football helmet. He told his family that X did the same thing, so it must be okay. After all, X was now the team's star quarterback.

Susie's parents were horrified by her behavior, and Jim's parents were worried sick about him. But the worst came when the twins, Joe and Peggy, decided to share everything with each other. Peggy used Joe's hockey skates, and his microscope, and took half his newspaper route. Joe used Peggy's needlepoint kit, and her cookbooks, and took two of her three baby-sitting jobs. Peggy started running the lawn mower, and Joe started running the vacuum cleaner.

Their parents weren't one bit pleased with Peggy's wonderful biology experiments, or with Joe's terrific needlepoint pillows. They didn't care that Peggy mowed the lawn better, and that Joe vacuumed the carpet better. In fact, they were furious. It's all that little X's fault, they agreed. Just because X doesn't know what it is, or what it's supposed to be, it wants to get everybody *else* mixed up, too!

Peggy and Joe were forbidden to play with X any more. So was Susie, and then Jim, and then *all* the Other Children. But it was too late; the Other Children stayed mixed up and happy and free, and refused to go back to the way they'd been before X.

Finally, Joe and Peggy's parents decided to call an emergency meeting of the school's Parents' Association, to discuss "The X Problem." They sent a report to the principal stating that X was a "disruptive influence." They demanded immediate action. The Joneses, they said, should be *forced* to tell whether X was a boy or a girl. And then X should be forced to behave like whichever it was. If the Joneses refused to tell, the Parents' Association said, then X must take an Xamination. The school psychiatrist must Xamine it physically and mentally, and issue a full report. If X's test

showed it was a boy, it would have to obey all the boys' rules. If it proved to be a girl, X would have to obey all the girls' rules.

And if X turned out to be some kind of mixed-up misfit, then X should be Xpelled from the school. Immediately!

The principal was very upset. Disruptive influence? Mixed-up misfit? But X was an Xcellent student. All the teachers said it was a delight to have X in their classes. X was president of the student council. X had won first prize in the talent show, and second prize in the art show, and honorable mention in the science fair, and six athletic events on field day, including the potato race.

Nevertheless, insisted the Parents' Association, X is a Problem Child. X is the Biggest Problem Child we have ever seen!

So the principal reluctantly notified X's parents that numerous complaints about X's behavior had come to the school's attention. And that after the psychiatrist's Xamination, the school would decide what to do about X.

The Joneses reported this at once to the scientists, who referred them to page 85,759 of the *Instruction Manual.* "Sooner or later," it said, "X will have to be Xamined by a psychiatrist. This may be the only way any of us will know for sure whether X is mixed up—or whether everyone else is."

The night before X was to be Xamined, the Joneses tried not to let X see how worried they were. "What if—?" Mr. Jones would say. And Ms. Jones would reply, "No use worrying." Then a few minutes later, Ms. Jones would say, "What if—?" and Mr. Jones would reply, "No use worrying."

X just smiled at them both, and hugged them hard and didn't say much of anything. X was thinking, What if—? And then X thought: No use worrying.

At Xactly 9 o'clock the next day, X reported to the school psychiatrist's office. The principal, along with a committee from the Parents' Association, X's teacher, X's classmates, and Ms. and Mr. Jones, waited in the hall outside. Nobody knew the details of the tests X was to be given, but everybody knew they'd be *very* hard, and that they'd reveal Xactly what everyone wanted to know about X, but were afraid to ask.

It was terribly quiet in the hall. Almost spooky. Once in a while, they would hear a strange noise inside the room. There were buzzes. And a beep or two. And several bells. An occasional light would flash under the door. The Joneses thought it was a white light, but the principal thought it was blue. Two or three children swore it was either yellow or green. And the Parents' Committee missed it completely.

Through it all, you could hear the psychiatrist's low voice, asking hundreds of questions, and X's higher voice, answering hundred of answers.

The whole thing took so long that everyone knew it must be the most complete Xamination anyone had ever had to take. Poor X, the Joneses thought. Serves X right, the Parents' Committee thought. I wouldn't like to be in X's overalls right now, the children thought.

At last, the door opened. Everyone crowded around to hear the results. X didn't look any different; in fact, X was smiling. But the psychiatrist looked terrible. He looked as if he was crying! "What happened?" everyone began shouting. Had X done something disgraceful? "I wouldn't be a bit surprised!" muttered Peggy and Joe's parents. "Did X flunk the *whole* test?" cried Susie's parents. "Or just the most important part?" yelled Jim's parents.

"Oh, dear," sighed Mr. Jones.

"Oh, dear," sighed Ms. Jones.

"*Sssh*," ssshed the principal. "The psychiatrist is trying to speak."

Wiping his eyes and clearing his throat, the psychiatrist began, in a hoarse whisper. "In my opinion," he whispered—

you could tell he must be very upset—"in my opinion, young X here—"

"Yes? Yes?" shouted a parent impatiently.

"*Sssh!*" ssshed the principal.

"Young *Sssh* here, I mean young X," said the doctor, frowning, "is just about—"

"Just about *what?* Let's have it!" shouted another parent. ". . . just about the *least* mixed-up child I've ever Xamined!" said the psychiatrist.

"Yay for X!" yelled one of the children. And then the others began yelling, too. Clapping and cheering and jumping up and down.

"*SSSH!*" SSShed the principal, but nobody did.

The Parents' Committee was angry and bewildered. How *could* X have passed the whole Xamination? Didn't X have an *identity* problem? Wasn't X mixed up at *all?* Wasn't X *any* kind of a misfit? How could it *not* be, when it didn't even *know* what it was? And why was the psychiatrist crying?

Actually, he had stopped crying and was smiling politely through his tears. "Don't you see?" he said. "I'm crying because it's wonderful! X has absolutely no identity problem! X isn't one bit mixed-up! As for being a misfit—ridiculous! X knows perfectly well what it is! Don't you, X?" The doctor winked. X winked back.

"But what *is* X?" shrieked Peggy and Joe's parents. "*We* still want to know what it is!"

"Ah, yes," said the doctor, winking again. "Well, don't worry. You'll all know one of these days. And you won't need me to tell you."

"What? What does he mean?" some of the parents grumbled suspiciously.

Susie and Peggy and Joe all answered at once. "He means that by the time X's sex matters, it won't be a secret any more!"

With that, the doctor began to push through the crowd toward X's parents. "How do you do," he said, somewhat stiffly.

And then he reached out to hug them both. "If I ever have an X of my own," he whispered, "I sure hope you'll lend me your instruction manual."

Needless to say, the Joneses were very happy. The Project Baby X scientists were rather pleased, too. So were Susie, Jim, Peggy, Joe, and all the Other Children. The Parents' Association wasn't, but they had promised to accept the psychiatrist's report, and not make any more trouble. They even invited Ms. and Mr. Jones to become honorary members, which they did.

Later that day, all X's friends put on their red-and-white checked overalls and went over to see X. They found X in the back yard, playing with a very tiny baby that none of them had ever seen before. The baby was wearing very tiny red-and-white checked overalls.

"How do you like our new baby?" X asked the Other Children proudly:

"It's got cute dimples," said Jim.

"It's got husky biceps, too," said Susie.

"What kind of baby is it?" asked Joe and Peggy.

X frowned at them. "Can't you tell?" Then X broke into a big, mischievous grin. *"It's a Y!"*

REFERENCES–THE SOCIAL CONSTRUCTION OF GENDER: WHAT MAKES A MAN?

ACKER, J. (1988). Class, gender, and the relations of distribution. *Signs* 13: 473–97.

ACKER, J. (1990). Hierarchies, jobs, and bodies: A theory of gendered organizations. *Gender & Society* 4: 139–158.

ALMQUIST, E.M. (1987). Labor market gendered inequality in minority groups. *Gender & Society* 1: 400–414.

AMADIUME, I. (1987). *Male daughters, female husbands: Gender and sex in an African society.* London: Zed Books.

AUSTAD, S.N. (1986). Changing sex nature's way. *International Wildlife,* May–June: 29

BARKALOW, C., with A. Raab. (1990). *In the men's house.* New York: Poseidon Press.

BARRETT, M. ([1980] 1988). *Women's oppression today: The Marxist/feminist encounter.* Rev. ed. London: Verso.

BEM, S.L. (1981). Gender schema theory: A cognitive account of sex typing. *Psychological Review* 88: 354–64.

BEM, S.L. (1983). Gender schema theory and its implications for child development: Raising gender-aschematic children in a gender-schematic society. *Signs* 8: 598–616.

BERNARD, J. *The female world.* New York: Free Press.

BERNSTEIN, R. (1986). France jails 2 in odd case of espionage. *New York Times,* May 11.

BIERSACK, A. (1984). Paiela "women-men": The reflexive foundations of gender ideology. *American Ethnologist* 11: 118–38.

BIRDWHISTELL, R.L. (1970). *Kinesics and context: Essays on body motion communication.* Philadelphia: University of Pennsylvania Press.

BLACKWOOD, E. (1984). Sexuality and gender in certain Native American tribes: The case of cross-gender females. *Signs* 10: 27–42.

BOLIN, A. (1987). Transsexualism and the limits of traditional analysis. *American Behavioral Scientist* 31: 41–65.

BOURDIEU, P. ([1980] 1990). *The logic of practice.* Stanford, CA: Stanford University Press.

BUTLER, J. (1990). *Gender trouble: Feminism and the subversion of identity.* New York and London: Routledge.

CARRIGAN, T., R.W. Connell, and J. Lee. (1987). Toward a new sociology of masculinity. In H. Brod, ed., *The making of masculinities.* Boston: Allen and Unwin.

CHAFETZ, J.S., and A.G. Dworkin. (1986). *Female revolt: Women's movements in world and historical perspective.* Totowa, NJ: Rowman and Allenheld.

CHODOROW, N. (1978). *The reproduction of mothering.* Berkeley: University of California Press.

CIXOUS, H., and C. Clément. ([1975] 1986). *The newly born woman,* trans. B. Wing. Minneapolis: University of Minnesota Press.

COCKBURN, C. (1985). *Machinery of dominance: Women, men, and technical knowhow.* London: Pluto Press.

COLLINS, P.H. (1989). The social construction of black feminist thought. *Signs* 14: 745–773.

COLLINS, P.H. (1990). *Black feminist thought: Knowledge, consciousness, and the politics of empowerment.* Boston: Unwin Hyman.

CONNELL, R.W. (1987). *Gender and power: Society, the person, and sexual politics.* Stanford, CA: Stanford University Press.

COSER, R.L. (1978). The principle of patriarchy: The case of *The Magic Flute. Signs* 4: 337–48.

DAVIES, C. (1982). Sexual taboos and social boundaries. *American Journal of Sociology* 87: 1032–1063.

DAVIS, N.J., and R.V. Robinson. (1991). Men's and women's consciousness of gender inequality: Austria, West Germany, Great Britain, and the United States. *American Sociological Review* 56: 72–84.

DE BEAUVOIR, S. (1953). *The second sex,* trans. H.M. Parshley. New York: Knopf.

DEVOR, H. (1987). Gender blending females: Women and sometimes men. *American Behavioral Scientist* 31: 12–40.

DEVOR, H. (1989). *Gender blending: Confronting the limits of duality.* Bloomington: Indiana University Press.

EICHLER, M. (1989). Sex change operations: The last bulwark of the double standard. In Richardson, L., and V. Taylor, eds., *Feminist Frontiers II.* New York: Random House.

EPSTEIN, C.F. (1988). *Deceptive distinctions: Sex, gender, and the social order.* New Haven: Yale University Press.

FAUSTO-STERLING, A. (2000). The five sexes, revisited. *The Sciences* 40 (July): 4.

FLAX, J. (1990). *Thinking fragments: Psychoanalysis, feminism, and postmodernism in the contemporary West.* Berkeley: University of California Press.

FOUCAULT, M. (1972). *The archaeology of knowledge and the discourse on language,* trans. A.M. Sheridan Smith. New York: Pantheon.

FREUD, S. ([1933] 1973). Femininity. *New Introductory Lectures on Psychoanalysis.* Harmondsworth, UK: Penguin.

GARBER, M. (1992). *Vested interests: Cross-dressing and cultural anxiety.* New York and London: Routledge.

GARFINKEL, H. (1967). *Studies in ethnomethodology.* Englewood Cliffs, NJ: Prentice-Hall.

GILMORE, D. (1990). *Manhood in the making: Cultural concepts of masculinity.* New Haven: Yale University Press.

GRAMSCI, A. (1971). *Selections from the prison notebooks,* trans. and ed. Q. House and G.N. Smith. New York: International Publishers.

HARAWAY, D. (1978a) Animal sociology and a natural economy of the body politic. Part I: A political physiology of dominance. *Signs* 4: 21–36.

HARAWAY, D. (1989). *Primate visions.* New York and London: Routledge.

HARAWAY, D. (1991). *Simians, cyborgs, and women: The reinvention of nature.* New York and London: Routledge.

HARTMANN, H.I. (1976). Capitalism, patriarchy, and job segregation by sex. *Signs* 1(3, pt. 2): 137–167.

HARTMANN, H.I. (1981b). The unhappy marriage of Marxism and feminism; Towards a more progressive union. In L. Sargent, ed., *Women and revolution: A discussion of the unhappy marriage of Marxism and feminism.* Boston: South End Press.

HARTSOCK, N. (1983). *Money, sex, and power: Toward a feminist historical materialism.* New York: Longman.

HESS, B.B. (1990). Beyond dichotomy: Drawing distinctions and embracing differences. *Sociological Forum* 5: 75–93.

HILBERT, R.A. (1987). Bureaucracy as belief, rationalization as repair: Max Weber in a post-functionalist age. *Sociology Theory* 5: 70–86.

HOOKS, B. (1984). *Feminist theory: From margin to center.* Boston: South End Press.

HOWARD, J.E. (1988). Crossdressing, the theater, and gender struggle in early modern England. *Shakespeare Quarterly* 39: 418–41.

HWANG, D.H. (1989). *M. Butterfly.* New York: New American Library.

IRIGARAY, L. ([1974] 1985). *Speculum of the other woman,* trans. G. C. Gill. Ithaca: Cornell University Press.

JAY, N. (1981). Gender and dichotomy. *Feminist Studies* 7: 38–56.

KANDIYOTI, D., ed. (1991). *Women, Islam, and the state.* Philadelphia: Temple University Press.

KANDO, T. (1973). *Sex change: The achievement of gender identity among feminized transsexuals.* Springfield, IL: Charles C. Thomas.

KESSLER, S., and W. MCKENNA. ([1978] 1985). *Gender: An ethnomethodological approach.* Chicago: University of Chicago Press.

KOLATA, G. (1992). Who is female? Science can't say. *New York Times.* February 16.

KOMAROVSKY, M. (1992). The concept of social role revisited. *Gender & Society* 6: 301–313.

KONDO, D.K. (1990b). *M. Butterfly:* Orientalism, gender, and a critique of essentialist identity. *Cultural Critique* 16 (Fall): 5–29.

LANCASTER, J.B. (1974). *Primate behavior and the emergence of human culture.* New York: Holt, Rinehart & Winston.

LE GUIN, U. (1969). *The left hand of darkness.* New York: Ace.

LÉVI-STRAUSS, C. (1956). The family. In *Man, culture, and society,* ed. H.L. Shapiro. New York: Oxford.

LÉVI-STRAUSS, C. ([1949] 1969). *The elementary structures of kinship,* trans. J.H. Bell and J.R. von Sturmer. Boston: Beacon Press.

MACKINNON, C. (1982). Feminism, Marxism, method and the state: An agenda for theory. *Signs* 7: 515–544.

MATTHAEI, J.A. (1982). *An economic history of women's work in America.* New York: Schocken.

MENCHER, J. (1988). Women's work and poverty: Women's contribution to household maintenance in South India. In Dwyer, D. and J. Bruce, eds., *A home divided: Women and income in the Third World.* Palo Alto, CA: Stanford University Press.

MILKMAN, R. (1987). *Gender at work.* Urbana: University of Illinois Press.

MITCHELL, J. (1975). *Psychoanalysis and feminism.* New York: Vintage.

MOGHADAM, V. (1989). Revolution, the state, Islam, and women: Sexual politics in Iran and Afghanistan. *Social Text* 22: 40–61.

MORRIS, J., (1975). *Conundrum.* New York: Signet.

Ms. Magazine (1991). Reinventing the wheel. March.

New York Times (1989). Musician's death at 74 reveals he was a woman. February 2.

PALMER, P. (1989). *Domesticity and dirt: Housewives and domestic servants in the United States, 1920–1945.* Philadelphia: Temple University Press.

PAPANEK, H. (1979). Family status production: The "work" and "non-work" of women. *Signs* 4: 775–781.

RESKIN, B.F. (1988). Bringing the men back in: Sex differentiation and the devaluation of women's work. *Gender & Society* 2: 58–81.

RICH, A. (1977). *Of woman born: Motherhood as experience and as institution.* New York: Norton.

ROWBOTHAM, S. (1989). *The past is before us: Feminism in action since the 1960s.* Boston: Beacon Press.

RUBIN, G. (1975). The traffic in women: Notes on the political economy of sex. In *Toward an anthropology of women,* ed. R.R. Reiter. New York: Monthly Review Press.

RUGH, A.B. (1986). *Reveal and conceal: Dress in contemporary Egypt.* Syracuse: Syracuse University Press.

SCOTT, J.W. (1988a). *Gender and the politics of history.* New York: Columbia University Press.

SMITH, D. (1987a). *The everyday world as problematic: A feminist sociology.* Toronto: University of Toronto Press.

SMITH, D. (1990). *The conceptual practices of power: A feminist sociology of knowledge.* Toronto: University of Toronto Press.

TANGRI, S.S. (1976). A feminist perspective on some ethical issues in population programs. *Signs* 1: 895–904.

VAN GENNEP, A. (1960). *The rites of passage,* trans. M.B. Vizedom and G.L. Caffee. Chicago: University of Chicago Press.

WALBY, S. (1986). *Patriarchy at work: Patriarchal and capitalist relations in employment.* Minneapolis: University of Minnesota Press.

WALBY, S. (1990). *Theorizing patriarchy.* Oxford and New York: Basil Blackwell.

WEST, C., and D. Zimmerman. (1987). Doing gender. *Gender & Society* 1: 125–151.

WILLIAMS, C.L. (1989). *Gender differences at work: Women and men in nontraditional occupations.* Berkeley: University of California Press.

YOUNG, K. et al., eds. (1981). *Of marriage and the market: Women's subordination in international perspective.* London: CSE Books.

Growing Up:
At Home, At School

The earliest producers of masculinities are perhaps the most powerful: the family and the school. In the everyday intimate interactions of caregivers and children are carried the cues and codes that shape our first understandings of masculinity and femininity. Even before birth, the prescriptions of gender come into play as nurseries are prepared and color-coded clothes are purchased. Later, in classroom and playground, the gendering continues among peers who share both the institutional context of the school and the commercial culture that begins courting future consumers almost as soon as they can walk.

Leslie Brody notes that a "primary goal that parents have for their children is that they be socially accepted by the culture in which they live" (165). Brody concludes that "Repeated patterns of interaction and gender-differentiated relationships within the family (and undoubtedly within a larger societal context) seem to be quite important for the emergence of gender differences in the intensity of expressed emotion. Gender differences in parents' socialization patterns are quite consistent with and are probably influenced by cultural gender roles concerning emotional expressiveness" (165). For a boy, this often means that school and home are places where he must stifle a range of emotions. Dan Kindlon and Michael Thompson believe that boys "are systematically steered away from their emotional lives toward silence, solitude, and distrust" (xv), and William Pollack has written of the urgent need to "unlearn the Boy Code" (25) that maintains the myths by which boys are too often constrained.

Recalling our own early schooling through the lens of awareness about gendering can lead to the surprising recognition of how pervasive gender has always been in our lives, influencing not only our choice of clothes, but of majors and careers too. The texts in this section look at early childhood from a number of different perspectives, including those of the psychologist, the sociologist, and the cultural critic. They explore and describe how children interact with parents and teachers, and with each other, in a variety of settings. Apart from the influences of school and home, children also grow up in a world conditioned by commerce and its products, a world in which they are positioned as consumers.

The Socialization Component

Eleanor E. Maccoby

TALK WITH CHILDREN ABOUT EMOTIONS

I have identified a tendency for parents to use a more power-assertive communication style with their sons than with their daughters. Recently, an additional difference has emerged in studies of the kinds of communications that occur between parents and children of the two sexes: a tendency for parents (perhaps especially mothers) to talk more with their young daughters about emotions. Judy Dunn and colleagues (Dunn, Bretherton, and Munn, 1987) recorded conversations between mothers and toddlers (aged 18 months or 24 months), and examined what kinds of things mothers talk about to these very young children. The researchers were particularly interested in talk about feeling states. A number of such states were considered: liking or disliking an event or person or object; being afraid, surprised, sad, upset, or angry; expressing sympathy or concern.

Dunn and colleagues give several examples of a mother's focusing on feeling states. In one instance, the child referred back to an argument with the mother at breakfast, when the child hadn't wanted to eat the cereal the mother had offered. The

mother said, "Crying, weren't you? We had quite a battle." In another case, the mother's feeling-state language came in response to the child's own introduction of such language: the child wanted some chocolate cake. When the mother refused, the child said: "Why? Tired!" The mother replied, "You tired? Ooh!"

Mothers' usage of feeling-state language to eighteen-month-old boys was only about two thirds as frequent as to girls of this age, and when the children were 24 months old, the difference was greater: now mothers initiated feeling-state talk with daughters 3.3 times per hour, compared with 1.6 times with sons. Reciprocally, girls used (and initiated) more feeling-state language than boys at the age of 24 months.

As children acquire more language, and conversations between parents and children become richer and more complex, the greater use of talk about emotions to girls continues. Radke-Yarrow and colleagues report that mothers of children in their third year use more emotion words with daughters than with sons.[1] There appears to be a difference not only in the *amount* of emotion-talk that takes place with sons and daughters, but in its nature as well. In two studies, Robyn Fivush (1993) told parents that she was interested in young children's memories, and asked them to discuss special novel events with their children (aged 30 to 35 months). In the first study, only mothers were involved, but in the second, fathers were included as well. Fivush found that parents sometimes attributed emotional states to a child, as for example:

Reprinted by permission of the publisher from "The Socialization Component" in *The Two Sexes: Growing Up Apart, Coming Together* by Eleanor E. Maccoby. Cambridge, Mass.: The Belknap Press of Harvard University Press, pp. 135–152. Copyright © 1998 by the President and Fellows of Harvard College.

MOTHER: You were so happy.

CHILD: Yeah.

Sometimes a parent elaborated on the emotion attributed to the child:

MOTHER: Were you scared?

CHILD: Yeah.

MOTHER: I had never seen you so scared.

Or, a parent might bring in causes or consequences of an emotional state.

In a third study conducted by Fivush (1993), mothers were asked to discuss four specific kinds of emotional events with their children: events involving the experience of happiness, sadness, anger, and fear. In all three studies, discussions of emotions were almost always initiated by the parent, and boys and girls did not differ in their use of emotion words. Parents, however, talked in somewhat different ways with sons and daughters: they talked more about sadness with daughters than sons, and were more likely to explore explanations of sadness and to try to resolve sad emotional states with daughters.[2]

With sons more than daughters, conversations were about anger or conflict. Boys sometimes introduced the idea of retaliation:

MOTHER: Who bites you?

BOY: Uh, ummm, Johnny bites me.

MOTHER: Yeah, and what do you think when Johnny bites you?

BOY: That I will shoot him.

MOTHER: You're gonna shoot him?

BOY: (nods yes)

MOTHER: When he bites you?

BOY: Yes.

There were no instances in which a girl introduced the possibility of retaliation. It is evident from these examples that the children themselves are contributing actively to the direction the conversation takes. But drawing upon these and many other examples, Fivush concludes that parents make their own contribution, partly through attributing certain emotions to their children, but more commonly through elaboration and explanation. Fivush says that the mothers in her study seemed more willing to accept anger and retaliation in boys than in girls. When the mothers attributed anger to boys, the boys tended to agree, and the mother would reconfirm, as in the sequence: Mother: "You were mad, weren't you?" Child: "Yeah." Mother: "Yeah . . . " With girls more than with boys, mothers focused on reestablishing harmony between the child and others with whom the child was in conflict. It is interesting, too, that in choosing what emotional episodes to discuss with their children in the third study, mothers more often referred to socio-emotional episodes with their daughters (episodes in which other people were involved or had caused the emotional states). With sons, by contrast, mothers more often chose to talk about something the child experienced alone.

The tendency of mothers to focus on socio-emotional themes with daughters is further underscored in Smetana's work. In her observations of children aged 26 and 37 months with their mothers at home, she noted that when children did something naughty (something that impacted on the rights or well-being of other family members), mothers tended to talk with girls about the distress they were causing for others, a parental technique sometimes called "other-oriented induction." With boys, the mothers were more likely just to raise their voices and tell them to stop.

It should be noted, too, that although it is true that parents talk about emotions more with girls, girls also talk about emotions more with their parents than boys do. Emotion talk is a two-way process, and it is sometimes difficult to say how much contribution each member of the dyad makes to initiating or sustaining parent-child conversation about emotions.

What are the implications of the fact that parent-daughter pairs appear to talk about emotional states more frequently than parent-son pairs? Could this make a difference in the kind of culture that girls develop among themselves in their playgroups? Clearly, it could. There is evidence from two longitudinal studies (Dunn, Brown, and Beardsall, 1991; Dunn, Brown, Slomkowski, Tesla, and Youngblade, 1991) that children who spend their early years in families with frequent parent-child talk about emotions are better able to recognize others' emotional states at a later age, and better able to take the perspective of other people, than are children who were not exposed so much to emotion-talk.[3] It seems that sensitivity to the emotional states of others should promote just the kind of cooperative, reciprocal discourse more often seen in girls' groups than in boys' groups. But we have no evidence that it is the very girls who experience the most emotion-talk with their mothers who are most active in establishing the cooperative norms of girls' discourse. Such evidence would greatly strengthen the case for a connection.

We should be aware, too, that understanding the emotions of others may not always lead to cooperative, empathic interaction. It might instead contribute to skill in teasing or manipulating others (see the discussion by Dunn, Brown, and Beardsall, 1991, p. 454). So far, we cannot be sure whether early emotion-talk is a factor that underlies girls' greater use of conflict-mitigating, collaborative discourse in their same-sex groups, though it is a strong possibility. Nor can we be sure whether it was girls' readiness for such talk at an early age, or the mother's greater readiness to engage in such talk with a daughter, or both, that carries over to subsequent relationships with peers.[4]

TEACHING BOYS NOT TO DISPLAY FEELINGS

Not only do parents talk less to boys about feelings. There is evidence that they actively suppress emotional displays in boys. Block (1978) summarized studies in a number of northern European countries as well as the United States, finding that boys were consistently more likely than girls to be the objects of parental pressure not to cry and not to express feelings. In a longitudinal study, Jeanne Block (1978) found that parents of preschoolers were quite active in trying to "down-regulate" their sons' emotional displays. In Chapter 5, we saw that girls were making somewhat greater progress, during the toddler and preschool years, in regulating their own emotional states than were boys, so it is likely that parents were applying added regulatory pressure to boys partly because their sons were more given to impulsive emotional outbursts. Still, parents deem it especially important for boys not to display the kind of weakness or vulnerability or "babyishness" that is implied by crying and other displays of poor emotional control. The fact that their extra pressure on boys is effective is indicated by Buck's (1975) report that by the age of 6, mothers can more easily "read" a daughter's than a son's emotional state.

THE RECIPROCATION OF EMOTIONAL STATES

Although parents talk more about emotions to daughters, this does not imply that they express different emotions toward daughters and sons. As noted earlier, parents appear to be as affectionate toward young sons as toward daughters, and equally kindly and helpful in the sense that they are equally responsive to bids for attention or help from daughters and sons. Most of the research on parental responsiveness to infants and toddlers has been done with mothers, but what is known about fathers indicates that they, too, are as much involved in care-taking with young daughters as with sons, and show similar amounts of affection toward them. However, measures of parental responsiveness and affection are one-way scores; they assess a parental behavior apart from the degree to which the behavior (or emotional states) of the parent and child are synchronized. Recently, there has been increasing interest in emotional reciprocity, especially in the sharing of *positive* emotional states between parent and child. There have been claims that mothers establish a more intimate or "enmeshed" emotional relationship with daughters than with sons (Chodorow, 1978), and such a view would be supported if a greater frequency of positive emotional reciprocity were shown in mother-daughter pairs.

A number of researchers have attempted to see whether mothers were in some way inducting children of one sex more than the other into a mutually empathic system of interaction. Using detailed observations of mothers interacting with infants or toddlers, researchers have watched to see whether mothers match their own emotional expressions to those of the child. Leaper (1995) suggests that such matching may indeed be greater between mothers and daughters than between mothers and sons, but only in the context of traditionally female activities.

In general, however, matching or reciprocation of affect has not been shown to be greater between mothers and daughters than between mothers and sons. Consider first studies of infants: Haviland and Malatesta (1982) reported that mothers matched an infant *son*'s expression of interest, surprise, or joy more than they did a girl's.[5] Tronick and Cohn (1989, p. 83) also found that there was greater matching/synchrony by mothers with infant sons than with infant

daughters. But Martin (1981), when he assessed the degree to which mothers matched the intensity (and changes in intensity) of an infant's arousal level, found no sex difference. In the Stanford longitudinal study, two cohorts of children aged 18 months were observed in interaction with their mothers, and in both samples the number of "positive exchanges" between mother and child was very similar (and not significantly different) for boys and girls.

Kochanska and colleagues (Kochanska, Askan, and Koenig, 1995; Kochanska, 1997) worked with somewhat older children, observing episodes of interaction between approximately 100 mothers and their children at ages 33 months and 46 months. They report that when a mother-child pair frequently show positive emotions at the same time, the child, in other situations, will show more of what Kochanska calls "committed compliance"—that is, will comply with a mother's directive willingly or spontaneously, with little pressure. Furthermore, these researchers suggest that when children have experienced high levels of reciprocated positive affect as toddlers, a year later they will more readily incorporate or "internalize" adult norms of behavior. The Kochanska group found that girls have consistently higher scores on both committed compliance and internalization. Does this mean that girls, more often than boys, have a history of having frequently shared positive emotional states with their mothers? Surprisingly, no, at least not in the Kochanska sample as this form of reciprocity was measured. Episodes of shared positive feeling states were equally common in mother-daughter pairs and mother-son pairs, at both 33 months and 46 months.

Cross-cultural studies also do not point to greater mother-daughter enmeshment. Dora Dien (1992) describes the mother-*son* relationship as more enmeshed in Chinese society than the relationship between mothers and daughters. Whiting and Edwards (1988) did not have an explicitly reciprocal score for mother-child pairs, but they did have a score called "sociability," which implies two-way positive affect. In the various cultures they studied, mothers were equally "sociable" with young sons and daughters. We see, then, that research indicates that an equal degree of affective synchrony prevails in the interactions of mothers with infants and toddlers of the two sexes. This may be true with preschoolers as well, although the evidence for this age is limited. Thus there is no support so far for the hypothesis (Chodorow, 1978) that mothers construct a more empathic or enmeshed relationship with daughters than with sons in the early years via the matching of emotional states in infancy and toddler-hood.

The Kochanska report echoes some earlier research indicating that when mothers are nurturant and empathic, and when there are high levels of positive mother-child interaction, this is associated with high levels of empathy and concern for others in their young daughters, but not in their young sons.[6] This is not a universal finding, but taken together with the more recent Kochanska work it underlines the possibility that young girls are more open than young boys to affective inputs from their parents (perhaps especially from mothers).[7] If, then, the mother-child bond were shown to be more intimate, more mutually responsive than the mother-son bond—and so far, this has not been shown—it would not necessarily imply that the mother has more actively drawn her daughter than her son into such a bond. Again and again, we seem to face the same chicken-and-egg question as to whether it is the mother's socialization pressures or the child's characteristics that first establish the trajectory that a mother-child relationship will follow.

ARE FATHERS MORE ACTIVE THAN MOTHERS IN GENDER SOCIALIZATION?

In some ways, fathers seem to play the role of a grown-up male peer to their sons: they sometimes react to a son the way they interacted with other boys when they themselves were young. Such paternal reactions can start when a boy is very young. Consider one father's response when his toddler boy falls and hurts himself:

MOTHER SAYS: "Come here, honey. I'll kiss it better."

FATHER: "Oh toughen up. Quit your bellyaching." (Gable, Belsky, and Crnic, 1993, p. 32)

This father might be thinking ahead to the time when his son will have to cope with the derision of other boys if he becomes a "crybaby." Or, the father may simply be reacting as he would to any male's signs of weakness. In either case, he is playing a more active role than the mother in trying to instill male-typical ways of behaving in his son. We see the same thing at work when we compare the reactions of mothers and fathers to their children of preschool age, when the children are enacting sex-appropriate or sex-inappropriate scripts. Langlois and Downs (1980) set up two playrooms, one equipped with "masculine" play materials (an army game; a tollbooth with cars; cowboy outfits) and the other with "feminine materials" (dollhouse; cooking equipment; dress-up clothes). When a child had begun playing with the materials in one of these rooms, either the mother or the father was brought in to join the child's play, and the parental reactions were observed. When a father saw his son engaged in feminine activities, he was five times more likely to show a negative reaction than if he saw a daughter playing with masculine materials. Mothers, by contrast, were much less negative than fathers about a boy's cross-sex behavior, and reacted similarly to a daughter or son's being engaged in "sex-inappropriate" behavior.[8]

Siegal (1987) summarized the findings of 39 studies in which it was possible to compare fathers and mothers with respect to their treatment of sons and daughters. The studies were not all consistent, but the trend was clear: that fathers were indeed more likely than mothers to differentiate between sons and daughters.[9] The fathers' differential parenting behavior often took the form of being stricter with boys, more negative or confrontational with them. But in some studies there were other trends as well: a few reported that fathers took more interest in boys, or played with them in more arousing or "physical" ways (see also Power, 1994). And when boys arrive at grade school age, their fathers are more likely to take them (rather than their daughters) to sporting events, or play ball with them. At the same time, fathers tend to be less sympathetic toward shows of dependency from a son than from a daughter (Russell and Russell, 1987).

Fathers may also play a stronger role than mothers in "feminizing" daughters, though this is less clear. In the 1960s, Hetherington (1967) examined the in-home conditions that were associated with a little girl's becoming especially "feminine." She found the fathers of such little girls liked women, and showed appreciation of pretty clothes and hair-dos, and sweet, appealing ways, in their little daughters. Since that time, there has been little interest in this aspect of fathering, but there is no reason to believe that the connection between fatherly appreciation of femininity and little girls' gender development would be any less strong now than it was 30 years ago.

My major conclusion is that fathers, more than mothers, do try to "toughen up" their sons. Fathers also maintain a stance of male dominance toward their sons, as an older boy might do. And fathers who share

the common pattern of male homophobia may distance themselves somewhat from emotional involvement with their sons.[10] To some extent, then, fathers appear to be participating in the induction of boys into male peer culture. At the same time, there are countervailing forces: fathers, of course, are aware that their sons, just like their daughters, are young and vulnerable. So fathers of sons play two roles: that of parent-to-child and that of male-to-male. It seems reasonable that the younger the child, the more the parent-to-child role must take precedence. In any case, fathers clearly feel powerful ties to both sons and daughters: ties of love and ties stemming from the need to provide teaching, protection, and daily care. These things depend very little on the sex of the child, and both parents are largely even-handed with respect to them.

We have seen that fathers, at least under some circumstances, are more power-assertive with sons than with daughters—the implication being that they are "softer" with daughters. This may mean that they think boys are inherently tougher—better able to withstand pain and harshness—or that they need to be treated as though they were tough in order to make them so. There is a fairly consistent pattern here: a tendency for fathers to put especially strong pressures on their sons not to show weakness or signs of effeminacy. In addition, as children grow into middle childhood, each parent is likely to draw a same-sex child into shared sex-typed activities: mothers involve girls more in the preparation of meals (Goodnow, 1988) and fathers involve their sons more in both active and spectator sports, and in non-industrialized societies, fathers involve their sons more in male occupational activities.

SUMMARY AND COMMENT

Childhood culture is different from adult culture in many ways. Childhood culture is far more gender-segregated than is adult culture. Also, the content of children's games is passed on from one generation of children to another, not from adults to children. And interaction styles are different, too: especially among younger children, interaction is more "physical" (particularly among boys) and briefer than it is among adults. We may expect to find, then, that there is much that happens in children's playgroups that probably will not be best understood as an outcome of socialization pressures exerted by adults.

When we try to understand the impact of adult socialization agents on gender differentiation in childhood, the next important point to remember is the fact, documented in this chapter, that in many respects adults treat children of the two sexes in very similar ways. We have seen that when people are reacting to an unfamiliar infant or toddler, their reactions do not depend consistently on whether they believe the child to be a boy or a girl. In most respects, the same may be said of the way parents deal with their own sons and daughters: they are equally responsive to boys and girls overall, equally affectionate toward them, and place similar restrictions or demands upon their activities. These conclusions emerge from a large body of research in which parents have been observed, either at home or in a laboratory playroom, as they interact with sons or daughters ranging in age from infancy to middle childhood.

We do not see, then, a process in which parents are fostering the development of different global sex-typed personality traits in sons and daughters: we do not see socialization patterns that would lead to girls becoming more passive or dependent or "sociable," or boys becoming more assertive. And indeed, children of the two sexes do not typically differ with respect to global personality traits.

Within this pattern of overall similarity, however, certain trends toward gender differentiation may be seen. Parents treat little daughters more gently in terms of the quality of physical handling, and are more likely to roughhouse with young sons. They also behave somewhat more power-assertively toward a son in situations where they need to obtain compliance to a demand. Parents talk more with girls about emotions and about interpersonal events and causes of events. And parents react more positively when they see their children behaving in "sex-appropriate" ways as fairly narrowly defined (not defined in terms of global personality traits). That is, many parents like to see a little girl playing with dolls, pretending to cook, putting on dress-up clothes or trying on her mother's high-heeled shoes; or to see a little boy playing cowboy, or playing with trucks or carpentry tools. Indeed, parents usually provide children with sex-typed toys (along with a range of sex-neutral toys), and as we have seen, this parental behavior supports different kinds of play activities in the two sexes. Also, many parents tend to react negatively when a child engages in activities that are thought to be sex-inappropriate. These negative reactions are especially directed toward boys: both parents are more accepting of "tomboy" tendencies in a daughter than of "sissy" tendencies in a son. Fathers react more strongly than mothers toward cross-sex activities in their children, particularly in their sons. Parents, then, give girls more leeway than boys when it comes to sex-typing.

I should note that most of the differences in parental reactions to sons and daughters are small in magnitude (though, of course, small effects may accumulate over time and snowball in their impact): the distributions for parental treatment of boys and girls overlap greatly, and studies are not consistent in their findings. The exception is emotion-talk to children, where research conducted so far is consistent from one study to another, but even for this feature of socialization, the sex difference does not begin to approach the binary pattern established in playmate preferences.

No evidence has emerged that shows parents exerting direct pressure on their young children to play mainly with others of their own sex. At least, parents in modern industrial societies do not appear to do so. Nor do parents exert influence by example; in the home setting, adults do not segregate by sex, and so do not provide a model for sex segregation as something that adult society expects. Of course, differential socialization by parents might lead to gender segregation by a different route: if all or most parents reinforced girls for one set of characteristics and boys for another, children would presumably begin to find other children of their own sex more compatible, by virtue of their shared characteristics. I noted earlier, for example, that being played with roughly by their parents might predispose boys to rough-and-tumble play with other boys, who presumably have been similarly socialized. But the small amount of correlational evidence available so far does not support this scenario. For example, research to date does not show that the amount of roughhousing parents do with a son is related to the amount of rough-and-tumble play that child will engage in with peers, or to the child's preference for male playmates.

When it comes to sex-typing pressures from parents, such as providing sex-appropriate toys, it is plausible that the children who are most subject to such pressures would be the ones most likely to adopt sex-typed preferences for toys and activities, and who would then in turn prefer to play with other children with similar preferences—children of their own sex. So far, efforts to uncover such connections have been disappointing. Individual children seem to move into mainly sex-segregated playgroups regardless of how strongly their parents have reinforced sex-appropriate behavior at home. Indeed, their playmate preferences appear to be quite independent of how sex-typed their choices of toys and activities are.

To summarize my first main point: In-home socialization probably plays only a minor role in gender segregation. Although there are certain respects in which parents do treat sons and daughters differently on the average, individual children's preferences for same-sex playmates appear to be unrelated to whether or not a child has been subjected to greater or lesser degrees of sex-typing pressure from parents.

When it comes to the interaction styles that develop in all-male versus all-female playgroups, in-home socialization probably has a greater impact, although, as I discuss below, it is difficult to be sure. In addition to the greater frequency of parents roughhousing with sons, and their somewhat more tolerant attitude toward boys' fighting with their peers, parents use a more power-assertive, imperative style—including more physical punishment—with sons than they do with daughters, and it is plausible that boys learn to use the interactive styles that their parents use toward them (see Carli, 1995). These sex-differentiated parental practices could foster the rough, imperative interaction styles that boys exhibit in their playgroups. Similarly, the greater frequency of emotion-talk between parents and daughters could impel girls toward the more other-oriented, conflict-mitigating styles seen in female playgroups.

To summarize my second main point: In-home socialization is probably a more important factor in the kinds of interaction styles children develop in their same-sex playgroups than it is in producing gender segregation per se. There are a number of respects in which the direction of the sex difference in parental treatment matches, or is consistent with, the direction of the difference in playgroup interaction styles. Thus the characteristics that children of the two sexes develop in the course of interaction with their parents may well carry over, to some degree, to the way the children behave in interaction with same-sex playmates.

And in relation to asymmetry, my third main point is: Parents, especially fathers, appear to put more pressure on boys to be "masculine" than they do on girls to be "feminine." This parental behavior could contribute to the asymmetries noted elsewhere: the fact that boys' groups are stronger, more active in policing gender boundaries, and more given to pressuring each other not to be effeminate. It is not so clear, however, how parents' putting greater sex-typing pressure on boys could lead boys to distance themselves from *adults*, as well as from girls.

Note the word "probably" in my second point. There are some unresolved issues that keep us from being confident about the connections between in-home socialization practices and peer-group interaction styles. A major difficulty is the question of who is influencing whom. In the case of parents' using more power-assertive types of pressure on boys, there is good reason to believe that this happens because boys get into mischief more often and are less responsive than girls to milder forms of parental pressure. Similarly, boys may be played with more roughly because they somehow invite such play. And in the case of emotion-talk to children, there may be something in girls' readiness to engage in such talk, or at least to listen to it, that encourages their mothers' greater use of such talk with daughters. If parents are adapting their behavior to the eliciting characteristics of their children, might it not be the children's initial characteristics, rather than any effects of the parents' response, that carry over to the peer group? I would argue that interaction is always a two-way street, with each participant in the parent-child interactive chain influencing the other. And the two participants may contribute different things. For example, though it may be the child's temperament that influences the parental response, it may be the parent's interaction style, rather than the child's temperament, that has the most important influence on the style that develops in the children's playgroup. The relative contributions of parent and child have not been sorted out, however, and my best guess is that both matter.

An additional problem: There are difficulties in translating children's individual characteristics into group process. Parents presumably influence only their own individual child. And families differ considerably in how strongly the parents teach, or model, sex-typed interaction styles. If parents are influencing the play styles that emerge in same-sex playgroups, it ought to be the very children whose parents have encouraged these styles who emerge as style-setters in the children's groups. There is very little research on the socialization histories of the children who emerge as leaders, or style-setters, in children's groups. We know from some work by Charlesworth and LaFreniere (1983) that when four-child groups are competing for a scarce resource, it is the boys who individually rank high in dominance in their preschool setting who win out in the competition, doing so by the use of male-style strategies: pushing, threatening, commanding. If we were able to show that these dominant boys had come from families who used more physical punishment than other parents, did more rough-housing with their children, gave them only masculine toys, or encouraged them to hold their own with other children even if this required fighting, we would have completed the chain of evidence leading from parental socialization to sex-differentiated interaction styles. So far, the evidence is lacking that would allow us to establish this chain. Existing correlational studies have not shown clear connections between what individual parents are doing in terms of sex-typing pressures and how strongly their own children contribute to the sex-typed interaction styles that characterize sex-segregated peer groups.

Judith Harris (1995) has proposed what she calls a *group-socialization* theory. Her claim is that elements of culture are passed on from parents *as a group* to children *as a group,* and then the group of children socialize each other. The characteristics of a peer group do derive from what the parent generation has taught them. But if a particular pair of parents are providing their children with models, or using socialization pressures, which do not conform to the practices of the larger culture, then the child will take on the characteristics prescribed by the larger culture. Harris illustrates this process by reference to an immigrant child learning a new language—a different language from the one spoken at home. This child picks up the language, or dialect, spoken in the peer group, a language or dialect which most members of the peer group learned from their parents. But the transmission is a group process, not an individual one.

Harris' formulation is intriguing. Can we really see the transmission of language and the transmission of sex-typed childhood culture as analogous? One problem is, as I noted earlier, that childhood culture is in many respects quite different from adult culture, so that whatever effects adult socialization agents are having on children's playgroups do not take the form of

the transmission of identical elements. And in the case of language, the whole group of parents in a given cultural group speak very nearly the same language and the same dialect. This uniformity does not hold true for the socialization of gender. As we have seen, parents differ very greatly in whether, and how much, they maintain one set of socialization practices for boys and another for girls. It is possible, though, that enough parents have roughhoused with their boys and talked about emotions with their girls that a majority of children, when they enter their same-sex peer groups, will have had these sex-differentiated experiences and will incorporate them into the group process.

We need to know more about the ways in which group interaction styles emerge from the characteristics of the individual children who make up the group. Is there a kind of critical mass, such that if there are enough children who share a certain style learned earlier, these children can succeed in socializing the other children so that their style comes to pervade the interactions of the whole group? Or is it the case that the children who become style-setters in a group are the ones who have been socialized so that the interaction style they display fits best with some underlying disposition that most members of a given sex share? Or fits best with stereotypes, widely held in a culture, as to what modes of behavior are sex-appropriate? Clearly, these issues are important ones for a research agenda.

It is time to note, again, that my account so far may very well be too culture-bound. Most of the research on which my account is based has been done with children in modern industrialized societies. In smaller, more traditional social groups, the differential training of boys and girls may start much earlier and be much more powerful. Consider some observations made in an African village, where little girls as young as age 2 were seen to step to the side of a path and lower their eyes whenever a male approached them along the path.[11] Clearly, they had been trained in deference to men and boys, and presumably boys had also been trained to expect deference from females—to believe that males are the favored or superior sex. Children presumably can make such inferences early in life if they live in a society where, for example, the two sexes do not eat together—where the men and boys eat first, being waited on by the women, who have prepared the food. Inferences concerning the relative status of the two sexes derived from experiencing such cultural practices obviously could contribute strongly to children's congregating almost exclusively with playmates of their own sex, and to some of the asymmetries favoring male playgroups that I have noted. Indeed, Whiting and Edwards (1988, p. 277) note that it is in the very societies where men most clearly have higher status than women that boys make the earliest and strongest efforts to distance themselves from women and girls—from their own mothers, as well as from other females. In less industrialized cultures, too, segregation can be fostered by the assignment of different chores to boys and girls, so that they are found in different spaces: domestic chores for girls keeping them close to home while boys' chores, such as herding animals, take them some distance from home. My account so far, then, has pointed to a smaller role for socialization pressures from adults in modern industrialized societies than may be valid for a number of other cultures.

Although I have stressed the different interaction styles that emerge in male and female playgroups, I have said very little about the *content of* children's play. Here the cultural impact is great. In India, little girls use whatever materials are at hand—mud, sand, dough—to pretend that they are preparing chapatis and cooking them over a make-believe fire in a stone hearth. Girls in Mexico play at grinding corn and making tortillas; girls in the United States pretend they are making chocolate-chip cookies and baking them in an electric or gas oven. The content of children's play obviously derives from the scripts that their adult culture provides, and parents may be a major—though not the only—providers of the scripts that are learned. Certain aspects of male play, such as dominance struggles and themes of heroic combat, may be cross-culturally universal, or nearly so, but the content of the scripts depends on what weapons are available in a given culture and on what kind of cultural heroes are known to children.

As we saw at the beginning of this chapter, a common view is that boys and girls diverge in their childhood social behavior because adults treat them differently, and thus instill different habits, preferences, and skills. This conception is part of a more general view about socialization of children: that it occurs through processes whereby adults pass on to each new generation of children the rules, values, and beliefs that govern social behavior in the culture where the child is growing up. In this view, socialization occurs through the training of individual children. The characteristics of groups are a kind of sum or average of the characteristics of the individual children that constitute them.

There are a number of reasons to be dissatisfied with this approach. For one thing, as we have seen, childhood culture is in many ways not a direct reflection of adult culture. Further, the phenomena which need explanation—gender segregation, the distinctive male and female childhood cultures—are *group* processes, and we have seen that within-family processes do not translate well to group peer processes. But most important, the common view of socialization is too static. It does not take account of culture change. In the twentieth century, we have seen extraordinary changes in sex roles and in the relations between the sexes. We know what some of the social forces are that have brought about these changes: the widespread availability of contraception; the education of women; the employment of women; and the ideological changes embodied in the women's rights movement. In systematic ways, each new generation has been different from its parent generation. We could almost see this situation as a *failure* of socialization, if we think mainly in terms of intergenerational transmission.

Does this mean that I am discounting "socialization" as a force for gender differentiation? No, although it does mean that I am claiming a more limited role for parents in this socialization than others have done. Peers clearly have a socialization role. Indeed, peers may be more effective carriers of social change than the parent generation is. (After all, many children acquire computer literacy, or skill in video games, from agemates and from somewhat older young people who are much closer to their own age than their computer-illiterate parents or grandparents are.) But there may also be forms of direct transmission of changing gender ideology and changing cultural gender-related practices that bypass both parents and peers.

We have already seen that children's behavior is governed not only by what they have been directly taught but also by what they have inferred through observing the culture around them. Certain cultural views about gender are embodied in myths, plays, and stories as well as in daily life. They are "in the air," and can be picked up by children from a host of sources.

NOTES

1. Radke-Yarrow and colleagues analyzed mothers' speech to children aged 25–36 months, and reported more use of emotion words with daughters (Radke-Yarrow, Belmont, Nottelman, and Bottomly, 1990). They did not find that mothers spoke more to one sex than the other about other topics, however.

2. See also Kuebil and Krieger (1991), who reported that mothers talk more about sadness with their preschool daughters than with their sons, and that fathers talk with daughters more about being scared.

3. In a review summarizing 16 studies that dealt specifically with sensitivity to the emotional states of others, Haviland and Malatesta (1981) found clear evidence of greater sensitivity among females. We should, however, be wary of assuming that this sensitivity translates into greater *sharing* of others' affective states (empathy), or greater helpfulness to others growing out of empathy, on the part of females. In their review of sex differences in altruism, Radke-Yarrow, Zahn-Waxler, and Chapman (1983) found no consistent sex difference in any aspect of altruism, including empathic responses to others' distress.

4. Dunn and colleagues (1991) found that the amount of the *child's* talk about emotions to the mother predicted subsequent sensitivity to the emotional states of others much more strongly than did the amount of the mother's emotion-talk to the child.

5. Haviland and Malatesta believe that this finding—along with the finding that mothers gave a wider range of emotional responses to daughters, including nonmatching responses—suggests a "greater sense of empathy between mother and daughter" (1982, p. 201), but clearly other interpretations are possible.

6. Research supporting this conclusion is reviewed by Zahn-Waxler, Cole, and Barrett (1991, p. 255).

7. See also Gunnar and Donahue (1980) for evidence of greater social responsiveness in infant girls at 6 and 12 months. In a similar vein, Martin (1981) reported that girls were less insistent (more compliant) at both 10 and 22 months than were boys.

8. See the summary of these findings in Maccoby (1980, p. 240).

9. In 20 of the 39 studies, a difference was found in fathers' treatment of sons and daughters; such a difference was almost never found for mothers.

10. I am acquainted with a family in which the strongly homophobic father refused to change his sons' diapers, but was willing and able to carry out this chore with his daughter.

11. Personal communication from Herbert Leiderman (and see Levine et al., 1994).

The "Act Like a Man" Box

Paul Kivel

How is gender constructed in Western society? From a very early age, most boys are told to "act like a man." Even though they have all the normal human feelings of love, excitement, sadness, confusion, anger, curiosity, pain, frustration, humiliation, shame, grief, resentment, loneliness, low self-worth, and self-doubt, most are taught to hide the feelings (except anger) and appear to be tough and in control. They are told to be aggressive, not to back down, not to make mistakes, and to take charge, have lots of sex, make lots of money, and be responsible. Most of all, they are told not to cry.

At the Oakland Men's Project, which I helped to start over 20 years ago, we've called this rigid set of expectations the "Act Like a Man" Box because it feels like a box—a 24-hour-a-day, seven-day-a-week box that society tells boys they must fit themselves into. One reason we know it's a box is because every time a boy tries to step out he's pushed back in with names like wimp, sissy, mama's boy, girl, fag, nerd, punk, mark, bitch, and others even more graphic. Behind those names is the threat of violence. Most boys end up in a fight sometime in their youth to prove they are in the Box. If another boy comes up to you in the hall at junior high school and calls you a wimp, a girl, or a fag, you have to fight him to prove you are in the Box.

The columns on either side of the Box show widespread expectations our society

holds for men. The abuse, pressure, and training boys receive to meet these expectations and stay in the Box produce a lot of feelings, some of which are listed in the middle of the Box. Yet they have to cover over those feelings and try to act like a man because one of the strictures of being a man is not to show your feelings. Some of the names that boys get called are listed on the left of the Box. On the right are listed some of the other kinds of abuse that come with the training to be in the Box.

There are cultural variations of this theme, but its prevalence in Western cultures is striking. Boys develop different strategies for trying to survive in the Box, some might even sneak out of it at times, but, for many, the scars from living within the walls of the Box are long-lasting and painful.

If we pay attention we can easily see the Box's effects on boys. Just watch a group of them together. They are constantly challenging each other, putting each other down, hitting each other, testing to see who is in the Box. They are never at ease, always on guard. At an early age, most start to hide their feelings, toughen up, and will make a huge emotional effort not to cry. Many boys stop wearing colorful clothing or participating in activities that they think might make them vulnerable to being labeled gay. They walk more stiffly, talk more guardedly, move more aggressively. Behind this bravura they are often confused, scared, angry, and wanting closeness with others. But being in the Box precludes closeness and makes intimacy less and less likely.

Our desire for closeness with them is often at odds with our desire to toughen them

Excerpted from Paul Kivel, *Boys Will Be Men* (1999) Gabriola Island, B.C., Canada: New Society Publishers, pp. 11–16.

up so they will not be vulnerable. We may fervently want them to get out of the Box, but there can be subtle and not-so-subtle ways we reinforce their training. For example, most of us stop holding boys when they are four, five, or six years old. We might say to ourselves that we don't want our sons to remain babies, that they need to grow up, that it's a tough world out there. But boys, young men—every single one—need respectful, physical affection from the adults around them. They do pull away from us as they get older and face peer pressure to be unemotional, particularly in public situations. But primarily it is our discomfort rather than theirs that deprives them of the hugs, kisses, and physical affection they need into their teen years.

We may become fearful for their safety and offer only lukewarm support if they show interest in activities that are not traditionally male. We may encourage them to participate in athletic or other competitive programs because we think it is good for them, without questioning the values they learn from their activities.

There are probably times that we give up, say "boys will be boys," and don't challenge the messages and training they receive from TV, movies, books, sports, and their peers. We can remind ourselves that "boys will be men" and they need our support in figuring out how to be men who are not trapped in the Box.

VERBAL ABUSE:

wimp ▲
girl ▲
sissy ▲
mama's boy ▲
nerd ▲
fag ▲
punk ▲
mark ▲
bitch ▲

tough

aggressive

competitive

in control

no feelings

don't cry

take charge

don't make mistakes

succeed

anger
sadness
love
connection
confusion
low self-worth
resentment
curiosity
excitement
isolation

have money

never ask for help

angry

yell

intimidate

responsible

take it

don't back down

have sex with women

PHYSICAL ABUSE:

▲ hit/beat up
▲ teased
▲ isolated
▲ rejected
▲ forced to play sports
▲ sexual assault

"Act Like a Man" Box

QUESTIONS TO ASK YOURSELF

Is there an age beyond which you find it hard to hold or hug boys? Why?

What damage did you think it would do if you continued?

Are there any ways you have withheld affection or nurturing from an older boy because you were worried about the effect it might have on him?

Are there any names that you use to refer to boys who are not in the Box?

Has there ever been a time when you worried that your son or another boy wasn't tough enough?

Are there any ways that you encourage boys to toughen up, get over their pain, or take it like a man?

Are there activities that you are uncomfortable having boys participate in—for example, playing with dolls, dancing, wearing bright colors, jumping rope?

The key to staying in the Box is control. Boys are taught to control their bodies, control their feelings, control their relationships—to protect themselves from being vulnerable. Although the Box is a metaphor for the social pressures all boys must learn to respond to, the possibility that a boy will have control over the conditions of his life varies depending on his race, class, and culture.

Being in control is not the same as being violent. In Western societies hitting people is frowned upon except in particular sports or military settings. It is deemed much more refined to retain control by using verbal, emotional, or psychological means rather than physical force. Financial manipulation, coercion and intimidation, and sexual pressure are also condoned as long as no one is physically injured.

Clearly, the more money, education, and connections a man has, the easier it is for him to buy or manipulate others to get what he wants. Wealthy and upper- or middle-class white men are generally promoted and cele-brated for being in control and getting what they want. Poor or working-class men and men of color are usually punished for these same behaviors, especially, but not only, if they use physical force.

Why are boys trained to be in control? Most boys will end up with one of three roles in society—to be workers, consumers, or enforcers. A small percentage of boys are trained to give orders—to be bosses, managers, or officers. The Box trains boys for the roles they will play, whether they will make decisions governing the lives of others or carry out the decisions made by those at the top. I will have more to say about this training, but I think it is clear that the Box prepares boys to be police officers, security guards, deans, administrators, soldiers, heads of families, probation officers, prison guards—the roles that many men, primarily white men, are being trained to fill. Men of color, along with women and young people, are the people more often being controlled.

Many men are under the illusion that being in the Box is like being in an exclusive club. No girls allowed. All men are equal. For working- and middle-class white men and for those men of color who aspire to be accepted by them, the Box creates a false feeling of solidarity with men in power and misleads many men into thinking they have more in common with corporate executives, political and religious leaders, generals, and bosses than they have with women.

In this book, I examine closely the training that boys receive to "act like a man" and offer suggestions for countering it because this training sustains and perpetuates an undemocratic and unjust social structure. Although many of us are not happy with how it works, few of us talk to our sons about the gender-role training they are receiving. We may not point it out to them or notice with them the consequences for themselves, other men, and women. We may not challenge them to think critically about that training and to develop the communication and problem-solving skills that would get them out of the Box.

It is essential for young men to discuss and reject the behavior outlined in the "Act Like a Man" Box. It is liberating for them to understand the reasons why they feel so pressured, the consequences of this male training for them and for those around them, and the roles they are being prepared to play in the larger society. . . .

WHAT KIND OF MEN DO WE NEED?

This book is not about raising boys to "act like men." Every boy who survives childhood becomes a man, a physically mature adult human male. So what are we raising boys for? This is not an easy question to answer. To some extent I don't think we can know yet. New roles and new responsibilities have to emerge out of the lived needs of new times. However, there are some common

values I think we need as a foundation for any progressive future we can imagine.

One of those values is the elimination of rigidly defined, mutually exclusive gender roles that lock men and women into expectations and behaviors that are limiting and distorted. We will have achieved little if we do not seriously undermine male and female gender roles and must be constantly vigilant to ensure we do not recreate them in new guises.

I want to raise children who are responsible, cooperative, caring, and competent, regardless of their biology. I think we need young people who understand and are willing to challenge all forms of social injustice based on economics, race, gender, sexual identity, and ability.

Finally, I want to raise boys differently because they demand it from us. They are constantly challenging our ideas and child-rearing practices—constantly asking if what we are doing is relevant, current, appropriate. We can gain a great deal if we heed their challenges and question our practices.

Through the Tunnel

Doris Lessing

Going to the shore on the first morning of the vacation, the young English boy stopped at a turning of the path and looked down at a wild and rocky bay, and then over to the crowded beach he knew so well from other years. His mother walked on in front of him, carrying a bright striped bag in one hand. Her other arm, swinging loose, was very white in the sun. The boy watched that white naked arm, and turned his eyes, which had a frown behind them, towards the bay and back again to his mother. When she felt he was not with her, she swung around. "Oh, there you are, Jerry!" she said. She looked impatient, then smiled. "Why, darling, would you rather not come with me? Would you rather—" She frowned, conscientiously worrying over what amusements he might secretly be longing for, which she had been too busy or too careless to imagine. He was very familiar with that anxious, apologetic smile. Contrition sent him running after her. And yet, as he ran, he looked back over his shoulder at the wild bay; and all morning, as he played on the safe beach, he was thinking of it.

Next morning, when it was time for the routine of swimming and sunbathing, his mother said, "Are you tired of the usual beach, Jerry? Would you like to go somewhere else?"

"Oh, no!" he said quickly, smiling at her out of that unfailing impulse of contrition—a sort of chivalry. Yet, walking down the path with her, he blurted out, "I'd like to go and have a look at those rocks down there."

She gave the idea her attention. It was a wild-looking place, and there was no one there; but she said, "Of course, Jerry. When you've had enough, come to the big beach. Or just go straight back to the villa, if you like." She walked away, that bare arm, now slightly reddened from yesterday's sun, swinging. And he almost ran after her again, feeling it unbearable that she should go by herself, but he did not.

She was thinking, Of course he's old enough to be safe without me. Have I been keeping him too close? He mustn't feel he ought to be with me. I must be careful.

He was an only child, eleven years old. She was a widow. She was determined to be neither possessive nor lacking in devotion. She went worrying off to her beach.

As for Jerry, once he saw that his mother had gained her beach, he began the steep descent to the bay. From where he was, high up among red-brown rocks, it was a scoop of moving blueish green fringed with white. As he went lower, he saw that it spread among small promontories and inlets of rough, sharp rock, and the crisping, lapping surface showed stains of purple and darker blue. Finally, as he ran sliding and scraping down the last few yards, he saw an edge of white surf and the shallow, luminous movement of water over white sand, and, beyond that, a solid, heavy blue.

He ran straight into the water and began swimming. He was a good swimmer.

He went out fast over the gleaming sand, over a middle region where rocks lay like discoloured monsters under the surface, and then he was in the real sea—a warm sea where irregular cold currents from the deep water shocked his limbs.

When he was so far out that he could look back not only on the little bay but past the promontory that was between it and the big beach, he floated on the buoyant surface and looked for his mother. There she was, a speck of yellow under an umbrella that looked like a slice of orange peel. He swam back to shore, relieved at being sure she was there, but all at once very lonely.

On the edge of a small cape that marked the side of the bay away from the promontory was a loose scatter of rocks. Above them, some boys were stripping off their clothes. They came running, naked, down to the rocks. The English boy swam towards them, but kept his distance at a stone's throw. They were of that coast; all of them were burned smooth dark brown and speaking a language he did not understand. To be with them, of them, was a craving that filled his whole body. He swam a little closer; they turned and watched him with narrowed, alert dark eyes. Then one smiled and waved. It was enough. In a minute, he had swum in and was on the rocks beside them, smiling with a desperate, nervous supplication. They shouted cheerful greetings at him; and then, as he preserved his nervous, uncomprehending smile, they understood that he was a foreigner strayed from his own beach, and they proceeded to forget him. But he was happy. He was with them.

They began diving again and again from a high point into a well of blue sea between rough, pointed rocks. After they had dived and come up, they swam around, hauled themselves up, and waited their turn to dive again. They were big boys—men, to Jerry. He dived, and they watched him; and when he swam around to take his place, they made way for him. He felt he was accepted and he dived again, carefully, proud of himself.

Soon the biggest of the boys poised himself, shot down into the water, and did not come up. The others stood about, watching. Jerry, after waiting for the sleek brown head to appear, let out a yell of warning; they looked at him idly and turned their eyes back towards the water. After a long time, the boy came up on the other side of a big dark rock, letting the air out of his lungs in a sputtering gasp and a shout of triumph. Immediately the rest of them dived in. One moment, the morning seemed full of chattering boys; the next, the air and the surface of the water were empty. But through the heavy blue, dark shapes could be seen moving and groping.

Jerry dived, shot past the school of underwater swimmers, saw a black wall of rock looming at him, touched it, and bobbed up at once to the surface, where the wall was a low barrier he could see across. There was no one visible; under him, in the water, the dim shapes of the swimmers had disappeared. Then one, and then another of the boys came up on the far side of the barrier of rock, and he understood that they had swum through some gap or hole in it. He plunged down again. He could see nothing through the stinging salt water but the blank rock. When he came up the boys were all on the diving rock, preparing to attempt the feat again. And now, in a panic of failure, he yelled up, in English, "Look at me! Look!" and he began splashing and kicking in the water like a foolish dog.

They looked down gravely, frowning. He knew the frown. At moments of failure, when he clowned to claim his mother's attention, it was with just this grave, embarrassed inspection that she rewarded him. Through his hot shame, feeling the pleading grin on his face like a scar that he could never remove, he looked up at the group of big brown boys on the rock and shouted "*Bonjour! Merci! Au revoir! Monsieur, monsieur!*" while he hooked his fingers round his ears and waggled them.

Water surged into his mouth; he choked, sank, came up. The rock, lately weighted with boys, seemed to rear up out of the water as their weight was removed. They were flying down past him now, into the water; the air was full of falling bodies. Then the rock was empty in the hot sunlight. He counted one, two, three . . .

At fifty, he was terrified. They must all be drowning beneath him, in the watery caves of the rock! At a hundred, he stared around him at the empty hillside, wondering if he should yell for help. He counted faster, faster, to hurry them up, to bring them to the surface quickly, to drown them quickly—anything rather than the terror of counting on and on into the blue emptiness of the morning. And then, at a hundred and sixty, the water beyond the rock was full of boys blowing like brown whales. They swam back to the shore without a look at him.

He climbed back to the diving rock and sat down, feeling the hot roughness of it under his thighs. The boys were gathering up their bits of clothing and running off along the shore to another promontory. They were leaving to get away from him. He cried openly, fists in his eyes. There was no one to see him, and he cried himself out.

It seemed to him that a long time had passed, and he swam out to where he could see his mother. Yes, she was still there, a yellow spot under an orange umbrella. He swam back to the big rock, climbed up, and dived into the blue pool among the fanged and angry boulders. Down he went, until he touched the wall of rock again. But the salt was so painful in his eyes that he could not see.

He came to the surface, swam to shore and went back to the villa to wait for his mother. Soon she walked slowly up the path, swinging her striped bag, the flushed, naked arm dangling beside her. "I want some swimming goggles," he panted, defiant and beseeching.

She gave him a patient, inquisitive look as she said casually, "Well, of course, darling."

But now, now, now! He must have them this minute, and no other time. He nagged and pestered until she went with him to a shop. As soon as she had bought the goggles, he grabbed them from her hand as if she were going to claim them for herself, and was off, running down the steep path to the bay.

Jerry swam out to the big barrier rock, adjusted the goggles, and dived. The impact of the water broke the rubber-enclosed vacuum, and the goggles came loose. He understood that he must swim down to the base of the rock from the surface of the water. He fixed the goggles tight and firm, filled his lungs, and floated, face down, on the water. Now he could see. It was as if he had eyes of a different kind—fish eyes that showed everything clear and delicate and wavering in the bright water.

Under him, six or seven feet down, was a floor of perfectly clean, shining white sand, rippled firm and hard by the tides. Two greyish shapes steered there, like long, rounded pieces of wood or slate. They were fish. He saw them nose towards each other, poise motionless, make a dart forward, swerve off, and come around again. It was like a water dance. A few inches above them the water sparkled as if sequins were dropping through it. Fish again—myriads of minute fish, the length of his fingernail—were drifting through the water, and in a moment he could feel the innumerable tiny touches of them against his limbs. It was like swimming in flaked silver. The great rock the big boys had swum through rose sheer out of the white sand—black, tufted lightly with greenish weed. He could see no gap in it. He swam down to its base.

Again and again he rose, took a big chestful of air, and went down. Again and again he groped over the surface of the rock, feeling it, almost hugging it in the desperate need to find the entrance. And then, once, while he was clinging to the black wall, his knees came up and he shot his feet out forward and they met no obstacle. He had found the hole.

He gained the surface, clambered about the stones that littered the barrier rock until he found a big one, and, with this in his arms, let himself down over the side of the rock. He dropped, with the weight, straight to the sandy floor. Clinging tight to the anchor of stone, he lay on his side and looked in under the dark shelf at the place where his feet had gone.

He could see the hole. It was an irregular, dark gap; but he could not see deep into it. He let go of his anchor, clung with his hands to the edges of the hole, and tried to push himself in.

He got his head in, found his shoulders jammed, moved them in sidewise, and was inside as far as his waist. He could see nothing ahead. Something soft and clammy touched his mouth; he saw a dark frond moving against the greyish rock, and panic filled him. He thought of octopuses, of clinging weed. He pushed himself out backward and caught a glimpse, as he retreated, of a harmless tentacle of seaweed drifting in the mouth of the tunnel. But it was enough. He reached the sunlight, swam to shore, and lay on the diving rock. He looked down into the blue well of water. He knew he must find his way through that cave, or hole, or tunnel, and out the other side.

First, he thought, he must learn to control his breathing. He let himself down into the water with another big stone in his arms, so that he could lie effortlessly on the bottom

of the sea. He counted. One, two, three. He counted steadily. He could hear the movement of blood in his chest. Fifty-one, fifty-two. . . . His chest was hurting. He let go of the rock and went up into the air. He saw that the sun was low. He rushed to the villa and found his mother at her supper. She said only "Did you enjoy yourself?" and he said "Yes."

All night the boy dreamed of the water-filled cave in the rock, and as soon as breakfast was over he went to the bay.

That night, his nose bled badly. For hours he had been underwater, learning to hold his breath, and now he felt weak and dizzy. His mother said, "I shouldn't overdo things, darling, if I were you."

That day and the next, Jerry exercised his lungs as if everything, the whole of his life, all that he would become, depended upon it. Again his nose bled at night, and his mother insisted on his coming with her the next day. It was a torment to him to waste a day of his careful self-training, but he stayed with her on that other beach, which now seemed a place for small children, a place where his mother might lie safe in the sun. It was not his beach.

He did not ask for permission, on the following day, to go to his beach. He went, before his mother could consider the complicated rights and wrongs of the matter. A day's rest, he discovered, had improved his count by ten. The big boys had made the passage while he counted a hundred and sixty. He had been counting fast, in his fright. Probably now, if he tried, he could get through that long tunnel, but he was not going to try yet. A curious, most unchildlike persistence, a controlled impatience, made him wait. In the meantime, he lay underwater on the white sand, littered now by stones he had brought down from the upper air, and studied the entrance to the tunnel. He knew every jut and corner of it, as far as it was possible to see. It was as if he already felt its sharpness about his shoulders.

He sat by the clock in the villa, when his mother was not near, and checked his time. He was incredulous and then proud to find he could hold his breath without strain for two minutes. The words "two minutes," authorised by the clock, brought close the adventure that was so necessary to him.

In another four days, his mother said casually one morning, they must go home. On the day before they left, he would do it. He would do it if it killed him, he said defiantly to himself. But two days before they were to leave—a day of triumph when he increased his count by fifteen—his nose bled so badly that he turned dizzy and had to lie limply over the big rock like a bit of seaweed, watching the thick red blood flow on to the rock and trickle slowly down to the sea. He was frightened. Supposing he turned dizzy in the tunnel? Supposing he died there, trapped? Supposing—his head went around, in the hot sun, and he almost gave up. He thought he would return to the house and lie down, and next summer, perhaps, when he had another year's growth in him—*then* he would go through the hole.

But even after he had made the decision, or thought he had, he found himself sitting up on the rock and looking down into the water; and he knew that now, this moment, when his nose had only just stopped bleeding, when his head was still sore and throbbing—this was the moment when he would try. If he did not do it now, he never would. He was trembling with fear that he would not go; and he was trembling with horror at the long, long tunnel under the rock, under the sea. Even in the open sunlight, the barrier rock seemed very wide and very heavy; tons of rock pressed down on where he would go. If he died there, he would lie until one day—perhaps not before next year—those big boys would swim into it and find it blocked.

He put on his goggles, fitted them tight, tested the vacuum. His hands were shaking. Then he chose the biggest stone he could carry and slipped over the edge of the rock until half of him was in the cool enclosing water and half in the hot sun. He looked up once at the empty sky, filled his lungs once, twice, and then sank fast to the bottom with the stone. He let it go and began to count. He took the edges of the hole in his hands and drew himself into it, wriggling his shoulders in sidewise as he remembered he must, kicking himself along with his feet.

Soon he was clear inside. He was in a small rock-bound hole filled with yellowish-grey water. The water was pushing him up against the roof. The roof was sharp and pained his back. He pulled himself along with his hands—fast, fast—and used his legs as levers. His head knocked against something; a sharp pain dizzied him. Fifty, fifty-one, fifty-two. . . . He was without light, and the water seemed to press upon him with the weight of rock. Seventy-one, seventy-two . . . There was no strain on his lungs. He felt like an inflated balloon, his lungs were so light and easy, but his head was pulsing.

He was being continually pressed against the sharp roof, which felt slimy as well as sharp. Again he thought of octopuses, and wondered if the tunnel might be filled with weed that could tangle him. He gave himself a panicky, convulsive kick forward, ducked his head, and swam. His feet and hands moved freely, as if in open water. The hole must have widened out. He thought he must be swimming fast, and he was frightened of banging his head if the tunnel narrowed.

A hundred, a hundred and one . . . The water paled. Victory filled him. His lungs were beginning to hurt. A few more strokes and he would be out. He was counting wildly; he said a hundred and fifteen, and then, a long time later, a hundred and fifteen again. The water was a clear jewel-green all around him. Then he saw, above his head, a crack running up through the rock. Sunlight was falling through it, showing the clean, dark rock of the tunnel, a single mussel shell, and darkness ahead.

He was at the end of what he could do. He looked up at the crack as if it were filled with air and not water, as if he could put his mouth to it to draw in air. A hundred and fifteen, he heard himself say inside his head—but he had said that long ago. He must go on into the blackness ahead, or he would drown. His head was swelling, his lungs cracking. A hundred and fifteen, a hundred and fifteen pounded through his head, and he feebly clutched at rocks in the dark, pulling himself forward leaving the brief space of sunlit water behind. He felt he was dying. He was no longer quite conscious. He struggled on in the darkness between lapses into unconsciousness. An immense, swelling pain filled his head, and then the darkness cracked with an explosion of green light. His hands, groping forward, met nothing; and his feet, kicking back, propelled him out into the open sea.

He drifted to the surface, his face turned up to the air. He was gasping like a fish. He felt he would sink now and drown; he could not swim the few feet back to the rock. Then he was clutching it and pulling himself up onto it. He lay face down, gasping. He could see nothing but a red-veined, clotted dark. His eyes must have burst, he thought; they were full of blood. He tore off his goggles and a gout of blood went into the sea. His nose was bleeding, and the blood had filled the goggles.

He scooped up handfuls of water from the cool, salty sea, to splash on his face, and did not know whether it was blood or salt water he tasted. After a time, his heart quieted, his eyes cleared, and he sat up. He could see the local boys diving and playing half a mile away. He did not want them. He wanted nothing but to get back home and lie down.

In a short while, Jerry swam to shore and climbed slowly up the path to the villa. He flung himself on his bed and slept, waking at the sound of feet on the path outside. His mother was coming back. He rushed to the bathroom, thinking she must not see his face with bloodstains, or tearstains, on it. He came out of the bathroom and met her as she walked into the villa, smiling, her eyes lighting up.

"Have a nice morning?" she asked, laying her hand on his warm brown shoulder a moment.

"Oh, yes, thank you," he said.

"You look a bit pale." And then, sharp and anxious, "How did you bang your head?"

"Oh, just banged it," he told her.

She looked at him closely. He was strained; his eyes were glazed-looking. She was worried. And then she said to herself, Oh, don't fuss! Nothing can happen. He can swim like a fish.

They sat down to lunch together.

"Mummy," he said, "I can stay underwater for two minutes—three minutes, at least." It came bursting out of him.

"Can you, darling?" she said. "Well, I shouldn't overdo it. I don't think you ought to swim any more today."

She was ready for a battle of wills, but he gave in at once. It was no longer of the least importance to go to the bay.

Girls and Boys Together . . . But Mostly Apart: Gender Arrangements in Elementary School

Barrie Thorne

Throughout the years of elementary school, children's friendships and casual encounters are strongly separated by sex. Sex segregation among children, which starts in preschool and is well established by middle childhood, has been amply documented in studies of children's groups and friendships (e.g., Eder & Hallinan, 1978; Schofield, 1981) and is immediately visible in elementary school settings. When children choose seats in classrooms or the cafeteria, or get into line, they frequently arrange themselves in same-sex clusters. At lunchtime, they talk matter-of-factly about "girls' tables" and "boys' tables." Playgrounds have gendered turfs, with some areas and activities, such as large playing fields and basketball courts, controlled mainly by boys, and others—smaller enclaves like jungle-gym areas and concrete spaces for hopscotch or jumprope—more often controlled by girls. Sex segregation is so common in elementary schools that it is meaningful to speak of separate girls' and boys' worlds.

Studies of gender and children's social relations have mostly followed this "two worlds" model, separately describing and comparing the subcultures of girls and of boys (e.g., Lever, 1976; Maltz & Borker, 1983). In brief summary: Boys tend to interact in larger, more age-heterogeneous groups

(Lever, 1976; Waldrop & Halverson, 1975; Eder & Hallinan, 1978). They engage in more rough and tumble play and physical fighting (Maccoby & Jacklin, 1974). Organized sports are both a central activity and a major metaphor in boys' subcultures; they use the language of "teams" even when not engaged in sports, and they often construct interaction in the form of contests. The shifting hierarchies of boys' groups (Savin-Williams, 1976) are evident in their more frequent use of direct command, insults, and challenges (Goodwin, 1980).

Fewer studies have been done of girls' groups (Foot, Chapman, & Smith, 1980; McRobbie & Garber, 1975), and—perhaps because categories for description and analysis have come more from male than female experience—researchers have had difficulty seeing and analyzing girls' social relations. Recent work has begun to correct this skew. In middle childhood, girls' worlds are less public than those of boys; girls more often interact in private places and in smaller groups or friendship pairs (Eder & Hallinan, 1978; Waldrop & Halverson, 1975). Their play is more cooperative and turn-taking (Lever, 1976). Girls have more intense and exclusive friendships, which take shape around keeping and telling secrets, shifting alliances, and indirect ways of expressing disagreement (Goodwin, 1980; Lever, 1976; Maltz & Borker, 1983). Instead of direct commands, girls more often use directives which merge speaker and hearer, e.g., "let's" or "we gotta" (Goodwin, 1980).

Willard W. Hartup and Zick Rubin, eds. *Relationships and Development* (1986). Mahwah, NJ: Lawrence Erlbaum Associates, pp. 61–73.

Although much can be learned by comparing the social organization and sub-cultures of boys' and of girls' groups, the separate worlds approach has eclipsed full, contextual understanding of gender and social relations among children. The separate worlds model essentially involves a search for group sex differences, and shares the limitations of individual sex difference research. Differences tend to be exaggerated and similarities ignored, with little theoretical attention to the integration of similarity and difference (Unger, 1979). Statistical findings of difference are often portrayed as dichotomous, neglecting the considerable individual variation that exists; for example, not all boys fight, and some have intense and exclusive friendships. The sex difference approach tends to abstract gender from its social context, to assume that males and females are qualitatively and permanently different (with differences perhaps unfolding through separate developmental lines). These assumptions mask the possibility that gender arrangements and patterns of similarity and difference may vary by situation, race, social class, region, and subculture.

Sex segregation is far from total, and is a more complex and dynamic process than the portrayal of separate worlds reveals. Erving Goffman (1977) has observed that sex segregation has a "with-then-apart" structure; the sexes segregate periodically, with separate spaces, rituals, and groups, but they also come together and are, in crucial ways, part of the same world. This is certainly true in the social environment of elementary schools. Although girls and boys do interact as boundaried collectivities—an image suggested by the separate worlds approach—there are other occasions when they work or play in relaxed and integrated ways. Gender is less central to the organization and meaning of some situations than others. In short,

sex segregation is not static, but is a variable and complicated process.

To gain an understanding of gender which can encompass both the "with" and the "apart" of sex segregation, analysis should start not with the individual, nor with a search for sex differences, but with social relationships. Gender should be conceptualized as a system of relationships rather than as an immutable and dichotomous given. Taking this approach, I have organized my research on gender and children's social relations around questions like the following: How and when does gender enter into group formation? In a given situation, how is gender made more or less salient or infused with particular meanings? By what rituals, processes, and forms of social organization and conflict do "with-then-apart" rhythms get enacted? How are these processes affected by the organization of institutions (e.g., different types of schools, neighborhoods, or summer camps), varied settings (e.g., the constraints and possibilities governing interaction on playgrounds vs. classrooms), and particular encounters?

METHODS AND SOURCES OF DATA

This study is based on two periods of participant observation. In 1976–1977 I observed for 8 months in a largely working-class elementary school in California, a school with 8% Black and 12% Chicana/o students. In 1980 I did fieldwork for 3 months in a Michigan elementary school of similar size (around 400 students), social class, and racial composition. I observed in several classrooms—a kindergarten, a second grade, and a combined fourth-fifth grade—and in school hallways, cafeterias, and playgrounds. I set out to follow the round of the school day as children experience it, recording their interactions with one another, and with adults, in varied settings.

Participant observation involves gaining access to everyday, "naturalistic" settings and taking systematic notes over an extended period of time. Rather than starting with preset categories for recording, or with fixed hypotheses for testing, participant-observers record detail in ways which maximize opportunities for discovery. Through continuous interaction between observation and analysis, "grounded theory" is developed (Glaser & Strauss, 1967).

The distinctive logic and discipline of this mode of inquiry emerges from: (1) theoretical sampling—being relatively systematic in the choice of where and whom to observe in order to maximize knowledge relevant to categories and analysis which are being developed; and (2) comparing all relevant data on a given point in order to modify emerging propositions to take account of discrepant cases (Katz, 1983). Participant observation is a flexible, open-ended and inductive method, designed to understand behavior within, rather than stripped from, social context. It provides richly detailed information which is anchored in everyday meanings and experience.

DAILY PROCESSES OF SEX SEGREGATION

Sex segregation should be understood not as a given, but as the result of deliberate activity. The outcome is dramatically visible when there are separate girls' and boys' tables in school lunchrooms, or sex-separated groups on playgrounds. But in the same lunchroom one can also find tables where girls and boys eat and talk together, and in some playground activities the sexes mix. By what processes do girls and boys separate into gender-defined and relatively boundaried collectivities? And in what contexts, and through what processes, do boys and girls interact in less gender-divided ways?

In the school settings I observed, much segregation happened with no mention of gender. Gender was implicit in the contours of friendship, shared interest, and perceived risk which came into play when children chose companions—in their prior planning, invitations, seeking-of-access, saving-of-places, denials of entry, and allowing or protesting of "cuts" by those who violated the rules for lining up. Sometimes children formed mixed-sex groups for play, eating, talking, working on a classroom project, or moving through space. When adults or children explicitly invoked gender—and this was nearly always in ways which separated girls and boys—boundaries were heightened and mixed-sex interaction became an explicit arena of risk.

In the schools I studied, the physical space and curricula were not formally divided by sex, as they have been in the history of elementary schooling (a history evident in separate entrances to old school buildings, where the words "Boys" and "Girls" are permanently etched in concrete). Nevertheless, gender was a visible marker in the adult-organized school day. In both schools, when the public address system sounded, the principal inevitably opened with: "Boys and girls . . . ," and in addressing clusters of children, teachers and aides regularly used gender terms ("Heads down, girls"; "The girls are ready and the boys aren't"). These forms of address made gender visible and salient, conveying an assumption that the sexes are separate social groups.

Teachers and aides sometimes drew upon gender as a basis for sorting children and organizing activities. Gender is an embodied and visual social category which roughly divides the population in half, and the separation of girls and boys permeates the history and lore of schools and playgrounds. In both schools—although through awareness of Title IX, many teachers had changed this practice—one could see separate girls' and boys' lines moving, like caterpillars, through the school halls. In the 4th–5th grade classroom the teacher frequently pitted girls against boys for spelling and math contests. On the playground in the Michigan school, aides regarded the space close to the building as girls' territory, and the playing fields "out there" as boys' territory. They sometimes shooed children of the other sex away from those spaces, especially boys who ventured near the girls' area and seemed to have teasing in mind.

In organizing their activities, both within and apart from the surveillance of adults, children also explicitly invoked gender. During my fieldwork in the Michigan school, I kept daily records of who sat where in the lunchroom. The amount of sex segregation varied: It was least at the first grade tables and almost total among sixth graders. There was also variation from classroom to classroom within a given age, and from day to day. Actions like the following heightened the gender divide:

> In the lunchroom, when the two second grade tables were filling, a high-status boy walked by the inside table, which had a scattering of both boys and girls, and said loudly, "Oooo, too many girls," as he headed for a seat at the far table. The boys at the inside table picked up their trays and moved, and no other boys sat at the inside table, which the pronouncement had effectively made taboo.

In the end, that day (which was not the case every day), girls and boys ate at separate tables.

Eating and walking are not sex-typed activities, yet in forming groups in lunchrooms and hallways children often separated by sex. Sex segregation assumed added dimensions on the playground, where spaces, equipment, and activities were infused with gender meanings. My inventories of activities and groupings on the playground showed similar patterns in both schools: Boys controlled the large fixed spaces designated for team sports (baseball diamonds, grassy fields used for football or soccer); girls more often played closer to the building, doing tricks on the monkey bars (which, for 6th graders, became an area for sitting and talking and using cement areas for jumprope, hopscotch, and group games like four-square. (Lever, 1976, provides a good analysis of sex-divided play.) Girls and boys most often played together in kickball, and in group (rather than team) games like four-square, dodgeball, and handball. When children used gender to exclude others from play, they often drew upon beliefs connecting boys to some activities and girls to others:

> A first grade boy avidly watched an all-female game of jump rope. When the girls began to shift positions, he recognized a means of access to the play and he offered, "I'll swing it." A girl responded, "No way, you don't know how to do it, to swing it. You gotta be a girl." He left without protest.

Although children sometimes ignored pronouncements about what each sex could or could not do, I never heard them directly challenge such claims.

When children had explicitly defined an activity or a group as gendered, those who crossed the boundary—especially boys who moved into female-marked space—risked being teased. ("Look! Mike's in the girls' line!" "That's a girl over there," a girl said loudly, pointing to a boy sitting at an otherwise all-female table in the lunchroom.) Children, and occasionally adults, used teasing—especially the tease of "liking" someone of the other sex, or of "being" that sex by virtue of being in their midst—to police gender boundaries. Much of the teasing drew upon heterosexual romantic definitions, making cross-sex interaction risky, and increasing social distance between boys and girls.

RELATIONSHIPS BETWEEN THE SEXES

Because I have emphasized the "apart" and ignored the occasions of "with," this analysis of sex segregation falsely implies that there is little contact between girls and boys in daily school life. In fact, relationships between girls and boys—which should be studied as fully as, and in connection with, same-sex relationships—are of several kinds:

1. "Borderwork," or forms of cross-sex interaction which are based upon and reaffirm boundaries and asymmetries between girls' and boys' groups;
2. Interactions which are infused with heterosexual meanings;
3. Occasions where individuals cross gender boundaries to participate in the world of the other sex; and
4. Situations where gender is muted in salience, with girls and boys interacting in more relaxed ways.

Borderwork

In elementary school settings boys' and girls' groups are sometimes spatially set apart. Same-sex groups sometimes claim fixed territories such as the basketball court, the bars, or specific lunchroom tables. However, in the crowded, multifocused, and adult-controlled environment of the school, groups form and disperse at a rapid rate and can never stay totally apart. Contact between girls and boys sometimes lessens sex segregation, but gender-defined groups also come together in ways which emphasize their boundaries.

"Borderwork" refers to interaction across, yet based upon and even strengthening gender boundaries. I have drawn this notion from Fredrik Barth's (1969) analysis

of social relations which are maintained across ethnic boundaries without diminishing dichotomized ethnic status.[1] His focus is on more macro, ecological arrangements; mine is on face-to-face behavior. But the insight is similar: Groups may interact in ways which strengthen their borders, and the maintenance of ethnic (or gender) groups can best be understood by examining the boundary that defines the group, "not the cultural stuff that it encloses" (Barth, 1969, p. 15). In elementary schools there are several types of borderwork: contests or games where gender-defined teams compete; cross-sex rituals of chasing and pollution; and group invasions. These interactions are asymmetrical, challenging the separate-but-parallel model of "two worlds."

Contests   Boys and girls are sometimes pitted against each other in classroom competitions and playground games. The 4th–5th grade classroom had a boys' side and a girls' side, an arrangement that reemerged each time the teacher asked children to choose their own desks. Although there was some within-sex shuffling, the result was always a spatial moiety system—boys on the left, girls on the right—with the exception of one girl (the "tomboy" whom I'll describe later), who twice chose a desk with the boys and once with the girls. Drawing upon and reinforcing the children's self-segregation, the teacher often pitted the boys against the girls in spelling and math competitions, events marked by cross-sex antagonism and within-sex solidarity:

> The teacher introduced a math game; she would write addition and subtraction problems on the board, and a member of each team would race to be the first to write the correct answer. She wrote two scorekeeping columns on the board. "Beastly Boys" . . . "Gossipy Girls." The boys yelled out, as several girls laughed, "Noisy girls! Gruesome

girls!" The girls sat in a row on top of their desks; sometimes they moved collectively, pushing their hips or whispering "pass it on." The boys stood along the wall, some reclining against desks. When members of either group came back victorious from the front of the room, they would do the "giving five" handslapping ritual with their team members.

On the playground a team of girls occasionally played against a team of boys, usually in kickball or team two-square. Sometimes these games proceeded matter-of-factly, but if gender became the explicit basis of team solidarity, the interaction changed, becoming more antagonistic and unstable:

> Two fifth-grade girls against two fifth-grade boys in a team game of two-square. The game proceeded at an even pace until an argument ensued about whether the ball was out or on the line. Karen, who had hit the ball, became annoyed, flashed her middle finger at the other team and called to a passing girl to join their side. The boys then called out to other boys, and cheered as several arrived to play. "We got five and you got three!" Jack yelled. The game continued, with the girls yelling, "Bratty boys! Sissy boys!" and the boys making noises—"weee haw" "ha-ha-ha!"—as they played.

Chasing   Cross-sex chasing dramatically affirms boundaries between girls and boys. The basic elements of chase and elude, capture and rescue (Sutton-Smith, 1971) are found in various kinds of tag with formal rules, and in informal episodes of chasing which punctuate life on playgrounds. These episodes begin with a provocation (taunts like "You can't get me!" or "Slobber monster!"; bodily pokes or the grabbing of possessions). A provocation may be ignored, or responded to by chasing. Chaser and chased may then alternate roles. In an ethno-

graphic study of chase sequences on a school playground, Christine Finnan (1982) observes that chases vary in number of chasers to chased (e.g., one chasing one, or five chasing two); form of provocation (a taunt or a poke); outcome (an episode may end when the chased outdistances the chaser, or with a brief touch, being wrestled to the ground, or the recapturing of a hat or a ball); and in use of space (there may or may not be safety zones).

Like Finnan (1982), and Sluckin (1981), who studied a playground in England, I found that chasing has a gendered structure. Boys frequently chase one another, an activity which often ends in wrestling and mock fights. When girls chase girls, they are usually less physically aggressive; they less often, for example, wrestle one another to the ground.

Cross-sex chasing is set apart by special names—"girls chase the boys"; "boys chase the girls"; "the chase"; "chasers"; "chase and kiss"; "kiss chase"; "kissers and chasers"; "kiss or kill"—and by children's animated talk about the activity. The names vary by region and school, but contain both gender and sexual meanings (this form of play is mentioned, but only briefly analyzed, in Finnan, 1981; Sluckin, 1981; Parrott, 1972; and Borman, 1979).

In "boys chase the girls" and "girls chase the boys" (the names most frequently used in both the California and Michigan schools) boys and girls become, by definition, separate teams. Gender terms override individual identities, especially for the other team ("Help, a girl's chasin' me!"; "C'mon Sarah, let's get that boy"; "Tony, help save me from the girls"). Individuals may call for help from, or offer help to, others of their sex. They may also grab someone of their sex and turn them over to the opposing team: "Ryan grabbed Billy from behind, wrestling him to the ground. 'Hey, girls, get 'im,' Ryan called."

Boys more often mix episodes of cross-sex with same-sex chasing. Girls more often have safety zones, places like the girls' rest-room or an area by the school wall, where they retreat to rest and talk (sometimes in animated postmortems) before new episodes of cross-sex chasing begin.

Early in the fall in the Michigan school, where chasing was especially prevalent, I watched a second grade boy teach a kindergarten girl how to chase. He slowly ran backwards, beckoning her to pursue him, as he called, "Help, a girl's after me." In the early grades chasing mixes with fantasy play, e.g., a first-grade boy who played "sea monster," his arms outflung and his voice growling, as he chased a group of girls. By third grade, stylized gestures—exaggerated stalking motions, screams (which only girls do), and karate kicks—accompany scenes of chasing.

Names like "chase and kiss" mark the sexual meanings of cross-sex chasing, a theme I return to later. The threat of kissing—most often girls threatening to kiss boys—is a ritualized form of provocation. Cross-sex chasing among sixth graders involves elaborate patterns of touch and touch avoidance, which adults see as sexual. The principal told the sixth graders in the Michigan school that they were not to play "pom-pom," a complicated chasing game, because it entailed "inappropriate touch."

Rituals of Pollution Cross-sex chasing is sometimes entwined with rituals of pollution, as in "cooties," where specific individuals or groups are treated as contaminating or carrying "germs." Children have rituals for transferring cooties (usually touching someone else and shouting "You've got cooties!"), for immunization (e.g., writing "CV" for "cootie vaccination" on their arms), and for eliminating cooties (e.g., saying "no gives" or using "cootie catchers" made of folded paper described in Knapp &

Knapp, 1976). While girls may give cooties to girls, boys do not generally give cooties to one another (Samuelson, 1980).

In cross-sex play, either girls or boys may be defined as having cooties, which they transfer through chasing and touching. Girls give cooties to boys more often than vice versa. In Michigan, one version of cooties is called "girl stain"; the fourth-graders whom Karkau, 1973, describes, used the phrase "girl touch." "Cootie queens," or "cootie girls" (there are no "kings" or "boys") are female pariahs, the ultimate school untouchables, seen as contaminating not only by virtue of gender, but also through some added stigma such as being overweight or poor.[2] That girls are seen as more polluting than boys is a significant asymmetry, which echoes cross-cultural patterns, although in other cultures female pollution is generally connected to menstruation, and not applied to prepubertal girls.

Invasions Playground invasions are another asymmetric form of borderwork. On a few occasions I saw girls invade and disrupt an all-male game, most memorably a group of tall sixth-grade girls who ran onto the playing field and grabbed a football which was in play. The boys were surprised and frustrated, and, unusual for boys this old, finally tattled to the aide. But in the majority of cases, boys disrupt girls' activities rather than vice versa. Boys grab the ball from girls playing foursquare, stick feet into a jump rope and stop an ongoing game, and dash through the area of the bars, where girls are taking turns performing, sending the rings flying. Sometimes boys ask to join a girls' game and then, after a short period of seemingly earnest play, disrupt the game:

> Two second-grade boys begged to "twirl" the jump rope for a group of second-grade girls who had been jumping for some time. The girls agreed, and the boys began to

twirl. Soon, without announcement, the boys changed from "seashells, cockle bells" to "hot peppers" (spinning the rope very fast), and tangled the jumper in the rope. The boys ran away laughing.

Boys disrupt girls' play so often that girls have developed almost ritualized responses: They guard their ongoing play, chase boys away, and tattle to the aides. In a playground cycle which enhances sex segregation, aides who try to spot potential trouble before it occurs sometimes shoo boys away from areas where girls are playing. Aides do not anticipate trouble from girls who seek to join groups of boys, with the exception of girls intent on provoking a chase sequence. And indeed, if they seek access to a boys' game, girls usually play with boys in earnest rather than breaking up the game.

A close look at the organization of borderwork—or boundaried interactions between the sexes—shows that the worlds of boys and girls may be separate but they are not parallel, nor are they equal. The worlds of girls and boys articulate in several asymmetric ways:

1. On the playground, boys control as much as ten times more space than girls, when one adds up the area of large playing fields and compares it with the much smaller areas where girls predominate. Girls, who play closer to the building, are more often watched over and protected by the adult aides.

2. Boys invade all-female games and scenes of play much more than girls invade boys. This, and boys' greater control of space, correspond with other findings about the organization of gender, and inequality, in our society: compared with men and boys, women and girls take up less space, and their space, and talk, are more often violated and interrupted (Greif, 1982; Henley, 1977; West & Zimmerman, 1983).

3. Although individual boys are occasionally treated as contaminating (e.g., a third grade boy who [to] both boys and girls was "stinky" and "smelled like pee"), girls are more often defined as polluting. This pattern ties to themes that I discuss later: It is more taboo for a boy to play with (as opposed to invade) girls, and girls are more sexually defined than boys.

A look at the boundaries between the separated worlds of girls and boys illuminates within-sex hierarchies of status and control. For example, in the sex-divided seating in the 4th–5th grade classroom, several boys recurringly sat near "female space": their desks were at the gender divide in the classroom, and they were more likely than other boys to sit at a predominantly female table in the lunchroom. These boys—two non-bilingual Chicanos and an overweight "loner" boy who was afraid of sports—were at the bottom of the male hierarchy. Gender is sometimes used as a metaphor for male hierarchies; the inferior status of boys at the bottom is conveyed by calling them "girls":

> Seven boys and one girl were playing basketball. Two younger boys came over and asked to play. While the girl silently stood, fully accepted in the company of players, one of the older boys disparagingly said to the younger boys, "You girls can't play."[3]

In contrast, the girls who more often travel in the boys' world, sitting with groups of boys in the lunchroom or playing basketball, soccer, and baseball with them, are not stigmatized. Some have fairly high status with other girls. The worlds of girls and boys are asymmetrically arranged, and spatial patterns map out interacting forms of inequality.

Heterosexual Meanings

The organization and meanings of gender (the social categories "woman/man," "girl/boy") and of sexuality vary cross-culturally (Ortner & Whitehead, 1981)—and, in our society, across the life course. Harriet Whitehead (1981) observed that in our (Western) gender system, and that of many traditional North American Indian cultures, one's choice of a sexual object, occupation, and one's dress and demeanor are closely associated with gender. However, the "center of gravity" differs in the two gender systems. For Indians, occupational pursuits provide the primary imagery of gender; dress and demeanor are secondary, and sexuality is least important. In our system, at least for adults, the order is reversed: heterosexuality is central to our definitions of "man" and "woman" ("masculinity"/"femininity"), and the relationships that obtain between them, whereas occupation and dress/demeanor are secondary.

Whereas erotic orientation and gender are closely linked in our definitions of adults, we define children as relatively asexual. Activities and dress/demeanor are more important than sexuality in the cultural meanings of "girl" and "boy." Children are less heterosexually defined than adults, and we have nonsexual imagery for relations between girls and boys. However, both children and adults sometimes use heterosexual language—"crushes," "like," "goin' with," "girlfriends," and "boyfriends"—to define cross-sex relationships. This language increases through the years of elementary school; the shift to adolescence consolidates a gender system organized around the institution of heterosexuality.

In everyday life in the schools, heterosexual and romantic meanings infuse some ritualized forms of interaction between groups of boys and girls (e.g., "chase and kiss") and help maintain sex segregation. "Jimmy likes Beth" or "Beth likes Jimmy" is a major form of teasing, which a child risks in choosing to sit by or walk with someone of the other sex. The structure of teasing, and children's sparse vocabulary for relationships between girls and boys, are evident in the following conversation which I had with a group of third-grade girls in the lunchroom:

Susan asked me what I was doing, and I said I was observing the things children do and play. Nicole volunteered, "I like running, boys chase all the girls. See Tim over there? Judy chases him all around the school. She likes him." Judy, sitting across the table, quickly responded, "I hate him. I like him for a friend." "Tim loves Judy," Nicole said in a loud, sing-song voice.

In the younger grades, the culture and lore of girls contain more heterosexual romantic themes than that of boys. In Michigan, the first-grade girls often jumped rope to a rhyme which began: "Down in the valley where the green grass grows, there sat Cindy (name of jumper), as sweet as a rose. She sat, she sat, she sat so sweet. Along came Jason, and kissed her on the cheek . . . first comes love, then comes marriage, then along comes Cindy with a baby carriage . . . " Before a girl took her turn at jumping, the chanters asked her "Who do you want to be your boyfriend?" The jumper always proffered a name, which was accepted matter-of-factly. In chasing, a girl's kiss carried greater threat than a boy's kiss; "girl touch," when defined as contaminating, had sexual connotations. In short, starting at an early age, girls are more sexually defined than boys.

Through the years of elementary school, and increasing with age, the idiom of heterosexuality helps maintain the gender divide. Cross-sex interactions, especially when children initiate them, are fraught with the risk of being teased about "liking" someone of the other sex. I learned of several close cross-sex friendships, formed and maintained in neighborhoods and church, which went underground during the school day.

By the fifth grade a few children began to affirm, rather than avoid, the charge of having a girlfriend or a boyfriend; they introduced the heterosexual courtship rituals of adolescence:

In the lunchroom in the Michigan school, as the tables were forming, a high-status fifth-grade boy called out from his seat at the table: "I want Trish to sit by me." Trish came over, and almost like a king and queen, they sat at the gender divide—a row of girls down the table on her side, a row of boys on his.

In this situation, which inverted earlier forms, it was not a loss, but a gain in status to publicly choose a companion of the other sex. By affirming his choice, the boy became unteasable (note the familiar asymmetry of heterosexual courtship rituals: the male initiated). This incident signals a temporal shift in arrangements of sex and gender.

Traveling in the World of the Other Sex

Contests, invasions, chasing, and heterosexually-defined encounters are based upon and reaffirm boundaries between girls and boys. In another type of cross-sex interaction, individuals (or sometimes pairs) cross gender boundaries, seeking acceptance in a group of the other sex. Nearly all the cases I saw of this were tomboys—girls who played organized sports and frequently sat with boys in the cafeteria or classroom. If these girls were skilled at activities central in the boys' world, especially games like soccer, baseball, and basketball, they were pretty much accepted as participants.

Being a tomboy is a matter of degree. Some girls seek access to boys' groups but are excluded; other girls limit their "crossing" to specific sports. Only a few—such as the tomboy I mentioned earlier, who chose a seat with the boys in the sex-divided fourth–fifth grade—participate fully in the boys' world. That particular girl was skilled at the various organized sports which boys played in different seasons of the year. She was also adept at physical fighting and at using the forms of arguing, insult, teasing, naming, and sports-talk of the boys' subculture. She was the only Black child in her classroom, in a school with only 8% Black students; overall that token status, along with unusual athletic and verbal skills, may have contributed to her ability to move back and forth across the gender divide. Her unique position in the children's world was widely recognized in the school. Several times, the teacher said to me, "She thinks she's a boy."

I observed only one boy in the upper grades (a fourth grader) who regularly played with all-female groups, as opposed to "playing at" girls games and seeking to disrupt them. He frequently played jumprope and took turns with girls doing tricks on the bars, using the small gestures—for example, a helpful push on the heel of a girl who needed momentum to turn her body around the bar—which mark skillful and earnest participation. Although I never saw him play in other than an earnest spirit, the girls often chased him away from their games, and both girls and boys teased him. The fact that girls seek, and have more access to boys' worlds than vice versa, and the fact that girls who travel with the other sex are less stigmatized for it, are obvious asymmetries, tied to the asymmetries previously discussed.

Relaxed Cross-Sex Interactions

Relationships between boys and girls are not always marked by strong boundaries, heterosexual definitions, or by interacting on the terms and turfs of the other sex. On some occasions girls and boys interact in relatively comfortable ways. Gender is not strongly salient nor explicitly invoked, and girls and boys are not organized into boundaries collectively. These "with" occasions have been neglected by those studying gender and children's relationships, who have emphasized either the model of separate worlds (with little attention to their articulation) or heterosexual forms of contact.

Occasions where boys and girls interact without strain, where gender wanes, rather than waxes in importance, frequently have one or more of the following characteristics:

1. The situations are organized around an absorbing task, such as a group art project or creating a radio show, which encourages cooperation and lessens attention to gender. This pattern accords with other studies finding that cooperative activities reduce group antagonism (e.g., Sherif & Sherif, 1953, who studied divisions between boys in a summer camp; and Aronson et al., 1978, who used cooperative activities to lessen racial divisions in a classroom).

2. Gender is less prominent when children are not responsible for the formation of the group. Mixed-sex play is less frequent in games like football, which require the choosing of teams, and more frequent in games like handball or dodgeball which individuals can join simply by getting into a line or a circle. When adults organize mixed-sex encounters—which they frequently do in the classroom and in physical education periods on the playground—they legitimize cross-sex contact. This removes the risk of being teased for choosing to be with the other sex.

3. There is more extensive and relaxed cross-sex interaction when principles of grouping other than gender are explicitly involved—for example, counting off to form teams for spelling or kickball, dividing lines by hot lunch or cold lunch, or organizing a work group on the basis of interests or reading ability.

4. Girls and boys may interact more readily in less public and crowded settings. Neighborhood play, depending on demography, is more often sex and age integrated than play at school, partly because with fewer numbers, one may have to resort to an array of social categories to find play partners or to constitute a game. And in less crowded environments there are fewer potential witnesses to "make something of it" if girls and boys play together.

Relaxed interactions between girls and boys often depend on adults to set up and legitimize the contact.[4] Perhaps because of this contingency—and the other, distancing patterns which permeate relations between girls and boys—the easeful moments of interaction rarely build to close friendship. Schofield (1981) makes a similar observation about gender and racial barriers to friendship in a junior high school.

IMPLICATIONS FOR DEVELOPMENT

I have located social relations within an essentially spatial framework, emphasizing the organization of children's play, work, and other activities within specific settings, and in one type of institution, the school. In contrast, frameworks of child development rely upon temporal metaphors, using images of growth and transformation over time. Taken alone, both spatial and temporal frameworks have shortcomings; fitted together, they may be mutually correcting.

Those interested in gender and development have relied upon conceptualizations of "sex role socialization" and "sex differences." Sexuality and gender, I have argued, are more situated and fluid than these individualist and intrinsic models imply. Sex and gender are differently organized and defined across situations, even within the same institution. This situational variation (e.g., in the extent to which an encounter heightens or lessens gender boundaries, or is infused with sexual meanings) shapes and constrains individual behavior. Features which a developmental perspective might attribute to individuals, and understand as relatively internal attributes unfolding over time, may, in fact, be highly dependent on context. For example, children's avoidance of cross-sex friendship may be attributed to individual gender development in middle-childhood: But attention to varied situations may show that this avoidance is contingent on group size, activity, adult behavior, collective meanings, and the risk of being teased.

A focus on social organization and situation draws attention to children's experiences in the present. This helps correct a model like "sex role socialization" which casts the present under the shadow of the future, or presumed "endpoints" (Speier, 1976). A situated analysis of arrangements of sex and gender among those of different ages may point to crucial disjunctions in the life course. In the fourth and fifth grades, culturally defined heterosexual rituals ("goin' with") begin to suppress the presence and visibility of other types of interaction between girls and boys, such as nonsexualized and comfortable interaction, and traveling in the world of the other sex. As "boyfriend/girlfriend" definitions spread, the fifth-grade tomboy I described had to work to sustain "buddy" relationships with boys. Adult women who were tomboys often speak of early adolescence as a painful time when they were pushed away from participation in boys' activities. Other adult women speak of the loss of intense, even erotic ties with other girls when they entered puberty and the rituals of dating, that is, when they became absorbed into the institution of heterosexuality (Rich, 1980). When Lever (1976) describes best-friend relationships among fifth-grade girls as preparation for dating, she imposes heterosexual ideologies onto a present which should be understood on its own terms.

As heterosexual encounters assume more importance, they may alter relations in same-sex groups. For example, Schofield (1981) reports that for sixth- and seventh-grade children in a middle school, the popularity of girls with other girls was affected by their popularity with boys, while boys' status with other boys did not depend on their relations with girls. This is an asymmetry familiar from the adult world; men's relationships with one another are defined through varied activities (occupations, sports), while relationships among women—and their public status—are more influenced by their connections to individual men.

A full understanding of gender and social relations should encompass cross-sex as well as within-sex interactions. "Borderwork" helps maintain separate, gender-linked subcultures, which, as those interested in development have begun to suggest, may result in different milieux for learning. Daniel Maltz and Ruth Borker (1983) for example, argue that because of different interactions within girls' and boys' groups, the sexes learn different rules for creating and interpreting friendly conversation, rules which carry into adulthood and help account for miscommunication between men and women. Carol Gilligan (1982) fits research on the different worlds of girls and boys into a theory of sex differences in moral development. Girls develop a style of reasoning, she argues, which is more personal and relational; boys develop a style which is more positional, based on separateness. Eleanor Maccoby (1982), also following the insight that because of sex segregation, girls and boys grow up in different environments, suggests implications for gender differentiated prosocial and antisocial behavior.

This separate worlds approach, as I have illustrated, also has limitations. The occasions when the sexes are together should also be studied, and understood as contexts for experience and learning. For example, asymmetries in cross-sex relationships convey a series of messages: that boys are more entitled to space and to the nonreciprocal right of interrupting or invading the activities of the other sex; that girls are more in need of adult protection, and are lower in status, more defined by sexuality, and may even be polluting. Different types of cross-sex interaction—relaxed, boundaried, sexualized, or taking place on the terms of the other sex—provide different contexts for development.

By mapping the array of relationships between and within the sexes, one adds complexity to the overly static and dichotomous imagery of separate worlds. Individual experiences vary, with implications for development. Some children prefer same-sex groupings; some are more likely to cross the gender boundary and participate in the world of the other sex; some children (e.g., girls and boys who frequently play "chase and kiss") invoke heterosexual meanings, while others avoid them.

Finally, after charting the terrain of relationships, one can trace their development over time. For example, age variation in the content and form of borderwork, or of cross and same-sex touch, may be related to differing cognitive, social, emotional, or physical capacities, as well as to age-associated cultural forms. I earlier mentioned temporal shifts in the organization of cross-sex chasing, for mixing with fantasy play in the early grades to more elaborately ritualized and sexualized forms by the sixth grade. There also appear to be temporal changes in same and cross-sex touch. In kindergarten, girls and boys touch one another more freely than in fourth grade, when children avoid relaxed cross-sex touch and instead use pokes, pushes, and other forms of mock violence, even when the touch clearly couches affection. This touch taboo is obviously related to the risk of seeming to *like* someone of the other sex. In fourth grade, same-sex touch begins to signal sexual meanings among boys, as well as between boys and girls. Younger boys touch one an-

other freely in cuddling (arm around shoulder) as well as mock violence ways. By fourth grade, when homophobic taunts like "fag" become more common among boys, cuddling touch begins to disappear for boys, but less so for girls.

Overall, I am calling for more complexity in our conceptualization of gender and of children's social relationships. Our challenge is to retain the temporal sweep, looking at individual and group lives as they unfold over time, while also attending to social structure and context, and to the full variety of experiences in the present.

ACKNOWLEDGMENT

I would like to thank Jane Atkinson, Nancy Chodorow, Arlene Daniels, Peter Lyman, Zick Rubin, Malcolm Spector, Avril Thorne, and Margery Wolf for comments on an earlier version of this paper. Conversations with Zella Luria enriched this work.

NOTES

1. I am grateful to Frederick Erickson for suggesting the relevance of Barth's analysis.

2. Sue Samuelson (1980) reports that in a racially mixed playground in Fresno, California, Mexican-American, but not Anglo children gave cooties. Racial, as well as sexual inequality may be expressed through these forms.

3. This incident was recorded by Margaret Blume, who, for an undergraduate research project in 1982, observed in the California school where I earlier did fieldwork. Her observations and insights enhanced my own, and I would like to thank her for letting me cite this excerpt.

4. Note that in daily school life, depending on the individual and the situation, teachers and aides sometimes lessened, and at other times heightened sex segregation.

Schools and Gender

R. W. Connell

Since schools are routinely blamed for social problems of every description, from unemployment to godlessness, it is not surprising that they should also be blamed for problems about boys. It is, therefore, important to say that the school is not the only institution shaping masculinities, and may not be the most important. Psychoanalysis has made us familiar with the emotional dynamics of the family as an influence on gender, an argument recently renewed—and carefully located in the history of gender relations—in Nielsen and Rudberg's (1994) developmental model of gender. The sociology of culture makes us aware of the importance of mass communications in the contemporary gender order. Media research documents what we know intuitively, that mass media are crammed with representations of masculinities—from rock music, beer commercials, sitcoms, action movies and war films to news programs—which circulate on a vast scale (Craig 1992).

Given these forces, why pay attention to the school? Teachers discussing problems about boys often suggest that they are confronting intractable patterns fixed outside the school. Certainly children bring conceptions of masculinity into the school with them. Jordan (1995) has wittily documented the "Warrior Narratives" brought into an Australian kindergarten, where some of the boys disrupted a carefully non-sexist regime

by playing games involving guns, fighting, and fast cars. This is hardly an isolated experience. Witness the Ninja Turtles and X-Men of the American Grade 2 classroom studied by Dyson (1994). Such a feeling among teachers is reinforced by the two most popular explanations of masculinity, biological determinism, which emphasizes the body, and sex-role theory, which emphasizes broad cultural expectations.

That the school is an important player in the shaping of modern masculinities can be suggested, but not demonstrated, by research within schools. It is more strongly demonstrated from outside, for instance by life-history studies of masculinity such as Messner's work on U.S. athletes, or my research with groups of Australian men. Schools figure significantly in autobiographical narratives, for instance in the preparation and choice of an athletic career.

Further, we should not ignore the practical judgment of parents about the importance of schooling, reflected in the demand for "boys' programs." Though we will never have a simple way of measuring the relative influence of different institutions, there seems to be good warrant for considering schools one of the major sites of masculinity formation.

A "site" can be understood in two ways. It can be examined as an institutional *agent* of the process. To understand this, we must explore the structures and practices by which the school forms masculinities among its pupils. Alternatively, we can examine the school as the *setting* in which other agencies are in play, especially the agency of the pupils themselves. Both aspects are explored later in this chapter.

Since almost all the discussion of gender focusses on gender difference, we should from the start be alert to gender *similarity*. Public controversies over gender differences in educational outcomes ("The girls are beating the boys.") persistently ignore the extent of overlap, focussing on small differences between statistical means and ignoring measures of dispersion.

Many educational practices iron out gender differences. A common curriculum, a shared timetable, and the experience of living daily in the same architecture with the same classroom routines are not trivial parts of boys' and girls' school experience. Teachers may deliberately set out to de-emphasize gender difference, laying their emphasis on individual growth, as King (1978) noted about British infants schools in the heyday of 1970s progressivism. The whole history of feminism shows that education systems can be a force for gender equity as well as inequity.

This issue can lead to serious problems in the interpretation of quantitative research of the very common kind which goes looking for statistical differences between groups of boys and girls. Schools may be having a gender *effect* without producing gender *difference*. The school is having a gender effect, for instance, when it changes gender relations so as to produce more similarity.

A key step in understanding gender in schools is to "think institutionally," as Hansot and Tyack (1988) have argued. As with corporations, workplaces and the state, gender is embedded in the institutional arrangements through which a school system functions: divisions of labour, authority patterns and so on. These are, as Lingard and Douglas (1999) have recently shown, the sites of a shifting gender politics which provides the context of gender relations in individual schools.

The totality of gender arrangements within a school is the school's *gender regime*. Gender regimes differ between schools, though within limits set by the broader culture and the constraints of the local education system (Kessler et al. 1985).

Theoretical work allows us to sort out the different components of a school's gender regime. Four types of relationship are involved:

Power relations

These include supervision and authority among teachers; and patterns of dominance, harassment, and control over resources among pupils. A familiar and important pattern is the association of masculinity with authority, and the concentration of men in supervisory positions in school systems. Among pupils, power relations may be equally visible. Prendergast's (1996) ethnography in a British working-class high school shows, for instance, how control over playground space for informal football games was crucial in maintaining the hegemony of an aggressive, physical masculinity in this school's peer group life.

Division of labour

This includes work specializations among teachers, such as concentrations of women in domestic science, language, and literature teaching, and men in science, mathematics, and industrial arts. It also includes the informal specializations among pupils, from the elementary classroom where a teacher asks for a "big strong boy" to help move a piece of furniture, to the gendered choice of electives in vocational education at secondary and post-secondary levels.

Patterns of emotion

What the sociologist Hochschild (1983) has called the "feeling rules" for occupations can be found in teaching, often associated with specific roles in a school: the tough deputy principal, the drama teacher, etc. Among the most important feeling rules in schools are those concerned with sexuality, and the prohibition on homosexuality may be particularly important in definitions of masculinity (Frank 1993, Mac an Ghaill 1994). Lingard and Douglas (1999) note how the "emotional economy" of education can be reconstructed, indeed is being reshaped now under the impact of neo-liberalism.

Symbolism

Schools import much of the symbolization of gender from the wider culture, but they have their own symbol systems too: uniforms and dress codes, formal and informal language codes, etc. A particularly important symbolic structure in education is the gendering of knowledge, the defining of certain areas of the curriculum as masculine and others as feminine. Activities such as sports may also be of great importance in the symbolism of gender.

Through these intersecting structures of relationships, schools create institutional definitions of masculinity. Such definitions are impersonal; they exist as social facts. Pupils participate in these masculinities simply by entering the school and living in its structures. The terms on which they participate, however, are negotiable—whether adjusting to the patterns, rebelling against them, or trying to modify them.

Gender regimes need not be internally coherent, and they are certainly subject to change. This is vividly shown in Draper's (1993) account of the "re-establishment of gender relations following a school merger" in Britain, an unusual study which catches gender arrangements in the midst of change. Draper shows how different groups of pupils and teachers involved in the merger had conflicting agendas and inter-

ests, with sometimes startling results—from boys wearing eyeshadow to girls subverting school uniform.

Teachers' autobiographies, especially those of feminist teachers, contain many narratives of encounters with oppressive gender regimes in schools and of attempts—sometimes successful—to change them. Children as well as teachers work on the gender regime. In the U.S. elementary schools studied by Thorne (1993), the meanings of gender were constantly being debated and revised by the children, the gender boundaries both enforced and challenged in the playground and classrooms.

Given this background, let us examine how schools influence the construction of masculinities.

SCHOOLS AS AGENTS IN THE MAKING OF MASCULINITIES

Masculinizing practices

There is no mystery about why some schools made masculinities: they were intended to. A fascinating historical study, Heward's *Making a Man of Him* (1988), reconstructs the interplay between Ellesmere College, a minor private school in Britain, and the class and gender strategies of the families who sent boys there. The school defined and enforced a suitable masculinity among its boys through rigidly enforced conventional dress, discipline (prefects having the authority to beat younger boys), academic competition and hierarchy (emphasized by constant testing), team games, and gender segregation among the staff. In the wake of the 1930s Depression, Ellesmere modified its formula, increasing its academic and vocational emphasis and decreasing its emphasis on sport.

The discipline, dress code, etc., can be considered a set of *masculinizing practices* governed by the gender regime of the school. Different circumstances produce a different formula. In another illuminating historical study, Morrell (1993–4) traces the production of "a rugged, rather than cerebral, masculinity" on the colonial frontier. The white boarding schools of Natal, South Africa, in the half-century to 1930, also used the prefect system and gender segregation. But these schools laid more emphasis on toughness and physical hierarchy among the boys, through masculinizing practices such as initiation, "fagging," physical punishment and spartan living conditions. This agenda was obviously connected with the context of colonial conquest, and the goal of maintaining racial power over colonized peoples.

These vehement gender regimes show the potential of the school as a masculinity-making device, but such cases are hardly the norm in contemporary public education. The masculinizing agenda has been muted by co-education—but has it been eliminated?

In some ways, co-educational settings make it easier to mark difference, that is, establish symbolic oppositions between girls and boys. School uniforms or conventions of dress, separate toilets, forms of address, practices such as lining boys and girls up separately, or creating classroom competitions of "the boys" against "the girls" all do this job. Formal texts may reinforce the lesson from popular culture that masculinity is defined by difference from femininity. As Sleeter and Grant (1991) have shown in a study of textbooks used in U.S. schools up to Grade 8, gender patterns have persisted despite a recent shift by writers and publishers to non-sexist language. Representations of men have remained more stereotyped than those of women.

Broad features of co-educational schools' gender regimes thus sustain particular definitions of masculinity. Does this turn into an active masculinizing practice?

Studies of particular areas of schools' work show that it does.

A case in point is the schools' treatment of sexuality. Sex education classes generally teach an unreflective heterosexual interpretation of students' desires, in which masculine sexuality is defined by a future of marriage and fatherhood. This can be seen in Trudell's (1993) detailed ethnography of sex education in a U.S. high school.

Since formal sex education is mostly ineffective, such classes will probably not be a major source of gender meanings for the pupils. But, as Mac an Ghaill's (1994) important British study of school sexuality and masculinity demonstrates, these ideas are backed by a much wider range of practices. A heterosexual construction of masculine and feminine as opposites (as in "the opposite sex," "opposites attract") runs through a great deal of the school's informal culture and curriculum content. Homosexual experience is generally blanked out from the official curriculum. Gay youth are liable to experience hostility from school officials and straight youth, while teachers experience heavy constraint in dealing with sexual diversity (Laskey & Beavis 1996).

Co-educational schools, then, typically operate with an informal but powerful ideology of gender difference, and do put pressure on boys to conform to it. In certain areas of the school's gender regime the pressure approaches that of the vehement regimes discussed above, and a regular vortex of masculinity formation can be seen.

Masculinity vortices

Boys' subjects. The first vortex arises in the realm of symbolism through the gender meanings of school knowledge. Most of the academic curriculum is common to girls and boys, and while conveying gender messages, does so diffusely. But in certain areas of study, pathways diverge and gender messages become more concentrated. Grant and Sleeter's (1986) study of "Five Bridges" junior high school in the United States found that while the school made an equal formal offer of learning to boys and girls, it allowed virtual segregation in some subject areas. These were especially practical subjects such as Shop (Industrial Arts) and Child Development. Indeed the school cued this segregation by its own gender division of labor among teachers.

This is a widespread pattern. System-wide data on enrolments in New South Wales secondary schools show certain subjects with marked gender differences in enrolment. In 1998, for instance, boys in Year 10 made up 90 percent of the candidates for the elective School Certificate subject Technics I, and 87 percent of the candidates for Technical Drawing—compared with 50 percent of the candidates for Science, a compulsory subject, and 26 percent of the candidates for Food Technology, a subject descended from the old "girls' subject" of cooking (Board of Studies 1998).

At the Higher School Certificate level, Year 12, there is more flexibility and the gender patterning is more pronounced. At this level in 1998, boys made up 94 percent of the candidates for Engineering Science, 73 percent of the candidates for Physics, 69 percent of the candidates for Design and Technology, and 61 percent of the candidates for Computing Studies—compared with 36 percent of Biology, 35 percent of Visual Arts, 25 percent of Drama, 21 percent of Food Technology and 1 percent of Textiles and Design (Board of Studies 1999).

This degree of segregation does not arise by chance. Particular curriculum areas are culturally gendered. Industrial Arts (Shop) teaching, for instance, is historically connected with manual trades where there was a strong culture of workplace masculinity and where women used to be excluded. As Mealyea's (1993) case study of new Industrial Arts teachers demonstrates, it can be difficult for men with backgrounds in such trades to accept the new policies of gender equity and inclusiveness.

Academic subjects may also have strong gender meanings. It has long been recognized that physical sciences are culturally defined as masculine and have a concentration of men teachers. Martino's (1994) sophisticated analysis of secondary classes in Western Australia shows how subject English, by contrast, is feminized. In the eyes of many of the boys, English classes are distanced by their focus on the expression of emotions, their apparent irrelevance to men's work, the lack of set rules and unique answers, and the contrast with activities defined as properly masculine, such as sport.

Discipline. The second vortex is closely linked to power relations. Adult control in schools is enforced by a disciplinary system which often becomes a focus of masculinity formation.

Teachers from infants to secondary level may use gender as a means of control, for instance shaming boys by saying they are "acting like a girl." Punishment too is liable to be gendered. When corporal punishment was legal, boys were much more often beaten than girls. Non-violent punishments still bear down more heavily on boys. A pioneering study of suspensions in a working-class area of Sydney found that 84 percent of the pupils suspended were boys, as were 87 percent of the pupils with repeat suspensions (White 1993).

These turn out to be typical percentages. A few years later the New South Wales public school system began to release system-wide discipline statistics. In 1998, of 35,755 short suspensions from schools, 81 percent were of boys. Of 5396 long suspensions, 85 percent were of boys (*Sydney Morning Herald,* 11 March 1999.) The highest rates were in working-class areas.

Where the hegemony of the school is secure, boys may learn to wield disciplinary power themselves as part of their learning of masculine hierarchy. This was the basis of the old prefect system.

Where hegemony is lacking, a "protest masculinity" may be constructed through defiance of authority, all too familiar in working-class schools. With corporal punishment, defiance requires bravery in the face of pain, a masculinity test of the crudest kind. Even with non-violent discipline, such as the "punishing room" in the African-American school studied by Ferguson (1994), the contest with authority can become a focus of excitement, labeling, and the formation of masculine identities.

Sport. The third vortex blends power, symbolism, and emotion in a particularly potent combination. Here the schools are using consumer society's key device for defining hegemonic masculinity.

Foley's (1990) superb ethnography of a high school in a south Texas town gives a vivid description of "the great American football ritual." He shows that not only the football team, but the school population as a whole, use the game for celebration and reproduction of the dominant codes of gender. The game directly defines a pattern of aggressive and dominating performance as the most admired form of masculinity; and indirectly, marginalizes others. The cheer-leaders become models of desirability among the girls; and their desirability further defines the hierarchy of masculinities among the boys, since only the most securely positioned boys will risk ridicule by asking them for a date.

The only thing wrong with Foley's account is the suggestion that this is peculiarly American. Ice hockey in Canada, rugby in South Africa and New South Wales, soccer in Britain, are heavily masculinized contact sports that play a similar cultural role

(Gruneau & Whitson 1993, Robins & Cohen 1978, Walker 1988).

Girls too participate in school sport, though not with the same frequency as boys. Typically the high-profile boys' sports are markedly more important in the cultural life of schools. The coaches of boys' representative teams can be important figures in a high school. Physical education teachers have an occupational culture that, on Skelton's (1993) autobiographical account, centers on a conventional masculinity that is "not only dominant, but neutralized as natural and good, part of the expected and unquestioned nature of things."

Selection and differentiation

The masculinizing practices of boys' subjects, discipline and sport each tend to produce, directly, a specific kind of masculinity. But this is not the only way that masculinities are produced in schools. Some aspects of the school's functioning shape masculinities indirectly, and may have the effect not of producing one masculinity but of emphasizing differences between masculinities. The most important case is, undoubtedly, educational selection.

The competitive academic curriculum, combined with tracking, streaming, or selective entry, is a powerful social mechanism that defines some pupils as successes and others as failures, broadly along social class lines. There are strong reactions among the pupils to this compulsory sorting-and-sifting, whose gender dimension has been visible (though not always noticed) since the early days of school ethnographies.

The most clearcut examples are from studies of boys' schools. The famous cases of the "lads" and the "ear'oles" in the British working-class school studied by Willis (1977) show a difference not only in conformity to school but in styles of masculinity. The "ear'oles," defined by the other group as effeminate, are using the school as a pathway to careers, while the "lads" are headed for the factory floor.

The pattern can also be traced in co-educational schools. Mac an Ghaill, for instance, distinguishes the "Academic achievers" from the "macho lads," the "new enterprisers" and the "real Englishmen," as subcultures of masculinity in the school he studied. Something like these differences can be seen as early as elementary school, as shown by Warren's (1997) study of boys and differing masculinities in an English classroom. As Garvey (1994) puts it, streaming itself becomes a masculinizing practice.

Sewell (1997), in an illuminating study of black youth in British schools, shows how the interplay of school with popular culture tends to push African-Caribbean boys into a dichotomy of rebellion or overconformity. The academic and disciplinary hierarchy of schools thus influences the making of masculinities, but by producing plural masculinities, in a structured gender order among boys, rather than a single pattern of masculinity.

PUPILS AS AGENTS, SCHOOL AS SETTING

Peer culture

One of the most important features of school as a social setting is its informal peer group life. The peer milieu has its own gender order, distinct though not fixed. There is turbulence and uncertainty as young people try to define their paths in life. With the approach of adolescence, interactions between boys and girls are liable to be sexualized, by flirting, innuendo, and teasing. The heterosexual "romance" pattern of gender relations persists through high school into college, where it can still dominate student life, as Holland and Eisenhart's (1990) intensive study shows.

The romance pattern defines masculinity in general through the masculine/feminine dichotomy. It also feeds into the hierarchy of masculinities, since heterosexual success is a formidable source of peer group prestige. Foley's study of a Texas high school gives an extended account of the parties and other social events at which masculinity is displayed and hierarchies reinforced. In this milieu the interplay of gender and ethnicity constructs several versions of masculinity: Anglo jocks, Mexican-American anti-authoritarian "vatos," and the "silent majority."

Peer culture is now closely linked with mass communication. Mass culture generates images and interpretations of masculinity which flow chaotically into school life and are reworked by the pupils through everyday conversation, ethnic tensions in the playground, sexual adventures and so on. Some are racially based, such as the image of uncontrollable, violent black masculinity that is familiar in white racism—and has now been seized by young black men (for instance in rap music) as a source of power. Some of these representations are at odds with school agendas. Others (such as interest in sports) are likely to mesh; we should not assume a constant tension between peer culture and school.

Adolescent boys' peer talk constantly uses sexuality to establish hierarchies: "fag," "slag," etc. Research in secondary schools in several countries has found widespread verbal harassment of girls by boys (Everhart 1983, Lees 1986, Milligan & Thomson 1992). Yet at this age sex is still being learnt. Wood's (1984) study of boys' sex talk in a London secondary school annexe emphasizes the element of fantasy, uncertainty, and boasting. The boys' pretensions can be punctured when a tough girl, or group of girls, pushes back. Wood notes the different registers of boys' sex talk, for instance, the greater hesitancy in a mixed group.

In these observations the collective dimension of masculinity is clear. The peer groups, not individuals, are the bearers of gender definitions. This is presumably the explanation for a familiar observation by parents and teachers that boys who create trouble in a group by aggression, disruption and harassment—that is, an exaggerated performance of hegemonic masculinity—can be cooperative and peaceable on their own.

Taking up the offer

Masculinities and femininities are actively constructed, not simply received. Society, school and peer milieu make boys an offer of a place in the gender order; but boys determine how they take it up.

Protest masculinity is a case in point. The majority of boys learn to negotiate school discipline with only a little friction. A certain number, however, take the discipline system as a challenge, especially in peer networks which make a heavy investment in ideas of toughness and confrontation. Jack Harley, described elsewhere, is a clear example. His expulsion from school and disrupted learning were consequences not of a passively suffered fate but of Jack's vigorous response to his situation.

"Taking up the offer" is a key to understanding disciplinary problems in schools and boys' involvement in violence and sexual harassment. Groups of boys engage in these practices, not because they are driven to it by raging hormones, but in order to acquire or defend prestige, to mark difference, and to gain pleasure. Rule-breaking becomes central to the making of masculinity when boys lack other resources for gaining these ends.

However, the active construction of masculinity need not lead to conflict with the school. There are forms of masculinity much more compatible with the school's educational program and disciplinary needs. This is especially true of middle-class masculinities organized around careers, which emphasize competition through expertise rather than physical confrontation. It seems likely that the construction of masculinities which emphasize responsibility and group cohesion, rather than aggression and individuality, has helped in the educational success of youth from Chinese and Japanese ethnic backgrounds in North America (Takagi 1992, Cheng 1996). Boys who launch themselves on such trajectories are likely to have a much smoother educational passage. The schools as currently organized are a resource for them, and they are an asset for their schools.

The active responses are collective as well as individual. Thorne's (1993) documentation of the gender "boundary work" done in elementary schools shows purposive group activity. So does the rejection by certain boys of a key part of hegemonic masculinity, heterosexual desire. For those boys who begin to think of themselves as gay, a vital step is finding a social network in which homosexual desire seems something other than the ghastly mistake that conventional gender ideology represents it to be.

The making of masculinities in schools, then, is far from the simple learning of norms suggested by "sex-role socialization." It is a process with multiple pathways, shaped by class and ethnicity, producing diverse outcomes. The process involves complex encounters between growing children, in groups as well as individually, with a powerful but divided and changing institution. In some areas of school life, masculinizing practices are conspicuous, even obtrusive. In other areas they are hardly visible at all. Some masculinizing effects are intended by the school, some are unintended, and some are not wanted at all—but still occur.

Two implications are very clear. There is a need for educational thinking about this situation, and there are many possibilities for educational work. Let us now consider the shape this work might take.

South Park, Blue Men, Anality, and Market Masculinity

Judith Kegan Gardiner

Recently, I joined a group of my young male cousins at a family gathering. They lounged around the television set for hours, laughing, drinking beer and soda, and watching a marathon compilation of *South Park* tapes. I joined them and was perplexed. I saw crude cartoon characters, the main ones being four primary school boys. One child kept getting killed, although he reappeared in later episodes. The tone was callous, even sadistic. The few adults, mostly parents and teachers, seemed irrelevant and ineffectual. There were hardly any women. Numerous jokes were about farting or getting things stuck up or blown out one's ass. I thought the program was stupid, obviously inferior to the elegantly allusive *Simpsons* cartoon series, and I did not understand its appeal.[1]

A few weeks ago, I went to a sold-out performance of "Tubes," or the Blue Man Group, a high-priced live entertainment that I saw at a Chicago theater.[2] To cheerful loud music, three men with blue-painted heads and faces, wearing full-body workmen's uniforms, splattered paint and spit up marshmallows and blew through plumbing pipes in a manic display of comic vaudeville. They ejected goop from their bodies, both from their mouths and from a new orifice in the chest of their uniforms. A large part of the fun of the show came from their making

messes, playing with messes, and using their bodies as instruments of art and pleasure, banging them rhythmically to make music. The three blue men did not speak, although the audience heard projected voices, which ostensibly belonged to videos that were displayed on a large screen on stage. In addition, the blue men riffled through flipboards filled with writing, and they bopped one another and drummed LED displays on which messages to the audience scrolled. It was a terrific show, entertaining, inventive, and energetic, which culminated with the audience reeling reams of toilet paper that scrolled out from multiple spindles on the back wall, over our collective heads, and onto a white snarly mass on the stage.[3]

The link that connected these two performances for me appeared in a video screened during the Blue Man Group show.[4] Its cartoonish, diagrammatic format and authoritative voiceover imitated the kind of educational videos used in schools and museums. First, it showed a plug-like form, then many such forms being connected by lines between them. The system became more complex until the screen looked like a wiring diagram or computer board. Still, the connections proliferated. Then, an authoritative voiceover announced, "We are all connected." Technology, computerization, the Internet, just as we expected. But the voice continued, "by plumbing." The lines turned to sewage pipes, the connectors to arrows, and all the arrows were marked, "away." "Sometimes there are blockages," said the

Judith Kegan Gardiner, *Men and Masculinities*, vol. 2, No. 3 (January 2000), pp. 251–271, © 2000 Sage Publications, Inc. Reprinted by Permission of Sage Publications, Inc.

voice, as the diagram pictured a bleeping red stoppage point on a pipeline, and arrows pointed up from the sketched outlines of a sink and a toilet. Everyone laughed.

Thus, a familiar diagram of circuit wizardry metamorphosed into a picture of plumbing embarrassments. Mind swerved into body; the endlessly hyped iconography of new-age technology was shown resisting, going backward, regressing into the irrefutable, funny materiality of intractable human waste. Anality, then, was not merely an incidental childish throwback in these entertainments. Rather, I saw it as connected with, shaping, and shaped by contemporary masculinity and consumer capitalism. These two cultural events, the *South Park* cartoon show and the Blue Man Group entertainment, exhibited anality in their raucous delight in noise, mess, evacuation, and expulsion. However, this was not the anality of the familiar compulsive character, retentive and controlling. Instead, it was an expulsive anality that I argue is related to the ambiguities of men's roles and identities in consumer society. That is, such anality is connected less with the breadwinner masculinity of the post-World War II era than specifically with the market masculinity of our media age. This new masculinity takes its shape from men's attempts to maintain personal autonomy both against the impersonal, overarching authority of the law of the father and against the more seductive, amorphous, and relentless power of corporate advertising, which I call the market of the mother.

THEORIES OF ANALITY

Freud's analyses of anality are rich and perverse. In Freud's theories of infantile sexuality, a stage of oral pleasure at the mother's breast is followed by anal erotism. Freud saw the anal character as a specific kind of neurotic who had compensated for a strong childhood anal erotism by becoming overcontrolled, hence "orderly, parsimonious, and obstinate" (Freud 1908, 169). Freud also connected anal erotism with both sadism and money; he believed the child unconsciously perceived feces as a gift to the mother that could be given or withheld, an ambivalence later transferred to money and also to the child's fantasy of a detachable penis, hence to fears of its loss. Thus, "anal defiance" was particularly male, a component and concomitant of "the castration complex" through which Freud believed boys are socialized into mature heterosexual masculinity in civilized societies (Freud 1917, 133; 1918, 122). Jack Nicholson's character in the recent film *As Good as It Gets* is a comic version of the Freudian anal neurotic personality type. He is rigid, obsessive, constantly swearing, aggressively homophobic, and rich, and he controls other people through his money, including the spunky yet sweetly maternal working-class woman who saves him from his childish and neurotic isolation.

Erik Erikson and other ego psychologists popularized this Freudian theory for the postwar United States. Erikson (1950) rationalized and harmonized Freud's stages into a psychology that charts the normal child's development as a fully social being in a typically middle-class, heterosexual nuclear family. Following Freud, Erikson's second stage is the anal one, stimulated by adults' efforts to get the child to control its bowels and bladder and be socialized into cleanliness. This stage is built on contradictions and ambivalence, since the child is being trained both to retain its bodily products and to eliminate them, depending on the time, place, and situation. Erikson says, "the anal zone lends itself more than any other to the display of stubborn adherence to contradictory impulses" (p. 77). The child at this stage will alternately hoard and discard things, people, and bodily products, alternately "letting go" and "holding on" (p. 78). Thus, success in this stage would show the child "withholding and expelling at will" and therefore developing its willpower as well as its senses of order and propriety (p. 76). However, because Erikson's generically male child feels "powerless in his own body," frightened of his own waste products, and powerless against the outside world, he may also experience shame at his lack of control and his exposure before others. On the other hand, he may assert such control with inflexible firmness. The anal child may also have messy fantasies and "violently hostile wishes of total elimination," in which he controls or destroys other people (p. 55). When this stage goes wrong, Freud and Erikson speak of obsessional neuroses, aggressive evacuation (or constipation), profanity, scatology, and paranoia, especially paranoid fantasies of evil substances within one's own body. Many of these symptoms find obvious analogues in the compulsive repetitions, comic scatology, and paranoid certainty of being attacked or invaded seen in *South Park* and, in more sublimated forms, in the Blue Man Group.

A more positive view of anality than Freud's, one that stresses its subversive potential, is found in Mikhail Bakhtin's (1984) glorification of the grotesque body as it appears in medieval and Renaissance European carnival and popular culture. For Bakhtin, the democratic spirit of folk humor contests authority and turns established hierarchies on their heads by using imagery from what he calls the "material body lower stratum" (p. 368). Such popular humor includes the "slinging of excrement" that signifies destruction and debasement but that also connotes "the area of the genital organs, the fertilizing and generating stratum. Therefore, in the images of urine and excre-

ment is preserved the essential link with birth, fertility, renewal, welfare" (p. 148). Folk anality is thus inseparable from ideas of the open and communal rather than the closed and individual body. Even the aggression, beatings, mock murders, and deaths found in folk ritual, in this view, serve to dethrone authority and defeat "fear by laughter" (p. 395). Insisting on their rights to pleasure and abundance, the common people ultimately recognize themselves in the grotesque body as "the historical, progressing body of mankind" (p. 367). Bakhtin thus emphasizes the specific class and historical contexts of the popular, precapitalist festive anality he describes and contrasts these conditions with the differing social formations under capitalism: "the material bodily principle in grotesque realism is offered in its all-popular festive and utopian aspect," he says, adding that "the material bodily principle is contained not in the biological individual, not in the bourgeois ego, but in the people, a people who are continually growing and renewed" (p. 19).

Like Freud, Erikson (1950) sees the repression of infantile anal erotism as a matter of "middle-class mores," a view that corresponds with Bakhtin's division between folk openness and middle-class closure and with, for example, the division between *South Park*'s child Kyle, who delights in playing with feces, and his middle-class parents' horrified response (p. 77). Some contemporary theorists of masculinity continue this line of reasoning. For example, Calvin Thomas (1996) deploys Lacanian theories to describe men's typical "scatontological anxiety" and "generalized anxiety of expenditure" as fears connected with the social prohibition against children receiving pleasure from anal activities (pp. 84–85). Such anxieties are then allayed and overlaid as the boy develops his identification with the father and the established social system of male mastery, domination, and production. Seeing the core of masculine anxiety as the fear of recognizing female subjectivity, both in the male self and in women, Thomas connects this psychology with the economic system so that the "capitalist deployment of masculinity through rationalized commodity formalism" becomes the means for men's "avoidance of that self-abjection by which the masculine subject becomes the turd of his own fantasy" (p. 96).

In this psychoanalytic schema, the adult middle-class man's psychology develops within a system of family relations that make him anxious and misogynistic, perhaps compulsive and retentive, ambivalent about authority but eager to identify with it. At the same time, men in capitalism generally are socialized into Oedipal competitions among men that render worker resistance intelligible. If a worker understands that his labor power is being taken from him, exploited, by capitalist bosses, he might well resist so as to take back his own. Marxist masculinity theorist Harry Brod (1995) appeals to this tradition, even as he claims we have now moved from private to public patriarchy, a form he calls "fratriarchy, the rule of the brothers, . . . a form of competitive bonding that keeps things in the family of men"; he urges men to resist this bonding and instead to participate "in a political movement to overthrow the capitalist patriarchal state, which is taking your power from you only to use it against you" (p. 92). Thus, Brod assumes a Freudian psychological model of men joining together to resist oppression as workers and as men, men organized as brothers in Oedipal rebellion against an authoritarian father. In profeminist Lacanian formulations of this paradigm like Thomas's, the name of the father stands symbolically for the whole system of patriarchal law and domination that must be fought (Thomas 1996, 49–51). In both

Freudian-Lacanian and Marxist systems, the generic individual is male, and the paradigmatic development is that from son to father, with mothers as objects of rivalry between them and daughters largely absent from the Oedipal scenario (see Brenkman 1993, 234). Like orthodox Marxist analyses of class relations, Freudian and Lacanian psychological systems assume a static division between work and family and so between male and female gender roles that is characteristic of Western industrialism. Thus, both domination and resistance in these systems of thought are primarily figured as male. Men are the active sex to Freud, while passivity is the defining mark of the feminine (Freud 1933). Masculinity is validated by activity in Western industrial societies like Freud's. Moreover, men are represented in modern society as independent actors, that is, as producers or workers making money as well as things. In contrast, women are represented as homebound, passive, and dependent, that is, as unpaid nurturers and consumers.[5]

MARKET MASCULINITY AND CONSUMER RESISTANCE

Now, I suggest we are seeing realigned configurations of gender and psychology through such entertainments as the Blue Man Group and *South Park*. Men's masculinity, especially the masculinity of young men, appears reshaped in contemporary representations in the directions of increased passivity, self-indulgence, and sexual objectification and also in resistance to these traits (see Beneke 1997; Pfeil 1995). Young men in front of television sets and computer consoles are being passified—that is, made more passive, not more peaceful—by a consumer culture that positions everyone as passive and incorporative, ready to absorb all "messages." This culture subjects everyone to constant intrusion and emotional manipulation by advertising. Unlike those past kinds of propaganda that appealed primarily to duty and patriotism, and so connected "manliness" with "civilization," current commercials appeal chiefly to private pleasures and ridicule group action (Bederman 1995). In *South Park*, adults as well as children are ineffectual or humiliated when they attempt to act. For example, the parents temporarily win a campaign to stop the scatological television program their children watch, but not because of their masochistic demonstration of immolating themselves against the program's corporate headquarters. Rather, the parents win concessions only because they are afflicted with aggressively smelly diarrhea (17 September 1997).

Like many entertainments in the television culture, the Blue Man Group and *South Park* both reflect this passivity and attempt to offset it by positioning their spectators as actively making individual choices—one of which is to attend this spectacle—not as workers or family members, then, but as consumers. Although the consumer is, of course, still bound by laws, they are as distant, remote, and perhaps useless as the auditorium voiceovers of Blue Man Group or the silly police officer, vain woman mayor, and inept school authorities portrayed in *South Park*, who are more interested in primping for press conferences than in saving the town from rampaging monsters (18 February 1998). Much more immediate than official authority is the constant pressure of advertising, of the market of the mother as an ever-present, seductive, and intrusive imperative to buy and consume, buy and consume, interrupting the television viewer every few minutes. Just such a saccharine insistence on something pleasant but unwholesome characterizes Mrs. Cartman on *South Park* as she offers her obese son yet another bag of "Cheesy Poofs" or plate of cookies as a solu-

tion to all his problems (27 August 1997). Commercial products echo such motifs. "Warm up to South Park," reads the catalog copy selling *South Park* coffee mugs: "Even if it's as cold as Kenny's corpse outside, you can warm up to some of Chef's sweet lovin'. . . . The perfect drinking vessel with Mrs. Cartman's cookie-dings!" (Brainstorms 1998, 25).

In each day's listening to commercial radio and television, Americans hear repeated and insistent voices of authority telling us what to do, voices often not visibly attached to bodies but supposed to emanate from doctors, scientists, and wizards of household cleanliness, while the authority of these "messages" is enforced through the audience's familiarity with the celebrity voices that impersonate them. Blue Man Group dramatizes the consumer's helplessness before an infantilizing onslaught of expert authority when it displays a film of lovely, colored fractal patterns with a voiceover telling the audience it cannot understand the mathematics involved in generating these patterns.[6] Similarly, the three Blue Men rapidly turn over flipboards that announce random facts and also warn the audience that it cannot keep up with the information overload of modern life and should not even try. In this way, scientific and sociological facts are presented not as information for use but already as indigestible waste, material that will pass right through us without nourishing us. The information overload is also connected with seductions to dumb down, to return to the preverbal and preoedipal simplicities of instinctual demand and its assuaging, perhaps even to the sensory simplifications of *South Park*'s visual animation style or Blue Man Group's childlike speechlessness.

According to Freud and Erikson, orality precedes anality in the infant's developing sense of self. Americans from childhood on have access to already-prepared food, drink, snacks, and even drugs and are constantly enticed to consume them. Many people believe that Americans are getting fatter and exercising less as we watch endless images of thin beautiful athletes, a combination that can create self-loathing and eating disorders, at present still primarily in young women. "Just saying no" is the road to autonomy for the two-year-old being toilet trained, and it seems appropriate that this strategy is also being mobilized against the even more infantile stage of oral temptation represented by passively succumbing to drugs.[7] Yet, inveighing against the passivity of consumer culture ignores its ambivalences. Many people feel that they are constantly monitoring everything they eat or drink, perpetually on a diet and exercising self-control many times a day as they pass the refrigerator or vending machine without taking a snack, even if their weight gradually increases from occasional small indulgences.

Advertising does create its own resistances, however. Its repetitions attempt to induce dependencies on its products at the same time that these repetitions raise the consumers' level of tolerance against them. Commercials repeat, sometimes within minutes, as if to defeat the people who left the room or diverted their attention during them. People now are exposed to barrages of repeated, seductively beautiful, well-made, and intrusive messages that are designed to get into our heads and make us buy things. It therefore seems likely that various forms of repetition compulsion and anal defiance will appear in the defenses against such onslaughts. The toilet break is so intimately connected with commercials that marketers can supposedly gauge programs' popularity by the changes in municipal water levels induced by simultaneous mass flushing, a resistance to passively receiving ads that operates by simple avoidance, even as it metaphorically mimes the active expulsion of indigestible matter.

Gender is related to the consumer culture in complex ways. Insofar as selfishness in boys is figured as perfectly appropriate, whereas women are to be nurturant and self-sacrificing, desires to consume can be supportive of masculinity: commercials that show young men running, jumping, and driving apparently seek to persuade men that they work and play hard and hence should "just do it" because they "deserve the best"—whatever the product is. Current advertising also sexually objectifies men, subjecting their bodies to the scrutiny of others. Margaret Morganroth Gullette (1997) indicts a capitalist system that seeks self-indulgent consumers and cheap workers unprotected by seniority rules, and she sees the current glorification of youth as decreasing gender difference by making men increasingly vulnerable to the "commercial packaging of youth" long aimed at women (p. 144). Men, as well as women, now see beautiful young specimens of their sex constantly displayed as sexual objects, a display that can provoke homophobic anxieties as well as envious identifications.

Men's resistance to these commercial forces, I contend—that is, their resistance to being positioned as passive, sexually objectified consumers—may take several forms in which the psychology of anality plays a part. These forms of resistance may be figured in terms of a realigned anality that is neither the obsessive, hoarding anality of the bourgeoisie nor the polymorphously sensual anality of the Bakhtinian folk. Instead, this new masculine psychology shares characteristics and symptoms with both. It also exceeds them and takes a new configuration that has many qualities at once—an apparently childish, homoerotic but homophobic, racist, cynical, and paranoid form of anal erotism. This masculine anality is dedicated to fighting against taking things in by pushing things out. The inputs it expels are not merely food products and sexual threats but also advertising, adults, and their authority. A poster advertised for college students, for example, features the always-victimized *South Park* child Kenny sitting on a toilet, behind which is a note reading "Excuse from being late. I have explosive diarrhea" (Globalprints 1998). Rejecting school, rejecting authority, the vulnerable boys of *South Park* signal a thoroughly ambivalent resistance to the conditions of their lives that also resists any politics of collective action.

Masculinity theorist Timothy Beneke (1997) argues that "virtually anything men experience as stressful can serve as an occasion to prove manhood, so long as it is also something experienced as stressful by women"; he gives the specific example that "boys and even men feel superior to women and other men through their greater capacity to handle 'grossness,' unpleasant sounds and smells, insects and rodents, dirt, and so on" (p. 39). This aggressive delight in "grossness" fits the expulsive anality I am describing here, an anality that also constructs masculinity as explicitly childish—before responsibility or adult sexuality though implicitly heterosexual, male-bonded rather than relating to women, potentially sadistic, acquiring only to spend, and compulsively participating in vicarious and symbolic violence (which may turn into active violence against people who are not perceived as fully persons or who are perceived as threatening to heterosexual masculinity, like gay men). So reviews of Blue Man Group commend its "childlike love of play" and compare its pleasures to those of finger painting, and the boys in *South Park* are eight-year-old third graders younger than their R-rated, late-evening watchers (Koren 1997; Richards 1998). The swaddled, hairless Blue Man Group members are all male, as the generic baby is still male and as blue clothing still signals a baby boy. Describing the popular 1994 Hollywood film *Forrest Gump*, Fred Pfeil

(1995) articulates a similar kind of contemporary masculinity that uses childishness as an alibi: the simple-minded hero Forrest, he says, is "warranted to take up the traditional functions of masculinity," those of the "protector-provider," but "only insofar as he remains a child in all other respects, immaculately innocent of any knowledge of or participation in the larger world" (p. 256).

Nothing in the Blue Man Group's performance alludes to sexual difference or, for that matter, sexual desire for either men or women. The *South Park* children, in contrast, frequently allude to sexual matters, but without understanding them, presumably to the delighted superiority of their young adult audience. (Their language reminds me of a schoolyard insult I heard, when one boy called another a "mother fucking doo-doo head," in which the children clearly understood the latter part of the insult but just tacked on the first half in imitation of what older kids said). The deliberate childishness and masculine anal passive aggression of *South Park* and Blue Man Group also recall the recent campus legend of fraternity men watching the Super Bowl on television while drinking and wearing diapers so that they would not have to leave the room for even a moment.

The same young male viewers may enjoy the increasing violence and emotional intensity of today's sports, video games, even television talk shows, which stoke the need for more aggression and competition to fulfill compensatory functions for increasingly passive male watchers. Pfeil (1995) details some analogous processes in reviewing the "soft-boiled dick" masculinities that connote both sensitivity and the ultimate resort to violence in contemporary movies, rock music, and detective fiction (p. 105). I think that the young male viewer may also reinforce his sense of active masculinity by spitting out epithets, so identifying with the verbal aggressivity of continual cursing on *South Park*. In fact, cursing and farting are the kinds of activities possible even to the child or couch potato to make him feel more rebellious, tough, and assertive as he sits before the television set—a situation itself dramatized and ridiculed in other television programs, like *Beavis and Butthead*.

Although the Freudian version of anal erotism makes much of feces as hard objects, products, or gifts, Blue Man Group favors colorful splatterings, and many of the *South Park* episodes feature symphonies of even more ethereal flatulence, pure performance without product, which may be taken as signs of the children's simultaneous abjection before, defiance of, and exclusion from adult producer culture and their cynical incorporation into the endless hot air of the information society. In fact, the favorite television program within the program watched by the boys of *South Park* consists entirely of two boys farting at one another and then laughing (17 September 1997). Similarly, such male-focused media personalities as Howard Stern and "Love Line's" Adam Corolla boast of farting over the broadcast air.[8]

Thus, a rebellious, expulsive, and apparently childish anality, I argue, works to shore up male autonomy in our consumer society by resisting the masculinity-undermining effects of consumer passivity, objectification, and other manipulations. This kind of anality may have both positive and negative potentials, psychologically and politically. Its positive potential is most manifest in the creativity and play based on making the body into matter and in the political possibilities of resisting and ejecting intrusive matter and so of contesting established authority and convention. Eve Sedgwick (1993), one of the few feminist theorists of anality, speaks of the "projective squeamishness" that adults impose on children's passions and perversities (p. 177). She implies that adults project their own squeamishness onto children, who are freer of such conventions, but the phrase also applies beautifully to performances like Blue Man Group and *South Park*, in which one might see squeamishness as spat or farted out of the performing child and toward the reluctant adult. The reverse may also be true, with adults projecting their squeamishly renounced aggressions and resistances onto children as their young adult audiences presumably do for *South Park*, with its scenes of combined "shame, exhibition, and misrecogized fury," to quote Sedgwick's description of infantile anal erotism (p. 211).[9] These negative emotions and projections also indicate some limits to the progressive potential of this anality, which affirms some men's autonomy at the expense of women and abjected categories of men. Moreover, this anality is narrowly defensive, confined to resisting the status quo rather than articulating alternatives to it. It contests consumer capitalism's specific incursions on the masculine self but not its continued allure for the young men who participate in it. Fundamentally, it does not contest consumer capitalism's monopoly of social power.

An explicit example of anal ambivalence about consumerism occurs in the 1997 *South Park* Christmas program, "Mr. Hankey the Christmas Poo."[10] Kyle, a Jewish boy who covets Christmas presents and conformity with his classmates, imagines a Santa-hatted piece of feces who welcomes him to the Christmas spirit, sings, leads him around, and makes terrible messes. Mr. Hankey disturbs Kyle's parents and all the other *South Park* adults except for the soulful African American school Chef, who is the only adult who believes in—and can see—Mr. Hankey (17 December 1997). Even funnier, and even nastier than killing Kenny, apparently, is smearing the walls with feces. Various teenagers that I know say that this is their favorite *South Park* program and the funniest one. This episode flings the strongest rejection and rebuke to the consumer culture in its fantasy of messing up Christmas. At the same time, it projects its rebellion onto a Jewish boy and indicates the longing, even for Jewish children, to become completely integrated into the American ruling religion of consumerism. Such consumerism now provides ideally fantasized substitutes for family, community, love, and liberal acceptance of difference: it does not matter what religion you are identified with so long as you participate in Christmas consumption. This sentiment is explicitly expressed in the 1995 "Spirit of Christmas" episode in which Jesus fights Santa Claus over the meaning of the holiday. Stan, one of the Christian children, summarizes the lesson of the program: "I learned something today. It doesn't matter if you're Christian or Jewish or atheist or Hindu, Christmas is still about one very important thing. . . . Presents."[11]

Young men's ambiguous resistances to being passively intruded upon and to the blandishments of the endless "buy and eat, my child," of advertising may also continue to take the familiar and unattractive forms of misogyny and homophobia. Currently, this homophobia is also anally inflected. It appears especially in attacks against men who are anally receptive in their sexual practices, a preoccupation that shows in young men's homophobic, often coprophilic, sometimes affectionately homoerotic abuse of one another with such terms as "buttfucker," "buttmunch," or "fudgepacker."[12] Although *South Park* speaks an official ideology of liberal tolerance for homosexuality, for instance in the program on "Big Gay Al's Big Gay Boat Ride," in which the children learn to accept Stan's homosexual dog, they still taunt each other in anal terms (3 September 1997). Freud (1908)

demurely says that "an invitation to a caress of the anal zone is still used today, as it was in ancient times, to express defiance or defiant scorn, and thus in reality signifies an act of tenderness that has been overtaken by repression" (p. 173). He believed that some of his disturbed male patients had experienced such tenderness toward men, based on identifications with their mothers as their fathers' sexual partners, and so developed and repressed fantasies of passive anal receptivity to other men (Freud 1918, 72). Thus, classical psychoanalysis connects anality with male passivity. When Erikson (1950) writes, "any anal fixation . . . is especially apt to prepare for a homosexual attitude with the implied idea of gaining love and control forever through anal incorporation" (p. 80), he assumes that an "anal fixation" will be receptive and incorporative rather than expulsive, although his own description of the anal stage of infantile sexuality describes both possibilities. Furthermore, Erikson localizes this mechanism to boys, who, he claims, are unlike women in that they can grasp or hoard only in this manner. Discussing the fantasies of anal rape held by one of Freud's patients, Peter Middleton (1992) adds his surmise that men's homophobia springs from their fear of other's men's penetrative violence against themselves, a violence he sees as constitutive of dominant masculinity (p. 98). Thus, anal preoccupations are intrinsic to the stability of contemporary heterosexual masculinity insofar as it defines itself in opposition to homosexual passivity and receptive effeminacy.

Contemporary queer studies, too, emphasize anality, with a particular focus on anal eroticism, abjection, and death. "Is the rectum a grave?" Leo Bersani (1988) asks in an essay that traces homophobic hatred of gay men to a repulsion toward and fascination with anal erotism that reveals men's unconscious fear of passivity and vulnerability, of a death of the masterful male self.

In the age of AIDS, he says, heterosexual men inhibit their compassion toward the victims of this terrible disease. Instead, they project its danger away from themselves through a fear of gay men, whom they imagine as sinister agents of death. Reversing this logic, Bersani argues, "if the rectum is the grave in which the masculine ideal (an ideal shared—differently—by men and women) of proud subjectivity is buried, then it should be celebrated for its very potential for death" (p. 222; also see Bersani 1995). As male homosexuality in popular culture is now chiefly ridiculed through jokes concerning anality rather than other sexual regions or practices, fantasies of anality color the perception of homosexuals by heterosexuals. On the other hand, the expulsive, market-resisting, childish, and passive-aggressive anality I have been describing here cannot simply be reduced to homophobia. Instead, I conjecture that the consumer culture connotes receptive passivity for both men and women. This passivity especially threatens masculine activity, mastery, and dominance, which can be reasserted and reinforced through proud resistance to anal intrusion and through scatological anal expulsion. Instead of finding this process constitutive of masculinity per se, however, I suggest that it has specific meanings and takes specific form in the young men of today's consumer culture.

One of these forms is the resistance to things coming into the body as feminizing intrusions into a masculine self. This resistance seems also to extend to empathy, in which the emotions and perceptions of others resonate feelingly within the self. Therefore, boys' training in masculinity is explicitly antiempathic, as Donna Eder (1995) found in her study of boys' teasing in middle school and as David Collinson (1995) discusses in his observations of working-class men's joking on the job. Beneke (1997), too, stresses that modern manhood requires resisting empathy with those weaker or in pain, remaining "cold-blooded when confronting suffering or horror" (p. 41). The Blue Man Group performance elaborately manages the audience's responses to emotion through official-looking LED sign displays. First, these innocuously remind everyone not to take flash photographs in the theater; then they instruct the audience to humiliate latecomers with applause. Explaining that a man picked arbitrarily out of the crowd looks sad and needs cheering up, the instructions command the audience to chant, "We love you" to him, which many people do, in unison. All know that they are completely unacquainted with the person that they are saying they "love." This produces a mutual complicity in superficial verbal conformity and a distancing of the self from expressions of emotion. Presumably, some men in the audience are on dates with their girlfriends, who thus hear them publicly and meaninglessly declaring a sentiment to a random man that they may have resisted uttering in private intimacy to a special woman. *South Park* is even more direct in training its audience to rebuff sentiment and empathy. One boy's egg-shaped baby brother is repeatedly kicked on the program after he has pleaded, "Don't kick the baby" in childish tones. The best-known repetition in the series is the death of the unintelligible, parka-hooded child Kenny in nearly every episode, followed by the cheerfully aggressive refrain from the other boys, "Oh my God, they've killed Kenny. You bastards," a situation reproduced on tee shirts available in my campus bookstore and more actively echoed in the instruction, "click here to kill Kenny" on an internet advertisement to buy *South Park* videotapes (yahoo.com 1998).

While young men are being trained to resist empathic feelings for others, and so to deny their own dependencies, they are also being socialized into perceiving their own bodies as the chief realm for the expression of both indulgence and discipline, of masculinity and its disparagements. As in other facets of American culture, liberal racism ambiguously heightens and denies attention to differences in men's appearance, and it also works to shore up consumer masculinity, with its anal reification of people as products. In the ads and myths of liberal consumerism, race is irrelevant; only talent counts. If former Chicago basketball star Michael Jordan and other superathletes are the perfect hypermasculine men in the eyes of many Americans, for example, they are also the best-known endorsers of products and supremely profitable products in themselves (Bigness and Hirsley 1999). Even when men of color are revered as such icons of masculinity, however, anally eroticized racist fears help create white consumer solidarity and consolidate white male heterosexuality: the African American prison rapist of other men is now a recurrent fixation of terrorized fascination for heterosexual men, including those with little likelihood of prison residence.[13]

While racial and ethnic divisions continue to be used to divide and separate workers, furthermore, ads build a false sense of unity and progress, a liberal hegemony of youthful solidarity through consumer taste so that the "Pepsi Generation" or rap music listeners are portrayed in advertisements showing beautiful, vigorous, multiethnic people. Blue Man Group personifies this liberal racism with its apparent indifference to skin tone. "He could be blue. He could be green"; whatever the discrimination, the discriminator states that skin color was not its cause (e.g., Jen 1996, 210). Masks of blue paint occlude the race of the performers in Blue Man Group so that they are colored like Muppets, Smurfs, or fantasies of multiethnic tolerance, not like any known group

of humans. Yet, blueface resembles blackface and operates similarly: the blue men are like clowns or children with rhythm; they represent primitive instincts; they are ostentatiously colored; they are not white (see Guber 1997, 72).

The pattern of liberal racism in *South Park* is more overt. Its one exemplary person of color is the African American Chef who feeds the children in their grade school cafeteria. Isolated from other adults, he is treated differently from other adult men in the community. With a face like the cook on an old Cream of Wheat box, the *South Park* Chef is a nurturing mammy and an eminently successful heterosexual lover, although he maintains no lasting ties with women and has no family of his own. Instead, he remains a reliable servant for the boys, ever ready to provide them with sexual information or run to their rescue. Among his other comically stereotypical attributes, he has rhythm, the singing, dancing soul represented by the voice of singer Isaac Hayes, and so he is also implicitly a celebrity in comparison with the other characters, whose voices were not familiar to listeners from other contexts. As both celebrity and image of a commercial product, Chef is the most reliable moral authority on the program. He is the adult closest to the children in terms of understanding them, a surrogate parental authority, and a model of fantastically overgendered masculinity—a hyperheterosexual phallic mother, a maternal dad to the boys, and the school football coach to boot.[14] Instinctive, rhythmic, and messy, the men of color in both Blue Man Group and *South Park* thus seem analogous to the stage of expulsive anal erotism in Freudian child development, to be enjoyed and outgrown, and they also represent the racist ambivalence of consumer masculinity by being simultaneously performers and products, contradictory objects of enjoyment and of deniable identification for their young white male viewers.

Another contradiction of the consumer culture is that each seller repeatedly incites people to believe in and act on its claims and to disbelieve the claims of others, thus heightening the listeners' tolerance for increasing levels of persuasion and disbelief. The resistance to intrusion by such lures to consume and believe may then take the twinned forms of cynicism and paranoia. The consumer cynic rejects, disbelieves, expels, or excretes political and advertising hype, frequently with little reasoned way of distinguishing among truer or falser premises or promises, yet continues to consume. The writers and producers of *South Park*, Trey Parker and Matt Stone (1992–99), introduce their commercial videotapes with ostentatiously false information and blatantly insincere professions, for example, the repeated statement that each program is their favorite. Similarly, the messages that the Blue Man Group displays tell the audience not to be anxious about their inability to assimilate, judge, or act on the information overload around them but merely to sit back and enjoy the show. The skepticism against constituted authority that the Left once was able to mobilize to debunk the ideology of rulers and bosses has now often turned into right-wing cynicism, the assurance to all by the popular media that we are being lied to—by the politicians if not by ads—and that the proper response is to trust the "free" and impartial laws of the corporate marketplace, since there can be no better alternatives to the system we now have. Thus, the disillusioned may leave government to those who profit from it personally, like the self-aggrandizing mayor on *South Park*, and mock consumer protestors, like Kyle's mother on the same program, who object to the "potty-mouthed toilet humor" of the cartoons that her son watches on television (17 September 1997).

This contemporary popular cynicism bears some analogy to the Freudian concept of the patient's resistance against the interpretations of the analyst. Freud (1918) says that doubt enables the patient "to lie entrenched behind a respectful indifference and to allow the efforts of the treatment to slip past him for years together," so remaining unchanged (p. 75). This skepticism, which in its current consumer shape is anything but "respectful," is also perversely connected with paranoia—for Freud, one of the signs of repressed anal erotism. In such paranoia, the skeptical distrust of other people increases into a certainty of their malevolence. The paranoid knows that "They" are trying to get him, and the enemy "They" depends on the times; in the fifties, for example, the evil intruders were often communists, whereas today's paranoia seems evidence of a crisis of authority without a clear alternative belief system. Now, the intruder may be the consumer culture itself, making the active self passive, compliant, needy, and vulnerable to the desires it incites. Such psychological mechanisms may help account for the popularity of the anally expulsive resistance and rebellion represented in the *South Park* characters or the twinned skepticism and credulity invoked and mimed by the Blue Man Group. These entertainments reify the forces of consumer capitalism's war against us from within our own bodies and our own society, then project them as internal evils and dangers that must be expelled—like the Blue Man Group's gagging mouthfuls of marshmallows or *South Park*'s bouts of raucously explosive diarrhea. *South Park* mocks this paranoid motif of the alien within when space invaders plant an anal probe in one child that makes him compulsively sing, dance, and fart flames until an eighty-foot satellite dish emerges out of his derriere (13 August 1997).

What are little boys being trained for in the United States today? Computer software, entertainment, and preparation for war are America's leading edge industries, what we export to other nations. Both Blue Man Group and *South Park* show the play and aggression in computerization, in the sadistic pleasures of blipping cartoon figures or smart-rocketing targets to oblivion, as the United States proudly replayed for the population during its Gulf War against Iraq. Both the creativity and the sadism of the expulsive masculine anality I have been describing are necessary for these new enterprises, the mess and the constraint, the inundating by voices of authority and the resistance to them, the computer, and the toilet.

So the anal humor of *South Park* and Blue Man Group is both paranoid and cynical, passive and aggressive, related to the productions of the culture while defined by its consumptions. It excretes the products of the material culture back at its audiences as well as at authority figures, and, at the same time, it disguises its aggression as natural, unwilled bodily process. Moreover, such humor identifies the viewer with the vulnerability and impotence of children, a vulnerability we all share against a market and state apparatus that we are led to believe lie beyond our control. It is in the open recognition of this vulnerability that this kind of anality may differ from the traditional scatology found in the Bakhtinian carnivalesque or in working-class irreverence to bosses. In the carnival, the low becomes high for a limited period until order and authority are restored. In *South Park,* as in many American situation comedies and cartoons, the adult world is without any authority worthy of respect, yet childish rule offers no comforts or possibilities for utopian transformation. The image of the "real world" is that of compulsively repeating commercials and a continual battle between the ambivalent gratifications of passive compliance and consumer resistance. Under such conditions, I speculate, the young adult male viewer of

these childish entertainments may feel consoled by being at least more in control of himself than the *South Park* children, less messy than the Blue Men, hence less dependent and more masculine.

FEMINIST IMPLICATIONS

In the summer of 1998, *South Park* was the most popular program on United States cable television (McDonald 1998; Van Meter 1998). Blue Man Group was then continuing its several-year open run of performances in New York, Boston, and Chicago. Throughout this article, I have assumed that these two apparently disparate popular performances are symptomatic of larger trends in contemporary culture, and I have analyzed their anal imagery seeking insights into the psychologies they imply about their audiences, particularly of young, white, heterosexual men. Such inferences are clearly conjectural. By connecting contemporary psychologies to specific facets of current consumer culture, however, they avoid essentializing masculinity as inalterably oppressive and misogynistic.

As we face new formations of capital and government, and so new formations of psychology and gender, realigned forms of organized rather than somaticized resistance may prove more effective. Traditionally, progressives organized working men in opposition to their bosses. Increasingly in relation to the consumer economy, however, workers are dispossessed as part time, temporary, or without specifically valued trade skills. Many people may identify their interests, even their gender and identities, as consumers of purchased goods and services more clearly than they identify their rights as workers. Leftists and progressives already fight for active control of our economic and political life and now sometimes integrate these battles with those for more active control of our consuming life as well, for example, as voters, environmental activists, or concerned shoppers. These battles have considerable potential for cross-class cooperation that should also include both sexes. For many Americans, hearing how Nike workers abroad or clothing sweatshop workers in the United States are exploited may motivate purchaser boycotts that can support workers' efforts and even modify corporate strategies. Consumer identification with the vulnerability of children may also make showing the exploitation of children an effective organizing strategy for men as well as for women. I have suggested in this article that the expulsive anality of such popular representations as *South Park* and the Blue Man Group itself indicates a kind of ambivalent resistance to the consumer culture, even though overt consumer activism—exactly in the campaign against scatological children's television—is self-referentially mocked in *South Park* (17 September 1997).

If there are, indeed, such realigned configurations of masculinity in contemporary consumer society as I have described, what are the implications for feminists? Many analyses of hegemonic masculinity in Western societies today, including those analyses that draw on the psychology of anality, paint masculinity as so powerfully oppressive that the only moral role for a profeminist human male is "Refusing to Be a Man" (Stoltenberg 1989; also see 1994). According to Thomas (1996), "at the core" of masculinist anxiety "concerning a mode of recognition in and by which [a man] is turned into shit" is the fear of recognizing women's subjectivity (p. 96). He describes this psychological dynamic as hopelessly polarized:

> within the confines of a strictly gendered and hierarchical subject/object polarity, to grant subjectivity and authority to the femi-

nine side of the equation is to objectify and deauthorize the masculine, thus accentuating not only the latter's lack of autonomy, its dependency and helplessness, but also its abjection, its inert and fecal passivity, (pp. 96–97).

In response, he recommends that men learn how to let the anxiety of "endless interpretive desire . . . remain productive," a hope especially targeted to writers and intellectuals (p. 194). Other theorists stress the difficulties of persuading men to give up their masculinity as it is traditionally constituted. For example, Bob Connell (1995) proposes "A Practical Politics of Gender for Heterosexual Men" that includes everything from sharing childcare and working for affirmative action to redistributing social wealth, an agenda for social justice that he concedes would be "highly stressful in the short run" for men (pp. 87–88). Clearly, masculinity is far too deeply a part of men's psyches and sense of self to be easily eradicated, nor is it obvious that the obliteration of masculinity is necessary to achieve gender justice. Michael Kimmel (1996) argues for the "full equality" of all people, which will only be "possible if we change the meaning of manhood," yet he insists his is "not a call for androgyny, for a blurring of masculinity and femininity into a mélange of some vaguely defined 'human' qualities" but rather a celebration of difference that assures all Americans "a secure and confident sense" of themselves (p. 334).

I have been arguing here that contemporary American masculinity is already changing in ways that merit feminist attention, and I have attempted to indicate some of these changes by looking at psychologies of anality in popular cultural performances involving young men. No feature of such consumer analities and masculinities is unique; all their components have appeared in other cultural forms, and obviously this analysis ignores empirical data on child rearing in favor of interpreting popular cultural representations. Nevertheless, these representations may indeed indicate new psychological configurations of gender, new anally inflected consumer masculinities. With their ambivalently progressive and regressive features, these masculinities do not easily align with dualistic judgments of what is oppressive and what is liberating for men or women, and I suggest that they might therefore usefully figure into feminist efforts to foster alternative, less sexist masculinities. For example, if young men today are developing traits like resistance to empathy, these may not be intrinsic to a circular reinforcement of masculinity at the inevitable expense of femininity and women. Instead, such personality formations may be better read as responses to specific, historical changes in the consumer economy that typically affect men's identities differently than women's (see Gardiner 1998). If my analyses of consumer masculinity provide some accurate insights here, many young men are likely to fight direct attempts to make them less sexist because they will perceive such campaigns as intrusive attacks on their inner male selves. In the popular imagination rather than in the women's movement, feminists constantly accuse men of sexism; such defensive projections may enable some young men to endorse sexism as a masculinity-affirming briar patch into which they are happy to be thrown.[15] In contrast, efforts simultaneously to develop men's empathy and to reinforce their resistance to corporate manipulation may prove to be more promising paths toward achieving the same, less sexist behavior (see Goleman 1995). For instance, feminists might successfully reinforce boys and men for status masculinity—"of course you're a real man"—while decrying as not manly all forms of bullying, unfairness, and personal and social violence. Men truly secure of their masculinity, we may believe, will be able to be gentle, tender, unafraid of other men, antiracist, and antihomophobic, and they might best gain a sense of active autonomy and control, of a developing and responsible masculinity, in joining with other men and women to fight for more just economic, political, and gender structures.

The transition from industrial to consumer capitalism apparently entails typically different difficulties for men and for women in maintaining a socially coherent sense of gender identity. By showing current forms of masculinity as functional, not merely to uphold male superiority over women but also to uphold male autonomy against the invasive, pervasive, and seductive consumer culture, I hope to indicate one specific historical variable in the construction of contemporary masculinity and therefore its susceptibility to change. Other connections than those I have described may also be developing among consumer culture, anality, masculinity, and the possibilities for progressive resistance, not only to sexism but also to the corporate domination of public and private life. As we have seen, Brod (1995) urged men to join "a political movement to overthrow the capitalist/patriarchal state, which is taking your power from you only to use it against you," a phrasing that attempts to mobilize men through a psychology of resistance to the intrusions of established power on the individual (p. 92). A nuanced, depolarized effort to find alternative nonsexist masculinities, I have suggested, may also benefit from understanding that young American men's masculinities are now forming in ambivalent resistance, not only to the law of the father, but also to the consumer culture's market of the mother.[16]

NOTES

1. Further viewing revealed allusions in *South Park* as well and some anal themes in *The Simpsons.* The themes outlined below are more prevalent in the early *South Park* programs.

2. Reviews posted on the Internet include those by Bowen (1998), Koren (1997), Narciso (1998), and Richards (1998).

3. According to its press releases, Blue Man Group was founded in New York by Matt Goldman, Phil Stanton, and Chris Wink in 1991 and currently performs in several cities with different actors. For information about Blue Man Group, I thank Marni Kamber, associate company manager of Blue Man Group Chicago, 1998.

4. This film was produced by the Blue Man Group.

5. For a materialist feminist review of some feminist responses in Freud, see Gardiner (1992).

6. "Fractal Film" is credited to Dr. Heinze-Otto Peitgen in Blue Man Group (1998, Stagebill, p.18).

7. The "Just Say No" campaign also collaborates with the tendency to discursive magic in our culture of representations, in which saying something often substitutes for doing it.

8. I received this information secondhand from friends who heard about my project. The Corolla broadcast was January 7, 1999. No date was reported for the Howard Stern reference.

9. *South Park* Web sites include grandiose and aggressive titles like "Buffest, Kickass Sites," "Kick the Baby Site," and "They killed Kenny" site. One site featuring a fan's own cartoon apparently identifies with both the abject child and with Mr. Hankey as an aggressive, homo-erotic, oral and anal castrator. The site is titled, "Mr. Hanky the Christmas Poo Ate My Balls" and shows Kyle as the victim. Mr. Hankey tells Kyle his "balls sure do smell . . . like flowers," asks to "munch" his "sack," eats one testicle and pursues the other saying, "I'm pissed. Give me your damn balls" (prosep5 1998).

10. An earlier episode, "The Spirit of Christmas" in 1995, showed a battle between Jesus and Santa Claus over the meaning of Christmas (Adequate Design 1997–98).

11. Kyle's dirty habits and fantasies also relate to older anti-semitic traditions. For example, Calvin

Thomas (1996) connects traditional anti-semitism with the abjection of anality: for the anti-semitic, Thomas says, "the Jews cannot recognize the truly messianic because of what he considers their abject association with the messy anus," an admittedly "atrocious pun" that Thomas uses to emphasize men's dangerous projections of their anxieties about bodily integrity onto women, homosexuals, Jews, and other marginalized figures (p. 63). The "South Park Episode Guide" attributes the character of Mr. Hankey to Trey Parker, whose closest child representative on the program, Stan, is not Jewish. Parker, it says, "started drawing Mr. Hankey in high school. One idea when Trey was offered a TV show was the Mr. Hankey Show, but people weren't too happy with the idea of a show about talking poo" (Adequate Design 1997–98).

12. "Big Gay Al's Big Gay Animal Farm" is featured in a *South Park* episode about tolerance and a homosexual dog (3 September 1997). Cartman, Kyle, and Santa call each other variants on "buttfucker" in the 1995 "Spirit of Christmas" program, and the term "buttmunch," apparently acceptable for cable television, is heard, for example, on the September 17, 1997, episode. I have heard all these terms used among teenaged boys from the Midwest and West Coast.

13. In popular culture, the prison rapist now appears as excitingly fearful icon, for both white and African American men, of an African American hypermasculinity whose anally penetrative homosexual desire is denied under the simplification, previously attributed to some feminists, that rape is a crime of violence, not of sex. Jokes about prison rapists now occur even on mainstream television programs like *The Tonight Show.*

14. hooks (1996, 84, 216) discusses representations of African American men as feminized helpers to white men. Pfeil (1995) describes popular representations of the "proto-sexual healing of the white man by the black" (p. 13).

15. I base this conjecture on student e-mails circulated in 1998 and from Internet jokes with titles like "If Men Really Ruled the World."

16. This article is part of a project on "Masculinity in Feminist Theory," which has been supported by the Institute for the Humanities at the University of Illinois at Chicago. A short version of this article was delivered to the Marxist Literary Group, June 1998. For helpful comments, I thank the anonymous reviewers for this journal.

The Ninjas, the X-Men, and the Ladies: Playing with Power and Identity in an Urban Primary School

Anne Haas Dyson

Children in our diverse society are not only learning to read and write texts; they are learning to read and write human possibilities. They read each other's faces and clothes as closely as they do any storybook, and they write each other's future in the stories they imagine. This article is an analytic narrative about children's use of stories to reveal and transform images of power and of gender in the local culture of an urban second-grade classroom. It is based on a qualitative study of children's symbolic and social use of superhero stories—popular media stories that vividly reveal societal beliefs about power and gender, which are themselves interwoven in complex ways with race, class, and physical demeanor. Through the writing and acting of stories, the children let each other witness their imaginations at work and then raise issues about who plays whom in whose story. The dialogic processes thus enacted allowed rigid images of gender relations and of glorified power to be rendered more complex. There is no simple classroom procedure that will allow children to achieve some sort of critical consciousness and a world of greater imagined possibilities for all. But there are processes, rooted in the social lives and play of childhood, that can help children deal with the contradictory pressures of growing up in a multicultural society where power (i.e., ability to

Teachers College Record 96, 2 (Winter 1994), pp. 219–39. Copyright © by Teachers College, Columbia University.

take action and influence that society) is not equitably distributed.

Holly and Tina, both second-graders, are talking over the latest news in the classroom grapevine: Thomas and Aloyse have just been suspended for hitting Monique. Holly states the moral of this true story:

HOLLY: You're not supposed to slap girls, 'cause girls are not that strong, like boys.

TINA: HUH! The yellow girls are. Like you. You just don't know. You can use your strength. But you just don't know you can. I used it before. (Tina is African-American; Holly is mixed race—African-American and European American—"yellow," in Tina's terms.)

HOLLY: I can beat up Aloyse. You saw me beat up Aloy—You saw me slap Aloyse twice.

TINA: You saw me beat that boy *up*. Right here. (Tina points to the upper part of her arm, bent at the elbow.) That's your strength. Right there. . . .

HOLLY: I know. I slapped Lawrence.

TINA: I slapped him and airpunched him. (Tina acts out her swift moves.)

HOLLY: I slapped him five times and punched him six times.

TINA: You must really *like* him. If you punch him and slap him, that means you like him.

HOLLY: I *hate* him! (distressed) I was just joking.

Stories, whether told or written, dramatized or sung, are universal cultural tools for evaluating past experiences and for participating in the social present. Within and through stories, we fashion our relationships with others, joining with them, separating from them, expressing in ways subtle and not our feelings about the world around us. As Bakhtin argued, the stories we tell not only shape a specific ongoing relationship (like that between Holly and Tina); they also dynamically reveal our response to broader, deeper cultural conversations (like the children's about gender, strength, and, in less explicit ways, race ["the yellow girls are"]).[1]

Stories have this capacity because threaded throughout any particular story are complex cultural "story lines" about relations between people—boys and girls, adults and children, rich people and poor, people of varied heritages, physical demeanor, and societal powers.[2] As one aspect or another of these relationships is foregrounded, the stories of any one individual reveal a self that is complex and contradictory.[3]

Thus, with her storytelling, Holly moves to join Tina in the world of tough girls who know their strength and say "HUH!" to societal beliefs about strength and gender. But she has to quickly deny her story when Tina invokes another belief, one that reflects child culture's long traditions of carefully guarding the borders between boys and girls.[4] Tina *airpunched* her victim; Holly did not—and her story left her vulnerable to the accusation of liking a boy.

Much of children's grappling with issues of social identity and cultural possibilities—with what a person of a certain sex, race, ethnicity, physical bearing, and appearance can do or be—happens beyond our direct control, in the social and cultural worlds of childhood.[5] In those worlds, children often seem to take as their guides Ninja Turtles, karate kids, and other figures of popular culture—often male superheroes and females needing saving.[6]

In this article, I draw on an ethnographic study in Holly and Tina's classroom to illustrate, first, the functional appeal of stories that permeate children's peer worlds, particularly popular superhero stories. Second, I aim to illustrate as well the cultural constraints and transformative possibilities of these stories. In Holly and Tina's classroom, the transformative power of stories was revealed in a classroom practice called "Author's Theater." Through this practice, the children themselves confronted the complex issues of identity and power embedded in superhero stories. Finally, I discuss the qualities of that practice that seemed critical to the transformation of cultural images. Thus, I hope to offer insights about popular culture and childhood that are useful for educators grappling with the beliefs, stories, and symbols of the children under their care.

THE APPEAL, THE PROBLEMS, AND THE POTENTIAL OF SUPERHEROES IN THE CLASSROOM

The desire to imagine oneself in a pleasurable world accounts, to at least some extent, for children's attraction to superheroes. Indeed, for both children and adults, the stories of popular culture may provide images and events that fuel imagination and interaction (e.g., the "trekkie" fan clubs, inspired by the television series *Star Trek*).[7] Young children seem especially drawn to popular media stories that tap into themes already deeply embedded in common kinds of child play, like boy/girl chasing games and the encounters between good guys and bad guys.[8]

The scripted roles and dramatic action of superhero stories provide familiar ground for the complex negotiations of childhood play. To enact a narrative world, children must share thematic material—they must agree, for example, that babies need mothers, the desired need suitors, and competitors need other competitors, most commonly, good guys need bad guys. Moreover, they must also negotiate their own rights to certain identities, to certain roles.[9]

Thus, the social enactment of stories involves complex negotiations of identity, which themselves raise issues of inclusion and exclusion. "We already have all the parts," the children in the story might say to an outsider wanting to play too. Through such rejections, children may protect their fragile story space from disruption.[10] But, as I will illustrate, they may also ward off others who do not fit their visions of who can and cannot play certain roles.

As adults, we worry that children are not imagining alternative roles for themselves, that they are appropriating stories with stereotypical relations between women and men, between people of different races, ethnicities, and social classes (e.g., see any issue of *Teaching Tolerance* magazine). And yet, the fluidity of children's individual and collective sense of self and others—their desire to both defy and conform to dominant images, evident in Tina's airpunches and Holly's "joking"—is a key to the transformation of limited and limiting visions. Those contradictions, though, need space for exploration and manipulation.

For example, children's desires to be powerful in some way, to feel strong, and the ways in which simplistic definitions of power and of gender relationships put them at odds with each other and, indeed, with themselves can be brought out in the open. The dialogic process of exploring contradictions and conflicts, of grappling with issues of inclusion and exclusion, allow the stories

of girls, boys, and powerful people to begin to be transformed.[11]

In Tina and Holly's classroom, the children explored their visions of themselves and others—not in the ways that adults might, by much explicit and critical talk about the meaning of social categories like "man" and "woman"—but by choosing playmates and then playing in front of each other. Tina, Holly, and their friends let each other witness their imaginations at work and then raised issues about who plays whom in whose story; they thus enacted and negotiated the organizational structures and routines their teacher offered, structures and routines named "Author's Theater."

AUTHOR'S THEATER: REVEALING PROBLEMS AND POSSIBILITIES

The Data Base

My own story is based on three months of observation at an East San Francisco Bay K–3 school located in the south central part of an urban area and serving a population diverse in race and social class. I observed primarily in Holly and Tina's second-grade classroom, a classroom guided by their skilled teacher, Kristen. (The Appendix provides demographic information on the twenty-eight second-grade children.)

When Kristen took over this classroom in March of the school year,[12] she initiated a daily writing time and, as an optional activity during that time, an Author's Theater. In this practice, related to one developed by Paley,[13] the children chose classmates to act out their "written" stories.[14] During writing time, there was much informal talk about who was doing an Author's Theater story— and about who would play what character in it. After each Author's Theater presentation, the children had an opportunity to comment on and ask questions of the author.

The children, as individuals and as a collective, wrote many kinds of stories with roots in experiences at home and at school. But one kind of story—the kind that led to the most explicit talk about issues of identity—had its roots in the popular media: the superhero story. Initially the children's popular media stories focused on Ninja Turtles but, in time, the turtles were overtaken by X-Men, superheroes with mutant powers found in comic books, videotapes and games, trading cards, and, most accessible of all, Saturday morning cartoons. The writing and acting of X-Men stories was a particularly rich source for the study of child representation and transformation of gender and power because X-Men are a collective (unlike single superheroes like Batman) and include males and females as both X-Men and arch rivals.

Although superhero stories were composed primarily by boys, both boys and girls knew about the X-Men characters and regularly watched the Saturday morning cartoon. However, knowledge of X-Men was class- and, therefore, race-related, at least in part because the middle-class parents generally did not encourage this form of entertainment. Thus, some interested children learned about X-Men from the talk, play, and story writing of their peers.[15]

I also learned about superheroes from the children's talk, play, and story writing. I visited Kristen's classroom for two to five hours each week, taking notes, audiotaping Author's Theater events, and collecting the children's written stories. As the project progressed, I talked with children about their attraction to these popular figures and also about whether their parents allowed them to watch the Saturday morning cartoon. I also talked extensively with Kristen, who confirmed and extended my own information through regular discussions with both parents and children. Finally, two research

assistants, Wanda Brooks and Elizabeth Scarboro, studied Ninja Turtle movies and X-Men videos, focusing especially on the roles of male and female characters.

From all this study, I constructed my own narrative about the appeal, the limits, and the transformative possibilities of superhero stories. My narrative has three central characters, each of whom played a key role in the classroom drama: Tina, Holly, and Sammy. Tina and Holly, like other girls, initially did not write about popular culture; they wrote about friends and family.[16] But they knew about Ninjas and X-Men, and, moreover, they wanted acting parts in the boys' stories. As I will illustrate, Tina and Holly were classroom change agents in part because they articulated their exclusion in sociopolitical, rather than personal, ways.

Sammy, who was also African-American, was new in the school and very much wanted friends. Fascinated by Ninjas and X-Men, he used Author's Theater to gain a foothold into what was initially the boys' domain; at the same time, he shared racial and cultural background, not to mention a neighborhood, with Holly and Tina. As I will also illustrate, his desire for the boys' approval and his vulnerability to pressure from the classroom social activists contributed to Sammy's role as a change agent.

The narrative itself unfolds in four sections (chapters, in a sense). In the first, the excluded girls seek access to the existent symbolic order—one where powerful boys save "foxy" girls. In the second, new symbolic possibilities for gender relations and for the portrayal of power are rendered null by social dynamics that maintain the cultural status quo. In the third, the symbolic order is complicated, as the excluded girls, especially Tina, take control of the story lines; they both pursue "male" power and engage the boys in "female" action. As the children declare and manipulate their sense of cultural possibilities, contradictory story lines interweave themselves in new fictions. Thus, rigid images of gender relations and of glorified power are challenged, rendered more fluid, more complex, as the fourth section illustrates.[17]

In short, this analytic narrative is about children's use of superhero stories to reveal and transform images of power and of gender in the local culture of a classroom, images that are themselves interwoven in complex ways with race, social class, physical appearance, and personality (including being relatively more sociable or reticent). The characters are energized by the desire to play and by complex issues of inclusion and exclusion; and the resulting plot line is dialogic, as competing visions conflict, coexist, and interweave.

The Ninjas and the "Lady": The Right to be Rescued

In the early spring of 1993, Ninjas were dominant cultural symbols in the second grade. In their most popular variant, they were four teen-age mutant turtles. The turtles, who were trained by a wise old Asian rat, used karate to fight bad guys and to help April, a young female reporter; this reporter was, in their words, a "babe," a real "fox."

Undergirding the Ninja stories, then, were narrow, clearly differentiated roles for males and females. Both boys and girls explicitly said, and implied by their play, that boys wrote Ninja stories because then they got to play karate. On the other hand, girls wanted to play April, because she "is cute," to quote Holly.

The Possibility of Being "Cute" No boy ever wrote April's name in a Ninja story; rather, they wrote the names of the turtles and then set up the action between the good guys (the turtles) and the bad guys (led by Shredder, an Asian human). Sammy's first Ninja Turtle story began in a typical way.

Ouse upon a time ther war Ninja turtle	[Once upon a time there were Ninja Turtles.
ther name war Michoagelo Leonardo	Their names were Michaelangelo, Leonardo,
raphal Donotelo and the war nice and they war friend and the mean was Shredder	Raphael, Donatello, and they were nice and they were friends and the mean (one) was Shredder.]

The possibility of a girl in a Ninja story, though, was common knowledge and a potential point of negotiation in the peer talk before an Author's Theater. Even if the author did not specifically mention April, a part for her could *potentially* be improvised by the author during the performance, and improvisations of plot were not uncommon.

Still, there was only *one* girl part. Moreover, when the boys discussed that girl, they emphasized her desirability, just as the turtles do in the original movie. Listen, for example, as Sammy talks to Seth, Jonathan, and Radha; the latter three boys have just agreed to play the Ninjas in his story.

> **SAMMY:** And you know who April is? Melissa.
>
> Radha smiles at this, eyes widening, being playfully dramatic. He turns and grins at Seth and Jonathan.

Sammy admired these boys, especially the competitive Seth, whose economically and socially privileged background was marked in his dress, in the objects he brought from home, in his stories of family trips, and in the polite but consistent ways in which he assumed positions of leadership. In the Ninja stories, Sammy, Seth, Jonathan, and Radha were all on the same male team, friends united in their toughness and in their admiration of a female.

Perhaps because the Ninja movies emphasize the physical features of the "babe" or "fox," the visual image of April herself—

slender, well-dressed, and white—seemed fixed. In contrast, the emphasis of all male superheroes (whether turtle, human, or mutant human) is on the enjoyment of aggressive, physical power; looking like the superhero was not necessary for the boys.

Thus, a girl like Tamara, a blue-eyed blond whose poverty was as marked as was Seth's privilege, could never be an April and, initially, neither could a girl of color. The role went to Melissa or Sarah, two friendly, attractive girls, both middle-class and white. Neither child was familiar with Ninja Turtles (or X-Men), because they were not allowed to watch shows with violence in them. And neither actively campaigned for the April role. These girls were *sought* for that role, and they pleasantly agreed when any boy asked.

Indeed, during composing time one day, Lawrence, who was biracial, commented to his peers that April *had* to be white—a statement that led to immediate and firm objections from Holly, Lettrice, and Aloyse (who told Kristen, who objected as well). At the very moment that he stated this rule, Lawrence was drawing Professor X—the bald, white leader of the X-Men superheroes—as a black man with a flat top. Moreover, Lawrence's regular school playmates were African-American and often included both girls and boys. Lawrence was making a specific statement about a specific story, and he seemed genuinely startled by the objections. (Lawrence, I should add, did hear these objections. He offered Monique, a dark-skinned African-American child, the role of April in his next Ninja production.)

The Possibility of Acting Well before Lawrence's statement, Holly, Tina, and other girls, black and white, had been complaining about not being allowed a part in the boys' Ninja stories or, in the case of Melissa and Sarah, of being allowed a part, but then having nothing to do. Moreover, Holly and Tina saw their exclusion, not as a matter of individual affront ("you never let me play"), but as a matter of collective exclusion ("you never let girls play").

Holly, Tina, and other girls wanting roles began to push hard whenever they noticed any boy offering roles in a superhero story. And they especially pushed Sammy, who wrote more Superhero stories than anyone else and who also very much wanted to be liked by everyone. Sammy was very vulnerable.

On the day Sammy chose Melissa for his Ninja Turtle story and secured Radha's approval, Holly and her classmate Johnetta asked over and over for a part to play. Sammy explained that there were no girl parts, other than April's. But the children continued to demand a role, and Johnetta even said she would be a boy. (Indeed, seven of the girls on varied occasions voiced their willingness to take boy parts, if need be.[18])

"OK, you can be a bad guy," said Sammy, but he immediately changed his mind. "You're Verna," he said. "She a lady. You're not no bad guy. You a lady. Verna. April friend. She [Holly] a lady too."

Although ostensibly successful in negotiating a role, the girls were *not* given a written part in Sammy's story; nor did Sammy, on his own, improvise a female role when he stood in front of the class. He concentrated on organizing for the display of physical power; he introduced the characters and set up the fight scene by having the bad guys invade the good guys' territory. All three girls—Holly, Johnetta, and Melissa—began complaining loudly that they had nothing to do. United in their discontent, they disrupted the play. In response, Sammy improvised:

SAMMY: (pretending to read) Verna and April was friends. They used to play with each other. [Johnetta and Melissa join hands and play ring-a-round-the-rosy, a common class metaphor for girl play.] They used to play with each other. And the lady [Holly]—I don't know who she is. She a lady—she a nice lady too. She April and Verna friend, and they play. [Holly joins the ring-a-round-the-rosy.] Until the Rat King is coming.

Sammy is now preparing to return to the boys and the fight scene, but Holly whispers frantically.

HOLLY: Say I got bit by a rat and the turtles have to help me.

Sammy obliges and, finally, the fight begins.

In brief, the Ninja stories typically excluded girls. There was some possibility of negotiation; however, to gain a role, a girl had to fit the specifications of a superhero script. And those specifications did not position males and females as equal members of the same team. Thus, Holly, a working-class girl of color, worked hard to gain the right to be rescued. When the X-Men arrived, however, the girls' ambitions changed notably, as I illustrate in the section to come.

On The Gender of X-Men: The Right to Be Tough

During the spring months, the X-Men craze grew in the classroom, just as it did in the entire Bay Area, from kindergarten through secondary school. A major Bay Area paper listed the X-Men as dominant "in" figures among youth—both boys *and* girls. Contributing to the appeal of the popular comic characters, first published in 1963, was the new X-Men cartoon show on Saturday mornings.

New Possibilities for Inclusion   The appeal of the X-Men to the second-grade girls seemed tied to the greater role of girls in superhero play. For example, second-grader Rhonda explained, "Most of the girls, they don't like [Ninja Turtles]. . . . It's meant for boys." When I asked why, Rhonda elaborated,

"Everybody want to be April, but—'cause—there's supposed to be *one* April." So, "kids really play cartoons like X-Men . . . [that have] Storm, Jean, and all that," that is, all those X-Men characters who, like Storm and Jean, are women.

Her peer Michael concurred, "You just hate Ninja Turtles because it's not that much girls on it. But you like X-Men because it's got X-Men girls on it." And first-grader Briana, whom I talked with regularly on the playground, explained further. The Ninjas only have "one girl that needs some help. . . . They have *girls* in that [X-Men] show. And they have some . . . black girls and some white girls. . . . The X-Men are friends and they help each other."

Indeed, all children familiar with the superhero stories agreed that both girls and boys are on the X-Men team. Moreover, they knew too that, in Sammy's words, the X-Men women are "as strong as men." Further, X-Men stories emphasize mental as well as physical strength; in fact, Professor X, the leader of the X-Men, is in a wheelchair. Thus, the girls had new grounds for demanding inclusion, as Holly made clear to Lawrence:

Lawrence is making a list of characters he plans to include in his X-Men story. He includes only one girl (the X-Men character Storm), which Holly finds quite irritating.

HOLLY: That's *all!* (with exasperation) You know some other girls in it. (with definitiveness)

A New Reason for Exclusion   Despite the new possibilities X-Men stories offered for gender relations, the *exclusion* of girls continued. And this exclusion had its roots in an X-Men theme that was, from an adult perspective, rather minor in the cartoon—that of romantic relationships. Certain X-Men males flirt with and, in some cases, have named relationships with X-Men females (e.g., Jean

Gray and Cyclops, two X-Men characters, are engaged). Thus, a boy including a "lady" was potentially making a public statement about romantic love.

In schoolchildren's social worlds, a boy and girl who *willingly* choose each other's company in public places (i.e., without adult coercion) are often victims of heterosexual teasing, particularly by boys.[19] Outside the context of Author's Theater and the public display of one's imagination, knowledgeable girls and boys, together and separately, talked about the powers of both male and female X-Men. But when the identities of powerful X-Men were assumed by boys and girls planning public performances, sexual border wars erupted, and the team disbanded.

This was dramatically illustrated by the fate of the X-Men characters Rogue and Gambit. The girls who watched X-Men preferred Rogue, a red-haired Southern woman, who is friendly, humorous, able to fly great distances and to absorb the power of others, and, moreover, is just plain "tough," as both girls and boys acknowledged. There was some sentiment for Storm, a black woman who can control the forces of the weather. But, as Tina explained, Storm "be getting knocked out too much." When Storm gets exhausted from controlling the weather—"knocked out"—Rogue regularly saves her.

For similar reasons, Sammy and many other boys liked Gambit, a Cajun who, like Rogue, is friendly, humorous, and powerful—able to convert matter's potential energy into explosive power. Nonetheless, both Rogue and Gambit, *powerful* characters, became pow*erless* in the X-Men play. In X-Men cartoons and comics, Rogue and Gambit sometimes flirt. They have no physical relationship—in fact, Rogue probably would kill anyone she kissed (as she did her first boyfriend). And yet, if a boy moved to put Rogue in his X-Men story, the romantic potential between Rogue and Gambit closed out the collaborative

meaning of a tough X-Men team—and the teasing that thus followed destroyed the team.

Sammy, in particular, seemed to exploit the romantic tension for peer group control. An enthusiastic X-Men fan, Sammy's first written X-Men story, like his Ninja stories, set up two teams (the good guys and the bad guys) and the possibility of a fight:

> Ouse upon a time
> ther was X-Man
> [and] the bad guys
> and they was try[ing] to destroy X-Man

As Sammy was writing this story, Tina and Holly began begging for the role of Rogue. Sammy said Tina could be Rogue—and then immediately proclaimed, "You [Tina] marry Radha, 'cause he Gambit." And, of course, both Tina and Radha immediately abandoned their roles to avoid the humiliation of being teased, and Holly lost all interest in her favorite character.

Sammy seemed to delight in the tensions he caused, but most boys simply left girls out. Indeed, boys sometimes assured potential players, as Nyem did Patrick, that "it ain't no girl gonna be in it." And, conversely, a boy being recruited might ask "Who don't got a girl friend in there?" as Thomas did when Sammy asked him to be in his story.

The X-Men play, then, raised the possibility of new images of gender and of power. But in child worlds, like adult worlds, meanings do not come in any direct way from stories themselves; meanings are constructed and reconstructed in the social world that takes up the story. And, in this classroom—as in many others in our society—boys' willing and public association with girls made both sexes vulnerable. Thus, a boy author, deeply attracted to the power of male superheroes, could use girls to gain power over both boys and girls. Or, he could avoid girls, and the usual good guy/bad guy play could proceed.

Refashioning X-Men: The Right to be Strong and Weak

Holly and Tina continued to be frustrated by the lack of access to superhero play. So the girls did what excluded but not defeated people often do—they wrote their own stories. Not surprisingly, these stories, composed by authors situated in the social world very differently, revealed a complex, contradiction-ridden response to the ongoing conversation about gender and power.

Tina was the first to declare her intention to write her own X-Men story. "And no boys," she said firmly to Holly, " 'cause the boys doesn't let us play."

Sitting side-by-side, Tina and Holly began to playfully plan their X-Men story. At first Tina said she would be Rogue. But then she became "the toughest guy in the world. . . . We're all Blobs!" (Blobs are huge, fleshy mutant humans, virtually indestructible and very bad guys.) " 'Cause if somebody threw a metal ball at me, the energy go right through me and I would never know. And we're sisters robbing the world. . . . And we'll never get sick. And we'll never die."

The sisters evolved, Tina becoming Uncle Blob, Holly niece Blob. The biological sex of Tina vacillated, as if she were struggling with the possibility of being tough and female. As the girls became more and more animated, they moved to the classroom rug, deep in play:

> TINA: I'm about to go get Rogue! And I'm tying her up and cutting her [red] hair off.
> HOLLY: 'Cause there's fire in there!

Uncle Blob (Tina) "drinks" Rogue's hair, absorbing her fire power—but leaving none for his poor niece Holly Blob, who seems to find herself once again in a weak role. Holly begs for the right to be like her Uncle, to be powerful:

> HOLLY: Why you drunk it all, Uncle? Why can't I be like you, uncle? I want to be like you, uncle.
> TINA: You're like your mother, not like me. (shooting fire)
> HOLLY: Can I be like you?

Uncle Blob (Tina) gives her a small bit of fire power in a (pretend) cup, just a bit, though.

> TINA: The only thing you can do is just shoot out fire at them [the X-men] and then just call me. (There are shades here of the Ninja Turtle stories and of April, who has to call for help.)

Tina was seemingly in revolt, trying on a role very different from that of a weak, desirable girl with a heart of gold. She was using her strength, this tiny child whose journal was entitled "The Peace Book" and who wrote, as did Holly, about family and friends and relationships. Although Holly was in the weaker role, she was entertaining the possibility of an alternative vision.

Class composing time ended before the children had put pencil to paper, but they intended to write their X-Men story the next day. Such a story, however, one where second-grade girls become unapologetic bad guys, would not survive in the public sphere of the classroom. It would be constrained by the social pressure of girls and boys seeking inclusion as powerful good guys and, then, by the sexual border work that threatened a team of women and men. Still, as Uncle Blob and her niece reentered the culture of the classroom, they did not go quietly into the realm of the more conventional superhero story.

Holly's Tired X-Men   The next day Tina was absent (Tina missed a great deal of school), so Holly tried to write the story herself. But as soon as the word was out that Holly was writing an X-Men story, the pressure began to add characters—good guys. And Holly, like Sammy, did not want to disappoint people, as she later explained to Kristen:

> **HOLLY:** I thinked about it, and um I said, I said there should be some other people then this. Then I— when I start asking people, Aloyse, he be all, and James kind of following me and saying, "OH! Can I be, Can I be Cyclops?" and all that stuff.

As Holly agreed to allow one character after another into her story, she abandoned the idea of the Blob family and decided to become the once again powerful Rogue (who, just the day before, had been rendered vulnerable by the Blobs). Unfortunately, Holly's friend Liliana also wanted to be Rogue, and a loud argument began. Rahda, Ricky, and Kevin, working nearby, looked over at the feuding friends:

> **RADHA:** What are you fighting over?
>
> **RICKY:** Do you both wanta be Rogue?

Without waiting for an answer, the three boys begin to chant in unison.

> **BOYS:** Rogue and Gambit, sitting in a tree. [Holly: Shut up!] K-I-S-S-I-N-G.

The rhyme goes on, graphically depicting female anatomy—despite the fact that physical contact between Rogue and Gambit is portrayed as impossible in the X-Men stories.

Both girls were immediately silenced, and both temporarily abandoned their ambitions to be Rogue. Holly adopted what she perceived as the weaker role of Storm. (Later Liliana reclaimed Rogue, and Radha confided to Holly that he had wanted to be Gambit, but since he could not get rid of Rogue, he would be the loveless X-Men character, Archangel.)

Despite the strong social pressures, Holly's final text portrayed a distinctly different X-Men team. Not only were her char-

acters predominantly female, they were also people with feelings about each other, just as was typically the case in girls' written worlds. Further, Holly's X-Men were ambivalent about their physical powers, as are the media's X-Men, who sometimes long to be "normal" and bemoan the destructiveness of physical violence. Holly, pressured into the role of Storm, depicted exhausted X-Men, complaining about their responsibilities:

> Once upon a time there was
> a grop of people it was the X-Men.
> Storm said I am tirde [tired] of
> changing the weather
> but you have to keep working
> Arckangel said. I'm tired
> of working too, rogue said.
> I have to save storm evre time
> she fall. I get tired of
> fighting bad guys. Ready to fight?
> and they all had fun. the end.

The last two sentences had been hastily added when Kristen said composing time was over—and one can wonder how much fun they all were having.

In this publicly enacted story, Holly was not a nameless nice lady in a superhero story, nor was she a little girl who alternately liked and fought with her girl friends (the dominant plot of her previous tales). Holly entered into the power politics of classroom superhero stories, armed with a pencil, and emerged a tired superhero, saved by another tired superhero. The dominant good guy/bad guy plot was intertextually linked with her history as a writer of relationships and with her present position as a pressured girl. Thus, that plot lost some of its "authority," as Bakhtin might say;[20] Holly brought to the public stage—and thereby involved the class as actors and audience members in—an alternative story. In that story, girls and boys could be on the same team; moreover, physical power was not necessarily such fun. Sometimes the good guys just wanted to leave the bad guys alone.

Tina's Grieving X-Men   The next day, when Tina returned, she also found herself embroiled in classroom power plays. At first, Tina was determined to continue to be Blob, even when pressure came from her former niece, Holly.

Tina is sitting during composing time with Holly, Liliana, Sarah, and James.

HOLLY: Can I be Rogue?

TINA: You're all bad guys. I got all the part of you all.

HOLLY: We're not bad guys.

TINA: But so! You can't beat me! Hey-hey-hey-hey! You can try to beat me all you want.

LILIANA: Are you Jean Gray [another X-Men character]?

TINA: No I'm Blob. You can't kill me.

LILIANA: A BOY.

TINA: So! I wanta be a boy.

Still, the pressure continued. Holly was determined to be Rogue, and Monique wanted Storm. Sarah said she would be any good-guy girl, and then James asked to be Wolverine. So Tina relented, with evident exasperation, "You don't want to be a bad guy? OK. Fine. You're not a bad guy."

These classroom negotiations resulted in a story without Blob. Indeed, during Author's Theater, Tina took no role; she read the following story herself:

ods tare wry 4 x-man	Once there were 4 X-Men
in the x-man fote othr	And the X-Men fought others.
own x-man died	One X-Men died.
and the rast uavy they wrey	And the rest of them were
sad they criyd	sad. They cried
Storm flow away	Storm flew away.
rogue stry to criy	Rogue started to cry.
Jeen Gray cam	Jean Gray came.
Black Momy cam to	Black Mommy [a bad guy] came too.
They all fote	They all fought
and the x-man won	And the X-Men won.
rogue found storm	Rogue found Storm.
She was making weather	She was making weather.
and they all lived	And they all lived
happy eave after the end.	happy ever after the end.

During the enactment of her play, Tina was particularly attentive to James's participation:

TINA: (reading) "One of the X-Men *died.*"

No one dies. So Tina repeats the sentence louder.

TINA: "ONE OF THE X-MEN DIED." Die! Die!

Finally a girl dies.

TINA: "And the rest were very sad. They cried." (Holly cries). Everybody cry now, even the *boys.*

Actually, neither James or Monique was pretending to cry. Moreover, in the real second-grade world, boys were as likely to cry as girls. But crying boys are not common in superhero stories. So Tina marked James's failure to participate as the failure of the cultural category of *boys.*

After the play was over, James complained that he had nothing to do in Tina's play.

JAMES: You didn't give me no part.

TINA: Your part was to cry and to fight.

JAMES: Uh uh.

TINA: I said *everybody,* including *you,* should cry. *Everybody,* including *you,* should fight.

Thus, in Holly's and Tina's visions, superhero teams were dominated by women of color who, nonetheless, served with women and men of different races. Moreover, power itself was tempered with human fragility: People fought, became tired, grieved, and died. These two activist girls—experienced writers of relationships—were changing the possibilities for superhero stories in the local culture of the classroom. While conventional male-exclusive superhero stories continued, they were "dialogized," to use Bakhtin's word; [21] that is, they were rendered a possibility among other possibilities. In fact, it was Sammy who put together the first well-integrated X-Men team.

The X-People: The Right to Play

During the last composing period of the school year, Sammy asked in an open way who wanted to be in his X-Men story. Moreover, Liliana and Aloyse ignored the teasing that began when their roles as Jean Gray and Cyclops (engaged characters) were known.

Thus, the children took the roles they wanted and stayed with them. The teasing stopped, the story was read, the drama enacted—an unusual X-Men drama. In Sammy's production, the X-Men were indeed gender-balanced: There were four girls and five boys. Moreover, of the two bad guys, one was a girl and one a boy. (And, while the children on the stage were predominantly African-American, the girls and boys were racially integrated too.)

After the play was over, Kristen asked if there were any comments. A number of children noted that acting out the story had been fun, and others noted that it had been fun to watch. And, indeed, it was an unusually pleasant superhero play—no teasing, no girls or boys stomping off the stage, no one complaining that somebody did not get to play or had nothing to do.

Then Sammy himself, with no prompting from anyone, said, "And there were really

more X-Men. The *X-people* were boys and girls, and the um bad guys were boys and girls"—a spontaneous semantic transformation to mark the cultural one. Thus Sammy seemed to know that, at its roots, the disruption of classroom superhero stories was about inclusion, exclusion, and the right to play.

ON READING AND WRITING THE FUTURE

I have told a story of children creating and recreating the meaning of superhero stories in the company of each other, opening up their own interpretations—their own pleasures—to the responses of others. Issues of cultural images literally played themselves out, yielding alternative visions of power and of gender. The relationships enacted were more diverse than the ones that stopped Tina and Holly's playful talk in the opening anecdote—images of romantic liking, passionate hating, and the strong male threatening or saving the lady "needing some help." In at least some of their stories, the children were more like supportive brothers and sisters confronting common dangers, sharing common emotions, than romantic lovers or unidimensional superheroes. [22]

Although individual children have been featured, their stories were shaping—and being reshaped within—the larger classroom drama produced by their teacher, Kristen. Her means, the composing and acting of stories, would not necessarily yield similar dynamics in all classrooms; but certain qualities of Author's Theater seem critical to promoting the dialogic process of confronting and interweaving conflicting story lines. [23]

First, the practice was consistent with children's ways of reflecting and it focused on children's issues, particularly, the right to play. Critical discussions of how stories represent women, men, and power may, in and of themselves, have limited impact on children's imaginations.[24] Children seem to examine gripping media stories from "inside the experience," by playing and replaying them, rather than by "holding them up as objects of scrutiny."[25]

The practice of Author's Theater allowed children to do just that, to be actively involved in each other's visions of pleasure and power. In some situations, it seems wise to tell young children "You can't say you can't play," as the master teacher Vivian Paley does in her moving book on "the habit of rejection."[26] And, in fact, sometimes Kristen did control the children's play and work partners, directing them, for example, to choose somebody they "don't know very well," somebody they "didn't usually play with," or even somebody "of a different race." But, in the context of Author's Theater, Kristen said, in effect, "You can say you can't play. But when you say that in this public place, you must face the consequences of your decisions. And I will help."

Second, the social practice of Author's Theater provided a routine where children could voice their comments and questions as individuals and as members of groups. And consciousness of groups (e.g., "You never let girls play") is required, for any one child's imagination is realized or constrained by the "sociological imagination" of the class as a whole, by the ways the community imagines the intersection of individual biographies with societal possibilities.[27] Importantly, in Kristen's room, the children most sensitive to issues of social inclusion and exclusion—and thus best posed to take action for social change—were *not* the most advanced child writers (i.e., they did not write the longest, most developed stories). Indeed, the principal considered retaining Tina because of her absences and her perceived skill limits. Potential for critical reflection and social action has not been a valued "skill" in our schools.

Third, the practice was under careful monitoring by the teacher. Kristen brought some of the children's play into the public sphere of formally composed, enacted, and discussed stories, and then she carefully monitored the interaction. She did not ignore the gender and power issues of the children's superhero stories. She did not ban these stories, but she also did not have the children simply publish and edit them.[28] She tapped and exploited the social dynamics of childhood to help the children examine them. To this end, she made sure the children listened to each other's opinions and feelings and, when need be, she spoke clearly and firmly for fairness, as in her response to Lawrence's assertion about the role of April.

However, an enriching of classroom cultural images came about, not only because of formal presentations and discussions, but also because of informal peer negotiations. And those negotiations were motivated by the desire to play. *Thus, a fourth critical feature of the Author's Theater practice was simply that it was fun.* Given the choice of watching other children play or actively participating in that play, many children bargained for a part in others' stories.

Superhero stories were particularly appealing, offering pleasurable roles informed by the larger society's messages. Open for public witnessing and, supposedly, for public participation, superhero stories engendered issues of the limited roles of girls, the heterosexual teasing that disrupted play, the desires of both boys and girls to get on with the business of being a superhero—and the conflicting images of what a superhero's life was like.

Thus, Holly, Tina, and their friends became intensely involved in exploring their relationships with each other, just as all children do, in one way or the other. They read each others' faces, clothes, and ways of talking; they write each other's futures in the stories they imagine. This sort of reading and writing happens at the same time, and through the same activities, that teach children to spell, to write on the line, to compose.[29] As educators, we must, I believe, help children discover the ways in which their reading and writing of each other limits their collective possibilities and prevents the play from going on.

NOTES

1. Mikhail M. Bakhtin, *The Dialogic Imagination: Four Essays by M. Bakhtin*, ed. Michael Holquist (Austin: University of Texas Press, 1981), pp. 259–422.

2. Pam Gilbert, "And They Lived Happily Ever After: Cultural Storylines and the Construction of Gender," in *The Need for Story: Cultural Diversity in Classroom and Community*, ed. Anne Haas Dyson and Celia Genishi (Urbana, Ill.: National Council of Teachers of English, 1994), p. 124.

3. Patricia J. Williams, *The Alchemy of Race and Rights* (Cambridge: Harvard University Press, 1991), p. 130.

4. The concept of "border" is based on the research of Fredrik Barth, ed., *Ethnic Groups and Boundaries: The Social Organization of Cultural Differences* (Boston: Little, Brown, 1969), pp. 9–38; he studied how interaction across ethnic group boundaries may strengthen, rather than weaken, those boundaries. Barth's work influenced Barrie Thorne, *Gender Play: Girls and Boys in School* (New Brunswick: Rutgers University Press, 1991), pp. 64–88; she developed the term "sexual borderwork": Boys and girls can strengthen, rather than reduce, their sense of difference through particular kinds of interactions (e.g., boy/girl chase games, teasing when gender expectations are violated). The same phenomenon is described as "category-maintenance work" by Bronwyn Davies, *Frogs and Snails and Feminist Tales: Preschool Children and Gender* (Boston: Allen and Unwin, 1989), pp. 28–29.

5. As numerous scholars have documented, groups of children construct social organizations and cultural meanings that are conceptually autonomous (i. e., that have their own integrity) even as they are dialectically embedded within adult worlds; see, for example, studies by William Corsaro, *Friendship and Peer Culture in the Early Years* (Norwood: Ablex, 1985), Anne Haas Dyson, *Social Worlds of Children Learning to Write in an Urban Primary School* (New York: Teachers College Press, 1993); and Thorne, *Gender Play*.

6. For a critical discussion of popular culture, see Henry A. Giroux and Roger I. Simon, "Popular Culture as a Pedagogy of Pleasure and Meaning," in *Popular Culture, Schooling, and Everyday life*, ed. Henry A. Giroux and Roger I. Simon (South Hadley, Mass.: Begin & Garvey, 1989), pp. 1–29.

7. Henry Jenkins, *Textual Poachers: Television Fans and Participatory Culture* (New York: Routledge, 1992), pp. 1–8.

8. For an illuminating study of Australian school children's use of television in their social interaction and play, see Patricia Palmer, *The Lively Audience: A Study of Children around the TV Set* (Sydney: Allen and Unwin, 1986).

9. Catherine Garvey, *Play*, enl. ed. (Cambridge: Harvard University Press, 1990), pp. 79–100.

10. Corsaro, *Friendship and Peer Culture*, pp. 122–49.

11. Maxine Greene provides a rich discussion of the connections between classroom dialogue and critical examination of societal relations in her *The Dialectic of Freedom* (New. York: Teachers College Press, 1988).

12. The children's original second-grade teacher left the school because of her pregnancy. When Kristen arrived, the class was experiencing racial tensions; for example, a number of white children and black children accused each other of liking only children of their own race. Kristen hoped opportunities to express themselves through writing, acting, and talking would help the children, not only become writers, but also come to know each other better. She noted also that interest in Ninja Turtles and X-Men cut across racial lines, and so she did not discourage popular culture stories. I stress, however, that many kinds of written texts were read, discussed, and written during the course of the school day.

13. Vivian G. Paley, *Wally's Stories* (Cambridge: Harvard University Press, 1980), pp. 162–67.

14. Although this practice was part of the daily composing period, certain children sometimes only pretended to have actually written a story. They would stand up to "read," having nothing at all on their papers. In addition, sometimes a child author would designate a reader (a designation requiring an actual text) and then assume a desired role in her or his own story.

15. Groups of children did play X-Men on the playground during morning and noon recess. Although I only observed mixed-race groups of boys engaged in such play (a variant of good guys/bad guys chase games), both girls and boys reported that sometimes the boys "let" the girls play the roles of female X-Men.

16. During the project, approximately 48 percent of all written products by girls centered on relationships with family and friends (30 of 63); 76 percent of all products included specific named emotions. Only 14 percent of the boys' products (9 of 65) were so centered and less than 1 percent included specific named emotions. In contrast, 46 percent of the boys' texts drew on media superheroes stories, but only 8 percent of the girls' did.

17. The complex nature of the girls' grappling with gender relations and power—their seeking of access to the existent order, their attempts to reverse that order, and, finally, to make more fluid the relationship between gender and identity—connects with

the multifaceted nature of the feminist movement in adult society. See especially Julia Kristeva, who called for new aesthetic practices to "bring out—along with the *singularity* of each person and, even more, along with the multiplicity of each person's possible identifications . . . the *relativity of his/her symbolic as well as biological existence*" (*The Kristeva Reader*, ed. Toril Moi [New York: Columbia University Press, 1986], p. 210; emphasis in the original).

18. Palmer reported that, in male superhero play, all "good guys" were boys; "baddies" were imagined or played by younger sisters and girls (*The Lively Audience*, p. 106).

19. See Thorne, *Gender Play*, pp. 54–55.

20. Bakhtin, *The Dialogic Imagination*, p. 424.

21. Ibid., p. 426.

22. For a discussion of the sibling metaphor, see Thorne, *Gender Play*, p. 172.

23. For practical suggestions for engaging young children in critical reflection on text, see Barbara Comber and Jennifer O'Brien, "Critical Literacy: Classroom Explorations," *Critical Pedagogy Networker* 6 (June 1993): 1–11.

24. See, for example, Davies, *Frogs and Snails and Feminist Tales*, pp. 43–69.

25. Palmer, *The Lively Audience*, p. 113.

26. Vivian G. Paley, *You Can't Say You Can't Play: The Habit of Rejection* (Cambridge: Harvard University Press, 1992), pp. 3–36.

27. C. Wright Mills, *The Sociological Imagination* (New York: Oxford University Press, 1959), pp. 5–8.

28. For critical perspectives on gender and currently popular writing pedagogies, see Gilbert, "And They Lived Happily Ever After"; and Barbara Kamler, "Constructing Gender in the Process Writing Classroom," *Language Arts* 70 (February 1993): 95–103.

29. For a rich discussion of the links between cultural identity, societal ideologies, and literacy learning, see Allan Luke, Joan Kale, and Michael G. Singh, with Tracey Hill and Favardin Daliri, "Talking Difference: Discourses on Aboriginal Identity in Grade One Classrooms," in *Power and Discourse in Education*, ed. D. Corson and A. Hargreaves (Clevedon: Multilingual Matters, in press).

Appendix
Sex and Ethnicity of Second-Grade Children

SEX	ETHNICITY
Female	
Holly	African American/European American
Johnetta	African American
LaShanda	African American/Native American
Lettrice	African American
Liliana*	European American
Lynn*	European American
Margaret*	European American
Makeda	African American
Melissa*	European American
Monique	African American
Rhonda	African American
Susan*	European American
Sarah*	European American
Tamara	European American
Tina	African American
Male	
Aloyse	Ethiopian American (immigrant)
James	Korean American
Jonathan*	European American
Kevin	European American
Lawrence	African American/European American
Michael	African American
Nyem	African American
Patrick	European American
Radha	Indian (Asian) American
Ricky	African American
Sammy	African American
Seth*	European American
Thomas	African American

*Children from homes in which at least one parent had a middle-class, white-collar job.

REFERENCES–GROWING UP: AT HOME, AT SCHOOL

ADEQUATE DESIGN. (1997–98). South Park *episode guide*. Available: www.adequate. com/ south_park.

ARONSON, F., et al. (1978). *The jigsaw classroom*. Beverly Hills, CA: Sage.

BAKHTIN, M. (1984). *Rabelais and his world*. Trans. H. Iswolsky. Bloomington: Indiana University Press.

BARTH, F., ed (1969). *Ethnic groups and boundaries*. Boston: Little, Brown.

BEDERMAN, G. (1995). *Manliness and civilization: A cultural history of gender and race in the United States, 1880–1917*. Chicago: University of Chicago Press.

BENEKE, T. (1997). *Proving manhood: Reflections on men and sexism*. Berkeley: University of California Press.

BERSANI, L. (1995). Loving men. In Berger, M., B., Wallis, and S. Watson, eds., *Constructing masculinity*. New York: Routledge.

BERSANI, L. (1998). Is the rectum a grave? In Crimp, D., ed., *AIDS: Cultural analysis/cultural activism*. Cambridge, MA: MIT Press.

BIGNESS, J., and M. HIRSLEY. (1999). Unparalleled value. *Chicago Tribune*. January 13, 3: 1.

BLOCK, J. H., 1978. Another look at sex differentiation in the socialization behaviors of mothers and fathers. In J. Sherman and F. L. Denmark, eds., *The psychology of women: Future directions of research*. New York: Psychological Dimensions.

BLUE MAN GROUP. (1998). *Stagebill*. (October 9–19).

BOARD OF STUDIES NSW (1998). Statistics—school certificate 1998, updated at 22.12.1998 *http://www.boardofstudies.nsw.edu.au/docs_stats/sc98_y10.html*.

BOARD OF STUDIES NSW (1999). 1998 higher school certificate examination statistics. Sydney: NSW Board of Studies.

BORMAN, K.M. (1979). Children's interactions in playgrounds. *Theory into Practice 18:* 251–257.

BOWEN, J. (1998). Blue Man group. Centerstage (Chicago). Available: centerstage.net/chicago.

BRAINSTORMS. (1998). Fall catalog. Reading, PA.

BREAKMAN, J. (1993). *Straight male modern: A cultural critique of psychoanalysis*. New York: Routledge.

BROD, H. (1995). The politics of the mythopoetic men's movement. In M. S. Kimmel, ed., *The politics of manhood: Profeminist men respond to the mythopoetic men's movement (and the mythopoetic leaders answer)*. Philadelphia: Temple University Press, pp. 89–96.

BUCK, R. 1975. Non-verbal communication of affect in children. *Journal of Personality and Social Psychology* 31: 644–653.

CARLI, L. L. 1995. No: biology does not create gender differences in personality. In M. R. Walsh, ed., *Women, men, and gender*. New Haven: Yale University Press.

CHARLESWORTH, W. R., and P. LAFRENIERE. 1983. Dominance, friendship utilization, and resource utilization in preschool children's groups. *Ethology and Sociobiology* 4: 175–186.

CHENG, C. (1996). "We choose not to compete": The merit discourse in the selection process, and Asian and Asian American men and their masculinity. In C. Cheng, ed., *Masculinities in organizations*. Thousand Oaks: Sage Publications.

CHODOROW, N. 1978. *The reproduction of mothering: Psychoanalysis and the sociology of gender*. Berkeley: University of California Press.

COLLINSON, D. (1995). "Engineering humor": Masculinity, joking and conflict in shop-floor relations. In Kimmel, M. S., and M. A. Messner, eds., *Men's lives*. 3rd ed. Boston: Allyn & Bacon.

CONNELL, R. W. (1995). Men at bay: The "men's movement" and its newest best-sellers. In M. Kimmel, ed., *The politics of manhood*. Philadelphia: Temple University Press, pp. 75–88.

CRAIG, S., ed. (1992). *Men, masculinity, and the media*. Thousand Oaks, CA: Sage Publications.

DIEN, D. (1992). Gender and individuation: China and the West. *Psychoanalytic Review* 79 (1): 105–119.

DRAPER, J. (1993). We're back with Gobbo: The re-establishment of gender relations following a school merger. In P. Woods, and M. Hammersley, eds., *Gender and ethnicity in schools: Ethnographic accounts.* London: Routledge/Open University.

DUNN, J., I. BRETHERTON, and P. MUNN. (1987). Conversations about feeling states between mothers and their young children. *Developmental Psychology* 23: 132–39.

DUNN, J., J. BROWN, and L. BEARDSALL. (1991). Family talk about feeling states and children's later understanding of others' emotions. *Developmental Psychology* 27: 448–455.

DUNN, J., J. BROWN, C. SLOMKOWSKI, C. TESLA, and L. YOUNGBLADE. (1991). Young children's understanding of other people's feelings and beliefs: Individual differences and their antecedents. *Child Development* 62: 1352–1366.

EDER, D., and M.T. HALLINAN. (1978). Sex differences in children's friendships. *American Sociological Review* 43: 237–250.

EDER, D., with C. EVANS, and S. PARKER. (1995). *School talk: Gender and adolescent culture.* New Brunswick: Rutgers University Press.

ERIKSON, E.H. (1950). *Childhood and society.* New York: Norton.

EVERHART, R.B. (1983). *Reading, writing and resistance: Adolescence and labor in a junior high school.* Boston: Routledge and Kegan Paul.

FERGUSON, A. (1994). "Boys will be boys: Defiant acts and the social construction of black masculinity." Draft Ph.D. dissertation, University of California, Berkeley.

FINNAN, C.R. (1982). The ethnography of children's spontaneous play. In G. Spindler, ed., *Doing the ethnography of schooling,* pp. 358–380. New York: Holt, Rinehart and Winston.

FIVUSH, R. (1993). Emotional content of parent-child conversations about the past. In C.A. Nelson, ed., *Memory and Affect in Development.* Minnesota Symposium on Child Psychology, vol. 26, pp. 39–78. Minneapolis: University of Minnesota.

FOLEY, D.E. (1990). *Learning capitalist culture: Deep in the heart of Texas.* Philadelphia: University of Pennsylvania Press.

FOOT, H.C., A.J. CHAPMAN, and J.R. SMITH. (1980). Introduction. *Friendship and social relations in children,* pp. 1–14. New York: Wiley.

FRANK, B. (1993). Straight/strait jackets for masculinities: Educating for "real men." *Atlantis* 18: 47–59.

FREUD, S. (1908). Character and anal eroticism. In *The standard edition of the complete psychological works,* trans. J. Strachey. London: Hogarth, 1953–74. Vol. 9, pp. 167–76.

FREUD, S. (1917). Of transformations of instinct as exemplified in anal eroticism. *Standard Edition* Vol. 17, pp. 125–134.

FREUD, S. (1918). From the history of an infantile neurosis. *Standard Edition* Vol. 17, pp. 3–122.

FREUD, S. (1933). New introductory lectures on psycho-analysis. Lecture XXIII: Femininity. *Standard Edition* Vol. 22, pp. 112–35.

GABLE, S., J. BELSKY, and K. CRNIC. (1993). Coparenting in the child's second year. Stability and change from 15 to 21 months. Paper presented at the biennial meeting of the Society for Research in Child Development, New Orleans, March.

GARDINER, J. (1992). Psychoanalysis and feminism: An American humanist's view. *Signs* 17(2): 437–454.

GARDINER, J. (1992). Feminism and the future of fathering. In T. Digby, ed., *Men doing feminism.* New York: Routledge.

GARVEY, T. (1994). Streaming as a masculinizing practice in the 1950s and 1960s. Paper presented to the Annual Conference on the Australian and New Zealand History of Education Society, Perth.

GILLIGAN, C. (1982). *In a different voice: Psychological theory and women's development.* Cambridge, MA: Harvard University Press.

GLASER, B. G., and A. L. STRAUSS. (1967). *The discovery of grounded theory.* Chicago: Aldine.

GLOBALPRINTS.COM. (1998). Advertisement for posters at the University of Illinois at Chicago bookstore.

GOFFMAN, E. (1977). The arrangement between the sexes. *Theory and Society* 4: 301–336.

GOLEMAN, D. (1995). *Emotional intelligence: Why it can matter more than I. Q.* London: Bloomsbury.

GOODWIN, M. H. (1980). Directive-response sequences in girls' and boys' task activities. In S. McConnell-Ginet, R. Borker, and N. Furman, eds., *Women and language in literature and society*, pp. 157–173. New York: Praeger.

GRANT, C. A., and C. E. SLEETER. (1986). *After the school bell rings.* Philadelphia: Falmer.

GRIEF, E. B. (1980). Sex differences in parent-child conversations. *Women's Studies International Quarterly 3:* 253–358.

GRUNEAU, R., and D. WHITSON. (1993). *Hockey night in Canada: Sport, identity and cultural politics.* Toronto: Garamond Press.

GUBAR, S. (1997). *Racechanges: White skin, black face in American culture.* New York: Oxford University Press.

GULLETTE, M. (1997). *Declining to decline: Cultural combat and the politics of the midlife.* Charlottesville: University Press of Virginia.

GUNNAR, M. R., and M. DONAHUE. (1980). Sex differences in responsiveness between six months and twelve months. *Child Development* 44: 678–681.

HANSOT, E., and D. TYACK. (1988). Gender in public schools: Thinking institutionally. *Signs* 13: 741–760.

HARRIS, J. (1995). Where is the child's environment? A group socialization theory of development. *Psychological Review* 102: 458–489.

HAVILAND, J. J., and C. Z. MALATESTA. (1981). The development of sex differences in nonverbal signals: Fallacies, facts, and fantasies. In C. Mayo and N. M. Henley, eds., *Gender and non-verbal behavior.* New York: Springer-Verlag.

HENLEY, N. (1977). *Body politics: Power, sex, and non-verbal communication.* Englewood Cliffs, NJ: Prentice-Hall.

HETHERINGTON, E. M. (1967). The effects of family variables on sex-typing, on parent-child similarity, and on imitation in children. In J. P. Hill, ed., *Minnesota symposium on child psychology*, Vol. 1. Minneapolis: University of Minnesota Press.

HEWARD, C. (1988). *Making a man of him: Parents and their sons' education at an English public school 1929–1950.* London: Routledge.

HOCHSCHILD, A. (1983). *The managed heart: Commercialization of human feeling.* Berkeley: University of California Press.

HOLLAND, D. C., and M. A. EISENHART. (1990). *Educated in romance: Women, achievement, and college culture.* Chicago: University of Chicago Press.

hooks, b. (1996). *Reel to real: Race, sex and class at the movies.* New York: Routledge.

JEN, G. (1996). *Mona in the promised land.* New York: Random House.

JORDAN, E. (1995). "Fighting boys and fantasy play" : The construction of masculinity in the early years of school. *Gender and Education* 7: 69–86.

KARBAU, K. (1973). *Sexism in the fourth grade.* Pittsburgh: KNOW, Inc (pamphlet).

KATZ, J. (1983). A theory of qualitative methodology: The social system of analytic fieldwork. In R. M. Emerson, ed., *Contemporary field research*, pp. 127–148. Boston: Little, Brown.

KESSLER, S. J., and W. MCKENNA. (1978). *Gender: An ethnomethodological approach.* New York: John Wiley.

KIMMEL, M. (1996). *Manhood in America: A cultural history.* New York: Free Press.

KING, R. (1978). *All things bright and beautiful? A sociological study of infants' classrooms.* Chichester: Wiley.

KNAPP, M., and H. KNAPP. (1976). *One potato, two potato: The secret education of American children.* New York: W. W. Norton.

KOCHANSKA, G., N. AKSAN, and A. L. KOENIG. (1995). A longitudinal study of the roots of preschoolers' conscience: Committed compliance and emerging internalization. *Child Development* 66 (6): 1752–1769.

KOCHANSKA, G. (1997). Mutually responsive orientation between mothers and their young children: Implications for early socialization. *Child Development* 68: 94–112.

KOREA, Y. (1997). Blue Man Group. *Theatre Review* (Boston) 117 (53): 6.

KUEBIL, J. and E. KRIEGER. (1991). Emotion and gender in parent-child conversations about the past. Paper presented at the biennial meeting of the Society for Research in Child Development, Seattle.

LANGLOIS, J.H., and A.C. DOWNS. (1980). Mothers, fathers, and peers as socialization agents of sex-typed play behaviors in young children. *Child Development* 51: 1217–1247.

LASKEY, L., and C. BEAVIS, eds., (1996). *Schooling and sexualities: Teaching for a positive sexuality.* Geelong: Deakin Centre for Education and Change.

LEAPER, C., L. LEVE, T. STRASSER, and R. SCHWARTZ. (1995). Mother-child communication sequences: Play activity, child gender, and marital status effects. *Merrill Palmer Quarterly* 41(3): 307–327.

LEES, S. (1986). *Losing out: Sexuality and adolescent girls.* London: Hutchinson.

LEVER, J. (1976). Sex differences in the games children play. *Social Problems* 23: 478–487.

LEVINE, R., S. Dixon, A. RICHMAN, P.H. LEIDERMAN, C.H. KEEFER, and T.B. BRAZELTON. (1994). *Child care and culture: Lessons from Africa.* New York: Cambridge University Press.

LINGARD, B., and P. DOUGLAS. (1999). *Men engaging feminisms: Pro-feminism, backlashes, and schooling.* Buckingham: Open University Press.

MAC AN GHAILL, M. (1994). *The making of men: Masculinities, sexualities, and schooling.* Buckingham: Open University Press.

MACCOBY, E. (1980). *Social development: Psychological growth and the parent-child relationship.* New York: Harcourt, Brace, Jovanovich.

MACCOBY, E. (1982). *Social groupings in childhood: Their relationship to prosocial and antisocial behavior in boys and girls.* Paper presented at conference on The Development of Prosocial and Antisocial Behavior. Voss, Norway.

MACCOBY, E., and C. JACKLIN. (1974). *The psychology of sex differences.* Stanford, CA: Stanford University Press.

MALTZ, D. N., and R. A. BORKER. (1983). A cultural approach to male-female miscommunication. In J. J. Gumperz, ed., *Language and social identity*, pp. 195–216. New York: Cambridge University Press.

MARTIN, J. A. (1981). A longitudinal study of the consequences of early mother-infant interaction: A microanalytic approach. *Monographs of the Society for Research in Child Development*, serial no. 190, 46 (3).

MARTINO, W. (1994). Masculinity and learning: Exploring boys' under-achievement and under-representation in subject English. *Interpretations* 27: 22–57.

McDONALD, S. (1998). 25 shocking secrets you need to know about *South Park. TV Guide* (March 28–April 3), 22–27.

McROBBIE, A., and J. GARBER. (1975). Girls and subcultures. In S. Hall and T. Jefferson, eds., *Resistance through rituals*, pp. 209–223. London: Hutchinson.

MEALYEA, R. (1993). Reproducing vocationalism in secondary schools: Marginalization in practical workshops. In L. Angas, ed., *Education, inequality and social identity.* London: Falmer.

MIDDLETON, P. (1992). *The inward gaze: Masculinity and subjectivity in modern culture.* London: Routledge.

MILLIGAN, S., and K. THOMSON. (1992). *Listening to girls.* Australia: Ashenden and Associates.

MORRELL, R. (1993–4). Masculinities and the white boys' boarding schools of Natal, 1880–1930. *Masculinities* 2 (2): 56–82.

NARCISO, A. (1998). Blue Man Group. *Theatre Review* (New York). Available: cogsum. com/review2. html.

NIELSEN, H.B., and M. RUDBERG. (1994). *Psychological gender and modernity.* Oslo: Scandinavian University Press.

ORTNER, S.B., and H. WHITEHEAD. (1981). *Sexual meanings.* New York: Cambridge University Press.

PARROTT, S. (1972). Games children play: Ethnography of a second-grade recess. In J.P. Spradley & D.W. McCurdy, eds., *The cultural experience,* pp. 206–219. Chicago: Science Research Associates.

PFEIL, P. (1995). *Wise guys: Studies in postmodern domination and difference.* London: Verso.

POWER, T.G., M.P. MCGRATH, S.O., HUGHES, and S.H. MANIRE. (1994). Compliance and self-assertion: Young children's responses to mothers versus fathers. *Developmental Psychology,* 30(6): 980–988.

PRENDERGAST, S. (1996). Boys, bodies and pedagogy: Constructing emotions in school. Paper delivered at Gender, Body and Love Seminar, Centre for Women's Research, University of Oslo.

PROSEP5 (1998). Mr. Hanky the Christmas poo ate my balls. Available members. aol.com/ prosep5/hankybal. htm.

RADKE-YARROW, M., B., BELMONT, E., NOTTELMAN, and L. BOTTOMLY. (1990). Young children's self-conceptions: Origins in the natural discourse of depressed and normal mothers and their children. In D. Cicchetti and M. Beeghly, eds., *The self in transition: Infancy to childhood.* Chicago: University of Chicago Press.

RADKE-YARROW, M., C. ZAHN-WAXLER, and M. CHAPMAN. (1993). Children's prosocial dispositions and behavior. In P.H. Mussen, ed., *Handbook of child psychology,* 4th ed., vol. 4, *Socialization, personality, and social development.* New York: John Wiley.

RICH, A. (1980). Compulsory heterosexuality and lesbian existence. *Signs* 5: 631–660.

RICHARDS, D. (1991). Broadway Theater Online. Available: www. Broadwaytheater. com.

ROBINS, D., and P. COHEN. (1978). *Knuckle sandwich: Growing up in the working-class city.* Harmondsworth: Penguin.

RUSSELL, G., and A. RUSSELL. (1987). Mother-child and father-child relationships in middle childhood. *Child Development* 58: 1573–1585.

SAMUELSON, S. (1980). The cooties complex. *Western Folklore* 39: 198–210.

SAVIN-WILLIAMS, R.C. (1976). An ethological study of dominance formation and maintenance in a group of human adolescents. *Child Development* 47: 972–979.

SCHOFIELD, J.W. (1981). Complementary and conflicting identities: Images and interaction in an interracial school. In S.R. Asher and J.M. Gottman, eds., *The development of children's friendships,* pp. 53–90. New York: Cambridge University Press.

SEDGWICK, E.K. (1993). *Tendencies.* Durham, NC: Duke University Press.

SEWELL, T. (1997). *Black masculinities and schooling: How black boys survive modern schooling.* Stoke-on-Trent: Trentham Books.

SHERIF, M., and C. SHERIF. (1953). *Groups in harmony and tension.* New York: Harper.

SIEGEL, M. (1987). Are sons and daughters treated more differently by fathers than mothers? *Developmental Review* 7: 183–209.

SKELTON, A. (1993). On becoming a male physical education teacher: The informal culture of students and the construction of hegemonic masculinity. *Gender and Education* 5: 289–303.

SLEETER, C.E., and C.A. GRANT. (1991). Race, class, gender and disability in current textbooks. In M.W. Apple and Christian-Smith, L.K., eds., *The politics of the textbook.* New York: Routledge.

SOUTH PARK (1992–1999). Writers T. Parker and M. Stone. Television series on Comedy Central channel: sales and rental videotapes are available for some episodes.

STOLTENBERG, J. (1989). *Refusing to be a man: Essays on sex and justice.* Portland, ME: Breitenbush.

STOLTENBERG, J. (1994). *The end of manhood. A book for men of conscience.* New York: Plume/Penguin.

TAKAGI, D. Y. (1992). *The retreat from race: Asian-American admissions and racial politics.* New Brunswick: Rutgers University Press.

THOMAS, C. (1996). *Male matters: Masculinity, anxiety, and the male body on the line.* Urbana: University of Illinois Press.

THORNE, B. (1993). *Gender play: Girls and boys in school.* New Brunswick: Rutgers University Press.

TRONICK, E.Z. and J.F. COHN. (1989). Infant-mother face to face interaction: Age and gender difference in coordination and the occurrence of miscoordination. *Child Development* 609: 85–92.

TRUDELL, B.N. (1993). *Doing sex education: Gender politics and schooling.* New York: Routledge.

VAN METER, J. (1998). Stupid Inc. *New York Times Magazine,* 26 July, 15–17.

WALKER, L. (1988a). Chivalrous masculinity among juvenile offenders in Western Sydney: A new perspective on young working-class men and crime. *Current Issues in Criminal Justice* 9(3): 279–293.

WALKER, L. (1988b). Under the bonnet: Car culture, technological dominance and young men of the working-class. *Journal of Interdisciplinary Gender Studies* 3(2): 23–43.

WARREN, S. (1997). Who do these boys think they are? An investigation into the construction of masculinities in a primary classroom. *International Journal of Inclusive Education* 1(2): 207–22.

WHITE, P.G., K. YOUNG, and W.G. McTEER. (1995). Sport, masculinity, and the injured body. In D. Sabo and D.F. Gordon, eds., *Men's health and illness.* Thousand Oaks: Sage Publications.

WHITING, B.B., and C.P. EDWARDS. (1988). *Children of different worlds: The formation of social behavior.* Cambridge, Mass: Harvard University Press.

WILLIS, P. (1977). *Learning to Labour.* Farnborough: Saxon House.

WOOD, J. (1984). Groping towards sexism: Boys' sex talk. In McRobbie, A., and M. Nava, eds., *Gender and Generation.* London: Macmillan.

YAHOO. (1998). Internet search engine. *South Park* material listed at yahoo.com/ new_ad_media/television/shows/cartoons?south_park.

ZAHN-WAXLER, C., P. COLE, and K.C. BARRETT. (1991). Guilt and empathy: Sex differences and implications for the development of depression. In J. Garber and K. Dodge, eds., *The development of emotion regulation and dysregulation.* New York: Cambridge University Press.

Playing Games, Learning Gender

Looking around any suburban playground, it can often seem that boys have but two options: to be soldiers or athletes. They wear miniature versions of professional players' uniforms, or some version of camouflage gear. The connection between certain sports—particularly football—and hegemonic masculinity is well documented (Barnett 2000; Davis 1997; McBride 1995). The masculinities produced by the culture of team sports are very often reinforced by whole communities of adults, as Bernard Lefkowitz detailed in his investigation of the high school football culture of Glen Ridge, New Jersey. Sports in the dominant culture emphasize a tough masculinity that can be dangerous not only to others, but to players themselves—when Minnesota Vikings tackle Korey Stringer died from heat stroke while training in the summer of 2001, no commentators questioned that a macho attitude to pain played a role in his death. Every boy, Michael Thompson wrote recently, "is defined by athletics, whether he likes it or not, whether he is good at them or not" (270).

There is no necessary relation between particular sports and hegemonic masculinity, but for two centuries their reciprocity has institutionalized a specific notion of manhood. The relationship is reinforced in the United States by the link made between certain sports and nationalism: In times of crisis, not to applaud baseball and football can be perceived as tantamount to a lack of patriotism. Football was the structuring metaphor of the Persian Gulf war, from the pilot who compared the lack of Iraqi air resistance to the other team not showing up for a big game, to General Schwarzkopf's description of the "Hail Mary play" that won the war (Hussey).

But there is also a profound conflict for many boys between the admonition to "take it like a man" on the field and later to talk about their feelings. Boys are "never at ease, always on guard" (Kivel 13), nervously comparing themselves to the norms of masculinity in their particular group. For parents, too, as Adatto explains in her piece in this section, the tension between raising nonviolent, nurturing sons and sons who are socially comfortable can be challenging.

Boyhood, Organized Sports,
and the Construction of Masculinities

Michael A. Messner

The rapid expansion of feminist scholarship in the past two decades has led to fundamental reconceptualizations of the historical and contemporary meanings of organized sport. In the nineteenth and twentieth centuries, modernization and women's continued movement into public life created widespread "fears of social feminization," especially among middle-class men (Hantover, 1978; Kimmel, 1987). One result of these fears was the creation of organized sport as a homosocial sphere in which competition and (often violent) physicality was valued, while "the feminine" was devalued. As a result, organized sport has served to bolster a sagging ideology of male superiority, and has helped to reconstitute masculine hegemony (Bryson, 1987; Hall, 1988; Messner, 1988; Theberge, 1981).

The feminist critique has spawned a number of studies of the ways that women's sport has been marginalized and trivialized in the past (Greendorfer, 1977; Oglesby, 1978; Twin, 1978), in addition to illuminating the continued existence of structural and ideological barriers to gender equality within sport (Birrell, 1987). Only recently, however, have scholars begun to use feminist insights to examine men's experiences in sport (Kidd, 1987; Messner, 1987; Sabo, 1985). This article explores the relationship between the construction of masculine identity and boyhood participation in organized sports.

I view gender identity not as a "thing" that people "have," but rather as a *process of construction* that develops, comes into crisis, and changes as a person interacts with the social world. Through this perspective, it becomes possible to speak of "gendering" identities rather than "masculinity" or "femininity" as relatively fixed identities or statuses.

There is an agency in this construction; people are not passively shaped by their social environment. As recent feminist analyses of the construction of feminine gender identity have pointed out, girls and women are implicated in the construction of their own identities and personalities, both in terms of the ways that they participate in their own subordination and the ways that they resist subordination (Benjamin, 1988; Haug, 1987). Yet this self-construction is not a fully conscious process. There are also deeply woven, unconscious motivations, fears, and anxieties at work here. So, too, in the construction of masculinity. Levinson (1978) has argued that masculine identity is neither fully "formed" by the social context, nor is it "caused" by some internal dynamic put into place during infancy. Instead, it is shaped and constructed through the interaction between the internal and the social. The internal gendering identity may set de-

Michael A. Messner, *Journal of Contemporary Ethnography*, Vol. 18, No. 4 (January 1990), pp. 416–444. Copyright © 1990 by Sage Publications Inc. Reprinted by permission of Sage Publications, Inc.

velopmental "tasks," may create thresholds of anxiety and ambivalence, yet it is only through a concrete examination of people's interactions with others within social institutions that we can begin to understand both the similarities and differences in the construction of gender identities.

In this study I explore and interpret the meanings that males themselves attribute to their boyhood participation in organized sport. In what ways do males construct masculine identities within the institution of organized sports? In what ways do class and racial differences mediate this relationship and perhaps lead to the construction of different meanings, and perhaps different masculinities? And what are some of the problems and contradictions within these constructions of masculinity?

DESCRIPTION OF RESEARCH

Between 1983 and 1985, I conducted interviews with 30 male former athletes. Most of the men I interviewed had played the (U.S.) "major sports"—football, basketball, baseball, track. At the time of the interview, each had been retired from playing organized sports for at least five years. Their ages ranged from 21 to 48, with the median, 33; 14 were black, 14 were white, and two were Hispanic; 15 of the 16 black and Hispanic men had come from poor or working-class families, while the majority (9 of 14) of the white men had come from middle-class or professional families. All had at some time in their lives based their identities largely on their roles as athletes and could therefore be said to have had "athletic careers." Twelve had played organized sports through high school, 11 through college, and 7 had been professional athletes. Though the sample was not randomly selected, an effort was made to see that the sample had a range of difference in terms of race and social class backgrounds, and that there

was some variety in terms of age, types of sports played, and levels of success in athletic careers. Without exception, each man contacted agreed to be interviewed.

The tape-recorded interviews were semi-structured and took from one and one-half to six hours, with most taking about three hours. I asked each man to talk about four broad eras in his life: (1) his earliest experiences with sports in boyhood, (2) his athletic career, (3) retirement or disengagement from the athletic career, and (4) life after the athletic career. In each era, I focused the interview on the meanings of "success and failure," and on the boy's/man's relationships with family, with other males, with women, and with his own body.

In collecting what amounted to life histories of these men, my overarching purpose was to use feminist theories of masculine gender identity to explore how masculinity develops and changes as boys and men interact within the socially constructed world of organized sports. In addition to using the data to move toward some generalizations about the relationship between "masculinity and sport," I was also concerned with sorting out some of the variations among boys, based on class and racial inequalities, that led them to relate differently to athletic careers. I divided my sample into two comparison groups. The first group was made up of 10 men from higher-status backgrounds, primarily white, middle-class, and professional families. The second group was made up of 20 men from lower-status backgrounds, primarily minority, poor, and working-class families.

BOYHOOD AND THE PROMISE OF SPORTS

Zane Grey once said, "All boys love baseball. If they don't they're not real boys" (as cited in Kimmel, 1990). This is, of course, an ideological statement; In fact, some boys do *not* love baseball, or any other sports, for that matter. There are millions of males who at an early age are rejected by, become alienated from, or lose interest in organized sports. Yet all boys are, to a greater or lesser extent, judged according to their ability, or lack of ability, in competitive sports (Eitzen, 1975; Sabo, 1985). In this study I focus on those males who did become athletes—males who eventually poured thousands of hours into the development of specific physical skills. It is in boyhood that we can discover the roots of their commitment to athletic careers.

How did organized sports come to play such a central role in these boy's lives? When asked to recall how and why they initially got into playing sports, many of the men interviewed for this study seemed a bit puzzled: after all, playing sports was "just the thing to do." A 42-year-old black man who had played college basketball put it this way:

> It was just what you did. It's kind of like, you went to school, you played athletics, and if you didn't, there was something wrong with you. It was just like brushing your teeth: it's just what you did. It's part of your existence.

Spending one's time playing sports with other boys seemed as natural as the cycle of the seasons: baseball in the spring and summer, football in the fall, basketball in the winter—and then it was time to get out the old baseball glove and begin again. As a black 35-year-old former professional football star said:

> I'd say when I wasn't in school, 95% of the time was spent in the park playing. It was the only thing to do. It just came as natural.

And a black, 34-year-old professional basketball player explained his early experiences in sports:

> My principal and teacher said, "Now if work at this you might be pretty dam good." So it was more or less a commu thing—everybody in the community "Boy, if you work hard and keep your clean, you gonna be good." Cause i natural instinct.

"It was natural instinct." "I was a natural." Several athletes used words such as these to explain their early attraction to sports. But certainly there is nothing "natural" about throwing a ball through a hoop, hitting a ball with a bat, or jumping over hurdles. A boy, for instance, may have amazingly dexterous inborn hand-eye coordination, but this does not predispose him to a career of hitting baseballs any more than it predisposes him to a life as a brain surgeon. When one listens closely to what these men said about their early experiences in sports, it becomes clear that their adoption of the self-definition of "natural athlete" was the result of what Connell (1990) has called "a collective practice" that constructs masculinities. The boyhood development of masculine identity and status—truly problematic in a society that offers no official rite of passage into adulthood—results from a process of interaction with people and social institutions. Thus, in discussing early motivations in sports, men commonly talk of the importance of relationships with family members, peers, and the broader community.

FAMILY INFLUENCES

Though most of the men in this study spoke of their mothers with love, respect, even reverence, their descriptions of their earliest experiences in sports are stories of an exclusively male world. The existence of older brothers or uncles who served as teachers and athletic role models—as well as sources of competition for attention and status within the family—was very common. An older brother, uncle, or even close friend of the family who was a successful athlete appears to have acted as a sort of standard of achievement against whom to measure oneself. A 34-year-old black man who had been a three-sport star in high school said:

> My uncles—my Uncle Harold went to the Detroit Tigers, played pro ball—all of 'em, everybody played sports, so I wanted to be better than anybody else. I knew that everybody in this town knew them—their names were something. I wanted my name to be just like theirs.

Similarly, a black 41-year-old former professional football player recalled:

> I was the younger of three brothers and everybody played sports, so consequently I was more or less forced into it. 'Cause one brother was always better than the next brother and then I came along and had to show them that I was just as good as them. My oldest brother was an all-city ballplayer, then my other brother comes along he's all-city and all-state, and then I have to come along.

For some, attempting to emulate or surpass the athletic accomplishments of older male family members created pressures that were difficult to deal with. A 33-year-old white man explained that he was a good athlete during boyhood, but the constant awareness that his two older brothers had been better made it difficult for him to feel good about himself, or to have fun in sports;

> I had this sort of reputation that I followed from the playgrounds through grade school, and through high school. I followed these guys who were all-conference and all-state.

Most of these men, however, saw their relationships with their athletic older brothers and uncles in a positive light; it was within these relationships that they gained experience and developed motivations that gave them a competitive "edge" within their same-aged peer group. As a 33-year-old black man describes his earliest athletic experiences:

> My brothers were role models. I wanted to prove—especially to my brothers—that I had heart, you know, that I was a man.

When asked, "What did it mean to you to be 'a man' at that age?" he replied:

> Well, it meant that I didn't want to be a so-called scaredy-cat. You want to hit a guy even though he's bigger than you to show that, you know, you've got this macho image. I remember that at that young an age, that feeling was exciting to me. And that carried over, and as I got older, I got better and I began to look around me and see, well hey! I'm competitive with these guys, even though I'm younger, you know? And then of course all the compliments come—and I began to notice a change, even in my parents—especially in my father—he was proud of that, and that was very important to me. He was extremely important . . . he showed me more affection, now that I think of it.

As this man's words suggest, if men talk of their older brothers and uncles mostly as role models, teachers, and "names" to emulate, their talk of their relationships with their fathers is more deeply layered and complex. Athletic skills and competition for status may often be learned from older brothers, but it is in boys' relationships with fathers that we find many of the keys to the emotional salience of sports in the development of masculine identity.

RELATIONSHIPS WITH FATHERS

The fact that boys' introductions to organized sports are often made by fathers who might otherwise be absent or emotionally distant adds a powerful emotional charge to these early experiences (Osherson, 1986). Although playing organized sports eventually came to feel "natural" for all of the men interviewed in this study, many needed to be "exposed" to sports, or even gently "pushed" by their fathers to become involved in activities like Little League baseball. A white, 33-year-old man explained:

> I still remember it like it was yesterday—Dad and I driving up in his truck, and I had my glove and my hat and all that—and I said, "Dad, I don't want to do it." He says, "What?" I says, "I don't want to do it." I was nervous. That I might fail. And he says, "Don't be silly. Lookit: There's Joey and Petey and all your friends out there." And so Dad says, "You're gonna do it, come on." And in my memory he's never said that about anything else; he just knew I needed a little kick in the pants and I'd do it. And once you're out there and you see all the other kids making errors and stuff, and you know you're better than those guys, you know: Maybe I do belong here. As it turned out, Little League was a good experience.

Some who were similarly "pushed" by their fathers were not so successful as the aforementioned man had been in Little League baseball, and thus the experience was not altogether a joyous affair. One 34-year-old white man, for instance, said he "inherited" his interest in sports from his father, who started playing catch with him at the age of four. Once he got into Little League, he felt pressured by his father, one of the coaches, who expected him to be the star of the team:

> I'd go 0-for-four sometimes, strike out three times in a Little League game, and I'd dread the ride home. I'd come home and he'd say, "Go in the bathroom and swing the bat in the mirror for an hour," to get my swing level . . . It didn't help much, though, I'd go out and strike out three or

four times again the next game too [laughs ironically].

When asked if he had been concerned with having his father's approval, he responded:

> Failure in his eyes? Yeah, I always thought that he wanted me to get some kind of [athletic] scholarship. I guess I was afraid of him when I was a kid. He didn't hit that much, but he had a rage about him—he'd rage, and that voice would just rattle you.

Similarly, a 24-year-old black man described his awe of his father's physical power and presence, and his sense of inadequacy in attempting to emulate him:

> My father had a voice that sounded like rolling thunder. Whether it was intentional on his part or not, I don't know, but my father gave me a sense, an image of him being the most powerful being on earth, and that no matter what I ever did I would never come close to him . . . There were definite feelings of physical inadequacy that I couldn't work around.

It is interesting to note how these feelings of physical inadequacy relative to the father lived on as part of this young man's permanent internalized image. He eventually became a "feared" high school football player and broke school records in weight-lifting, yet,

> As I grew older, my mother and friends told me that I had actually grown to be a larger man than my father. Even though in time I required larger clothes than he, which should have been a very concrete indication, neither my brother nor I could ever bring ourselves to say that I was bigger. We simply couldn't conceive of it.

Using sports activities as a means of identifying with and "living up to" the power and status of one's father was not always such a painful and difficult task for the men I interviewed. Most did not describe fathers who "pushed" them to become sports stars. The relationship between their athletic strivings and their identification with their fathers was more subtle. A 48-year-old black man, for instance, explained that he was not pushed into sports by his father, but was aware from an early age of the community status his father had gained through sports. He saw his own athletic accomplishments as a way to connect with and emulate his father:

> I wanted to play baseball because my father had been quite a good baseball player in the Negro leagues before baseball was integrated, and so he was kind of a model for me. I remember, quite young, going to a baseball game he was in—this was before the war and all—I remember being in the stands with my mother and seeing him on first base, and being aware of the crowd . . . I was aware of people's confidence in him as a serious baseball player. I don't think my father ever said anything to me like "play sports . . ." [But] I knew he would like it if I did well. His admiration was important . . . he mattered.

Similarly, a 24-year-old white man described his father as a somewhat distant "role model" whose approval mattered:

> My father was more of an example . . . he definitely was very much in touch with and still had very fond memories of being an athlete and talked about it, bragged about it. . . . But he really didn't do that much to teach me skills, and he didn't always go to every game I played like some parents. But he approved and that was important, you know. That was important to get his approval. I always knew that playing sports was important to him, so I knew implicitly that it was good and there was definitely a value on it.

First experiences in sports might often come through relationships with brothers or older male relatives, and the early emotional salience of sports was often directly related to a boy's relationship with his father. The sense of commitment that these young boys eventually made to the development of athletic careers is best explained as a process of development of masculine gender identity and status in relation to same-sex peers.

MASCULINE IDENTITY AND EARLY COMMITMENT TO SPORTS

When many of the men in this study said that during childhood they played sports because "it's just what everybody did," they of course meant that it was just what *boys* did. They were introduced to organized sports by older brothers and fathers, and once involved, found themselves playing within an exclusively male world. Though the separate (and unequal) gendered worlds of boys and girls came to appear as "natural," they were in fact socially constructed. Thorne's observations of children's activities in schools indicated that rather than "naturally" constituting "separate gendered cultures," there is considerable interaction between boys and girls in classrooms and on playgrounds. When adults set up legitimate contact between boys and girls, Thorne observed, this usually results in "relaxed interactions." But when activities in the classroom or on the playground are presented to children as sex-segregated activities and gender is marked by teachers and other adults ("boys line up here, girls over there"), "gender boundaries are heightened, and mixed-sex interaction becomes an explicit arena of risk" (Thorne, 1986; 70). Thus sex-segregated activities such as organized sports as structured by adults, provide the context in which gendered identities and separate "gendered cultures" develop and come to appear natural. For the boys in this study, it became "natural" to equate masculinity with competition, physical strength, and skills. Girls simply did not (could not, it was believed) participate in these activities.

Yet it is not simply the separation of children, by adults, into separate activities that explains why many boys came to feel such a strong connection with sports activities, while so few girls did. As I listened to men recall their earliest experiences in organized sports, I heard them talk of insecurity, loneliness, and especially a need to connect with other people as a primary motivation in their early sports strivings. As a 42-year-old white man stated, "The most important thing was just being out there with the rest of the guys—being friends." Another 32-year-old interviewee was born in Mexico and moved to the United States at a fairly young age. He never knew his father, and his mother died when he was only nine years old. Suddenly he felt rootless, and threw himself into sports. His initial motivations, however, do not appear to be based on a need to compete and win:

> Actually, what I think sports did for me is it brought me into kind of an instant family. By being on a Little League team, or even just playing with all kinds of different kids in the neighborhood, it brought what I really wanted, which was some kind of closeness. It was just being there, and being friends.

Clearly, what these boys needed and craved was that which was most problematic for them: connection and unity with other people. But why do these young males find *organized sports* such an attractive context in which to establish "a kind of closeness" with others? Comparative observations of young boys' and girls' game-playing behaviors yield important insights into this question. Piaget (1965) and Lever (1976) both observed that girls tend to have more "pragmatic" and "flexible" orientations to the rules of games; they are more prone to make exceptions and innovations in the middle of a game in order to make the game more "fair." Boys,

on the other hand, tend to have a more firm, even [in]flexible orientation to the rules of a game; to them, the rules are what protects any fairness. This difference, according to Gilligan (1982), is based on the fact that early developmental experiences have yielded deeply rooted differences between males' and females' developmental tasks, needs, and moral reasoning. Girls, who tend to define themselves primarily through connection with others, experience highly competitive situations (whether in organized sports or in other hierarchical institutions) as threats to relationships, and thus to their identities. For boys, the development of gender identity involves the construction of positional identities, where a sense of self is solidified through separation from others (Chodorow, 1978). Yet feminist psychoanalytic theory has tended to oversimplify the internal lives of men (Lichterman, 1986). Males do appear to develop positional identities, yet despite their fears of intimacy, they also retain a human need for closeness and unity with others. This ambivalence toward intimate relationships is a major thread running through masculine development throughout the life course. Here we can conceptualize what Craib (1987) calls the "elective affinity" between personality and social structure: For the boy who both seeks and fears attachment with others, the rule-bound structure of organized sports can promise to be a safe place in which to seek nonintimate attachment with others within a context that maintains clear boundaries, distance, and separation.

COMPETITIVE STRUCTURES AND CONDITIONAL SELF-WORTH

Young boys may initially find that sports gives them the opportunity to experience "some kind of closeness" with others, but the structure of sports and athletic careers often undermines the possibility of boys learning to transcend their fears of intimacy, thus becoming able to develop truly close and intimate relationships with others (Kidd, 1990; Messner, 1987). The sports world is extremely hierarchical, and an incredible amount of importance is placed on winning, on "being number one." For instance, a few years ago I observed a basketball camp put on for boys by a professional basketball coach and his staff. The youngest boys, about eight years old (who could barely reach the basket with their shots) played a brief scrimmage. Afterwards, the coaches lined them up in a row in front of the older boys who were sitting in the grandstands. One by one, the coach would stand behind each boy, put his hand on the boy's head (much in the manner of a priestly benediction), and the older boys in the stands would applaud and cheer, louder or softer, depending on how well or poorly the young boy was judged to have performed. The two or three boys who were clearly the exceptional players looked confident that they would receive the praise they were due. Most of the boys, though, had expressions ranging from puzzlement to thinly disguised terror on their faces as they awaited the judgments of the older boys.

This kind of experience teaches boys that it is not "just being out there with the guys—being friends," that ensures the kind of attention and connection that they crave; it is being *better* than the other guys—*beating them*—that is the key to acceptance. Most of the boys in this study did have some early successes in sports, and thus their ambivalent need for connection with others was met, at least for a time. But the institution of sport tends to encourage the development of what Schafer (1975) has called "conditional self-worth" in boys. As boys become aware that acceptance by others is contingent upon being good—a "winner"—narrow definitions of success, based upon

performance and winning become increasingly important to them. A 33-year-old black man said that by the time he was in his early teens:

> It was expected of me to do well in all my contests—I mean by my coaches, my peers, and my family. So I in turn expected to do well, and if I didn't do well, then I'd be very disappointed.

The man from Mexico, discussed above, who said that he had sought "some kind of closeness" in his early sports experiences began to notice in his early teens that if he played well, was a *winner*, he would get attention from others:

> It got to the point where I started realizing, noticing that people were always there for me, backing me all the time—sports got to be really fun because I always had some people there backing me. Finally my oldest brother started going to all my games, even though I had never really seen who he was [laughs]—after the game, you know, we never really saw each other, but he was at all my baseball games, and it seemed like we shared a kind of closeness there, but only in those situations. Off the field, when I wasn't in uniform, he was never around.

By high school, he said, he felt "up against the wall." Sports hadn't delivered what he had hoped it would, but he thought if he just tried harder, won one more championship trophy, he would get the attention he truly craved. Despite his efforts, this attention was not forthcoming. And, sadly, the pressures he had put on himself to excel in sports had taken most of the fun out of playing.

For many of the men in this study, throughout boyhood and into adolescence, this conscious striving for successful achievement became the primary means through which they sought connection with other people (Messner, 1987). But it is important to recognize that young males' internalized ambivalences about intimacy do not fully determine the contours and directions of their lives. Masculinity continues to develop through interaction with the social world—and because boys from different backgrounds are interacting with substantially different familial, educational, and other institutions, these differences will lead them to make different choices and define situations in different ways. Next, I examine the differences in the ways that boys from higher- and lower-status families and communities related to organized sports.

STATUS DIFFERENCES AND COMMITMENTS TO SPORTS

In discussing early attractions to sports, the experiences of boys from higher- and lower-status backgrounds are quite similar. Both groups indicate the importance of fathers and older brothers in introducing them to sports. Both groups speak of the joys of receiving attention and acceptance among family and peers for early successes in sports. Note the similarities, for instance, in the following descriptions of boyhood athletic experiences of two men. First, a man born in a white, middle-class family:

> I loved playing sports so much from a very early age because of early exposure. A lot of the sports came easy at an early age, and because they did, and because you were successful at something, I think that you're inclined to strive for that gratification. It's like, if you're good, you like it, because it's instant gratification. I'm doing something that I'm good at and I'm gonna keep doing it.

Second, a black man from a poor family:

> Fortunately I had some athletic ability, and, quite naturally, once you start doing good in whatever it is—I don't care if it's jacks—you show off what you do. That's your ability, that's your blessing, so you show it off as much as you can.

For boys from both groups, early exposure to sports, the discovery that they had some "ability," shortly followed by some sort of family, peer, and community recognition, all eventually led to the commitment of hundreds and thousands of hours of playing, practicing, and dreaming of future stardom. Despite these similarities, there are also some identifiable differences that begin to explain the tendency of males from lower-status backgrounds to develop higher levels of commitment to sports careers. The most clear-cut difference was that while men from higher-status backgrounds are likely to describe their earliest athletic experiences and motivations almost exclusively in terms of immediate family, men from lower-status backgrounds more commonly describe the importance of a broader community context. For instance, a 46-year-old man who grew up in a "poor working class" black family in a small town in Arkansas explained:

> In that community, at the age of third or fourth grade, if you're a male, they expect you to show some kind of inclination, some kind of skill in football or basketball. It was an expected thing, you know? My mom and my dad, they didn't push at all. It was the general environment.

A 48-year-old man describes sports activities as a survival strategy in his poor black community:

> Sports protected me from having to compete in gang stuff, or having to be good with my fists. If you were an athlete and got into the fist world, that was your business, and that was okay—but you didn't have to if you didn't want to. People would generally defer to you, give you your space away from trouble.

A 35-year-old man who grew up in "a poor black ghetto" described his boyhood relationship to sports similarly:

Where I came from, either you were one of two things: you were in sports or you were out on the streets being a drug addict, or breaking into places. The guys who were in sports, we had it a little easier, because we were accepted by both groups. . . . So it worked out to my advantage, cause I didn't get into a lot of trouble—some trouble, but not a lot.

The fact that boys in lower-status communities faced these kinds of realities gave salience to their developing athletic identities. In contrast, sports were important to boys from higher-status backgrounds, yet the middle-class environment seemed more secure, less threatening, and offered far more options. By the time most of these boys got into junior high or high school, many had made conscious decisions to shift their attentions away from athletic careers to educational and (nonathletic) career goals. A 32-year-old white college athletic director told me that he had seen his chance to pursue a pro baseball career as "pissing in the wind," and instead, focused on education. Similarly, a 33-year-old white dentist who was a three-sport star in high school, decided not to play sports in college, so he could focus on getting into dental school. As he put it,

> I think I kind of downgraded the stardom thing. I thought it was small potatoes. And sure, that's nice in high school and all that, but on a broad scale. I didn't think it amounted to all that much.

This statement offers an important key to understanding the construction of masculine identity within a middle-class context. The status that this boy got through sports had been *very* important to him, yet he could see that "on a broad scale," this sort of status was "small potatoes." This sort of early recognition is more than a result of the oft-noted middle-class tendency to raise "future-oriented" children (Rubin, 1976; Sennett and Cobb, 1973). Perhaps more important, it

is that the *kinds* of future orientations developed by boys from higher-status backgrounds are consistent with the middle-class context. These men's descriptions of their boyhoods reveal that they grew up immersed in a wide range of institutional frameworks, of which organized sports was just one. And—importantly—they could see that the status of adult males around them was clearly linked to their positions within various professions, public institutions, and bureaucratic organizations. It was clear that access to this sort of institutional status came through educational achievement, not athletic prowess. A 32-year-old black man who grew up in a professional-class family recalled that he had idolized Wilt Chamberlain and dreamed of being a pro basketball player, yet his father discouraged his athletic strivings:

> He knew I liked the game. I loved the game. But basketball was not recommended; my dad would say, "That's a stereotyped image for black youth. . . . When your basketball is gone and finished, what are you gonna do? One day, you might get injured. What are you gonna look forward to?" He stressed education.

Similarly, a 32-year-old man who was raised in a white, middle-class family, had found in sports a key means of gaining acceptance and connection in his peer group. Yet he was simultaneously developing an image of himself as a "smart student," and becoming aware of a wide range of non-sports life options:

> My mother was constantly telling me how smart I was, how good I was, what a nice person I was, and giving me all sorts of positive strokes, and those positive strokes became a self-motivating kind of thing. I had this image of myself as smart, and I lived up to that image.

It is not that parents of boys in lower-status families did not also encourage their boys to work hard in school. Several reported that their parents "stressed books first, sports second." It's just that the broader social context—education, economy, and community—was more likely to *narrow* lower-status boys' perceptions of real-life options, while boys from higher-status backgrounds faced an expanding world of options. For instance, with a different socioeconomic background, one 35-year-old black man might have become a great musician instead of a star professional football running back. But he did not. When he was a child, he said, he was most interested in music:

> I wanted to be a drummer. But we couldn't afford drums. My dad couldn't go out and buy me a drum set or a guitar even—it was just one of those things; he was just trying to make ends meet.

But he *could* afford, as could so many in his socioeconomic condition, to spend countless hours at the local park, where he was told by the park supervisor

> that I was a natural—not only in gymnastics or baseball—whatever I did, I was a natural. He told me I shouldn't waste this talent, and so I immediately started watching the big guys then.

In retrospect, this man had potential to be a musician or any number of things, but his environment limited his options to sports, and he made the best of it. Even within sports, he, like most boys in the ghetto, was limited:

> We didn't have any tennis courts in the ghetto—we used to have a lot of tennis balls, but no racquets. I wonder today how good I might be in tennis if I had gotten a racquet in my hands at an early age.

It is within this limited structure of opportunity that many lower-status young boys found sports to be *the* place, rather than *a* place, within which to construct masculine identity, status, the relationships. A 36-year-old white man explained that his father left the family when he was very young and his mother faced a very difficult struggle to make ends meet. As his words suggest, the more limited a boy's options, and the more insecure his family situation, the more likely he is to make an early commitment to an athletic career:

> I used to ride my bicycle to Little League practice—if I'd waited for someone to pick me up and take me to the ball park I'd have never played. I'd get to the ball park and all the other kids would have their dad bring them to practice or games. But I'd park my bike to the side and when it was over I'd get on it and go home. Sports was the way for me to move everything to the side—family problems, just all the embarrassments—and think about one thing, and that was sports . . . In the third grade, when the teacher went around the classroom and asked everybody, "What do you want to be when you grow up?," I said, "I want to be a major league baseball player," and everybody laughed their heads off.

This man eventually did enjoy a major league baseball career. Most boys from lower-status backgrounds who make similar early commitments to athletic careers are not so successful. As stated earlier, the career structure of organized sports is highly competitive and hierarchical. In fact, the chances of attaining professional status in sports are approximately 4:100,000 for a white man, 2:100,000 for a black man, and 3:1 million for a Hispanic man in the United States (Leonard and Reyman, 1988). Nevertheless, the immediate rewards (fun, status, attention), along with the constricted (nonsports) structure of opportunity, attract disproportionately large numbers of boys from lower-status backgrounds to athletic careers as their major means of constructing a masculine identity. These are the boys who later, as young men, had to struggle with "conditional self-worth," and, more often than not, occupational dead ends. Boys from higher-status backgrounds, on the other hand, bolstered their boyhood, adolescent, and early adult status through their athletic accomplishments. Their wider range of experiences and life chances led to an early shift away from sports careers as the major basis of identity (Messner, 1989).

CONCLUSION

The conception of the masculinity-sports relationship developed here begins to illustrate the idea of an "elective affinity" between social structure and personality. Organized sports is a "gendered institution"—an institution constructed by gender relations. As such, its structure and values (rules, formal organization, sex composition, etc.) reflect dominant conceptions of masculinity and femininity. Organized sports is also a "gendering institution"—an institution that helps to construct the current gender order. Part of this construction of gender is accomplished through the "masculinizing" of male bodies and minds.

Yet boys do not come to their first experiences in organized sports as "blank slates," but arrive with already "gendering" identities due to early developmental experiences and previous socialization. I have suggested here that an important thread running through the development of masculine identity is males' ambivalence toward intimate unity with others. Those boys who experience early athletic successes find in the structure of organized sport an affinity with this masculine ambivalence toward intimacy: The rule-bound, competitive, hierarchical world of sport offers boys an attractive means of establishing an emotionally distant

(and thus "safe") connection with others. Yet as boys begin to define themselves as "athletes," they learn that in order to be accepted (to have connection) through sports, they must be winners. And in order to be winners, they must construct relationships with others (and with themselves) that are consistent with the competitive and hierarchical values and structure of the sports world. As a result, they often develop a "conditional self-worth" that leads them to construct more instrumental relationships with themselves and others. This ultimately exacerbates their difficulties in constructing intimate relationships with others. In effect, the interaction between the young male's preexisting internalized ambivalence toward intimacy with the competitive hierarchical institution of sport has resulted in the construction of a masculine personality that is characterized by instrumental rationality, goal-orientation, and difficulties with intimate connection and expression (Messner, 1987).

This theoretical line of inquiry invites us not simply to examine how social institutions "socialize" boys, but also to explore the ways that boys' already-gendering identities interact with social institutions (which, like organized sport, are themselves the product of gender relations). This study has also suggested that it is not some singular "masculinity" that is being constructed through athletic careers. It may be correct, from a psychoanalytic perspective, to suggest that all males bring ambivalences toward intimacy to their interactions with the world, but "the world" is a very different place for males from different racial and socioeconomic backgrounds. Because males have substantially different interactions with the world, based on class, race, and other differences and inequalities, we might expect the construction of masculinity to take on different meanings for boys and men from differing backgrounds (Messner,

1989). Indeed, this study has suggested that boys from higher-status backgrounds face a much broader range of options than do their lower-status counterparts. As a result, athletic careers take on different meanings for these boys. Lower-status boys are likely to see athletic careers as *the* institutional context for the construction of their masculine status and identities, while higher-status males make an early shift away from athletic careers toward other institutions (usually education and nonsports careers). A key line of inquiry for future studies might begin by exploring this irony of sports careers: Despite the fact that "the athlete" is currently an example of an exemplary form of masculinity in public ideology, the vast majority of boys who become most committed to athletic careers are never well-rewarded for their efforts. The fact that class and racial dynamics lead boys from higher-status backgrounds, unlike their lower-status counterparts, to move into nonsports careers illustrates how the construction of different kinds of masculini*ties* is a key component of the overall construction of the gender order.

"All-American Guys"

Bernard Lefkowitz

The game of choice for most of the jocks coming out of middle school was football. Some planned to go out for other sports, such as wrestling and baseball, in the winter and spring. Paul, Richie, and Bryant would also wrestle, and Kyle would play baseball. But football was the high-profile one; history and tradition in Glen Ridge trained the spotlight on the football players.

So there they all were, grinding out the yardage, pounding away at each other in jayvee football practice: Paul Archer, Bryant Grober, Richie Corcoran, Kyle and Kevin Scherzer, and Peter Quigley. (Chris Archer, a year behind his friends, was in the eighth grade. He planned to play football and wrestle.) They would all play on the jayvee team for a year or so and then, barring setbacks such as failing grades, would move on to the varsity.

Barely a couple of weeks into the school year, the walls of Glen Ridge High vibrated with a rumble that built day by day into a huge roar. The approach of Homecoming Day. On the horizon: the big game. Time to stomp Glen Ridge's hated rival, Mountain Lakes.

On the Friday before the game, Kyle and Kevin and Paul and Richie and the other freshman jocks would pass the houses of the varsity players, checking out the decorations on the fences and doorways, pre-

pared with loving care by the cheerleaders. It was a tradition for the girls to decorate the homes of the varsity players before a big game; the guys also knew that the girls gave special attention to decorating the bedrooms of the senior players.

You couldn't get much algebra done this Friday. The varsity players wore their jerseys in school. The teachers couldn't miss the group of seniors dressed in red and white, acting smugly superior in the back of the classroom. On this day everybody seemed to know who ran the school, and it sure wasn't the grown-up in front of the blackboard.

Between classes the students got other reminders of whom the day belonged to. For example, each locker assigned to a varsity football player was decorated by a cheerleader. There would be signs exhorting the player to heroics on the field and drawings of hearts pierced by arrows. In front of the lockers, the cheerleaders and other fans would leave their offerings: mounds of candies, slices of cake covered with Saran Wrap. Some favored players would find in their lockers more personal messages—"I love your body"—and even some intimate garments, including bras and panties. The tie between sex and football heroics was very strong in Glen Ridge.

In the afternoon the entire school settled into the gym bleachers for sports assembly. Most of the rhetoric and applause were directed toward the varsity football players who paraded across the stage one by one in their game jerseys, flashing their toothiest smiles at their adoring public. Perhaps not all adoring. Sizable numbers of students sat on their hands, sneering at the attention the school was lavishing on a mediocre bunch of jocks. But they were the marginals, the ones who listened to the Grateful Dead and joined the chess club. "Catch the Spirit," the sign stretched above the stage said—and most students did.

The freshman players didn't really mind that right now they were lower than scrubs, not even bench-warmers. In another year or so, if everything worked out, they'd be out on the stage, too, waving to their fans.

That night before the game, the Homecoming dance was held in the school cafeteria. It wasn't a dress-up dance the way the Candy Cane Ball was later in the winter, but the kids caught the spirit, sweating through their shirts and tops after a half hour of dancing under the red-and-white streamers. Standing at the edge of the dance floor, Peter and Paul and the Scherzer twins and Bryant watched as the King and Queen of Homecoming, usually the football captain and the most popular cheerleader, were crowned. These first-year kids still looked so young in their pullover shirts and khakis. They didn't have varsity jackets yet, but already they were attracting a following—the girls who had been their friends since grade school and the guys who wanted to invest in a friendship that would assure them of popularity by proximity during the next four years.

In the town the football clan gathered. Homecoming was taken seriously in Glen Ridge. People came home from out of town and out of state for the game. Older brothers and sisters relived past glories at their parents' dinner tables and even older Ridgers camped at friends' and relatives' houses, delighted to show their old game slides against any bare wall.

Before game time hundreds of people were already in the stands, waving their Ridger pennants, roaring "Down the Lake."

Now the Red and White galloped onto Hurrell Field to do battle. The marching-band members, red-and-white sashes pinned to their chests as though they were conventioneers, paraded to the fifty-yard line at halftime, clutching their wide-brimmed, conquistador-like hats and white plumes against the breeze. The preening, cartwheeling cheerleaders chanted the fight song, while the junior varsity cheerleaders hawked programs and the booster mothers dispensed hot dogs and grape juice at the refreshment stand.

Soaking up the scene, the freshmen knew they were about to enter the celebrity phase of Glen Ridge athletics. The hearty camaraderie of their fathers and brothers and friends, the frankly appraising looks from the hottest girls in the school, the pampering from their mothers and sisters—this was the payoff. This was what they had been priming themselves for ever since they were five and six years old and had stepped up to the plate in Bandbox softball. The 5 A.M. wake-up calls for morning practice, wallowing in the mud during a Cobra League football game—now it all was paying off. For a moment you felt like you had the town in the palm of your hand. Ridger proud.

After the game ended, as soon as the players showered and changed, one honking motorcade wound its way to Bloomfield, to the Town Pub, where parents of the players and just plain boosters reconstructed every scoring drive.

Other groups went to the homes of senior players, where a huge spread of food and drinks had been laid out. The football players, the cheerleaders, and assorted hangers-on joined friends, neighbors, and relatives. The parties flowed out onto the porches and backyards. The kids drank their sodas decorously as the parents got red-faced and misty-eyed with nostalgia. Then when the old folks started yawning, the players said their goodbyes and headed for their own parties, as the royal retinue, the cheerleaders and other girls, trailed in their wake.

The whole weekend was one big dream, even for the freshmen kiddos. They were reveling in the attention they received as heirs apparent to the football royalty of Glen Ridge. But for a bunch of guys who hadn't even started to earn their varsity letters, the high-stakes competition they were entering had to provoke some anxiety as well. What if they didn't live up to everybody's expectations? You couldn't miss the real meaning of Homecoming weekend: To the sports-obsessed crowd of Glen Ridge, you were a jock or you were nothing.

.   .   .

Were the Jocks comfortable with the roles they were asked to play in the culture of Glen Ridge? A compelling argument can be made that the hyper-masculine style they were asked to assume by parents and brothers and sports enthusiasts was a heavy burden for a kid to carry through adolescence.

Most of these boys did not demonstrate great talent for athletics. They were kids who liked to throw a ball around or wrestle in the mud with their buddies. Yet they were touted by everyone who counted in their world as future stars. More than once, they asked themselves, What if I don't meet my father's expectations? What if I'm not even as good as my older brother—or, worse, my younger brother? When the school upped the ante, when it staked its reputation on their performance on the playing fields, it added significantly to the already outsized image that had been superimposed on a group of young and immature boys.

Then there was the matter of the social role that Glen Ridge conferred on its young athletes. That role decreed that they had to be popular, handsome, desirable to girls. But how many insecure adolescent boys believe, deep down, that they can live up to all that? They must have asked themselves: What if that cheerleader turns me down? What if I'm left out the next time the crowd has a party?

They also might wonder whether the love and respect they received from adults and peers was conditioned largely on their athletic performance. If I fail, they might ask, will anyone love me?

The swagger they affected—the Jock swagger—was a handy way to camouflage their doubts. It served three purposes: It compensated for their limitations as athletes by allowing them to pretend they were stars. It was a distorted exaggeration of how they thought dominant men—real men—were supposed to behave. And, conversely, their defiance of authority may well have been a disguised growl of resistance against being programmed to conform to the myths nurtured by the community.

Young men have many social, psychological, and sexual insecurities. The myth of the future jock king added to the list. If they sensed they weren't going to be great athletes, they might try to conceal their insecurity through a show of childish bravado; they might try to lead by intimidation, not merit. If they weren't allowed to grow into their own masculine identity, they could develop their own grotesque version of manhood.

The Making of a Bully

Susan Douglas

The man was screaming at a teenage boy. "Why are you being so nice to him?" he yelled. "*Why?*"

The boy looked sheepish, and was silent.

"You hit him, and you hit him *hard* next time," the older man insisted.

I was out walking the dog on a trail that surrounds the local high school, and I had stumbled upon football practice—blocking practice, to be precise. I didn't know this at first. I heard only the man's voice, serrated and alien, cutting though the sounds of crickets and rustling leaves and disrupting my rich inner thoughts about what to make for dinner and where to get my daughter's school supplies.

She and I had just reviewed "Promoting Responsible Behavior," a flier sent home with her on the first day of school that listed "guidelines for a respectful, self-disciplined, and caring school community." Hitting, pushing, and any other forms of physical aggression are *verboten*, and now children as young as six can be overheard talking about respecting others' "personal space."

The young man berated for being a wuss was probably drilled in the school district's "conflict-management curriculum," also touted in the flier. What was he to do? Should he learn to hit as hard as possible? Or would he be nice and fail? How would he manage to be peaceable yet a brute?

The coach's instructions caught me at the height of the police scandal in New York. White male officers holding positions of enormous power and authority conducted a sexually monstrous invasion of a black man's body. At the time, I was also reading *Our Guys* by Bernard Lefkowitz, his disturbing account of the 1989 rape of a retarded girl in Glen Ridge, New Jersey. The stars of the school's football team attacked her with a baseball bat and broom handle, no less. Like the cops in New York, these guys assumed they'd never get caught, or that such things would be tolerated.

The cops were "rogues," "renegades," according to New York officials. But Lefkowitz's account is much more chilling. It was the revered jock culture of Glen Ridge—one that reigns supreme in high schools throughout the land—that produced and then sought to dismiss the despicable acts against the girl in the basement.

Feminists get into trouble when we suggest that there might be a deep and pathological crisis surrounding masculinity in this country. We get into even bigger trouble when we ask about the relationship between cherished male institutions—football teams, military academies, police squads, frat houses—and brutal, criminal behavior. We are male-bashers, or we are making glib causal associations, ignoring the good these institutions do. No matter that as macho an institution as the FBI documented, in the mid-1980s, that athletes in sports in which aggressiveness and physical force are prided—most notably football and basketball players—were reported to the police for sexual assault 38 percent more often than the average male college student.

But all too many news stories—from the scandals in the military to the epidemic of police brutality and the rapes by athletes—point to the truth that much of our culture is built upon a tolerance, even a reverence, for an aggressive, above-the-law, bullying version of manhood.

Many feminists, for good reason, have emphasized the loss of self-esteem that all too many girls experience when they hit adolescence. But it is time now to start focusing on the boys as well. Too many boys are growing up in a culture that compels them to suppress their fundamental humanity. When that happens, those they have power over suffer, sometimes brutally.

Trigger-Happy Birthday

Kiku Adatto

Some months ago, my 12-year-old son received a brightly colored invitation to a friend's birthday party, which was being held someplace called Boston Paintball. A few days later, I received a more somber missive: "This is a Release of Liability—read before signing."

A couple of clauses stood out. No. 1: "The risk of injury from the activity and weaponry involved in paintball is significant, including the potential for permanent disability and death." No. 4: "I, for myself and on behalf of my heirs, assigns, personal representatives and next of kin, *hereby release . . . the American Paintball League (A.P.L.), Boston Paintball . . . with respect to any and all injury, disability, death. . . .*"

Welcome to today's birthday party. And by the way, if your kid is killed at the party, it's not our fault. Call me an old-fashioned mother, but I just couldn't sign. Apparently all the other parents did, however; my son's friends told him that everyone had a great time.

I decided to visit Boston Paintball to check it out. Located in an old converted warehouse, the place was teeming with white suburban boys. Over at one end, I found another birthday party, for a kid named Max and 10 or so friends.

With their parents' help, the kids were putting on safety gear—chest protectors, neck guards and "Star Wars"-style masks. "It's fun," said Max's mom encouragingly, "like a video game." Then a referee held up a paintball gun (which looked like a real semiautomatic) and shot off a few rounds. The boys quickly lined up to get their weapons.

Next came the safety orientation. "First rule: don't lift off the masks on the field. We shoot balls at 100 miles an hour. Lift a mask, you'll lose an eye. Second rule: on the field, no shooting point-blank. No taking hostages. No using dead guys as shields. No hitting with fists or with gun butts." Max's dad snapped a few photos and handed out the ammunition.

The referee gave the signal, and the game began.

But nothing happened. The boys huddled behind the bunkers. Eventually some of them poked their heads out; sporadic shots were fired. A few brave souls ventured into the open.

I was watching with the other parents from behind a window in the viewing area. Suddenly a paintball bullet hit the window with a dull thud. I started back. My adrenaline was pumping, but my mind said, "Trust the plexiglass." More bullets splattered the window. It sounded like real gunfire. "Hey, it looks like one of the kids is shooting at us," joked one of the mothers. We all laughed. And moved back from the window.

There was a release of tension after the first game. Max appeared in the lobby flushed and jubilant. "It was awesome," he said. "I hit someone." Max's parents laid out pizza. Spirits were high. "I killed a person," a boy said as he downed a Coke.

While they ate, I visited the gift shop. Along the back wall were racks of paintball looking like assault weapons— e Sniper II at \$249.99 to the Express utococker at \$749.99. Even without souvenirs, paintball is pricey: \$29 for (\$39 for adults), with numerous extra es. A birthday party for 10 boys with pizza can run \$450.

Back at Max's party, one boy was pressing a cold Coke can against a welt. I asked Max's mom about the cost. "Max has contributed a hundred bucks of his birthday money to help pay for the party," she said fondly. Suddenly she spotted a welt on another boy's chin. "Oh, my God. How did that happen?" She turned back to me. "He's a little warrior," she said.

When paintball was invented 19 years ago in New Hampshire, it was played by adults who focused less on simulated violence than on self-reliant survival. Today, it is reportedly a billion-dollar business in North America alone, with outdoor theme parks featuring mock Vietcong villages and bases named the Rambo Hotel. It's a business that proudly markets itself as an all-purpose sport: the Boston Paintball Web site said it was great for "stress relief, confidence, company outings, morale boosting" and, of course, "birthdays."

Some of the mothers in attendance that day said that paintball is no different from the war games their brothers played a generation ago. I disagree. True, when I was a kid, my friends and I spun violent fantasies, some (like cowboys and Indians) as troubling as the new high-tech games. But there were differences. We didn't pay for admission. The guns weren't lethal. We used our imaginations. And our parents didn't open the paper several times a year to read about kids firing guns in school.

As I was pulling out of the paintball parking lot, the attendant, a guy in his 40's, asked if I had played. I said no. "I don't think it's good, kids and paintball," he said. "They don't realize that they can hurt somebody with those guns."

Well, I'm with the parking-lot attendant. And as for the contract, I still couldn't sign.

REFERENCES—PLAYING GAMES, LEARNING GENDER

BARNETT, N.D., with M. DiSabato. (2000). Training camp: Lessons in masculinity. In J. Gold, and S. Villari. *Just sex.* Lanham, MD: Rowman and Littlefield.

BENJAMIN, J. (1988). *The bonds of love: Psychoanalysis, feminism, and the problem of domination.* New York: Pantheon.

BIRRELL, S. (1987). The woman athlete's college experience: Knowns and unknowns. *Journal of Sport and Social Issues* 11: 82–96.

BRYSON, L. (1987). Sport and the maintenance of masculine hegemony. *Women's Studies International Forum* 10: 349–360.

CHODOROW, N. (1978). *The reproduction of mothering.* Berkeley: University of California Press.

CONNELL, R.W. (1987). *Gender and power.* Stanford, CA: Stanford University Press.

CONNELL, R.W. (1990). An iron man: The body and some contradictions of hegemonic masculinity. In M.A. Messner and D.F. Sabo, eds., *Sport, men and the gender order: Critical feminist perspectives.* Champaign, IL: Human Kinetics.

CRAIB, I. (1987). Masculinity and male dominance. *Sociology Review* 38: 721–43.

DAVIS, L. (1997). *The swimsuit issue and sport: Hegemonic masculinity in* Sports Illustrated. Albany: SUNY Press.

EITZEN, D.S. (1975). Athletics in the status system of male adolescents: A replication of Coleman's *The adolescent society. Adolescence* 10: 268–276.

GILLIGAN, C. (1982). *In a different voice: Psychological theory and women's development.* Cambridge: Harvard University Press.

GREENDORFER, S.L. (1977). The role of socializing agents in female sport involvement. *Research Q* 48: 304–310.

HALL, M.A. (1988). The discourse on gender and sport: From femininity to feminism. *Sociology of Sport Journal* 5: 330–340.

HANTOVER, J. (1978). The boy scouts and the validation of masculinity. *Journal of Social Issues* 34: 184–95.

HAUG, F. (1987). *Female sexualization.* London: Verso.

HUSSEY, M. (1991). Warwatching. *Central Park*, 19/20, 184–191.

KIDD, B. (1987). Sports and masculinity. In M. Kaufman, ed., *Beyond patriarchy: Essays by men on pleasure, power, and change*, pp. 250–265. Toronto: Oxford University Press.

KIDD, B. (1990). The men's cultural centre: sports and the dynamic of women's oppression/men's repression. In M.A. Messner and D.F. Sabo, eds., *Sport, men and the gender order: Critical feminist perspectives.* Champaign, IL: Human Kinetics.

KIMMEL, M.S. (1987). Men's response to feminism at the turn of the century. *Gender & Society* 1: 261–283.

KIMMEL, M.S. (1990). Baseball and the reconstitution of American masculinity: 1880–1920. In M.A. Messner and D.F. Sabo, eds., *Sport, men and the gender order: Critical feminist perspectives.* Champaign, IL: Human Kinetics.

KIVEL, P. (1999). *Boys will be men: Raising our sons for courage, caring and community.* Gabriola Island: New Society Publishers.

LEONARD, W.M. II and J.M. Reyman. (1988). The odds of attaining professional athletic status: Refining the computations. *Sociology of Sport Journal* 5: 162–169.

LEVER, J. (1976). Sex differences in the games children play. *Social Problems* 23: 478–487.

LEVINSON, D.J. et al. (1978). *The seasons of a man's life.* New York: Ballantine.

LICHTERMAN, P. (1986). Chodorow's psychoanalytic sociology: A project half-completed. *California Sociologist* 9: 147–166.

McBride, J. (1995). *War, battering and other sports.* Atlantic Highlands, NJ: Humanities Press International.

Messner, M. (1987). The meaning of success: The athletic experience and the development of male identity. In H. Brod, ed., *The making of masculinities: The new men's studies,* pp. 193–210. Boston: Allen and Unwin.

Messner, M. (1988). Sports and male domination: The female athlete as contested ideological terrain. *Sociology of Sport Journal* 5: 197–211.

Messner, M. (1989). Masculinities and athletic careers. *Gender & Society* 3: 71–88.

Oglesby, C.A., ed. (1978). *Women and sport: From myth to reality.* Philadelphia: Lea and Farber.

Osherson, S. (1986). *Finding our fathers: How a man's life is shaped by his relationship with his father.* New York: Fawcett Columbine.

Piaget, J.H. (1965). *The moral judgment of the child.* New York: Free Press.

Rubin, L.B. (1976). *Worlds of pain: Life in the working-class family.* New York: Basic Books.

Sabo, D. (1985). Sport, patriarchy and male identity: New questions about men and sport. *Arena Review* 9: 2.

Schafer, W.E. (1975). Sport and male sex role socialization. *Sport Sociology Bulletin* 4: 47–54.

Sennett, R., and J. Cobb. (1973). *The hidden injuries of class.* New York: Random House.

Theberge, N. (1981). A critique of critiques: Radical and feminist writings on sport. *Social Forces* 60: 2.

Thompson, M. (2000). *Speaking of boys: Answers to the most-asked questions about raising sons.* New York: Ballantine.

Thorne, B. (1986). Girls and boys together . . . but mostly apart: Gender arrangements in elementary school. In W.W. Hartup and Z. Rubin, eds., *Relationships and development,* pp. 167–184. Hillsdale, NJ: Lawrence Erlbaum.

Twin, S.L., ed. (1978). *Out of the bleachers: Writings on women and sport.* Old Westbury, NY: Feminist Press.

Husbands, Sons, and Fathers

Periodically, "crises of masculinity" have led western societies to worry that men are straying from their proper manhood. For the Victorians, the essences of masculinity and femininity were sharply divided. The English critic John Ruskin lectured in 1864 on the proper roles of men and women: "The man's power is active, progressive, defensive. He is eminently the doer, the creator, the discoverer, the defender. . . . The man, in his rough work in the open world, must encounter all peril and trial: . . . But he guards the woman from all this" (90–91). In the 1880s the fear of feminization focused on the influence of schools, where boys spent their days indoors being taught by women. The formation in 1910 of the Boy Scouts of America was one organized response to a perceived need for boys to experience outdoor life and regain the autonomy they had supposedly lost through the sedentary nature of modern, urban life (Hantover). Popular ideals of manhood received another severe blow in the trenches of World War I: Thousands of men succumbed to what was then termed "male hysteria" (later shell shock, and now post-traumatic stress disorder), causing panic in the military high command and leading to harsh treatments intended to shock the men back into their "proper" manly state of courage (McLaren 1997; Showalter 1985).

In the 1950s, *Playboy* magazine exhorted its readers "to resist marriage and 'enjoy the pleasures the female has to offer without becoming emotionally involved'" (Ehrenreich 47). The magazine's airbrushed nudes were there "to prove that a playboy didn't have to be a husband to be a man" (Ehrenreich 51). Post-World War II American men, too, were warned against the loss of that rugged autonomy that supposedly was the essence of masculinity. More recently, a similar lament for what anthropologist Lionel Tiger calls "the decline of males" has been heard. "The more I consider what men have lost," writes journalist Susan Faludi, "—a useful role in public life, a way of earning a decent and reliable living, appreciation in the home, respectful treatment in the culture—the more it seems that men of the late twentieth century are falling into a status oddly similar to that of women at mid-century" (Faludi 40). Faludi documents how frequently at the heart of contemporary movements that appeal to masses of men—Promise Keepers, the Million Man March, the "Wild Man" movement—is the figure of the "prodigal father" (Faludi 274), the man who was not there for his son.

This father is in many ways rooted in a caricature, however. Historian Thomas Laqueur believes that "we lack a history of fatherhood," in the sense that the story of fathers has been "subsumed under the history of a pervasive patriarchy" (205). The parodic figure of the domestic autocrat has dominated our cultural narratives, and, indeed, it can often seem that the entire western literary tradition is the endlessly repeated story of the struggle between father and son.

"Can a good father only ever feel he is an inadequate mother?" asks Naomi Segal. "Can our husband push a supermarket trolley in the morning and turn us on twelve hours later?" A last gasp defense of patriarchy, according to Allan Johnson, argues that rather than men being dominant, "motherhood makes women the most powerful and valued gender" (Johnson 181). It is easy, he continues, "for men to see themselves as outsiders to the mystery of life and reproduction" (182) if their sense of masculinity is centered on control. But notions of fatherhood are changing. Gordon Churchwell thinks that "Right now we're at a weird juncture in the history of the family" (284). "There is not the slightest doubt in my mind," he says, "that men who experience pregnancy and birth are marked permanently by a biological transformation" (283–284). The work of making gender visible, then, must include new stories about men as fathers, as husbands, as sons—stories that illuminate how these social categories produce masculinities, stories told from many different points of view.

Who Needs Men?

Harper's *Forum with Barbara Ehrenreich and Lionel Tiger.*

DE-GENDERED MAN?

HARRISON: Lionel, you mentioned that your male college students seem quite confused about what is expected of them. Is it that they don't want to fulfill traditional expectations or that they feel that they *can't* fulfill those expectations? In other words, does the idea of supporting a family terrify them?

TIGER: Young people are absolutely terrified about their futures. They're very, very concerned about earning a living. They're very aware of the profound competition in the job market, that companies are not keeping people forever. Personal economic stability is the first order of business. And now women are the majority in the universities, so the men are competing not only with one another, which they've always had to do, but now with women, and women generally do better.

EHRENREICH: So you cite that as another example of male decline, what we could call the feminizing of the university?

TIGER: I wouldn't use that word, "feminizing."

EHRENREICH: One of the reasons why fewer men are going to college may be because they suspect that they can make a living just as well without a college education; in other words, they still have such an advantage over women in the non-professional workforce that they don't require an education. I would explore that possibility before advertising the point that the relative decline of men in the student body represents male decline. It may represent male *advantage.*

TIGER: I can't treat that idea seriously, because, for example, we know from the black community that women go into the university far more than men. And it's not because black men are getting jobs as orthodontists; it's because they're not getting any jobs at all. They're not going into any higher education because they just feel doomed. So yours is a capricious analysis. Furthermore, let's assume that men are now staying out of the university and earning fortunes doing I don't know what, but let's assume that they are. When push comes to shove, ten years from now, it's the women who are going to get the good jobs because they've got the credentials. Those are the emergent outlines of our community. When I talk about the decline of males, I'm merely trying to point out something that's quite astonishing; if any of us had been told thirty years ago that men would now be the minority at universities and that universities would now be having affirmative action for *men*, we'd have been shocked. Even fifteen years ago, we wouldn't have believed it. Events have happened so rapidly that we've lost an analytical lever to try to understand them. That's all I'm trying to say. Paternity certainty is not the only thing that's involved. Nonetheless, in most cases, most men still do what they are supposed to do about their children, and they work their asses off for them. Some of them leave, as you yourself characterize, but it's now much more permissible to leave, not, please, just because of *Playboy* but because of some sense of equity: the idea that I do not have to provide money to another organism. Marriage is no longer a sacred ritual, legislated and denoted by God, but yet another contract. The rise of the prenuptial contract is merely a leading indicator of the prenuptial agreements emotionally, which are that we go into this relationship until severe irritation do us part.

EHRENREICH: You are romanticizing marriage in the past. Marriage, if anything, has become much more about romantic love than it was in past centuries, when it was a contract between two families, an economic relationship. You'll concede that—

TIGER: I don't want to concede that point. What I want to concede is that marriage has always been seen as a difficult phenomenon involving male and female sexuality that was likely to yield children. Therefore it required a composed preparation called the wedding, in which you bring the two families together, in some cultures actually exchanging money through the wedding feast and the wedding gifts. I agree totally that it has never been a romantic matter. The more romantic it's become, the less it's had to do with kinship and the more it's had to do with psychology.

EHRENREICH: I want to get at another level here. I want to explore your feelings about these things. You say the "decline" of males—there's a sad tone to that. I would feel sad, as a mother of a son, if males suddenly started "declining" in some serious way. Do you feel loss and regret and nostalgia? Why call it a decline? Why not say, Let's go boldly forth in this more egalitarian and somewhat de-gendered world?

TIGER: A more attractive picture to be sure, but not, however, I think, quite as accurate a rendition of the emotional consequences of what's happening. I'm not interested in characterizing my own personal psyche in this matter, solely because I think it's of zero interest to anyone. What is of interest is the fact that, as you suggested, young men and women are very concerned about these matters, one reason being that they no longer have a set of rules that they think are emotionally and morally worthwhile. Now, why should people have rules? If you study anthropology, you realize that human beings generally try to have rules, notions of how to behave. What we saw in the Clinton-Lewinsky business was some astonishing confusion between personal and public life.

EHRENREICH: You certainly got away from the issue of how *you* feel about it. See, *I'm* willing to say how I feel.

TIGER: I'm wholly uninterested in your feelings.

EHRENREICH: But I think it lends energy to what I say here, because I *do* feel strongly about this. A good deal of my adult life has been given to the struggle for gender equity. I don't want males to decline, I want females to rise up. I think you have some powerful nostalgia here, perhaps not only for patriarchy but for more hierarchical and feudalistic ways of life in general.

TIGER: I could not object more strongly to your characterization of me as moving toward patriarchy and—what was the other calumny? Feudalism?

EHRENREICH:z That's left open unless you—

TIGER: You don't leave it open. I don't think the intellectual is the personal. I think the personal is the personal and the intellectual is the intellectual. We shouldn't confuse psychodrama with analysis. And I happen to think, as a matter of formal principle, that one's personal position is not necessarily connected to one's intellectual position.

EHRENREICH: You come to this discussion of men and women, and you have no particular stake in the kind of world we're heading toward?

TIGER: I have a stake in getting the argument right. I have a stake in trying to ensure that when people live their lives they do so with a measure of information that is as uncorrupted as possible by sentiment, cant, and ideology. I have a personal stake that is anti-ideological, I will concede that. Ideology is a form of brain damage, and too much of the world makes easy judgments based on ideology rather than the harder work of going through each case on its merits. So to that extent, yes, I do have a personal position, but it's a functional position, not, I have to assure you, out of some nostalgia for the Montreal of the 1940s in which I grew up working in my father's economic colossus, Martin's Herring Store. This was presumably where I learned the elegant privilege of patriarchy. You must be joking. Be a little kinder to the messenger.

EHRENREICH: But there's a nostalgia to the phrase "the decline of males." I'm willing to be generous on this point and take you as just a neutral, nonideological, disembodied presence commenting on things very distant from you. But these things are not distant from me, or from a lot of people trying to figure out their lives. When is the decline of males going to get to the point when, say, the Senate is mostly women?

TIGER: Oh, I don't think it's going to, because women understand perfectly well that the best thing to do is to vote for the appropriate senators. Which is what they've figured out now to do in the last two elections, and they've done all through Europe too.

EHRENREICH: If men are declining so fast, why aren't there more women in the Senate?

TIGER: They should be if they want. I don't think it's necessarily a sign of progress to be in the Senate, given most of the people there.

EHRENREICH: How about CEOs? Women have made very little progress at the top of the corporate hierarchy.

TIGER: Again, that's a complicated question about who wants those jobs.

EHRENREICH: A lot of women do.

TIGER: Then they should try to get them. They're going to have as much trouble getting them as men do. Most men, virtually *all* men, don't get those jobs. Yes, there's a disproportionate number of men who have those jobs, because a disproportionate number of men have been in the system over the years. It will change. But not totally. A lot of women will simply not be prepared to do what men are prepared to do, which is essentially to deny themselves any inner private life in order to achieve this status.

EHRENREICH: Wait, wait. I hope you're not saying that the reason women aren't in those positions of power is that they just haven't tried. You're going to have trouble convincing a lot of women that men are on the decline when we haven't seen much of a change in the positions of power in the world. And so I would say, yeah, they may be declining, but not fast enough.

TIGER: Regarding the dramatic spots, the CEO positions, I agree. I don't think that's going to change very quickly. That will depend on people being willing to be unmarried, on women being unmarried.

EHRENREICH: Wait, why doesn't it depend on men being willing to be unmarried? We don't have celibate male CEOs.

TIGER: No, because they have wives.

EHRENREICH: So it would seem to me that men are still holding their own pretty well, that there's still quite a bit of advantage in being a man.

TIGER: I never said there was a disadvantage.

EHRENREICH: Well, I'm just pointing out that the decline hasn't been very dramatic.

TIGER: It hasn't been yet. But when I use the general term "males," I'm not so interested in the elite CEOs. I'm much more interested in the broad mass of the population and how people in general are living, much more interested in the one third of babies born to single mothers who, I think, get a raw deal at the outset—because there's no father. And that fact seems to me to be vital in any effort to look at the future.

HARRISON: Barbara, you mentioned your son. How do you think these changes affect him?

EHRENREICH: He's twenty-six and in a long-term relationship. He's not married. And the deal between him and his girlfriend is that when she's making more money she supports the two of them and when he's making more he supports the two of them. There doesn't seem to be any fuss about it. I think it'll be the same way if they have children, that they'll divide the child raising that way. I don't think he's unique to his generation in being pretty laid-back about the traditional male sex role. He's just not interested.

TIGER: I was once asked by a major magazine principally devoted to women to do a story about women married to men whom the women felt were not working hard enough. One man had gone off to Seattle to express himself, and another had decided to take up bookbinding. The men were doing just what they felt like doing. The women were *deeply* irritated. And I think one consequence of this kind of quest for non-traditional male identity is that a lot of women will say, I'm not going to even bother getting married.

HARRISON: But Lionel, how could women possibly complain about men simply expressing themselves, when, in fact, that freedom is what women have worked for so hard for thirty years?

TIGER: I remember that one woman came to our place for dinner—and she's got a very important job—and the first thing she said was, "I can't work this hard anymore." Now, she had a job of such envious status that most people would be thrilled with it. What she was saying was that she wanted her spouse to actually do more than what he was doing. And he was doing the best he could. But that was her response. When you look at what's going on in Japan, in Germany, in France, in England, at the marriage patterns, you see real changes. In Japan, for example, the women have decided they simply cannot bear these men who go off to work and come back drunk at night and expect them to have dinner ready and all of that. The women are simply not getting married. And if they are getting married they're not having any children, so the Japanese government has been trying to stimulate the birth rate, and in Singapore they actually pay people with high IQs to have babies. It's a kind of high comedy. But the women are realizing that they have to be able to do it themselves. So one reason that there are more women in college than men is that they're working for two, because they're going to have to support children.

HARRISON: Barbara, if your son has a child with this woman, in or out of wedlock, do you expect that he'll support that child?

EHRENREICH: Well, he'll do his best, yes.

HARRISON: Do you *expect* him to support that child?

EHRENREICH: Well, with his girlfriend, yes. I would expect them both to support that child. Who else? You want me to do it?

HARRISON: What if he didn't?

EHRENREICH: And he just goofed off? Well, I guess I'd have to take that baby in.

TIGER: You know what? You're now part of the emerging kinship system.

EHRENREICH: I'm part of a family. It's a family responsibility.

TIGER: That's right, which is what marriage always has been. Kinship responsibility.

EHRENREICH: Why, what are you getting at? Are you saying my son is a no-good, a deadbeat?

HARRISON: I am trying to find the point of conflict. Earlier you referred to men being freed from their roles. If your son decided to move to Seattle and put earrings in his ears and do something crazy—

EHRENREICH: He already has earrings.

HARRISON: Okay, what I mean is, what if he did not want to support the child? At what point do you say, Your freedom ends—

EHRENREICH: Of course I believe in responsibility to children when they come along, but I was trying to talk very sympathetically toward men who reject this kind of role. I'm not, however, sympathetic to deadbeat dads. Kids are an absolute, lifelong responsibility. Spouses, girlfriends come and go. A kid, that's who the contract should be with. And I would say all this to my son if he were to be so rotten. But he's actually one of the most responsible people on earth.

TIGER: Obviously he's had a decent mother in this matter, but the fact is, for a lot of young men, their mothers don't know what to tell them.

EHRENREICH: What about the women, though? Women have spent far more of their time raising children, having children, and if any sex has been radically displaced from its traditional work, it's women. My great-grandmothers had four, five, six pregnancies. A tremendous investment of a woman's life. *This* is what has changed. Now, in my generation, it might be two or three pregnancies. In my daughter's, it'll be one or two. So if any sex has been quickly tossed out of what apparently was its prehistorically ordained job, it's females. So please don't now toss us out of the colleges and better jobs.

TIGER: You obviously are not getting the tone of the argument, because women can still do what they've always done.

EHRENREICH: Which is?

TIGER: Which is if they want, they can have a child or two. They're not exempt from or kept out of the reproductive system, and that's what's happening with a third of the babies in the industrial world.

EHRENREICH: Men aren't either. I'm saying both sexes have been pushed out of older roles.

TIGER: Oh, no question about it.

EHRENREICH: Women certainly more so, and all the more radically so without welfare. Now you can't even say, Oh, I think I'm going to have a baby and let the government support it.

TIGER: But women still have the opportunity to experience a good part of the life cycle. I see the life cycle as something you really want to protect, in that you want to give every organism the opportunity to do as full a range of its endowed genetic capabilities as possible. In this sense I have a zookeeper's mentality. You want to create a societal zoo in which the conditions are as close to the evolutionary nature of the animals' conditions as you possibly can. Therefore I think that forcing people not to have children is wrong. I think it's morally wrong. It's biologically wrong also. And we evaluate zoos by how well the animals reproduce in them.

EHRENREICH: But there's no need for us to keep reproducing at a rapid clip. From the vantage point of economic elites, there's even a surplus of humans on earth.

TIGER: No, there's not a surplus.

EHRENREICH: But the population is high. You can't so easily convince the elite in some particular country that their businesses will come to a halt if they don't campaign to provide charity for starving babies. We have a trend away from social welfare, toward dismantling it, because there's no reason on the part of the elite to keep those little children alive. This is what's new, I would say, about the human situation. We have overfilled the earth, or at least filled it up pretty well. And some of the visions of family that you have, which I sense that you are nostalgic for, belong to a more sparsely populated earth, and are implicitly pro-natalist.

TIGER: The earth that we're talking about, the industrial earth, is becoming, in fact, more and more sparsely populated. The birth rates all through Europe and Russia are declining, and Italy will have about half its population in sixty years if the current birth rate stays as it is.

EHRENREICH: But the overall global population is expected to go up for several more decades.

TIGER: That's a conjectural issue, because then the basic political question becomes immigration.

EHRENREICH: Huh? My point is that biologically this is a new situation. Maybe there was a time when women had to stay at home or at the hearth, and produce baby after baby, and just fill up the earth. God said, Go forth and multiply, and we took that commandment very seriously, this species. That's been done. You could still argue against feminists in the nineteenth century and say, Well, if you want to have these jobs and do this and that, what's going to happen to the species? Now we can say, as women, Wait a minute, we did our work, we overstocked the earth with human beings. We can take a rest now. We can be gay if we want. We can be asexual. The change may be terrifying in some ways, but it's also wonderful.

TIGER: As I mentioned, in many of the European countries and eventually in the United States, absent Hispanic immigration, populations will begin to decline. It doesn't feel as if it ever will, but there is a declining birth rate in many of the European countries, and it's serious enough for governments to pay attention.

EHRENREICH: My point is that for the first time on earth, that's something to applaud.

TIGER: Yes, except that in terms of the life cycles of the men and women involved, it is a form of sentimentally enforced infertility. Look at fertility clinics now, which are among the most prosperous part of the medical industry because people have delayed having children. A community enjoys itself better if it engages in reproduction, simply because reproduction is so rich, such an important part of life.

EHRENREICH: Right, but it's no longer a necessity.

TIGER: I never said it was.

EHRENREICH: I know. I'm making a huge, sweeping biological point.

TIGER: I wouldn't dream of doing that.

EHRENREICH: (Laughing) Come *on*. I feel comfortable making huge sweeping biological points with you because you have done so much of it in your life—and very intriguingly. But the fact is that now women can live different ways. That is the biological turning point. The burden is not on every woman to keep her womb stuffed with the next baby.

TIGER: Then the question remains—and you're rephrasing the question that's implicit in our discussion—what the hell do the males do?

LEVITTOWN IN THE PALEOLITHIC ERA

EHRENREICH: You know, Lionel, it's funny to me that you haven't mentioned the crisis for males that took place about 12,000 years ago—just on the eve of the transition to agriculture, as hunting was ceasing to be a viable way of life, and largely, I would conjecture, because of depleted game stocks in the world. What men did at that point was pretty scary. They invented war. They found something for themselves to do. It was glorious, it flattered their egos, those of them that lived through it. Then there were those poor guys who had to make the much less glamorous adaptation to pushing a plow, to agriculture. I'm just saying you haven't mentioned the first big decline of males 12,000 years ago.

TIGER: It was a decline, but it involved a change. That crisis of movement from hunting and gathering to agriculture and pastoralism generated all our moral systems. The Lord is my Shepherd, the Buddhist ethic—all these are the ethics of small farmers and shepherds, part of an effort to deal with precisely the problem of what the hell do we do with the males. So we make up a religion, we tell them that they're going to have to do this on pain of hell. And if they happen to get involved sexually with someone and a baby is born, then they're married de facto, full stop, end of story. All the organized religions come out of that crisis of transition. Warfare, yes. Warfare happened, however, before, and it happens in the chimps.

EHRENREICH: The first evidence of war, as opposed to individual homicides, is from around 12,000 years ago, which is long after our evolutionary divergence from chimps.

TIGER: That's when the population started to get large enough.

EHRENREICH: Maybe. But I want to take this opportunity to take issue with the whole view of gender and evolution you have been associated with for decades: the "man the hunter" theory, in which the males are the hunters and the females just wait around for them to bring the meat home. I think my real anger at you, Lionel, is that—I have to say it—is that by creating this mythical view of our past—and I don't think you did it all that convincingly—you made it impossible for anybody to talk interestingly about prehistory for a long, long time.

TIGER: I did this?

EHRENREICH: Yep. I'm blaming you and a few other sociobiologists who said, here's how it was millions and hundreds of thousands and tens of thousands of years ago, this is what it was like in the gender sense, here is what the two sexes did. It turned a lot of women off from looking back at our evolutionary history. And it's not well founded, not at all. That whole "man the hunter" idea is a strange vision of human evolution. For one thing, it would make us the only predatory species in which only one sex hunted. Very odd.

TIGER: What about the chimps?

EHRENREICH: Female chimps hunt, too.

TIGER: But hardly at all. Occasionally and opportunistically, but they don't go out and—

EHRENREICH: But the male chimps don't either. They are not exactly a predatory species.

TIGER: But they do conduct warfare.

EHRENREICH: Not anywhere near as intelligently—or as often—as ants do. My point is that we are beginning to understand that hunting, until about 15,000 years ago, was probably a communal activity. It was not done by small bands of guys going off and leaving the gals back at the campsite. It was done by a whole community driving herd animals over a cliff, into a cul-de-sac, into a net (a net often made by women, we assume, but we don't really know). So, you, Lionel, gave us a very funny picture. You gave us a picture of evolution in which only one sex was really being acted on by natural selection, and that was the male sex. Because males were hunting, the male sex was naturally selected for intelligence, for the ability to cooperate with others, for everything.

TIGER: My central argument in *Men in Groups* was that hunting was cooperative among humans, who do cooperate to acquire food, unlike the other primates, who do not. In *Imperial Animal*, Fox and I asserted that it was biologically better to give than to receive. But the hunters were and largely are male. It was women who were selecting the hunters. That's how prestige in sexual selection goes. You're accusing me of having made an argument based on a relatively small database, which I concede, but I wasn't there, and neither were you; you don't know who was making nets, you don't know who was killing the animals. The genetic evidence we have shows that this hunting business went on for nearly the entire history of our species. At the time of Christ half the people were still hunting and gathering. Was there a difference between men and women and their hunting patterns? If a bunch of guys are going out hunting and you, the woman, are carrying a bowling ball in the hot tropical sun, namely a baby, are you going to go with them? No.

EHRENREICH: You're not following my distinction between the communal strategy of hunting and the stalking strategy of hunting. This is important, because the stalking of individual animals probably becomes more important only as the supply of animals begins to shrink—more recently than 15,000, 12,000 years ago—on the verge of the Neolithic revolution. All I'm saying is that "man the hunter" is basically an exciting macho fantasy of human evolution.

TIGER: It's a macho fantasy to hunt a pig? Those are your words.

EHRENREICH: Yeah, they're my words! Because *your* words really shut off any useful discussion of gender and human evolution. Because I share your respect for biology. I *do* believe there is a human nature. I do believe there are some things about us that we share that come from that long prehistory. I further believe that some of them are ill-served by, or contradicted by, the arrangements in which we now live. Not just men or women— I'm talking about all humans. For example, I think we're a sociable species. Sociality is central to us. You created the term "male

bonding." You threw us way off the track with that. It's not male bonding that's at issue, it's human sociality. It's a desire to bond with other people in generous, exciting, adventurous, convivial ways. We may not be set up to live in a socially isolated capitalist society. It would be important to talk about that. I personally resent the fact that I can't even open up the subject of human evolution with my feminist friends without wasting half an hour refuting you.

TIGER: Look, I'm either flattered or deeply depressed by the power I retroactively had in these matters. It comes as a great surprise to me. But let's assume that you're correct and that I had this negative impact, along with a few other chums. I'm certainly not alone in this malefaction. We were dealing with the comparative primate data such as they were, which show remarkable sex differences. When we do a genotype of humans and chimps, we're just like them, except for possibly as few as fifty genes—fifty genes out of a hundred thousand. So you cannot then tell me that this Paleolithic history is in the realm of nostalgia alone.

EHRENREICH: Of course, I'm not. I'm agreeing with you on that.

TIGER: Maybe some of us were a little intrepid in trying to specify these ideas rather early on, but then what was the alternative? To go on yammering about sex roles and gender and all of these contemporary sorts of things?

EHRENREICH: But you essentially made up a story. And what made it so suspect, even to those of us who didn't have a grip on the data, is that the picture you created of prehistory looks so much like Levittown in 1957. The guys went out in the morning and worked, the women stayed at home with the babies. That made it suspect to some of us right from the start.

TIGER: You may have been unduly constrained by Levittown, because if you also look at the hill towns of Italy 3,000 or 5,000 or 7,000 years ago, you'd find that the men would go out into the fields and the women would remain at the hearth.

EHRENREICH: What made it suspect is that it looked all too much like you were finding Paleolithic justifications for the hierarchy that existed in 1957.

TIGER: I'm sorry, Barbara, I don't think that's a strong argument. I can appreciate—

EHRENREICH: No, it's not a strong argument. It's just a reason for suspicion. I'm saying it would have been odd if people 25,000 years ago had sex role relationships very much like people in Levittown in 1957.

HARRISON: If that's true, Barbara, how would you redescribe 25,000 years ago? What were the differences between men and women then?

EHRENREICH: Well, we don't know how much difference there was. You'd have to be pretty foolish to extrapolate back to 25,000 years ago.

TIGER: Why?

EHRENREICH: Or you could be Lionel and do it. But I would not. I would say that there's reason to believe, as I already said, that the economy was based on communal hunting, which requires everybody in the group. You need the pack.

TIGER: Barbara, that's not what happens with contemporary hunter-gatherers.

EHRENREICH: Of course not. Contemporary hunter-gatherers live in a world that's been depleted of game. Today, you have to stalk individual animals.

TIGER: I understand—

EHRENREICH: It s my turn to explain all of pre-history, Lionel, you've *had* your turn. I'll give you a guess, a speculation. That era of communal hunting comes to an end when the game supply is diminishing globally—for whatever reasons, perhaps because of human hunting. Then humans change sometime, much closer to now than 25,000 years ago, maybe 15,000 years ago, 12,000 years ago, to the other hunting strategy, which is hunting by stalking. That requires quiet, and, no, you can't be carrying a baby. That's when hunting gets more specialized, with bands of men. That and the Neolithic revolution really transform the relationship between the sexes. For one thing, pro-natalism enters in with the Neolithic. You need those babies to be field hands. So I would say the downfall for both sexes may have come with that transition. We got locked into a mode of production that only became worse and more constraining with industrialization.

TIGER: Again, none of us was there. I'm not so displeased as you appear to be with retrodiction; that is, by looking at what happens now and describing what might have happened in the past. Or looking at a contemporary chimp and asking, What is the chimp likely to have been 50,000 years ago? I think there's some genuine continuity between those two figures—chimp then, chimp now. I think the same is true with humans. And if one looks at what men now do recreationally, they hunt and fish. Generally women do not. Some women do, but the overwhelming numbers of hunters and fisherpeople are men. They do sports. They pay attention to sports. They do the proto-aggression sort of thing that one would expect a captive chimp to do.

EHRENREICH: But whenever women have gotten a chance to hunt and fish, and when those things have been appealing, socially prestigious things to do, they have done it. And women are hunting and participating in sports more and more now. You're neglecting the increasing participation of women not only in sports but as sports fans. The number of women who watch the NFL is amazing. As restrictions have been lifted off women, we become boxers, we become—

HARRISON: Let me interrupt you right there. Boxing seems to be a useful compression of everything we're talking about, since it's combat. A woman friend recently said to me, "Women are boxers now. We should pay attention to this." And my response was that when the first woman kills another woman boxing, then I'll believe that women are boxers. Perhaps that is a prototypically male point of view.

EHRENREICH: Perhaps, but Lionel just said we can extrapolate back from what people do as hobbies to what they did in the Paleolithic. I'm saying that once you give women a chance, they do some amazing things. I would not have predicted, twenty years ago, that women would be so eager to get into combat in the military. Another little touchy subject we—

TIGER: They're still not, as a matter of fact, if you ask the ones who are actually in the military. It's fine if you ask all the theorists.

EHRENREICH: But women have been beating on the door, they want the military promotions.

TIGER: Who? Who? Who? Who? Who?

EHRENREICH: Female officers, for example. And remember that women are already allowed in combat in two branches of the service—the Navy and the Air Force. Anyway, my point is that as barriers have been removed from women's lives, things happen that even I, as a very feminist, liberated woman, would not have imagined. So if you're going to say, Well, in 1973 men liked sports and women liked needlepoint, and we can extrapolate back to 25,000 years ago from that, I'd say, no, no way.

TIGER: I'm not suggesting that these differences are so absolute you will never find a man doing anything a woman does and vice versa. That's simply not an acceptable argument. But just because you will find some women playing sports is not then necessarily to say that all of those differences that may have existed in the past are therefore theoretical.

EHRENREICH: Well, I'm just questioning your little methodology of going back from what people like to do now to what they were doing 25,000 years ago.

TIGER: What you call my "little methodology" has to do with an effort to understand the nature of the species from what it actu-

ally chooses to do. It seems to me that there is a kind of listening that one does, as you did in your report on working in restaurants ["Nickel-and-Dimed," January], that you can do only if you're not making judgments. What I'm talking about here is a species-wide ethnography based on a commitment to the notion that human beings are more or less all the same, that there are some differences between men and women that tend to recur. You will get a lot of women at bullfights, but you will get more men interested in *being* bullfighters. So to try to invalidate a broad argument about the nature of a reproductive species and its sex roles on the basis of who goes to NFL games doesn't seem to be an appropriate position.

EHRENREICH: Right, but to make any arguments on the basis of what people have been doing, according to their sex, for the last twenty, thirty, forty years, is also ridiculous. A woman couldn't *be* a woman bullfighter in 1940. In many parts of the country a woman couldn't walk down the street smoking a cigarette. Women have been so constrained in so many societies, and still are in many societies, that I would not want to extrapolate from their behavior in these sexist societies to whatever might be "natural" to us.

Why Can't a Good Man Be Sexy?
Why Can't a Sexy Man Be Good?

Naomi Segal

The paper that follows arose out of both personal and theoretical preoccupations. Given as the first talk in a well-publicized series with a challenging overall theme, its title drew an audience of a size that shocked even the organizers. More than a hundred people—most of them fresh-faced undergraduates—crowded into a room half the required size, hoping perhaps to hear the problem solved or see a Gordian knot sliced before their eyes. The paper, like the title, however, consists almost entirely of questions. It is written overtly from the position of a feminist mother, and it offers no advice. It does not pretend to debate anything but subjective problems, but it assumes that subjectivities coexisting in an institution bring objectively real and generally relevant problems into existence. These are questions of rights and boundaries but also of desire. Desire is what we do not control; goodwill and desire are perhaps, peculiarly and sadly, twins that sit incompatibly in the domestic nest.

Re-editing the paper a year after I first delivered it, I approach it with a certain sense of the uncanny—last year's news both distant and too familiar. The question on which the paper ended—where is the space where the two men can be one man?—may

be read as utopian or merely pessimistically rhetorical. I shall return, in some closing remarks, to my more recent thoughts on the subject. For now, I shall suggest that one cause for the split between the good and the sexy may simply be the natural invidiousness of habit: Living with anyone or anything leads to the familiarity that breeds if not contempt, at least inattention. Sexual desire must be attentive. The kind of attention it requires is both other-directed and narcissistic—and daily contact may blur both of these in a way that conscious effort could remedy. Yet how is it that our children continue to be beautiful in a way wholly other than sexual and which develops through trials and errors but without fading away? What is it about adults living together that can blunt the mutual gaze of two equals with good intentions? Are we simply the slaves of the history of our institutions or our psychology? Knowing what is wrong can be the crucial first step to change—or it can be recognition that only dissolution may allow something new to begin. Either way, the next step must be knowing what we want, and hoping they and we might want in the same ways. . . . .

The problem of feminism was and remains men. The problem I have in mind here is not that of men as oppressors but—the personal being as much political as ever—rather that of the men we love, and how we love them. (When I use the term "love" I do it in the full awareness of how old-fashioned it sounds—this need not detain us—and how complicated it is; but it is love that is at issue here, along with the apparently more simple problem of desire.)

Homosexual love is, of course, no easier to work out in this respect—in fact within feminism the moral debates that rage most urgently at present are those among lesbians about their modes of desire, fantasy and behaviour—and perhaps homosexual love is both clearer and more irresoluble as an issue. But the issue of desire for heterosexual feminists, and how to live that desire in love (and whether these two are necessarily, as the Romantics told us, mutually contradictory), is compounded by the problems of living in a conventionally endorsed institution. Whether actually married or cohabiting as parents, men and women who try to live feminism together seem driven up against a set of massive problems. Let's take marriage as our paradigm, for in it the institution is fully in place. However little we might change our names, when feminist women enter into that partnership that is supposed (and that we expect) to provide support of several kinds and a continued kind of loving, how do we reckon to make it consistent with our ideology? Can marriage take in equality? What do we mean by equality? Are there some aspects of our wifehood that we want intact, along with our outdoor freedoms? Do we, in any case, get enough of these freedoms not to resent the token man we choose to live with? And as for children—how can we, as strange as this may sound, combine heterosexuality with maternity? Can we combine motherhood with parenthood? Who is the father of our children?

My title is not just a good hook for audience or reader. It is, I think, the crucial issue now for men and women who are feminists. How are desire and work to be combined in the home? Can they be? If not, why can't they be?

More questions. Who *are* the men we call good? Who are the men we call sexy? Where do they come from? What parenting (what mothering) made them as they are—or as they seem to us, because of course the good and the sexy may only be in the eyes of the beholder, it may be the case that one woman's good man is another woman's sexy man, and if this is so, perhaps parenting has a less inexorable effect than the institutions we live in in adulthood. By "goodness"—another wonderfully old-fashioned term—I mean feminist goodness, what we sixties children call "right-on-ness," the political scruples we expect of men we choose to live with, something that may, common sense tells us, be more readily found in certain gay men than in heterosexual men—but *why*? Is there something wrong with heterosexual desire? Is there something wrong with the work-sharing institution we mean by marriage? Yes, of course, both. But what are we to do about it?

Is goodness incompatible with masculinity—and if it is, for whom? For us in our modes of desire? For men in their sense of self? Can a good father only ever feel he is an inadequate mother? We may laugh at his tussling with this, but if we do it is unkind and evasive laughter, evasive of something jealous in ourselves. Do we really want our children's father to take over those aspects of motherhood—sensuality and passion—that we most prize? (There are, of course, real dangers of a predatory incestuous interest if they do, something we feel easily innocent of, even though predatoriness and incest may both come in various forms.) If we don't want our men to get this close to our children, what kind of fatherhood are we leaving them? What kind of sensuality and passion are we leaving them?

What is the difference between being a wife (despised and painful term) and a mother? Is the husband of a feminist doomed to perceive himself between these two metaphorical poles? And there is more—for we all know how difficult it is to have a son. How are we to bring up our sons—how are their fathers to bring up our sons—in such a way that they can be both good and sexy?

The split in my title is shocking in part because, with a quick reverse of gender, we can see it as the mainstay of the patriarchal ideology: *maman* or *putain*, virgin (that is, desexualized mother) or whore, it is the crudest of political snares. For a feminist to propose a similar split, she has first to be clear that we are not, of course, in control of our desiring imaginations (this is the not-so-secret secret of any committed politics) and secondly to try and show that when this dichotomy is spoken from the point of view of the subordinated group it has quite new connotations. Or has it? Can we always rely on the virtue of the victim to get us by morally? Or are we oppressors in that place so long assigned to us and to which we, like all working people, inevitably return, the hearth and home? Or again, if we accuse ourselves, are we too succumbing to the temptation of seeing the mother as that force of nature that has too uncanny a power not to be, by very definition, destructive?[1] Why should the bad habit of mother-blaming stop, after all, when the mother is myself? To leave blame aside for the moment, let us try and divide these issues as my title divides them. First, desire.

Desire is never simply a private experience: feminist or not, we live in a relation to the socially constructed masculinity that has its base in men's relative public power. But I want here to look indoors and to suggest five elements in which I think a woman's heterosexual desire consists—some of these may be common to both sexes, others perhaps are not, and sexual experience is perhaps (thus far) the kind of information least easy to compare. What I shall not describe is anything about excitement or satisfaction: these are both too general and too particular to be relevant to my question.

The first element is something like aesthetic play—purposeless purposiveness: there is an aim but no end. The second is a recovery of childhood which consists in indulging the original polymorphous perversity, or whatever version of it you allow into adult consciousness: a special freedom in this regard that does not get experienced in other ways. It is what a woman friend of mine called being "dirty," but she meant a "dirtiness" that is more or less the same as innocence. It is access to one's own body via the other's body.

The third element is something to do with nurturance. In Proust, the protagonist finds in his lover Albertine's kiss (however hopelessly his passion is based on a dialectic of contempt and evasiveness) a restored copy of the mother's goodnight kiss—a mixture of ceremony and habit on which as a child his security depended. This is a physical form of sustenance which has echoes of breastfeeding, whichever sex receives it from which.

Now something political: There is, I think, a pleasure in having power over the powerful. Any virgin, however repressed, sees the powerful effect her choices have on the desire of the man. Something of this is, I think, at the base of the pride taken by conventional women in having a son—temporarily in possession of a dependent phallus (as we are in another sense in bed), these mothers indulge in a combination of pride and contempt for the imitation man. The sexual version of this may be fleeting or symbolic, unless a sadomasochistic explicitness both aestheticizes and literalizes the power structure, but I think it exists in one form or other in every heterosexual encounter—not necessarily oppressively—for it remains also play and innocence. Another way of understanding such power-play as benign is to read it through the fifth element, which is narcissism. If a man in bed recovers the mother in one way—aggressively, perhaps, if he has never accepted the pains of separation—the woman recovers her in another. The mother is first love-object, first toy and world to both sexes. The woman in bed watching herself watched (is this what they mean by passivity?) is worshipping at the shrine of the mother via her own body; she both has and is.[2] The only similar moment of plenitude (and I have no idea if there is some similar moment for men) that I know of—but this latter is, strikingly, an *intellectual* plenitude, a plenitude of knowledge experienced via the body—is in pregnancy.

The man with whom the woman experiences this range of pleasures is, for her, sexy. If I have described this combination of elements as an experience of femininity, then by corollary the perception of these five potentials in the person of the lover is an experience of the masculine.

If desire is risk—love being the possibility of the impossible, the impossible being found to exist, now (in psychoanalytic terms, the achievement of the object)—then there is something in that plenitude of being that we could call phallic. It might be objected that of my list of five elements, only one—the political one—suggests a male object. It could also be objected that in the fifth element, the plenitude of narcissism, no other of either sex is needed—but this would not be so, since the narcissistic experience has to do with being *other to an other* for which sexuality is a necessary element (it is not the same with one's children). This otherness is sexual in that it proceeds from/produces gender difference.[3] By contrast, a woman's unsexual relationships with other women tend to be structured as a subject–subject encounter. Talking together, women create a weave of

agreements. There is something more quarrelsome and differently self-conscious about heterosexual love, structured as it is both by the genderedness of desire and the social patterns of power. And by that very token, existentially if you like, the endorsement that comes from being desired by the other sex is uniquely risky and distinctively based on being his object. Heterosexual love can be (when it is what we wish it to be) a dangerously balanced endorsement via the position of object—object of his sentence, that is, not of his reification.

What then, if this need is a need of the masculine? Feminism exists to decenter the phallus as political instrument of magic—to argue for the danger and arbitrariness of that myth. Feminist marriage must decenter the power of the phallus in two crucial ways: in career equality and in equality of parenting. Both these equalities are based in the aim to make a home based on feminist values and "women's skills."

These two equalities are both practical and ideological: they appear in day-to-day choices (nights, rather, with breast or bottle, mornings waking to the radio-alarm not to lovemaking) but they represent our principles as they are embodied in economic reality. Here is the dilemma:

If we both want equal careers, where do we live? (And how rare any version of equality really is.) If one commutes—usually the man—the other is a single parent all week and at weekends they pass each other in the hall (this has been nicely termed a "telegamous partnership"). Or her career, conventionally, lags some paces behind. Then what is she to do with her rightful anger, reproached by others as "competitiveness"? If she lags behind, the phallus is in place all right in the household, as the fetish of power, even though it may embarrass them both.

As for equal parenting—suppose it is possible—do we reasonably define it by the dirtiness, the boringness and stressfulness of the work the father does? But if so, what about the fragrant bits—do we want to share those? Don't we insist after all (because this has something to do with our sexuality) on keeping for ourselves the passion between mother and child that begins at conception?

Feminist motherhood is woman-centered. How many of us have come to think we'd rather have women than men at the birth—not just holding the medical but the personal hand too? And not only because we have suspected they stop desiring us once they have seen this. Or how many of us have dreaded having sons because, as truly matrilinear women,[4] we carry our ideology as well as our desire in our wombs? What place is there in all this for a father?

In the mythology of patriarchal tradition, the mother is just the seedbed, the link in a chain that gives sons to fathers, passing on a name; the Oedipus complex, too, makes the "desire of the mother" a temporary, childish stage. But feminism looks back to nature to rediscover that males have a minuscule and brief part in reproduction. And if we need women as friends, children to give us value, work to prove our creativity, what need is left for men? Simply to help provide a home and to give us the seed so that we can make and keep our children? But coming to this point, perhaps we are unintentionally reproducing an old pattern after all: If we keep men out of the center of parenthood it may be because we fear *but thereby make easier* their ability to separate from the family, consecrating their inessential place in it.

The phallus we need to become pregnant by is not the phallus of desire. Just short of expendable, it makes us culture's praying mantises. This is the man from whom we require work, not love. But we want to love him too . . .

Where does this leave his desire—that essential element in ours, if we are to be turned on by his otherness? Is the whole process inevitably going to take away his pride, and if it does will shame emasculate? Will he, left with the service side, become our wife? If we want him to nurture, provide and protect, are we feminizing him? If we are (and consider this a compliment, as we consider it for our sons—who wants a masculine boy?), then perhaps he can only in any case fail: For if we want women, we have our friends, and if our children want mothers, they have us.

And who are these good men? Are they the husbands we want because their parents have raised them repressively, to suffer, feel obligation and by the feminizing structures of guilt efface their wishes for the sake of the family? Can there be another way? If we insist that there can be new ways of being a good mother, for us now, do we allow them other ways of being a good father as well? For if we don't, then our sons will not know how to do it at all.

(Let me not be misunderstood—I am not arguing for the sexiness of *bad* men. I am assuming that the women I am thinking of will not have allied themselves with crass or unthinking men. The sexiness I have outlined is anything but macho, just as the goodness is the goodness of simple reason, however rare these qualities may be to find.)

How are our sons to become good men by day and sexy men at night? Can our husband push a supermarket trolley in the morning and turn us on twelve hours later? Must work preclude play? Will we inevitably move ever closer to a version of the invidious split men have made among women, with two possible results: either that my good man is your sexy man and vice versa, a tragi-comic chain with everyone facing two ways; or else two types of maleness are being produced, one good and one sexy.

If this split is really happening, a possible cause is this: over the centuries men have divided women into two types, building up

Western culture on this unadmitted neurosis; now we have a little bit of power, very fragile and barely enjoyed, never self-justifying enough to go underground into psychosexual development—and with this insecure little bit of power we cannot (thank goodness) split the world but concentrate instead on our very small domestic/political patch.

Then we see the destructive result (and take the guilt on ourselves) in the husband who finds himself being a wife. We follow through the familiar logic that marriage is an institution which cannot support more than one whole person. If the man holds the reins (purse-strings, heartstrings) then sexuality is intact—someone is frustrated but no one is shamed. If it is the woman, if their time is her time, then something shocking is exposed, something neither men nor women can easily admit. The good man and the sexy man perhaps grow out of the two alternative structures—a depressing thought. If he wants to change from one mode to another, he will need to change beds. And then what happens?

Returning to the psychoanalytic angle, we might find another version of the cause. Let me propose that, rather than the phallus, the mother is the first whole object of desire. In the loving man of heterosexual desire (with whom we play, in whom we can see ourselves desirably reflected), do we find the mother who will exercise her power by lending us her phallus? Is our pleasure something to do with a moment of completeness thus entirely shared? But in that other man, the good husband, do we not take the phallus away to make our children, incorporating its virtue into a greater one? If so, we are refusing to let the plenitude be shared—no one may be mother but us.

Once again, can the man we choose for his genes also give pleasure? Can he continue to give pleasure? Can we be *la mère jouissante*? One reason why not might be that

we have discovered pregnancy, childbirth, lactation and nurturing to be the real buzz. But it isn't *jouissance* because it isn't becoming the child again ourselves. Where is the space where our body can be at once sexual and maternal? Where is the space where the two men can be one man?

I return to the image of the son. We want to be something other than a momentary and despicable Jocasta. Look at a three-year-old (male or female), affectionate without guilt and happy in its body without vanity. Yes, they are already gendered at three, but need they grow into the split men and women of my title?

A year later the questions remain.[5] Looking at my generation of feminist women, I note the frequency of separation and divorce, telegamous partnerships being those (ironically, predictably) in which the split is effected with least scarring: for the children especially, the new structure of separate parenting runs on smoothly from the old. Wise heads nod at the inevitability of dual-career partnerships falling into separation, considering that was how they always were; we read in the failure of our monogamy and the success of our autonomy something both burdensome and pleasant—would we really rather be alone *without* the child-care demands that fill evenings, coupled with the "free" weekends to catch up with everything else in a house where objects briefly stay where we put them? But we also reflect on the abandonment of a girlish hope that mature partnership might after all have been possible.

A few weeks ago I saw a film released from censorship after almost a decade: Nagisa Oshima's *Ai No Corrida* (*In the Realm of the Senses*) (1976). The intense and exclusive sexual passion of Kichi and Sada, which takes them indoors into an ever narrower private/artificial space heavily scented with their shared pleasure, ends in his slow strangulation by her followed by a careful castration that had most of the audience hiding their eyes. What was most seductive, and most unusual for a film portraying desire and violence in a heterosexual context, was the extent to which the man and his pleasure were the willing instrument of the woman's pleasure. As she strangles Kichi, Sada is co-opting his orgasm as her own (he, after all, dies as it happens); at the instant of his death, his phallus,[6] which hitherto she has borrowed in a mutual *jouissance,* becomes hers. We see the clothed body of Sada curved against the naked body of Kichi, he smiling peacefully, gashed red in the place where a woman is said to have "no sex," and carrying on his chest the avowal of their love that she has written with his blood, while the director's voice-over announces the historical facts: the original Sada wandered through Tokyo for four days with the severed genitals in her hands, "radiantly happy," and her case inspired a strange sympathy. Why is this woman happy with her lover's castrated remains? Why do the public and private systems of censure allow her both her passion and her gesture?

I recently spoke to a man who, after fifteen years of loving a woman at a distance, agreed enthusiastically to have a child with her saying he understood that, if he were to die, she wanted to have something (someone) that would keep the relationship incarnate. After changing his mind, he was appalled by her grief at the loss of that potential child, almost as if the now-broken promise was proved a mistake by the woman's transfer of bereavement from him to a child. Similarly, the logic of *Ai No Corrida* suggests that the woman cannot have both Kichi and his phallus; male-made and male-conceived, the film, of course, forms her wish out of his ambivalent wish, representing in his cheerful willingness a man's desire to be separated

whole from part, and in her violence his wish to remain undivided. The relation of man to penis is one of peculiar mutual dependence; thus Freud, in a revealingly casual metonymy, refers to a boy as "the small bearer of the penis" [*der kleine Penisträger*],[7] involuntarily evoking a kind of Obélix whose bearing is never done. What, in such a semi-joined pair, supports what, who depends on whom? If a man is (in his own phantasm, perhaps in ours) the metonym of a metonym, is castration not the logical desire and fear that motivates his relation to us?

If, at this drastic estimate, the lover is metonym to his metonym, servant to the phallus that may serve the woman better than himself, remaining finally in her body or her hands, are all men similarly dependent on, afraid of and *necessarily* separable from their children? Then, when they leave us, must they experience the shock of endorsing, in anger or gratitude, the proof of their voluntary redundancy now that they have left us with child? We know how nearly expendable the male is in sexual reproduction, how entirely redundant in the thousands of species that reproduce asexually, how, to rephrase Samuel Butler, a man is simply a woman's way of making another woman.[8] A male lion entering a pride consisting of females and young will clear the decks for the greatest reproduction of his genes by killing the cubs and causing abortion in any pregnant female. Unlike lions, human men can be deeply attached to their children, loving them in a passionate responsible way indistinguishable from the mother's way, except that they go and we stay.

Are there, finally, as Irigaray and Cixous suggest, two economies, one tendentiously tied to the masculine, the other to the feminine? The first, an economics of scarcity, reasons by either/or, by separation, competition and jealousy: it institutes the harem and *gynaeceum,* adultery as the normal mode of passion, the womb unable to hold both child and man at once, and culture as a great *trompe l'oeil* that imitates our reproduction, assigning it to nature, dividing us from other, conscious creativities and turning our blood magic into scarlet letters.[9] The second is an economics of plenty, a logic of both/and, passing beyond both Romanticism and Freudianism; by this latter reasoning, more demand produces more supply and there is, I should like to argue, nothing intrinsically feminine or even gendered in it (though indeed its contrary is clearly patriarchal). Its mode can be seen reflected in the two least bloody of secretions, breast-milk and semen, both of which are supplied more generously as demand increases in strength or frequency. But nowadays we are rightly fearful of mixing body fluids; by reason of death, our heterosexuality has lost its traditional tie to penetration, and the surface becomes the place where pleasure ought instead to be written. What I have spoken of in this paper is the question of an internal event (love, gestation, the doubly desiring womb, the moment of shared pleasure) turning into an external one (marriage, politics, the separable phallus, the once-born child). Intimacy is surely something to do with a penetration without violence, cutting off neither the inside nor the outside. Can the economics of plenty allow a combination, against the constraints of our bad old habits, of male and female, lovers and parents, good and sexy?

NOTES

1. See Dorothy Dinnerstein, *The Mermaid and the Minotaur* (published in the UK as *The Rocking of the Cradle and the Ruling of the World*), New York: Harper and Row, 1977; London: The Women's Press, 1978. The feminist literature on motherhood is massive and speedily increasing. Most influential, though very different, are, on the one hand, Dinnerstein and Nancy Chodorow, *The Reproduction of Mothering*, Berkeley: University of California Press, 1978; and on the other, the work of French theorists such as Julia Kristeva, Hélène Cixous and Luce Irigaray. For useful recent summaries of changing views on motherhood in the last thirty years of feminism, see Lynne Segal, *Is the Future Female?* London: Virago, 1987; Marianne Hirsch, *The Mother-Daughter Plot*, Bloomington: University of Indiana Press, 1989; and my own entry on "Motherhood" in ed. Elizabeth Wright *et al.*, *Psychoanalysis and Feminism: A Critical Dictionary*, Oxford: Blackwell 1992.

2. See Dinnerstein, Women's Press edition, pp. 61–63.

3. I use the term "gender" here to refer to a subject/object difference leaning on an axis of desire and power, whether or not the two subjects in the encounter (ideally a seesaw structure of balance and exchange) are sexed differently, male and female. Genet's male homosexuals are, in this sense, sharply distinguished by gender—even if such gendering may occasionally be reversible, his most muscular thugs carrying such delicious names as "Mignon-les-Petits-Pieds" and "Notre-Dame-des-Fleurs."

4. For a development of this term, see my *The Adulteress's Child*, Cambridge: Polity, 1992, especially the introduction.

5. The following remarks are borrowed from the Conclusion of *The Adulteress's Child*.

6. I am using the term "phallus" in this section with a shameless lack of reference to Lacan. What I have in mind is the already sufficiently phantasmatic organ attached to the body of a male lover making love.

7. Sigmund Freud, "The Dissolution of the Oedipus Complex" (1924), *The Pelican Freud Library*, vol. 7, Harmondsworth: Penguin; 1977, p. 321.

8. The original ("it has, I believe, been often remarked that a hen is only an egg's way of making another egg") is from Samuel Butler, *Life and Habit* (Trübner, London, 1878), p.134; it is quoted in Jeremy Cherfas and John Gribbin, *The Redundant Male*, London: Bodley Head, 1984, p.11. I am indebted to them also for the attractive formula: "Males are simply modified females tailored to a particular role in the reproductive process" (54). Their book is, however, a slide from an excitingly modest title to a grotesquely sociobiologized analysis: in the chapter where they finally speak of human women, one might think culture had never existed. For a more useful presentation of the facts and arguments from nature, see Sarah Blaffer Hrdy, *The Woman Who Never Evolved*, Cambridge, Mass.: Harvard University Press, 1981; and Irene Elia, *The Female Animal*, Oxford: Oxford University Press, 1985.

9. See ed. Thomas Buckley and Alma Gottlieb, *Blood Magic*, Berkeley: University of California Press, 1988, and especially the wonderful Chris Knight, "Menstrual Synchrony and the Australian Rainbow Snake," pp. 232–55.

A Father's Story

Andre Dubus

My name is Luke Ripley, and here is what I call my life: I own a stable of thirty horses, and I have young people who teach riding, and we board some horses too. This is in northeastern Massachusetts. I have a barn with an indoor ring, and outside I've got two fenced-in rings and a pasture that ends at a woods with trails. I call it my life because it looks like it is, and people I know call it that, but it's a life I can get away from when I hunt and fish, and some nights after dinner when I sit in the dark in the front room and listen to opera. The room faces the lawn and the road, a two-lane country road. When cars come around the curve northwest of the house, they light up the lawn for an instant, the leaves of the maple out by the road and the hemlock closer to the window. Then I'm alone again, or I'd appear to be if someone crept up to the house and looked through a window: a big-gutted grey-haired guy, drinking tea and smoking cigarettes, staring out at the dark woods across the road, listening to a grieving soprano.

My real life is the one nobody talks about anymore, except Father Paul LeBoeuf, another old buck. He has a decade on me: he's sixty-four, a big man, bald on top with grey at the sides; when he had hair, it was black. His face is ruddy, and he jokes about being a whiskey priest, though he's not. He gets outdoors as much as he can, goes for a long walk every morning, and hunts and fishes with me. But I can't get him on a horse anymore. Ten years ago I could badger him into a trail ride; I had to give him a western saddle, and he'd hold the pommel and bounce through the woods with me, and be sore for days. He's looking at seventy with eyes that are younger than many I've seen in people in their twenties. I do not remember ever feeling the way they seem to; but I was lucky, because even as a child I knew that life would try me, and I must be strong to endure, though in those early days I expected to be tortured and killed for my faith, like the saints I learned about in school.

Father Paul's family came down from Canada, and he grew up speaking more French than English, so he is different from the Irish priests who abound up here. I do not like to make general statements, or even to hold general beliefs, about people's blood, but the Irish do seem happiest when they're dealing with misfortune or guilt, either their own or somebody else's, and if you think you're not a victim of either one, you can count on certain Irish priests to try to change your mind. On Wednesday nights Father Paul comes to dinner. Often he comes on other nights too, and once, in the old days when we couldn't eat meat on Fridays, we bagged our first ducks of the season on a Friday, and as we drove home from the marsh, he said: For the purposes of Holy Mother Church, I believe a duck is more a creature of water than land, and is not rightly meat. Sometimes he teases me about never putting anything in his Sunday collection, which he would not know about if I hadn't told him years ago. I would like to believe I told him so we could have philosophical talk at dinner, but probably the truth is I suspected he knew, and I did not want him to think I so loved money that I would not even give his church a coin on Sunday. Certainly the ushers who pass the baskets know me as a miser.

I don't feel right about giving money for buildings, places. This starts with the Pope, and I cannot respect one of them till he sells his house and everything in it, and that church too, and uses the money to feed the poor. I have rarely, and maybe never, come across saintliness, but I feel certain it cannot exist in such a place. But I admit, also, that I know very little, and maybe the popes live on a different plane and are tried in ways I don't know about. Father Paul says his own church, St. John's, is hardly the Vatican. I like his church: it is made of wood, and has a simple altar and crucifix, and no padding on the kneelers. He does not have to lock its doors at night. Still it is a place. He could say Mass in my barn. I know this is stubborn, but I can find no mention by Christ of maintaining buildings, much less erecting them of stone or brick, and decorating them with pieces of metal and mineral and elements that people still fight over like barbarians. We had a Maltese woman taking riding lessons, she came over on the boat when she was ten, and once she told me how the nuns in Malta used to tell the little girls that if they wore jewelry, rings and bracelets and necklaces, in purgatory snakes would coil around their fingers and wrists and throats. I do not believe in frightening children or telling them lies, but if those nuns saved a few girls from devotion to things, maybe they were right. That Maltese woman laughed about it, but I noticed she wore only a watch, and that with a leather strap.

The money I give to the church goes in people's stomachs, and on their backs, down in New York City. I have no delusions about the worth of what I do, but I feel it's better to feed somebody than not. There's a priest in Times Square giving shelter to runaway kids, and some Franciscans who run a bread line; actually it's a morning line for coffee and a roll, and Father Paul calls it the continental breakfast for winos and bag ladies. He is curious about how much I am sending, and I know why: he guesses I send a lot, he has said probably more than tithing, and he is right; he wants to know how much because he believes I'm generous and good, and he is wrong about that; he has never had much money and does not know how easy it is to write a check when you have everything you will ever need, and the figures are mere numbers, and represent no sacrifice at all. Being a real Catholic is too hard; if I were one, I would do with my house and barn what I want the Pope to do with his. So I do not want to impress Father Paul, and when he asks me how much, I say I can't let my left hand know what my right is doing.

He came on Wednesday nights when Gloria and I were married, and the kids were young; Gloria was a very good cook (I assume she still is, but it is difficult to think of her in the present), and I liked sitting at the table with a friend who was also a priest. I was proud of my handsome and healthy children. This was long ago, and they were all very young and cheerful and often funny, and the three boys took care of their baby sister, and did not bully or tease her. Of course they did sometimes, with that excited cruelty children are prone to, but not enough so that it was part of her days. On the Wednesday after Gloria left with the kids and a U-Haul trailer, I was sitting on the front steps, it was summer, and I was watching cars go by on the road, when Father Paul drove around the curve and into the driveway. I was ashamed to see him because he is a priest and my family was gone, but I was re- lieved too. I went to the car to greet him. He got out smiling, with a bottle of wine, and shook my hand, then pulled me to him, gave me a quick hug, and said: "It's Wednesday, isn't it? Let's open some cans."

With arms about each other we walked to the house, and it was good to know he was doing his work but coming as a friend too, and I thought what good work he had. I have no calling. It is for me to keep horses.

In that other life, anyway. In my real one I go to bed early and sleep well and wake at four forty-five, for an hour of si- lence. I never want to get out of bed then, and every morning I know I can sleep for an- other four hours, and still not fail at any of my duties. But I get up, so have come to be- lieve my life can be seen in miniature in that struggle in the dark of morning. While mak- ing the bed and boiling water for coffee, I talk to God: I offer Him my day, every act of my body and spirit, my thoughts and moods, as a prayer of thanksgiving, and for Gloria and my children and my friends and two women I made love with after Gloria left. This morning offertory is a habit from my boyhood in a Catholic school; or then it was a habit, but as I kept it and grew older it be- came a ritual. Then I say the Lord's Prayer, trying not to recite it, and one morning it occurred to me that a prayer, whether re- cited or said with concentration, is always an act of faith.

I sit in the kitchen at the rear of the house and drink coffee and smoke and watch the sky growing light before sunrise, the trees of the woods near the barn taking shape, becoming single pines and elms and oaks and maples. Sometimes a rabbit comes out of the treeline, or is already sitting there, invisible till the light finds him. The birds are awake in the trees and feeding on the ground, and the little ones, the purple finches and titmice and chickadees, are at

the feeder I rigged outside the kitchen win- dow; it is too small for pigeons to get a pur- chase. I sit and give myself to coffee and tobacco, that get me brisk again, and I watch and listen. In the first year or so after I lost my family, I played the radio in the morn- ings. But I overcame that, and now I rarely play it at all. Once in the mail I received a questionnaire asking me to write down everything I watched on television during the week they had chosen. At the end of those seven days I wrote in *The Wizard of Oz* and returned it. That was in winter and was actually a busy week for my television, which normally sits out the cold months without once warming up. Had they sent the ques- tionnaire during baseball season, they would have found me at my set. People at the stables talk about shows and performers I have never heard of, but I cannot get inter- ested; when I am in the mood to watch tele- vision, I go to a movie or read a detective novel. There are always good detective nov- els to be found, and I like remembering them next morning with my coffee.

I also think of baseball and hunting and fishing, and of my children. It is not painful to think about them anymore, be- cause even if we had lived together, they would be gone now, grown into their own lives, except Jennifer. I think of death too, not sadly, or with fear, though something like excitement does run through me, some- thing more quickening than the coffee and tobacco. I suppose it is an intense interest, and an outright distrust: I never feel certain that I'll be here watching birds eating at to- morrow's daylight. Sometimes I try to think of other things, like the rabbit that is warm and breathing but not there till twilight. I feel on the brink of something about the life of the senses, but either am not equipped to go further or am not interested enough to concentrate. I have called all of this think- ing, but it is not, because it is unintentional;

what I'm really doing is feeling the day, in silence, and that is what Father Paul is doing too on his five-to-ten-mile walks.

When the hour ends I take an apple or carrot and I go to the stable and tack up a horse. We take good care of these horses, and no one rides them but students, instructors, and me, and nobody rides the horses we board unless an owner asks me to. The barn is dark and I turn on lights and take some deep breaths, smelling the hay and horses and their manure, both fresh and dried, a combined odor that you either like or you don't. I walk down the wide space of dirt between stalls, greeting the horses, joking with them about their quirks, and choose one for no reason at all other than the way it looks at me that morning. I get my old English saddle that has smoothed and darkened through the years, and go into the stall, talking to this beautiful creature who'll swerve out of a canter if a piece of paper blows in front of him, and if the barn catches fire and you manage to get him out he will, if he can get away from you, run back into the fire, to his stall. Like the smells that surround them, you either like them or you don't. I love them, so am spared having to try to explain why. I feed one the carrot or apple and tack up and lead him outside, where I mount, and we go down the driveway to the road and cross it and turn northwest and walk then trot then canter to St. John's.

A few cars are on the road, their drivers looking serious about going to work. It is always strange for me to see a woman dressed for work so early in the morning. You know how long it takes them, with the makeup and hair and clothes, and I think of them waking in the dark of winter or early light of other seasons, and dressing as they might for an evening's entertainment. Probably this strikes me because I grew up seeing my father put on those suits he never wore on weekends or his two weeks off, and so am accustomed to the men, but when I see these women I think something went wrong, to send all those dressed-up people out on the road when the dew hasn't dried yet. Maybe it's because I so dislike getting up early, but am also doing what I choose to do, while they have no choice. At heart I am lazy, yet I find such peace and delight in it that I believe it is a natural state, and in what looks like my laziest periods I am closest to my center. The ride to St. John's is fifteen minutes. The horses and I do it in all weather; the road is well plowed in winter, and there are only a few days a year when ice makes me drive the pickup. People always look at someone on horseback, and for a moment their faces change and many drivers and I wave to each other. Then at St. John's, Father Paul and five or six regulars and I celebrate the Mass.

Do not think of me as a spiritual man whose every thought during those twenty-five minutes is at one with the words of the Mass. Each morning I try, each morning I fail, and know that always I will be a creature who, looking at Father Paul and the altar, and uttering prayers, will be distracted by scrambled eggs, horses, the weather, and memories and daydreams that have nothing to do with the sacrament I am about to receive. I can receive, though: the Eucharist, and also, at Mass and at other times, moments and even minutes of contemplation. But I cannot achieve contemplation, as some can; and so, having to face and forgive my own failures, I have learned from them both the necessity and wonder of ritual. For ritual allows those who cannot will themselves out of the secular to perform the spiritual, as dancing allows the tongue-tied man a ceremony of love. And, while my mind dwells on breakfast, or Major or Duchess tethered under the church eave, there is, as I take the Host from Father Paul and place it on my tongue and return to the pew, a feeling that I am thankful I have not lost in the forty-eight years since my first Communion. At its center is excitement; spreading out from it is the peace of certainty. Or the certainty of peace. One night Father Paul and I talked about faith. It was long ago, and all I remember is him saying: Belief is believing in God; faith is believing that God believes in you. That is the excitement, and the peace; then the Mass is over, and I go into the sacristy and we have a cigarette and chat, the mystery ends, we are two men talking like any two men on a morning in America, about baseball, plane crashes, presidents, governors, murders, the sun, the clouds. Then I go to the horse and ride back to the life people see, the one in which I move and talk, and most days I enjoy it.

It is late summer now, the time between fishing and hunting, but a good time for baseball. It has been two weeks since Jennifer left, to drive home to Gloria's after her summer visit. She is the only one who still visits; the boys are married and have children, and sometimes fly up for a holiday, or I fly down or west to visit one of them. Jennifer is twenty, and I worry about her the way fathers worry about daughters but not sons. I want to know what she's up to, and at the same time I don't. She looks athletic, and she is: she swims and runs and of course rides. All my children do. When she comes for six weeks in summer, the house is loud with girls, friends of hers since childhood, and new ones. I am glad she kept the girl friends. They have been young company for me and, being with them, I have been able to gauge her growth between summers. On their riding days, I'd take them back to the house when their lessons were over and they had walked the horses and put them back in the stalls, and we'd have lemonade or Coke, and cookies if I had some, and talk until their parents came to drive them home. One year their breasts grew, so I wasn't startled when I saw Jennifer in July. Then they were driving cars to the stable, and beginning to look like young women, and I was passing out beer and ashtrays and they were talking about college.

When Jennifer was here in summer, they were at the house most days. I would say generally that as they got older they became quieter, and though I enjoyed both, I sometimes missed the giggles and shouts. The quiet voices, just low enough for me not to hear from wherever I was, rising and falling in proportion to my distance from them, frightened me. Not that I believed they were planning or recounting anything really wicked, but there was a female seriousness about them, and it was secretive, and of course I thought: love, sex. But it was more than that: it was womanhood they were entering, the deep forest of it, and no matter how many women and men too are saying these days that there is little difference between us, the truth is that men find their way into that forest only on clearly marked trails, while women move about in it like birds. So hearing Jennifer and her friends talking so quietly, yet intensely, I wanted very much to have a wife.

But not as much as in the old days, when Gloria had left but her presence was still in the house as strongly as if she had only gone to visit her folks for a week. There were no clothes or cosmetics, but potted plants endured my neglectful care as long as they could, and slowly died; I did not kill them on purpose, to exorcise the house of her, but I could not remember to water them. For weeks, because I did not use it much, the house was as neat as she had kept it, though dust layered the order she had made. The kitchen went first: I got the dishes in and out of the dishwasher and wiped the top of the stove, but did not return cooking spoons and pot holders to their hooks on the wall, and soon the burners and oven were caked with spillings, the refrigerator had more space and was spotted with juices. The living room and my bedroom went next; I did not go into the children's rooms except on bad nights when I went from room to room and looked and touched and smelled, so they did not lose their order until a year later when the kids came for six weeks. It was three months before I ate the last of the food Gloria had cooked and frozen: I remember it was a beef stew, and very good. By then I had four cookbooks, and was boasting a bit, and talking about recipes with the women at the stables, and looking forward to cooking for Father Paul. But I never looked forward to cooking at night only for myself, though I made myself do it; on some nights I gave in to my daily temptation, and took a newspaper or detective novel to a restaurant. By the end of the second year, though, I had stopped turning on the radio as soon as I woke in the morning, and was able to be silent and alone in the evening too, and then I enjoyed my dinners.

It is not hard to live through a day, if you can live through a moment. What creates despair is the imagination, which pretends there is a future, and insists on predicting millions of moments, thousands of days, and so drains you that you cannot live the moment at hand. That is what Father Paul told me in those first two years, on some of the bad nights when I believed I could not bear what I had to: the most painful loss was my children, then the loss of Gloria, whom I still loved despite or maybe because of our long periods of sadness that rendered us helpless, so neither of us could break out of it to give a hand to the other. Twelve years later I believe ritual would have healed us more quickly than the repetitious talks we had, perhaps even kept us healed. Marriages have lost that, and I wish I had known then what I know now, and we had

performed certain acts together every day, no matter how we felt, and perhaps then we could have subordinated feeling to action, for surely that is the essence of love. I know this from my distractions during Mass, and during everything else I do, so that my actions and feelings are seldom one. It does happen every day, but in proportion to everything else in a day, it is rare, like joy. The third most painful loss, which became second and sometimes first as months passed, was the knowledge that I could never marry again, and so dared not even keep company with a woman.

On some of the bad nights I was bitter about this with Father Paul, and I so pitied myself that I cried, or nearly did, speaking with damp eyes and breaking voice. I believe that celibacy is for him the same trial it is for me, not of the flesh, but the spirit: the heart longing to love. But the difference is he chose it, and did not wake one day to a life with thirty horses. In my anger I said I had done my service to love and chastity, and I told him of the actual physical and spiritual pain of practicing rhythm: nights of striking the mattress with a fist, two young animals lying side by side in heat, leaving the bed to pace, to smoke, to curse, and too passionate to question, for we were so angered and oppressed by our passion that we could see no further than our loins. So now I understand how people can be enslaved for generations before they throw down their tools or use them as weapons, the form of their slavery— the cotton fields, the shacks and puny cupboards and untended illnesses—absorbing their emotions and thoughts until finally they have little or none at all to direct with clarity and energy at the owners and legislators. And I told him of the trick of passion and its slaking: how during what we had to believe were safe periods, though all four children were conceived at those times, we were able with some coherence to question the tradition and reason and justice of the law against birth control, but not with enough conviction to soberly act against it, as though regular satisfaction in bed tempered our revolutionary as well as our erotic desires. Only when abstinence drove us hotly away from each other did we receive an urge so strong it lasted all the way to the drugstore and back; but always, after release, we threw away the remaining condoms; and after going through this a few times, we knew what would happen, and from then on we submitted to the calendar she so precisely marked on the bedroom wall. I told him that living two lives each month, one as celibates, one as lovers, made us tense and short-tempered, so we snapped at each other like dogs.

To have endured that, to have reached a time when we burned slowly and could gain from bed the comfort of lying down at night with one who loves you and whom you love, could for weeks on end go to bed tired and peacefully sleep after a kiss, a touch of the hands, and then to be thrown out of the marriage like a bundle from a moving freight car, was unjust, was intolerable, and I could not or would not muster the strength to endure it. But I did, a moment at a time, a day, a night, except twice, each time with a different woman and more than a year apart, and this was so long ago that I clearly see their faces in my memory, can hear the pitch of their voices, and the way they pronounced words, one with a Massachusetts accent, one midwestern, but I feel as though I only heard about them from someone else. Each rode at the stables and was with me for part of an evening; one was badly married, one divorced, so none of us was free. They did not understand this Catholic view, but they were understanding about my having it, and I remained friends with both of them until the married one left her husband and went to Boston, and the divorced one

moved to Maine. After both those evenings, those good women, I went to Mass early while Father Paul was still in the confessional, and received his absolution. I did not tell him who I was, but of course he knew, though I never saw it in his eyes. Now my longing for a wife comes only once in a while, like a cold: on some late afternoons when I am alone in the barn, then I lock up and walk to the house, daydreaming, then suddenly look at it and see it empty, as though for the first time, and all at once I'm weary and feel I do not have the energy to broil meat, and I think of driving to a restaurant, then shake my head and go on to the house, the refrigerator, the oven; and some mornings when I wake in the dark and listen to the silence and run my hand over the cold sheet beside me; and some days in summer when Jennifer is here.

Gloria left first me, then the Church, and that was the end of religion for the children, though on visits they went to Sunday Mass with me, and still do, out of a respect for my life that they manage to keep free of patronage. Jennifer is an agnostic, though I doubt she would call herself that, any more than she would call herself any other name that implied she had made a decision, a choice, about existence, death, and God. In truth she tends to pantheism, a good sign, I think; but not wanting to be a father who tells his children what they ought to believe, I do not say to her that Catholicism includes pantheism, like onions in a stew. Besides, I have no missionary instincts and do not believe everyone should or even could live with the Catholic faith. It is Jennifer's womanhood that renders me awkward. And womanhood now is frank, not like when Gloria was twenty and there were symbols: high heels and cosmetics and dresses, a cigarette, a cocktail. I am glad that women are free now of false modesty and all its attention paid the flesh; but, still, it is difficult to see so much of your daughter, to hear her talk as only men and bawdy women used to, and most of all to see in her face the deep and unabashed sensuality of women, with no tricks of the eyes and mouth to hide the pleasure she feels at having a strong young body. I am certain, with the way things are now, that she has very happily not been a virgin for years. That does not bother me. What bothers me is my certainty about it, just from watching her walk across a room or light a cigarette or pour milk on cereal.

She told me all of it, waking me that night when I had gone to sleep listening to the wind in the trees and against the house, a wind so strong that I had to shut all but the lee windows, and still the house cooled; told it to me in such detail and so clearly that now, when she has driven the car to Florida, I remember it all as though I had been a passenger in the front seat, or even at the wheel. It started with a movie, then beer and driving to the sea to look at the waves in the night and the wind, Jennifer and Betsy and Liz. They drank a beer on the beach and wanted to go in naked but were afraid they would drown in the high surf. They bought another six-pack at a grocery store in New Hampshire, and drove home. I can see it now, feel it: the three girls and the beer and the ride on country roads where pines curved in the wind and the big deciduous trees swayed and shook as if they might leap from the earth. They would have some windows partly open so they could feel the wind; Jennifer would be playing a cassette, the music stirring them, as it does the young, to memories of another time, other people and places in what is for them the past.

She took Betsy home, then Liz, and sang with her cassette as she left the town west of us and started home, a twenty-minute drive on the road that passes my house. They had each had four beers; but now there were twelve empty bottles in the bag on the floor at the passenger seat, and I keep focusing on their sound against each other when the car shifted speeds or changed directions. For I want to understand that one moment out of all her heart's time on earth, and whether her history had any bearing on it, or whether her heart was then isolated from all it had known, and the sound of those bottles urged it. She was just leaving the town, accelerating past a night club on the right, gaining speed to climb a long, gradual hill, then she went up it, singing, patting the beat on the steering wheel, the wind loud through her few inches of open window, blowing her hair as it did the high branches alongside the road, and she looked up at them and watched the top of the hill for someone drunk or heedless coming over it in part of her lane. She crested to an open black road, and there he was: a bulk, a blur, a thing running across her headlights, and she swerved left and her foot went for the brake and was stomping air above its pedal when she hit him, saw his legs and body in the air, flying out of her light, into the dark. Her brakes were screaming into the wind, bottles clinking in the fallen bag, and with the music and wind inside the car was his sound, already a memory but as real as an echo, that car-shuddering thump as though she had struck a tree. Her foot was back on the accelerator. Then she shifted gears and pushed it. She ejected the cassette and closed the window. She did not start to cry until she knocked on my bedroom door, then called: 'Dad?'

Her voice, her tears, broke through my dream and the wind I heard in my sleep, and I stepped into jeans and hurried to the door, thinking harm, rape, death. All were in her face, and I hugged her and pressed her cheek to my chest and smoothed her blown hair, then led her, weeping, to the kitchen and sat her at the table where still she could not speak, nor look at me; when she raised her face it fell forward again, as of its own weight, into her palms. I offered tea and she shook her head, so I offered beer twice, then she shook her head, so I offered whiskey and she nodded. I had some rye that Father Paul and I had not finished last hunting season, and I poured some over ice and set it in front of her and was putting away the ice but stopped and got another glass and poured one for myself too, and brought the ice and bottle to the table where she was trying to get one of her long menthols out of the pack, but her fingers jerked like severed snakes, and I took the pack and lit one for her and took one for myself. I watched her shudder with her first swallow of rye, and push hair back from her face, it is auburn and gleamed in the overhead light, and I remembered how beautiful she looked riding a sorrel; she was smoking fast, then the sobs in her throat stopped, and she looked at me and said it, the words coming out with smoke: 'I hit somebody. With the *car.*'

Then she was crying and I was on my feet, moving back and forth, looking down at her, asking *Who? Where? Where?* She was pointing at the wall over the stove, jabbing her fingers and cigarette at it, her other hand at her eyes, and twice in horror I actually looked at the wall. She finished the whiskey in a swallow and I stopped pacing and asking and poured another, and either the drink or the exhaustion of tears quieted her, even the dry sobs, and she told me; not as I tell it now, for that was later as again and again we relived it in the kitchen or living room, and, if in daylight, fled it on horseback out on the trails through the woods and, if at night, walked quietly around in the moonlit pasture, walked around and around it, sweating through our clothes. She told it in bursts, like she was a child again, running to me, injured from play. I put on boots and

a shirt and left her with the bottle and her streaked face and a cigarette twitching between her fingers, pushed the door open against the wind, and eased it shut. The wind squinted and watered my eyes as I leaned into it and went to the pickup.

When I passed St. John's I looked at it, and Father Paul's little white rectory in the rear, and wanted to stop, wished I could as I could if he were simply a friend who sold hardware or something. I had forgotten my watch but I always know the time within minutes, even when a sound or dream or my bladder wakes me in the night. It was nearly two; we had been in the kitchen about twenty minutes; she had hit him around one-fifteen. Or her. The road was empty and I drove between blowing trees; caught for an instant in my lights, they seemed to be in panic. I smoked and let hope play its tricks on me: it was neither man nor woman but an animal, a goat or calf or deer on the road; it was a man who had jumped away in time, the collision of metal and body glancing not direct, and he had limped home to nurse bruises and cuts. Then I threw the cigarette and hope both out the window and prayed that he was alive, while beneath that prayer, a reserve deeper in my heart, another one stirred: that if he were dead, they would not get Jennifer.

From our direction, east and a bit south, the road to that hill and the night club beyond it and finally the town is, for its last four or five miles, straight through farming country. When I reached that stretch I slowed the truck and opened my window for the fierce air; on both sides were scattered farmhouses and barns and sometimes a silo, looking not like shelters but like unsheltered things the wind would flatten. Corn bent toward the road from a field on my right, and always something blew in front of me: paper, leaves, dried weeds, branches. I slowed approaching the hill, and went up it in second, staring through my open window at the ditch on the left side of the road, its weeds alive, whipping, a mad dance with the trees above them. I went over the hill and down and, opposite the club, turned right onto a side street of houses, and parked there, in the leaping shadows of trees. I walked back across the road to the club's parking lot, the wind behind me, lifting me as I strode, and I could not hear my boots on pavement. I walked up the hill, on the shoulder, watching the branches above me, hearing their leaves and the creaking trunks and the wind. Then I was at the top, looking down the road and at the farms and fields; the night was clear, and I could see a long way; clouds scudded past the half-moon and stars, blown out to sea.

I started down, watching the tall grass under the trees to my right, glancing into the dark of the ditch, listening for cars behind me; but as soon as I cleared one tree, its sound was gone, its flapping leaves and rattling branches far behind me, as though the greatest distance I had at my back was a matter of feet, while ahead of me I could see a barn two miles off. Then I saw her skid marks: short, and going left and downhill, into the other lane. I stood at the ditch, its weeds blowing; across it were trees and their moving shadows, like the clouds. I stepped onto its slope, and it took me sliding on my feet, then rump, to the bottom, where I sat still, my body gathered to itself, lest a part of me should touch him. But there was only tall grass, and I stood, my shoulders reaching the sides of the ditch, and I walked uphill, wishing for the flashlight in the pickup, walking slowly, and down in the ditch I could hear my feet in the grass and on the earth, and kicking cans and bottles. At the top of the hill I turned and went down, watching the ground above the ditch on my right, praying my prayer from the truck again, the first one, the one I would admit,

that he was not dead, was in fact home, and began to hope again, memory telling me of lost pheasants and grouse I had shot, but they were small and the colors of their home, while a man was either there or not; and from that memory I left where I was and while walking in the ditch under the wind was in the deceit of imagination with Jennifer in the kitchen, telling her she had hit no one, or at least had not badly hurt anyone, when I realized he could be in the hospital now and I would have to think of a way to check there, something to say on the phone. I see now that, once hope returned, I should have been certain what it prepared me for: ahead of me, in high grass and the shadows of trees, I saw his shirt. Or that is all my mind would allow itself: a shirt, and I stood looking at it for the moments it took my mind to admit the arm and head and the dark length covered by pants. He lay face down, the arm I could see near his side, his head turned from me, on its cheek.

'Fella?' I said. I had meant to call, but it came out quiet and high, lost inches from my face in the wind. Then I said, 'Oh God,' and felt Him in the wind and the sky moving past the stars and moon and the fields around me, but only watching me as He might have watched Cain or Job, I did not know which, and I said it again, and wanted to sink to the earth and weep till I slept there in the weeds. I climbed, scrambling up the side of the ditch, pulling at clutched grass, gained the top on hands and knees, and went to him like that, panting, moving through the grass as high and higher than my face, crawling under that sky, making sounds too, like some animal, there being no words to let him know I was here with him now. He was long; that is the word that came to me, not tall. I kneeled beside him, my hands on my legs. His right arm was by his side, his left arm straight out from the shoulder, but turned, so his palm was open to the tree above us. His left cheek was cleanshaven, his eye closed, and there was no blood. I leaned forward to look at his open mouth and saw the blood on it, going down into the grass. I straightened and looked ahead at the wind blowing past me through grass and trees to a distant light, and I stared at the light, imagining someone awake out there, wanting someone to be, a gathering of old friends, or someone alone listening to music or painting a picture, then I figured it was a night light at a farm-yard whose house I couldn't see. *Going*, I thought. *Still going*. I leaned over again and looked at dripping blood.

So I had to touch his wrist, a thick one with a watch and expansion band that I pushed up his arm, thinking *he's left-handed*, my three fingers pressing his wrist, and all I felt was my tough fingertips on that smooth underside flesh and small bones, then relief, then certainty. But against my will, or only because of it, I still don't know, I touched his neck, ran my fingers down it as if petting, then pressed, and my hand sprang back as from fire. I lowered it again, held it there until it felt that faint beating that I could not believe. There was too much wind. Nothing could make a sound in it. A pulse could not be felt in it, nor could mere fingers in that wind feel the absolute silence of a dead man's artery. I was making sounds again; I grabbed his left arm and his waist, and pulled him toward me, and that side of him rose, turned, and I lowered him to his back, his face tilted up toward the tree that was groaning, the tree and I the only sounds in the wind. Turning my face from his, looking down the length of him at his sneakers, I placed my ear on his heart, and heard not that but something else, and I clamped a hand over my exposed ear, heard something liquid and alive, like when you pump a well and after a few strokes you hear air and water moving in the pipe, and I knew I must

raise his legs and cover him and run to a phone, while still I listened to his chest, thinking *raise with what? cover with what?* and amid the liquid sound I heard the heart, then lost it, and pressed my ear against bone, but his chest was quiet, and I did not know when the liquid had stopped, and do not know now when I heard air, a faint rush of it, and whether under my ear or at his mouth or whether I heard it at all. I straight-ened and looked at the light, dim and yel-low. Then I touched his throat, looking him full in the face. He was blond and young. He could have been sleeping in the shade of a tree, but for the smear of blood from his mouth to his hair, and the night sky, and the weeds blowing against his head, and the leaves shaking in the dark above us.

I stood. Then I kneeled again and prayed for his soul to join in peace and joy all the dead and living; and, doing so, con-fronted my first sin against him, not stop-ping for Father Paul, who could have given him the last rites, and immediately then my second one, or I saw then, my first, not call-ing an ambulance to meet me there, and I stood and turned into the wind, slid down the ditch and crawled out of it, and went up the hill and down it, across the road to the street of houses whose people I had left be-hind forever, so that I moved with stealth in the shadows to my truck.

When I came around the bend near my house, I saw the kitchen light at the rear. She sat as I had left her, the ashtray filled, and I looked at the bottle, felt her eyes on me, felt what she was seeing too: the dirt from my crawling. She had not drunk much of the rye. I poured some in my glass, with the water from melted ice, and sat down and swallowed some and looked at her and swal-lowed some more, and said: 'He's dead.'

She rubbed her eyes with the heels of her hands, rubbed the cheeks under them, but she was dry now.

'He was probably dead when he hit the ground. I mean, that's probably what killed—'

'Where was he?'

'Across the ditch, under a tree.'

'Was he—did you see his face?'

'No. Not really. I just felt. For life, pulse. I'm going out to the car.'

'What for? Oh.'

I finished the rye, and pushed back the chair, then she was standing too.

'I'll go with you.'

'There's no need.'

'I'll go.'

I took a flashlight from a drawer and pushed open the door and held it while she went out. We turned our faces from the wind. It was like on the hill, when I was walking, and the wind closed the distance behind me: after three or four steps I felt there was no house back there. She took my hand, as I was reaching for hers. In the garage we let go, and squeezed between the pickup and her little car, to the front of it, where we had more room, and we stepped back from the grill and I shone the light on the fender, the smashed headlight turned into it, the concave chrome staring to the right, at the garage wall.

'We ought to get the bottles,' I said.

She moved between the garage and the car, on the passenger side, and had room to open the door and lift the bag. I reached out, and she gave me the bag and backed up and shut the door and came around the car. We sidled to the doorway, and she put her arm around my waist and I hugged her shoulders.

'I thought you'd call the police,' she said.

We crossed the yard, faces bowed from the wind, her hair blowing away from her neck, and in the kitchen I put the bag of bottles in the garbage basket. She was working at the table: capping the rye and putting

it away, filling the ice tray, washing the glasses, emptying the ashtray, sponging the table.

'Try to sleep now,' I said.

She nodded at the sponge circling under her hand, gathering ashes. Then she dropped it in the sink and, looking me full in the face, as I had never seen her look, as perhaps she never had, being for so long a daughter on visits (or so it seemed to me and still does: that until then our eyes had never seriously met), she crossed to me from the sink and kissed my lips, then held me so tightly I lost balance, and would have stumbled forward had she not held me so hard.

I sat in the living room, the house darkened, and watched the maple and the hemlock. When I believed she was asleep I put on *La Boheme*, and kept it at the same volume as the wind so it would not wake her. Then I listened to *Madame Butterfly*, and in the third act had to rise quickly to lower the sound: the wind was gone. I looked at the still maple near the window, and thought of the wind leaving farms and towns and the coast, going out over the sea to die on the waves. I smoked and gazed out the window. The sky was darker, and at daybreak the rain came. I listened to *Tosca*, and at six-fifteen went to the kitchen where Jennifer's purse lay on the table, a leather shoulder purse crammed with the things of an adult woman, things she had begun accumulating only a few years back, and I nearly wept, thinking of what sandy foundations they were: driver's license, credit card, disposable lighter, cigarettes, checkbook, ballpoint pen, cash, cosmetics, comb, brush, Kleenex, these the rite of passage from childhood, and I took one of them—her keys—and went out, remembering a jacket and hat when the rain struck me, but I kept going to the car, and squeezed and lowered myself into it, pulled the seat belt over my shoulder and fastened it and backed out, turning in the drive, going forward into the road, toward St. John's and Father Paul.

Cars were on the road, the workers, and I did not worry about any of them noticing the fender and light. Only a horse distracted them from what they drove to. In front of St. John's is a parking lot; at its far side, past the church and at the edge of the lawn, is an old pine, taller than the steeple now. I shifted to third, left the road, and, aiming the right headlight at the tree, accelerated past the white blur of church, into the black trunk growing bigger till it was all I could see, then I rocked in that resonant thump she had heard, had felt, and when I turned off the ignition it was still in my ears, my blood, and I saw the boy flying in the wind. I lowered my forehead to the wheel. Father Paul opened the door, his face white in the rain.

'I'm all right.'

'What happened?'

'I don't know. I fainted.'

I got out and went around to the front of the car, looked at the smashed light, the crumpled and torn fender.

'Come to the house and lie down.'

'I'm all right.'

'When was your last physical?'

'I'm due for one. Let's get out of this rain.'

'You'd better lie down.'

'No. I want to receive.'

That was the time to say I want to confess, but I have not and will not. Though I could now, for Jennifer is in Florida, and weeks have passed, and perhaps now Father Paul would not feel that he must tell me to go to the police. And, for that very reason, to confess now would be unfair. It is a world of secrets, and now I have one from my best, in truth my only, friend. I have one from Jennifer too, but that is the nature of fatherhood.

Most of that day it rained, so it was only in early evening, when the sky cleared, with a setting sun, that two little boys, leaving their confinement for some play before dinner, found him. Jennifer and I got that on the local news, which we listened to every hour, meeting at the radio, standing with cigarettes, until the one at eight o'clock; when she stopped crying, we went out and walked on the wet grass, around the pasture, the last of sunlight still in the air and trees. His name was Patrick Mitchell, he was nineteen years old, was employed by CETA, lived at home with his parents and brother and sister. The paper next day said he had been at a friend's house and was walking home, and I thought of that light I had seen, then knew it was not for him; he lived on one of the streets behind the club. The paper did not say then, or in the next few days, anything to make Jennifer think he was alive while she was with me in the kitchen. Nor do I know if we—I—could have saved him.

In keeping her secret from her friends, Jennifer had to perform so often, as I did with Father Paul and at the stables, that I believe the acting, which took more of her than our daylight trail rides and our night walks in the pasture, was her healing. Her friends teased me about wrecking her car. When I carried her luggage out to the car on that last morning, we spoke only of the weather for her trip—the day was clear, with a dry cool breeze—and hugged and kissed, and I stood watching as she started the car and turned it around. But then she shifted to neutral and put on the parking brake and unclasped the belt, looking at me all the while, then she was coming to me, as she had that night in the kitchen, and I opened my arms.

I have said I talk with God in the mornings, as I start my day, and sometimes as I sit with coffee, looking at the birds, and the woods. Of course He has never spoken to me, but that is not something I require. Nor does He need to. I know Him, as I know the part of myself that knows Him; that felt Him watching from the wind and the night as I knelt over the dying boy. Lately I have taken to arguing with Him, as I can't with Father Paul, who, when he hears my monthly confession, has not heard and will not hear anything of failure to do all that one can to save an anonymous life, of injustice to a family in their grief, of deepening their pain at the chance and mystery of death by giving them nothing—no one—to hate. With Father Paul I feel lonely about this, but not with God. When I received the Eucharist while Jennifer's car sat twice-damaged, so redeemed, in the rain, I felt neither loneliness nor shame, but as though He were watching me; even from my tongue, intestines, blood, as I have watched my sons at times in their young lives when I was able to judge but without anger, and so keep silent while they, in the agony of their youth, decided how they must act; or found reasons, after their actions, for what they had done. Their reasons were never as good or as bad as their actions, but they needed to find them, to believe they were living by them, instead of the awful solitude of the heart.

I do not feel the peace I once did: not with God, nor the earth, or anyone on it. I have begun to prefer this state, to remember with fondness the other one as a period of peace I neither earned nor deserved. Now in the mornings while I watch purple finches driving larger titmice from the feeder, I say to Him: I would do it again. For when she knocked on my door, then called me, she woke what had flowed dormant in my blood since her birth, so that what rose from the bed was not a stable owner or a Catholic or any other Luke Ripley I had lived with for a long time, but the father of a girl.

And He says: I am a Father too.

Yes, I say, as You are a Son Whom this morning I will receive; unless You kill me on the way to church, then I trust You will receive me. And as a Son You made Your plea.

Yes, He says, but I would not lift the cup.

True, and I don't want You to lift it from me either. And if one of my sons had come to me that night, I would have phoned the police and told them to meet us with an ambulance at the top of the hill.

Why? Do you love them less?

I tell Him no, it is not that I love them less, but that I could bear the pain of watching and knowing my sons' pain, could bear it with pride as they took the whip and nails. But You never had a daughter and, if You had, You could not have borne her passion.

So, He says, you love her more than you love Me.

I love her more than I love truth.

Then you love in weakness, He says.

As You love me, I say, and I go with an apple or carrot out to the barn.

So I Guess You Know What I Told Him

Stephen Dobyns

FLOYD BEEFUS was picking a tick off one of the springers when the gas man slipped on a cracked dinner plate on the cellar stairs and went bump, bump, bump, right to the bottom. "Yow!" went the gas man. The springer jumped but Floyd kept gripping him tight between his knees until he had cracked the tick between his forefinger and thumb, then he limped slowly to the cellar door.

The gas man lay in a heap at the bottom. He was a well-fed-looking fellow in a green shirt, green pants, and a little green cap. He was moaning and rubbing his leg.

"You hurt yourself?" called Floyd Beefus.

The gas man stared up the stairs at him with a confused look, as if his eyes had gone loose in his head. He was about forty, maybe twenty years younger than Floyd himself. "I think I broke my leg. I need an ambulance. You got a phone?"

"Nope," said Floyd. "No phone." He limped back to the springer and let him into the pen in the backyard before he peed on the rug. The springer had picked up the tick when they had been out hunting pheasants that morning. Floyd had thought the frost would have killed the ticks. It was early September and Floyd had a small farm outside of Montville, about twenty miles from Belfast. As he put the springer into his pen, he glanced around at the maples just beginning to turn color under the bright blue sky. Soon it would be hunting season and Floyd might get himself a nice buck. Frieda would appreciate that if she was still with them. After a moment, he went back inside to check on the gas man.

"You want an aspirin or maybe a Coca-Cola?" he called. He understood that the gas man posed a problem but he wasn't yet sure how to deal with it.

"Jesus, I'm in pain. You got to call a doctor." The gas man had stretched himself out a little with his head on the bottom step. He had a thick, red face. Floyd Beefus thought the man looked excitable and it made Floyd suck his teeth.

"I already told you I don't have no phone." Floyd had had a phone but he lost track of the bill and the phone had been temporarily disconnected. Frieda used to take care of all that. Floyd Beefus lowered himself onto the top step and gazed down at the gas man. He guessed he'd have to step over him if he went into the basement to fetch any of his tools.

"Then use a neighbor's phone. This is an emergency!"

"The nearest neighbor's two miles," said Floyd. "That'd be Harriet Malcomb in the mobile unit. Course I just call it a trailer. I'd be surprised if she had a phone. She don't even have a car. If you'd done this a week ago, then you would have caught some summer people, but the last of them left on Tuesday: Mike Prescott, a lawyer from Boston. Sometimes he has parties. I'd hate to tell what goes on."

"You can use my car."

"I can't drive no more on account of the Dewey."

"Dewey?"

"DWI."

The gas man was staring at him in a way that Floyd Beefus thought bordered on the uncivil. "You sure you don't want that aspirin?" added Floyd. "Or maybe a pillow?"

"I can't just lie here," said the gas man, letting the whine grow in his voice. "I could be bleeding internally!"

Floyd scratched the back of his neck. He saw cobwebs on the stairs that would never have been allowed to settle before his wife got sick. "I don't like to leave Frieda. She's up in bed." He started to say more, then didn't.

"Jesus," said the gas man, "don't you see this is a crisis situation? I'm a supervisor. I can't just lie here in your cellar. I could die here."

"Oh, you won't die," said Floyd. He considered the gas man's excitability. "If you're a supervisor, how come you're reading my meter?"

"We're understaffed. You got to get a doctor!"

Floyd pulled his pocket watch out of the pocket of his dungarees and opened the lid. It was shortly past ten-thirty.

"The visiting nurse should be here in a while. She usually shows up a little after lunchtime. Billy, that's my son, he took the Ford down to Rockland this morning. He said he'd be back by late afternoon. Had to go to the pharmacy down there. I don't see why they don't sell the damn stuff in Belfast. You'd think bedsores'd be the same in both places."

"After lunchtime?" said the gas man.

"Around one, one-thirty. Loretta likes to stop for the blue plate special out at the Ten-Four Diner. And if they have blueberry pie, she generally takes a slice. She's a fat old thing. She'll fix you right up."

"That could be three hours," said the gas man.

"Just about. You want to think again about that aspirin?"

"It upsets my stomach. You have any Tylenol?"

"Nope," said Floyd. "Course Frieda's got some morphine. I could give you a shot if you like. I've become practiced at it."

The gas man had big blue eyes and Floyd found himself thinking: Googly eyes.

"Morphine?"

"The visiting nurse brings it. A month ago Frieda only needed two shots a day. Now she needs four. Loretta, that's the nurse, she said she's seen patients taking six and even eight shots before their time's up. You sure you don't want a little shot? Loretta will be giving us some more."

The gas man shut his eyes. "I don't take morphine. Perhaps you could get me a glass of water. And I'll have some aspirin after all. God, it'd be just my luck to start puking."

The aspirin was above the bathroom sink. Before getting it, Floyd looked in on Frieda. She was sleeping. Her gray hair was spread out on the pillow around her face. Floyd thought of the tumor in her stomach. It didn't sleep; it just got bigger. The bedroom was full of medicines and an oxygen tank. It had a sweet hospital smell. Floyd himself had been sleeping in the spare room for six weeks and he still couldn't get used to it. He got the aspirin, then went downstairs for the water. One of the springers was barking but he was just being conversational.

Floyd had to wash out a glass. Since Frieda had been sick, he and Billy had been doing the cooking and cleaning up but it didn't come easy. A pot on the stove was still crusted with spaghetti sauce from two nights earlier.

Floyd descended the cellar stairs, watching out for the stuff that was on the steps: newspapers and empty Ball jars. He sat down above the gas man and handed him the water and bottle of aspirin. "You married?" he asked.

The gas man pried the top off the bottle of aspirin. "I got a wife," he said.

"Kids?"

"Two."

"I been married forty years," said Floyd. "We done it right after Frieda finished high school. I didn't graduate myself. Didn't need it back then."

The gas man didn't say anything. He took two aspirin, then took two more. There was sweat on his forehead. Floyd thought his face looked unhealthy but maybe it was the pain. The gas man drank some water, then shut his eyes.

"You like your wife?" asked Floyd.

The gas man opened his eyes. "Sure, I mean, she's my wife."

"How'd you feel if you didn't have her anymore?"

"What do you mean?"

"Well, if she died or went away."

"She wouldn't do that. Go away, I mean." The gas man's voice had an impatient edge.

"But what if she died?"

"I guess I'd be surprised."

"Is that all? Just surprised?"

"Well, she's thirty-eight. There's nothing wrong with her." The man took off his green cap and pushed a hand through his hair. It was dark brown with some gray at the temples.

"A car could hit her," said Floyd. "She could be struck down when crossing the street. It happens all the time."

"She pays attention. She looks both ways."

"It could still happen."

The gas man thought a moment, then got angry. "Can't you see I don't want to talk! I hurt and you won't even get help!"

Floyd pursed his lips. He sat above the gas man and looked down on his bald spot. "I already explained about that." He thought how the gas man's bald spot would get bigger and bigger till it ate up his whole head. "You live around here?" he asked.

"I live in Augusta."

"They got a lot of dangerous streets in Augusta," said Floyd. "I seen them."

The gas man sighed.

"Wouldn't you mind if your wife was hit by a car?"

"Mind, of course I'd mind! Jesus, what are you saying?"

"I'm just trying to get the picture," said Floyd.

"We got two kids, like I say. They're both still in school. Who'd take care of them?"

"My two oldest are grown up," said Floyd. "A daughter in Boston and my older boy in Portland. But they'd be here in a minute if Frieda got took worse. You sleep with your wife?"

"Of course I sleep with my wife. What are you getting at?" The gas man turned his head but it was hard to see Floyd seated behind him. Floyd had his arms folded across his knees and was resting his chin on his wrist.

"Me and Frieda, we can't sleep together no more. At first without her there I could hardly sleep at all. The bed seemed hollow, like it was no more than an empty shoe. She'd move around a lot in the night and she'd cry. She's scared but she won't say anything. I would've stayed right there in the old double bed but the visiting nurse said it would be better if I moved. At first I sat up in a chair with her but I couldn't do that for too many nights. Sleeping in the spare room feels like I done something wrong."

The gas man didn't speak for a moment. Then he said, "Can you get me a pillow for my head?"

Floyd got a pillow upstairs from Billy's room. His knee hurt from walking around the fields that morning and he moved slowly. Frieda was still asleep. He stood a moment in the doorway and watched her breathe. After she exhaled there was a pause that seemed to stretch on and on. Then she would breathe again and Floyd would relax a little. Her skin was the color of old egg cartons. He took the pillow back down to the gas man, who was rubbing his leg below the knee.

"I can feel the bone pressing against the skin," said the gas man. "It's sure to be bleeding inside. I could lose my whole leg." He had pulled up the green pant leg and showed Floyd the red bump in his skin where the bone was pressing.

Floyd put the pillow behind the gas man's head. "I broke my leg falling off the tractor once. I lay in the field for two hours and no harm was done except for the pain. It's not like cancer. The body can take a lot."

"It hurts," said the gas man.

"That's just your body telling you there's something wrong. You want me to haul you upstairs and put you on the couch?"

The gas man considered that. When he thought, he moved his tongue around in his mouth. "I think I better stay right here until the rescue squad shows up."

Floyd wasn't sure he could get the gas man up the stairs in any case. "You pray?" he asked.

"I'm not much for church," said the gas man.

"Me neither, but there's a Bible around somewheres if you need it. Frieda likes to look at it. Right up to last March she'd never been took sick. Never complained, always kept us going with her jokes. You ever been unfaithful to your wife?"

The gas man's head jerked on his pillow. "Jesus, what kind of question is that?"

"I just wanted to know."

"My affairs are none of your business, absolutely none of your business."

Floyd settled himself more comfortably on the step. He was sorry that the gas man was so unforthcoming. "You know Belfast?"

"I been there."

"You know how it used to have those two chicken-processing plants? Penobscot Poultry and the other one. I forget its name. A guy named Mendelsohn run it. Every summer Belfast used to have a poultry festival with rides and activities in the city park. It used to be something special and high school bands would come from all over. And the Shriners, too."

The gas man didn't speak. He began rubbing his leg again. There was a bend in it that Floyd didn't think looked right.

"There was a woman who worked upstairs at Penobscot. She had a job putting the little piece of paper between the chicken parts and Styrofoam. Her name was Betsy. My, she liked to make trouble. She was never buttoned clear to the neck. About twelve years ago me and Frieda went to that poultry fair. The kids were young enough to still like it. I was drinking beer. That's always a mistake with me. After dark I got Betsy back on a tree stump. I was just unbuttoning myself when Frieda found me. Jesus, I already had Betsy's shorts off under her dancing skirt."

"Why are you telling me this?" The gas man stretched his neck to get a glimpse of Floyd.

"I was just thinking about it, that's all," said Floyd.

"Don't you see I don't care what you've done?"

"Then what do you want to talk about?" asked Floyd.

"I don't want to talk at all."

Floyd sat for a moment. The gas man had a fat gold wedding ring, then another ring with a blue stone on his right pinkie finger. He had shiny teeth and Floyd thought it was the kind of mouth that was used to eating a lot, the kind of mouth that enjoyed itself.

"How's your leg?" asked Floyd.

"It hurts."

"That aspirin help any?"

"It makes my stomach queasy."

"You sure you don't want a Coke?"

"I just want to get out of here. You got to take my car."

"The Dewey'd get me for sure," said Floyd, "and then there's Frieda. If she woke up, you couldn't do anything."

Floyd leaned back with his elbows on a step. The cellar was filled with evidence of forty years in this house: broken chairs, old bikes, tools, canning equipment, a dog bed for Bouncer, who had been dead fifteen years. The cellar had a musty smell. He wondered what he would do with this stuff when Frieda died. The thought of her death was like a pain in his body.

"You ever think," said Floyd, "that a bad thing happens to you because of some bad thing you've done?"

"What do you mean?" asked the gas man suspiciously.

"Well, that time I fell off the tractor and broke my leg was right after I'd been with Betsy at the poultry festival. Even when I fell I had the sense that something was giving me a shove. If I'd had two more seconds I'd've stuck it into her . . . "

"I don't want to hear about this," said the gas man.

"What I was wondering is maybe you've been doing something you shouldn't. You always play straight with your wife?"

"This is none of your business."

"You never felt temptation?"

"I only wanted to read your meter," said the gas man. "That's all, just your meter."

"You're a better man than I am. I felt temptation. I felt it every time I went into town. It wasn't that I don't love my wife. I was just exercising myself, so to speak. I'd go into Barbara's Lunch and just breathe heavily. Going into houses like you do, you must of felt temptation a whole lot."

"I don't want to talk about it. I'm a supervisor."

"But younger, when you were a plain gas man. Didn't some woman look at you and smile?"

"Why are you saying this?" asked the gas man. He spoke so forcefully that little drops of spit exploded from his lips. He tried to turn but couldn't quite see Floyd sitting behind him.

"You know," said Floyd, "after Frieda caught me behind the beer tent with Betsy McCollough, she'd look at me with such . . . disappointment. I don't mean right at the time. Then she was just angry. But later, at dinner or just walking across the room, she'd look up at me and I could see the wounding in her face. She still loved me and I loved her, too. It was eleven, almost twelve years later the cancer took hold of her, but I find myself thinking that my time with Betsy had opened the cancer to her. It made a little door for the cancer to enter."

The gas man had his face in his hands. He didn't say anything. The tips of his ears were all red.

"We were married right in Montville," said Floyd. "All our families were there, most of them dead now. We planned to be so happy. Even now, lying in bed, Frieda will look at me with that look of disappointment. Maybe that's too strong a word. She doesn't regret her marriage or regret having met me. It's like she thought I was a certain size and then she found out I was a little smaller. And I can never say she's wrong. I can't make myself bigger. When she was first sick, I used to make her dinners and bring her stuff and she appreciated it but it never made me as big a person as she used to think I was. And soon, you know, she'll be gone, and then I won't be able to explain anything or fix anything. All our time will be over."

The gas man didn't say anything.

"What d'you think about that?" asked Floyd.

"I just want a doctor," said the gas man.

"If you're so good," said Floyd, "then why won't you talk to me about it?"

"About what?"

"About what I done."

"Because I don't care," said the gas man. "Don't you understand it? I don't care."

"Fine gas man you are," said Floyd. He sat without speaking. He rubbed his knee and the gas man rubbed his leg.

"I don't mean to hurt your feelings," said the gas man.

"That's okay," said Floyd, "I'm not worth much."

"It's not what you're worth," said the gas man. "My leg's broken. I hurt. I'm preoccupied."

"You think I'm not preoccupied?" said Floyd. "My wife's dying upstairs and I can't do anything about it. I look in her face and I see the memories there. I see how I hurt her and how I said the wrong things and how I got angry and how I wasn't the man she hoped I'd be. I see that in her face and I see she's going to die with that. You think I'm not preoccupied?"

The gas man put his cap back on his head and pulled down the brim. "I don't know what to say. I come into this place. All I want is to read your meter. Why the hell can't you keep that stuff off the stairs? You think it's nice to be a gas man going into strange basements all the time? All I want is to get in and get out. Then I go home, eat dinner, watch some TV, and go to bed. Is

that too much to ask? Instead, I slip on a dinner plate and you say I must've deserved it. I must've been cheating on my wife. All I want is to get my leg fixed. I'm sorry your wife's dying. I can't do anything about it. I'm just a gas man."

Floyd leaned back and sighed. He heard one of the springers howling. Frieda had a buzzer that sounded off in the kitchen if she needed anything. Apart from the springer, the house was silent except for the gas man's heavy breathing. Floyd felt dissatisfied somehow, like finishing a big meal and still being hungry. He looked at his watch. It was almost eleven-thirty.

"Old Loretta should be reaching the Ten-Four Diner in another hour," he said. "My, she loves to eat. I've known her even to have two pieces of pie with ice cream. If they got blueberry and if they got rhubarb, then I bet she'll have both."

"What's the latest she's gotten here?"

"Three o'clock."

The gas man groaned "I hurt, I hurt a lot."

"There's still that morphine," said Floyd.

"No morphine," said the gas man.

"Anything else you want? Maybe a tuna fish sandwich?"

"You got any whiskey?"

"There might be some White Horse somewheres."

"Maybe a shot of that, maybe a double."

Floyd made his way back upstairs. He was sorry the gas man didn't want a tuna fish sandwich. He wanted to feed him, to have the gas man think well of him. Looking in on Frieda, he saw she had turned her head but that was all. She said the morphine gave her bright-colored dreams. She dreamt about being a kid or going to school or having children again. Rich, vigorous dreams and Floyd Beefus envied her for them. When he went to bed he was just grinding and grinding all night long like a tractor motor.

He poured the gas man half a glass of whiskey, then poured himself some as well. Floyd made his way back down the cellar stairs. He handed the gas man the bigger glass.

"Here you go," he said.

The gas man gripped it with both hands and took a drink, then he coughed. He had fingers like little sausages.

"You like being a supervisor?" asked Floyd.

"Sure."

"What do you like about it?"

"It commands respect."

"You ever fired anybody?"

"Well, sometimes you have to let somebody go."

"You feel bad about that?"

"I feel my duty is to the company and to the trust they put in me." The gas man took another drink.

Floyd couldn't imagine being a gas man or what it would be like going into people's houses. He had been a farmer all his life.

"You ever stole anything from them?"

The gas man cranked his head around. The whiskey had brought a little color to his nose. "Of course not!"

"Not even a ballpoint pen or a couple of paper clips?"

"They trust me."

"How long you worked for the company?"

"Almost twenty-three years."

"That's a big chunk of time. You must've done a lot of stuff for them."

"I've had a wide variety of experience." The gas man talked about the sort of things he had done: office work, fieldwork, repairing broken equipment. He finished his whiskey and Floyd gave him another. The gas man took two more aspirins. It was just after twelve o'clock.

"You won't change your mind about that sandwich?"

"I don't like tuna fish," said the gas man. "Maybe some toast with a little butter. Not too brown."

Floyd went back up to the kitchen. The bread had a little mold but he cut it off. He checked the toaster to make sure no mice had gotten electrocuted. Sometimes they crept inside and got caught like lobsters in a trap. Floyd wiped a plate off on his pant leg, then he buttered the toast using a clean knife. Through the kitchen window he saw four cows moseying in a line across the field. He and Billy had milked all thirty before sunup. Floyd took the toast back down to the gas man.

"How many houses can you go into in a single day as a gas man?" asked Floyd.

"Maybe sixty out in the country, double that in the city." He had his mouth full of toast and he wiped his lips with the back of his hand.

"And nothing strange ever happens?"

"In and out, that's all I want. Sometimes a dog gives you some trouble. I'm like a shadow in people's lives."

"And you've never felt temptation?"

The gas man drank some whiskey. "Absolutely never."

"No women give you the eye?"

"Their lives don't concern me. It's their meters I'm after." The gas man put the empty plate on the step. He was still chewing slowly, getting a few last crumbs, running his tongue along the gap between his teeth and his lower lip. "It's my duty not to get involved."

"But people must talk to you. A woman must give you a friendly look."

"Oh, it's there all right," said the gas man. "I could be bad if I wanted."

"You seen things."

"I seen a lot."

"It must be a burden sometimes."

"My duty's to the gas company, like I say. That's why they made me supervisor, because I make the right decisions, or try to. They appreciate my loyalty."

"What kind of things have you seen?" asked Floyd.

The gas man drank some more whiskey, then rested the glass on his thigh. "There was a woman in Augusta, a divorcée, who had it in mind to make trouble. I seen that."

"Good-looking?"

"A little thick, but good-looking. This was ten years ago."

"What'd she do?"

The gas man took off his cap again and wiped his brow. He set his cap carefully on the step beside him. "Well, the first time I went by her house she offered me a cup of coffee. I know that doesn't sound like much but it was just the beginning. She asked if I wanted a cup of coffee and if I wanted to sit down and rest a little. She was wearing a bathrobe, a cream-colored bathrobe. She had thick brown hair past her shoulders and it was nicely brushed."

"You take the coffee?"

"I always make a point of never taking anything."

"Then what happened?"

"A month later, I went by her house again. She was waiting for me. She followed me down to the basement when I went to read her meter. I turned around and she was standing right in front of me, still in her bathrobe, like she'd been wearing it for the entire month. I said howdy and she asked if I'd like to rest a little and I said I had to keep moving. Then she asked if I liked to dance and I said I didn't, that I hadn't danced since high school. So I walked around her and left."

"You think she wanted to dance right then?" asked Floyd. He liked dancing but he hadn't had much occasion in his life. When he was younger, there had been barn dances during the summer and sometimes he still recalled the smell of perfume and hay.

"I don't know if she wanted to dance," said the gas man. "I didn't think about it. I was in a hurry."

"She must have been lonely."

"A gas man doesn't socialize. It's like being a priest but you deal with meters instead. One time a man asked me for five dollars so he could feed his family. I didn't even answer him. I don't even like it when people ask me the time of day or what the weather is like outside. In and out, that's my motto."

"So what happened with the woman?" asked Floyd.

"So the third month I check her meter she doesn't follow me down to the basement. She was still wearing her robe and I thought she'd been drinking a little. She greeted me heartily, like I was an old friend. People have done that before trying to get around me. I just nodded. I go down in the basement and check her meter. When I start back up the basement stairs, she's standing at the top. She's taken off her bathrobe and she's wearing only this pink underwear, pink panties. Her titties are completely bare and she's pushing them up at me. Big, pink titties. She was blocking the door so I couldn't get through. 'Take me,' she says, like she thinks she's a cab or something."

"What did you do?" asked Floyd.

"I asked her to get out of my way, that I was in a hurry. She still didn't move. So I yelled at her. I told her I was a busy man and I didn't have time to waste. She took her hands away from her titties pretty quick, I can tell you. I said her behavior was awful and she should be ashamed."

"Then what happened?"

"She stepped aside and I left."

"And the next month?"

"The next month she was gone and the house was shut up. I didn't think much of it but a month later I asked one of her neighbors if she'd moved. I don't know why I asked but I kept thinking of her. Maybe it was because the woman seemed crazy. Anyway, the neighbor told me the woman was dead. One morning she just hadn't woken up. The neighbor said it was pills. She just took all the pills she could find. It was the neighbor who told me that the woman was a divorcée. She said the husband had gotten the kids and married someone else. I don't know when she died, just sometime during the month."

Floyd finished his whiskey. One of the springers was barking again. Floyd thought that no woman in his entire life had ever looked at him and said, "Take me," not even his wife. "You could have kept her alive," he said.

"What d'you mean?"

"You could have talked to her. She might still be around."

"She wanted sex. She was crazy."

"But you could have talked to her. She probably only wanted a little conversation."

"That's not my job. To me, she was only a person with a gas meter. In and out, like I say."

"What if you'd found her bleeding on the floor?"

"I would have called the cops."

"But the stuff she told you, it was like she was bleeding." Floyd regretted he had given the gas man any of his White Horse.

"It's not my job to deal with bleeding."

"You should've danced with her," said Floyd. "I would've danced with her. I would've danced till my feet fell off."

"We already know about you," said the gas man. "You and that woman behind the beer tent."

"You as good as killed her," said Floyd. He felt angry but knew that only a piece of his anger was connected to the gas man. The rest seemed a blanket over everything else. He didn't like the whole setup: people

coming into and going out of this life and none of it being by choice.

Floyd heard Frieda's buzzer and he got to his feet. He felt dizzy from the whiskey. He made his way upstairs holding on to the banister. The gas man kept saying something but Floyd didn't pay any mind.

Frieda's eyes were only half open. "I would like some more water." Her voice was very soft.

Floyd got the water from the kitchen and put in a couple of cubes of ice. When he handed it to Frieda, he said, "There's a real jerk in the basement."

"Tell him to go away."

"I can't. He's broken his leg."

Frieda nodded solemnly. The morphine and her approaching death made her more accepting of the world's peculiarities.

"Then give him something to eat."

"I already did."

"Then just bear with it," she said.

When Floyd looked back down the basement stairs, he saw the gas man was holding his head in his hands. "More aspirin?" He found it hard to be polite.

"Leave me alone."

"Any food? Maybe a blanket?" It was approaching one o'clock. Loretta could be arriving in as little as half an hour.

"I don't want anything from you," said the gas man.

Floyd was about to turn away and fix himself some lunch, then he changed his mind. "That's why you fell," he said. "Because of that woman who wanted to dance. That's the punishment you got, busting your dancing leg. Ten years ago, you said. That punishment's been coming after you for a long time, just creeping along waiting for its chance."

"Shut up!" said the gas man. "Shut up, shut up!"

Floyd told Billy about the gas man that night at dinner. Billy was a thin, heavily freckled youngster in his late teens who wore old dungarees and a gray University of Maine sweatshirt. His mother's illness was like an awful noise in his ears.

"So the rescue squad is carrying this fellow out of the house," said Floyd. "His hands were over his face but you could tell he was crying. I was standing there holding the dog. The guy sees me. 'Damn you,' he says, 'Goddamn you to hell!'"

"After you'd been taking care of him and fed him?" asked Billy. They were eating beans and franks.

"Some people have no sense of how to behave," said Floyd. "Some people would act bad even in front of St. Peter. 'Damn you,' he kept saying. Well, I wasn't going to take that in front of the rescue squad. A man can be provoked only so far."

"I can't believe you kept your trap shut," said Billy.

"I don't like being messed with." Floyd paused with his fork halfway to his mouth. "I guess you know what I told him."

"I bet you gave him the very devil."

"That's just the least of it," said Floyd.

REFERENCES—HUSBANDS, SONS, AND FATHERS

CHURCHWELL, G. (2000). *Expecting: One man's uncensored memoir of pregnancy.* New York: HarperCollins.

EHRENREICH, B. (1983). Playboy joins the battle of the sexes. In *The hearts of men.* New York: Doubleday.

FALUDI, S. (1999). *Stiffed: The betrayal of the American man.* New York: William Morrow.

HANTOVER, J. (1978). The Boy Scouts and the validation of masculinity. *Journal of Social Issues 34*(1): 184–195.

JOHNSON, A.G. (1997). *The gender knot: Unraveling our patriarchal legacy.* Philadelphia: Temple University Press.

LAQUEUR, T.W. (1990). The facts of fatherhood. In M. Hirsch and E. Fox Keller, eds., *Conflicts in feminism,* pp. 205–221. New York: Routledge.

MCLAREN, A. (1997). *The trials of masculinity: Policing sexual boundaries, 1870–1930.* Chicago: University of Chicago Press.

RUSKIN, John. (1886). *Sesame and lilies.* New York: John Wiley & Sons.

SHOWALTER, E. (1985). *The English malady: Women, madness, and English culture, 1830–1980.* New York: Pantheon.

TIGER, L. (1999). *The decline of males.* New York: Golden Books.

Working Lives, Gendered Institutions

Women have always worked, but men's sense of self has long been intimately tied to their work. Polls conducted in the 1970s and 1980s consistently found that both men and women defined the primary quality of masculinity as being able to provide for one's family. The very word "work" was itself for a long time gendered to exclude the work that went on in homes; the term "working mother" still does this (and who ever heard of a "working father"?). Work outside the home is gendered still: Roughly half the world's workers are in sex-stereotyped occupations, according to the International Labor Office (*Economist*).

In her groundbreaking book *Men and Women of the Corporation,* Rosabeth Moss Kanter argued that the emergence of corporations that replaced family-owned and -run businesses in the early twentieth century promoted a highly masculinized form of management. Lee Chalmers has drawn on the work of Kanter and others to explain that "management has been reproduced as a male activity not only through the process of males recruiting males but also through the recruits becoming attached to, and disciplined by, the sense of identity and purpose derived from committing to the practices and definitions of organisational reality offered by, for example, the managerial discourse of rationality" (47). Rational, dispassionate decision making has been the valued style for the workplace, in contrast to stereotypical notions about women's inherent emotionality. It is a style that can be deadly, as James Messerschmidt demonstrates in his discussion of the *Challenger* explosion in this section.

Cultural notions about masculinity and femininity often lag behind the realities of people's daily lives, and gender is still frequently institutionalized in the workplace in ways that maintain masculinities our public discourse about work claims to have left behind. To judge from recent reports from the workplace, gender confusion reigns. Men, according to one commentator, now recognize that "it is smart office politics to be seen as a sensitive family man" (Dowd 1998), but for women to succeed in business, they must now "ditch the hardball styles of the 1980s of being assertive and standing firm" and be "ladies first" (Banerjee 2001). The gendered nature of many occupations can be both an advantage and a disadvantage for men, as Jim Allan and Christine L. Williams discuss in this section. For Scott Russell Sanders, the work men do with their hands must be distinguished from work that allows men to preserve their bodies from the predations of labor. His essay eloquently implies the pitfalls of any generalizations about men and work, and brings into the foreground the axis of class that must also always inflect any discussion of gender.

Advantages and Disadvantages of "Being a Man"

Jim Allan

The fact that men are especially underrepresented in the elementary sector of the teaching profession offers them both advantages and disadvantages related to their gender. In this chapter, I focus on the importance of gender in hiring decisions. Many of those I interviewed perceived that men received preferential treatment in hiring. Some remembered job interviews in which principals told them outright they were particularly interested in hiring men.

> When I went to college, I heard that superintendents wanted and needed male elementary teachers. Talking to principals, they told me they needed more male teachers in elementary schools. (Ross, sixth-grade science teacher)

> Going into the interview for elementary education, I was more sure of myself, from all the people telling me that you're . . . you have a good shot at getting this job because you're a man. . . . I was more confident going into elementary teaching being a male. It's just what everybody's been telling you. (Curt, fourth-grade social studies teacher)

> I had an interview just this last spring in the Chicago area where that was, I think, one of the main aspects. The woman principal told me there were no males in the school

and they felt it was important to hire one. (Tom, 17-year veteran art teacher)

Three sets of reasons were offered to explain this apparent preference for men in elementary school teaching. Respondents claimed that men were preferred due to (a) their institution's commitment to affirmative action; (b) the desire of male principals for male companionship and support; and (c) the public's demand for male role models in the classroom. I will discuss each of these reasons, focusing on the contradictions they create for male elementary school teachers.

The first reason given for the preference for men was the institution's commitment to affirmative action or principles of "gender fairness." They compared their elementary school's initiative in hiring men to programs aimed at increasing women's participation in traditionally male occupations or to the hiring of racial or ethnic minorities. Some went further in suggesting that the purpose of affirmative action in hiring men was to *prove* something: to "show kids that a man can do this work." They implied that behind affirmative action was the objective of enlarging children's understandings of opportunities in the world of work, in addition to combating gender stereotypes.

As a second explanation for the apparent preference for men, some respondents suggested that elementary school principals—the majority of whom are men—seek gender alliances in otherwise all-female institutions by hiring other men as teachers. This is particularly the case when principals and male teachers share an interest in sports or a background in coaching. Men in this situation implied that a shared socialization in sports and male teamwork assures principals of male friends as well as male allies and assistants, whose loyalty, authority, assumptions, and tacit understandings they can count on. Duane, a sixth-grade math teacher and high school coach, in his 18th year of teaching, explained:

> Administrators are looking for male teachers. We had 200 applicants for three jobs in this district with only a handful of males. And those men were looked at a little bit longer in the interviewing process. My administrator told me that male teachers are easier to get along with, more receptive to administrative decisions, a little bit easier going, not liable to get as excited as easily . . . that's why he was looking. . . . Now that's not true in every case, I'm sure. . . . I think administrators feel some pressure from the public that they would like to see possibly more male influence. I think the public would like to see more men at all levels. . . . A lot of administrators are ex-coaches. They relate to men. There's a tendency to hire somebody that you can relate to. In my case, the day I interviewed, the principal was a coach at the time I was playing for a nearby college. The first half of the interview was spent discussing basketball in the sixties. You know there's kind of a bond there that develops.

Where a bond of common interest and experience existed, particularly in sports, men elementary teachers formed special relationships with male principals, often socializing together in the principal's office or the lounge as part of their daily routine. Thus, men teachers themselves perceived both affirmative action and stereotypically masculine interests male teachers shared with principals as giving some men an initial advantage in being hired.

However, this hiring preference for men was often accompanied by conflict with the female staff. Some men reported that women colleagues questioned the qualifications of men who appear to have been hired—whether through affirmative action or because of shared interests with principals—"just because they are men." The men felt challenged to prove to women the sincerity of their motivation, their aptitude for teaching, and sensitivity in human relations. Curt, the fourth-grade teacher who was also a high school coach, put it this way:

> I think sometimes female teachers will look at you, especially at first, and say, "Okay, let's see if you as a male can handle this." Especially me being a coach. And I don't know—they never said anything to me, but they kind of look at you like "are you going to be able to handle this situation?" . . . It's kind of a challenge to me. I want to show them that I can. I'm a competitive person.

Bill, a fifth-grade science teacher, one of two men working in a school with 20 women colleagues, saw a clear connection between his interest in athletics and "prejudgment" on the part of some women colleagues:

> When I started in elementary education I was the only male teacher, and my reactions were always looked at a little differently, and they were judging me, I think, a little differently because I was a man. They wanted to see how I would handle the young kids' emotions . . . or if I'd be too macho. You know, I've had contact with a number of prejudging teachers as I've entered the field as an elementary teacher. . . . People think the reason I'm doing the teaching is because I'm in athletics, and I think I've proven myself, at least in this school system, that my first priority is teaching. I *love* to teach.

Thus, the very reason for their advantage in hiring (their masculinity) raised suspicion and doubt on the part of some female teachers about the men's ability to do their job.

Some men recounted experiences that indicated to them women colleagues' opposition in principle to men teaching young children. Bill described such an encounter with a senior woman colleague at an end-of-the-school-year party:

> She finally just said, "You know, I do not believe in men in the elementary ed system. I truly just, I see no purpose for men in this part of the system." And I was offended at that point, and then she said, "But you've been able," she said, "I'm impressed. I've got to say you're an exception." Now, I was both pleased to hear that comment, complimented by it, but I was offended that she had stereotyped me, that she didn't feel men should be in that realm of teaching. She truly did not feel there was a place for men in elementary ed.

David, a fifth- and six-grade team teacher who at first had been the only male teacher in his building, recalled what he perceived as women colleagues' perplexity and suspicion:

> [What do they suspect you of? What do you have to prove to them?] You're not making enough money, for one thing. Men are "supposed" to make more money. You don't know how to interact with people. You don't have people's emotional needs up front as your consideration. You don't have enough rapport with parents—this, I think is often an attitude. You really don't have the people skills to be working at the elementary level . . . you aren't smart enough. [Okay. So these are things you feel you have to prove?] Yeah. If you're a male in the first place, some women view you not exactly as a threat, but as a fish out of water. "Why are you teaching in grade school?" This has been a female domain, and it really still is. And you're suspect just because of your maleness. Well, just the way females are suspect at the university level. Their femaleness is suspect. They aren't objective enough, or they're not intelligent enough

or something. . . . It's like being black in the white world. [Okay.] That sort of isolation that you are, you're not self-defined. You are defined by the environment and by the women in the environment.

Although women teachers do not control hiring, they have considerable influence on persistence. Since teaching on the elementary level requires a high degree of flexibility, collegiality, and cooperation, men who don't "prove themselves," or don't "get along," don't get rehired.

> [Anything else that might make an unfortunate situation for beginning male teachers?] The ability to get along with the other teachers, the women teachers. That's a big item. You've got to be able to work together. You've got to be willing to take your place and follow suit. (Mark, third-grade teacher)

> [Tell me about this man who was not rehired.] The biggest thing was not getting along with other staff members. He got off on the wrong foot with some . . . mainly women. They didn't like him; he didn't like them. . . . They let him go. (Curt, fourth-grade social studies teacher)

> [How do you avoid offending them (women teachers)? How important is that for a man?] If you are going to survive in grade school! Yeah, nobody ever talks about that. I don't think, from what I've ever heard, that anyone acknowledges to undergrads in ed school that this sort of thing exists. . . . But it's absolutely essential. . . . Your edges get ground off if you're going to survive. (Steve, a fifth-grade teacher, one of two men working in a building with 26 women colleagues)

Thus two advantages men perceived in getting hired—affirmative action and interests shared with principals—were accompanied by initial disadvantages in establishing the trust and cooperation of women colleagues, which men saw as essential to success. Men are placed in a double bind: While their presumed "masculine" interests in sports and male bonding may have given them initial hiring advantages, these same characteristics can alienate men from their female colleagues.

However, not all the men interviewed experienced preference in hiring or close bonding with their male principals once on the job. Some encountered ambivalence and conflict, especially if they asserted professional autonomy or questioned school procedures. Mark, a 41-year-old teacher with 15 years of experience in elementary schools, discussed his experience with "patronizing principals":

> Generally the principals I have worked with, well, they all have been male except one. The women didn't really do this sort of behavior, but I think some men who become principals get into it because they want the authority and the power and the privilege of dominating other people. . . . It's more of a power issue. So what I've seen go on is the "rooster in the hen house" sort of thing, where you have the one special male and a collection of women. And even if the teachers are men, they are treated like women. . . . [Have you had other experiences that would add to my understanding of this?] Right. Whenever I question this principal, or I'm thinking of another male principal, at a staff meeting, there would never be agreement. Whatever I would say would be viewed as a disagreement or a threat. Whereas a woman could get away with it. With some of the principals there is never the freedom to question their judgment in public. . . . [Do you think other men also perceive this about principals as "rooster in the hen house"?] Definitely! Absolutely. I don't know how they would word it, but they would work around to it. . . .
> [What is the principal thinking if he finds men a threat to his authority, but he

is hiring them?] Well, I think it's the same way that you hire blacks. You don't have a choice. You have to hire them because of affirmative action or it's just a politically correct thing to do. You can't avoid it. You just have to do it.
> [What kind of a man would your principal prefer to hire?] Someone who doesn't question his authority, even in private.

In the above example, female teachers are preferred because they are supposedly more docile and tractable than men. Male teachers can represent a threat to the authority of the male principal, especially if they ally themselves with their female colleagues. Stan, a fifth-grade teacher with 7 years of experience, after one year at a new school where he is the only male, concurred:

> On all-school policy issues . . . I think my principals expected teachers to just accept the announced policy and go along, don't expect teachers as a matter of course to engage in debate. I think it's very much my business and something I should have input on. This causes more conflict for me than some women teachers because they're more apt not to speak up, even though they too may disagree. . . . My women colleagues were intimidated, I think, and I was supposed to be too. There was a lot of discontent in the staff. But I was the only one to speak out. I spoke out as a professional, but I got a lot of resistance. Now I'm more apt to keep my mouth shut and just go along. Why fight it?

Thus, being male is a potential source of simultaneous advantage and disadvantage within the gendered structure of power in elementary schools. Men elementary teachers, in forming alliances either with male principals or female colleagues, present an implicit challenge to institutionalized relationships between men and women. Men perceived themselves surrounded by conflict in structures of authority and control. Gender alliances with male administrators were offset by challenges to men's legitimacy as teachers, posed by women, who, as a majority, defined work norms and to some extent controlled men's ability to succeed and continue. On the other hand, men's discovery of and resistance to "women's work," as low-status, rationalized, and "deskilled" labor, put them in conflict with other men who were administrators. Participants in this study revealed that *both* conflicts in the gendered structure of school authority and control were sources of frustration for them.

The third and most frequently given rationale men perceived as a hiring advantage in elementary teaching was the need for male role models for young children. Almost without exception, the men I interviewed sensed public perceptions of an important need for increased involvement of adult men in the lives of children, owing to the increasing number of single-parent families, or families in which fathers have limited interaction with their children.

> I don't know what it means to be a male role model as a teacher. I say I do it, but I don't know what it means. I guess I say I do it because I have so many parents who say I do it. [Let me see if I understand. They think they need you because there isn't a father at home, and they think you're going to do something that otherwise a father would do.] Right. [But you aren't really sure you're doing it?] Right. [But they're hiring you to do it and valuing you for doing it?] Right. Yes, absolutely. (Mark, third-grade teacher)

> [You sense that others, particularly parents and administrators, expect you to do something called male role modeling?] Yes. And I don't think that those parents or administrators have a clear view as to what they want. Their perceptions are, "We've had a tradi-

tional family pattern that looks like this. We don't have that any more, but we *should* still have it." . . . You see more and more studies, children born into single-parent families are much more likely to be poor. Are much more likely to have emotional problems. Much more likely to have discipline problems at school. A lot of these things. And I think this is the one thing a principal or whoever is hiring can have control over. "Well I can hire a man. I can't do much else. But perhaps hire a male and maybe that will magically help alleviate things." (Mike, a young, unmarried, "Talented and Gifted" teacher)

Thus, many men felt they were given a hiring preference because of the public's demands for more male role models, but were at a loss to identify exactly what this work consisted of.

This reason for the preferential treatment of men placed them in a very paradoxical position. For even as they were expected to be male role models, they were simultaneously stereotyped as feminine—because of the kind of work they do. A recurring theme among the men I interviewed was their awareness of public perceptions, shared in some cases by women colleagues at their level and by male colleagues at higher grade levels, that teaching children was not an occupation a competent "real man" would willingly choose. Steve, a fifth-grade teacher expressed this view:

> [I want to return to your comment that elementary teachers are perceived as being feminine. You believe that there is such a public perception?] Oh, there *is*. [There's no question in your mind about that.] Oh, no. I mean it's like saying George Bush is the President. [What does that mean, being more feminine?] When men do what women usually do, people think it's a sissy activity. [How does that perception affect you?] I think you just develop a thick-skinned attitude. What makes me angry is not so much this perception, as the low status and pay associated with work women typically do.

This public perception is a deterrent to men teaching in the lower school grades.

[How would it be different for you if you were teaching in first or third grade rather than in fifth?] It would be tough for me. Maybe that's where the stereotype comes in. It would be hard for me. I guess it's not that I couldn't relate to the kids. I've taught them in summer school. I know I *can* teach them. But I'd have a difficult time. [Why?] People look at a male first-grade teacher as being a little bit . . . *different*. You know what I mean. Family acquaintances might see this as strange. [So it would be difficult for you to work at that level?] Oh, yes. Very difficult. (Duane, veteran fifth-grade math teacher)

Females are the motherly type that can get down with little kids, but males seem like . . . some of the men don't want to admit that they can go down to that level. That's what I feel from some of the people in town. I don't know if it's ego or what. . . . Sometimes males have the feeling that they have to act like a male; it's society's expectation, and you have to be tougher and stronger— handle big kids and big discipline problems. I think some men might *want* to. I think there are male teachers who would want to. But they won't, because of the reactions they expect from other people. (Curt, fourth-grade social studies)

The men in my study used different strategies to negotiate this paradox. Some responded to the feminine stereotypes by defining their work as different from "what women do." Duane, the fifth-grade math teacher who also coached high school sports, noted that being a coach, because of the association of athletics with masculinity, helped men establish their legitimacy. But he sensed that for others, the feminine stereotype was problematic.

[Are there things that if a man is *not* a coach, but he wants to be a successful elementary teacher and get along, that he can do that give him the same kind of entry?] He had best not be the least bit feminine. I mean they expect a male teacher to be a man, whether he is a coach or not. If a man were perceived as feminine, I'm sure it would be a problem. [Why?] You need to be a male role model. Be the opposite of being feminine. Now that's pretty subjective. I guess I see it as a man who is willing to be involved in male-related activities. That is not to say that involvement in female-related activities is wrong . . . but sports, fishing, rather than cooking. I don't think it's wrong to do the cooking and things that are traditionally feminine, but yet the kids need foremost from you the male . . . the traditional male-type things need to be more preeminent.

But if a man emphasized masculinity *too* much, then he would undermine his legitimacy as a teacher. So, in addition to demonstrating stereotypical male attributes, men elementary teachers felt challenged to show sincere motivation in working with children, and sensitivity to children's limitations and needs.

[Do you detect any assumptions parents or others may have about you before they get to know you?] Well, maybe thinking a male is more of a disciplinarian. Maybe they might think that I'm meaner. Maybe they don't think I'm as sensitive. Maybe they think sometimes a man is not as sensitive as a woman. . . . Then you've got to prove to them that you're just as sensitive as the female. [Sensitive?] Yes. Like in "I care about kids' problems." (Curt)

Many men who successfully modeled what they perceived to be expected male attributes sensed fear, uncertainty, and intimidation in children, which they needed to work consciously to overcome. Yet, ways of demonstrating sensitivity that are "natural" and available to women are foreclosed for men.

At this age, kids hug more. They go up and hug their female teachers more. [Than they do the male teachers?] Yes. And I don't really mind that, because they tell us not to even show any affection, because nowadays people think a man is molesting kids if it happens. And . . . but it hurts. You see a little kid going up and hugging one of the women teachers and you're saying, "That'd be nice to get that hug," because it makes you feel better. Then they'll come up and they do surprise you and hug you and you feel better about it. (Ross, a beginning fourth-grade teacher)

It seems to me easier for a woman teacher to become involved in and comment on a child's emotional state, than it is for men. It's easier for a woman to be more supportive than it is for a male. [Are you saying that in dealing with children's emotional issues, men feel more constrained?] More constrained, *definitely*. Both can tell when a child is upset, but the male's range of appropriate responses is narrower. . . . An example is on the playground when a child is hurt. A male teacher in contact with a child . . . those gestures are always smaller. They convey just as much meaning, but they can't be on the same scale as a female's. (Mike, "Talented and Gifted" teacher)

Men felt they must overtly demonstrate care for children and sensitivity to their emotional needs. But behaviors, that are perceived as natural demonstrations of these qualities in women, are off-limits to men, who feel them as equally natural but as inviting suspicion of abuse. The vehemence with which men expressed this constraint was surprising. One participant recalled the indelible impression of his first awareness of this danger to men in elementary teaching.

I had a mentor in college, and he told me one time, I remember our conversation about my decision to change my major to elementary education. He cautioned me in a very serious manner about what devastation it could have on my career if this ever happened to me. [If what ever happened?] If there were any false charges against me in regard to sexual molestation or anything. And I had to be really careful of it, and that I needed to think of that. . . . I don't know why he told me this, but it had an incredible . . . I've never forgotten the conversation. And I have a policy. I never touch a girl unless it's on the top of the head. I never touch them. I never touch them anywhere. I never even hand them anything. . . . Boys, I don't have any rules about boys. . . . I don't have any concerns there, but the girls I do. I used to resent it, but now I just see it as a sort of fact of life— never let a girl stay after school alone. If I'm taking kids home, make sure I leave the boys off last. You know, just normal precautions. (David, fifth and sixth grade)

Several men were fearful about demonstrating caring or giving special attention to children.

[To what extent do you think men elementary teachers become aware that when they give extra attention, or whatever the child needs, that that can be misconstrued?] Oh, *definitely*. It's much easier for a woman to give a gift to a student and not have it misinterpreted. . . . I read about people losing jobs. I used to have kids sit on my lap, little kids. I don't touch anybody now, and I know this other man I work with is very much the same way. [So this has definitely constrained your practice.] Absolutely. It puts a real cramp on the teacher-student relationship. And women don't have to be afraid of that. [How do you feel about not being able to touch kids as a teacher?] I guess I haven't touched anybody for so long that I don't think about it anymore. But I had to consciously, oh, maybe 10 years ago, step back, very . . . very consciously stop doing certain things. [You never give a child a hug?] No. Especially not if I was a single man. (Terry, fourth-grade social studies teacher)

Young single men, whose time and energy are not shared with their own children, and who might therefore have more enthusiasm for as well as commitment to children at work are particularly suspect.

> [How is being an elementary teacher different for a single man and a married man?] You need to be a lot more careful as a single man. All grade school men have broken the male stereotype somehow. [Married men, because they have a spouse, give more assurance? They're not going to be risky with children?] Right. Definitely. (Duane, fifth-grade math)

> Parents are generally more leery of male teachers. If this was a young woman staying after school [to offer special help or extra activities], it would be no big deal at all. She would be "dedicated." "Isn't this great? She's willing to give this time, and do these things, clubs and athletics, and so forth." But this young single guy, who does a great job, he should be commended for all the time he is putting in. But it makes people a little nervous. (David, fifth- and sixth-grade team teacher)

Nearly all men interviewed perceived male role modeling as an unwritten but crucial component of their job description, a widely held expectation and criterion of success. Many men were uncertain, when asked, how to role model beyond "doing what men do." They sensed others' conflicting definitions of the male role itself: the disciplinarian surrogate father engaged only in "unfeminine" activities, or the feminine, nurturing, empathic companion of children. The men in this study were forced to steer a course between these two equally dangerous extremes, either of which could result in suspicions and ultimate dismissal. The man who is too "masculine" would be suspected of being an incompetent and insensitive teacher, while the man who is nurturing and empathic would be stereotyped as feminine and "unnatural." Thus, paradoxically, an initial hiring advantage to men carries with it certain disadvantages, insofar as it places men in an untenable situation.

CONCLUSION

In spite of the initial advantages offered by affirmative action, welcoming male principals, and widespread public perception of the need for more male role models in the socialization of children, men who choose elementary teaching experience stressful disadvantages, posed by conflict and contradiction focused on their maleness. In fact, each advantage is itself potentially a disadvantage or source of uneasiness.

If men are hired simply because they are men, they raise suspicions among their female colleagues about their suitability as teachers. Conversely, some men encounter hostility from male principals, who perceive male teachers as a threat to their authority. Forming alliances with either the male principal or the female teachers entails high potential costs—all because these are men working in female-identified jobs.

The hiring preference based on the need for male role models also presents a series of dilemmas for male teachers. Conforming too closely to traditional definitions of masculinity again raises doubts about men's competence as teachers, while emphasizing nurturance and sensitivity opens men to the charges of effeminacy, or even worse.

The elementary school is a thoroughly gendered institution in which being male or female is an unspoken basis of power (Apple, 1990; Clifford, 1989). Understanding the organization of schools and the lives of those who work in them requires analysis of what Hansot and Tyack (1988) called "the absent presence" of gender: "organizational cultures in which many gender practices are implicit (often all the more powerful for being taken for granted)." Proportions of men and women in both elementary administration and teaching are particularly skewed, compared to middle schools or high schools. Men elementary school teachers often feel isolated and vulnerable, because they upset the gendered ordering of the institution. These interviews suggest that the fewness of men contributes to both their advantages and disadvantages. Future research might explore the extent to which disadvantages so outweigh advantages that men are, in effect, forestalled or forced out, thus conserving the current division of labor.

Managing to Kill: Masculinities and the Space Shuttle *Challenger* Explosion

James W. Messerschmidt

THE LAUNCH DECISION

On January 27, 1986, NASA scrubbed the scheduled flight due to high crosswinds at the launch site and rescheduled *Challenger* for the following morning (President's Commission, 1986, p. 17). By the early afternoon of January 27, 1986, MTI engineers became increasingly concerned over the predicted low temperature of 29° F for the rescheduled launch time, especially in light of the near disaster one year earlier at 53° F. This concern led ultimately to a teleconference between Marshall and MTI officials on the issue of temperature. Data regarding the effect of low temperature on the O-rings and the joint seal were presented by MTI engineers, along with an opinion that launch should be delayed until the temperature was at least 53° F. Marshall requested that MTI prepare and telefax a more formal presentation to both Marshall and Kennedy Space Center officials (in Florida) for a full-fledged teleconference later that evening (p. 106).

At approximately 8:45 P.M. EST, the second teleconference commenced. The telefax presented a history of the O-ring erosion in the SRB joints of previous flights. Roger Boisjoly, the leading engineering specialist at MTI, expressed deep concern about launching at such a low temperature (President's Commission, 1986, p. 88). Boisjoly argued

Excerpted From Cliff Cheng, *Masculinities in Organizations,* pp. 37–49. © 1996 by Sage Publications, Inc. Reprinted by Permission of Sage Publications, Inc.

that the Shuttle should not be launched below a temperature of 53° F, because such temperature would result in the O-rings becoming less resilient and, therefore, incapable of sealing the joint before hot gases ignited to cause an explosion. As Boisjoly stated to the President's Commission (p. 89), it would be "like trying to shove a brick into a crack versus a sponge." Indeed, by now both MTI management and engineers agreed that the Shuttle should not launch until temperatures reached at least 53° F. Notwithstanding, Marshall managers "were not pleased" with MTI's conclusions and recommendations (p. 90).

Marshall challenged MTI's data and conclusions primarily by accusing MTI of trying to establish new launch-commit criteria based on a 53° F standard. Eventually, Lawrence Mulloy, SRB manager at Kennedy, responded to MTI's concern about temperature by stating, "My God, Thiokol, when do you want me to launch, next April?" (President's Commission, 1986, p. 96). Mulloy (p. 1529) insisted that MTI's position was irrationally qualitative, based simply on experience rather than rational, quantifiable evidence. A further exchange between MTI and NASA representatives continued for quite sometime, MTI maintaining that launch should not occur outside the 53° F database. George Hardy, deputy director of science and engineering at Marshall, responded by stating, "I'm appalled at your recommendation" (p. 94).

Thus, MTI found itself on the defensive and experienced formidable coaxing to reverse their no-launch recommendation.

MTI was placed in a social situation where they had to demonstrate convincingly it was not safe to launch, whereas in all previous preflight conferences, MTI was required to verify it was safe to launch. In other words, they had to prove the launch would fail![1]

Eventually the debate reached an impasse. Overwhelmed at having to prove that the joint would fail, MTI management sought a 5-minute, off-line recess to reevaluate the effect of temperature on the O-rings (President's Commission, 1986). The caucus (lasting at least 30 minutes) began with Jerry Mason, senior vice president at MTI, stating to the three managers around him, "We have to make a management decision" (p. 92). Assuming that management was about to consider reversing the earlier no-launch decision, the MTI engineers (especially Roger Boisjoly and Arnie Thompson) attempted a last-minute explanation of the effects of low temperature on O-ring resiliency. Boisjoly explained this attempt to the President's Commission:

> Arnie actually got up from his position which was down the table, and walked up the table and put a quarter pad down in front of the management folks, and tried to sketch out once again what his concern was with the joint, and when he realized he wasn't getting through, he just stopped.
>
> I tried one more time with the photos. I grabbed the photos, and I went up and discussed the photos once again and tried to make the point that it was my opinion from actual observations that temperature was indeed a discriminator and we should not ignore the physical evidence that we had observed. . . . I also stopped when it was apparent that I couldn't get anybody to listen. (pp. 92–93)

In short, these two engineers ardently tried to stop management from reversing their earlier unanimous no-launch decision.

During this exchange, it was clear that three of the four managers supported a launch but that Bob Lund, vice president of engineering, remained committed to the earlier no-launch decision (p. 108). After some further discussion of the data, with Lund remaining the sole holdout among the managers, Mason turned to Lund and instructed him "to take off his engineering hat and put on his management hat" (p. 93). The managers then agreed they had to make a management decision, as Mason states, "in order to conclude what we needed to conclude" (p. 1383). At this point, the engineers were excluded from the decision-making process and a final management review was conducted by the four managers only. The MTI managers, then, with Lund concurring, decided to reverse the decision of the engineers and approve the launch for the next morning. As the President's Commission put it,

> At approximately 11 P.M. EST, the Thiokol-NASA tele-conference resumed, the Thiokol management stating that they had reassessed the problem, that the temperature effects were a concern, but that the data were admittedly inconclusive. Kilminster read the rationale recommending launch and stated that that was Morton Thiokol's recommendation. (p. 96)

MANAGING TO KILL

How can we begin to understand the fact that, in the face of a strong possibility of risk to human life, MTI engineers recognized this threat and argued against the launch, whereas, MTI managers yielded to Marshall pressure and voted unanimously to launch?[2] It is now well established in the sociological literature that gender is embedded in corporations, and that gender is accomplished through concrete corporate activities, resulting not only in gender divisions (e.g., gender divisions of labor, "male" and "female" jobs) but also in situationally specific gendered images, symbols, and practices (Acker, 1992). More specifically, corporations often are defined through metaphors of masculinity. As Joan Acker (1992) puts it,

> Today, organizations are lean, mean, aggressive, goal oriented, efficient, and competitive but rarely empathetic, supportive, kind and caring. Organizational participants actively create these images in their efforts to construct organizational cultures that contribute to competitive success. (p. 253)

The gendering of corporations involves a presentation of self as a gendered member of the corporation and, for the corporate manager, this means specific practices—such as rationality, instrumentalism, careerism, decisiveness, productivism, and risk taking—that help the corporation be successful (Kerfoot and Knights, 1993, p. 671). Indeed, as we have known for almost 20 years, corporate-managerial masculinity is measured by success in reaching corporate goals; accordingly, managerial gendered practices align themselves with corporate needs (Acker, 1990; Kanter, 1977; Tolson, 1977).

MTI managers, like other corporate managers, pursued such gendered practices to assist MTI in attaining its goals. Like other corporate managers, MTI managers consistently faced economic pressures that focused on the present and the near future: "the *next* milestone, the *next* contract, and the *next* stockholders' report are 'real' near-terms subjects that a manager must always address" (Dubinskas, 1988, p. 195). As indicated, the immediate situational goal of MTI was to preserve a lucrative government contract. Given the social situation of uncertainty in reaching this goal caused by the O-ring problem, rather than "hang tough" and continue to oppose the launch, MTI management engaged in risk-taking behavior to achieve their corporate objective. MTI managers rationalized giving greater weight to the advantage

of risk-taking practices over halting Shuttle flights until the O-ring problem could be fixed. They chose the risk-taking path as more likely to advance both their individual masculine performance (gender) as well as corporate success (social class).[3]

When managers talk about "what is at stake" in their jobs, the answer invariably is "the growth of the organization" and, hence, their ultimate status (Dubinskas, 1988, p. 199). Interviews with corporate managers show that they regard a manager who fails to take risks as one who should not be in the business of managing, and risk taking is especially warranted when faced with possible failure to meet corporate goals (March & Shapira, 1987, pp. 1408–1409). To be sure, for managers faced with such uncertainty in meeting goals, "the desire to reach the target focuses attention in a way that leads generally to risk taking. In this case, the opportunities for gain receive attention, rather than the dangers" (p. 1413). Thus, we should not be surprised that the MTI managers reversed the decision of the engineers and approved the launch. Indeed, prestige accompanies the advocacy of such risk-taking and advocates of risk are perceived as especially capable managers, particularly when successful on the previous occasion (p. 1414).[4]

In this context, then, for MTI managers risk taking became the situational defining feature of managerial masculinity. Risk taking is widely documented as a masculine practice, where risk-ladened social situations are responded to more often by men or boys than women or girls as a challenge, an opportunity to "prove" one's worth and demonstrate prowess to others (Arch, 1993, p. 4).[5] The MTI managers were no different from many other men confronted with a risk-ladened situation; doing risk taking for them was, simultaneously, doing masculinity. What is different is that this risk-taking masculine practice was specific to the particular social situation of this corporation. Clearly, the unique social conditions surrounding *Challenger* flights—preserving a lucrative government contract—created a context for MTI managers to push the limits of SRB technology. Because these managers had to demonstrate that the SRBs could survive a rigorous flight schedule, rather than acknowledge design flaws, they demonstrated corporate-managerial competence by supporting the necessity for remaining on schedule. Thus, risk taking became an available resource for achieving corporate goals, because they "got away with it last time." As one member of the President's Commission (1986) observed,

> [The Shuttle] flies [with O-ring erosion] and nothing happens. Then it is suggested, therefore, that the risk is no longer so high for the next flights. We can lower our standards a little bit because we got away with it last time. (p. 148)

In other words, because flight after flight was "successful" (an explosion did not occur), this rationalized further risk taking. Having survived the challenge, MTI managers became increasingly comfortable continuing the risk-taking behavior; thus, risk taking became a practice not only for securing corporate goals but for solving the gender accountability problem at "the job." Doing risk taking was not solely a practice for demonstrating corporate loyalty but simultaneously for rendering such action accountable in terms of the normative conceptions and activities appropriate to the male sex category in this corporation. Because threats to profit making are concurrent threats to corporate-manager masculine accomplishment, risk taking is an acceptable means of resolving both problems: Risk taking is a resource in this particular setting for accomplishing profit (class) and masculinity (gender). Accordingly, risk taking was nor-

malized among MTI management, permitting these men to draw on previously formed risk-taking behavior as a resource for doing masculinity. In short, managerial risk taking became an institutionalized practice, a masculine resolution to the spectacle of technological uncertainty.

Thus, MTI managers gave Marshall the green light to launch to, as the President's Commission (p. 104) stated, "accommodate a major customer." Indeed, throughout "the first 3 weeks of January 1986, NASA and Thiokol conducted negotiations over a one-billion-dollar contract," and extremely important contract discussions were scheduled for January 28—"the day after Thiokol managers made their recommendation to proceed with the launch, the day the *Challenger* was destroyed" (McConnell, 1987, p. 60). Given this milieu, agreeing to take the risk demonstrated not only loyalty to the corporation but, simultaneously, provided MTI managers with a resource for doing masculinity—and, simultaneously, corporate crime—in that specific social setting.

Moreover, the attraction to risk taking by these corporate managers had as much to do with the social action itself as with what it produced in terms of corporate goals. The validation of manager effectiveness at MTI was one's proclivity to "go to the limit" in bringing a flight to "successful" fruition (President's Commission, 1986, p. 110). Each victorious challenge reconfirmed for others one's identity as an accomplished, proficient manager. Fervently effectuating risk-taking social practices provided these managers with the opportunity to exercise diligent control over the situation and bring it to a triumphant conclusion. This is consistent with other research on corporate-manager masculinity that indicates that such managers are ranked "in terms of their capacity to display attributes of control over the definition of the reality of events" and are "constantly preoccupied with purposive action in the drive to be 'in control'" (Kerfoot & Knights, 1993, pp. 671–672). Thus, every successful launch was taken as proof that one was "in control" and, therefore, possessed "the right stuff" to be a *man*(ager).[6] Indeed, the "enterprise of winning" by overcoming danger is for managers "life consuming" and results in "an inward turned competitiveness, focused on the self, creating, in fact, an instrumentality of the personal" (Donaldson, 1993, p. 665). As Kerfoot and Knights (1993) argue, at the level of embodied experience, this corporate-manager masculinity results

> in the position whereby individuals feel "driven" for no discernible reason, other than as a part of what it means, and how it feels, to subscribe to an ideal of competence, and where the display of vulnerability is to threaten the image of that competence. (p. 672)

This translates into the denial or suppression of emotionality, fear, and uncertainty and, therefore, in the social situation of the off-line caucus, it should not be surprising to find MTI managers unanimously supporting launch; to do otherwise would mean exhibiting fear and uncertainty. These corporate-managers displayed, as Rosabeth Moss Kanter (1977) put it in her discussion of managerial masculinity, "a capacity to set aside personal, emotional considerations in the interests of task accomplishments" (p. 22). Indeed, MTI managers disregarded (at least publicly) during the entire teleconference and off-line caucus the fact that human beings were on *Challenger*. The task was to "get *Challenger* up," and all factors antagonistic to that goal—including human life—were deemed irrelevant.

This masculine discourse on the part of MTI managers is similar to the "techno-strategic" discourse outlined by Carol Cohn (1987, 1995) in her important research on nuclear defense intellectuals. Cohn (1995) found that during professional meetings, these men systematically suppressed

> the emotional, the concrete, the particular, the human bodies and their vulnerability, human lives and their subjectivity—all of which are marked as feminine in the binary dichotomies of gender discourse. In other words, gender discourse informs and shapes nuclear and national security discourse. (pp. 134–135)

Similarly, MTI managers eschewed any discussion of human beings (the flight crew) and their vulnerability to the risky technology. And clearly, it was the masculine discourse that generated this *indifference* to the human consequences of managerial decisions. In short, being more attentive to the survival of their lucrative contract rather than the survival of human beings was a means of "doing masculinity" and, as a result, corporate crime.[7]

The decision to launch by MTI managers can be understood, then, in terms of its captivating and enticing masculine appeal—a social practice that had become normalized in MTI managerial relationships. And because masculinity is constantly renegotiated and "made," voting to launch (and, therefore, changing their earlier no-launch position) was an acceptable (that is, accountable) practice for its making in that particular social situation; a practice that "allowed" these managers to live up to a particular masculine ideal.

It is tempting to end the analysis here simply by reasoning that risk-taking masculinity "gave rise" to this corporate crime. Although this conclusion is attractive and not without substance, it disregards the diversity of masculinities actually constructed in corporations and, thus, their relation to corporate crime. Consequently, we must consider the varieties of masculinities at MTI, not just one type. Indeed, analyzing masculinities places us in a position to address why some men at MTI (engineers), despite the institutionalized and heavy emphasis on risk taking, ardently opposed the launch. It is to the engineers that we now turn.

RESISTING LAUNCH

"Of all the major professions," Judy Wajcman (1991) writes, "engineering contains the smallest proportion of females" and, like management, "projects a heavily masculine image" (p. 145). However, corporate managers validate masculinity by success at securing corporate economic goals, while engineers are concerned primarily with technical competence and achievements and tend to devalue economic goals (Cockburn & Ormrod, 1993, p. 161; Vaughan, 1989, p. 337). Indeed, managers and engineers "identify themselves as being in—and 'from'—different 'worlds'" (Dubinskas, 1988, p. 185). Consequently, both managers and engineers weave gendered distinctions into their everyday understanding of "the job," and thus construct masculinity differently.

The relationship between "technical competence" and the social construction of gender difference is well documented in the literature; as Cynthia Cockburn (1985) puts it, "femininity is incompatible with technological competence; to feel technically competent is to feel manly" (p. 12). Nevertheless, to argue that technical competence is "manly" is not to infer only one type of technical masculinity. Indeed, working-class and middle-class men construct masculinity differently, depending on their relation to technology in the workplace. For working-class men, the work environment of the shop floor is given significance by associating manual work with a physically strong and active type of masculinity. In other words, the masculinity of the shop floor stresses the presentation and celebration of physical prowess (Clatterbaugh, 1990; Cockburn, 1983, 1985; Willis, 1979).

Professional engineers, however, do not claim physical prowess but construct masculinity through their possession of abstruse and "expert" technical knowledge (Wajcman, 1991, p. 39). As Cockburn (1985) shows, for professional engineers, "intellectuality and analytical power are appropriated for masculinity" (p. 196). Wajcman (1991) further points out that this knowledge bestows masculine power on engineers "in relation to other men and women who lack this expertise, in terms of the material rewards this skill brings, and even in terms of their popular portrayal as 'heroes' at the frontiers of technological progress" (p. 144). Thus, technical competence is a key source of masculine power among men and "doing engineering" is simultaneously "doing" a particular type of technically competent masculinity. Indeed, being in control of the very latest technology (such as the Space Shuttle *Challenger*) "signifies being involved in directing the future" and so is a highly esteemed activity, whereas, mastery over other kinds of technology (such as machines on the shop floor) does not accord the same status or power (pp. 144–145). Professional engineering not only increases for engineers "their sense of the greatness of their sex," but in addition inculcates "a sense of being special" among the technically competent (Cockburn, 1985, p. 172).

Clearly, then, a major part of engineer masculinity is to be in command of the particular technology and, therefore, to know the limits of that technology. Consequently, engineers (relative to managers) place a very high priority on quality and safety (Starbuck & Milliken, 1988, p. 333). Indeed, Cockburn (1985) stresses the emotional investment engineers lodge in "their" technology:

> In the main these men identify themselves with technology and identify technology with masculinity. . . . Engineers identify so closely with the technology with which they are involved that many will choose their employment less by the salary it offers than by the complexity of the technology it opens up to them. (pp. 171, 172)

Anticipating Cockburn 20 years earlier, Samuel Florman (1976) emphasized the sensual pleasures secured from "doing engineering," and, most recently, Sally Hacker (1989) speaks of a "masculine eroticization of engineering," in which technological innovation is realized as exhilarating and a source of intense pleasure and arousal.

Given this emotional charge, engineers have a direct interest in the technology succeeding as planned and, concurrently, technological success delivers a virile status on engineers, thereby ensuring a claim to "engineer masculinity" (Wajcman, 1991). As a result, risk taking is *not* the appealing masculine practice to engineers that it is to managers. Indeed, for engineers, inasmuch as technical failure threatens their masculinity, it should not be surprising that MTI engineers would exhibit greater caution regarding O-ring capability and argue against launch. Thus, although managers see themselves as "realists" struggling with immediate economic crises that sometimes demand risk taking, engineers attempt to protect their work from myopic managers and are more inclined to disdain risk taking (Dubinskas, 1988, p. 201). Indeed, these strikingly different practices were accomplished situationally during the off-line caucus and brilliantly illustrate the relational character of masculinities. They demonstrate how the definition of masculinity is not

only the collective work of a group of people—in this case, corporate managers and engineers—but is constructed differently through social interaction. Both groups exhibit the different ways in which masculinity is defined and sustained, and how this proprietary masculinity relates to their definition of work-related issues; managers and engineers actively confront the work situation and shape practices for solving problems. Yet they do this in distinctly different ways, and it is this contrasting social action that is central to the production of different masculinities. From essentially similar starting points—class, race, and gender privilege, as well as engagement in "mental labor"— two divergent masculinities are produced. Both groups of men pick up the theme of hegemonic masculinity regarding the importance of work in the paid labor market (and clearly both have benefited from the subordination of women), yet they rework that hegemonic theme in situationally specific ways.

In addition, the *relationship* between these masculinities is in part the basis of MTI organization. As with other male-dominated organizations (such as the military—general/soldier [Connell, 1995b]—and the police—office cop/street cop [Messerschmidt, 1993]), it is the relationship between engineer and manager masculinities—technically competent but subordinate to managerial authority on the one hand, dominating and economically competent on the other—that is, in part, the foundation of MTI organization. Yet as indicated, this relationship is far from one of simple complementarity but, rather, is embedded in a power hierarchy.[8] At MTI, a difference in corporate masculinities was constructed in practice by the asymmetry of power between managers and engineers. "Decisions" were ultimately in the hands of management; yet as we have seen, the power to manage is not always easily exercised.

Engineers can and do wield the weapon of "technical competence," at least to some degree, to make their collective voice heard. During the off-line caucus, two MTI engineers attempted to protect "their technology" by challenging managerial authority. There was a contest of masculinities, in which both managers and engineers were attempting to control the SRB technology. Nevertheless, there are limits to oppositional practices by the less powerful, as noted by the engineers themselves. For example, Boisjoly stated to the President's Commission, "I had my say, and I never take any management right to take the input of an engineer and then make a decision based upon that input, and I truly believe that" (p. 1421). Similarly, Brian Russell, another MTI engineer told the commission, "It was a management decision at the vice president's level, and they had heard all they could hear, and I felt there was nothing more to say" (p. 1487)[9]

What these statements reveal is that power is a relationship that structures social interaction between men in the corporation. By engaging in practices that reproduce the division of labor and power, managers and engineers are not only doing their job and, therefore, reproducing corporate organization, they are also constructing masculinities. Both managers and engineers are acknowledging through practice that the lopsided power relationships are indeed "fair."

In addition, the comment by Jerry Mason to Bob Lund during the off-line caucus—to take off his "engineering hat" and put on his "management hat"—is key to understanding the social construction of, and relationship between, masculinities. Lund was vice president of engineering, making him both an engineer and a manager. Initially, Lund put on his engineering hat and argued against launch. However, once he entered the social situation of the off-line caucus, Lund followed instructions, put on his management hat, and concurred with the other managers to approve launch.

What this reveals is that through the exchange of hats, Lund reestablished a corporate-manager masculinity that had been diminished by his earlier opposition to launch. The problem for Lund was to produce configurations of behavior that could be seen by others as normative. Yet as the social setting changed—from outside to inside the caucus—so did the conceptualization of what is normative masculine behavior. In short, Lund formed different types of masculinity that could be assessed and approved in both social settings as normal.

The case of Lund demonstrates how we maintain different gender identities that may be emphasized or avoided, depending on the social setting. Men construct their gendered action in relation to how such actions might be interpreted by others (that is, their accountability) in the particular social context in which they occur. Given the power relation prevalent in the off-line caucus, Lund did masculinity differently, because the setting and the available resources changed.[10]

Overall, the disparate degree of power among men significantly affects the varieties of masculinities constructed and therefore support for, or rejection of, the launch as a resource for doing masculinity. Engineers were able to oppose the launch, because such a practice was—in this particular situation—a resource for doing gender; attempting to prevent the launch was an accountable practice for doing engineer masculinity. Thus, MTI managers (including Lund) advocated an unsafe launch, whereas engineers resisted such a launch, because of different masculine meanings attaching to the particular practice.

CONCLUSION

Gender is one of the most significant ways in which we make sense of our daily work environment, and work in the paid labor market is a crucial milieu for the *construction of masculinities*. Both managers and engineers construct masculinity at the workplace, but the way in which they do so reveals a fundamental difference. And this diversity is strikingly apparent in support for or rejection of the *Challenger* launch. Indeed, as David Morgan (1992) argues, the kind of work determines "the material out of which certain masculinities are shaped" (p. 86). The corporation sets limits for the type of masculinities that might be constructed and one's position in the corporate division of labor and power determines the resources available for masculine practices. The *Challenger* illustration reveals how the corporate division of labor and power is constituted by social action and, in turn, provides resources for doing masculinity. In this way, social structures both constrain and enable social action and, therefore, masculinities and corporate crime. In short, the data on the Space Shuttle *Challenger* explosion provides empirical support for structured action theory and, therefore, how in the same social situation, one type of masculinity (manager) was constructed through the commission of corporate crime, while contemporaneously another type of masculinity (engineer) was constructed through resisting that crime.

Thus, managers and engineers experience their corporate world from a specific position in the organization and, accordingly, construct masculinity in a uniquely appropriate way. Indeed, conceptualizing the *Challenger* explosion from a structured action perspective demonstrates that we are able now to explore sociologically which males commit which crimes in which social situa-tions. In other words, why some men in corporations "manage to kill," whereas other men do not.

NOTES

1. As Bob Lund (1986), vice president of engineering at MTI, stated in testimony to the President's Commission, "We have dealt with Marshall for a long time and have always been in the position of defending our position that we were ready to fly . . . [now] we had to prove to them we *weren't* ready" (pp. 1456–1457). And as Roger Boisjoly put it, "This was a meeting where the determination was to launch, and it was up to us to prove beyond a shadow of a doubt that it was not safe to do so. This is in total reversal to what the position usually is in a pre-flight conversation" (p. 1421).

2. Due to space limitations, I concentrate my analysis in the remaining sections exclusively on the corporate (MTI) decision to launch.

3. Although all the major MTI managerial decision makers were Caucasian, the social construction of "whiteness" was not the salient feature to this situation as gender and class. In other words, class and gender were directly threatened by the O-ring problem but not race. Moreover, this socially injurious act conforms to the definition of corporate crime outlined earlier, because the decision to launch helped further MTI's corporate goal of preserving a lucrative contract.

4. The importance of risk taking in the corporate-managerial world was recently highlighted in a book on women managers. According to Driscoll and Goldberg (1993), to gain entry to the masculine corporate-managerial "club," "women would do well to become risk-takers" because "risk-taking pays off . . . the greater the risk, the greater the reward" (p. 46)

5. The sociology-of-risk literature has shockingly ignored this important link with gender. See, for example, Short and Clarke (1992) and Luhman (1993).

6. It should therefore not be surprising to find that interview data of corporate managers shows that they "care about their reputations for risk taking and are eager to expound on their sentiments about the deficiencies of others" (March & Shapira, 1987, p. 1413).

7. Bob Lund, vice president of engineering at MTI, stated the following to the President's Commission (1986) when asked why he initially opposed launch: "You know this program has people on it, and so I am very concerned about that, and I want to make sure that if there is any hint of a problem, that we are not extending that" (p. 1459). However, though he is the only person to acknowledge such a concern to the Commission, there is no evidence that he announced this concern at any time during the launch decision process and, finally, he eventually voted—with the other managers—to launch *Challenger*. Thus, although MTI managers did not intend harm to the seven crew

members, they clearly were indifferent to the human consequences of their actions and, therefore, committed corporate crime. Moreover, I must stress that it was the gendered interaction and discourse within the particular social situation of the teleconference and off-line caucus that generated this indifference.

8. Due to space limitations, I am able to consider only power relations at MTI. However, we also observe power relations between managers of the two organizations. MTI's reversal from a no-launch to a launch decision clearly must be understood in terms of its relatively powerless position vis-à-vis Marshall. That is, MTI must be responsive to its major customer or potentially suffer dire economic consequences. Marshall managers, by reason of their powerful position, had the resources to pressure MTI to prove that it was unsafe to launch. Consequently, a full understanding of the power dynamics involved in this event—something clearly beyond the scope of this chapter—must consider this relationship between the "men at Marshall" and the "men at MTI."

9. This comment by Brian Russell indicates that the two engineers—Roger Boisjoly and Arnie Thompson—who challenged the authority of management during the off-line caucus were acting as spokespersons for the other eight engineers.

10. Lund simply was not "jumping" from one masculinity to another. To "do" manager masculinity in this setting required Lund to actively demasculinize what had previously been an acceptable masculine practice for him (opposing the launch). When asked by the President's Commission (pp. 1568–1569) why he changed his mind when he changed his hat, Lund responded by supporting Mulloy's gendered dichotomy discussed above: irrational-qualitative (wimpish) versus rational-quantitative (masculine). In short, by supporting the launch, Lund was able to patently separate himself from what the particular situation of the caucus defined as "wimpish" and, therefore, be assessed as normatively masculine.

The Men We Carry in Our Minds

Scott Russell Sanders

"This must be a hard time for women," I say to my friend Anneke. "They have so many paths to choose from, and so many voices calling them."

"I think it's a lot harder for men," she replies.

"How do you figure that?"

"The women I know feel excited, innocent, like crusaders in a just cause. The men I know are eaten up with guilt."

We are sitting at the kitchen table drinking sassafras tea, our hands wrapped around the mugs because this April morning is cool and drizzly. "Like a Dutch morning," Anneke told me earlier. She is Dutch herself, a writer and midwife and peacemaker, with the round face and sad eyes of a woman in a Vermeer painting who might be waiting for the rain to stop, for a door to open. She leans over to sniff a sprig of lilac, pale lavender, that rises from a vase of cobalt blue.

"Women feel such pressure to be everything, do everything," I say. "Career, kids, art, politics. Have their babies and get back to the office a week later. It's as if they're trying to overcome a million years' worth of evolution in one lifetime."

"But we help one another. We don't try to lumber on alone, like so many wounded grizzly bears, the way men do." Anneke sips her tea. I gave her the mug with owls on it, for wisdom. "And we have this deepdown sense that we're in the *right*—we've been held back, passed over, used—while men feel they're in the wrong. Men are the ones who've been discredited, who have to search their souls."

I search my soul. I discover guilty feelings aplenty—toward the poor, the Vietnamese, Native Americans, the whales, an endless list of debts—a guilt in each case that is as bright and unambiguous as a neon sign. But toward women I feel something more confused, a snarl of shame, envy, wary tenderness, and amazement. This muddle troubles me. To hide my unease I say, "You're right, it's tough being a man these days."

"Don't laugh." Anneke frowns at me, mournful-eyed, through the sassafras steam. "I wouldn't be a man for anything. It's much easier being the victim. All the victim has to do is break free. The persecutor has to *live* with his past."

How deep is that past? I find myself wondering after Anneke has left. How much of an inheritance do I have to throw off? Is it just the beliefs I breathed in as a child? Do I have to scour memory back through father and grandfather? Through St. Paul? Beyond Stonehenge and into the twilit caves? I'm convinced the past we must contend with is deeper even than speech. When I think back on my childhood, on how I learned to see men and women, I have a sense of ancient, dizzying depths. The back roads of Tennessee and Ohio where I grew up were probably closer, in their sexual patterns, to the campsites of Stone Age hunters than to the genderless cities of the future into which we are rushing.

The first men, besides my father, I remember seeing were black convicts and white guards, in the cottonfield across the road from our farm on the outskirts of Memphis. I must have been three or four. The prisoners wore dingy gray-and-black zebra suits, heavy as canvas, sodden with sweat. Hatless, stooped, they chopped weeds in the fierce heat, row after row, breathing the acrid dust of boll-weevil poison. The overseers wore dazzling white shirts and broad shadowy hats. The oiled barrels of their shotguns flashed in the sunlight. Their faces in memory are utterly blank. Of course those men, white and black, have become for me an emblem of racial hatred. But they have also come to stand for the twin poles of my early vision of manhood—the brute toiling animal and the boss.

When I was a boy, the men I knew labored with their bodies. They were marginal farmers, just scraping by, or welders, steelworkers, carpenters; they swept floors, dug ditches, mined coal, or drove trucks, their forearms ropy with muscle; they trained horses, stoked furnaces, built tires, stood on assembly lines wrestling parts onto cars and refrigerators. They got up before light, worked all day long whatever the weather, and when they came home at night they looked as though somebody had been whipping them. In the evenings and on weekends they worked on their own places, tilling gardens that were lumpy with clay, fixing brokendown cars, hammering on houses that were always too drafty, too leaky, too small.

The bodies of the men I knew were twisted and maimed in ways visible and invisible. The nails of their hands were black and split, the hands tattooed with scars. Some had lost fingers. Heavy lifting had given many of them finicky backs and guts weak from hernias. Racing against conveyor belts had given them ulcers. Their ankles and knees ached from years of standing on concrete. Anyone who had worked for long around machines was hard of hearing. They squinted, and the skin of their faces was creased like the leather of old work gloves. There were times, studying them, when I dreaded growing up. Most of them coughed, from dust or cigarettes, and most of them drank cheap wine or whiskey, so their eyes looked bloodshot and bruised. The fathers of my friends always seemed older than the mothers. Men wore out sooner. Only women lived into old age.

As a boy I also knew another sort of men, who did not sweat and break down like mules. They were soldiers, and so far as I could tell they scarcely worked at all. During my early school years we lived on a military base, an arsenal in Ohio, and every day I saw GIs in the guardshacks, on the stoops of barracks, at the wheels of olive drab Chevrolets. The chief fact of their lives was boredom. Long after I left the Arsenal I came to recognize the sour smell the soldiers gave off as that of souls in limbo. They were all waiting—for wars, for transfers, for leaves, for promotions, for the end of their hitch—like so many braves waiting for the hunt to begin. Unlike the warriors of older tribes, however, they would have no say about when the battle would start or how it would be waged. Their waiting was broken only when they practiced for war. They fired guns at targets, drove tanks across the churned-up fields of the military reservation, set off bombs in the wrecks of old fighter planes. I knew this was all play. But I also felt certain that when the hour for killing arrived, they would kill. When the real shooting started, many of them would die. This was what soldiers were *for*, just as a hammer was for driving nails.

Warriors and toilers: those seemed, in my boyhood vision, to be the chief destinies for men. They weren't the only destinies, as I learned from having a few male teachers, from reading books, and from watching television. But the men on television—the politicians, the astronauts, the generals, the savvy lawyers, the philosophical doctors, the bosses who gave orders to both soldiers and laborers—seemed as remote and unreal to me as the figures in tapestries. I could no more imagine growing up to become one of these cool, potent creatures than I could imagine becoming a prince.

A nearer and more hopeful example was that of my father, who had escaped from a red-dirt farm to a tire factory, and from the assembly line to the front office. Eventually he dressed in a white shirt and tie. He carried himself as if he had been born to work with his mind. But his body, remembering the earlier years of slogging work, began to give out on him in his fifties, and it quit on him entirely before he turned sixty five. Even such a partial escape from man's fate as he had accomplished did not seem possible for most of the boys I knew. They joined the Army, stood in line for jobs in the smoky plants, helped build highways. They were bound to work as their fathers had worked, killing themselves or preparing to kill others.

A scholarship enabled me not only to attend college, a rare enough feat in my circle, but even to study in a university meant for the children of the rich. Here I met for the first time young men who had assumed from birth that they would lead lives of comfort and power. And for the first time I met women who told me that men were guilty of having kept all the joys and privileges of the earth for themselves. I was baffled. What privileges? What joys? I thought about the maimed, dismal lives of most of the men back home. What had they stolen from their wives and daughters? The right to go five days a week, twelve months a year, for thirty or forty years to a steel mill or a coal mine? The right to drop bombs and die in war? The right to feel every leak in the roof, every gap in the fence, every cough in the engine, as a wound they must mend? The right to

feel, when the lay-off comes or the plant shuts down, not only afraid but ashamed?

I was slow to understand the deep grievances of women. This was because, as a boy, I had envied them. Before college, the only people I had ever known who were interested in art or music or literature, the only ones who read books, the only ones who ever seemed to enjoy a sense of ease and grace were the mothers and daughters. Like the menfolk, they fretted about money, they scrimped and made-do. But, when the pay stopped coming in, they were not the ones who had failed. Nor did they have to go to war, and that seemed to me a blessed fact. By comparison with the narrow, ironclad, days of fathers, there was an expansiveness, I thought, in the days of mothers. They went to see neighbors, to shop in town, to run errands at school, at the library, at church. No doubt, had I looked harder at their lives, I would have envied them less. It was not my fate to become a woman, so it was easier for me to see the graces. Few of them held jobs outside the home, and those who did filled thankless roles as clerks and waitresses. I didn't see, then, what a prison a house could be, since houses seemed to me brighter, handsomer places than any factory. I did not realize—because such things were never spoken of—how often women suffered from men's bullying. I did learn about the wretchedness of abandoned wives, single mothers, widows; but I also learned about the wretchedness of lone men. Even then I could see how exhausting it was for a mother to cater all day to the needs of young children. But if I had been asked, as a boy, to choose between tending a baby and tending a machine, I think I would have chosen the baby. (Having now tended both, I know I would choose the baby.)

So I was baffled when the women at college accused me and my sex of having cornered the world's pleasures. I think something like my bafflement has been felt by other boys (and by girls as well) who grew up in dirt-poor farm country, in mining country, in black ghettos, in Hispanic barrios, in the shadows of factories, in Third World nations—any place where the fate of men is as grim and bleak as the fate of women. Toilers and warriors. I realize now how ancient these identities are, how deep the tug they exert on men, the undertow of a thousand generations. The miseries I saw, as a boy, in the lives of nearly all men I continue to see in the lives of many—the body-breaking toil, the tedium, the call to be tough, the humiliating powerlessness, the battle for a living and for territory.

When the women I met at college thought about the joys and privileges of men, they did not carry in their minds the sort of men I had known in my childhood. They thought of their fathers, who were bankers, physicians, architects, stockbrokers, the big wheels of the big cities. These fathers rode the train to work or drove cars that cost more than any of my childhood houses. They were attended from morning to night by female helpers, wives and nurses and secretaries. They were never laid off, never short of cash at month's end, never lined up for welfare. These fathers made decisions that mattered. They ran the world.

The daughters of such men wanted to share in this power, this glory. So did I. They yearned for a say over their future, for jobs worthy of their abilities, for the right to live at peace, unmolested, whole. Yes, I thought, yes yes. The difference between me and these daughters was that they saw me, because of my sex, as destined from birth to become like their fathers, and therefore as an enemy to their desires. But I knew better. I wasn't an enemy, in fact or in feeling. I was an ally. If I had known, then, how to tell them so, would they have believed me? Would they now?

The Glass Escalator: Hidden Advantages for Men in the "Female" Professions

Christine L. Williams

The sex segregation of the U.S. labor force is one of the most perplexing and tenacious problems in our society. Even though the proportion of men and women in the labor force is approaching parity (particularly for younger cohorts of workers) (U.S. Department of Labor 1991:18), men and women are still generally confined to predominantly single-sex occupations. Forty percent of men or women would have to change major occupational categories to achieve equal representation of men and women in all jobs (Reskin and Roos 1990:6), but even this figure underestimates the true degree of sex segregation. It is extremely rare to find specific jobs where equal numbers of men and women are engaged in the same activities in the same industries (Bielby and Baron 1984).

Most studies of sex segregation in the work force have focused on women's experiences in male-dominated occupations. Both researchers and advocates for social change have focused on the barriers faced by women who try to integrate predominantly male fields. Few have looked at the "flip-side" of occupational sex segregation: the exclusion of men from predominantly female occupations (exceptions include Schreiber 1979; Williams 1989; Zimmer 1988). But the fact is that men are less likely to enter female sex-typed occupations than women are to enter

male-dominated jobs (Jacobs 1989). Reskin and Roos, for example, were able to identify 33 occupations in which female representation increased by more than nine percentage points between 1970 and 1980, but only three occupations in which the proportion of men increased as radically (1990:20–21).

In this paper, I examine men's underrepresentation in four predominantly female occupations—nursing, librarianship, elementary school teaching, and social work. Throughout the twentieth century, these occupations have been identified with "women's work"—even though prior to the Civil War, men were more likely to be employed in these areas. These four occupations, often called the female "semi-professions" (Hodson and Sullivan 1990), today range from 5.5 percent male (in nursing) to 32 percent male (in social work). (See Table 1.) These percentages have not changed substantially in decades. In fact, as Table 1 indicates, two of these professions—librarianship and social work—have experienced declines in the proportions of men since 1975. Nursing is the only one of the four experiencing noticeable changes in sex composition, with the proportion of men increasing 80 percent between 1975 and 1990. Even so, men continue to be a tiny minority of all nurses.

Although there are many possible reasons for the continuing preponderance of women in these fields, the focus of this paper is discrimination. Researchers examining the integration of women into "male fields" have identified discrimination as a major

TABLE 1
Percent Male in Selected Occupations, Selected Years

PROFESSION	1990	1980	1975
Nurses	5.5	3.5	3.0
Elementary teachers	14.8	16.3	14.6
Librarians	16.7	14.8	18.9
Social workers	31.8	35.0	39.2

Source: U.S. Department of Labor. Bureau of Labor Statistics.
Employment and Earnings 38:1 (January 1991), Table 22 (Employed
civilians by detailed occupation), 185; 28:1 (January 1981), Table
23 (Employed persons by detailed occupation), 180; 22:7 (January
1976), Table 2 (Employed persons by detailed occupation), 11.

barrier to women (Jacobs 1989; Reskin 1988; Reskin and Hartmann 1986). This discrimination has taken the form of laws or institutionalized rules prohibiting the hiring or promotion of women into certain job specialties. Discrimination can also be "informal," as when women encounter sexual harassment, sabotage, or other forms of hostility from their male coworkers resulting in a poisoned work environment (Reskin and Hartmann 1986). Women in nontraditional occupations also report feeling stigmatized by clients when their work puts them in contact with the public. In particular, women in engineering and blue-collar occupations encounter gender-based stereotypes about their competence which undermine their work performance (Epstein 1988; Martin 1980). Each of these forms of discrimination—legal, informal, and cultural—contributes to women's underrepresentation in predominantly male occupations.

The assumption in much of this literature is that any member of a token group in a work setting will probably experience similar discriminatory treatment. Kanter (1977), who is best known for articulating this perspective in her theory of tokenism, argues that when any group represents less than 15 percent of an organization, its members will be subject to predictable forms of discrimination. Likewise, Jacobs argues that "in some ways, men in female-dominated occu-

pations experience the same difficulties that women in male-dominated occupations face" (1989:167), and Reskin contends that any dominant group in an occupation will use their power to maintain a privileged position (1988:62).

However, the few studies that have considered men's experience in gender atypical occupations suggest that men may not face discrimination or prejudice when they integrate predominantly female occupations. Zimmer (1988) and Martin (1988) both contend that the effects of sexism can outweigh the effects of tokenism when men enter nontraditional occupations. This study is the first to systematically explore this question using data from four occupations. I examine the barriers to men's entry into these professions; the support men receive from their supervisors, colleagues and clients; and the reactions they encounter from the public (those outside their professions).

METHODS

I conducted in-depth interviews with 76 men and 23 women in four occupations from 1985–1991. Interviews were conducted in four metropolitan areas: San Francisco/Oakland, California; Austin, Texas; Boston, Massachusetts; and Phoenix, Arizona. These four areas were selected because they show considerable variation in the proportions of men in the four professions. For example, Austin has one of the highest percentages of men in nursing (7.7 percent), whereas Phoenix's percentage is one of the lowest (2.7 percent) (U.S. Bureau of the Census 1980). The sample was generated using "snowballing" techniques. Women were included in the sample to gauge their feelings and responses to men who enter "their" professions.

Like the people employed in these professions generally, those in my sample were predominantly white (90 percent).[1] Their ages ranged from 20 to 66 and the average age was 38. The interview questionnaire consisted of several open-ended questions on four broad topics: motivation to enter the profession; experiences in training; career progression; and general views about men's status and prospects within these occupations. I conducted all the interviews, which generally lasted between one and two hours. Interviews took place in restaurants, my home or office, or the respondent's home or office. Interviews were tape-recorded and transcribed for the analysis.

Data analysis followed the coding techniques described by Strauss (1987). Each transcript was read several times and analyzed into emergent conceptual categories. Likewise, Strauss' principle of theoretical sampling was used. Individual respondents were purposively selected to capture the array of men's experiences in these occupations. Thus, I interviewed practitioners in every specialty, oversampling those employed in the *most* gender atypical areas (e.g., male kindergarten teachers). I also selected respondents from throughout their occupational hierarchies—from students to administrators to retirees. Although the data do not permit within group comparisons, I am reasonably certain that the sample does capture a wide range of experiences common to men in these female-dominated professions. However, like all findings based on qualitative data, it is uncertain whether the findings

generalize to the larger population of men in nontraditional occupations.

In this paper, I review individuals' responses to questions about discrimination in hiring practices, on-the-job rapport with supervisors and co-workers, and prejudice from clients and others outside their profession.

DISCRIMINATION IN HIRING

Contrary to the experience of many women in the male-dominated professions, many of the men and women I spoke to indicated that there is a *preference* for hiring men in these four occupations. A Texas librarian at a junior high school said that his school district "would hire a male over a female."

I: Why do you think that is?

R: Because there are so few, and the . . . ones that they do have, the library directors seem to really . . . think they're doing great jobs. I don't know, maybe they just feel they're being progressive or something, [but] I have had a real sense that they really appreciate having a male, particularly at the junior high. . . . As I said, when seven of us lost our jobs from the high schools and were redistributed, there were only four positions at junior high, and I got one of them. Three of the librarians, some who had been here longer than I had with the school district, were put down in elementary school as librarians. And I definitely think that being male made a difference in my being moved to the junior high rather than an elementary school.

Many of the men perceived their token status as males in predominantly female occupations as an *advantage* in hiring and promotions. I asked an Arizona teacher whether his specialty (elementary special education) was an unusual area for men compared to other areas within education. He said,

Much more so. I am extremely marketable in special education. That's not why I got into the field. But I am extremely marketable because I am a man.

In several cases, the more female-dominated the specialty, the greater the apparent preference for men. For example, when asked if he encountered any problem getting a job in pediatrics, a Massachusetts nurse said,

> No, no, none.... I've heard this from managers and supervisory-type people with men in pediatrics: "It's nice to have a man because it's such a female-dominated profession."

However, there were some exceptions to this preference for men in the most female-dominated specialties. In some cases, formal policies actually barred men from certain jobs. This was the case in some rural Texas school districts, which refused to hire men in the youngest grades (K–3). Some nurses also reported being excluded from positions in obstetrics and gynecology wards, a policy encountered more frequently in private Catholic hospitals.

But often the pressures keeping men out of certain specialties were more subtle than this. Some men described being "tracked" into practice areas within their professions which were considered more legitimate for men. For example, one Texas man described how he was pushed into administration and planning in social work, even though "I'm not interested in writing policy; I'm much more interested in research and clinical stuff." A nurse who is interested in pursuing graduate study in family and child health in Boston said he was dissuaded from entering the program specialty in favor of a concentration in "adult nursing." A kindergarten teacher described the difficulty of finding a job in his specialty after graduation: "I was recruited immediately to start getting into a track to become an administrator. And it was men who recruited me. It was men that

ran the system at that time, especially in Los Angeles."

This tracking may bar men from the most female-identified specialties within these professions. But men are effectively being "kicked upstairs" in the process. Those specialties considered more legitimate practice areas for men also tend to be the most prestigious, better paying ones. A distinguished kindergarten teacher, who had been voted city-wide "Teacher of the Year," told me that even though people were pleased to see him in the classroom, "there's been some encouragement to think about administration, and there's been some encouragement to think about teaching at the university level or something like that, or supervisory-type position." That is, despite his aptitude and interest in staying in the classroom, he felt pushed in the direction of administration.

The effect of this "tracking" is the opposite of that experienced by women in male-dominated occupations. Researchers have reported that many women encounter a "glass ceiling" in their efforts to scale organizational and professional hierarchies. That is, they are constrained by invisible barriers to promotion in their careers, caused mainly by sexist attitudes of men in the highest positions (Freeman 1990).[2] In contrast to the "glass ceiling," many of the men I interviewed seem to encounter a "glass escalator." Often, despite their intentions, they face invisible pressures to move up in their professions. As if on a moving escalator, they must work to stay in place.

A public librarian specializing in children's collections (a heavily female-dominated concentration) described an encounter with this "escalator" in his very first job out of library school. In his first six-months' evaluation, his supervisors commended him for his good work in storytelling and related activities, but they criticized him for "not shooting high enough."

> Seriously. That's literally what they were telling me. They assumed that because I was a male—and they told me this—and that I was being hired right out of graduate school, that somehow I wasn't doing the kind of management-oriented work that they thought I should be doing. And as a result, really they had a lot of bad marks, as it were, against me on my evaluation. And I said I couldn't believe this!

Throughout his ten-year career, he has had to struggle to remain in children's collections.

The glass escalator does not operate at all levels. In particular, men in academia reported some gender-based discrimination in the highest positions due to their universities' commitment to affirmative action. Two nursing professors reported that they felt their own chances of promotion to deanships were nil because their universities viewed the position of nursing dean as a guaranteed female appointment in an otherwise heavily male-dominated administration. One California social work professor reported his university canceled its search for a dean because no minority male or female candidates had been placed on their short list. It was rumored that other schools on campus were permitted to go forward with their searches—even though they also failed to put forward names of minority candidates—because the higher administration perceived it to be "easier" to fulfill affirmative action goals in the social work school. The interviews provide greater evidence of the "glass escalator" at work in the lower levels of these professions.

Of course, men's motivations also play a role in their advancement to higher professional positions. I do not mean to suggest that the men I talked to all resented the in-

formal tracking they experienced. For many men, leaving the most female-identified areas of their professions helped them resolve internal conflicts involving their masculinity. One man left his job as a school social worker to work in a methadone drug treatment program not because he was encouraged to leave by his colleagues, but because "I think there was some macho shit there, to tell you the truth, because I remember feeling a little uncomfortable there . . . ; it didn't feel right to me." Another social worker, employed in the mental health services department of a large urban area in California, reflected on his move into administration:

> The more I think about it, through our discussion, I'm sure that's a large part of why I wound up in administration. It's okay for a man to do the administration. In fact, I don't know if I fully answered a question that you asked a little while ago about how did being male contribute to my advancing in the field. I was saying it wasn't because I got any special favoritism as a man, but . . . I think . . . because I'm a man, I felt a need to get into this kind of position. I may have worked harder toward it, may have competed harder for it, than most women would do, even women who think about doing administrative work.

Elsewhere I have speculated on the origins of men's tendency to define masculinity through single-sex work environments (Williams 1989). Clearly, personal ambition does play a role in accounting for men's movement into more "male-defined" arenas within these professions. But these occupations also structure opportunities for males independent of their individual desires or motives.

The interviews suggest that men's underrepresentation in these professions cannot be attributed to discrimination in hiring or promotions. Many of the men indicated that they received preferential treatment because they were men. Although men mentioned gender discrimination in the hiring process, for the most part they were channelled into the more "masculine" specialties within these professions, which ironically meant being "tracked" into better paying and more prestigious specialties.

SUPERVISORS AND COLLEAGUES: THE WORKING ENVIRONMENT

Researchers claim that subtle forms of work place discrimination push women out of male-dominated occupations (Jacobs 1989; Reskin and Hartmann 1986). In particular, women report feeling excluded from informal leadership and decision-making networks, and they sense hostility from their male co-workers, which makes them feel uncomfortable and unwanted (Carothers and Crull 1984). Respondents in this study were asked about their relationships with supervisors and female colleagues to ascertain whether men also experienced "poisoned" work environments when entering gender atypical occupations.

A major difference in the experience of men and women in nontraditional occupations is that men in these situations are far more likely to be supervised by a member of their own sex. In each of the four professions I studied, men are overrepresented in administrative and managerial capacities, or, as is the case of nursing, their positions in the organizational hierarchy are governed by men (Grimm and Sterm 1974; Phenix 1987; Schmuck 1987; Williams 1989; York, Henley and Gamble 1987). Thus, unlike women who enter "male fields," the men in these professions often work under the direct supervision of other men.

Many of the men interviewed reported that they had good rapport with their male supervisors. Even in professional school,

some men reported extremely close relationships with their male professors. For example, a Texas librarian described an unusually intimate association with two male professors in graduate school:

> I can remember a lot of times in the classroom there would be discussions about a particular topic or issue, and the conversation would spill over into their office hours, after the class was over. And even though there were . . . a couple of the other women that had been in on the discussion, they weren't there. And I don't know if that was preferential or not . . . it certainly carried over into personal life as well. Not just at the school and that sort of thing. I mean, we would get together for dinner . . .

These professors explicitly encouraged him because he was male:

> I: Did they ever offer you explicit words of encouragement about being in the profession by virtue of the fact that you were male? . . .
>
> R: Definitely. On several occasions. Yeah. Both of these guys, for sure, including the Dean who was male also. And it's an interesting point that you bring up because it was, oftentimes, kind of in a sign, you know. It wasn't in the classroom, and it wasn't in front of the group, or if we were in the student lounge or something like that. It was . . . if it was just myself or maybe another one of the guys, you know, and just talking in the office. It's like . . . you know, kind of an opening-up and saying, "You know, you are really lucky that you're in the profession because you'll really go to the top real quick, and you'll be able to make real definite improvements and changes. And you'll have a real influence," and all this sort of thing. I mean, really, I can remember several times.

Other men reported similar closeness with their professors. A Texas psychotherapist recalled his relationships with his male professors in social work school:

I made it a point to make a golfing buddy with one of the guys that was in administration. He and I played golf a lot. He was the guy who kind of ran the research training, the research part of the master's program. Then there was a sociologist who ran the other part of the research program. He and I developed a good friendship.

This close mentoring by male professors contrasts with the reported experience of women in nontraditional occupations. Others have noted a lack of solidarity among women in nontraditional occupations. Writing about military academies, for example, Yoder describes the failure of token women to mentor succeeding generations of female cadets. She argues that women attempt to play down their gender difference from men because it is the source of scorn and derision.

> Because women felt unaccepted by their male colleagues, one of the last things they wanted to do was to emphasize their gender. Some women thought that, if they kept company with other women, this would highlight their gender and would further isolate them from male cadets. These women desperately wanted to be accepted as cadets, not as women cadets. Therefore, they did everything from not wearing skirts as an option with their uniforms to avoiding being a part of a group of women. (Yoder 1989:532)

Men in nontraditional occupations face a different scenario—their gender is construed as a *positive* difference. Therefore, they have an incentive to bond together and emphasize their distinctiveness from the female majority.

Close, personal ties with male supervisors were also described by men once they were established in their professional careers. It was not uncommon in education, for example, for the male principal to informally socialize with the male staff, as a Texas special education teacher describes:

Occasionally I've had a principal who would regard me as "the other man on the campus" and "it's us against them," you know? I mean, nothing really that extreme, except that some male principals feel like there's nobody there to talk to except the other man. So I've been in that position.

These personal ties can have important consequences for men's careers. For example, one California nurse, whose performance was judged marginal by his nursing supervisors, was transferred to the emergency room staff (a prestigious promotion) due to his personal friendship with the physician in charge. A Massachusetts teacher acknowledged that his principal's personal interest in him landed him his current job.

> I: You had mentioned that your principal had sort of spotted you at your previous job and had wanted to bring you here [to this school]. Do you think that has anything to do with the fact that you're a man, aside from your skills as a teacher?
>
> R: Yes, I would say in that particular case, that was part of it. . . . We have certain things in common, certain interests that really lined up.
>
> I: Vis-à-vis teaching?
>
> R: Well, more extraneous things—running specifically, and music. And we just seemed to get along real well right off the bat. It is just kind of a guy thing; we just liked each other . . .

Interviewees did not report many instances of male supervisors discriminating against them, or refusing to accept them because they were male. Indeed, these men were much more likely to report that their male bosses discriminated against the *females* in their professions. When asked if he thought physicians treated male and female nurses differently, a Texas nurse said:

> I think yeah, some of them do. I think the women seem like they have a lot more trouble with the physicians treating them in a

derogatory manner. Or, if not derogatory, then in a very paternalistic way than the men [are treated]. Usually if a physician is mad at a male nurse, he just kind of yells at him. Kind of like an employee. And if they're mad at a female nurse, rather than treat them on an equal basis, in terms of just letting their anger out at them as an employee, they're more paternalistic or there's some sexual harassment component to it.

A Texas teacher perceived a similar situation where he worked:

> I've never felt unjustly treated by a principal because I'm a male. The principals that I've seen that I felt are doing things that are kind of arbitrary or not well thought out are doing it to everybody. In fact, they're probably doing it to the females worse than they are to me.

Openly gay men may encounter less favorable treatment at the hands of their supervisors. For example, a nurse in Texas stated that one of the physicians he worked with preferred to staff the operating room with male nurses exclusively—as long as they weren't gay. Stigma associated with homosexuality leads some men to enhance, or even exaggerate their "masculine" qualities, and may be another factor pushing men into more "acceptable" specialties for men.

Not all men who work in these occupations are supervised by men. Many of the men interviewed who had female bosses also reported high levels of acceptance—although levels of intimacy with women seemed lower than with other men. In some cases, however, men reported feeling shut-out from decision making when the higher administration was constituted entirely by women. I asked an Arizona librarian whether men in the library profession were discriminated against in hiring because of their sex:

> Professionally speaking, people go to considerable lengths to keep that kind of thing

out of their [hiring] deliberations. Personally, is another matter. It's pretty common around here to talk about the "old girl network." This is one of the few libraries that I've had any intimate knowledge of which is actually controlled by women.... Most of the department heads and upper level administrators are women. And there's an "old girl network" that works just like the "old boy network," except that the important conferences take place in the women's room rather than on the golf course. But the political mechanism is the same, the exclusion of the other sex from decision making is the same. The reasons are the same. It's somewhat discouraging . . .

Although I did not interview many supervisors, I did include 23 women in my sample to ascertain their perspectives about the presence of men in their professions. All of the women I interviewed claimed to be supportive of their male colleagues, but some conveyed ambivalence. For example, a social work professor said she would like to see more men enter the social work profession, particularly in the clinical specialty (where they are underrepresented). Indeed, she favored affirmative action hiring guidelines for men in the profession. Yet, she resented the fact that her department hired "another white male" during a recent search. I questioned her about this ambivalence:

> I: I find it very interesting that, on the one hand, you sort of perceive this preference and perhaps even sexism with regard to how men are evaluated and how they achieve higher positions within the profession, yet, on the other hand, you would be encouraging of more men to enter the field. Is that contradictory to you, or . . . ?
>
> R: Yeah, it's contradictory.

It appears that women are generally eager to see men enter "their" occupations. Indeed, several men noted that their female colleagues had facilitated their careers in various ways (including mentorship in college). However, at the same time, women often resent the apparent ease with which men advance within these professions, sensing that men at the higher levels receive preferential treatment which closes off advancement opportunities for women.

But this ambivalence does not seem to translate into the "poisoned" work environment described by many women who work in male-dominated occupations. Among the male interviewees, there were no accounts of sexual harassment. However, women do treat their male colleagues differently on occasion. It is not uncommon in nursing, for example, for men to be called upon to help catheterize male patients, or to lift especially heavy patients. Some librarians also said that women asked them to lift and move heavy boxes of books because they were men. Teachers sometimes confront differential treatment as well, as described by this Texas teacher:

> As a man, you're teaching with all women, and that can be hard sometimes. Just because of the stereotypes, you know. I'm real into computers . . . and all the time people are calling me to fix their computer. Or if somebody gets a flat tire, they come and get me. I mean, there are just a lot of stereotypes. Not that I mind doing any of those things, but it's . . . you know, it just kind of bugs me that it is a stereotype, "A man should do that." Or if their kids have a lot of discipline problems, that kiddo's in your room. Or if there are kids that don't have a father in their home, that kid's in your room. Hell, nowadays that'd be half the school in my room (laughs). But you know, all the time I hear from the principal or from other teachers, "Well, this child really needs a man . . . a male role model" (laughs). So there are a lot of stereotypes that . . . men kind of get stuck with.

This special treatment bothered some respondents. Getting assigned all the "discipline problems" can make for difficult working conditions, for example. But many men claimed this differential treatment did not cause distress. In fact, several said they liked being appreciated for the special traits and abilities (such as strength) they could contribute to their professions.

Furthermore, women's special treatment sometimes enhanced—rather than poisoned—the men's work environments. One Texas librarian said he felt "more comfortable working with women than men" because "I think it has something to do with control. Maybe it's that women will let me take control more than men will." Several men reported that their female colleagues often cast them into leadership roles. Although not all savored this distinction, it did enhance their authority and control in the work place. In subtle (and not-too-subtle) ways, then, differential treatment contributes to the "glass escalator" men experience in nontraditional professions.

Even outside work, most of the men interviewed said they felt fully accepted by their female colleagues. They were usually included in informal socializing occasions with the women—even though this frequently meant attending baby showers or Tupperware parties. Many said that they declined offers to attend these events because they were not interested in "women's things," although several others claimed to attend everything: The minority men I interviewed seemed to feel the least comfortable in these informal contexts. One social worker in Arizona was asked about socializing with his female colleagues:

> I: So in general, for example, if all the employees were going to get together to have a party, or celebrate a bridal shower or whatever, would you be invited along with the rest of the group?
>
> R: They would invite me, I would say, somewhat reluctantly. Being a black male, working with all white females, it

did cause some outside problems. So I didn't go to a lot of functions with them . . .

I: You felt that there was some tension there on the level of your acceptance . . . ?

R: Yeah. It was OK working, but on the outside, personally, there was some tension there. It never came out, that they said, "Because of who you are we can't invite you" (laughs), and I wouldn't have done anything anyway. I would have probably respected them more for saying what was on their minds. But I never felt completely in with the group.

Some single men also said they felt uncomfortable socializing with married female colleagues because it gave the "wrong impression." But in general, the men said that they felt very comfortable around their colleagues and described their work places as very congenial for men. It appears unlikely, therefore, that men's underrepresentation in these professions is due to hostility towards men on the part of supervisors or women workers.

DISCRIMINATION FROM "OUTSIDERS"

The most compelling evidence of discrimination against men in these professions is related to their dealings with the public. Men often encounter negative stereotypes when they come into contact with clients or "outsiders"—people they meet outside of work. For instance, it is popularly assumed that male nurses are gay. Librarians encounter images of themselves as "wimpy" and asexual. Male social workers describe being typecast as "feminine" and "passive." Elementary school teachers are often confronted by suspicions that they are pedophiles. One kindergarten teacher described an experience that occurred early in his career which was related to him years afterwards by his principal:

He indicated to me that parents had come to him and indicated to him that they had a

problem with the fact that I was a male. . . . I recall almost exactly what he said. There were three specific concerns that the parents had: One parent said, "How can he love my child; he's a man." The second thing that I recall, he said the parent said, "He has a beard." And the third thing was, "Aren't you concerned about homosexuality?"

Such suspicions often cause men in all four professions to alter their work behavior to guard against sexual abuse charges, particularly in those specialties requiring intimate contact with women and children.

Men are very distressed by these negative stereotypes, which tend to undermine their self-esteem and to cause them to second-guess their motivations for entering these fields. A California teacher said,

If I tell men that I don't know, that I'm meeting for the first time, that that's what I do, . . . sometimes there's a look on their faces that, you know, "Oh, couldn't get a real job?"

When asked if his wife, who is also an elementary school teacher, encounters the same kind of prejudice, he said,

No, it's accepted because she's a woman. . . . I think people would see that as a . . . step up, you know. "Oh, you're not a housewife, you've got a career. That's great . . . that you're out there working. And you have a daughter, but you're still out there working. You decided not to stay home, and you went out there and got a job." Whereas for me, it's more like I'm supposed to be out working anyway, even though I'd rather be home with [my daughter].

Unlike women who enter traditionally male professions, men's movement into these jobs is perceived by the "outside world" as a step down in status. This particular form of discrimination may be most significant in explaining why men are underrepresented in these professions. Men who otherwise might show interest in and aptitudes for such careers are probably discouraged from pursuing them because of the negative popular stereotypes associated with the men who work in them. This is a crucial difference from the experience of women in nontraditional professions: "My daughter, the physician," resonates far more favorably in most people's ears than "My son, the nurse."

Many of the men in my sample identified the stigma of working in a female-identified occupation as the major barrier to more men entering their professions. However, for the most part, they claimed that these negative stereotypes were not a factor in their own decisions to join these occupations. Most respondents didn't consider entering these fields until well into adulthood, after working in some related occupation. Several social workers and librarians even claimed they were not aware that men were a minority in their chosen professions. Either they had no well-defined image or stereotype, or their contacts and mentors were predominantly men. For example, prior to entering library school, many librarians held part-time jobs in university libraries, where there are proportionally more men than in the profession generally. Nurses and elementary school teachers were more aware that mostly women worked in these jobs, and this was often a matter of some concern to them. However, their choices were ultimately legitimized by mentors, or by encouraging friends or family members who implicitly reassured them that entering these occupations would not typecast them as feminine. In some cases, men were told by recruiters there were special advancement opportunities for men in these fields, and they entered them expecting rapid promotion to administrative positions.

I: Did it ever concern you when you were making the decision to enter nursing school, the fact that it is a female-dominated profession?

R: Not really. I never saw myself working on the floor. I saw myself pretty much going into administration, just getting the background and then getting a job someplace as a supervisor and then working, getting up into administration.

Because of the unique circumstances of their recruitment, many of the respondents did not view their occupational choices as inconsistent with a male gender role, and they generally avoided the negative stereotypes directed against men in these fields.

Indeed, many of the men I interviewed claimed that they did not encounter negative professional stereotypes until they had worked in these fields for several years. Popular prejudices can be damaging to self-esteem and probably push some men out of these professions altogether. Yet, ironically, they sometimes contribute to the "glass escalator" effect I have been describing. Men seem to encounter the most vituperative criticism from the public when they are in the most female-identified specialties. Public concerns sometimes result in their being shunted into more "legitimate" positions for men. A librarian formerly in charge of a branch library's children's collection, who now works in the reference department of the city's main library, describes his experience:

R: Some of the people [who frequented the branch library] complained that they didn't want to have a man doing the storytelling scenario. And I got transferred here to the central library in an equivalent job . . . I thought that I did a good job. And I had been told by my supervisor that I was doing a good job.

I: Have you ever considered filing some sort of lawsuit to get that other job back?

R: Well, actually, the job I've gotten now . . . well, it's a reference librarian; it's what I wanted in the first place. I've got a whole lot more authority here. I'm also in charge of the circulation

desk. And I've recently been promoted because of my new stature, so
. . . no, I'm not considering trying to
get that other job back.

The negative stereotypes about men who do
"women's work" can push men out of specific jobs. However, to the extent that they
channel men into more "legitimate" practice
areas, their effects can actually be positive.
Instead of being a source of discrimination,
these prejudices can add to the "glass escalator effect" by pressuring men to move *out* of
the most female-identified areas, and *up* to
those regarded more legitimate and prestigious for men.

CONCLUSION: DISCRIMINATION AGAINST MEN

Both men and women who work in nontraditional occupations encounter discrimination, but the forms and consequences of this
discrimination are very different. The interviews suggest that unlike "nontraditional"
women workers, most of the discrimination
and prejudice facing men in the "female
professions" emanates from outside those
professions. The men and women interviewed for the most part believed that men
are given fair—if not preferential—treatment in hiring and promotion decisions, are
accepted by supervisors and colleagues, and
are well-integrated into the work place subculture. Indeed, subtle mechanisms seem to
enhance men's position in these professions—a phenomenon I refer to as the "glass
escalator effect."

The data lend strong support for Zimmer's (1988) critique of "gender neutral
theory" (such as Kanter's [1977] theory of
tokenism) in the study of occupational segregation. Zimmer argues that women's occupational inequality is more a consequence
of sexist beliefs and practices embedded in
the labor force than the effect of numerical
underrepresentation per se. This study sug-

gests that token status itself does not diminish men's occupational success. Men take
their gender privilege with them when they
enter predominantly female occupations:
this translates into an advantage in spite of
their numerical rarity.

This study indicates that the experience of tokenism is very different for men
and women. Future research should examine how the experience of tokenism varies
for members of different races and classes as
well. For example, it is likely that informal
work place mechanisms similar to the ones
identified here promote the careers of token
whites in predominantly black occupations.
The crucial factor is the social status of the
token's group—not their numerical rarity—
that determines whether the token encounters a "glass ceiling" or a "glass escalator."

However, this study also found that
many men encounter negative stereotypes
from persons not directly involved in their
professions. Men who enter these professions are often considered "failures," or sexual deviants. These stereotypes may be a
major impediment to men who otherwise
might consider careers in these occupations. Indeed, they are likely to be important
factors whenever a member of a relatively
high status group crosses over into a lower
status occupation. However, to the extent
that these stereotypes contribute to the
"glass escalator effect" by channeling men
into more "legitimate" (and higher paying)
occupations, they are not discriminatory.

Women entering traditionally "male"
professions also face negative stereotypes suggesting they are not "real women" (Epstein
1981; Lorber 1984; Spencer and Podmore
1987). However, these stereotypes do not
seem to deter women to the same degree that
they deter men from pursuing nontraditional
professions. There is ample historical evidence that women flock to male-identified
occupations once opportunities are available
(Cohn 1985; Epstein 1988). Not so with men.

Examples of occupations changing from predominantly female to predominantly male are very rare in our history. The few existing cases—such as medicine—suggest that redefinition of the occupations as appropriately "masculine" is necessary before men will consider joining them (Ehrenreich and English 1978).

Because different mechanisms maintain segregation in male- and female-dominated occupations, different approaches are needed to promote their integration. Policies intended to alter the sex composition of male-dominated occupations—such as affirmative action—make little sense when applied to the "female professions." For men, the major barriers to integration have little to do with their treatment once they decide to enter these fields. Rather, we need to address the social and cultural sanctions applied to men who do "women's work" which keep men from even considering these occupations.

One area where these cultural barriers are clearly evident is in the media's representation of men's occupations. Women working in traditionally male professions have achieved an unprecedented acceptance on popular television shows. Women are portrayed as doctors ("St. Elsewhere"), lawyers ("The Cosby Show," "L.A. Law"), architects ("Family Ties"), and police officers ("Cagney and Lacey"). But where are the male nurses, teachers and secretaries? Television rarely portrays men in nontraditional work roles, and when it does, that anomaly is made the central focus—and joke—of the program. A comedy series (1991–92) about a male elementary school teacher ("Drexell's Class") stars a lead character who *hates children!* Yet even this negative portrayal is exceptional. When a prime time hospital drama series ("St. Elsewhere") depicted a male orderly striving for upward mobility, the show's writers made him a "physician's assistant," not a nurse or nurse practitioner—the much more likely "real life" possibilities.

Presenting positive images of men in nontraditional careers can produce limited effects. A few social workers, for example, were first inspired to pursue their careers by George C. Scott, who played a social worker in the television drama series, "Eastside/Westside." But as a policy strategy to break down occupational segregation, changing media images of men is no panacea. The stereotypes that differentiate masculinity and femininity, and degrade that which is defined as feminine, are deeply entrenched in culture, social structure, and personality (Williams 1989). Nothing short of a revolution in cultural definitions of masculinity will effect the broad-scale social transformation needed to achieve the complete occupational integration of men and women.

Of course, there are additional factors besides societal prejudice contributing to men's underrepresentation in female-dominated professions. Most notably, those men I interviewed mentioned as a deterrent the fact that these professions are all underpaid relative to comparable "male" occupations, and several suggested that instituting a "comparable worth" policy might attract more men. However, I am not convinced that improved salaries will substantially alter the sex composition of these professions unless the cultural stigma faced by men in these occupations diminishes. Occupational sex segregation is remarkably resilient, even in the face of devastating economic hardship. During the Great Depression of the 1930s, for example, "women's jobs" failed to attract sizable numbers of men (Blum 1991:154). In her study of American Telephone and Telegraph (AT&T) workers, Epstein (1989) found that some men would rather suffer unemployment than accept relatively high paying "women's jobs" because of the damage to their identities this would cause. She quotes one unemployed man who refused to apply for a female-identified telephone operator job:

> I think if they offered me $1000 a week tax free, I wouldn't take that job. When I . . . see those guys sitting in there [in the telephone operating room], I wonder what's wrong with them. Are they pansies or what? (Epstein 1989: 577)

This is not to say that raising salaries would not affect the sex composition of these jobs. Rather, I am suggesting that wages are not the only—or perhaps even the major—impediment to men's entry into these jobs. Further research is needed to explore the ideological significance of the "woman's wage" for maintaining occupational stratification.[3]

At any rate, integrating men and women in the labor force requires more than dismantling barriers to women in male-dominated fields. Sex segregation is a two-way street. We must also confront and dismantle the barriers men face in predominantly female occupations. Men's experiences in these nontraditional occupations reveal just how culturally embedded the barriers are, and how far we have to travel before men and women attain true occupational and economic equality.

This research was funded in part by a faculty grant from the University of Texas at Austin. I also acknowledge the support of the sociology departments of the University of California, Berkeley; Harvard University; and Arizona State University. I would like to thank Judy Auerbach, Martin Button, Robert Nye, Teresa Sullivan, Debra Umberson, Mary Waters, and the reviewers at *Social Problems* for their comments on earlier versions of this paper.

NOTES

1. According to the U.S. Census, black men and women comprise 7 percent of all nurses and librarians, 11 percent of all elementary school teachers, and 19 percent of all social workers (calculated from U.S. Census 1980: Table 278, 1–197). The proportion of blacks in social work may be exaggerated by these statistics. The occupational definition of "social worker" used by the Census Bureau includes welfare workers and pardon and parole officers, who are not considered "professional" social workers by the National Association of Social Workers. A study of degreed professionals found that 89 percent of practitioners were white (Hardcastle 1987).

2. In April 1991, the Labor Department created a "Glass Ceiling Commission" to "conduct a thorough study of the underrepresentation of women and minorities in executive, management, and senior decision-making positions in business" (U.S. House of Representatives 1991:20).

3. Alice Kessler-Harris argues that the lower pay of traditionally female occupations is symbolic of a patriarchal order that assumes female dependence on a male breadwinner. She writes that pay equity is fundamentally threatening to the "male worker's sense of self, pride, and masculinity" because it upsets his individual standing in the hierarchical ordering of the sexes (1990:125). Thus, men's reluctance to enter these occupations may have less to do with the actual dollar amount recorded in their paychecks, and more to do with the damage that earning "a woman's wage" would wreak on their self-esteem in a society that privileges men. This conclusion is supported by the interview data.

REFERENCES–WORKING LIVES, GENDERED INSTITUTIONS

ACKER, J. (1990). Hierarchies, jobs, bodies: A theory of gendered organizations. *Gender & Society, 4*(2): 139–158.

APPLE, M.W. (1990). *Teachers and texts.* New York: Routledge.

ARCH, E.C. (1993). Risk-taking: A motivational basis for sex differences. *Psychological Reports, 73:* 3–11.

BANERJEE, N. (2001). Some "bullies" seek ways to soften up: Toughness has risks for women executives. *New York Times.* August 10.

BIELBY, W.T., and J.N. Baron. (1984). A woman's place is with other women: Sex segregation within organizations. In B. Reskin, Ed., *Sex segregation in the workplace: Trends, explanations, remedies,* pp. 27–55. Washington, DC: National Academy Press.

BLUM, L.M. (1991). *Between feminism and labor: The significance of the comparable worth movement.* Berkeley, CA: University of California Press.

CARROTHERS, S., and P. Crull. (1984). Contrasting sexual harassment in female-dominated and male-dominated occupations. In K.B. Sacks and D. Remy, Eds., *My troubles are going to have trouble with me: Everyday trials and triumphs of women workers,* pp. 220–227. New Brunswick, NJ: Rutgers University Press.

CHALMERS, L.V. (2001). *Marketing masculinities: Gender and management politics in marketing work.* Westport, CT: Greenwood Press.

CLATTERBAUGH, K. (1990). *Contemporary perspectives on masculinity.* Boulder, CO: Westview.

CLIFFORD, G.J. (1989). Man/woman/teacher: Gender, family, and career in American educational history. In D. Warren, Ed., *American teachers: History of a profession at work.* New York: Macmillan.

COCKBURN, C. (1983). *Brothers: Male dominance and technological change.* London: Pluto.

COCKBURN, C. (1985). *Machinery of dominance: Women, men and technical knowhow.* London: Pluto.

COCKBURN, C., and S. Ormrod. (1993). *Gender and technology in the making.* Newbury Park, CA: Sage.

COHN, C. (1987). Sex and death in the rational world of defense intellectuals. *Signs, 12*(4): 687–718.

COHN, C. (1985). War, wimps, and women: Talking gender and thinking war. In M.S. Kimmel and M.A. Messner, eds., *Men's Lives,* pp. 131–143. Boston: Allyn & Bacon.

COHN, S. (1985). *The process of occupational sex-typing.* Philadelphia: Temple University Press.

CONNELL, R.W. (1995b) Masculinity, violence, and war. In M.S. Kimmel and M.A. Messner, eds., *Men's Lives,* pp. 125–130. Boston: Allyn & Bacon.

DONALDSON, M. (1993). What is hegemonic masculinity? *Theory and Society, 22:* 643–657.

DOWD, M. (1998). Pass the Midol. *New York Times.* April 15.

DUBINSKAS, F.A. (1988). Janus organizations: Scientists and managers in genetic engineering firms. In F.A. Dubinskas, Ed., *Making time: Ethnographies of high technology organizations,* pp. 170–232. Philadelphia: Temple University Press.

Economist. (1998). July 18.

EHRENREICH, B. (1978). *For her own good: 100 years of expert advice to women.* Garden City, NY: Anchor Books.

EPSTEIN, C.F. (1981). *Women in law.* New York: Basic Books.

EPSTEIN, C.F. (1988). *Deceptive distinctions: Sex, gender and the social order.* New Haven: Yale University Press.

EPSTEIN, C.F. (1989). Workplace boundaries: Conceptions and creations. *Social Research, 56,* 571–590.

FLORMAN, S.C. (1976). *The existential pleasures of engineering.* New York: St. Martin's.

FREEMAN, S.J.M. (1990). *Managing lives: Corporate women and social change.* Amherst, MA: University of Massachusetts Press.

GRIMM, J.W., and R.N. Stern. (1974). Sex roles and internal labor market structures: The female semi-professions. *Social Problems,* 21: 690–705.

HACKER, S. (1989) *Pleasure, power and technology: Some tales of gender, engineering, and the cooperative workplace.* Boston: Unwin Hyman.

HANSOT, E., and D. Tyack. (1988). Gender in American public schools: Thinking institutionally. *Signs,* 13(4): 741–760.

HARDCASTLE, D.A. (1987). The social work labor force. Austin, TX: School of Social Work, University of Texas.

HODSON, R., and T. Sullivan. (1990). *The social organization of work.* Belmont, CA: Wadsworth Publishing Co.

JACOBS, J. (1989). *Revolving doors: Sex segregation and women's careers.* Stanford, CA: Stanford University Press.

KANTER, R.M. (1977). *Men and women of the corporation.* New York: Basic Books.

KERFOOT, D., and D. Knights. (1993). Management, masculinity, and manipulation: From paternalism to corporate strategy in financial services in Britain. *Journal of Management Studies,* 30(4): 659–677.

KESSLER-HARRIS, A. (1990). *A Woman's Wage: Historical meanings and social consequences.* Lexington, KY: Kentucky University Press.

LORBER, J. (1984). *Women Physicians: Careers, status, and power.* New York: Tavistock.

MARCH, J.G., and Z. Shapira. (1987). Managerial perspectives on risk and risk-taking. *Management Science,* 33(11): 1404–1418.

MARTIN, S.E. (1980). *Breaking and entering: Police women on patrol.* Berkeley, CA: University of California Press.

MARTIN, S.E. (1988). Think like a man, work like a dog, and act like a lady: Occupational dilemmas of policewomen. In A. Statham, E.M. Miller, and H.O. Mauksch. Eds., *The worth of women's work: A qualitative synthesis,* pp. 205–223. Albany, NY: State University of New York Press.

MCCONNELL, M. (1987). Challenger: *A major malfunction.* Garden City, NY: Doubleday.

MESSERSCHMIDT, J.W. (1993) *Masculinities and crime: Critique and reconceptualization of theory.* Lanham, MD: Rowman & Littlefield.

MORGAN, D.H.J. (1992). *Discovering men.* New York: Routledge.

PHENIX, K. (1987). The status of women librarians. *Frontiers,* 9: 36–40.

President's Commission. (1986). *Report* of *the Presidential Commission on the Space Shuttle* Challenger *accident.* Washington, DC: Governmental Printing Office.

RESKIN, B., and H. Hartmann. (1986). *Women's work, men's work: Sex segregation on the job.* Washington, DC: National Academy Press.

RESKIN, B., and P. Roos. (1990). *Job queues, gender queues: Explaining women's inroads into male occupations.* Philadelphia: Temple University Press.

SCHMUCK, P.A. (1987). Women school employees in the United States. In P.A. Schmuck, Ed., *Women educators: Employees of schools in western countries,* pp. 75–97. Albany, NY: State University of New York Press.

SCHRIEBER, C. (1979). *Men and women in transitional occupations.* Cambridge, MA: MIT Press.

SPENCER, A., and D. Podmore. (1987). *In a man's world: Essays on women in male-dominated professions.* London: Tavistock.

STARBUCK, W.H., and F.J. Milliken. (1988). *Challenger:* Fine-tuning the odds until something breaks. *Journal of Management Studies,* 25(4):319–340.

STRAUSS, A.L. (1987). *Qualitative analysis for social scientists.* Cambridge, England: Cambridge University Press.

TOLSON, A. (1977). *The limits of masculinity.* New York: Harper and Row.

U.S. Bureau of the Census. (1980). *Detailed population characteristics,* vol. 1, ch. D. Washington, DC: Government Printing Office.

U.S. Congress. House (1991). *Civil rights and women's equity in employment act of 1991.* Report. (Report 102–40, Part I.) Washington, DC: Government Printing Office.

U.S. Department of Labor, Bureau of Labor Statistics. (1991). *Employment and earnings.* January. Washington, DC: Government Printing Office.

WACJMAN, J. (1991). *Feminism confronts technology.* University Park, PA: Pennsylvania State University Press.

WILLIAMS, C.L. (1989). *Gender differences at work: Women and men in nontraditional occupations.* Berkeley, CA: University of California Press.

WILLIS, P.E. (1979). Shop floor culture, masculinity, and the wage form. In J. Clarke, C. Crichter, and R. Johnson, Eds., *Working-class culture,* pp. 185–198. London: Hutchinson.

YODER, J.D. (1989). Women at West Point: Lessons for token women in male-dominated occupations. In Freeman, J., Ed., *Women: A feminist perspective,* pp. 523–537. Mountain View, CA: Mayfield Publishing Company.

YORK, R.O., H.C. Henley, and D.N. Gamble. (1987). Sexual discrimination in social work: Is it salary or advancement? *Social Work,* 32: 336–340.

ZIMMER, Lynn (1988). Tokenism and women in the workplace. *Social Problems,* 35: 64–77.

Sex, Love, and Power

When Michael Moffat had Rutgers University students write sexual self-reports in the mid-1980s, he noted that although a "new sexual orthodoxy" prevailed on campus that held that both women and men have a "right" to sexual pleasure, a "modern variant of the older double standard was also articulated" (Moffat 204). The students he dubbed "neotraditionalists" were struggling with the contradictions between a new discourse about sexuality that was becoming common in schools and colleges, and the traditional beliefs they had absorbed from popular culture, peers, and home.

Today, college women expect "equality in the classroom and in the bedroom" (Gold and Villari xx). For the generation who were in high school when the President of the United States publicly acknowledged having sex with an intern in the Oval Office and several prominent men were charged with rape, the "nineties will be remembered as a national chat room on sex, violence, equality, and power" (Gold and Villari xxiii). It has become difficult to separate sex from power, despite the efforts of a new wave of widely publicized neotraditionalist women to return heterosexuality to the world of romantic fiction (Fein and Schneider).

The concept of "sexual politics" gained currency in the 1960s (Millett 1970, Firestone 1971) and quickly transformed thinking about rape (Brownmiller 1975) and pornography (Dworkin 1981). The feminist critique of pornography in the 1970s—a time when explicitly violent content increased, ascribed by some to a backlash against the prominence of the women's movement—defined it as less to do with sexual arousal than with the subordination of women. This gender analysis had a corollary in the analysis of rape as a crime of power rather than of sexual desire. The hydraulic model of male sexuality—men "need" sex as release—began to give way to an understanding of the politics of sexuality, the recognition that all sexual relationships take place within a gendered context. Given our heterosexist culture, gay relationships also are constrained by confused perceptions about homosexuality and masculinity, as Nardi explains in this section. In a culture in which sexuality is a primary currency of identity, the arguments continue to be complex and challenging.

The editors of *Transforming a Rape Culture* write that "Rape is a pervasive fact of American life, and its incidence is growing dramatically" (Buchwald et al. 9). A movement against sexual violence has been growing steadily on college campuses across the United States since the end of the 1980s: "Today," as one of that movement's chroniclers writes, "everyone knows by junior high school about date or acquaintance rape, but in 1989 we had no name for it" (Gold and Villari xviii). Duke University students belonging to a group called Men Acting for Change "present programs about gender and sexuality, focusing on sexual violence and homophobia, to fraternities and other campus groups" (Stoltenberg 89). For this generation of college men, the experience of being perceived by their female peers as a potential rapist has had a profound effect (Stoltenberg 91), creating new masculinities.

But of course, the neotraditionalists still exist. The students of the anti-sexual violence movement may be in the vanguard, but they are still the minority. Anyone who has received by e-mail one of those "100 Great Reasons to Be a Guy" lists or watched television in the last few years will be aware that nineteenth-century norms of heterosexual relations still pervade the culture.

Lust

Susan Minot

LEO was from a long time ago, the first one I ever saw nude. In the spring before the Hellmans filled their pool, we'd go down there in the deep end, with baby oil, and like that. I met him the first month away at boarding school. He had a halo from the campus light behind him. I flipped.

Roger was fast. In his illegal car, we drove to the reservoir, the radio blaring, talking fast, fast, fast. He was always going for my zipper. He got kicked out sophomore year.

By the time the band got around to playing "Wild Horses," I had tasted Bruce's tongue. We were clicking in the shadows on the other side of the amplifier, out of Mrs. Donovan's line of vision. It tasted like salt, with my neck bent back, because we had been dancing so hard before.

Tim's line: "I'd like to see you in a bathing suit." I knew it was his line when he said the exact same thing to Annie Hines.

You'd go on walks to get off campus. It was raining like hell, my sweater as sopped as a wet sheep. Tim pinned me to a tree, the woods light brown and dark brown, a white house half-hidden with the lights already on. The water was as loud as a crowd hissing. He made certain comments about my forehead, about my cheeks.

We started off sitting at one end of the couch and then our feet were squished against the armrest and then he went over to turn off the TV and came back after he had taken off his shirt and then we slid onto the floor and he got up again to close the door, then came back to me, a body waiting on the rug.

You'd try to wipe off the table or to do the dishes and Willie would untuck your shirt and get his hands up under in front, standing behind you, making puffy noises in your ear.

He likes it when I wash my hair. He covers his face with it and if I start to say something, he goes, "Shush."

For a long time, I had Philip on the brain. The less they noticed you, the more you got them on the brain.

My parents had no idea. Parents never really know what's going on, especially when you're away at school most of the time. If she met them, my mother might say, "Oliver seems nice" or "I like that one" without much of an opinion. If she didn't like them, "He's a funny fellow, isn't he?" or "Johnny's perfectly nice but a drink of water." My father was too shy to talk to them at all, unless they played sports and he'd ask them about that.

The sand was almost cold underneath because the sun was long gone. Eben piled a mound over my feet, patting around my ankles, the ghostly surf rumbling behind him in the dark. He was the first person I ever knew who died, later that summer, in a car crash. I thought about it for a long time.

"Come here," he says on the porch.

I go over to the hammock and he takes my wrist with two fingers.

"What?"

He kisses my palm then directs my hand to his fly.

Songs went with whichever boy it was. "Sugar Magnolia" was Tim, with the line "Rolling in the rushes/down by the riverside." With "Darkness Darkness," I'd picture Philip with his long hair. Hearing "Under my Thumb" there'd be the smell of Jamie's suede jacket.

We hid in the listening rooms during study hall. With a record cover over the door's window, the teacher on duty couldn't look in. I came out flushed and heady and back at the dorm was surprised how red my lips were in the mirror.

One weekend at Simon's brother's, we stayed inside all day with the shades down, in bed, then went out to Store 24 to get some ice cream. He stood at the magazine rack and read through *MAD* while I got butterscotch sauce, craving something sweet.

I could do some things well. Some things I was good at, like math or painting or even sports, but the second a boy put his arm around me, I forget about wanting to do anything else, which felt like a relief at first until it became like sinking into a muck.

It was different for a girl.

When we were little, the brothers next door tied up our ankles. They held the door of the goat house and wouldn't let us out till we showed them our underpants. Then they'd

forget about being after us and when we played whiffle ball, I'd be just as good as them.

Then it got to be different. Just because you have on a short skirt, they yell from the cars, slowing down for a while and if you don't look, they screech off and call you a bitch.

"What's the matter with me?" they say, point-blank.

Or else, "Why won't you go out with me? I'm not asking you to get married," about to get mad.

Or it'd be, trying to be reasonable, in a regular voice, "Listen, I just want to have a good time."

So I'd go because I couldn't think of something to say back that wouldn't be obvious, and if you go out with them, you sort of have to do something.

I sat between Mack and Eddie in the front seat of the pickup. They were having a fight about something. I've a feeling about me.

Certain nights you'd feel a certain surrender, maybe if you'd had wine. The surrender would be forgetting yourself and you'd put your nose to his neck and feel like a squirrel, safe, at rest, in a restful dream. But then you'd start to slip from that and the dark would come in and there'd be a cave. You make out the dim shape of the windows and feel yourself become a cave, filled absolutely with air, or with a sadness that wouldn't stop.

Teenage years. You know just what you're doing and don't see the things that start to get in the way.

Lots of boys, but never two at the same time. One was plenty to keep you in a state.

You'd start to see a boy and something would rush over you like a fast storm cloud and you couldn't possibly think of anyone else. Boys took it differently. Their eyes perked up at any little number that walked by. You'd act like you weren't noticing.

The joke was that the school doctor gave out the pill like aspirin. He didn't ask you anything. I was fifteen. We had a picture of him in assembly, holding up an IUD shaped like a T. Most girls were on the pill, if anything, because they couldn't handle a diaphragm. I kept the dial in my top drawer like my mother and thought of her each time I tipped out the yellow tablets in the morning before chapel.

If they were too shy, I'd be more so. Andrew was nervous. We stayed up with his family album, sharing a pack of Old Golds. Before it got light, we turned on the TV. A man was explaining how to plant seedlings. His mouth jerked to the side in a tic. Andrew thought it was a riot and kept imitating him. I laughed to be polite. When we finally dozed off, he dared to put his arm around me but that was it.

You wait till they come to you. With half fright, half swagger, they stand one step down. They dare to touch the button on your coat then lose their nerve and quickly drop their hand so you—you'd do anything for them. You touch their cheek.

The girls sit around in the common room and talk about boys, smoking their heads off.
"What are you complaining about?" says Jill to me when we talk about problems.
"Yeah," says Giddy. "You always have a boyfriend."
I look at them and think, As if.

I thought the worst thing anyone could call you was a cockteaser. So, if you flirted, you had to be prepared to go through with it. Sleeping with someone was perfectly normal once you had done it. You didn't really worry about it. But there were other problems. The problems had to do with something else entirely.

Mack was during the hottest summer ever recorded. We were renting a house on an island with all sorts of other people. No one slept during the heat wave, walking around the house with nothing on which we were used to because of the nude beach. In the living room, Eddie lay on top of a coffee table to cool off. Mack and I, with the bedroom door open for air, sweated and sweated all night.

"I can't take this," he said at 3 A.M. "I'm going for a swim." He and some guys down the hall went to the beach. The heat put me on edge. I sat on a cracked chest by the open window and smoked and smoked till I felt even worse, waiting for something—I guess for him to get back.

One was on a camping trip in Colorado. We zipped our sleeping bags together, the coyotes' hysterical chatter far away. Other couples murmured in other tents. Paul was before sunrise, starting a fire for breakfast. He wasn't much of a talker in the daytime. At night, his hand leafed about in the hair at my neck.

There'd be times when you overdid it. You'd get carried away. All the next day, you'd be in a total fog, delirious, absent-minded, crossing the street and nearly getting run over.

The more girls a boy has, the better. He has a bright look, having reaped fruits, blooming. He stalks around, sure–shouldered, and you have the feeling he's got more in him, a fatter heart, more stories to tell. For a girl, with each boy it's like a petal gets plucked each time.

Then you start to get tired. You begin to feel diluted, like watered-down stew.

Oliver came skiing with us. We lolled by the fire after everyone had gone to bed. Each creak you'd think was someone coming downstairs. The silver-loop bracelet he gave me had been a present from his girl-friend before.

On vacations, we went skiing, or you'd go south if someone invited you. Some people had apartments in New York that their families hardly ever used. Or summer houses, or older sisters. We always managed to find some place to go.

We made the plan at coffee hour. Simon snuck out and met me at Main Gate after lights-out. We crept to the chapel and spent the night in the balcony. He tasted like onions from a submarine sandwich.

The boys are one of two ways: either they can't sit still or they don't move. In front of the TV, they won't budge. On weekends they play touch football while we sit on the sidelines, picking blades of grass to chew on, and watch. We're always watching them run around. We shiver in the stands, knocking our boots together to keep our toes warm and they whizz across the ice, chopping their sticks around the puck. When they're in the rink, they refuse to look at you, only eyeing each other beneath low helmets. You cheer for them but they don't look up, even if it's a face-off when nothing's happening, even if they're doing drills before any game has started at all.

Dancing under the pink tent, he bent down and whispered in my ear. We slipped away to the lawn on the other side of the hedge. Much later, as he was leaving the buffet with two plates of eggs and sausage, I saw the grass stains on the knees of his white pants.

Tim's was shaped like a banana, with a graceful curve to it. They're all different. Willie's like a bunch of walnuts when nothing was happening, another's as thin as a thin hot dog. But it's like faces; you're never really surprised.

Still, you're not sure what to expect.

I look into his face and he looks back. I look into his eyes and they look back at mine. Then they look down at my mouth so I look at his mouth, then back to his eyes then, backing up, at his whole face. I think, Who? Who are you? His head tilts to one side.

I say, "Who are you?"

"What do you mean?"

"Nothing."

I look at his eyes again, deeper. Can't tell who he is, what he thinks.

"What?" he says. I look at his mouth.

"I'm just wondering," I say and go wandering across his face. Study the chin line. It's shaped like a persimmon.

"Who are you? What are you thinking?"

He says, "What the hell are you talking about?"

Then they get mad after when you say enough is enough. After, when it's easier to explain that you don't want to. You wouldn't dream of saying that maybe you weren't really ready to in the first place.

Gentle Eddie. We waded into the sea, the waves round and plowing in, buffalo-headed, slapping our thighs. I put my arms around his freckled shoulders and he held me up, buoyed by the water, and rocked me like a sea shell.

I had no idea whose party it was, the apartment jam-packed, stepping over people in the hallway. The room with the music was practically empty, the bare floor, me in red shoes. This fellow slides onto one knee and takes me around the waist and we rock to jazzy tunes, with my toes pointing heavenward, and waltz and spin and dip to "Smoke Gets in Your Eyes" or "I'll Love You Just for Now." He puts his head to my chest, runs a sweeping hand down my inside thigh and we go loose-limbed and sultry and as smooth as silk and I stamp my red heels and he takes me into a swoon. I never saw him again after that but I thought, I could have loved that one.

You wonder how long you can keep it up. You begin to feel like you're showing through, like a bathroom window that only lets in grey light, the kind you can't see out of.

They keep coming around. Johnny drives up at Easter vacation from Baltimore and I let him in the kitchen with everyone sound asleep. He has friends waiting in the car.

"What are you crazy? It's pouring out there," I say.

"It's okay," he says. "They understand."

So he gets some long kisses from me, against the refrigerator, before he goes because I hate those girls who push away a boy's face as if she were made out of Ivory soap, as if she's that much greater than he is.

The note on my cubby told me to see the headmaster. I had no idea for what. He had received complaints about my amorous displays on the town green. It was Willie that spring. The headmaster told me he didn't care what I did but that Casey Academy had a reputation to uphold in the town. He lowered

his glasses on his nose. "We've got twenty acres of woods on this campus," he said. "Smooch with your boyfriend there."

Everybody'd get weekend permissions for different places then we'd all go to someone's house whose parents were away. Usually there'd be more boys than girls. We raided the liquor closet and smoked pot at the kitchen table and you'd never know who would end up where, or with whom. There were always disasters. Ceci got bombed and cracked her head open on the bannister and needed stitches. Then there was the time Wendel Blair walked through the picture window at the Lowe's and got slashed to ribbons.

He scared me. In bed, I didn't dare look at him. I lay back with my eyes closed, luxuriating because he knew all sorts of expert angles, his hands never fumbling, going over my whole body, pressing the hair up and off the back of my head, giving an extra hip shove, as if to say *There*. I parted my eyes slightly, keeping the screen of my lashes low because it was too much to look at him, his mouth loose and pink and parted, his eyes looking through my forehead, or kneeling up, looking through my throat. I was ashamed but couldn't look him in the eye.

You wonder about things feeling a little off-kilter. You begin to feel like a piece of pounded veal.

At boarding school, everyone gets depressed. We go in and see the housemother, Mrs. Gunther. She got married when she was eighteen. Mr. Gunther was her high-school sweetheart, the only boyfriend she ever had.

"And you knew you wanted to marry him right off?" we ask her. She smiles and says, "Yes."

"They always want something from you," says Jill, complaining about her boyfriend.

"Yeah," says Giddy. "You always feel like you have to deliver something."

"You do," says Mrs. Gunther. "Babies."

After sex, you curl up like a shrimp, something deep inside you ruined, slammed in a place that sickens at slamming, and slowly you fill up with an overwhelming sadness, an elusive gaping worry. You don't try to explain it, filled with the knowledge that it's nothing after all, everything filling up finally and absolutely with death. After the briskness of loving, loving stops. And you roll over with death stretched out alongside you like a feather boa, or a snake, light as air, and you . . . you don't even ask for anything or try to say something to him because it's obviously your own damn fault. You haven't been able to—to what? To open your heart. You open your legs but can't, or don't dare anymore, to open your heart.

It starts this way:

You stare into their eyes. They flash like all the stars are out. They look at you seriously, their eyes at a low burn and their hands no matter what starting off shy and with such a gentle touch that the only thing you can do is take that tenderness and let yourself be swept away. When, with one attentive finger they tuck the hair behind your ear, you—

You do everything they want.

Then comes after. After when they don't look at you. They scratch their balls, stare at the ceiling. Or if they do turn, their gaze is altogether changed. They are surprised. They turn casually to look at you, distracted, and get a mild distracted surprise. You're gone. Their black look tells you that the girl they were fucking is not there anymore. You seem to have disappeared.

Men-Only Spaces as Effective Sites for Education and Transformation in the Battle to End Sexual Assault

Stephen Montagna

When the axe came into the forest,
the trees said "The handle is one of us . . . "

I believe we all suffer from divisionary and polarizing thinking, are all out of balance in different degrees at different times particularly because of win-lose ethics, from which in the long run everyone suffers. Developing a non-enemy ethic in my life means refusing to hate and refusing to win at a cost to others. I am trying to look for the human face behind the enemy image and in this find a possible transformation of relationship.

—K. Louise Schmidt,
Transforming Abuse: Nonviolent Resistance and Recovery

Six years ago I moved to Madison, Wisconsin, from the East Coast to pursue my master of fine arts degree, and to get away from the East Coast. In a certain sense, I was also trying to get away from Nancy.

Nancy and I had dated, quite briefly, at the end of my senior year of undergrad. Our charming, promising, and nonsexual (though physical) relationship was punctuated with the discovery that she had been cheating on me with another man. Under any circumstances this would be upsetting;

Excerpted from Jodi Gold and Susan Villari, eds. *Just Sex: Students Rewrite the Rules on Sex, Violence, Activism, and Equality,* pp. 181–88. Copyright © 2000 Rowman & Littlefield.

my frustration was enhanced by the fact that we had specifically held back from becoming intimate sexually because her previous partner had focused so much of that relationship on intercourse. This former partner, our argument would reveal, was in fact the man she had been sleeping with behind my back. In the wake of that catastrophic scene in my kitchen, with tears rolling down cheeks and the threat of dishes being thrown, I fell back on the support and comfort of friends. The conclusion arrived upon by my little clan of coed compatriots was unanimous. I had been too nice to her in the relationship: "She's a bitch . . . you shouldn't take that stuff from a woman . . . be more aggressive . . . go out and get it."

Getting "it" was, after all, a man's central occupation.

These phrases ran around inside my head, ricocheting like a mantra, and amplifying until the original sentiment, their desire for me not to be hurt, became the seed of the twisted promise to myself to obtain sexual satisfaction—even if it meant hurting someone else. Fate lent a hand, with an offer to teach and get my graduate degree halfway across the country. It was perfect: Moving far away would help me forget the hurt Nancy had caused me. Furthermore, in the Midwest I would meet thousands of available women and "get what I wanted" from them.

The summer passed. I moved. I started grad school on a campus nearly ten times larger than the one I had spent my undergrad years on; the amount of potentially available females was staggering. Despite this, I was terrified of actually asking someone out, and completely confused about the language my friends had passed along to me. It was language that inferred a kind of aggression that wasn't really inside me. It felt foreign. One day in the student union, I happened upon a brochure for the organization Men Stopping Rape. The pamphlet spoke not only about avoiding bad behavior with women in your life, but also of reaching out and connecting with other men. I decided to attend a meeting and check them out; I thought, if nothing else, it will impress the girls.

The environment of the MSR meeting was so welcoming and transformational, that I not only returned for subsequent meetings but went on to partake in the workshop presenter training, and eventually moved into presenting workshops both on the UW campus and in the Dane County community. My life, as they say, has never been the same.

"Just what do men talk about?" I don't want to explain that yet; I like to leave a little mystery, create a little cliff-hanger: What exactly happened in those mysterious MSR meetings? My withholding this information is a little tongue-in-cheek gibe, an in-joke if you will, with many of the women I've come into contact with in my six years with Men Stopping Rape who want to know what exactly it is we do.

This question has become quite controversial, in fact. Recently, a debate arose on the electronic forum CCOAR (Coalition of Campus Organizations Addressing Rape) over what men's participation in the anti-rape education movement should be (if any!?). Further compounding this controversy is the fact that we at MSR specifically advocate "men only" spaces for most of our workshops; men, in a room alone, talking about rape.

For a number of reasons, many women feel threatened when they hear about men working in the area of sexual assault prevention education. On one level, they feel cheated because after working so hard to raise awareness for women's rights and issues, here come the men trying to shine the spotlight back on themselves. Also, since sexual assault crosses borders of gender, orientation, and physical space, it is easy to fear anyone who mounts a soapbox: Just what do they stand for? What is their definition of assault? Where do they stand politically? What is their prescribed cure?

The most potent threat posed by men doing work with men, is that we are, statistically speaking, the "perpetrating class." The predominant number of assaults, regardless of the gender of the victim, are perpetrated by males. There is a long history of assaults taking place in, or being informed by activities in, traditionally male-only environments (Peggy Reeves Sanday has already so eloquently and bravely researched fraternity traditions—if you haven't read her work you are missing something[1]). As one person explained to a fellow MSR presenter, "Men collude"; in other words, when men are alone together, sexism rules.

Now, I want to be perfectly clear that I am not (repeat: not, not, not) saying that the agenda of the feminist movement is to attack men. From my perspective what most feminists out there are trying to do is deconstruct the system of patriarchy—the institutionalized implementation of a bias against anything perceived to be weak (that is, anything female or effeminate, or any display of dependence). The difficult thing is that most men have a hard time understanding feminism. While most feminists are addressing bad behavior, men hear it as an attack on their biology. They cannot separate a feminist critique of "the system of patriarchy" from a criticism of themselves as men.

One of the reasons this is true is that, in my experience, men's issues have been absent from rape prevention programs. On college campuses, in particular, sexual assault prevention education is done "quick and painlessly" during freshman orientation, never to be revisited, unless the student willingly takes a women's studies course. Higher education's rallying cry for preventing assault is that old standard: "No means No." The recipe is simple: Teach women how to say no and how to defend themselves (against what?—why, against men of course . . .), throw in a little lesson to the men on how to respect women. Add a warning about alcohol. Mix.

The message is still about women, though. Men are not taught how to respect each other, how to be safe around other men, or that men have boundaries too. Absent from sexual assault prevention education is the realization that perpetrator behavior is a result of misinformation handed down from generation to generation through the popular culture (movies, magazines, music), and further, that this misinformation can be unlearned.

On the CCOAR list one person posted an inquiry as to what others were doing across the country to educate men. Several people responded, including myself, describing the programming we do in MSR. The ensuing dialogue was skeptical. An educator from the University of Washington commented that at her school, "no matter what group was being presented to, there would *always* be a female presenter present." Her assumption seemed to be that men in a room together, alone, would simply talk about sex, while sexism would go unchallenged. Furthermore, she proclaimed that men's resistance to rape prevention training in coed settings with female presenters was a ~~result~~ of their inability to accept women as ~~autho~~rity figures.

Another list member submitted a number of questions, including "What kinds of things are men more comfortable talking about if women aren't present that need to be talked about in rape education?" and "Do you see a danger in supporting male-only rape education groups, given that this may be extended to arguments to exclude women from other arenas of male bonding (such as fraternities, which research data demonstrates are such frequent sites for sexual abuse)? How do you negotiate the contradiction effectively?"

It is true that male-only environments have been at the root of many sexist acts and beliefs, and it is specifically for that reason that male-only environments must be used in unlearning those habitual behaviors. Popular science so far hasn't found sexism to be buried in the Y chromosome. It comes from behavior and attitudes passed on across generations and cultures. Why have such attitudes permeated male-only spaces? Simple: We are terrified of each other.

Men's exchanges are fraught with the underlying threat of violence, and informed by homophobia (for our purposes, homophobia is not just the fear of homosexuals—it is the institutional belief that men cannot be intimate with each other—emotionally or otherwise). In a culture where we are shamed for showing feelings, men learn to express any type of feeling as rage. If we feel threatened, we do everything we can to pose a larger threat. In such an arena women become both targets of criticism and objects we use; the stories we tell each other about what we do with women on dates (or claim to have done) become tools used to maintain status among our circle of men.

At Men Stopping Rape, we feel our job is to reconstruct the male-only space as one where sexism can be identified and challenged. More important, we seek to create a space where men can build trust and safety with each other in a way that would no longer require women or their bodies to be used as a means of maintaining status. For men to see and hear another man talking about sex, sexuality, and sexual assault is radical; no one has ever talked to them about this stuff before in a clear, informative way.

Regarding the comment that men resist female presenters because they cannot accept women as authority figures, while it is certainly true that men have such a problem, resistance is not absent in a male-only workshop. Truth be told, their resistance is not so much against the woman as it is against the feminine. For instance, when I go in to present a workshop, I am not an authority figure in their eyes at first; I am an "other." Their homophobia is in place, so I'm automatically gay to them (debased to the "level of the feminine") because, after all, aren't all sensitive men gay? They perceive that I have come simply to chastise them and slap their wrists.

There are several benefits to having a male facilitator and a male-only environment. In a coed workshop with a female presenter, the men would be less likely actually to say some of the things on their minds. They are too busy trying to avoid being called on, and too busy posturing for the benefit of the other females present. When women are absent, their agenda is to assert themselves; they do not censor themselves. Second, I myself was raised as a man, and can address on that fundamental level the ways in which our culture teaches aggression and coercion.

Men need to hear about sexual assault in a context that does not automatically place them in the role of perpetrator simply based on gender. While the concept of "No Means No" is important for men to hear, and while they do need to learn about respecting women as human beings—as individuals—they further need to hear that they them-

selves have a right to set boundaries. In other words, men cannot possibly be taught how to respect women when they have no concept of what it means to have the right to control their own physical boundaries. All their lives men are taught that their masculine identities are dependent upon their ability to put their bodies at risk. They are expected to excel in athletics; they are expected to develop muscular, strong physiques; they are taught that anything emotional makes them weak. If we really want to reach men on the issue of sexual assault, a starting point must be to relearn masculinity; if we really want women to be safe around men, we must teach men to be caring, communicative, and supportive with each other.

"No Means No" is further compounded by the fact that men are told that our masculinity, our sexuality, and our identity as men are directly connected to our ability to get a woman to say yes. Men's ability to grapple with the concepts of no and yes is impaired by the culturally taught bias against communication. For decades these men have been bombarded with images in print and in the movies of men who simply "make their move," "don't ask, take," and, the definitive slogan, "just do it." Where does communication fit into such a paradigm? In workshops I lead men in an exploration of these stereotypes. "How many of you have seen a movie in which two people have sex?" I ask. All of their hands go up. "How many of you have seen films in which they actually talked while they were having sex?" Almost every hand goes down.

Men have had no models to show how communication can improve sex—not just make it more safe, but also more enjoyable. When I facilitate a workshop, one of my goals is to take "No Means No" to the next level—or, perhaps more accurately, flip it around. As a man, I am responsible for only two things: *my* feelings and *my* needs. It is my responsibility to myself to let the person I'm with know what I'm feeling, what I would like to do; how that person reacts is not my responsibility. By working against the grain of society, which historically has viewed asking as "unromantic" because it "ruins the mood," I present communication as part of a package of my taking responsibility for myself. By asking I am not ruining the mood, I am in fact creating the mood; I am letting my partner know my sexual desires. I am presuming no privilege to it, nor any power over her/him to get what I want.

All this is done in an effort to get men to reject the myth that our avoidance of communication goes beyond fear of being uncool; men don't ask because they are afraid of rejection. ("Rejection!" I call out to the workshop participants. "The number one cause of death among men!") My initial question to the workshop participants is "How do you know she wants a kiss?" which yields the typical stereotypes of our pop culture: "She looks at you in a certain way," "She moves closer to you," or some intricate combination in which she looks at you, then away, then down, then back at you. The irony is that many men take this as "yes" and never bother to ask what their partner may actually feel like doing. "If all this body language is in place, and you're telling me that you know she wants a kiss," I ask them, "then you have your answer. Where is the risk in asking?"

There is nothing buried deep in the male soul that impels us to force someone to pleasure us. It is the pressure from without, from our male peers, from our cultural teaching, that pushes us constantly to score (to find a way, as the old frat phrase goes, to "work out a yes"). To live in a world ruled by the principles of patriarchy means a constant repression of feelings, a commitment to being violent, to putting your body at risk, to expressing affection either by slapping your male friends' backsides, or, with women,

scoring. Men have been denied that middle ground: affection, compassion, sensuality, compatibility, cooperation.

In coed workshops it is very effective to have a male-female presenter team; it is very important to model a positive, cooperative male-female dynamic, and it has been very effective in such workshops I've done in the past. However, I feel the work is incomplete if both genders don't get some time in the workshop in a same-sex-only setting. Female presenters are often unable to deal with the topic from a man's perspective. This is not meant to sound like a criticism; the fact is, it is not their job to deal with our oppression and pain—they have their own to work on, and that is plenty.

However, as a community invested in ending sexual assault—not just avoiding it but ending it—we must involve and engage men. We negotiate the contradiction of men-only spaces as sites for sexism, assault, and collusion by giving them a directly contradictory experience: a men-only space that challenges them to be accountable for their actions, while at the same time provides a forum for expressing their feelings of oppression. Much of the debate around the issue of men-only spaces has been caused by lack of understanding between men and women of each other's processes. So I am trying to paint an accurate picture of what occurs in one of our workshops so that we can move beyond generalizations (and the fear caused by our assumptions) and into more focused critique.

Thus, we arrive back at my little cliffhanger. It was in such a men-only meeting, my third MSR meeting, in fact, in which a conversation took place that changed my life. In a discussion being led by Michael, one of MSR's founders, we came upon the topic of consent. In response to a question Michael was tossing around the circle of six men, I said, "Yes, of course you ask the woman [you] are with—up to a point." Michael encouraged me to go further with my comment: What was that "point"? I launched into a detailed explanation of "failsafe"—the point at which a man is so committed to orgasm that, like our B-52 bombers (notice the military allusions in our sexual discourse), he cannot be called back to base. In other words, I reiterated, "I reach that certain point at which I cannot stop."

Michael leaned back in his chair and nodded with a skeptical squint in his eyes. After a moment he offered: "Let's play a little game . . . it's just an exercise, just to think about. You've gone on a date with a woman. You've talked and asked questions, you've gone back to your place, and you've both consented to having sex. Along the way you're asking and checking in and everything is fine; you start having intercourse, you're inside her, and everything feels great. The woman suddenly says, 'Stephen, wait . . . I'm not feeling well, I don't know, maybe something I ate . . . . Could we just hold up for a second?' Does she have the right?"

With that last question he leaned forward in his chair with a penetrating, inviting expression on his face; the inference was that it was a question to be answered not out loud, but in my own heart. My brain raced; the only possible answer to that question kept bumping into the brick wall of my social programming—"No . . . no, she can't . . . how can she . . . ," or even better, "How dare she?" The feeling was one of being cheated, having my power taken away; and yet my conscience could not accept any other answer but yes. To answer any other way is to put that woman in a category one step removed from human being.

None of the other men in the circle reacted with anger toward me; instead they sat silently nodding. The profound quality of that moment sticks with me to this day. To move beyond the superficial "We shouldn't rape, I know it's bad" to recognizing that what perpetuates a culture of rape is the inability of society to grant a woman the most fundamental of human rights: sovereignty over her own person. Further, then to make the connection that such a right was exactly what I wanted for myself—sovereignty over my own body, my own life.

Ultimately, the most effective sexual assault prevention education programming must allow for coed workshops copresented by male and female facilitators to be augmented by separate single-sex discussions. Too often men's sexism is reaffirmed because they imagine feminism as a great big ax coming at them to remove their sexuality, to empower women at the expense of men. As a man reaching out into my community of men, I am spreading the message that the true intent of feminism is equality. For men that means being accountable for our actions; it also means empowering ourselves to reconstruct masculinity in a way that allows us to be caring, communicative, and supportive, not only with intimate partners, but with each other as well. A true ending to the rape culture in which we now live will come only when we can educate men about how much more rewarding consensual relationships can be, not only for the women in our lives, but for ourselves.

NOTE

1. Peggy Reeves Sanday, *Fraternity Gang Rape: Sex, Brotherhood, and Privilege on Campus.* New York: New York University Press, 1990.

Using Pornography

Robert Jensen

MY NARRATIVE

> History gets written with the mind holding the pen. What would it look like, what would it read like, if it got written with the body holding the pen?
>
> (Berman, 1990, p. 110).

In this section of the chapter, I want to let my body hold the pen.

First, the potentially relevant facts about who "I" am include, in no particular order: white and of northern European ancestry, born in 1958, Midwestern born and currently living in the south, raised in the lower-middle to middle class and now residing in the middle class, married for six years until a recent divorce, father of a 5-year-old boy, living as a heterosexual most of my life until recently coming out (more on that later), anti-sexist/pro-feminist, anti-racist, anti-capitalist, the third of four children from a typically dysfunctional American family with one alcoholic parent.

I have spent much time in the past decade trying to be in my body as I have researched and written about pornography. In conjunction with many other sources of information presented in this chapter, I-in-my-body have insights into the role of pornography in the construction of male sexuality in contemporary U.S. culture.

Part of the authority for that claim comes from a simple observation: I get erections from pornography. I take that to be epistemologically significant; my body understands the charge of pornography. Because I was raised in a sexist culture with few (if any) influences that mitigated that sexism, I am in a position to explore how that sexual charge is connected to the ideology of male dominance and female submission that structures contemporary commercial pornography.

I focus on this embodied, personal approach partly in reaction to the scholarly literature on pornography, so much of which is written by men and is distinctly disembodied (for exceptions, see Abbott, 1990; Baker, 1992; and Kimmel, 1990). Political tracts, law review articles, and reports of social science studies written by men rarely include any acknowledgment of the position of the author in a pornographic world, let alone an examination of what it means for how one comes to know about pornography. That kind of embodied exploration is rare because, as feminist theorists have long pointed out, in all those areas—philosophy, law, social science—emotional detachment and objectivity are seen as virtues. But that stance actually has repressed much of what we might know about pornography. As Morris Berman (1990, p. 110) puts it, "[T]o leave your body and believe that you can still know anything at all is quite literally a form of madness." In that sense, many of the scholarly works on pornography are quite mad—misguided attempts to sever mind and body, reason and emotion—that lead to less, not more, trustworthy knowledge.

In the remainder of this chapter I will say a bit more about the value of embodied narratives, describe my own pornography use, and offer observations on pornography's effects on me and men.

Embodied Narratives

Consciousness-raising for men is loaded with potential problems if done in isolation from women, a problem that can be seen in various parts of the contemporary men's movement, especially the mythopoetic wing, where a focus on the personal often impedes social analysis and liberatory politics (Jensen, 1995a; Kimmel & Kaufman, 1994). For men, the process must include women; that is, we have to pay attention to feminist criticism to help us make sense of our experience. Men must acknowledge that women have some epistemic privilege—the idea that "members of an oppressed group have a more immediate, subtle and critical knowledge about the nature of their oppression than people who are nonmembers of the oppressed group" (Narayan, 1988, p. 35). My goal is to examine my life and compare it with the narratives of other men, using feminist insights to make sense of it all. Of course, there is never a unified feminist or women's stance on any question. My job is not simply to listen to women and do what they say, since "they" do not speak with one voice and I have to remain responsible for my choices. In my work in feminist theory, I have tried to listen to the many voices speaking on the issue of pornography and have made commitments to a radical feminist position (and to particular women in feminism) that I think best explains the world as I understand it. This process is always ongoing; at the same time, one must make choices between conflicting accounts of the world and act on those choices (Jensen, 1997b).

So, this writing is an attempt at the "critical story-telling" that Jeff Hearn (1987, p. 182) calls for in the project of "collective self-reflective theorising." To reiterate points made earlier in this chapter, I do not assert that my experience with pornography can be generalized to all men. Instead, I view this as a contribution to an ongoing conversation about pornography. Such work is difficult to do with integrity, but my hope is, following Joseph Boone, that:

> if the male critic can discover a position from which to speak that neither elides the importance of feminism to his work nor ignores the specificity of his gender, he may also find that his voice no longer exists as an abstraction, but that it in fact inhabits a body: its own sexual/textual body (Boone, 1990, p. 12).

As introduction to my story, I need to explain my own journey to this position. My early work on legal aspects of the pornography debate used traditional methods, which allowed me to distance myself from my personal experience with pornography. But a growing sense of dissatisfaction with that work led me to a project designed to confront the content of pornography in 20 pornographic paperback novels analyzed in the previous chapter. I read the books, taking detailed notes about scenes, themes, portrayals, and language used. In the role of detached investigator, I tried to move through the books using my "rational" faculties, but I found that my body kept making its presence known; I kept getting erections.

Before I started that project I was aware that pornography still could produce intense sexual reactions in me, even though at that time it had been several years since my last contact with pornography (I stopped using pornography after returning to graduate school and coming into contact with the feminist critique). Yet, in my pursuit of intellectual knowledge I had detached from the emotional, embodied knowledge of my past experience with pornography; the scholarly endeavor insulated me from those other ways of knowing about pornography. The deeper I got into the scholarly work, the further I got from that embodied knowledge until, finally, I was forced to confront it through the reaction of my body. As I read the books, intellectually I was able to identify and analyze the misogynistic images and messages, but physically, my body responded the way it had been trained.

That reaction threw into question assumptions that I had been smugly comfortable with. This had, and continues to have, an important effect on my sexuality and my personal life. My concern here, however, is with the equally important effect that experience has had on my scholarly work. I realized that I could no longer deny that part of what I knew about pornography was personal and embodied, and that I would have to explore those issues if I wanted to be [a] competent and ethical researcher. As I planned the interviews with pornography users, I knew I would have to write my own story as well as theirs.

A Personal History of Pornography Use

I begin this account with the understanding that my interpretation of my experiences can be challenged. Clearly, I have a kind of access to my emotions and sexual reactions that others do not. But in invoking the personal, I don't claim I am exempt from critique; experience is not a guarantee of insightful interpretation. This is my narrative, my reconstruction of experience. At various points in my life there will be varying personal and political factors that shape my understanding of self. There is no experience of self unmediated by culture, no pretheoretical knowledge of the self. My interpretations have changed over time, and what I offer is the best reading I have of them at this time, a reading that others may have grounds to challenge.

From my research and informal discussions with men, I believe that my use of pornography is fairly typical for a United States male born after World War II, what I call the *Playboy* generation. My exposure to pornography began around second grade. I have hazy memories of a soft-core motorcycle magazine, which included pictures of women naked from the waist up, that a friend had found and hid in his backyard. Using the magazine was always a group project; we would pass it around and comment on the women's bodies. After that, someone in my circle of friends almost always had a copy of *Playboy*, *Penthouse*, or some similar magazine that had been found, stolen from a store, or taken from dad. One friend had a hiding place in his attic, where we occasionally would go to look at them.

In my first year of high school, I had a friend who had perfected the art of getting into movie theaters through exit doors. Usually we went into mainstream films, but when we felt bold we made a run at X-rated movies. I also remember having access to pornographic novels in my high school years and finding them as intense an experience as the visual material.

In college I saw a few X-rated movies with friends (both all-male and mixed-gender groups), who treated the outings as campy fun, and I went to a couple of those movies on my own. When I would go with friends from our small-town college to Minneapolis, we often would stop at pornography shops to see what the big city had to offer. In my 20s, my use of pornography was episodic. At various times I would feel drawn to pornographic movies, and in a six- or seven-year period, I probably saw 10 to 15 of them, once or twice with someone else, but usually alone. I saw some of these movies at mainstream theaters, but more typically at adult theaters and bookstores, where I would browse among other material. The movies were what is most often called hard-core pornography: graphic sex scenes built around a contrived story line. I typically stayed for no more than 15 to 30 minutes; after the initial excitement wore off, feelings of guilt and shame made it uncomfortable to be in those theaters.

I typically did not purchase pornography to use at home, although through the years I occasionally bought magazines such as *Playboy* and *Penthouse*. I never showed pornography to women with whom I was involved, with the exception of one trip to an adult theater with a girlfriend in college. I never made homemade pornography or recorded sexual activity.

Although I did not actively use pornography with partners, pornography was central to my sex life at various times. From grade school on, I masturbated to pornographic images, either those in front of me or those retained in my mind from earlier consumption. I focused on certain kinds of images (women performing oral sex on men, men penetrating women anally, group sex involving a woman and more than one man), and I could summon up those images easily.

This brief summary of my past pornography use leaves out some details that are too painful to recount in a public forum. Even though I no longer use pornography, this still was difficult to write. In my anxiety and fear is a lesson about pornography. At the macro level, pornography works to create, maintain, and reinforce a system of male control. But for each individual who uses pornography, the story is more complicated and not just an expression of the desire to control women. I feel a kind of residual guilt and shame over my use of pornography, even though I realize most men have had similar experiences. Some of the pornography users I interviewed expressed the same feelings. Others expressed no regrets over their use and were proud of what they saw as a transcendence of sexual inhibitions. While it is difficult to generalize about these emotions, I believe that, like me, most men who use pornography struggle with the mixed messages from society. On the one hand, pornography is widely accepted and can be used for male bonding; in other situations, a man's use of it can be turned against him with the charge that he can't get a "real woman." Men who were raised in sexually or emotionally repressed families, again like me, may use pornography but then confront those early internalized proscriptions.

Although I have been arguing for the importance of narratives, these differences in men's reactions to their own pornography use highlight how important it is to remember that no single narrative is the whole story. That does not mean that no coherent account of pornography in this society can be constructed. It need not be shown that all men use pornography in exactly the same way for pornography to be a key component of a system of male dominance. In this case, for instance, whether a pornography user feels guilt and shame or is proud of his use, the result is generally the same: The use of pornography continues.

Pornography and I

I focus now on the effects pornography had on me. In my experience:

1. Pornography was an important means of sex education.
2. Pornography constructed women as objects, which encouraged me to see women in real life in that same way.

3. Pornography created or reinforced desires for specific acts, most of which focused on male pleasure and can cause female pain.
4. Rather than unlocking sexual creativity, pornography shaped and constrained my sexual imagination with its standardized scripts.
5. Race was an important aspect of pornography, reinforcing my view of women of color as the "exotic primitive."
6. Viewing a large amount of overtly violent pornography was not necessary for pornography to have the effect of eroticizing violence for me.
7. That eroticization of violence had a tangible effect on my sex life.
8. Pornography is most centrally about control, and I was attracted to it by my need for a sense of control over women and their sexuality.

Sex Education

Sex was not openly discussed in my home and at the time I was growing up sex education in the schools was limited or nonexistent. So, most of my sexual education came on the streets with peers and was rooted in pornography. It was in that material that I first saw nude adult women and figured out the mechanics of sex.

There is nothing inherently problematic about learning about sexuality from a publication. The problem is when those publications construct sexuality in a male-dominant framework and present women as sexual objects. These images were incredibly powerful for me and my childhood friends. They helped plant in me some basic assumptions about sex: that a certain kind of female appearance was most desirable, that women could be used for sex in ways portrayed in the magazines and movies (as well as through my use of those materials), that women's resistance to certain kinds of sexual activity was the result of prudish inhibitions that could, and should, be overcome.

Those messages were transmitted by other cultural products and institutions as well, but it was in pornography that I found them most explicitly expressed.

Objectification of Women

Women are objectified not only in pornography, of course, but in numerous other sites in the culture. For me, pornography intensified that tendency to see women first and foremost not so much as sexual beings but as sexual objects for men to view and use. For me, the immediate "sizing up" of a woman is institutionalized; that is, it takes active effort on my part to interrupt the process and refuse to objectify. The reality is, of course, that I often let the process continue, even though I am aware of what I am doing. That is one of the most basic privileges of being a man; I always have the option of ignoring my own convictions and using a woman for my own fantasy.

Is this really an act of male supremacy, or simply an appreciation of female beauty or an acknowledgment of human sexuality? I do not mean to suggest that sexual attraction is inherently corrupt; to raise these issues is not to advocate a prudish repression of sexuality. But it is crucial to examine the power at work in sexual situations. Heterosexual men's sexuality in this culture is constructed around the domination of women. In some other world, one not structured by sexism, my concerns perhaps could be minimized. But in a culture that for centuries has defined woman as object, it is essential that men be aware of, and honest about, the way in which we see women.

Again, pornography is not the only element in this construction of women. But my use of pornography was a central component of it. In my case, I have seen women on the street and created sexual scenes with them that were taken directly from pornography I had seen. That has not happened in some time; it's one thing I no longer allow myself. But the fact that it was once a routine part of my sexual imagination tells me something about how pornography has affected my view of women.

Although some commentators have suggested that such objectification is unavoidable, even natural, I believe that resisting it is a fundamental step for men trying to avoid sexist behavior. As Susanne Kappeler (1986, p. 61) writes:

> The fundamental problem at the root of men's behavior in the world, including sexual assault, rape, wife battering, sexual harassment, keeping women in the home and in unequal opportunities and conditions, treating them as objects for conquest and protection—the root problem behind the reality of men's relations with women, is the way men see women, is Seeing.

Desire

As the testimony of women has pointed out, men's desire for certain kinds of sexual activity can be taken directly from pornography. The question of the causal chain likely cannot be answered definitively: Do the desires exist independently and then get represented in pornography, or does pornography help create the desires? One convention of pornography that we discussed previously leads me to think that in some ways, pornography can construct desire. Since the mid-1970s, the cum shot—showing the man ejaculating onto the woman's body—has been a standard of explicit pornography to provide visual proof of men's pleasure (Williams, 1989). As a veteran pornographic movie actor put it, "The cum shot in the face is the stock-in-trade of orgasms. It's the ejaculation into a woman's waiting face that gets the audience off more than anything else" (Bill Margold, quoted in Hebditch and Anning, 1988, p. 31).

Some of the men I interviewed said they enjoyed that type of climax, and I can recall similar desires in the past. Consider this comment from a man's response to a sex survey:

> Nude pictures from men's magazines turn me on, and when I finally ejaculate, I aim right at the girl's breasts, pubic hair, or buttocks, whichever pleases me most. The more copious my output of sperm, the more satisfied I am (Hite, 1982, p. 781).

Did that desire arise from some "natural" source? From a social construction view of sexuality, the concept of authentic sexual desire is problematic; there is no pure, natural sexuality that isn't mediated by culture. Here I simply contend that pornography is a force that can shape desire and that we should be concerned with how men may be conditioned to desire sexual acts that are humiliating, degrading, or painful for women.

Scripting Sex

Several men I interviewed argued that sexually explicit material helped open up their sexual horizons. For me, pornography constricted, not expanded, my sexual imagination. Looking back on my experiences, I see no evidence that pornography fueled sexual creativity or sparked creative fantasies. Fantasy, in this sense, implies a flight of imagination, a letting go of oneself, the possibility of transcending the ordinary. For me, pornography did none of those things. It constrained my imagination, helped keep me focused on sexual activity that was rooted in male dominance, and hindered me from moving beyond the ordinary misogyny of the culture. Instead of my imagination running wild, my imagination was locked into a film loop, reproducing scripts and scenes from pornography. Pornographic sexuality—as reproduced in pornography and throughout our culture—crippled my erotic imagination, and I have only recently begun the long project of recovering the erotic, in the expanded sense the term is used by such writers as Carter Heyward (1989) and Audre Lorde (1984).

A validation of this view comes, ironically, from the pornographic actor Bill Margold, who saw no harm in pornography but understood the way it restricts the erotic. In discussing why people need pornographic films, he said: "We're drowning in our own sexual quicksand because there's a lack of imagination" (quoted in Hebditch and Anning, 1988, p. 27).

Race

For me, racial differences had erotic potential. Some of the men I interviewed, all of whom were white, said that they did not like pornography that used women of color and fast-forwarded past it in videotapes or passed over it in magazines. There was no pattern to these judgments; some men liked Asian women but not black women, while for others the opposite was true. Some men only wanted to watch white women. In the pornography market, there are publications and films that cater to all these tastes.

Those two responses—fascination with, or distaste for, women of color—are flip sides of the same racist coin. For white consumers, women of color can be even more sexually stimulating. For some, such as me, that connected to the stereotype of the "exotic primitive" and conjured up images of a wild sexuality. So, I found pornography that used women of color especially attractive and have specific memories of pornographic magazines that featured black women and Asian women. That reaction, of course, is hardly progressive. The pornography that highlighted nonwhite women played on stereotypes of the subservient Asian woman, the hot-blooded Latina, and

the sexually promiscuous black woman. Although I did not consider myself racist at the time, my interest in such material grew out of the racism I had learned (and continue to struggle to unlearn), just expressed in a manner less overtly racist than those men who told me they found women of color in pornography to be unattractive to them.

Violence and Pornography

As in the previous chapter, I use the terms "violent" and "nonviolent" hesitantly, because there is no clear line between the two categories in a misogynistic culture. But in the common use of those terms, violent pornography is usually taken to mean depictions of sexual activity that include overt violence, such as physical abuse, the use of restraints, the presence of weapons, or strong verbal coercion. Nonviolent pornography usually describes depictions of sexual activity without those elements. The feminist claim that pornography fuses sex and violence is often rejected by men who say they do not use or enjoy violent pornography. But pornography does not need to be overtly violent to be part of a process by which violence is eroticized. I was never interested in overtly violent pornography, yet I was conditioned, in part by "nonviolent" pornography, to accept violence as erotic. Again, this is one of those claims that is difficult to prove because we live in a culture that, in general, sexualizes violence; no one can say for sure what specific images or influences create an appetite for sexualized violence. But my sense from my life is that pornography played an important role.

I realized that violence had been eroticized for me when reading the novels previously mentioned. At the time, I would have vigorously denied any claim that I found sexual violence erotic. But as I read those books, I was aroused by descriptions of sexual violence, such as a description of a man's sexual torture of a woman with whips and other paraphernalia. No matter what I thought about sexual violence, the eroticization of violence had taken place in my body; it worked on me. I responded sexually not only to the descriptions of sex, but also to those portions that used explicit violence and coercion. I found myself becoming sexually aroused by material that violated what I thought was my own sense of what was appropriate and healthy sex. I wanted to reject any experience of pleasure from those images, but my body accepted them.

What I had learned to find arousing was a basic power dynamic of male dominance and female subordination, which is much the same in violent and nonviolent pornography. Once male dominance is eroticized, male violence becomes at least potentially erotic. I could have denied that, as I think many men do, but my sexual reaction to the novels uncovered the reality of my erotic imagination.

Sex and Violence in the World

In defense of pornography, F.M. Christensen (1990, p. 41) argues that "the existence of violent sex in no way impugns nonviolent sex or its portrayal." I disagree. When the sex depicted in pornography is conditioned by male dominance, the line between the violent and nonviolent isn't nearly as crucial as many would like to believe. The hierarchical structure of nonviolent pornography trained my body to understand the erotic potential that this culture has assigned to rape. During my study of pornography I learned that rape was sexy to me. That reality had been living in my body for some time, but it was disturbing to admit. It led to the inescapable conclusion that I am capable of rape, even if I can't imagine ever committing such an act. The simple truth is that in this culture, men have

to make a conscious decision not to rape, because rape is so readily available to us and so rarely results in sanctions of any kind.

If that claim about violence I just made is true—that both the sex offenders and I learned to eroticize violence—then why have I never committed a sex crime? First, to repeat earlier assertions, it is not my contention, nor the contention of anyone in the feminist anti-pornography movement, that pornography alone causes rape or that all pornography users commit rape. A complex network of factors lead a man to rape, and while pornography can be an important component, it obviously is not the only one.

But it also is important to remember that while I say I have never committed a sex crime, all I can really say is that I have not committed a sex crime under the male-defined sexual standards of this culture, which are similar to the standards set out in pornography. My own sexual definitions were framed by my use of pornography, and according to those definitions I have not raped. Yet, I do not know if that is an opinion that would be shared by every woman I have known (Jensen, 1995a). After trying to examine my sexual history from a non-pornographic perspective, I still come to the conclusion that I never crossed the line into coerced sex. But the final answer to that question would have to come from those women.

Control

The single most important thing I have learned from analyzing my own history and from the interviews is how central the concept of control—of women by men—is to pornography. In my life, that is most clear from the period in which I used pornography the most heavily. It came in my mid-20s after the break-up of an intense relationship with a woman. One reason I found the relationship, and its unraveling, so troublesome was that I was not in control. In most of my intimate relationships before and after, I retained most of the power to make basic decisions about the nature of the relationship. But in that situation, for a variety of reasons, I gave up control to the woman. That left me in a particularly volatile emotional state after the break-up, which I believe made pornography even more attractive.

In pornography, control remains in male hands in two ways. First, the magazines and movies that I can recall seeing depicted sexual encounters in which men were in control, guiding women's actions to produce male pleasure. The images that stay with me from that period are those in which the woman was completely subordinate, performing sexual acts on, and for, the man. Second, by making female sexuality a commodity, pornography allowed me to control when and where I used it, and therefore used the women in it. Barry Brummett makes this point in his analysis of pornographic movies viewed on a home VCR,

pointing out how the control offered by the text is reinforced by the control offered by the medium (the ability to fast-forward and rewind to play back):

> VCRs never say no to their users; neither do characters in pornographic films. People agree to requests for sex with the same instant and uncritical willingness shown by the television and the VCR (Brummett, 1988, p. 209).

Technological advances continue to offer consumers even more control. In a story about the growing market in pornographic CD-ROMs, a sex shop manager explained, "They're good for releasing a little tension. CD-ROMs are great because you can control everything, all the action" (quoted in Marriott, 1995, B7). But all pornography offers that control to the consumer at some level. For me, retreating to a pornographic world allowed me to regain a sense of control over female sexuality that I had lost in real life.

Sex, Friendship, and Gender Roles Among Gay Men

Peter M. Nardi

The connection between sexual orientation and gender roles has been confused by many people. Too often, assumptions about homosexuality or heterosexuality have led to assumptions about masculinity or femininity. Altman (1982, p. 55) states it succinctly:

> [T]he belief that homosexuality is somehow a reflection of a blurred sense of masculinity/femininity remains central to the Western imagination, and to the extent that our concepts of gender have implied a heterosexual norm, this is important in understanding the development of homosexual identity.

Understanding the differences between sexual identity and gender roles is enhanced when focusing on the issues of friendship and sex among gay men. For many people, being gay has been interpreted in terms of not being masculine or, more specifically, being seen as feminine. In fact, this attribution is arguably at the core of why homosexuality in men is feared by many and why many men fear expressions of intimacy and emotional closeness (Segal, 1990). Not only does a culture ascribe certain traits to men and women and then label those traits in terms of masculine or feminine social roles, but those roles are also attributed to sexual desire, especially among homosexuals (Altman, 1982).

Peter M. Nardi, *Men's Friendships,* pp. 173–185. © 1992 by Sage Publications, Inc. Reprinted by Permission of Sage Publications, Inc.

What results, then, is a belief that gay men can act in some areas in traditionally masculine ways (primarily in the sexual arena) and in other areas in traditionally feminine ways (such as emotional relationships, temperament, or sometimes body language). Over the past several decades, this belief has evolved as American society experienced the transformation of much of gay subculture from feminine to masculine to androgynous images.

Throughout the 1970s, as the contemporary gay movement developed, a new style of homosexual manliness was constructed (Humphreys, 1971). Partly in compensatory reaction to the stigma of femininity and passivity imposed on gay men, a macho and hypermasculine look evolved (Levine, 1988). But it was also partly an expression of traditional male gender roles that existed all along for most gay men who had been socialized into masculinity and lived in gender conformity as children. In fact, one could interpret the changes dialectically: Pre-Stonewall imagery of gay men was primarily feminine; post-Stonewall and pre-AIDS semiotics of gay men were primarily masculine; and the AIDS years have synthesized these images into an androgynous look, on one hand eschewing the iconography of masculine gay clones (no facial hair, less macho clothing), and on the other hand adopting a combination of both masculine and feminine images (earrings, ponytails, for some, and masculine but stylish clothes).

The distinctions between such concepts as *masculinity* and *gay* are highlighted when discussing the role of friendship in gay men's lives. While evidence exists that many gay men relate to their friends in gender non-conforming ways that are not typical of the ways heterosexual men interact with their friends (Sherrod & Nardi, 1988), other data about the role of sex in their friendships support how much traditional male roles persist. In some ways, gay men's friendships are a good example of a combination of traditionally defined masculine and feminine gender roles that appear to characterize some of contemporary gay male subcultures. And by focusing attention on the role of sex in friendship, many of these issues are highlighted.

SEX AND FRIENDSHIP

Perhaps the least studied area in the friendship literature is the role sex and sexual attraction play in the development of friendship, and when it is discussed, it is primarily about heterosexual opposite-sex friendships. Seiden and Bart (1975, p. 220) speculate that "There is probably an erotic component in most close friendships. . . . but this appears to be disturbing to many people and is denied or repressed." Rubin (1985, p. 179) similarly argues:

> More than others, best friends are drawn together in much the same way as lovers— by something ineffable, something to which, most people say, it is almost impossible to give words. . . . [P]eople often talk as if something happened to them in the same way they "happened" to fall in love and marry.

Although Rubin (p. 180) also says that in friendship "the explicitly sexual is muted, if not fully out of consciousness," she does acknowledge the "appeal of the physical" in the process of friendship initiation and development. She feels that "most friends come together out of some combination of attraction to the other and their internal psychological needs and desires."

The sexual component in friendships typically emerges when discussing cross-sex friendships among heterosexuals. O'Meara (1989, p. 530) concludes:

> [C]ross-sex friendship is an ambiguous relationship in American culture in the sense that it has a deviant status reflected in a lack of instructive role models and appropriate terminology to capture its unique qualities, lacks coherent cultural scripts for guiding everyday interaction, and is influenced by gender-based schematic processing. . . . [C]ross-sex friends must continuously negotiate the private rules that guide their everyday behavior in a context that treats their existence as deviant and even threatening.

However, the more the social environment provides a context for initiating and maintaining cross-gender friendships while minimizing the relevance of the sexual dimension, the more likely such friendships can occur (Allan, 1989). So, when work situations are no longer dependent on a gender division of labor, when the age and marital status of the people involved are young and single, and when the potential friends are not constrained by traditional gender-role proscriptions, then the possibilities for a nonsexual cross-gender friendship increase.

When a sexual friendship does occur, "the basis of the solidarity of the friendship is altered and usually it is difficult to revert to the previous state once the sexual relationship ends" (Allan, p. 83). O'Meara (p. 534) similarly reports that for many men sex in friendship with women often destroys the friendship and, thus, passion and sexual attraction must be "continually monitored, contended with, and regulated through negotiation."

An interesting test case of the role of sex, gender roles, and sexual attraction in friendship is available when studying the friendships among gay men. O'Meara (p. 529) boldly states (without data to support it) that "this factor of sexual attraction appears nonexistent in friendships among gays." But given the sociological argument that "different 'boundaries' are constructed around friendships" in part due to personal choice and the sociocultural context (Allan, p. 15), the friendships of gay men might have a very different sexual component to them than cross-gender heterosexual friendships.

Sonenschein (1968), in an early ethnography of a gay male community, develops a typology of relationships based on duration and level of sexuality. Essentially, he argues that first order friendships (best and really close friends) and second order friendships (good friends but not permanent) were entirely nonsexual. Extended encounters (sexual affairs) were often unstable and not characterized by strongly committed social support, while brief encounters were typically nonpermanent sexual relationships. Permanent partners (lovers) are sociosexual relationships akin to heterosexual marriages in terms of commitment and stability. For the most part, Sonenschein concludes, gay men tend to separate those individuals who serve their social needs from those who serve their sexual needs.

A similar argument was made in an interview with a gay man in his twenties:

> I will not and have never had sex with any friend. I've either dated the person or became friends with them. Once I went out with this guy for 2 months and there was no physical relationship yet. We had agreed to take it slowly. But one day I realized I didn't want to sleep with him, so we talked about it. He's now my closest friend in the city.

On the other hand, sex and friendship may be more connected for other gay men. White (1983, p. 16) discusses the role of sex and friendship in his essay about gay men in the 1980s by comparing it to Japanese court life of the tenth century:

> Friendship . . . intertwines with sexual adventure and almost always outlasts it; a casual encounter can lead to a lifelong, romantic but sexless friendship. . . . [S]ex, love and friendship may overlap but are by no means wholly congruent. In this society, moreover, it is friendship that provides the emotional and social continuity, whereas sexuality is not more and no less than an occasion for gallantry.

In some cases, gay men are acquaintances first and then become sexual partners; in general, though, people seem to be clearly distinguished as sexual partners or social partners, but rarely both simultaneously. Sonenschein (p. 72) speculates as to whether the category of "friends" is "really a residual category of individuals who did not work out as sexual partners or whether there are differential expectations through which individuals are initially screened to become either 'friends' or 'partners.'" The evidence from his observations and from our own data indicates that both processes operate: Many gay men have had sex with their best friends, but many have been sexually attracted without sex taking place.

One 34-year-old male we interviewed said:

> The best close friends I had were from when I was sexually active. . . . I would date for a few weeks and when they got too "amorous," I was very good at stopping the sex and turning it into a friendship. . . . It upsets me to realize that I cannot make new friends unless I work with them or have sex with them.

Given the dearth of studies on gay friendship, rather than develop research to test specific hypotheses, we designed an exploratory study to assess the relationship between sex and friendship among gay men. What follows, then, is both a speculative essay on the possibilities of sex and friendship among gay men and also a presentation of data from a survey of 161 gay men that explores these issues.

What guides this exploratory research is an attempt to understand the role masculinity plays in contributing to the relationship between sex and friendship among men. While a study of white, middle-class gay men does not directly answer such questions about heterosexual men or men in various ethnic and racial subcultures, it does introduce some insights and research questions about the interaction of gender, sexual orientation, and the structure of friendships.

SPECULATIONS AND POSSIBILITIES

While there is evidence that some gay men recollect playing gender non-conforming roles and games as children (see Harry, 1982), there is no reason to conclude that all gay men were socialized without the traditional and normative values and roles of what the culture defines as masculine. Those traditional norms typically include the expectation that men be sexually assertive in relationships and initiate sexual activity. Furthermore, evidence from research on teenage sexuality often indicates that boys are sexual before intimacy is achieved with a partner (in fact, they try to gain intimacy through the sexual act), while girls more often seek intimacy prior to a sexual act.

Whether such patterns hold among homosexual boys and girls is rarely studied. But if one assumes a typical male socialization pattern, then we might conclude that gay men—being true to their gender roles—are likely to have sexual experiences with friends, perhaps as a way of achieving friendship. On the other hand, if we assume that gay men as boys were different in the enactment of traditional gender roles, then friendship might precede sexuality as a pattern in their lives.

Another avenue of research might concern the topic of attraction and friendship, independent of sexual behavior. If indeed attraction plays a part in the formation of all friendships, attraction (and the willingness to admit it) may emerge as an even more salient factor in gay men's friendships, since the potentiality for sexual interaction is much more likely.

In addition, the notion of falling in love with a friend can also be explored more directly with a gay male sample. Unlike any reluctance to discuss this subject among heterosexual cross-sex and same-sex friendships, gay friendships can address this topic clearly. In short, by using a sample of gay men, the issues of sexual attraction, being in love, and sexual behavior among friends can be investigated. In so doing, we can get a sharper understanding of the contextual nature of friendship and gender roles and the variations that exist among different subgroups of men.

METHODOLOGY

Subjects

One hundred and sixty-one gay men and 122 lesbians responded to a questionnaire survey, representing a response rate of 48% of the 620 subjects who were contacted through gay and lesbian organizations in the greater Los Angeles metropolitan area. For the purposes of this article, only the data from the gay men are discussed, except where information about gay men's friendships is clarified by comparison with the lesbians. (For further details about this study and additional data from the questionnaires, see Sherrod & Nardi, 1988.)

Because of the topic of this research, snowball sampling techniques—typically used in studies of stigmatized and hard-to-locate subjects where random sampling is impossible—was not used to obtain respondents. The built-in bias of sampling friends of friends with snowball methods might have produced a distorted picture of friendship patterns. Therefore, respondents were obtained by contacting gay and lesbian organizations, including political, social, religious, and professional organizations. Admittedly, the sample we obtained through this "social outcropping" technique may also be a biased sample of the population, but given the choices, we decided that the biases associated with the social outcropping technique would be less than those associated with the snowball method. As a result, the current study focuses on friendship among a sample of white, educated, middle- and upper-middle-class, urban gay men and lesbians who are open and attending gay-identified organizations. Consequently, the results may not be generalizable to nonurban, nonwhite, working-class, closeted gay men and lesbians who are not affiliated with gay-identified political and social organizations.

QUESTIONNAIRE

A 19-page questionnaire was developed and pilot-tested on a small sample of gay men and lesbians. A revised form took approximately 30 minutes to complete. Questionnaires were preaddressed and stamped for easy return. The questionnaire asked respondents to provide information about three types of friendship: *casual friends, close friends,* and a *best friend.* These three categories of friendship were selected because previous research had demonstrated that people typically employ such categories when describing their friends (Caldwell & Peplau, 1982; Wright, 1982). The questionnaire included the following definitions of each type of friendship: A *casual friend* is "someone who is more than an acquaintance, but not a close friend; your commitment to the friendship would probably not extend beyond the circumstances that bring you together; for example, a work friend or neighbor." A *close friend* is "someone to whom you feel a sense of mutual commitment and continuing closeness; a person

with whom you talk fairly openly and feel comfortable spending time." A *best friend* is "the friend to whom you feel the greatest commitment and closeness; the one who accepts you 'as you are,' with whom you talk the most openly and feel the most comfortable spending time." A question was also asked to determine whether the best friend was a current lover or partner of the respondents; if so, respondents were instructed to select another best friend for this section of the questionnaire, someone other than the lover/partner, if one existed. If someone had more than one best friend, respondents were instructed to select only one when answering this section of the questionnaire.

Respondents were asked to report whether they (a) had ever been sexually attracted to their best friend, (b) were sexually involved with their best friend, and (c) were ever in love with their best friend both "in the past" and "currently." We also asked them if they had sex with their casual friends and with their close friends (using a 5-point scale from "None" to "Most").

In addition, respondents were asked to indicate (using a 5-point Likert scale where 1 = lowest and 5 = highest): (a) how much they have *actually* discussed their own sexual behavior with their casual, close, and best friends, and (b) how *important* it is to talk about sexual issues or concerns with their casual, close, and best friends.

RESULTS

When we asked respondents to rate how important it was to have friends who they can talk with about sex, the percentage who answered "very important" or "extremely important" (4 and 5 on the scale) increased as they referred to casual, close, and best friends. As Table 1 (A) illustrates, 18.6% of the gay men said they felt it was either very important or extremely important to talk to their casual friends about sex; 56% said so about their close friends; and 76.2% said that about their best friend. Conversely, the percentage of those who feel it is not at all important (1 on the scale), decreased across the three categories of friendship from 32% to 4% to 2%. In brief, gay men expect to be able to talk about sex with their friends, especially their best friend and close friends.

Likewise (see Table 1, B), we find that 71.2% of the gay men have discussed with their best friend all or almost all details about sex; 53.4% have with their close friends; and fewer than 18% have with their casual friends. Fewer than 1% responded that they never discussed anything about sex with their best friend, around 10% said that about their close friends, and 36% of the gay men did not discuss sex at all with their casual friends. In short, one of the characteristics about best and close friends is that they are the people gay men talk to about sex.

When respondents were asked to indicate with how many of their casual and close same-sex friends they actually had sex over the years, 37.5% said with none of their casual friends, and 24.2% said with none of their close friends (see Table 1, C). In comparison to lesbians, gay men were much more likely to have had sex with their casual friends (66.4% of the lesbians said they did not have sex with any of their casual friends) and to have had sex with their close friends (41.3% of the lesbians said with none of their close friends).

Despite some popular literature that suggests that gay men have many straight female friends, about 82% of our sample said their best friend was a gay or bisexual male, and fewer than 10% said their best friend was a straight female. This lends support to Altman's (1982, p. 60) observation that the gay male proclamation that "all my friends are women" is more likely today to be "'*None* of my friends are not gay': the new identity/community/culture is producing a separatism that tends to isolate gay men from straight men, from women, and from children."

With this in mind, the following responses for the questions about best friend are tabulated only for those whose best friend was a gay or bisexual male. Recall, also, that subjects in relationships were asked to select a person other than their lover.

TABLE 1
Discussing Sex with Friends (N = 161)

A. How important is it for you to talk about sex with your friends?

	Casual	Close	Best
Not at all important	31.7%	3.8%	2.2%
Very important	14.3%	38.4%	39.6%
Extremely important	4.3%	17.6%	36.6%
Mean (scale of 1 to 5)	2.29	3.57	4.05

B. How much have you discussed sex with your friends?

	Casual	Close	Best
Not discussed at all	36.1%	9.4%	0.8%
Discussed almost all	10.8%	35.2%	28.0%
Discussed all	7.0%	18.2%	43.2%
Mean (scale of 1 to 5)	2.28	3.37	3.97

C. With how many of your casual and close same-sex friends have you had sex?

	Casual	Close
None	37.5%	24.2%
One or two	28.8%	42.2%
Some	26.9%	24.2%
Many	5.6%	5.6%
Most	1.3%	3.7%

As Table 2 shows, almost 80% of the gay men said they were attracted to their best friend in the past, and 52% continue to be attracted to him. Around 60% said they had sex with their best friend in the past, and 20% continue to do so. About 57% were in love with their best friend in the past, and 48% still are. Thus, in this particular sample, attraction clearly plays an important role in selection of a friend, and sex was once a part of that early friendship, as were feelings of love. Over time attraction and love have diminished for many, but almost half still maintain those emotions. However, few remain sexually involved any longer with their best friend. Approximately 20% of the gay men also said their current best friend is an ex-lover (in contrast to 45% of the lesbians).

DISCUSSION

Since this was an exploratory project, it is difficult to answer specific questions about the reasons why these findings exist. What does emerge, however, illustrates that sexual attraction and sexual involvement are salient components in the early stages of friendship for most gay men in this sample. This should not be too surprising since many gay men meet their potential friends in situations where sexual attraction is a relevant factor for initiating interactions. Furthermore, sexual involvement is often the next step for men in getting to know someone, in contrast to a model, especially for women, where sex follows a period of getting to know a person. As the men get to know each other, decisions are made to continue in a romantic manner or to "let's just be friends"—a statement that signifies the end of a sexual relationship and the start of a nonsexual friendship relationship.

While attraction and feelings of love may still persist, sexual involvement ceases, suggesting the emergence of an "incest taboo" among the "family" of friends (see Nardi, 1992; Weston, 1991). If the men continue to see each other, a friendship may develop, evolving from a casual one to a close one and, perhaps, into a best friendship. This would explain the higher percentage of men (in comparison to women who, in general, tend not to initiate interactions sexually) who said they had sex with casual friends. One might argue (given the percentage of lesbians whose best friends are ex-lovers and the fewer number who had sex with casual friends) that gay men are more likely to have had sex first and then develop a social intimacy with their friends. As they become more intimate and disclosing, sexual involvement decreases. So that when the sex ends, the friendship can continue if some degree of closeness and sharing has been established. But if the relationship was based primarily on sex, when that ends, the friendship does also. The fact that lesbians are significantly more likely to continue to maintain friendship with an ex-lover might suggest that their relationships were established first on a basis of intimacy and sharing, rather than on one of sex.

TABLE 2
Sexual Behavior and Attraction with Same-Sex Best Friend
(N = 118) (percentage answering Yes)

	In the past	Currently
A. Sexually attracted to best friend	79.4%	51.5%
B. Sexually involved with best friend	58.8%	20.4%
C. In love with best friend	57.4%	47.6%
D. Best friend is an ex-lover	18.8%	

Again, since the data don't address these questions directly, they are provided as hypotheses for future research. What needs to be explored further, then, is whether sexual orientation or traditional gender roles prevail in explaining how gay men connect sex and friendship. As men, they see sex as the way to intimacy. But as gay people, they develop a strong emotional intimacy with other men, unlike what research shows about how heterosexual men relate to other men (Sherrod & Nardi, 1988).

So while gay men are often seen as challengers to the hegemonic masculinity of white, heterosexual men (Segal, 1990), perhaps when it comes to sexual behavior they are conforming to traditional masculine gender roles. While same-sex friendships among gay men are not directly comparable to other-sex friendships among straight men, they do illustrate the potential for both breaking down traditional gender roles and maintaining them. They show how men perpetuate the traditional masculine image of sex as the means to intimacy while, at the same time, they subvert the norm of masculinity by showing that men can be intimate with one another at an emotional, sharing level.

This contradiction may not be all that unusual. An examination of extraordinary social conditions and crises often allows men a wider range of behaviors than regularly expressed. Segal (1990, p. 103), for example, argues that, in the "constant pressure to confirm masculinity in its difference from femininity," when men are at their most powerfully masculine selves, such as in combat, "they can embrace, weep, display what Western manhood depicts as more feminine feelings and behaviour."

With gay men, the social conditions of marginalization, oppression, and exclusion have contributed to this duality of traditional masculine roles and expressive, caring intimacy with friends. Or, in other words, sexual orientation and gender roles do not necessarily predict one another with consistency.

Thus, it is in the area of friendship and sex that one can seek some answers to how gender and sexual orientation are constructed in our culture and, in particular, how concepts of masculinity are shaped by concepts of homosexuality and heterosexuality. Owens (1987, p. 230) quotes Foucault, who said in an interview: "The disappearance of friendship as a social institution, and the declaration of homosexuality as a social/political/medical problem, are the same process." This is so, Segal (p. 139) agrees, because masculinity has been defined by its opposition to femininity and homosexuality: "The possible imputation of homosexual interest to any bonds between men ensured that men had constantly to be aware of and assert their difference from both women and homosexuals." And it is with the emergence of concepts of homosexuality in terms of a social identity and not just a sexual act that Rotundo (1989, p. 21) concludes that "Romantic male friendship is an artifact of the nineteenth century."

Thus, by understanding how gay men today organize their friendships and the role it plays in their lives, the tenuous connections between gender and sexual orientation grow even weaker and the various ways masculinity is constructed in a culture get uncovered. For it is in the area of sex and friendship among gay men that the issues of traditional masculine roles and traditional feminine roles are clarified for all people in contemporary American society.

AUTHOR'S NOTE: Many of the ideas discussed in this paper came from conversations, collaboration, and friendship with Drury Sherrod, who helped design the questionnaire and collect the original data used in this article.

The Heterosexual Questionnaire

M. Rochlin

1. What do you think caused your heterosexuality?

2. When and how did you decide you were a heterosexual?

3. Is it possible that your heterosexuality is just a phase you may grow out of?

4. Is it possible that your heterosexuality stems from a neurotic fear of others of the same sex?

5. If you have never slept with a person of the same sex, is it possible that all you need is a good Gay lover?

6. Do your parents know that you are straight? Do your friends and/or roommate(s) know? How did they react?

7. Why do you insist on flaunting your heterosexuality? Can't you just be who you are and keep it quiet?

8. Why do heterosexuals place so much emphasis on sex?

9. Why do heterosexuals feel compelled to seduce others into their lifestyle?

10. A disproportionate majority of child molesters are heterosexual. Do you consider it safe to expose children to heterosexual teachers?

11. Just what do men and women *do* in bed together? How can they truly know how to please each other, being so anatomically different?

12. With all the societal support marriage receives, the divorce rate is spiraling. Why are there so few stable relationships among heterosexuals?

13. Statistics show that lesbians have the lowest incidence of sexually transmitted diseases. Is it really safe for a woman to maintain a heterosexual lifestyle and run the risk of disease and pregnancy?

14. How can you become a whole person if you limit yourself to compulsive, exclusive heterosexuality?

15. Considering the menace of overpopulation, how could the human race survive if everyone were heterosexual?

16. Could you trust a heterosexual therapist to be objective? Don't you feel s/he might be inclined to influence you in the direction of her/his own leanings?

17. There seem to be very few happy heterosexuals. Techniques have been developed that might enable you to change if you really want to. Have you considered trying aversion therapy?

18. Would you want your child to be heterosexual, knowing the problems that s/he would face?

M. Rochlin, *Changing Men*, Spring 1982. © 1982 Sage Publications, Inc. Reprinted by Permission of Sage Publications, Inc.

REFERENCES—SEX, LOVE, AND POWER

ABBOTT, F., ed. (1990). *Men and intimacy: Personal accounts of exploring the dilemmas of modern male sexuality.* Freedom, CA: Crossing Press.

ALLAN, G. (1989). *Friendship: Developing a sociological perspective.* Boulder, CO: Westview.

ALTMAN, D. (1982). *The homosexualization of America.* Boston: Beacon.

BAKER, P. (1992). Maintaining male power: Why heterosexual men use pornography. In Catherine Itzin, ed., *Pornography, women, violence and civil liberties,* pp. 124–144. Oxford: Oxford University Press.

BERMAN, M. (1990). *Coming to our senses: Body and spirit in the hidden history of the west.* New York: Bantam.

BOONE, J.A. (1990). Of me(n) and feminism: Who(se) is the sex that writes? In J.A. Boone and M. Cadden, eds., *Engendering men: The question of male feminist criticism,* pp. 11–25. New York: Routledge.

BROWNMILLER, S. (1975). *Against our will: Men, women and rape.* New York: Simon & Schuster.

BRUMMETT, Barry. (1988). The homology hypothesis: Pornography on the VCR. *Critical Studies in Mass Communication,* 5(3): 202–216.

BUCHWALD, E., P.R. Fletcher, and M. Roth, eds. (1993). *Transforming a rape culture.* Minneapolis, MN: Milkweed Editions.

CALDWELL, M., and L. Peplau. (1982). Sex differences in same-sex friendships. *Sex Roles,* 8(7): 721–732.

CHRISTENSEN, F.M. (1990). *Pornography: The other side.* New York: Praeger.

DWORKIN, A. (1981). *Pornography: Men possessing women.* London: The Women's Press.

FEIN, E., and S. Schneider. (1995). *The rules: Time-tested secrets for capturing the heart of Mr. Right.* New York: Warner Books.

FIRESTONE, S. (1971). *The dialectic of sex.* London: Jonathan Cape.

GOLD, J., and S. Villari. (2000). *Just sex: Students rewrite the rules on sex, violence, activism, and equality.* Lanham, MD: Rowman & Littlefield.

HARRY, J. (1982). *Gay children grown up: Gender culture and gender deviance.* New York: Praeger.

HEARN, J. (1987). *The gender of oppression: Men, masculinity, and the critique of marxism.* New York: St. Martin's Press.

HEBDITCH, D., and N. Anning. (1988). *Porn gold: inside the pornography business.* London: Faber and Faber.

HEYWARD, C. (1995). *Staying power: Reflections on gender, justice, and compassion.* Cleveland: Pilgrim Books.

HITE, S. (1982). *The Hite report on male sexuality.* New York: Ballantine Books.

HUMPHREYS, L. (1971, March/April). New styles in homosexual manliness. *Transaction:* 38–46, 64–65.

JENSEN, R. (1995a). Feminist theory and men's lives. *Race, Gender and Class,* 2(2): 111–125.

JENSEN, R. (1997b). Privilege, power, and politics in research: A response to "Crossing sexual orientations." *Qualitative Studies in Education,* 10(1): 25–30.

KAPPELER, S. (1987). *The pornography of representation.* Minneapolis: University of Minnesota Press.

KIMMEL, M.S., ed. (1990). *Men confront pornography.* New York: Crown.

KIMMEL, M.S., and M. Kaufman. (1994). Weekend warriors: The new men's movement. In Harry Brod, ed., *Theorizing Masculinities,* pp. 259–288. Thousand Oaks: Sage.

LEVINE, M. (1988). *Gay macho: Ethnography of the homosexual clone.* Doctoral dissertation. New York University.

LORDE, A. *Sister outsider.* Freedom, CA: Crossing Press.

MARRIOTT, Michel. (1995). Virtual porn: Ultimate tease. *New York Times.* October 4: Bl, B7.

MILLETT, K. ([1970] 1977). *Sexual politics.* London: Virago.

MOFFATT, M. (1989). *Coming* of *age in New Jersey: College and American culture.* New Brunswick: Rutgers University Press.

NARAYAN, U. (1988). Working together across difference: Some considerations on emotions and political practice. *Hypatia,* 3(2): 31–47.

NARDI, P.M. (1992). That's what friends are for: Friends as family in the gay and lesbian community. In K. Plummer, ed., *Modern homosexualities: Fragments of lesbian and gay experience.* London: Routledge.

O'MEARA, J.D. (1989). Cross-sex friendship: Four basic challenges of an ignored relationship. *Sex Roles,* 21(7/8): 525–543.

OWENS, C. (1987). Outlaws: Gay men in feminism. In A. Jardine and P. Smith, eds., *Men in feminism,* pp. 219–232. New York: Methuen.

ROTUNDO, A. (1989). Romantic friendships: Male intimacy and middle-class youth in the northern United States, 1800–1900. *Journal of Social History,* 23(1): 1–25.

RUBIN, L. (1985). *Just friends: The role of friendship in our lives.* New York: Harper and Row.

SEGAL, L. *Slow motion: Changing masculinities.* New Brunswick, NJ: Rutgers University Press.

SEIDEN, A., and P. Bart. (1975). Woman to woman: Is sisterhood powerful? In N. Glazer-Malbin, ed., *Old family/new family* (pp. 189–228). New York: Van Nostrand.

SHERROD, D., and P.M. Nardi. (1988). *The nature and function of friendship in the lives of gay men and lesbians.* Paper presented at the American Sociological Association, Atlanta.

SONNENSCHEIN, D. (1968). The ethnography of male homosexual relationships. *Journal* of *Sex Research,* 4(2): 69–83.

STOLTENBERG, J. (1998). "I am not a rapist!": Why college guys are confronting sexual violence. In S.P. Schacht, and D.W. Ewing, eds., *Feminism and men: Reconstructing gender relations.* New York: New York University Press.

WESTON, K. (1991). *Families we choose: Gays, lesbians, and kinship.* New York: Columbia University Press.

WHITE, E. (1983, June). Paradise found: Gay men have discovered that there is friendship after sex. *Mother Jones,* pp. 10–16.

WILLIAMS, L. (1989). *Hard core: Power, pleasure and the "frenzy of the visible.* Berkeley: University of California Press.

WRIGHT, P. (1982). Men's friendships, women's friendships and the alleged inferiority of the latter. *Sex Roles,* 8(1): 1–20.

Black Masculinities: A Unique History

Recognizing that masculinity is not monolithic can assist us in seeing that not all men benefit equally from that gendered social hierarchy sometimes termed patriarchy. Racism and sexism intersect: For example, the gendered norm that men are "breadwinners" creates particular stress for those who are denied this role through institutionalized racism (Le Espiritu 37). Manning Marable describes the "essential tragedy of being Black and male" as "our inability as men and as people of African descent, to define ourselves without the stereotypes the larger society imposes upon us, and through various institutional means perpetuates and permeates within our entire culture" (70).

Different ethnic groups in the United States have individual histories (Takaki) that contribute to ideologies of masculinity different from the Eurocentric, white, heterosexual ideologies from which the invisible norm of hegemonic masculinity stems (see Stecopolous and Uebel). But the singular history of Black men is perhaps of particular relevance to a focus on masculinities because it has been so intertwined with myths of sexuality. Henry Louis Gates refers to

> our weird double confinement: we were to be black—and what did it mean to be black? We were to be men—and what did it mean to be men? At the overlap of these two categories, black and male, wasn't there an amalgamation-effect that was more than simply additive? (xiii–xiv).

In the 1991 hearings about Anita Hill's charge of sexual harassment against Supreme Court nominee Clarence Thomas, the nominee opportunistically used stereotypes about Black men's sexuality. "I cannot shake off these accusations," he announced, "because they play to the worst stereotypes we have about black men in this country" (Allen 27).

Those stereotypes aided Thomas in winning sympathy from his white supporters, but for the majority of Black men, particularly those of school age, the myths of "natural" tendencies to violence and untrammeled sexuality have been debilitating and often deadly. Discussion of an "achievement gap" in schools across the United States has led to the illumination of both overt and unconscious racism on the part of teachers and guidance counselors, and attention is also being paid to the discrimination institutionalized in standardized tests (Schiele). For African-American boys, however, the pressures of oppositional masculinities coupled with the perceptions fostered by a long history of oppression are a unique and painful burden.

Between Apocalypse and Redemption: John Singleton's *Boyz N the Hood*

Michael Eric Dyson

By now the dramatic decline in black male life has become an unmistakable feature of our cultural landscape—though of course the causes behind the desperate condition of black men date much further back than its recent popular discovery. Every few months, new reports and conferences attempt to explain the poverty, disease, despair, and death that shove black men toward social apocalypse.

If these words appear too severe or hyperbolic, the statistics testify to the trauma. For black men between the ages of 18 and 29, suicide is the leading cause of death. Between 1980 and 1985, the life expectancy for white males increased from 63 to 74.6 years, but only from 59 to 65 years for black males. Between 1973 and 1986, the real earnings of black males between the ages of 18 and 29 fell 31 percent as the percentage of young black males in the workforce plummeted 20 percent. The number of black men who dropped out of the workforce altogether doubled from 13 to 25 percent.

By 1989, almost 32 percent of black men between 16 and 19 were unemployed, compared to 16 percent of white men. And while blacks comprise only 12 percent of the nation's population, they make up 48 percent of the prison population, with men ac-counting for 89 percent of the black prison population. Only 14 percent of the white males who live in large metropolitan areas have been arrested, but the percentage for black males is 51 percent. And while 3 percent of white men have served time in prison, 18 percent of black men have been behind bars.[1]

Most chillingly, black-on-black homicide is the leading cause of death for black males between the ages of 15 and 34. Or to put it another way: "One out of every 21 black American males will be murdered in their lifetime. Most will die at the hands of another black male." These words appear in stark white print on the dark screen that opens John Singleton's masterful new film, *Boyz N The Hood* (1991). These words are both summary and opening salvo in Singleton's battle to reinterpret and redeem the black male experience. With *Boyz N The Hood* we have the most brilliantly executed and fully realized portrait yet of the coming-of-age odyssey that black boys must undertake in the suffocating conditions of urban decay and civic chaos.

Singleton adds color and depth to Michael Schultz's groundbreaking *Cooley High* (1975), extends the narrative scope of the Hudlin Brothers' important and humorous *House Party* (1990), and creates a stunning complement to Gordon Parks's pioneering *The Learning Tree* (1969), which traced the painful pilgrimage to maturity of a rural black male. Singleton's treatment of the various elements of contemporary black urban experience—gang violence, drug addiction, black male-female relationships, domestic joys and pains, friendships—is subtle and complex. He layers narrative textures over gritty and compelling visual slices of black culture that show us what it means to come to maturity, or die trying, as a black male.

Singleton's noteworthy attempt to present a richly hued, skillfully nuanced portrait of black male life is rare in the history of American film. Along with the seminal work of Spike Lee, and the recently expanded body of black film created by Charles Burnett, Robert Townsend, Keenan Wayans, Euhzan Palcy, Matty Rich, Mario Van Peebles, Ernest Dickerson, Bill Duke, Charles Lane, Reginald and Warrington Hudlin, Doug McHenry and George Jackson, and Julie Dash, Singleton symbolizes a new generation of black filmmakers whose artistic visions of African-American and American life may influence understandings of black worldviews, shape crucial perceptions of the sheer diversity of black communities, and address substantive racial, social, and political issues.

A major task, therefore, of African-American film criticism is to understand black film production in its historical, political, socio-economic, ideological, and cultural contexts. Such critical analysis has the benefit of generating plausible explanations of how black film developed; what obstacles it has faced in becoming established as a viable and legitimate means of representing artistic, cultural, and racial perspectives on a range of personal and social issues; the ideological and social conditions which stunted its growth, shaped its emergence and enabled its relatively recent success; the economic and political forces which limited the material and career options of black filmmakers, and constrained the opportunities for black artists to flourish and develop in a social environment hostile to black artistic production.

Another task of African-American film criticism is to provide rigorous tools of analysis, categories of judgment, and modes of evaluation that view the artistic achievements of black filmmakers in light of literary criticism, moral philosophy, feminist theory, intellectual history, cultural studies, and poststructuralist theory. African-American film criticism is not a hermetically sealed intellectual discourse that generates insight by limiting its range of intellectual reference to film theory, or to African-American culture, in interpreting the themes, ideas, and currents of African-American film. Rather, African-American film criticism draws from the seminal insights of a variety of intellectual traditions in understanding and explaining the genealogy, scope, and evolution of black artistic expression. In short, black film criticism does not posit or constitute a rigidly defined sphere of academic analysis or knowledge production, but calls into question regimented conceptions of disciplinary boundaries while promoting the overlapping and interpenetration of diverse areas of intellectual inquiry.

Finally, African-American film criticism is related to the larger task of sustaining a just, enabling, but rigorous African-American cultural criticism that revels in black culture's virtues, takes pleasure in its achievements, laments its failed opportunities, and interrogates its weaknesses. African-American cultural criticism is intellectually situated to disrupt, subvert, and challenge narrow criticisms or romantic celebrations of black culture. A healthy African-American cultural criticism views black folk not as mere victims in and of history, but as its resourceful co-creators and subversive regenerators. It understands black people as agents of their own jubilation and pain. It sees them, in varying degrees and in limited manner, as crafters of their own destinies, active participants in the construction of worlds of meaning through art, thought, and sport that fend off threatening enclosure by the ever-enlarging kingdom of absurdity. In this light, African-American film criticism pays attention to, and carefully evaluates, the treatment of crucial aspects of black culture in black films. Singleton's film addresses one of the most urgent and complex problems facing African-American communities: the plight of black men.

We have only begun to understand the pitfalls that attend the path of the black male. Social theory has only recently fixed its gaze on the specific predicament of black men in relation to the crisis of American capital, positing how their lives are shaped by structural changes in the political economy, for instance, rather than viewing them as the latest examples of black cultural pathology.[2] And social psychology has barely explored the deeply ingrained and culturally reinforced self-loathing and chronic lack of self-esteem that characterizes black males across age group, income bracket, and social location.

Even less have we understood the crisis of black males as rooted in childhood and adolescent obstacles to socio-economic stability, and moral, psychological, and emotional development. We have just begun to pay attention to specific rites of passage, stages of personality growth, and milestones of psycho-emotional evolution that measure personal response to racial injustice, social disintegration, and class oppression.

James P. Comer and Alvin F. Poussaint's *Black Child Care*, Marian Wright Edelman's *Families in Peril*, and Darlene and Derek Hopson's foundational *Different and Wonderful* are among the exceptions which address the specific needs of black childhood and adolescence. Jewelle Taylor Gibb's edited work, *Young, Black and Male in America: An Endangered Species* has recently begun to fill a gaping void in social–scientific research on the crisis of the black male.

In the last decade, however, alternative presses have vigorously probed the crisis of the black male. Like their black independent film peers, authors of volumes published by black independent presses often rely on lower budgets for advertising, marketing, and distribution. Nevertheless, word-of-mouth discussion of several books has sparked intense debate. Nathan and Julia Hare's *Bringing the Black Boy to Manhood: The Passage*, Jawanza Kunjufu's trilogy *The Conspiracy to Destroy Black Boys*, Amos N. Wilson's *The Development Psychology of The Black Child*, Baba Zak A. Kondo's *For Homeboys Only: Arming and Strengthening Young Brothers for Black Manhood*, and Haki Madhubuti's *Black Men: Obsolete, Single, Dangerous?* have had an important impact on significant subsections of literate black culture, most of whom share an Afrocentric perspective.

Such works remind us that we have too infrequently understood the black male crisis through coming-of-age narratives, and a set of shared social values that ritualize the process of the black adolescent's passage into adulthood. Such narratives and rites serve a dual function: they lend meaning to childhood experience, and they preserve and transmit black cultural values across the generations. Yet such narratives evoke a state of maturity—rooted in a vital community—that young black men are finding elusive or all too often, impossible to reach. The conditions of extreme social neglect that besiege urban black communities—in every realm from health care to education to poverty and joblessness—make the black male's passage into adulthood treacherous at best.

One of the most tragic symptoms of the young black man's troubled path to maturity is the skewed and strained state of gender relations within the black community. With alarming frequency, black men turn to black women as scapegoats for their oppression, lashing out—often with physical violence at those closest to them. It is the singular achievement of Singleton's film to redeem the power of the coming-of-age narrative while also adapting it to probe many of the very tensions that evade the foundations of the coming-of-age experience in the black community.

While mainstream American culture has only barely begun to register awareness of the true proportions of the crisis, young black males have responded on the last decade primarily in a rapidly flourishing independent popular culture, dominated by two genres: rap music and black film. The rap music of Run D.M.C., Public Enemy, Boogie Down Productions, Kool Moe Dee, N.W.A., Ice Cube and Ice T., and the films of Spike Lee, Robert Townsend, and now Matty Rich and Mario Van Peebles, have afforded young black males a medium to visualize and verbalize their perspectives on a range of social, personal, and cultural issues, to tell their stories about themselves and each other while the rest of America consumes and eavesdrops.

John Singleton's new film makes a powerful contribution to this enterprise. Singleton filters his brilliant insights, critical comments, and compelling portraits of young black male culture through a film that reflects the sensibilities, styles, and attitudes of rap culture.[3] Singleton's shrewd casting of rapper Ice Cube as a central character allows him to seize symbolic capital from a real life rap icon, while tailoring the violent excesses of Ice Cube's rap persona into a jarring visual reminder of the cost paid by black males for survival in American society. Singleton skillfully integrates the suggestive fragments of critical reflections on the black male predicament in several media and presents a stunning vision of black male pain and possibility in a catastrophic environment: South Central Los Angeles.

Of course, South Central Los Angeles is an already storied geography in the American social imagination. It has been given cursory—though melodramatic—treatment by news anchor Tom Brokaw's glimpse of gangs in a highly publicized 1988 TV special, and mythologized in Dennis Hopper's film about gang warfare, *Colors* (1988). Hopper, who perceptively and provocatively helped probe the rough edges of anomie and rebellion for a whole generation of outsiders in 1969's *Easy Rider*, less successfully traces the genealogy of social despair, postmodern urban absurdity and longing for belonging that provides the context for understanding gang violence. Singleton's task in part, therefore, is a filmic demythologization of the reigning tropes, images, and metaphors that have expressed the experience of life in South Central Los Angeles. While gangs are a central part of the urban landscape, they are not its exclusive reality. And though gang warfare occupies a looming periphery in Singleton's film, it is not the defining center.

Unquestionably, the 1991 urban rebellions in Los Angeles following the Rodney King verdict have given new poignancy to Singleton's depiction of the various personal, social and economic forces which shape the lives of the residents of South Central L.A. His film was an incandescent and prescient portrait of the simmering stew of social angers—aimed at police brutality, steeply declining property values, poverty and virile racism—which aggravate an already aggrieved community and which force hard social choices on neighborhoods (do we riot in our own backyards; do we maliciously target Korean businesses, especially since the case of Latasha Harlins, a black teenager murdered by a Korean grocer, who was simply given five years' probation; and do we destroy community businesses and bring the charge of senseless destruction of resources in our own community when in reality, before the riots, we were already desperate, poor and invisible, and largely unaided by the legitimate neighborhood business economy?) amounting to little more than communal triage. Singleton's film proves, in retrospect, a powerful meditation upon the blight of gang violence, hopelessness, familial deterioration and economic desperation which conspire to undermine and slowly but surely destroy the morale and structure of many urban communities, particularly those in South Central L.A.

Boyz N The Hood is a painful and powerful look at the lives of black people, mostly male, who live in a lower middle-class neighborhood in South Central Los Angeles. It is a story of relationships—of kin, friendship, community, love, rejection, contempt, and fear. At the story's heart are three important relationships: a triangular relationship between three boys, whose lives we track to mature adolescence; the relationship between one of the boys and his father; and the relationship between the other two boys and their mother.

Tre (Cuba Gooding, Jr.) is a young boy whose mother Reva Devereaux (Angela Bassett), in an effort to impose discipline upon him, sends him to live with his father across town. Tre has run afoul of his elementary school teacher for challenging both her authority and her Eurocentric curriculum. And Tre's life in his mother's neighborhood makes it clear why he is not accommodating well to school discipline. By the age of ten, he has already witnessed the yellow police tags that mark the scene of crimes and viewed the blood of a murder victim. Fortunately for Tre, his mother and father both love him more than they loved each other.

Doughboy (Former N.W.A. rapper Ice Cube, in a brilliant cinematic debut) and Ricky (Morris Chestnut) are half-brothers who live with their mother Brenda (Tyra Fer-

ell) across the street from Tre and his father. Brenda is a single black mother—a member of a much-maligned group that, depending on the amateurish social theory that wins the day, is vilified with charges of promiscuity, judged to be the source of all that is evil in the lives of black children, or at best stereotyped as the helpless beneficiaries of the state. Singleton artfully avoids these caricatures by giving a complex portrait of Brenda, a woman plagued by her own set of demons, but who tries to provide the best living she can for her sons.

Even so, Brenda clearly favors Ricky over Doughboy—and this favoritism will bear fatal consequences for both boys. Indeed in Singleton's cinematic worldview both Ricky and Doughboy seem doomed to violent deaths because—unlike Tre—they have no male role models to guide them. This premise embodies one of the film's central tensions—and one of its central limitations. For even as he assigns black men a pivotal role of responsibility for the fate of black boys, Singleton also gives rather uncritical "precedence" to the impact of black men, even in their absence, over the efforts of present and loyal black women who more often prove to be at the head of strong black families.

While this foreshortened view of gender relations within the black community arguably distorts Singleton's cinematic vision, he is nonetheless remarkably perceptive in examining the subtle dynamics of the black family and neighborhood, tracking the differing effects that the boys' siblings, friends, and environment have on them. There is no bland nature versus nurture dichotomy here: Singleton is too smart to render life in terms of a Kierkegaardian either/or. His is an Afrocentric world of both/and.

This complex set of interactions—between mother and sons, between father and son, between boys who benefit from paternal wisdom or maternal ambitions, between brothers whose relationship is riven by primordial passions of envy and contempt, between environment and autonomy, between the larger social structure and the smaller but more immediate tensions of domestic life—define the central shape of *Hood*. We see a vision of black life that transcends insular preoccupations with "positive" or "negative" images and instead presents at once the limitations and virtues of black culture.

As a result, Singleton's film offers a plausible perspective on how people make the choices they do—and on how choice itself is not a property of autonomous moral agents acting in an existential vacuum, but rather something that is created and exercised within the interaction of social, psychic, political, and economic forces of everyday experience. Personal temperament, domestic discipline, parental guidance (or its absence), all help shape our understanding of our past and future, help define how we respond to challenge and crisis, and help mold how we embrace success or seem destined for failure.

Tre's developing relationship with his father, Furious Styles (Larry Fishburne), is by turns troubled and disciplined, sympathetic and compassionate—finely displaying Singleton's open-ended evocation of the meaning of social choice as well as his strong sensitivity to cultural detail. Furious Styles's moniker vibrates with double meaning, a semiotic pairing that allows Singleton to signify in speech what Furious accomplishes in action: a wonderful amalgam of old-school black consciousness, elegance, style, and wit, linked to the hip-hop fetish of "dropping science" (spreading knowledge) and staying well informed about social issues.

Only seventeen years Tre's senior, Furious understands Tre's painful boyhood growth and identifies with his teen aspirations. But more than that, he possesses a sin-

cere desire to shape Tre's life according to his own best lights. Furious is the strong presence and wise counselor who will guide Tre through the pitfalls of reaching personal maturity in the chaos of urban childhood—the very sort of presence denied to so many in *Hood*, and in countless black communities throughout the country.

Furious, in other words, embodies the promise of a different conception of black manhood. As a father he is disciplining but loving, firm but humorous, demanding but sympathetic. In him, the black male voice speaks with an authority so confidently possessed and equitabl[y] wielded that one might think it is strongly supported and valued in American culture, but of course that is not so. The black male voice is rarely heard without the inflections of race and class domination that distort its power in the home and community, mute its call for basic respect and common dignity, or amplify its ironic denial of the very principles of democracy and equality that it has publicly championed in pulpits and political organizations.

Among the most impressive achievements of Singleton's film is its portrayal of the neighborhood as a "community." In this vein Singleton implicitly sides with the communitarian critique of liberal moral autonomy and atomistic individualism.[4] In *Hood* people love and worry over one another, even if they express such sentiments roughly. For instance, when the older Tre crosses the street and sees a baby in the path of an oncoming car, he swoops her up, and takes her to her crack-addicted mother. Tre gruffly reproves her for neglecting her child and insists that she change the baby's diapers before the baby smells as bad as her mother. And when Tre goes to a barbecue for Doughboy, who is fresh from a jail sentence, Brenda beseeches him to talk to Doughboy, hoping that Tre's intangible magic will "rub off on him."

But Singleton understands that communities embody resistance to the anonymity of liberal society as conceived in Aristotle via MacIntyre. His film portrays communities as more heterogenous, complex, and diverse, however, than the ideal of consensus that grounds MacIntyre's conception of communities, which is at least partially mediated through a common moral vocabulary. Singleton's neighborhood is a community precisely because it turns on the particularity of racial identity, and the contradictions of class location, that are usually muted or eradicated in mainstream accounts of moral community. Such accounts tend to eliminate racial, sexual, gender, and class difference in positing the conditions that make community possible, and in specifying the norms, values, and mores which regulate moral discourse and that structure communal behavior. Singleton's film community is an implicit argument for the increased visibility of a politics of difference within American culture, a solemn rebuke to the Capraesque representation of a socially and economically homogenous community.[5]

The quest for community represented in Singleton's film is related to the quest for intellectual community facilitated by certain modes of African-American cultural criticism. By taking black folk seriously, by taking just measure of their intellectual reflections, artistic perceptions, social practices, and cultural creations, the black cultural critic is seeking both to develop fair but forceful examination of black life, and to establish a community of interlocutors, ranging from high-brow intellectuals to everyday folk, whites and people of color alike, who are interested in preserving black culture's best features, ameliorating its weakest parts, and eradicating its worst traits.

Of course, specific moments of black cultural criticism also help shed light on aspects of black artistic production that may be overlooked or underestimated in much of mainstream criticism. A crucial role for African-American cultural criticism is to reveal historical connections, and thematic continuities and departures between black films and issues debated over time and space in African-American society. By doing so, the black cultural critic illumines the material interests of black filmmakers, while drawing attention to the cultural situation of black film practice. Singleton's depiction of community provides a colorful lens on problems which have long plagued black neighborhoods.

Singleton understands that communities, besides embodying the virtuous ends of their morally prudent citizens, also reflect the despotic will of their fringe citizens who threaten the civic pieties by which communities are sustained. *Hood*'s community is fraught with mortal danger, its cords of love and friendship under the siege of gang violence, and by what sociologist Mike Davis calls the political economy of crack.[6] Many inner-city communities live under what may be called a "juvenocracy": the economic rule and illegal tyranny exercised by young black men over significant territory in the black urban center. In the social geography of South Central L.A., neighborhoods are reconceived as spheres of expansion where urban space is carved up according to implicit agreements, explicit arrangements, or lethal conflicts between warring factions.

Thus, in addition to being isolated from the recognition and rewards of the dominant culture, inner-city communities are cut off from sources of moral authority and legitimate work, as underground political economies reward consenting children and teens with quick cash, faster cars, and sometimes, still more rapid death.[7] Along with the reterritorialization of black communal space through gentrification, the hegemony of the suburban mall over the inner city and downtown shopping complex, and white flight and black track to the suburbs and exurbs, the inner city is continually devastated.

Such conditions rob the neighborhood of one of its basic social functions and defining characteristics: the cultivation of a self-determined privacy in which residents can establish and preserve their identities. Police helicopters constantly zoom overhead in *Hood's* community, a mobile metaphor of the ominous surveillance and scrutiny to which so much of poor black life is increasingly subjected. The helicopter also signals another tragedy that *Hood* alludes to throughout its narrative: Ghetto residents must often flip a coin to distinguish Los Angeles' police from its criminals. After all, this was Darryl Gates's L.A.P.D., and the urban rebellion following the Rodney King verdict, with the thousand tales of social misery reported by black men of every age and economic group across the country, only underscores a long tradition of extreme measures that police have used to control crime and patrol neighborhoods.[8] As Singleton wrote after the rebellion:

> Anyone who has a moderate knowledge of African-American culture knows this was foretold in a thousand rap songs and more than a few black films. When Ice Cube was with NWA (Niggas With Attitude), he didn't write the lyrics to "Fuck tha Police" just to be cute. He was reciting a reflection of reality as well as fantasizing about what it would be like to be on the other end of the gun when it came to police relations. Most white people don't know what it is like to be stopped for a traffic violation and worry more about getting beat up or shot than paying the ticket. So imagine, if you will, growing up with this reality regardless of your social or economic status. Fantasize about what it is to be guilty of a crime at birth. The crime? Being born black . . . By issuing that verdict, the jury violated not only Rodney King's civil rights, not only the rights of all African Americans, but also showed a lack of respect

for every law-abiding American who believes in justice. (Singleton, 75)

Furious's efforts to raise his son in these conditions of closely surveilled social anarchy reveal the galaxy of ambivalence that surrounds a conscientious, community-minded brother who wants the best for his family, but who also understands the social realities that shape the lives of black men. Furious's urban cosmology is three-tiered: at the immediate level, the brute problems of survival are refracted through the lens of black manhood; at the abstract level, large social forces such as gentrification and the military's recruitment of black male talent undermine the black man's role in the community; at the intermediate level, police brutality contends with the ongoing terror of gang violence.

Amid these hostile conditions, Furious is still able to instruct Tre in the rules of personal conduct and to teach him respect for his community, even as he schools him in how to survive. Furious says to Tre, "I know you think I'm hard on you. I'm trying to teach you how to be responsible. Your friends across the street don't have anybody to show them how to do that. You gon' see how they end up, too." His comment, despite its implicit self-satisfaction and sexism (Ricky and Doughboy, after all, do have their mother Brenda), is meant to reveal the privilege of a young boy learning to face life under the shadow of fatherly love and discipline.

While Tre is being instructed by Furious, Ricky and Doughboy receive varying degrees of support and affirmation from Brenda. Ricky and Doughboy have different fathers, both of whom are conspicuously absent. In Doughboy's case, however, his father is symbolically present in that peculiar way that damns the offspring for their resemblance in spirit or body to the despised, departed father. The child becomes the vicarious sacrifice for the absent father, though he can never atone for the father's sins. Doughboy learns to see himself through his mother's eyes, her words ironically recreating Doughboy in the image of his invisible father. "You ain't shit," she says. "You just like yo' Daddy. You don't do shit, and you never gonna amount to shit."

Brenda is caught in a paradox of parenthood, made dizzy and stunned by a vicious cycle of parental love reinforcing attractive qualities in the "good" and obedient child, while the frustration with the "bad" child reinforces his behavior. Brenda chooses to save one child by sacrificing the other—lending her action a Styronian tenor, Sophie's choice in the ghetto. She fusses *over* Ricky; she fusses *at* Doughboy. When a scout for USC's football team visits Ricky, Brenda can barely conceal her pride. When the scout leaves, she tells Ricky, "I always knew you would amount to something."

In light of Doughboy's later disposition toward women, we see the developing deformations of misogyny. Here Singleton is on tough and touchy ground, linking the origins of Doughboy's misogyny to maternal mistreatment and neglect. Doughboy's misogyny is clearly the elaboration of a brooding and extended *ressentiment*, a deeply festering wound to his pride that infects his relationship with every woman he encounters.

For instance, at the party to celebrate his homecoming from his recent incarceration, Brenda announces that the food is ready. All of the males rush to the table, but immediately before they begin to eat, Tre, sensing that it will be to his advantage, reproves the guys for not acting gentlemanly and allowing the women first place in line. Doughboy chimes in, saying, "Let the ladies eat; 'ho's gotta eat too," which draws laughter, both from the audience with which I viewed the film, and the backyard male

crowd. The last line is a sly sample of Robert Townsend's classic comedic sendup of fast-food establishments in *Hollywood Shuffle* (1987). When his girlfriend (Regina King) protests, saying she isn't a "ho," Doughboy responds, "Oops, I'm sorry bitch," which draws even more laughter.

In another revealing exchange with his girlfriend, Doughboy is challenged to explain why he refers to women exclusively as "bitch, or 'ho, or hootchie." In trying to reply, Doughboy is reduced to the inarticulate hostility (feebly masquerading as humor) that characterizes misogyny in general: " 'cause that's what you are."

"Bitch" and "ho," along with "skeezer" and "slut," have by now become the standard linguistic currency that young black males often use to demonstrate their authentic machismo. "Bitch" and equally offensive epithets compress womanhood into one indistinguishable whole, so that all women are the negative female, the seductress, temptress, and femme fatale all rolled into one. Hawthorne's scarlet A is demoted one letter and darkened; now an imaginary black B is emblazoned on the forehead of every female.

Though Singleton's female characters do not have center stage, by no means do they suffer male effrontery in silent complicity. When Furious and Reva meet at a trendy restaurant to discuss the possibility of Tre returning to live with his mother, Furious says "I know you wanna play the mommy and all that, but it's time to let go." He reminds her that Tre is old enough to make his own decisions, that he is no longer a little boy because "that time has passed sweetheart, you missed it." Furious then gets up to fetch a pack of cigarettes as if to punctuate his self-satisfied and triumphant speech, but Tre's mother demands that he sit down.

As the camera draws close to her face, she subtly choreographs a black [woman's] grab-you-by-the-collar-and-set-you-straight demeanor with just the right facial gestures, and completes one of the most honest, mature, and poignant exchanges between black men and women in film history.

> It's my turn to talk. Of course you took in your son, my son, our son and you taught him what he needed to be a man, I'll give you that, because most men ain't man enough to do what you did. But that gives you no reason, do you hear me, no reason to tell me that I can't be a mother to my son. What you did is no different from what mothers have been doing from the beginning of time. It's just too bad more brothers won't do the same. But don't think you're special. Maybe cute, but not special. Drink your café au lait. It's on me.

Singleton says that his next film will be about black women coming of age, a subject left virtually unexplored in film. In the meantime, within its self-limited scope, *Hood* displays a diverse array of black women, taking care not to render them as either mawkish or cartoonish: a crack addict who sacrifices home, dignity, and children for her habit; a single mother struggling to raise her sons; black girlfriends hanging with the homeboys but demanding as much respect as they can get; Brandi (Nia Long), Tre's girlfriend, a Catholic who wants to hang on to her virginity until she's sure it's the right time; Tre's mother, who strikes a Solomonic compromise and gives her son up rather than see him sacrificed to the brutal conditions of his surroundings.

But while Singleton ably avoids flat stereotypical portraits of his female characters, he is less successful in challenging the logic that at least implicitly blames single black women for the plight of black children.[9] In Singleton's film version, it is not institutions like the Church that save Tre, but a heroic individual—his father Furious. But this leaves out far too much of the picture.

What about the high rates of black female joblessness; the sexist job market which continues to pay women at a rate that is seventy percent of the male wage for comparable work; the further devaluation of the "pink collar" by lower rates of medical insurance and other work-related benefits, all of which severely compromise the ability of single black mothers to effectively rear their children?[10] It is the absence of much more than a male role model and the strength he symbolizes that makes the life of a growing boy difficult and treacherous in communities such as South Central L.A.

The film's focus on Furious's heroic individualism fails, moreover, to account fully for the social and cultural forces that prevent more black men from being present in the home in the first place. Singleton's powerful message, that more black men must be responsible and present in the home to teach their sons how to become men, must not be reduced to the notion that those families devoid of black men are necessarily deficient and ineffective. Neither should Singleton's critical insights into the way that many black men are denied the privilege to rear their sons be collapsed to the idea that all black men who are present in their families will necessarily produce healthy, well-adjusted black males. So many clarifications and conditions must be added to the premise that *only* black men can rear healthy black males, that it dies the death of a thousand qualifications.

In reality, Singleton's film works off the propulsive energies that fuel deep, and often insufficiently understood tensions between black men and black women. A good deal of pain infuses relations between black men and women, recently dramatized with the publication of Shahrazad Ali's infamous and controversial underground best-seller, *The Blackman's Guide to Understanding the Blackwoman*. The book, which counseled black women to be submissive to black men, and which endorsed black male violence toward women under specific circumstances, touched off a furious debate that drew forth the many unresolved personal, social, and domestic tensions between black men and women.[11]

This pain follows a weary pattern of gender relations that has privileged concerns defined by black men over feminist or womanist issues. Thus, during the civil rights movement, feminist and womanist questions were perennially deferred, so that precious attention would not be diverted from racial oppression and the achievement of liberation.[12] But this deference to issues of racial freedom is a permanent pattern in black male-female relations; womanist and feminist movements continue to exist on the fringe of black communities.[13] And even in the Afrocentric worldview that Singleton advocates, the role of black women is often subordinate to the black patriarch.

Equally as unfortunate, many contemporary approaches to the black male crisis have established a rank hierarchy that suggests that the plight of black men is infinitely more lethal, and hence more important, than the conditions of black women. The necessary and urgent focus on the plight of black men, however, must not come at the expense of understanding its relationship to the circumstances of black women.

At places, Singleton is able to subtly embody a healthy and redemptive vision of black male-female relations. For instance, after Tre has been verbally abused and physically threatened by police brutality, he seeks sanctuary at Brandi's house, choreographing his rage at life in South Central by angrily swinging at empty space. As Tre breaks down in tears, he and Brandi finally achieve an authentic moment of spiritual and physical consummation previously denied them by the complications of peer pressure, and

religious restraint. After Tre is assured that Brandi is really ready, they make love, achieving a fugitive moment of true erotic and spiritual union.

Brandi is able to express an unfettered and spontaneous affection that is not a simplistic "sex-as-proof-of-love" that reigns in the thinking of many teen worldviews. Brandi's mature intimacy is both the expression of her evolving womanhood and a vindication of the wisdom of her previous restraint. Tre is able at once to act out his male rage and demonstrate his vulnerability to Brandi, thereby arguabl[y] achieving a synthesis of male and female responses, and humanizing the crisis of the black male in a way that none of his other relationships—even his relationship with his father—are able to do. It is a pivotal moment in the development of a politics of alternative black masculinity that prizes the strength of surrender and cherishes the embrace of a healing tenderness.

As the boys mature into young men, their respective strengths are enhanced, and their weaknesses exposed. The deepening tensions between Ricky and Doughboy break out into violence when a petty argument over who will run an errand for Ricky's girlfriend provokes a fistfight. After Tre tries unsuccessfully to stop the fight, Brenda runs out of the house, divides the two boys, slaps Doughboy in the face and checks Ricky's condition. "What you slap me for?," Doughboy repeatedly asks her after Ricky and Tre go off to the store. She doesn't answer, but her choice, again, is clear. Its effect on Doughboy is clearer still.

Such everyday variations on the question of choice are, again, central to the world Singleton depicts in *Hood*. Singleton obviously understands that people are lodged between social structure and personal fortune, between luck and ambition. He brings a nuanced understanding of choice to each character's large and small acts of valor, courage, and integrity that reveal what contemporary moral philosophers call virtue.[14] But they often miss what Singleton understands: character is not only structured by the choices we make, but by the range of choices we have to choose from—choices for which individuals alone are not responsible.

Singleton focuses his lens on the devastating results of the choices made by *Hood*'s characters, for themselves and for others. *Hood* presents a chain of choices, a community defined in part by the labyrinthine array of choices made and the consequences borne, to which others must then choose to respond. But Singleton does not portray a blind fatalism or a mechanistic determinism; instead he displays a sturdy realism that shows how communities affect their own lives, and how their lives are shaped by personal and impersonal forces.

Brenda's choice to favor Ricky may not have been completely her own—all the messages of society say that the good, obedient child, especially in the ghetto, is the one to nurture and help—but it resulted in Doughboy's envy of Ricky, and contributed to Doughboy's anger, alienation, and gradual drift into gang violence. Ironically and tragically, this constellation of choices may have contributed to Ricky's violent death when he is shot by members of a rival gang as he and Tre return from the neighborhood store.

Ricky's death, in turn, sets in motion a chain of choices and consequences. Doughboy feels he has no choice but to pursue his brother's killers, becoming a more vigilant keeper to his brother in Ricky's death than he could be while Ricky lived. Tre, too, chooses to join Doughboy, thereby repudiating everything his father taught, and forswearing every virtue he has been trained to observe. When he grabs his father's gun, but is met at the door by Furious, the collision

between training and instinct is dramatized on Tre's face, wrenched in anguish and tears.

Though Furious convinces him to relinquish the gun, Furious's victory is only temporary. The meaning of Tre's manhood is at stake; it is the most severe test he has faced, and he chooses to sneak out of the house to join Doughboy. All Furious can do is tensely exercise his hands with two silver balls, which in this context are an unavoidable metaphor for [how] black men view their fate through their testicles, which are constantly up for grabs, attack, or destruction. Then sometime during the night, Tre's impassioned choice finally rings false, a product of the logic of vengeance he has desperately avoided all these years; he insists that he be let out of Doughboy's car before they find Ricky's killers.

Following the code of male honor, Doughboy kills his brother's killers. But the next morning, in a conversation with Tre, he is not so sure of violence's mastering logic anymore, and says that he understands Tre's choice to forsake Doughboy's vigilante mission, even as he silently understands that he is in too deep to be able to learn any other language of survival.

Across this chasm of violence and anguish, the two surviving friends are able to extend a final gesture of understanding. As Doughboy laments the loss of his brother, Tre offers him the bittersweet consolation that "you got one more brother left." Their final embrace in the film's closing moment is a sign of a deep love that binds brothers; a love that, however, too often will not save brothers.

The film's epilogue tells us that Doughboy is murdered two weeks later, presumably to avenge the deaths of Ricky's killers. The epilogue also tells us that Tre and Brandi manage to escape South Central as Tre pursues an education at Morehouse College, with Brandi at neighboring Spelman College. It is testimony to the power of

Singleton's vision that Tre's escape is no callow Hollywood paean to the triumph of the human spirit (or, as some reviewers have somewhat perversely described the film, "life-affirming"). The viewer is not permitted to forget for a moment the absurd and vicious predictability of the loss of life in South Central Los Angeles, a hurt so colossal that even Doughboy must ask: "If there was a God, why he let motherfuckers get smoked every night?" Theodicy in gangface.

Singleton is not about to provide a slick or easy answer. But he does powerfully juxtapose such questions alongside the sources of hope, sustained in the heroic sacrifice of everyday people who want their children's lives to be better. The work of John Singleton embodies such hope by reminding us that South Central Los Angeles, by the sheer power of discipline and love, sends children to college, even as its self-destructive rage sends them to the grave.

NOTES

1. These statistics, as well as an examination of the social, economic, political, medical, and educational conditions of young black men, and public policy recommendations for the social amelioration of their desperate circumstances, are found in a collection of essays edited by Jewelle Taylor Gibbs, *Young, Black, And Male in America: An Endangered Species.*

2. William Julius Wilson has detailed the shift in the American political economy from manufacturing to service employment, and its impact upon the inner city and the ghetto poor, particularly upon black males who suffer high rates of joblessness (which he sees as the source of many problems in the black family) in *The Truly Disadvantaged.* For an analysis of the specific problems of black males in relation to labor force participation, see Gerald David Jaynes and Robin M. Williams, Jr., eds., *A Common Destiny* (pp. 301, 308–312).

3. I have explored the cultural expressions, material conditions, creative limits, and social problems associated with rap, in "Rap, Race and Reality" (pp. 98–100); "The Culture of Hip-Hop" (pp. 44–50), "2 Live Crew's Rap: Sex, Race and Class" (pp. 7–8) "As Complex As They Wanna Be: 2 Live Crew" (pp. 76–78), "Tapping Into Rap" (pp. 32–35), "Performance, Protest and Prophecy in the Culture of Hip-Hop" (pp. 12–24), and in Jim Gardner, "Taking Rap Seriously: Theomusicologist Michael Eric Dyson on the New Urban Griots and Peripatetic Preachers (An Interview)" (pp. 20–23).

4. I have in mind here the criticism of liberal society, and the forms of moral agency it both affords and prevents, that has been gathered under the rubric of communitarianism, ranging from MacIntyre's *After Virtue* to Bellah, et al.'s *Habits of the Heart.*

5. I am indebted to Christine Stansell for this characterization of how Singleton departs from Capra's depictions of community in his films.

6. See Mike Davis's and Sue Riddick's brilliant analysis of the drug culture in "Los Angeles: Civil Liberties between the Hammer and the Rock" (pp. 37–60).

7. For an insightful discussion of the relationship between the underground or illegitimate economy, and people exercising agency in resisting the worse injustices and effects of the legitimate economy, see Don Nonini, "Everyday Forms of Popular Resistance" (pp. 25–36).

8. For a recent exploration of the dynamics of social interaction between police as agents and symbols of mainstream communal efforts to regulate the behavior and social place of black men, and black men in a local community, see Elijah Anderson, *Streetwise* (pp. 163–206).

9. According to this logic, as expressed in a familiar saying in many black communities, black women "love their sons and raise their daughters." For a valiant, though flawed attempt to get beyond a theoretical framework that implicitly blames black women for the condition of black men, see Clement Cottingham, "Gender Shift in Black Communities" (pp. 521–525). Cottingham attempts to distance himself from arguments about a black matriarchy that stifles black male social initiative and moral responsibility. Instead he examines the gender shifts in black communities fueled by black female educational mobility and the marginalization of lower-class black males. But his attempt is weakened, ironically, by a prominently placed quotation by James Baldwin, which serves as a backdrop to his subsequent discussions of mother/son relationships, black male/female relationships, and black female assertiveness. Cottingham writes:

"Drawing on Southern black folk culture, James Baldwin, in his last published work, alluded to black lower-class social patterns which, when set against the urban upheaval among the black poor from the 1960s onward, seem to encourage this gender shift. He characterizes these lower-class social patterns as 'a disease peculiar to the Black community' called 'sorriness.' 'It is,' Baldwin observes, 'a disease that attacks black males. It is transmitted by Mama, whose instinct is to protect the Black male from the devastation that threatens him from the moment he declares himself a man.'

Apart from its protectiveness toward male children, Baldwin notes another dimension of 'worriness.' 'Mama,' he writes, 'lays this burden on Sister from whom she expects (or indicates she expects) far more than she expects from Brother; but one of the results of this all too comprehensible dynamic is that Brother may never grow up—in which case the community has become an accomplice to the Republic.' Perceptively,

Baldwin concludes that the differences in the socialization of boys and girls eventually erode the father's commitment to family life. (p. 522).

When such allusive but isolated ethnographic comments are not placed in an analytical framework that tracks the social, political, economic, religious, and historical forces that shape black (female) rearing practices and circumscribe black male/female relations, they are more often than not employed to blame black women for the social failure of black children, especially boys. The point here is not to suggest that black women have no responsibility for the plight of black families. But most social theory has failed to grapple with the complex set of forces that define and delimit black female existence, too easily relying upon anecdotal tales of black female behavior that prevents black males from flourishing, and not examining the shifts in the political economy, the demise of low-skilled, high-waged work, the deterioration of the general moral infrastructure of many poor black communities, the ravaging of black communities by legal forces of gentrification and illegal forces associated with crime and drugs, etc. These forces, and not black women, are the real villains.

10. For a perceptive analysis of the economic conditions which shape the lives of black women, see Julianne Malveaux, "The Political Economy of Black Women" (pp. 53–73).

11. The peculiar pain that plagues the relationships between black men and black women across age, income, and communal strata was on bold and menacing display in the confrontation between Clarence Thomas and Anita Hill during Senate hearings to explore claims by Hill that Thomas sexually harassed her while she worked for him at two governmental agencies. Their confrontation was facilitated and constructed by the televisual medium, a ready metaphor for the technological intervention into contemporary relations between significant segments of the citizenry. Television also serves as the major mediator between various bodies of public officials and the increasingly narrow publics at whose behest they perform, thus blurring the distinctions between public good and private interest. The Hill/Thomas hearings also helped expose the wide degree to which the relations between black men and black women are shaped by a powerful white male gaze. In this case, the relevant criteria for assessing the truth of claims about sexual harassment and gender oppression were determined by white senatorial surveillance.

12. Thus, it was unexceptional during the civil rights movement for strong, articulate black women to be marginalized, or excluded altogether, from the intellectual work of the struggle. Furthermore, concerns about feminist liberation were generally overlooked, and many talented, courageous women were often denied a strong or distinct institutional voice about women's liberation in the racial liberation movement. For a typical instance of such sexism within civil rights organizations, see Carson's discussion of black female dissent within SNCC, in Clayborne Carson, *In Struggle* (pp. 147–148).

13. For insightful claims and descriptions of the marginal status of black feminist and womanist concerns in black communities, and for helpful explorations of the complex problems faced by black feminists and womanists, see bell hook's *Ain't I A Woman?* Michele Wallace's *Invisibility Blues*, Audre Lorde's *Sister/Outsider*, and Alice Walker's *In Search of Our Mother's Garden*.

14. Of course, many traditional conceptions of virtue display a theoretical blindness to structural factors which circumscribe and influence the acquisition of traditional moral skills, habits, and dispositions, and the development of alternative and non-mainstream moral skills. What I mean here is that the development of virtues, and the attendant skills which must be deployed in order to practice them effectively, is contingent upon several factors: where and when one is born, the conditions under which one must live, the social and communal forces which limit and define one's life, etc. These factors color the character of moral skills which will be acquired, shape the way in which these skills will be appropriated, and even determine the list of skills required to live the good life in different communities. Furthermore, these virtues reflect the radically different norms, obligations, commitments, and socio-ethical visions of particular communities. For a compelling critique of MacIntyre's contextual universalist claim for the prevalence of the virtues of justice, truthfulness, and courage in all cultures, and the implications of such critique for moral theory, see Alessandro Ferrara's essay, "Universalisms: Procedural, Contextual and Prudential" (pp. 11–38). For an eloquent argument that calls for the authors of the communitarian social vision articulated in *Habits of the Heart* to pay attention to the life, thought, and contributions of people of color, see Vincent Harding. "Toward a Darkly Radiant Vision of America's Truth: A Letter of Concern. An Invitation to Re-Creation" (pp. 67–83).

Reconstructing Black Masculinity

bell hooks

Black and white snapshots of my childhood always show me in the company of my brother. Less than a year older than me, we looked like twins and for a time in life we did everything together. We were inseparable. As young children, we were brother and sister, comrades, in it together. As adolescents, he was forced to become a boy and I was forced to become a girl. In our southern black Baptist patriarchal home, being a boy meant learning to be tough, to mask one's feelings, to stand one's ground and fight— being a girl meant learning to obey, to be quiet, to clean, to recognize that you had no ground to stand on. I was tough, he was not. I was strong willed, he was easygoing. We were both a disappointment. Affectionate, full of good humor, loving, my brother was not at all interested in becoming a patriarchal boy. This lack of interest generated a fierce anger in our father.

We grew up staring at black and white photos of our father in a boxing ring, playing basketball, with the black infantry he was part of in World War II. He was a man in uniform, a man's man, able to hold his own. Despising his one son for not wanting to become the strong silent type (my brother loved to talk, tell jokes, and make us happy), our father let him know early on that he was no son to him, real sons wanted to be like their fathers. Made to feel inadequate, less than male in his childhood, one boy in a house full of six sisters, he became forever

"Reconstructing Black Masculinity" from bell hooks, *Black Looks*. Boston: South End Press, 1992.

haunted by the idea of patriarchal masculinity. All that he had questioned in his childhood was sought after in his early adult life in order to become a man's man—phallocentric, patriarchal, and masculine. In traditional black communities when one tells a grown male to "be a man," one is urging him to aspire to a masculine identity rooted in the patriarchal ideal. Throughout black male history in the United States there have been black men who were not at all interested in the patriarchal ideal. In the black community of my childhood, there was no monolithic standard of black masculinity. Though the patriarchal ideal was the most esteemed version of manhood, it was not the only version. No one in our house talked about black men being no good, shiftless, trifling. Head of the household, our father was a "much man," a provider, lover, disciplinarian, reader, and thinker. He was introverted, quiet, and slow to anger, yet fierce when aroused. We respected him. We were in awe of him. We were afraid of his power, his physical prowess, his deep voice, and his rare unpredictable but intense rage. We were never allowed to forget that, unlike other black men, our father was the fulfillment of the patriarchal masculine ideal.

Though I admired my father, I was more fascinated and charmed by black men who were not obsessed with being patriarchs: by Felix, a hobo who jumped trains, never worked a regular job, and had a missing thumb; by Kid, who lived out in the country and hunted the rabbits and coons that came to our table; by Daddy Gus, who spoke in hushed tones, sharing his sense of spiritual mysticism. These were the men who touched my heart. The list could go on. I remember them because they loved folks, especially women and children. They were caring and giving. They were black men who chose alternative lifestyles, who questioned the *status quo*, who shunned a ready made patriarchal identity and invented themselves. By knowing them, I have never been tempted to ignore the complexity of black male experience and identity. The generosity of spirit that characterized who they were and how they lived in the world lingers in my memory. I write this piece to honor them, knowing as I do now that it was no simple matter for them to choose against patriarchy, to choose themselves, their lives. And I write this piece for my brother in hopes that he will recover one day, come back to himself, know again the way to love, the peace of an unviolated free spirit. It was this peace that the quest for an unattainable life-threatening patriarchal masculine ideal took from him.

When I left our segregated southern black community and went to a predominately white college, the teachers and students I met knew nothing about the lives of black men. Learning about the matriarchy myth and white culture's notion that black men were emasculated, I was shocked. These theories did not speak to the world I had most intimately known, did not address the complex gender roles that were so familiar to me. Much of the scholarly work on black masculinity that was presented in the classroom then was based on material gleaned from studies of urban black life. This work conveyed the message that black masculinity was homogenous. It suggested that all black men were tormented by their inability to fulfill the phallocentric masculine ideal as it has been articulated in white supremacist capitalist patriarchy. Erasing the realities of black men who have diverse understandings of mas-

culinity, scholarship on the black family (traditionally the framework for academic discussion of black masculinity) puts in place of this lived complexity a flat, one-dimensional representation.

The portrait of black masculinity that emerges in this work perpetually constructs black men as "failures" who are psychologically "fucked up," dangerous, violent, sex maniacs whose insanity is informed by their inability to fulfill their phallocentric masculine destiny in a racist context. Much of this literature is written by white people, and some of it by a few academic black men. It does not interrogate the conventional construction of patriarchal masculinity or question the extent to which black men have historically internalized this norm. It never assumes the existence of black men whose creative agency has enabled them to subvert norms and develop ways of thinking about masculinity that challenge patriarchy. Yet, there has never been a time in the history of the United States when black folks, particularly black men, have not been enraged by the dominant culture's stereotypical, fantastical representations of black masculinity. Unfortunately, black people have not systematically challenged these narrow visions, insisting on a more accurate "reading" of black male reality. Acting in complicity with the *status quo*, many black people have passively absorbed narrow representations of black masculinity, perpetuated stereotypes, myths, and offered one-dimensional accounts. Contemporary black men have been shaped by these representations.

No one has yet endeavored to chart the journey of black men from Africa to the so called "new world" with the intent to reconstruct how they saw themselves. Surely the black men who came to the American continent before Columbus saw themselves differently from those who were brought on slave ships, or from those few who freely immigrated to a world where the majority of their brethren were enslaved. Given all that we know of the slave context, it is unlikely that enslaved black men spoke the same language, or that they bonded on the basis of shared "male" identity. Even if they had come from cultures where gender difference was clearly articulated in relation to specific roles that was all disrupted in the "new world" context. Transplanted African men, even those who were coming from cultures where sex roles shaped the division of labor, where the status of men was different and most often higher than that of females, had imposed on them the white colonizer's notions of manhood and masculinity. Black men did not respond to this imposition passively. Yet it is evident in black male slave narratives that black men engaged in racial uplift were often most likely to accept the norms of masculinity set by white culture.

Although the gendered politics of slavery denied black men the freedom to act as "men" within the definition set by white norms, this notion of manhood did become a standard used to measure black male progress. Slave narratives document ways black men thought about manhood. The narratives of Henry "Box" Brown, Josiah Henson, Frederick Douglass, and a host of other black men reveal that they saw "freedom" as that change in status that would enable them to fulfill the role of chivalric benevolent patriarch. Free, they would be men able to provide for and take care of their families. Describing how he wept as he watched a white slave overseer beat his mother, William Wells Brown lamented, "Experience has taught me that nothing can be more heart-rending than for one to see a dear and beloved mother or sister tortured, and to hear their cries and not be able to render them assistance. But such is the position which an American slave occupies." Frederick Douglass did not feel his man-

hood affirmed by intellectual progress. It was affirmed when he fought man to man with the slave overseer. This struggle was a "turning point" in Douglass' life: "It rekindled in my breast the smoldering embers of liberty. It brought up my Baltimore dreams and revived a sense of my own manhood. I was a changed being after that fight. I was nothing before—I was a man now." The image of black masculinity that emerges from slave narratives is one of hardworking men who longed to assume full patriarchal responsibility for families and kin.

Given this aspiration and the ongoing brute physical labor of black men that was the backbone of slave economy (there were more male slaves than black female slaves, particularly before breeding became a common practice), it is really amazing that stereotypes of black men as lazy and shiftless so quickly became common in public imagination. In these 19th and early 20th-century representations, black men were cartoon-like creatures only interested in drinking and having a good time. Such stereotypes were an effective way for white racists to erase the significance of black male labor from public consciousness. Later on, these same stereotypes were evoked as reasons to deny black men jobs. They are still evoked today.

Male "idleness" did not have the same significance in African and Native American cultures that it had in the white mindset. Many 19th-century Christians saw all forms of idle activity as evil, or at least a breeding ground for wrong-doing. For Native Americans and Africans, idle time was space for reverie and contemplation. When slavery ended, black men could once again experience that sense of space. There are no studies which explore the way Native American cultures altered notions of black masculinity, especially for those black men who lived as Indians or who married Indian wives.

Since we know there were many tribes who conceived of masculine roles in ways that were quite different from those of whites, black men may well have found African ideas about gender roles affirmed in Native traditions.

There are also few confessional narratives by black men that chronicle how they felt as a group when freedom did not bring with it the opportunity for them to assume a "patriarchal" role. Those black men who worked as farmers were often better able to assume this role than those who worked as servants or who moved to cities. Certainly, in the mass migration from the rural south to the urban north, black men lost status. In southern black communities there were many avenues for obtaining communal respect. A man was not respected solely because he could work, make money, and provide. The extent to which a given black man absorbed white society's notion of manhood likely determined the extent of his bitterness and despair that white supremacy continually blocked his access to the patriarchal ideal.

Nineteenth century black leaders were concerned about gender roles. While they believed that men should assume leadership positions in the home and public life, they were also concerned about the role of black women in racial uplift. Whether they were merely paying lip-service to the cause of women's rights or were true believers, exceptional individual black men advocated equal rights for black women. In his work, Martin Delaney continually stressed that both genders needed to work in the interest of racial uplift. To him, gender equality was more a way to have greater involvement in racial uplift than a way for black women to be autonomous and independent. Black male leaders like Martin Delaney and Frederick Douglass were patriarchs, but as benevolent dictators they were willing to share power with women, especially if it meant they did not have to surrender any male privilege. As co-editors of the *North Star*, Douglass and Delaney had a masthead in 1847 which read "right is of no sex—truth is of no color . . ." The 1848 meeting of the National Negro Convention included a proposal by Delaney stating: "Whereas we fully believe in the equality of the sexes, therefore, resolved that we hereby invite females hereafter to take part in our deliberation." In Delaney's 1852 treatise *The Condition, Elevation, Emigration, and Destiny of the Colored People of the United States, Politically Considered,* he argued that black women should have full access to education so that they could be better mothers, asserting:

> The potency and respectability of a nation or people, depends entirely upon the position of their women; therefore, it is essential to our elevation that the female portion of our children be instructed in all the arts and sciences pertaining to the highest civilization.

In Delaney's mind, equal rights for black women in certain public spheres such as education did not mean that he was advocating a change in domestic relations whereby black men and women would have co-equal status in the home.

Most 19th-century black men were not advocating equal rights for women. On one hand, most black men recognized the powerful and necessary role black women had played as freedom fighters in the movement to abolish slavery and other civil rights efforts, yet on the other hand they continued to believe that women should be subordinate to men. They wanted black women to conform to the gender norms set by white society. They wanted to be recognized as "men," as patriarchs, by other men, including white men. Yet they could not assume this position if black women were not willing to conform to prevailing sexist gender norms. Many black women who had endured white supremacist patriarchal domination during slavery did not want to be dominated by black men after manumission. Like black men, they had contradictory positions on gender. On one hand they did not want to be "dominated," but on the other hand they wanted black men to be protectors and providers. After slavery ended, enormous tension and conflict emerged between black women and men as folks struggled to be self-determining. As they worked to create standards for community and family life, gender roles continued to be problematic.

Black men and women who wanted to conform to gender role norms found that this was nearly impossible in a white racist economy that wanted to continue its exploitation of black labor. Much is made, by social critics who want to further the notion that black men are symbolically castrated, of the fact that black women often found work in service jobs while black men were unemployed. The reality, however, was that in some homes it was problematic when a black woman worked and the man did not, or when she earned more than he, yet, in other homes, black men were quite content to construct alternative roles. Critics who look at black life from a sexist standpoint advance the assumption that black men were psychologically devastated because they did not have the opportunity to slave away in low paying jobs for white racist employers when the truth may very well be that those black men who wanted to work but could not find jobs, as well as those who did not want to find jobs, may simply have felt relieved that they did not have to submit to economic exploitation. Concurrently, there were black women who wanted black men to assume patriarchal roles and there were some who were content to be autonomous,

independent. And long before contemporary feminist movement sanctioned the idea that men could remain home and rear children while women worked, black women and men had such arrangements and were happy with them.

Without implying that black women and men lived in gender utopia, I am suggesting that black sex roles, and particularly the role of men, have been more complex and problematized in black life than is believed. This was especially the case when all black people lived in segregated neighborhoods. Racial integration has had a profound impact on black gender roles. It has helped to promote a climate wherein most black women and men accept sexist notions of gender roles. Unfortunately, many changes have occurred in the way black people think about gender, yet the shift from one standpoint to another has not been fully documented. For example: To what extent did the civil rights movement, with its definition of freedom as having equal opportunity with whites, sanction looking at white gender roles as a norm black people should imitate? Why has there been so little positive interest shown in the alternative lifestyles of black men? In every segregated black community in the United States there are adult black men married, unmarried, gay, straight, living in households where they do not assert patriarchal domination and yet live fulfilled lives, where they are not sitting around worried about castration. Again it must be emphasized that the black men who are most worried about castration and emasculation are those who have completely absorbed white supremacist patriarchal definitions of masculinity.

Advanced capitalism further changed the nature of gender roles for all men in the United States. The image of the patriarchal head of the household, ruler of this mini-state called the "family," faded in the 20th century. More men than ever before worked for someone else. The state began to interfere more in domestic matters. A man's time was not his own; it belonged to his employer, and the terms of his rule in the family were altered. In the old days, a man who had no money could still assert tyrannic rule over family and kin, by virtue of his patriarchal status, usually affirmed by Christian belief systems. Within a burgeoning capitalist economy, it was wage-earning power that determined the extent to which a man would rule over a household, and even that rule was limited by the power of the state. In *White Hero, Black Beast,* Paul Hoch describes the way in which advanced capitalism altered representations of masculinity:

> The concept of masculinity is dependent at its very root on the concepts of sexual repression and private property. Ironically, it is sexual repression and economic scarcity that give masculinity its main significance as a symbol of economic status and sexual opportunity. The shrinkage of the concept of man into the narrowed and hierarchical conceptions of masculinity of the various work and consumption ethics also goes hand in hand with an increasing social division of labor, and an increasing shrinkage of the body's erogenous potentials culminating in a narrow genital sexuality. As we move from the simpler food-gathering societies to the agricultural society to the urbanized work and warfare society, we notice that it is a narrower and narrower range of activities that yield masculine status.

In feminist terms, this can be described as a shift from emphasis on patriarchal status (determined by one's capacity to assert power over others in a number of spheres based on maleness) to a phallocentric model, where what the male does with his penis becomes a greater and certainly a more accessible way to assert masculine status. It is easy to see how this served the inter-

ests of a capitalist state which was indeed depriving men of their rights, exploiting their labor in such a way that they only indirectly received the benefits, to deflect away from a patriarchal power based on ruling others and to emphasize a masculine status that would depend solely on the penis.

With the emergence of a fierce phallocentrism, a man was no longer a man because he provided care for his family, he was a man simply because he had a penis. Furthermore, his ability to use that penis in the arena of sexual conquest could bring him as much status as being a wage earner and provider. A sexually defined masculine ideal rooted in physical domination and sexual possession of women could be accessible to all men. Hence, even unemployed black men could gain status, could be seen as the embodiment of masculinity, within a phallocentric framework. Barbara Ehrenreich's *The Hearts of Men* chronicles white male repudiation of a masculine ideal rooted in a notion of patriarchal rule requiring a man to marry and care for the material well-being of women and children and an increasing embrace of a phallocentric "playboy" ideal. At the end of the chapter "Early Rebels," Ehrenreich describes rites of passage in the 1950s which led white men away from traditional nonconformity into a rethinking of masculine status:

> . . . not every would-be male rebel had the intellectual reserves to gray gracefully with the passage of the decade. They drank beyond excess, titrating gin with coffee in their lunch hours, gin with Alka-Seltzer on the weekends. They had stealthy affairs with secretaries, and tried to feel up their neighbors' wives at parties. They escaped into Mickey Spillane mysteries, where naked blondes were routinely perforated in a hail of bullets, or into Westerns, where there were no women at all and no visible sources of white-collar employment. And

some of them began to discover an alternative, or at least an entirely new style of male rebel who hinted, seductively, that there was an alternative. The new rebel was the playboy.

Even in the restricted social relations of slavery black men had found a way to practice the fine art of phallocentric seduction. Long before white men stumbled upon the "playboy" alternative, black vernacular culture told stories about that non-working man with time on his hands who might be seducing somebody else's woman. Blues songs narrate the "playboy" role. Ehrenreich's book acknowledges that the presence of black men in segregated black culture and their engagement in varied expressions of masculinity influenced white men:

> The Beat hero, the male rebel who actually walks away from responsibility in any form, was not a product of middle-class angst. The possibility of walking out, without money or guilt, and without ambition other than to see and do everything, was not even imminent in the middle-class culture of the early fifties. . . The new bohemianism of the Beats came from somewhere else entirely, from an underworld and an underclass invisible from the corporate "crystal palace" or suburban dream houses.

Alternative male lifestyles that opposed the *status quo* were to be found in black culture.

White men seeking alternatives to a patriarchal masculinity turned to black men, particularly black musicians. Norman Podhoretz's 1963 essay "My Negro Problem— And Ours" names white male fascination with blackness, and black masculinity:

> Just as in childhood I envied Negroes for what seemed to me their superior masculinity, so I envy them today for what seems to be their superior physical grace and beauty. I have come to value physical grace very highly and I am now capable of

aching with all my being when I watch a Negro couple on the dance floor, or a Negro playing baseball or basketball. They are on the kind of terms with their own bodies that I should like to be on with mine, and for that precious quality they seem blessed to me.

Black masculinity, as fantasized in the racist white imagination, is the quintessential embodiment of man as "outsider" and "rebel." They were the ultimate "traveling men" drifting from place to place, town to town, job to job.

Within segregated black communities, the "traveling" black man was admired even as he was seen as an indictment of the failure of black men to achieve the patriarchal masculine ideal. Extolling the virtues of traveling black men in her novels, Toni Morrison sees them as "truly masculine in the sense of going out so far where you're not supposed to go and running toward confrontations rather than away from them." This is a man who takes risks, what Morrison calls a "free man":

> This is a man who is stretching, you know, he's stretching, he's going all the way within his own mind and within whatever his outline might be. Now that's the tremendous possibility for masculinity among black men. And you see it a lot. . . They may end up in sort of twentieth-century, contemporary terms being also unemployed. They may be in prison. They may be doing all sorts of things. But they are adventuresome in that regard.

Within white supremacist capitalist patriarchy, rebel black masculinity has been idolized and punished, romanticized yet vilified. Though the traveling man repudiates being a patriarchal provider, he does not necessarily repudiate male domination.

Collectively, black men have never critiqued the dominant culture's norms of masculine identity, even though they have reworked those norms to suit their social situation. Black male sociologist Robert Staples argues that the black male is "in conflict with the normative definition of masculinity," yet this conflict has never assumed the form of complete rebellion. Assuming that black men are "crippled emotionally" when they cannot fully achieve the patriarchal ideal, Staples asserts: "This is a status which few, if any, black males have been able to achieve. Masculinity, as defined in this culture, has always implied a certain autonomy and mastery of one's environment." Though Staples suggests, "the black male has always had to confront the contradiction between the normative expectation attached to being male in this society and proscriptions on his behavior and achievement of goals," implicit in his analysis is the assumption that black men could only internalize this norm and be victimized by it. Like many black men, he assumes that patriarchy and male domination is not a socially constructed social order but a "natural" fact of life. He therefore cannot acknowledge that black men could have asserted meaningful agency by repudiating the norms white culture was imposing.

These norms could not be repudiated by black men who saw nothing problematic or wrong minded about them. Staples, like most black male scholars writing about black masculinity, does not attempt to deconstruct normative thinking, he laments that black men have not had full access to patriarchal phallocentrism. Embracing the phallocentric ideal, he explains black male rape of women by seeing it as a reaction against their inability to be "real men" (i.e., assert legitimate domination over women). Explaining rape, Staples argues:

> In the case of black men, it is asserted that they grow up feeling emasculated and powerless before reaching manhood. They often encounter women as authority figures and teachers or as the head of their household. These men consequently act out their feelings of powerlessness against black women in the form of sexual aggression. Hence, rape by black men should be viewed as both an aggressive and political act because it occurs in the context of racial discrimination which denies most black men a satisfying manhood.

Staples does not question why black women are the targets of black male aggression if it is white men and a white racist system which prevents them from assuming the "patriarchal" role. Given that many white men who fully achieve normal masculinity rape, his implied argument that black men would not rape if they could be patriarchs seems ludicrous. And his suggestion that they would not rape if they could achieve a "satisfying manhood" is pure fantasy. Given the context of this paragraph, it is safe to assume that the "satisfying manhood" he evokes carries with it the phallocentric right of men to dominate women, however benevolently. Ultimately, he is suggesting that if black men could legitimately dominate women more effectively they would not need to coerce them outside the law. Growing up in a black community where there were individual black men who critiqued normative masculinity, who repudiated patriarchy and its concomitant support of sexism, I fully appreciate that it is a tremendous loss that there is little known of their ideas about black masculinity. Without documentation of their presence, it has been easier for black men who embrace patriarchal masculinity, phallocentrism, and sexism to act as though they speak for all black men. Since their representations of black masculinity are in complete agreement with white culture's assessment, they do not threaten or challenge white domination, they reinscribe it.

Contemporary black power movement made synonymous black liberation and the effort to create a social structure wherein

black men could assert themselves as patriarchs, controlling community, family, and
kin. On one hand, black men expressed
contempt for white men yet they also envied
them their access to patriarchal power.
Using a "phallocentric" stick to beat white
men, Amiri Baraka asserted in his 1960s
essay "american sexual reference: black
male":

> Most American white men are trained to
> be fags. For this reason it is no wonder that
> their faces are weak and blank, left without
> the hurt that reality makes—anytime. That
> red flush, those silk blue faggot eyes...
> They are the "masters" of the world, and
> their children are taught this as God's fin-
> gerprint, so they can devote most of their
> energies to the nonrealistic, having no use
> for the real. They devote their energies to
> the nonphysical, the nonrealistic, and be-
> come estranged from them. Even their
> wars move to the stage where whole popu-
> lations can be destroyed by pushing a but-
> ton... can you, for a second imagine the
> average middle class white man able to do
> somebody harm? Alone? Without the tech-
> nology that at this moment still has him
> rule the world: Do you understand the soft-
> ness of the white man, the weakness...

This attack on white masculinity, and others
like it, did not mean that black men were attacking normative masculinity, they were
simply pointing out that white men had not
fulfilled the ideal. It was a case of "will the
real man please stand up." And when he
stood up, he was, in the eyes of black power
movement, a black male.

This phallocentric idealization of masculinity is most powerfully expressed in the
writings of George Jackson. Throughout
Soledad Brother, he announces his uncritical
acceptance of patriarchal norms, especially
the use of violence as a means of social control. Critical of nonviolence as a stance that
would un-man black males, he insisted:

> The symbol of the male here in North
> America has always been the gun, the knife,
> the club. Violence is extolled at every ex-
> change: the TV, the motion pictures, the
> best-seller lists. The newspapers that sell
> best are those that carry the boldest, blood-
> iest headlines and most sports coverage. To
> die for king and country is to die a hero.

Jackson felt black males would need to embrace this use of violence if they hoped to
defeat white adversaries. And he is particularly critical of black women for not embracing these notions of masculinity:

> I am reasonably certain that I draw from
> every black male in this country some com-
> ments to substantiate that his mother, the
> black female, attempted to aid his survival
> by discouraging his violence or by turning it
> inward. The blacks of slave society, U.S.A.,
> have always been a matriarchal subsociety.
> The implication is clear, black mama is
> going to have to put a sword in that
> brother's hand and stop that "be a good
> boy" shit.

A frighteningly fierce misogyny informs
Jackson's rage at black women, particularly
his mother. Even though he was compelled
by black women activists and comrades to
reconsider his position on gender, particularly by Angela Davis, his later work, *Blood
In My Eye*, continues to see black liberation
as a "male thing," to see revolution as a task
for men:

> At the end of this massive collective strug-
> gle, we will uncover a new man, the unpre-
> dictable culmination of the revolutionary
> process. He will be better equipped to
> wage the real struggle, the permanent
> struggle after the revolution—the one for
> new relationships between men.

Although the attitudes expressed by
Baraka and Jackson appear dated, they have
retained their ideological currency among

black men through time. Black female critiques of black male phallocentrism and sexism have had little impact on black male consciousness. Michele Wallace's *Black Macho and the Myth of the Super Woman* was the first major attempt by a black woman to speak from a feminist standpoint about black male sexism. Her analysis of black masculinity was based primarily on her experience in the urban northern cities, yet she wrote as if she were speaking comprehensively about collective black experience. Even so, her critique was daring and courageous. However, like other critics she evoked a monolithic homogenous representation of black masculinity. Discussing the way black male sexism took precedence over racial solidarity during Shirley Chisolm's presidential campaign, Wallace wrote:

> The black political forces in existence at the time—in other words, the black male political forces—did not support her. In fact, they actively opposed her nomination. The black man in the street seemed either outraged that she dared to run or simply indifferent.
>
> Ever since then it has really baffled me to hear black men say that black women have no time for feminism because being black comes first. For them, when it came to Shirley Chisholm, being black no longer came first at all. It turned out that what they really meant all along was that the black man came before the black woman.

Chisholm documented in her autobiography that sexism stood in her way more than racism. Yet she also talks about the support she received from her father and her husband for her political work. Commenting on the way individuals tried to denigrate this support by hinting that there was something wrong with her husband, Chisholm wrote: "Thoughtless people have suggested that my husband would have to be a weak man who enjoys having me dominate him. They are

wrong on both counts." Though fiercely critical of sexism in general and black male sexism in particular, Chisholm acknowledged the support she had received from black men who were not advancing patriarchy. Any critique of "black macho," of black male sexism, that does not acknowledge the actions of black men who subvert and challenge the *status quo* cannot be an effective critical intervention. If feminist critics ignore the efforts of individual black men to oppose sexism, our critiques seem to be self-serving, appear to be anti-male rather than anti-sexist. Absolutist portraits that imply that all black men are irredeemably sexist, inherently supportive of male domination, make it appear that there is no way to change this, no alternative, no other way to be. When attention is focused on those black men who oppose sexism, who are disloyal to patriarchy, even if they are exceptions, the possibility for change, for resistance is affirmed. Those representations of black gender relationships that perpetually pit black women and men against one another deny the complexity of our experiences and intensify mutually destructive internecine gender conflict.

More than ten years have passed since Michele Wallace encouraged black folks to take gender conflict as a force that was undermining our solidarity and creating tension. Without biting her tongue, Wallace emphatically stated:

> I am saying, among other things, that for perhaps the last fifty years there has been a growing distrust, even hatred, between black men and black women. It has been nursed along not only by racism on the part of whites but also by an almost deliberate ignorance on the part of blacks about the sexual politics of their experience in this country.

The tensions Wallace describes between black women and men have not abated, if anything they have worsened. In more recent years they have taken the public form of black women and men competing for the attention of a white audience. Whether it be the realm of job hunting or book publishing, there is a prevailing sense within white supremacist capitalist patriarchy that black men and women cannot both be in the dominant culture's limelight. While it obviously serves the interests of white supremacy for black women and men to be divided from one another, perpetually in conflict, there is no overall gain for black men and women. Sadly, black people collectively refuse to take seriously issues of gender that would undermine the support for male domination in black communities.

Since the 1960s black power movement had worked over-time to let sisters know that they should assume a subordinate role to lay the groundwork for an emergent black patriarchy that would elevate the status of black males, women's liberation movement has been seen as a threat. Consequently, black women were and are encouraged to think that any involvement with feminism was/is tantamount to betraying the race. Such thinking has not really altered over time. It has become more entrenched. Black people responded with rage and anger to Wallace's book, charging that she was a puppet of white feminists who were motivated by vengeful hatred of black men, but they never argued that her assessment of black male sexism was false. They critiqued her harshly because they sincerely believed that sexism was not a problem in black life and that black female support of black patriarchy and phallocentrism might heal the wounds inflicted by racist domination. As long as black people foolishly cling to the rather politically naive and dangerous assumption that it is in the interests of black liberation to support sexism and male domination, all our efforts to decolonize our minds and transform society will fail.

Perhaps black folks cling to the fantasy that phallocentrism and patriarchy will provide a way out of the havoc and wreckage wreaked by racist genocidal assault because it is an analysis of our current political situation that places a large measure of the blame on the black community, the black family, and, most specifically, black women. This way of thinking means that black people do not have to envision creative strategies for confronting and resisting white supremacy and internalized racism. Tragically, internecine gender conflict between black women and men strengthens white supremacist capitalist patriarchy. Politically behind the times where gender is concerned, many black people lack the skills to function in a changed and changing world. They remain unable to grapple with a contemporary reality where male domination is consistently challenged and under siege. Primarily it is white male advocates of feminist politics who do the scholarly work that shows the crippling impact of contemporary patriarchy on men, particularly those groups of men who do not receive maximum benefit from this system. Writing about the way patriarchal masculinity undermines the ability of males to construct self and identity with their well-being in mind, creating a life-threatening masculinist sensibility, these works rarely discuss black men.

Most black men remain in a state of denial, refusing to acknowledge the pain in their lives that is caused by sexist thinking and patriarchal, phallocentric violence that is not only expressed by male domination over women but also by internecine conflict among black men. Black people must question why it is that, as white culture has responded to changing gender roles and feminist movement, they have turned to black culture and particularly to black men for articulations of misogyny, sexism, and phallocentrism. In popular culture, representations of black masculinity equate it with brute phallocentrism, woman-hating, a pugilistic "rapist" sexuality, and flagrant disregard for individual rights. Unlike the young George Jackson who, however wrong-minded, cultivated a patriarchal masculinist ethic in the interest of providing black males with a revolutionary political consciousness and a will to resist race and class domination, contemporary young black males espousing a masculinist ethic are not radicalized or insightful about the collective future of black people. Public figures such as Eddie Murphy, Arsenio Hall, Chuck D., Spike Lee, and a host of other black males blindly exploit the commodification of blackness and the concomitant exotification of phallocentric black masculinity.

When Eddie Murphy's film *Raw* (which remains one of the most graphic spectacles of black male phallocentrism) was first shown in urban cities, young black men in the audience gave black power salutes. This film not only did not address the struggle of black people to resist racism, Murphy's evocation of homosocial bonding with rich white men against "threatening" women who want to take their money conveyed his conservative politics. *Raw* celebrates a pugilistic eroticism, the logic of which tells young men that women do not want to hear declarations of love but want to be "fucked to death." Women are represented strictly in misogynist terms—they are evil; they are all prostitutes who see their sexuality solely as a commodity to be exchanged for hard cash, and after the man has delivered the goods they betray him. Is this the "satisfying masculinity" black men desire or does it expose a warped and limited vision of sexuality, one that could not possibly offer fulfillment or sexual healing? As phallocentric spectacle, *Raw* announces that black men are controlled by their penises ("it's a dick thing") and asserts a sexual politic that is fundamentally anti-body.

If the black male cannot "trust" his body not to be the agent of his victimization, how can he trust a female body? Indeed, the female body, along with the female person, is constructed in *Raw* as threatening to the male who seeks autonomous self-hood since it is her presence that awakens phallocentric response. Hence her personhood must be erased; she must be like the phallus, a "thing." Commenting on the self-deception that takes place when men convince themselves and one another that women are not persons, in her essay on patriarchal phallocentrism "The Problem That Has No Name," Marilyn Frye asserts:

> The rejection of females by phallists is both morally and conceptually profound. The refusal to perceive females as persons is conceptually profound because it excludes females from that community whose conceptions of things one allows to influence one's concepts—it serves as a police lock on a closed mind. Furthermore, the refusal to treat women with the respect due to persons is in itself a violation of a moral principle that seems to many to be the founding principle of all morality. This violation of moral principle is sustained by an active manipulation of circumstances that is systematic and habitual and unacknowledged. The exclusion of women from the conceptual community simultaneously excludes them from the moral community.

Black male phallocentrism constructs a portrait of woman as immoral, simultaneously suggesting that she is irrational and incapable of reason. Therefore, there is no need for black men to listen to women or to assume that women have knowledge to share.

It is this representation of womanhood that is graphically evoked in Murphy's film *Harlem Nights*. A dramatization of black male patriarchal fantasies, this film reinvents the history of Harlem so that black men do not appear as cowards unable to confront racist white males but are reinscribed as tough, violent; they talk shit and take none. Again, the George Jackson revolutionary political paradigm is displaced in the realm of the cultural. In this fantasy, black men are as able and willing to assert power "by any means necessary" as are white men. They are shown as having the same desires as white men; they long for wealth, power to dominate others, freedom to kill with impunity, autonomy, and the right to sexually possess women. They embrace notions of hierarchal rule. The most powerful black man in the film, Quick (played by Murphy), always submits to the will of his father. In this world where homosocial black male bonding is glorified and celebrated, black women are sex objects. The only woman who is not a sex object is the post-menopausal mama/matriarch. She is dethroned so that Quick can assert his power, even though he later (again submitting to the father's will) asks her forgiveness. *Harlem Nights* is a sad fantasy, romanticizing a world of misogynist homosocial bonding where everyone is dysfunctional and no one is truly cared for, loved, or emotionally fulfilled.

Despite all the male bluster, Quick, a quintessential black male hero, longs to be loved. Choosing to seek the affections of an unavailable and unattainable black woman (the mistress of the most powerful white man), Quick does attempt to share himself, to drop the masculine mask and be "real" (symbolized by his willingness to share his real name). Yet the black woman he chooses rejects him, only seeking his favors when she is ordered to by the white man who possesses her. It is a tragic vision of black heterosexuality. Both black woman and black man are unable to respond fully to one another because they are so preoccupied with the white power structure, with the white man. The most valued black woman "belongs" to a white man who willingly exchanges her sexual favors in the interest of business. Desired by black and white men alike (it is their joint lust that renders her more valuable, black men desire her because white men desire her and *vice versa*), her internalized racism and her longing for material wealth and power drive her to act in complicity with white men against black men. Before she can carry out her mission to kill him, Quick shoots her after they have had sexual intercourse. Not knowing that he has taken the bullets from her gun, she points it, telling him that her attack is not personal but "business." Yet when he kills her he makes a point of saying that it is "personal." This was a very sad moment in the film, in that he destroys her because she rejects his authentic need for love and care.

Contrary to the phallocentric representation of black masculinity that has been on display throughout the film, the woman-hating black men are really shown to be in need of love from females. Orphaned, Quick, who is "much man" seeking love, demonstrates his willingness to be emotionally vulnerable, to share only to be rejected, humiliated. This drama of internecine conflict between black women and men follows the conventional sexist line that sees black women as betraying black men by acting in complicity with white patriarchy. This notion of black female complicity and betrayal is so fixed in the minds of many black men they are unable to perceive any flaws in its logic. It certainly gives credence to Michele Wallace's assertion that black people do not have a clear understanding of black sexual politics. Black men who advance the notion that black women are complicit with white men make this assessment without ever invoking historical documentation. Indeed, annals of history abound that document the opposite assumption, showing that black women have typically acted in solidarity with black men. While it may be accurate to argue that sexist black women are complicit with white supremacist capitalist patriarchy, so are sexist black men. Yet most black men continue to deny their complicity.

Spike Lee's recent film *Mo' Better Blues* is another tragic vision of contemporary black heterosexuality. Like *Harlem Nights*, it focuses on a world of black male homosocial bonding where black women are seen primarily as sex objects. Even when they have talent, as the black female jazz singer Clarke does, they must still exchange their sexual favors for recognition. Like Quick, Bleek, the black hero, seeks recognition of his value in heterosexual love relations. Yet he is unable to see the "value" of the two black women who care for him. Indeed, scenes where he makes love to Clarke and alternately sees her as Indigo and *vice versa* suggest the dixie cup sexist mentality (i.e., all women are alike). And even after his entire world has fallen apart he never engages in a self-critique that might lead him to understand that phallocentrism (he is constantly explaining himself by saying "it's a dick thing") has blocked his ability to develop a mature adult identity, has rendered him unable to confront pain and move past denial. Spike Lee's use of Murphy's phrase establishes a continuum of homosocial bonding between black men that transcends the cinematic fiction.

Ironically, the film suggests that Bleek's nihilism and despair can only be addressed by a rejection of a playboy, "dick thing" masculinity and the uncritical acceptance of the traditional patriarchal role. His life crisis is resolved by the reinscription of a patriarchal paradigm. Since Clarke is no longer available, he seeks comfort with Indigo, pleads with her to "save his life." Spike Lee, like Murphy to some extent, exposes the essential self-serving narcissism and denial of community that is at the heart of phallocentrism. He does not, however, envision a radical alternative. The film suggests Bleek has no choice and can only reproduce the same family narrative from which he has emerged, effectively affirming the appropriateness of a nuclear family paradigm where women as mothers restrict black masculinity, black male creativity, and fathers hint at the possibility of freedom. Domesticity represents a place where one's life is "safe" even though one's creativity is contained. The nightclub represents a world outside the home where creativity flourishes and with it an uninhibited eroticism, only that world is one of risk. It is threatening.

The "love supreme" (Coltrane's music and image is a motif throughout the film) that exists between Indigo and Bleek appears shallow and superficial. No longer sex object to be "boned" whenever Bleek desires, her body becomes the vessel for the reproduction of himself *via* having a son. Self-effacing, Indigo identifies Bleek's phallocentrism by telling him he is a "dog," but ultimately she rescues the "dog." His willingness to marry her makes up for dishonesty, abuse, and betrayal. The redemptive love Bleek seeks cannot really be found in the model Lee offers and as a consequence this film is yet another masculine fantasy denying black male agency and capacity to assume responsibility for their personal growth and salvation. The achievement of this goal would mean they must give up phallocentrism and envision new ways of thinking about black masculinity.

Even though individual black women adamantly critique black male sexism, most black men continue to act as though sexism is not a problem in black life and refuse to see it as the force motivating oppressive exploitation of women and children by black men. If any culprit is identified, it is racism. Like Staples' suggestion that the explanation of why black men rape is best understood in a context where racism is identified as the problem, any explanation that evokes a critique of black male phallocentrism is avoided. Black men and women who espouse cultural nationalism continue to see the struggle for black liberation largely as a struggle to recover black manhood. In her essay "Africa On My Mind: Gender, Counter Discourse and African-American Nationalism," E. Frances White shows that overall black nationalist perspectives on gender are rarely rooted purely in the Afrocentric logic they seek to advance, but rather reveal their ties to white paradigms:

> In making appeals to conservative notions of appropriate gender behavior, African-American nationalists reveal their ideological ties to other nationalist movements, including European and Euro-American bourgeois nationalists over the past 200 years. These parallels exist despite the different class and power base of these movements.

Most black nationalists, men and women, refuse to acknowledge the obvious ways patriarchal phallocentric masculinity is a destructive force in black life, the ways it undermines solidarity between black women and men, or how it is life-threatening to black men. Even though individual black nationalists like Haki Madhubuti speak against sexism, progressive Afrocentric thinking does not have the impact that the old guard message has. Perhaps it provides sexist black men with a sense of power and agency (however illusory) to see black women, and particularly feminist black women, as the enemy that prevents them from fully participating in this society. For such fiction gives them an enemy that can be confronted, attacked, annihilated, an enemy that can be conquered, dominated.

Confronting white supremacist capitalist patriarchy would not provide sexist black men with an immediate sense of agency or victory. Blaming black women, however, makes it possible for black men to negotiate with white people in all areas of their lives without vigilantly interrogating those interactions. A good example of this displacement is evident in Brent Staples' essay "The White Girl Problem." Defending his "politically incorrect taste in women" (i.e., his preference for white female partners), from attacking black women, Staples never interrogates his desire. He does not seek to understand the extent to which white supremacist capitalist patriarchy determines his desire. He does not want desire to be politicized. And of course his article does not address white female racism or discuss the fact that a white person does not have to be anti-racist to desire a black partner. Many inter-racial relationships have their roots in racist constructions of the Other. By focusing in a stereotypical way on black women's anger, Staples can avoid these issues and depoliticize the politics of black and white female interactions. His essay would have been a needed critical intervention had he endeavored to explore the way individuals maintain racial solidarity even as they bond with folks outside their particular group.

Solidarity between black women and men continues to be undermined by sexism and misogyny. As black women increasingly oppose and challenge male domination, internecine tensions abound. Publicly, many of the gender conflicts between black women and men have been exposed in recent years with the increasingly successful commodification of black women's writing. Indeed, gender conflict between sexist black male writers and those black female writers who are seen as feminists has been particularly brutal. Black male critic Stanley Crouch has been one of the leading voices mocking and ridiculing black women. His recently published collection of essays, *Notes of A Hanging Judge,* includes articles that are particularly scathing in their attacks on black women.

His critique of Wallace's *Black Macho* is mockingly titled "Aunt Jemima Don't Like Uncle Ben" (notice that the emphasis is on black women not liking black men, hence the caption already places accountability for tensions on black women). The title deflects attention away from the concrete critique of sexism in *Black Macho* by making it a question of personal taste. Everyone seems eager to forget that it is possible for black women to love black men and yet unequivocally challenge and oppose sexism, male domination, and phallocentrism. Crouch never speaks to the issues of black male sexism in his piece and works instead to make Wallace appear an "unreliable" narrator. His useful critical comments are thus undermined by the apparent refusal to take seriously the broad political issues Wallace raises. His refusal to acknowledge sexism, expressed as "black macho," is a serious problem. It destroys the possibility of genuine solidarity between black women and men, makes it appear that he is really angry at Wallace and other black women because he is fundamentally anti-feminist and unwilling to challenge male domination. Crouch's stance epitomizes the attitude of contemporary black male writers who are either uncertain about their political response to feminism or are adamantly anti-feminist. Much black male anti-feminism is linked to a refusal to acknowledge that the phallocentric power black men wield over black women is "real" power, the assumption being that only the power white men have that black men do not have is real.

If, as Frederick Douglass maintained, "power concedes nothing without a demand," the black women and men who advocate feminism must be ever vigilant, critiquing and resisting all forms of sexism. Some black men may refuse to acknowledge that sexism provides them with forms of male privilege and power, however relative.

They do not want to surrender that power in a world where they may feel otherwise quite powerless. Contemporary emergence of a conservative black nationalism which exploits a focus on race to both deny the importance of struggling against sexism and racism simultaneously is both an overt attack on feminism and a force that actively seeks to reinscribe sexist thinking among black people who have been questioning gender. Commodification of blackness that makes phallocentric black masculinity marketable makes the realm of cultural politics a propagandistic site where black people are rewarded materially for reactionary thinking about gender. Should we not be suspicious of the way in which white culture's fascination with black masculinity manifests itself? The very images of phallocentric black masculinity that are glorified and celebrated in rap music, videos, and movies are the representations that are evoked when white supremacists seek to gain public acceptance and support for genocidal assault on black men, particularly youth.

Progressive Afrocentric ideology makes this critique and interrogates sexism. In his latest book, *Black Men: Obsolete, Single, Dangerous*, Haki Madhubuti courageously deplores all forms of sexism, particularly black male violence against women. Like black male political figures of the past, Madhubuti's support of gender equality and his critique of sexism is not linked to an overall questioning of gender roles and a repudiation of all forms of patriarchal domination, however benevolent. Still, he has taken the important step of questioning sexism and calling on black people to explore the way sexism hurts and wounds us. Madhubuti acknowledges black male misogyny:

> The "fear" of women that exists among many Black men runs deep and often goes unspoken. This fear is cultural. Most men

are introduced to members of the opposite sex in a superficial manner, and seldom do we seek a more in depth or informed understanding of them. . . Women have it rough all over the world. Men must become informed listeners.

Woman-hating will only cease to be a norm in black life when black men collectively dare to oppose sexism. Unfortunately, when all black people should be engaged in a feminist movement that addresses the sexual politics of our communities, many of us are tragically investing in old gender norms. At a time when many black people should be reading Madhubuti's *Black Men, Sister Outsider, The Black Women's Health Book, Feminist Theory: From Margin to Center,* and a host of other books that seek to explore black sexual politics with compassion and care, folks are eagerly consuming a conservative tract, *The Blackman's Guide To Understanding The Blackwoman* by Shahrazad Ali. This work actively promotes black male misogyny, coercive domination of females by males, and, as a consequence, feeds the internecine conflict between black women and men. Though many black people have embraced this work there is no indication that it is having a positive impact on black communities, and there is every indication that it is being used to justify male dominance, homophobic assaults on black gay people, and rejection of black styles that emphasize our diasporic connection to Africa and the Caribbean. Ali's book romanticizes black patriarchy, demanding that black women "submit" to black male domination in lieu of changes in society that would make it possible for black men to be more fulfilled.

Calling for a strengthening of black male phallocentric power (to be imposed by force if need be), Ali's book in no way acknowledges sexism. When writing about black men, her book reads like an infantile caricature of the Tarzan fantasy. Urging black

men to assert their rightful position as patriarchs, she tells them: "Rise Blackman, and take your rightful place as ruler of the universe and everything in it. Including the black woman." Like *Harlem Nights*, this is the stuff of pure fantasy. That black people, particularly the underclass, are turning to escapist fantasies that can in no way adequately address the collective need of African Americans for renewed black liberation struggle is symptomatic of the crisis we are facing. Desperately clinging to ways of thinking and being that are detrimental to our collective well-being obstructs progressive efforts for change.

More black men have broken their silence to critique Ali's work than have ever offered public support of feminist writing by black women. Yet it does not help educate black people about the ways feminist analysis could be useful in our lives for black male critics to act as though the success of this book represents a failure on the part of feminism. Ali's sexist, homophobic, self-denigrating tirades strike a familiar chord because so many black people who have not decolonized their minds think as she does. Though black male critic Nelson George critiques Ali's work, stating that it shows "how little Afrocentrism respects the advances of African-American women," he suggests that it is an indication of how "unsuccessful black feminists have been in forging alliance with this ideologically potent community." Statements like this one advance the notion that feminist education is the sole task of black women. It also rather neatly places George outside either one of these potent communities. Why does he not seize the critical moment to bring to public awareness the feminist visions of Afrocentric black women? All too often, black men who are indirectly supportive of feminist movement act as though black women have a personal stake in eradicating sexism that men do not have.

Black men benefit from feminist thinking and feminist movement too.

Any examination of the contemporary plight of black men reveals the way phallocentrism is at the root of much black-on-black violence, undermines family relations, informs the lack of preventive health care, and even plays a role in promoting drug addiction. Many of the destructive habits of black men are enacted in the name of "manhood." Asserting their ability to be "tough," to be "cool," black men take grave risks with their lives and the lives of others. Acknowledging this in his essay "Cool Pose: The Proud Signature of Black Survival," Richard Majors argues that "cool" has positive dimensions even though it "is also an aggressive assertion of masculinity." Yet, he never overtly critiques sexism. Black men may be reluctant to critique phallocentrism and sexism, precisely because so much black male "style" has its roots in these positions; they may fear that eradicating patriarchy would leave them without the positive expressive styles that have been life-sustaining. Majors is clear, however, that a "cool pose" linked to aggressive phallocentrism is detrimental to both black men and the people they care about:

> Perhaps black men have become so conditioned to keeping up their guard against oppression from the dominant white society that this particular attitude and behavior represents for them their best safeguard against further mental or physical abuse. However, this same behavior makes it very difficult for these males to let their guard down and show affection. . .

Elsewhere, he suggests "that the same elements of cool that allow for survival in the larger society may hurt black people by contributing to one of the more complex problems facing black people today—black-on-black crime." Clearly, black men need to employ a feminist analysis that will address

the issue of how to construct a life-sustaining black masculinity that does not have its roots in patriarchal phallocentrism.

Addressing the way obsessive concern with the phallus causes black men stress in *No Name in the Street*, James Baldwin explains:

> Every black man walking in this country pays a tremendous price for walking: for men are not women, and a man's balance depends on the weight he carries between his legs. All men, however they may face or fail to face it, however they may handle, or be handled by it, know something about each other, which is simply that a man without balls is not a man . . .

What might black men do for themselves and for black people if they were not socialized by white supremacist capitalist patriarchy to focus their attention on their penises? Should we not suspect the contemporary commodification of blackness orchestrated by whites that once again tells black men not only to focus on their penis but to make this focus their all consuming passion? Such confused men have little time or insight for resistance struggle. Should we not suspect representations of black men like those that appear in a movie like *Heart Condition*, where the black male describes himself as "hung like a horse" as though the size of his penis defines who he is? And what does it say about the future of black liberation struggles if the phrase "it's a dick thing" is transposed and becomes "its a black thing?" If the "black thing," i.e., black liberation struggle, is really only a "dick thing" in disguise, a phallocentric play for black male power, then black people are in serious trouble.

Challenging black male phallocentrism would also make a space for critical discussion of homosexuality in black communities. Since so much of the quest for phallocentric manhood as it is expressed in black nationalist circles rests on a demand for compulsory heterosexuality, it has always promoted the persecution and hatred of homosexuals. This is yet another stance that has undermined black solidarity. If black men no longer embraced phallocentric masculinity, they would be empowered to explore their fear and hatred of other men, learning new ways to relate. How many black men will have to die before black folks are willing to look at the link between the contemporary plight of black men and their continued allegiance to patriarchy and phallocentrism?

Most black men will acknowledge that black men are in crisis and are suffering. Yet they remain reluctant to engage those progressive movements that might serve as meaningful critical interventions, that might allow them to speak their pain. On the terms set by white supremacist patriarchy, black men can name their pain only by talking about themselves in crude ways that reinscribe them in a context of primitivism. Why should black men have to talk about themselves as an "endangered species" in order to gain public recognition of their plight? And why are the voices of colonized black men, many of whom are in the spotlight, drowning out progressive voices? Why do we not listen to Joseph Beam, one such courageous voice? He had no difficulty sharing the insight that "communism, socialism, feminism and, homosexuality pose far less of a threat to America than racism, sexism, heterosexism, classism, and ageism." Never losing sight of the need for black men to name their realities, to speak their pain and their resistance, Beam concluded his essay "No Cheek To Turn" with these prophetic words:

I speak to you as a black gay pr ist man moving in a world wh wants to know my name, voice. In prison, I'm just a r army, I'm just a rank; on the j the hospital, I'm just a statistic; street, I'm just a suspect. My head reels. I didn't have access to print, I, too, would write on walls. I want my life's passage to be acknowledged for at least the length of time it takes pain to fade from brick. With that said I serve my notice: I have no cheek to turn.

Changing representations of black men must be a collective task. Black people committed to renewed black liberation struggle, the de-colonization of black minds, are fully aware that we must oppose male domination and work to eradicate sexism. There are black women and men who are working together to strengthen our solidarity. Black men like Richard Majors, Calvin Hernton, Cornel West, Greg Tate, Essex Hemphill, and others address the issue of sexism and advocate feminism. If black men and women take seriously Malcolm's charge that we must work for our liberation "by any means necessary," then we must be willing to explore the way feminism as a critique of sexism, as a movement to end sexism and sexist oppression, could aid our struggle to be self-determining. Collectively we can break the life-threatening choke-hold patriarchal masculinity imposes on black men and create life sustaining visions of a reconstructed black masculinity that can provide black men ways to save their lives and the lives of their brothers and sisters in struggle.

Like a Winding Sheet

Ann Petry

He had planned to get up before Mae did and surprise her by fixing breakfast. Instead he went back to sleep and she got out of bed so quietly he didn't know she wasn't there beside him until he woke up and heard the queer soft gurgle of water running out of the sink in the bathroom.

He knew he ought to get up but instead he put his arms across his forehead to shut the afternoon sunlight out of his eyes, pulled his legs up close to his body, testing them to see if the ache was still in them.

Mae had finished in the bathroom. He could tell because she never closed the door when she was in there and now the sweet smell of talcum powder was drifting down the hall and into the bedroom. Then he heard her coming down the hall.

"Hi, babe," she said affectionately.

"Hum," he grunted, and moved his arms away from his head, opened one eye.

"It's a nice morning."

"Yeah." He rolled over and the sheet twisted around him, outlining his thighs, his chest. "You mean afternoon, don't ya?"

Mae looked at the twisted sheet and giggled. "Looks like a winding sheet," she said. "A shroud—" Laughter tangled with her words and she had to pause for a moment before she could continue. "You look like a huckleberry—in a winding sheet—"

"That's no way to talk. Early in the day like this," he protested.

He looked at his arms silhouetted against the white of the sheets. They were inky black by contrast and he had to smile in spite of himself and he lay there smiling and savoring the sweet sound of Mae's giggling.

"Early?" She pointed a finger at the alarm clock on the table near the bed and giggled again. "It's almost four o'clock. And if you don't spring up out of there, you're going to be late again."

"What do you mean 'again'?"

"Twice last week. Three times the week before. And once the week before and—"

"I can't get used to sleeping in the daytime," he said fretfully. He pushed his legs out from under the covers experimentally. Some of the ache had gone out of them but they weren't really rested yet. "It's too light for good sleeping. And all that standing beats the hell out of my legs."

"After two years you oughta be used to it," Mae said.

He watched her as she fixed her hair, powdered her face, slipped into a pair of blue denim overalls. She moved quickly and yet she didn't seem to hurry.

"You look like you'd had plenty of sleep," he said lazily. He had to get up but he kept putting the moment off, not wanting to move, yet he didn't dare let his legs go completely limp because if he did he'd go back to sleep. It was getting later and later but the thought of putting his weight on his legs kept him lying there.

When he finally got up he had to hurry, and he gulped his breakfast so fast that he

Reprinted by the permission of Russell & Volkening as agents for the author. Copyright © 1945 by Ann Petry, renewed in 1973 by Ann Petry. Story originally appeared in *The Crisis*, 1945.

wondered if his stomach could possibly use food thrown at it at such a rate of speed. He was still wondering about it as he and Mae were putting their coats on in the hall.

Mae paused to look at the calendar. "It's the thirteenth," she said. Then a faint excitement in her voice, "Why, it's Friday the thirteenth." She had one arm in her coat sleeve and she held it there while she stared at the calendar. "I oughta stay home," she said. "I shouldn't go outa the house."

"Aw, don't be a fool," he said "Today's payday. And payday is a good luck day everywhere, any way you look at it." And as she stood hesitating he said, "Aw, come on."

And he was late for work again because they spent fifteen minutes arguing before he could convince her she ought to go to work just the same. He had to talk persuasively, urging her gently, and it took time. But he couldn't bring himself to talk to her roughly or threaten to strike her like a lot of men might have done. He wasn't made that way.

So when he reached the plant he was late and he had to wait to punch the time clock because the day-shift workers were streaming out in long lines, in groups and bunches that impeded his progress.

Even now just starting his workday his legs ached. He had to force himself to struggle past the outgoing workers, punch the time clock, and get the little cart he pushed around all night, because he kept toying with the idea of going home and getting back in bed.

He pushed the cart out on the concrete floor, thinking that if this was his plant he'd make a lot of changes in it. There were too many standing-up jobs for one thing. He'd figure out some way most of 'em could be done sitting-down and he'd put a lot more benches around. And this job he had—this job that forced him to walk ten hours a night, pushing this little cart, well, he'd turn it into a sitting-down job. One of

those little trucks they used around railroad stations would be good for a job like this. Guys sat on a seat and the thing moved easily, taking up little room and turning in hardly any space at all, like on a dime.

He pushed the cart near the foreman. He never could remember to refer to her as the forelady even in his mind. It was funny to have a white woman for a boss in a plant like this one.

She was sore about something. He could tell by the way her face was red and her eyes were half-shut until they were slits. Probably been out late and didn't get enough sleep. He avoided looking at her and hurried a little, head down, as he passed her though he couldn't resist stealing a glance at her out of the corner of his eyes. He saw the edge of the light-colored slacks she wore and the tip end of a big tan shoe.

"Hey, Johnson!" the woman said.

The machines had started full blast. The whirr and the grinding made the building shake, made it impossible to hear conversations. The men and women at the machines talked to each other but looking at them from just a little distance away, they appeared to be simply moving their lips because you couldn't hear what they were saying. Yet the woman's voice cut across the machine sounds—harsh, angry.

He turned his head slowly. "Good evenin', Mrs. Scott," he said, and waited.

"You're late again."

"That's right. My legs were bothering me."

The woman's face grew redder, angrier looking. "Half this shift comes in late," she said. "And you're the worst one of all. You're always late. Whatsa matter with ya?"

"It's my legs," he said. "Somehow they don't ever get rested. I don't seem to get used to sleeping days. And I just can't get started."

"Excuses. You guys always got excuses," her anger grew and spread. "Every guy comes in here late always has an excuse. His wife's sick or his grandmother died or somebody in the family had to go to the hospital," she paused, drew a deep breath. "And the niggers is the worse. I don't care what's wrong with your legs. You get in here on time. I'm sick of you niggers—"

"You got the right to get mad," he interrupted softly. "You got the right to cuss me four ways to Sunday but I ain't letting nobody call me a nigger."

He stepped closer to her. His fists were doubled. His lips were drawn back in a thin narrow line. A vein in his forehead stood out swollen, thick.

And the woman backed away from him, not hurriedly but slowly—two, three steps back.

"Aw, forget it," she said. "I didn't mean nothing by it. It slipped out. It was an accident." The red of her face deepened until the small blood vessels in her cheeks were purple. "Go on and get to work," she urged. And she took three more slow backward steps.

He stood motionless for a moment and then turned away from the sight of the red lipstick on her mouth that made him remember that the foreman was a woman. And he couldn't bring himself to hit a woman. He felt a curious tingling in his fingers and he looked down at his hands. They were clenched tight, hard, ready to smash some of those small purple veins in her face.

He pushed the cart ahead of him, walking slowly. When he turned his head, she was staring in his direction, mopping her forehead with a dark blue handkerchief. Their eyes met and then they both looked away.

He didn't glance in her direction again but moved past the long work benches, carefully collecting the finished parts, going slowly and steadily up and down, back and forth the length of the building, and as he walked he forced himself to swallow his anger, get rid of it.

And he succeeded so that he was able to think about what had happened without getting upset about it. An hour went by but the tension stayed in his hands. They were clenched and knotted on the handles of the cart as though ready to aim a blow.

And he thought he should have hit her anyway, smacked her hard in the face, felt the soft flesh of her face give under the hardness of his hands. He tried to make his hands relax by offering them a description of what it would have been like to strike her because he had the queer feeling that his hands were not exactly a part of him anymore—they had developed a separate life of their own over which he had no control. So he dwelt on the pleasure his hands would have felt—both of them cracking at her, first one and then the other. If he had done that his hands would have felt good now—relaxed, rested.

And he decided that even if he'd lost his job for it, he should have let her have it and it would have been a long time, maybe the rest of her life, before she called anybody else a nigger.

The only trouble was he couldn't hit a woman. A woman couldn't hit back the same way a man did. But it would have been a deeply satisfying thing to have cracked her narrow lips wide open with just one blow, beautifully timed and with all his weight in back of it. That way he would have gotten rid of all the energy and tension his anger had created in him. He kept remembering how his heart had started pumping blood so fast he had felt it tingle even in the tips of his fingers.

With the approach of night, fatigue nibbled at him. The corners of his mouth drooped, the frown between his eyes deepened, his shoulders sagged; but his hands stayed tight and tense. As the hours dragged by he noticed that the women workers had started to snap and snarl at each other. He couldn't hear what they said because of the sound of machines but he could see the quick lip movements that sent words tumbling from the sides of their mouths. They gestured irritably with their hands and scowled as their mouths moved.

Their violent jerky motions told him that it was getting close on to quitting time but somehow he felt that the night still stretched ahead of him, composed of endless hours of steady walking on his aching legs. When the whistle finally blew he went on pushing the cart, unable to believe that it had sounded. The whirring of the machines died away to a murmur and he knew then that he'd really heard the whistle. He stood still for a moment, filled with a relief that made him sigh.

Then he moved briskly, putting the cart in the storeroom, hurrying to take his place in the line forming before the paymaster. That was another thing he'd change, he'd thought. He'd have the pay envelopes handed to the people right at their benches so there wouldn't be ten or fifteen minutes lost waiting for the pay. He always got home about fifteen minutes late on payday. They did it better in the plant where Mae worked, brought the money right to them at their benches.

He stuck his pay envelope in his pants' pocket and followed the line of workers heading for the subway in a slow-moving stream. He glanced up at the sky. It was a nice night, the sky looked packed full to running over with stars. And he thought if he and Mae would go right to bed when they got home from work they'd catch a few hours of darkness for sleeping. But they never did. They fooled around—cooking and eating and listening to the radio and he always stayed in a big chair in the living room and went almost but not quite to sleep and when they finally got to bed it was five or six in the morning and daylight was already seeping around the edges of the sky.

He walked slowly, putting off the moment when he would have to plunge into the crowd hurrying toward the subway. It was a long ride to Harlem and tonight the thought of it appalled him. He paused outside an all-night restaurant to kill time, so that some of the first rush of workers would be gone when he reached the subway.

The lights in the restaurant were brilliant, enticing. There was life and motion inside. And as he looked through the window be thought that everything within range of his eyes gleamed—the long imitation marble counter, the tall stools, the white porcelain-topped tables and especially the big metal coffee urn right near the window. Steam issued from its top and a gas flame flickered under it—a lively, dancing, blue flame.

A lot of the workers from his shift—men and women—were lining up near the coffee urn. He watched them walk to the porcelain-topped tables carrying steaming cups of coffee and he saw that just the smell of the coffee lessened the fatigue lines in their faces. After the first sip their faces softened, they smiled, they began to talk and laugh.

On a sudden impulse he shoved the door open and joined the line in front of the coffee urn. The line moved slowly. And as he stood there the smell of the coffee, the sound of the laughter and of the voices, helped dull the sharp ache in his legs.

He didn't pay any attention to the white girl who was serving the coffee at the urn. He kept looking at the cups in the hands of the men who had been ahead of him. Each time a man stepped out of the line with one of the thick white cups the fragrant steam got in his nostrils. He saw that they walked carefully so as not to spill a single drop. There was a froth of bubbles at the top of each cup and he thought about how he would let the bubbles break against his lips before he actually took a big deep swallow.

Then it was his turn. "A cup of coffee," he said, just as he had heard the others say.

The white girl looked past him, put her hands up to her head and gently lifted her hair away from the back of her neck, tossing her head back a little. "No more coffee for a while," she said.

He wasn't certain he'd heard her correctly and he said, "What?" blankly.

"No more coffee for a while," she repeated.

There was silence behind him and then uneasy movement. He thought someone would say something, ask why or protest, but there was only silence and then a faint shuffling sound as though the men standing behind him had simultaneously shifted their weight from one foot to the other.

He looked at the girl without saying anything. He felt his hands begin to tingle and the tingling went all the way down to his finger tips so that he glanced down at them. They were clenched tight, hard, into fists. Then he looked at the girl again. What he wanted to do was hit her so hard that the scarlet lipstick on her mouth would smear and spread over her nose, her chin, out toward her cheeks, so hard that she would never toss her head again and refuse a man a cup of coffee because he was black.

He estimated the distance across the counter and reached forward, balancing his weight on the balls of his feet, ready to let the blow go. And then his hands fell back down to his sides because he forced himself to lower them, to unclench them and make them dangle loose. The effort took his breath away because his hands fought against him. But he couldn't hit her. He couldn't even now bring himself to hit a woman, not even this one, who had refused him a cup of coffee with a toss of her head. He kept seeing the gesture with which she had lifted the length of her blond hair from the back of her neck as expressive of her contempt for him.

When he went out the door he didn't look back. If he had he would have seen the flickering blue flame under the shiny coffee urn being extinguished. The line of men who had stood behind him lingered a moment to watch the people drinking coffee at the tables and then they left just as he had without having had the coffee they wanted so badly. The girl behind the counter poured water in the urn and swabbed it out and as she waited for the water to run out, she lifted her hair gently from the back of her neck and tossed her head before she began making a fresh lot of coffee.

But he had walked away without a backward look, his head down, his hands in his pockets, raging at himself and whatever it was inside of him that had forced him to stand quiet and still when he wanted to strike out.

The subway was crowded and he had to stand. He tried grasping an overhead strap and his hands were too tense to grip it. So he moved near the train door and stood there swaying back and forth with the rocking of the train. The roar of the train beat inside his head, making it ache and throb, and the pain in his legs clawed up into his groin so that he seemed to be bursting with pain and he told himself that it was due to all that anger-born energy that had piled up in him and not been used and so it had spread through him like a poison—from his feet and legs all the way up to his head.

Mae was in the house before he was. He knew she was home before he put the key in the door of the apartment. The radio was going. She had it tuned up loud and she was singing along with it.

"Hello, babe," she called out, as soon as he opened the door.

He tried to say 'hello' and it came out half grunt and half sigh.

"You sure sound cheerful," she said.

She was in the bedroom and he went and leaned against the doorjamb. The denim overalls she wore to work were carefully draped over the back of a chair by the bed. She was standing in front of the dresser, tying the sash of a yellow housecoat around her waist and chewing gum vigorously as she admired her reflection in the mirror over the dresser.

"Whatsa matter?" she said. "You get bawled out by the boss or somep'n?"

"Just tired," he said slowly. "For God's sake, do you have to crack that gum like that?"

"You don't have to lissen to me," she said complacently. She patted a curl in place near the side of her head and then lifted her hair away from the back of her neck, ducking her head forward and then back.

He winced away from the gesture. "What you got to be always fooling with your hair for?" he protested.

"Say, what's the matter with you anyway?" She turned away from the mirror to face him, put her hands on her hips. "You ain't been in the house two minutes and you're picking on me."

He didn't answer her because her eyes were angry and he didn't want to quarrel with her. They'd been married too long and got along too well and so he walked all the way into the room and sat down in the chair by the bed and stretched his legs out in front of him, putting his weight on the heels of his shoes, leaning way back in the chair, not saying anything.

"Lissen," she said sharply. "I've got to wear those overalls again tomorrow. You're going to get them all wrinkled up leaning against them like that."

He didn't move. He was too tired and his legs were throbbing now that he had sat down. Besides the overalls were already wrinkled and dirty, he thought. They couldn't help but be for she'd worn them all week. He leaned farther back in the chair.

"Come on, get up," she ordered.

"Oh, what the hell," he said wearily, and got up from the chair. "I'd just as soon

live in a subway. There'd be just as much place to sit down."

He saw that her sense of humor was struggling with her anger. But her sense of humor won because she giggled.

"Aw, come on and eat," she said. There was a coaxing note in her voice. "You're nothing but an old hungry nigger trying to act tough and—" she paused to giggle and then continued, "You—"

He had always found her giggling pleasant and deliberately said things that might amuse her and then waited, listening for the delicate sound to emerge from her throat. This time he didn't even hear the giggle. He didn't let her finish what she was saying. She was standing close to him and that funny tingling started in his finger tips, went fast up his arms and sent his fist shooting straight for her face.

There was the smacking sound of soft flesh being struck by a hard object and it wasn't until she screamed that he realized he had hit her in the mouth—so hard that the dark red lipstick had blurred and spread over her full lips, reaching up toward the tip of her nose, down toward her chin, out toward her cheeks.

The knowledge that he had struck her seeped through him slowly and he was appalled but he couldn't drag his hands away from her face. He kept striking her and he thought with horror that something inside him was holding him, binding him to this act, wrapping and twisting about him so that he had to continue it. He had lost all control over his hands. And he groped for a phrase, a word, something to describe what this thing was like that was happening to him and he thought it was like being enmeshed in a winding sheet—that was it—like a winding sheet. And even as the thought formed in his mind, his hands reached for her face again and yet again.

Theorists on Constructions of Black Masculinities: Identity, Consumerism, and Agency

Khaula Murtadha-Watts

What shapes the social, political and cultural realities for African-American males in central cities? What factors define and maintain these realities and how do they contribute to the construction of masculinities that are different for white, middle-class males in schools? There are many responses as cultural critics and activists struggle with these issues, yet there is usually agreement that poverty and the racist structuring of urban spaces has a dramatic impact on day-to-day existence. In many urban, poverty-ridden neighborhoods, the collapse of structures of meaning and feeling can be seen in the "sense of community" breakdown. To Marable (1992), this discontinuity is striking. Young blacks act as competitors within a culture of consumption, often relating to each other out of mistrust and fear. Cultural and religious critic Michael Dyson draws attention to how many inner-city communities (code words for poor, black, and brown) live under what may be called a "juvenocracy": the economic rule and illegal tyranny exercised by young black men over significant urban territory. His point is that in addition to being detached from the recognition and rewards of the dominant society, inner-city communities are continually devastated and cut off from sources of moral authority and legitimate work, as underground political economies reward both young children and teens with quick cash.

Dyson (1993) explores not only the cultural expressions, but the material conditions and social problems associated with rap music. His work is useful in this chapter about the constructions of black masculinities because, as he points out, rap culture represents to a great extent "the voice and vision of a significant segment of young black culture" (p. 281).

> Rap also mirrors the varieties of sexism that persist in many poor black communities, themselves reflections of the patriarchal tendencies that are dispersed throughout our culture. Only by confronting the powerful social criticism that rap culture articulates can we hope to understand its appeal. ... And by examining its weaknesses and blindnesses, we are encouraged to critically confront our similar shortcomings, which do not often receive the controversial media coverage given to rap culture. (p. 281)

Kitwana (1994) points out that what is in part problematic about many rap artists' message is that black women and men are objectified and dehumanized with distorted images bought and sold by black youth who lack an understanding of African American culture and historical struggles. For this reason I draw attention to rap's impact on constructions of

Excerpted from "Theorizing Urban Black Masculinity Construction in an African–Centered School" in Nancy Lesko, *Masculinities at School*, pp. 52–57. © 2000 by Sage Publications, Inc. Reprinted by Permission of Sage Publications, Inc.

masculinity in schools. Children do not leave their socially constructed knowledges at the school door. Not to examine the cultural forms that greatly impact their lives is to miss the engagement of black youth culture's values, attitudes, and concerns. For the most part, black males do not limit or confine themselves to the representations and images of white cultural productions, particularly television, film, and advertising. This is an issue of agency. Nevertheless, dominant white representations of black males may socialize black males to see themselves as always inadequate, as always "subordinated to more powerful white males whose approval they need to survive" (hooks, 1994, p. 103). The existing popular dominant representations of black masculinity are continuously reproduced, serving to reinforce and sustain particular power relationships.

In response to young listeners and others defending rap with an insistence that words such as "bytch, hoe, and nigga" are being reclaimed and redefined, cultural critic Madhubuti (cited in Kitwana, 1994) argues,

> There are certain words . . . that are debilitating to us, no matter how often they are used. Such a word is nigger. . . . A nigger which is a pitiful and shameful invention of Europeans, cannot be de-stereotyped by using it in another context, even if the users are black and supposedly politically correct (they are mostly young and unaware). (p. 27)

The "gangsta" rap word/world that dehumanizes women subsists within violence and is a master teacher of the very young. Visually stimulating music videos, appealing to the joy of rhythms and rhyme, powerfully suggest values that inform what it means to be masculine and to act in ways that are unquestioned or rethought as to their usefulness.

Stephen Haymes (1995) creates a different context for exploring the pedagogy of place in the urban environment by exploring how socially constructed mythologies about black people are

> realized in the material landscapes of the city, in its racialization of black residential space through the imagery of racial segregation. This imagery along with the racialization of crime portrays black residential space as natural "spaces of pathology," and in need of social control through policing and residential dispersion and displacement. (back cover)

For Haymes, black popular cultural forms act as points of resistance. His work draws attention to black masculinity construction as a response to geo-political manipulation and commodification of culture. His views are worth quoting at length:

> What is important about the concepts of decolonization, emancipation, and hooks' notion of "radical black subjectivity" is that they provide us with a way to talk about black public spaces in the city not simply as "spaces of opposition" but as "spaces of self actualization." In this way, defining black public spaces as "spaces of self actualization" is understanding the centrality of black popular urban culture in constructing such places . . . it is through black popular culture that black people in the city resist mainstream white culture's racializing and therefore biologization of their spaces, bodies, and personalities. (p. 138)

Representational politics, the struggle over identity, and the fashioning of images is at issue here. Madhubuti's and Haymes's differing points give rise to questions about the usefulness of rap for naming who we are in the black community and the problematics of reclaiming a language used to degrade and oppress women and people of color. The narrative complexity and vitality of "hip hop," "gangsta," and "righteous teaching" rap on the one hand represents desires and shifting attitudes, values, and definitions of social relationships that black youth claim for themselves. At the same time, it represents historical amnesia, a lack of political and pedagogical insight. Haymes (1995) argues,

> This is important in the early twentieth-century construction of the city as jungle—an image that preceded the emergence of large-scale black urban settlements—is now connoted with black people's dark skin. In other words, the urban has become a metaphor for race, and in white supremacist culture, like ours, race does not mean white, but black. So, in the city, urban problems, such as poverty, homelessness, joblessness, crime, violence, single-parent households, and drugs, are seen as racial problems, the problems of blacks, not of whites. And in a white supremacist culture, where race is biologized, racial problems are reduced to black people's bodies. (p. 138)

Both Haymes's and Madhubuti's points raise questions about the significance of rap to black communities' ability to name who they are and how they relate to the larger society and across gendered discourses. I would argue that, even within black communities, the association of "blackness" and urban problems has been uncritically accepted, particularly by the black middle classes (a pool from which, in conjunction with commuting whites, most inner-city teachers are drawn). Because they identify themselves as being black, everything in black culture is not seen as horrible and bad. Therefore, a tension exists that pits a desire to impart positive role modeling (and save individuals) against the terrifying menace of the urban "jungle." The perception—commercially manipulated and promoted—of black males as dangerous should not be dismissed easily. Prejudged by many, there is a fear that potentially wild animals, violent destructive gangsters, or sexual deviants lurk in the young bodies of black

males who, if left alone in their environments, would endanger the safety of American culture. It is important to recognize that this view of the urban context suggests a typology of black youthful masculinities that, early on, must be tamed and trained in elementary schools. A culture and implicit curriculum of physical restriction permeates many urban schools, and the explicit curriculum disassociates student learning from engaging black urban cultures and any possible constructivist notion of a culturally responsive pedagogy.[1]

Franklin's (1994) work identifies at least five distinct categories of black masculinity construction: *conforming, ritualistic, innovative, retreatist,* and *rebellious black masculinity. Conforming* masculinity is the acceptance of "mainstream society's prescriptions and proscriptions for heterosexual males." Black males follow the rules, according to Franklin, despite the fact that when society teaches men to work hard, set high goals, and strive for success, it does not teach black men that their probability of failure is high because glass ceilings and limited opportunities for them are endemic to U.S. society. Resembling conforming masculinity, *ritualistic* masculinity for blacks is following the prescriptions and rules but not really believing one will win—it's playing without really believing, without purpose or commitment. *Innovative* black masculinity distances itself from conforming or ritualistic by exaggerating traits of hegemonic masculinity in that the pursuit of material success leads to black-on-black crime and debases women, as a means of making money (as do some forms of rap music). *Retreatist* black masculinity reflects a giving up of all hope and may be seen in those men who are alcoholics, drug addicts, or who have given up looking for a meaningful existence. Franklin further suggests that a *rebellious* black masculinity is exhibited by those who work in organizations committed to black liberation.

Franklin's work is not about black boys in schools. However, I use his framework, taking into consideration that black masculinities are more accurately understood in terms of complex associations on more than one level of social arrangement. Thus we begin to recognize the differences between older black masculine identities—middle class, middle age, and single—on impoverished youth in cities. Schooling after the elementary level is highly ambivalent and much less hopeful about the outcomes for secondary black students. White males can be educationally and therefore socially hopeful. They can get back on track if they temporarily get out of line. Black masculinities are seen as determined and set at a very early stage. This complexity of associations is conspicuous in the case of schools.

In his study of African-American males, Lemelle (1995) is concerned with what he calls a teacher's role to make black male students conform to the hegemonic vision of people of color: "the students are on the scene to establish an improved quality of life for themselves and their families" (p. 53). Black males become "bad" to express individual autonomy in the school in much the same way that slaves became "criminals" through lying, cheating, and "stealing away" to obtain freedom. In his discussion of urbanization, Lemelle points out that black males are labeled as "unprepared for education, good jobs and promotions. Because of their deviance, they are in need of reform and rehabilitation." Thus, teachers, many of whom live outside of urban, predominantly black, low-income or impoverished communities, act as diplomats of prevailing values and become the means by which dominant white, middle-class values are supported and unquestioned.

NOTE

1. A number of texts theorize African-American constructions of masculinity outside of the African-centered framework. See, for example, *Black Men Speaking* by Charles Johnson and John McCluskey (1997). Popular culture is significant and insightfully taken up in the analysis offered by Michael Dyson (1993) in *Reflecting Black: African American Cultural Criticism.*

REFERENCES—BLACK MASCULINITIES: A UNIQUE HISTORY

ALLEN, E., Jr. (1992). Race and gender stereotyping in the Thomas confirmation hearings. *The Black Scholar* (Ed.). *Court of Appeal: The black community speaks out on the racial and sexual politics of Thomas vs. Hill.* New York: Ballantine Books.

ANDERSON, E. (1991). *Streetwise.* Chicago: University of Chicago Press.

BELLAH, R., R. Madsen, W.N. Sullivan, A. Swidler, and S.M. Tipton. (1985). *Habits of the heart: Individualism and commitment in American life.* Berkeley: University of California Press.

CARSON, C. (1981). *In struggle: SNCC and the black awakening of the 1960s.* Cambridge, MA: Harvard University Press.

COTTINGHAM, C. (1989, Fall). Gender shift in black communities. *Dissent* (Fall): 521–525.

DAVIS, M., and S. Riddick. (1988). Los Angeles: Civil liberties between the hammer and the rock. *New Left Review* (July–August): 37–60.

DYSON, M. (1993). *Reflecting black: African American cultural criticism.* Minneapolis: University of Minnesota Press.

DYSON, M. (1991). Performance, protest and prophecy in the culture of hip-hop. In J.M. Spencer, ed., *The Emergency of Black and the Emergence of Rap.* Durham: Duke University Press, pp. 12–24.

DYSON, M. (1987, March 16). Rap, race, and reality. *Christianity and Crisis*: 98–100.

DYSON, M. (1989, June). The culture of hip-hop. *Zeta Magazine*: 44–50.

DYSON, M. (1991, January). As complex as they wanna be: 2 Live Crew. *Z Magazine*: 76–78.

DYSON, M. (1991, May-June). Tapping into rap. *New World Outlook*: 32–35.

DYSON, M. (1991, January 2–9). 2 Live Crew's rap: Sex, race, and class. *The Christian Century*: 7–8.

FERRARA, A. (1990). Universalisms: Procedural, contextual, and prudential. In D. Rasmussen, ed., *Universalism vs. communitarianism: Contemporary debates in ethics.* Cambridge, MA: MIT Press, pp. 11–38.

FRANKLIN, C.W. (1994). Men's studies, the men's movement, and the study of black masculinities in the 1990s. In R.G. Majors and J.U. Gordon, eds., *The American black male: His present status and his future,* pp. 271–283. Chicago: Nelson Hall.

GARDNER, J. (1991, Spring). Taking rap seriously: Theomusicologist Michael Eric Dyson on the new urban griots and peripatetic preachers (an interview). *Artvu*: pp. 20–23.

GATES, H.L., Jr. (1997). *Thirteen ways of looking at a black man.* New York: Vintage.

GIBBS, J.T. (1988). *Young, black, and male in America: An endangered species.* Dover, MA: Auburn House.

HARDING, V. (1988). Toward a darkly radiant vision of America's truth: A letter of concern, an invitation to re-creation. In C.H. Reynolds, and R.V. Norman, eds., *Community in America: The challenge of habits of the heart.* Berkeley: University of California Press, pp. 67–83.

HAYMES, S. (1995). *Race, culture, and the city: A pedagogy for urban black struggle.* Albany: State University of New York Press.

hooks, b. (1981). *Ain't I a woman?: Black women and feminism.* Boston: South End Press.

hooks, b. (1994, February). Sexism and misogyny: Who takes the rap? Misogyny, gangsta rap and the piano. *Z Magazine*: 26–29.

JAYNES, G.D., and R. Williams, Jr., eds. (1989). *A common destiny: Blacks and American society.* Washington, DC: National Academy Press.

KITWANA, B. (1994). The rap on gangsta rap. Chicago: Third World Press.

LE ESPIRITU, Y. (1989). All Men are *not* created equal: Asian men in U. S. history. In M.S. Kimmel, and M.A. Messner, eds., *Men's lives.* Boston: Allyn & Bacon, pp. 35–44.

LEMELLE, A. (1995). *Black male deviance.* Westport, CT: Praeger.

LORDE, A. (1984). *Sister/outsider.* Freedom, CA: The Crossing Press.

MACINTYRE, A. (1984). *After virtue.* Notre Dame: University of Notre Dame Press.

MALVEAUX, J. (1987). The political economy of black women. In M. Davis, M. Marable, F. Pfeil, and M. Sprinker, eds., *The year left 2—Toward a rainbow socialism: Essays on race, ethnicity, class and gender.* London: Verso, pp. 52–72.

MARABLE, M. (1992, November). Black America in search of itself. *Progressive Magazine.* 18–23.

MARABLE, M. (1994). The Black male: Searching beyond stereotypes. In R. Majors, and J. Gordon, eds., *The American Black male.* Chicago: Nelson-Hall.

NONINI, D. (1988, November). Everyday forms of popular resistance. *Monthly review: An independent socialist magazine,* pp. 25–36.

SCHIELE, J.H. (1991, Spring). An epistemological perspective on intelligence assessment among African American children. *The Journal of Black Psychology,* 17(2): 23–36.

SINGLETON, J. (1992). The fire this time. (July), pp. 74–75.

STECOPOLOUS, H., and M. Uebel. (1997). *Race and the subject of masculinities.* Chapel Hill: Duke University Press.

TAKAKI, R. (1993). *A different mirror: A history of multicultural America.* Boston: Little, Brown and Company.

WALKER, A. (1983). *In search of our mother's garden.* New York: Harcourt, Brace and Jovanovich.

WALLACE, M. (1990). *Invisibility blues: From pop to theory.* London: Verso.

WILSON, W.J. (1987). *The truly disadvantaged: The inner city, the underclass, and public policy.* Chicago: The University of Chicago Press.

At War: The Shadow of a Soldier

"Does the shadow of a soldier's life fall over every man?" (Griffin 60). Although technology has made sexual difference obsolete in the conduct of modern warfare, war remains a highly gendered social institution. Women may have gone off to war in the Persian Gulf in 1991, but they were not officially permitted to engage in combat. A woman soldier's participation in combat during the U.S. invasion of Panama a year earlier had led to extended debate (Gordon), but the ancient myth that war is manly has been contradicted in recent times by the presence of enlisted women (Stiehm 224–232).

From the Homeric epics to our contemporary televised conflicts, war has provided the starkest manifestation of gendered and gendering culture as the figure of the soldier and hegemonic masculinity coincide in the cultural imagination. Commenting on the military establishment's homophobia, James McBride cites Lieutenant General Bernard E. Trainor, director of the National Security Program at Harvard University, who "openly stressed that the American armed forces ground military effectiveness in an 'ethos' of masculinity. It is deemed that the admission of openly homosexual men to the services threatens to undermine that masculinity and, with it, military preparedness" (McBride 68). Readying soldiers to fight necessitates not only desensitization, but also the *feminizing* of opponents. Cultural scholar Susan Jeffords has explained how popular representations of the war in Vietnam in film, oral history, novels, and short stories contributed in the 1980s to what she terms the "remasculinization of America," in the wake of the humiliation experienced by the United States in the 1970s. "The male Vietnam veteran—primarily the white male—was used as an emblem for a fallen and emasculated American male, one who had been falsely scorned by society and unjustly victimized by his own government" (Jeffords 168–169). The culmination of this process of remasculinization was the war against Iraq. On March 2, 1991, President Bush announced that "The specter of Vietnam has been buried forever in the desert sands of the Arabian peninsula."

But as writers such as James Garbarino and James William Gibson point out, the culture of war pervades civilian life also. Citing military psychologist David Grossman, Garbarino describes the way our entertainment culture prepares children for war:

> There is strong evidence to indicate that the indiscriminate civilian application of combat conditioning techniques as entertainment may be a key factor in the worldwide skyrocketing violent crime rates, including a seven-fold increase in per capita aggravated assault (Garbarino 115).

The shadow of the soldier's life falls across every boy, offering an approved masculinity that can be enacted in the schoolyard, on the athletic field, and in the home. Through war toys and the idioms of everyday speech, the masculinity of the soldier is naturalized.

In this section, Carol Cohn makes visible the unconscious gendering of the language of those who make war. Gregory Orfalea offers another, equally important aspect of the war story: the poignancy of the son whose father cannot speak about the battles of his youth. What World War I poet Wilfred Owen called "the old lie"— that it is sweet and fitting to die for one's country—is a narrative that has an especially powerful lure for many young men.

Wars, Wimps, and Women:
Talking Gender and Thinking War

Carol Cohn

I start with a true story, told to me by a white male physicist:

> Several colleagues and I were working on modeling counterforce attacks, trying to get realistic estimates of the number of immediate fatalities that would result from different deployments.[1] At one point, we remodeled a particular attack, using slightly different assumptions, and found that instead of there being thirty-six million immediate fatalities, there would only be thirty million. And everybody was sitting around nodding, saying, "Oh yeah, that's great, only thirty million," when all of a sudden, I *heard* what we were saying. And I blurted out, "Wait, I've just *heard* how we're talking—*Only* thirty million! *Only* thirty million human beings killed instantly?" Silence fell upon the room. Nobody said a word. They didn't even look at me. It was awful. I felt like a woman.

The physicist added that henceforth he was careful to never blurt out anything like that again.

.   .   .

During the early years of the Reagan presidency, in the era of the Evil Empire, the cold war, and loose talk in Washington about the possibility of fighting and "prevailing" in a nuclear war, I went off to do participant observation in a community of North American nuclear defense intellectuals and security af-

fairs analysts—a community virtually entirely composed of white men. They work in universities, think tanks, and as advisers to government. They theorize about nuclear deterrence and arms control, and nuclear and conventional war fighting, about how to best translate military might into political power; in short, they create the discourse that underwrites American national security policy. The exact relation of their theories to American political and military practice is a complex and thorny one; the argument can be made, for example, that their ideas do not so much shape policy decisions as legitimate them after the fact. But one thing that is clear is that the body of language and thinking they have generated filters out to the military, politicians, and the public, and increasingly shapes how we talk and think about war. This was amply evident during the Gulf War: Gulf War "news," as generated by the military briefers, reported by newscasters, and analyzed by the television networks' resident security experts, was marked by its use of the professional language of defense analysis, nearly to the exclusion of other ways of speaking.

My goal has been to understand something about how defense intellectuals think, and why they think that way. Despite the parsimonious appeal of ascribing the nuclear arms race to "missile envy,"[2] I felt certain that masculinity was not a sufficient explanation of why men think about war in the ways that they do. Indeed, I found many ways to understand what these men were doing that had little or nothing to do with gender.[3] But ultimately, the physicist's story and others like it made confronting the role of gender unavoidable. Thus, in this paper I will explore gender discourse, and its role in shaping nuclear and national security discourse.

I want to stress, this is not a paper about men and women, and what they are or are not like. I will not be claiming that men are aggressive and women peace loving. I will not even address the question of how men's and women's relations to war may differ, nor of the different propensities they may have to committing acts of violence. Neither will I pay more than passing attention to the question which so often crops up in discussions of war and gender, that is, would it be a more peaceful world if our national leaders were women? These questions are valid and important, and recent feminist discussion of them has been complex, interesting, and contentious. But my focus is elsewhere. I wish to direct attention away from gendered individuals and toward gendered discourses. My question is about the way that civilian defense analysts think about war, and the ways in which that thinking is shaped not by their maleness (or, in extremely rare instances, femaleness), but by the ways in which gender discourse intertwines with and permeates that thinking.[4]

Let me be more specific about my terms. I use the term *gender* to refer to the constellation of meanings that a given culture assigns to biological sex differences. But more than that, I use gender to refer to a symbolic system, a central organizing discourse of culture, one that not only shapes how we experience and understand ourselves as men and women, but that also interweaves with other discourses and shapes *them*—and therefore shapes other aspects of our world—such as how nuclear weapons are thought about and deployed.[5]

So when I talk about "gender discourse," I am talking not only about words or language but about a system of meanings, of ways of thinking, images and words that first shape how we experience, understand, and represent ourselves as men and women, but that also do more than that; they shape many other aspects of our lives and culture. In this symbolic system, human characteristics are dichotomized, divided into pairs of polar opposites that are supposedly mutually exclusive: mind is opposed to body; culture to nature; thought to feeling; logic to intuition; objectivity to subjectivity; aggression to passivity; confrontation to accommodation; abstraction to particularity; public to private; political to personal, ad nauseam. In each case, the first term of the "opposites" is associated with male, the second with female. And in each case, our society values the first over the second.

I break it into steps like this—analytically separating the *existence* of these groupings of binary oppositions, from the association of each group with a gender, from the valuing of one over the other, the so-called male over the so-called female, for two reasons: first, to try to make visible the fact that this system of dichotomies is encoding many meanings that may be quite unrelated to male and female bodies. Yet once that first step is made—the association of each side of those lists with a gender—gender now becomes tied to many other kinds of cultural representations. If a human activity, such as engineering, fits some of the characteristics, it becomes gendered.

My second reason for breaking it into those steps is to try to help make it clear that the meanings can flow in different directions; that is, in gender discourse, men and women are supposed to exemplify the characteristics on the lists. It also works in reverse, however; to evidence any of these characteristics—to be abstract, logical or dispassionate, for example—is not simply to be those things, but also to be manly. And to be manly is not simply to be manly, but also to be in the more highly valued position in the discourse. In other words, to exhibit a trait on that list is not neutral—it is not simply displaying some basic human characteristic. It also positions you in a discourse of gender. It associates you with a particular gender, and also with a higher or lower valuation.

In stressing that this is a *symbolic* system, I want first to emphasize that while real women and men do not really fit these gender "ideals," the existence of this system of meaning affects all of us, nonetheless. Whether we want to or not, we see ourselves and others against its templates, we interpret our own and others' actions against it. A man who cries easily cannot avoid in some way confronting that he is likely to be seen as less than fully manly. A woman who is very aggressive and incisive may enjoy that quality in herself, but the fact of her aggressiveness does not exist by itself; she cannot avoid having her own and others' perceptions of that quality of hers, the meaning it has for people, being in some way mediated by the discourse of gender. Or, a different kind of example: Why does it mean one thing when George Bush gets teary-eyed in public, and something entirely different when Patricia Shroeder does? The same act is viewed through the lens of gender and is seen to mean two very different things.

Second, as gender discourse assigns gender to human characteristics, we can think of the discourse as something we are positioned *by*. If I say, for example, that a corporation should stop dumping toxic waste because it is damaging the creations of mother earth (i.e., articulating a valuing and sentimental vision of nature), I am speaking in a manner associated with women, and our cultural discourse of gender positions me as female. As such I am then associated with the whole constellation of traits—irrational, emotional, subjective, and so forth—and I am in the devalued position. If, on the other-hand, I say the corporation should stop dumping toxic wastes because I have calculated that it is causing $8.215 billion of damage to eight nonrenewable resources, which should be seen as equivalent to lowering the GDP by 0.15 percent per annum (i.e., using a rational, calculative mode of thought), the discourse positions me as masculine—rational, objective, logical, and so forth—the dominant, valued position.

But if we are positioned *by* discourses, we can also take different positions *within* them. Although I am female, and thus would "naturally" fall into the devalued term, I can choose to "speak like a man"—to be hardnosed, realistic, unsentimental, dispassionate. Jeanne Kirkpatrick is a formidable example. While we can choose a position in a discourse, however, it means something different for a woman to "speak like a man" than for a man to do so. It is heard differently.

One other note about my use of the term *gender discourse*: I am using it in the general sense to refer to the phenomenon of symbolically organizing the world in these gender-associated opposites. I do not mean to suggest that there is a single discourse defining a single set of gender ideals. In fact, there are many specific discourses of gender, which vary by race, class, ethnicity, locale, sexuality, nationality, and other factors. The masculinity idealized in the gender discourse of new Haitian immigrants is in some ways different from that of sixth-generation white Anglo-Saxon Protestant business executives, and both differ somewhat from that of white-male defense intellectuals and security analysts. One version of masculinity is mobilized and enforced in the armed forces in order to enable men to fight wars, while a somewhat different version of masculinity is drawn upon and expressed by abstract theoreticians of war.[6]

Let us now return to the physicist who felt like a woman: what happened when he "blurted out" his sudden awareness of the "only thirty million" dead people? First, he was transgressing a code of professional conduct. In the civilian defense intellectuals' world, when you are in professional settings you do not discuss the bloody reality behind the calculations. It is not required that you be completely unaware of them in your outside life, or that you have no feelings about them, but it is required that you do not bring them to the foreground in the context of professional activities. There is a general awareness that you *could not* do your work if you did; in addition, most defense intellectuals believe that emotion and description of human reality distort the process required to think well about nuclear weapons and warfare.

So the physicist violated a behavioral norm, in and of itself a difficult thing to do because it threatens your relationships to and your standing with your colleagues.

But even worse than that, he demonstrated some of the characteristics on the "female" side of the dichotomies—in his "blurting" he was impulsive, uncontrolled, emotional, concrete, and attentive to human bodies, at the very least. Thus, he marked himself not only as unprofessional but as feminine, and this, in turn, was doubly threatening. It was not only a threat to his own sense of self as masculine, his gender identity, it also identified him with a devalued status—of a woman—or put him in the devalued or subordinate position in the discourse.

Thus, both his statement, "I felt like a woman," and his subsequent silence in that and other settings are completely understandable. To have the strength of character and courage to transgress the strictures of both professional and gender codes *and* to associate yourself with a lower status is very difficult.

This story is not simply about one individual, his feelings and actions; it is about

the role of gender discourse. The impact of gender discourse in that room (and countless others like it) is that some things get left out. Certain ideas, concerns, interests, information, feelings, and meanings are marked in national security discourse as feminine, and are devalued. They are therefore, first, very difficult to *speak*, as exemplified by the physicist who felt like a woman. And second, they are very difficult to *hear*, to take in and work with seriously, even if they *are* said. For the others in the room, the way in which the physicist's comments were marked as female and devalued served to delegitimate them. It is almost as though they had become an accidental excrescence in the middle of the room. Embarrassed politeness demanded that they be ignored.

I must stress that this is not simply the product of the idiosyncratic personal composition of that particular room. In other professional settings, I have experienced the feeling that something terribly important is being left out and must be spoken; and yet, it has felt almost physically impossible to utter the words, almost as though they could not be pushed out into the smooth, cool, opaque air of the room.

What is it that cannot be spoken? First, any words that express an emotional awareness of the desperate human reality behind the sanitized abstractions of death and destruction—as in the physicist's sudden vision of thirty million rotting corpses. Similarly, weapons' effects may be spoken of only in the most clinical and abstract terms, leaving no room to imagine a seven-year-old boy with his flesh melting away from his bones or a toddler with her skin hanging down in strips. Voicing concern about the number of casualties in the enemy's armed forces, imagining the suffering of the killed and wounded young men, is out of bounds. (Within the military itself, it is permissible, even desirable, to attempt to minimize immediate civilian casualties if it is possible to do so without compromising military objectives, but as we learned in the Persian Gulf War, this is only an extremely limited enterprise; the planning and precision of military targeting does not admit of consideration of the cost in human lives of such actions as destroying power systems, or water and sewer systems, or highways and food distribution systems.)[7] Psychological effects—on the soldiers fighting the war or on the citizens injured, or fearing for their own safety, or living through tremendous deprivation, or helplessly watching their babies die from diarrhea due to the lack of clean water—all of these are not to be talked about.

But it is not only particular subjects that are out of bounds. It is also tone of voice that counts. A speaking style that is identified as cool, dispassionate, and distanced is required. One that vibrates with the intensity of emotion almost always disqualifies the speaker, who is heard to sound like "a hysterical housewife."

What gets left out, then, is the emotional, the concrete, the particular, the human bodies and their vulnerability, human lives and their subjectivity—all of which are marked as feminine in the binary dichotomies of gender discourse. In other words, gender discourse informs and shapes nuclear and national security discourse, and in so doing creates silences and absences. It keeps things out of the room, unsaid, and keeps them ignored if they manage to get in. As such, it degrades our ability to think *well* and *fully* about nuclear weapons and national security, and shapes and limits the possible outcomes of our deliberations.

What becomes clear, then, is that defense intellectuals' standards of what constitutes "good thinking" about weapons and security have not simply evolved out of trial and error; it is not that the history of nuclear discourse has been filled with exploration of other ideas, concerns, interests, information, questions, feelings, meanings and stances which were then found to create distorted or poor thought. It is that these options have been *preempted* by gender discourse, and by the feelings evoked by living up to or transgressing gender codes.

To borrow a term from defense intellectuals, you might say that gender discourse becomes a "preemptive deterrent" to certain kinds of thought.

Let me give you another example of what I mean—another story, this one my own experience:

One Saturday morning I, two other women, and about fifty-five men gathered to play a war game designed by the RAND Corporation.[8] Our "controllers" (the people running the game) first divided us up into three sets of teams; there would be three simultaneous games being played, each pitting a Red Team against a Blue Team (I leave the reader to figure out which color represents which country). All three women were put onto the same team, a Red Team.

The teams were then placed in different rooms so that we had no way of communicating with each other, except through our military actions (or lack of them) or by sending demands and responses to those demands via the controllers. There was no way to negotiate or to take actions other than military ones. (This was supposed to simulate reality.) The controllers then presented us with maps and pages covered with numbers representing each side's forces. We were also given a "scenario," a situation of escalating tensions and military conflicts, starting in the Middle East and spreading to Central Europe. We were to decide what to do, the controllers would go back and forth between the two teams to relate the other team's actions, and periodically the controllers themselves would add something that would rachet up the conflict—an announcement of an "intercepted intelligence report" from the other side, the authenticity of which we had no way of judging.

Our Red Team was heavily into strategizing, attacking ground forces, and generally playing war. We also, at one point, decided that we were going to pull our troops out of Afghanistan, reasoning that it was bad for us to have them there and that the Afghanis had the right to self-determination. At another point we removed some troops from Eastern Europe. I must add that later on my team was accused of being wildly "unrealistic," that this group of experts found the idea that the Soviet Union might voluntarily choose to pull troops out of Afghanistan and Eastern Europe so utterly absurd. (It was about six months before Gorbachev actually did the same thing.)

Gradually our game escalated to nuclear war. The Blue Team used tactical nuclear weapons against our troops, but our Red Team decided, initially at least, against nuclear retaliation. When the game ended (at the end of the allotted time) our Red Team had "lost the war" (meaning that we had political control over less territory than we had started with, although our homeland had remained completely unviolated and our civilian population safe).

In the debriefing afterwards, all six teams returned to one room and reported on their games. Since we had had absolutely no way to know why the other team had taken any of its actions, we now had the opportunity to find out what they had been thinking. A member of the team that had played against us said, "Well, when he took his troops out of Afghanistan, I knew he was weak and I could push him around. And then, when we nuked him and he didn't nuke us back, I knew he was just such a wimp, I could take him for everything he's got and I nuked him again. He just wimped out."

There are many different possible comments to make at this point. I will restrict myself to a couple. First, when the man from the Blue Team called me a wimp (which is what it felt like for each of us on the Red Team—a personal accusation), I felt silenced. My reality, the careful reasoning that had gone into my strategic and tactical choices, the intelligence, the politics, the morality—all of it just disappeared, completely invalidated. I could not explain the reasons for my actions, could not protest, "Wait, you idiot, I didn't do it because I was weak, I did it because it made *sense* to do it that way, given my understandings of strategy and tactics, history and politics, my goals and my values." The protestation would be met with knowing sneers. In this discourse, the coding of an act as wimpish is hegemonic. Its emotional heat and resonance is like a bath of sulfuric acid: it erases everything else.

"Acting like a wimp" is an *interpretation* of a person's acts (or, in national security discourse, a country's acts, an important distinction I will return to later). As with any other interpretation, it is a selection of one among many possible different ways to understand something—once the selection is made, the other possibilities recede into invisibility. In national security discourse, "acting like a wimp," being insufficiently masculine, is one of the most readily available interpretive codes. (You do not need to do participant observation in a community of defense intellectuals to know this—just look at the "geopolitical analyses" in the media and on Capitol Hill of the way in which George Bush's military intervention in Panama and the Persian Gulf War finally allowed him to beat the "wimp factor.") You learn that someone is being a wimp if he perceives an international crisis as very dangerous and urges caution; if he thinks it might not be important to have just as many weapons that are just as big as the other guy's; if he suggests that an attack should not necessarily be answered by an even more destructive counterattack; or, until recently, if he suggested that making unilateral arms reductions might be useful for our own security.[9] All of these are "wimping out."

The prevalence of this particular interpretive code is another example of how gender discourse affects the quality of thinking within the national security community, first, because, as in the case of the physicist who "felt like a woman," it is internalized to become a self-censor; there are things professionals simply will not *say* in groups, options they simply will not argue nor write about, because they know that to do so is to brand themselves as wimps. Thus a whole range of inputs is left out, a whole series of options is foreclosed from their deliberations.

Equally, if not more damagingly, is the way in which this interpretive coding not only limits what is *said*, but even limits what is *thought*. "He's a wimp" is a phrase that *stops* thought.[10] When we were playing the game, once my opponent on the Blue Team "recognized the fact that I was a wimp," that is, once he interpreted my team's actions through the lens of this common interpretive code in national security discourse, he *stopped thinking*; he stopped looking for ways to understand what we were doing. He did not ask, "Why on earth would the Red Team do that? What does it tell me about them, about their motives and purposes and goals and capabilities? What does it tell me about their possible understandings of *my* actions, or of the situation they're in?" or any other of the many questions that might have enabled him to revise his own conception of the situation or perhaps achieve his goals at a far lower level of violence and destruction. Here, again, gender discourse acts as a preemptive deterrent to thought.

"Wimp" is, of course, not the only gendered pejorative used in the national secu-

rity community; "pussy" is another popular epithet, conjoining the imagery of harmless domesticated (read demasculinized) pets with contemptuous reference to women's genitals. In an informal setting, an analyst worrying about the other side's casualties, for example, might be asked, "What kind of pussy are you, anyway?" It need not happen more than once or twice before everyone gets the message; they quickly learn not to raise the issue in their discussions. Attention to and care for the living, suffering, and dying of human beings (in this case, soldiers and their families and friends) is again banished from the discourse through the expedient means of gender-bashing.

Another disturbing example comes from our relationship with what was then the Soviet Union. Former President Gorbachev was deeply influenced by a (mostly) young group of Soviet civilian defense intellectuals known as "new thinkers." The new thinkers questioned many of the fundamental bases of security policy as it has been practiced by both the United States and the USSR, and significant elements of Soviet defense policy were restructured accordingly. Intellectually, their ideas posed a profound challenge to the business-as-usual stance of American policy analysts; if taken seriously, they offered an exceptional opportunity to radically reshape international security arrangements. And yet, in at least one instance, American security specialists avoided serious consideration of those ideas through mindless masculinity defamation; for example, "I've met these Soviet 'new thinkers' and they're a bunch of pussies."[11]

Other words are also used to impugn someone's masculinity and, in the process, to delegitimate his position and avoid thinking seriously about it. "Those Krauts are a bunch of limp-dicked wimps" was the way one U.S. defense intellectual dismissed the West German politicians who were concerned about popular opposition to Euromissile deployments. [12] I have heard our NATO allies referred to as "the Euro-fags" when they disagreed with American policy on such issues as the Contra War or the bombing of Libya. Labeling them "fags" is an effective strategy; it immediately dismisses and trivializes their opposition to U.S. policy by coding it as due to inadequate masculinity. In other words, the American analyst need not seriously confront the Europeans' arguments, since the Europeans' doubts about U.S. policy obviously stem not from their reasoning but from the "fact" that they "just don't have the stones for war." Here, again, gender discourse deters thought.

"Fag" imagery is not, of course, confined to the professional community of security analysts; it also appears in popular "political" discourse. The Gulf War was replete with examples. American derision of Saddam Hussein included bumper stickers that read "Saddam, Bend Over." American soldiers reported that the "U.S.A." stenciled on their uniforms stood for "Up Saddam's Ass." A widely reprinted cartoon, surely one of the most multiply offensive that came out of the war, depicted Saddam bowing down in the Islamic posture of prayer, with a huge U.S. missile, approximately five times the size of the prostrate figure, about to penetrate his upraised bottom. Over and over, defeat for the Iraqis was portrayed as humiliating anal penetration by the more powerful and manly United States.

Within the defense community discourse, manliness is equated not only with the ability to win a war (or to "prevail," as some like to say when talking about nuclear war); it is also equated with the willingness (which they would call courage) to threaten and use force. During the Carter administration, for example, a well-known academic security affairs specialist was quoted as saying that "under Jimmy Carter the United States is spreading its legs for the Soviet

Union."[13] Once this image is evoked, how does rational discourse about the value of U.S. policy proceed?

In 1989 and 1990, as Gorbachev presided over the withdrawal of Soviet forces from Eastern Europe, I heard some defense analysts sneeringly say things like, "They're a bunch of pussies for pulling out of Eastern Europe." This is extraordinary. Here they were, men who for years railed against Soviet domination of Eastern Europe. You would assume that if they were politically and ideologically consistent, if they were rational, they would be applauding the Soviet actions. Yet in their informal conversations, it was not their rational analyses that dominated their response, but the fact that for them, the decision for war, the willingness to use force, is cast as a question of masculinity—not prudence, thoughtfulness, efficacy, "rational" cost-benefit calculation, or morality, but masculinity.

In the face of this equation, genuine political discourse disappears. One more example: After Iraq invaded Kuwait and President Bush hastily sent U.S. forces to Saudi Arabia, there was a period in which the Bush administration struggled to find a convincing political justification for U.S. military involvement and the security affairs community debated the political merit of U.S. intervention.[14] Then Bush set the deadline, January 16, high noon at the OK Corral, and as the day approached conversations changed. More of these centered on the question compellingly articulated by one defense intellectual as "Does George Bush have the stones for war?"[15] This, too, is utterly extraordinary. This was a time when crucial political questions abounded: Can the sanctions work if given more time? Just what vital interests does the United States actually have at stake? What would be the goals of military intervention? Could they be accomplished by other means? Is the difference between what sanctions might accomplish and what military violence might accomplish worth the greater cost in human suffering, human lives, even dollars? What will the long-term effects on the people of the region be? On the ecology? Given the apparent successes of Gorbachev's last-minute diplomacy and Hussein's series of nearly daily small concessions, can and should Bush put off the deadline? Does he have the strength to let another leader play a major role in solving the problem? Does he have the political flexibility to not fight, or is he hell-bent on war at all costs? And so on, ad infinitum. All of these disappear in the sulfuric acid test of the size of Mr. Bush's private parts.[16]

I want to return to the RAND war simulation story to make one other observation. First, it requires a true confession: *I was stung by being called a wimp.* Yes, I thought the remark was deeply inane, and it infuriated me. But even so, I was also stung. Let me hasten to add, this was not because my identity is very wrapped up with not being wimpish—it actually is not a term that normally figures very heavily in my self-image one way or the other. But it was impossible to be in that room, hear his comment and the snickering laughter with which it was met, and not to feel stung, and humiliated.

Why? There I was, a woman and a feminist, not only contemptuous of the mentality that measures human beings by their degree of so-called wimpishness, but also someone for whom the term *wimp* does not have a deeply resonant personal meaning. How could it have affected me so much?

The answer lies in the role of the context within which I was experiencing myself—the discursive framework. For in that room I was not "simply me," but I was a participant in a discourse, a shared set of words, concepts, symbols that constituted not only the linguistic possibilities available to us but also constituted *me* in that situation. This is

not entirely true, of course. How I experienced myself was at least partly shaped by other experiences and other discursive frameworks—certainly those of feminist politics and antimilitarist politics; in fact, I would say my reactions were predominantly shaped by those frameworks. But that is quite different from saying "I am a feminist, and that individual, psychological self simply moves encapsulated through the world being itself"—and therefore assuming that I am unaffected. No matter who else I was at that moment, I was unavoidably a participant in a discourse in which being a wimp has a meaning, and a deeply pejorative one at that. By calling me a wimp, my accuser on the Blue Team *positioned* me in that discourse, and I could not but feel the sting.

In other words, I am suggesting that national security discourse can be seen as having different positions within it—ones that are starkly gender coded; indeed, the enormous strength of their evocative power comes from gender.[17] Thus, when you participate in conversation in that community, you do not simply choose what to say and how to say it; you advertently or inadvertently choose a position in the discourse. As a woman, I can choose the "masculine" (tough, rational, logical) position. If I do, I am seen as legitimate, but I limit what I can say. Or, I can say things that place me in the "feminine" position—in which case no one will listen to me.

Understanding national security discourse's gendered positions may cast some light on a frequently debated issue. Many people notice that the worlds of war making and national security have been created by and are still "manned" by men, and ask whether it might not make a big difference if more women played a role. Unfortunately, my first answer is "not much," at least if we are talking about relatively small numbers of women entering the world of defense experts and national security elites as it is presently constituted. Quite apart from whether you believe that women are (biologically or culturally) less aggressive than men, every person who enters this world is also participating in a gendered discourse in which she or he must adopt the masculine position in order to be successful. This means that it is extremely difficult for anyone, female *or male*, to express concerns or ideas marked as "feminine" and still maintain his or her legitimacy.

Another difficulty in realizing the potential benefits of recruiting more women in the profession: the assumption that they would make a difference is to some degree predicated on the idea that "the feminine" is absent from the discourse, and that adding it would lead to more balanced thinking. However, the problem is not that the "female" position is totally absent from the discourse; parts of it, at least, albeit in a degraded and undeveloped form, are already present, named, delegitimated, and silenced, all in one fell swoop. The inclusion and delegitimation of ideas marked as "feminine" acts as a more powerful censor than the total absence of "feminine" ideas would be.

So it is not simply the presence of women that would make a difference. Instead, it is the commitment and ability to develop, explore, rethink, and revalue those ways of thinking that get silenced and devalued that would make a difference. For that to happen, men, too, would have to be central participants.

But here, the power of gender codes' policing function in the thought process is again painfully obvious. The gender coding not only marks what is out of bounds in the discourse and offers a handy set of epithets to use to enforce those rules. It also links that "subjugated knowledge" to the deepest sense of self-identity. Thus, as was evident with the physicist who felt like a woman, when men in the profession articulate those ideas, it not only makes them mavericks or intellectually

"off base"; it challenges their own gender identity. To the degree that a woman does not have the same kind of gender identity issue at stake, she may have stronger sources of resistance to the masculinity defamation that is used to police the thoughts and actions of those in the defense community. She does not have the power to change the fact that her actions will be interpreted and evaluated according to those gender codes, however. And in the defense community, the only thing worse than a man acting like a woman is a woman acting like a woman.

Finally, I would like to briefly explore a phenomenon I call the "unitary masculine actor problem" in national security discourse. During the Persian Gulf War, many feminists probably noticed that both the military briefers and George Bush himself frequently used the singular masculine pronoun "he" when referring to Iraq and Iraq's army. Someone not listening carefully could simply assume that "he" referred to Saddam Hussein. Sometimes it did; much of the time it simply reflected the defense community's characteristic habit of calling opponents "he" or "the other guy."[18] A battalion commander, for example, was quoted as saying "Saddam knows where we are and we know where he is. We will move a lot now to keep him off guard."[19] In these sentences, "he" and "him" appear to refer to Saddam Hussein. But, of course, the American forces had *no idea* where Saddam Hussein himself was; the singular masculine pronouns are actually being used to refer to the Iraqi military.

This linguistic move, frequently heard in discussions within the security affairs and defense communities, turns a complex state and set of forces into a singular male opponent. In fact, discussions that purport to be serious explorations of the strategy and tactics of war can have a tone which sounds more like the story of a sporting match, a fistfight, or a personal vendetta.

I would want to suck him out into the desert as far as I could, and then pound him to death.[20]

Once we had taken out his eyes, we did what could be best described as the "Hail Mary play" in football.[21]

[I]f the adversary decides to embark on a very high roll, because he's frightened that something even worse is in the works, does grabbing him by the scruff of the neck and slapping him up the side of the head, does that make him behave better or is it plausible that it makes him behave even worse?[22]

Most defense intellectuals would claim that using "he" is just a convenient shorthand, without significant import or effects. I believe, however, that the effects of this usage are many and the implications far-reaching. Here I will sketch just a few, starting first with the usage throughout defense discourse generally, and then coming back to the Gulf War in particular.

The use of "he" distorts the analyst's understanding of the opposing state and the conflict in which they are engaged. When the analyst refers to the opposing state as "he" or "the other guy," the image evoked is that of a person, a unitary actor; yet states are not people. Nor are they unitary and unified. They comprise complex, multifaceted governmental and military apparatuses, each with opposing forces within it, each, in turn, with its own internal institutional dynamics, its own varied needs in relation to domestic politics, and so on. In other words, if the state is referred to and pictured as a unitary actor, what becomes unavailable to the analyst and policy-maker is a series of much more complex truths that might enable him to imagine many more policy options, many more ways to interact with that state.

If one kind of distortion of the state results from the image of the state as a person, a unitary actor, another can be seen to stem from the image of the state as a specifically *male* actor.[23] Although states are almost uniformly run by men, states are not men; they are complex social institutions, and they act and react as such. Yet, when "he" and "the other guy" are used to refer to states, the words do not simply function as shorthand codes; instead, they have their own entailments, including assumptions about how men act, which just might be different from how states act, but which invisibly become assumed to be isomorphic with how states act.[24]

It also entails emotional responses on the part of the speaker. The reference to the opposing state as "he" evokes male competitive identity issues, as in, "I'm not going to let him push me around," or, "I'm not going to let him get the best of me." While these responses may or may not be adaptive for a barroom brawl, it is probably safe to say that they are less functional when trying to determine the best way for one state to respond to another state. Defense analysts and foreign policy experts can usually agree upon the supreme desirability of dispassionate, logical analysis and its ensuing rationally calculated action. Yet the emotions evoked by the portrayal of global conflict in the personalized terms of male competition must, at the very least, exert a strong pull in exactly the opposite direction.

A third problem is that even while the use of "he" acts to personalize the conflict, it simultaneously abstracts both the opponent and the war itself. That is, the use of "he" functions in very much the same way that discussions about "Red" and "Blue" do. It facilitates treating war within a kind of game-playing model, A against B, Red against Blue, he against me. For even while "he" is evocative of male identity issues, it is also just an abstract piece to moved around on a game board, or, more appropriately, a computer screen.

That tension between personalization and abstraction was striking in Gulf War discourse. In the Gulf War, not only was "he" frequently used to refer to the Iraqi military, but so was "Saddam," as in "Saddam really took a pounding today," or "Our goal remains the same: to liberate Kuwait by forcing Saddam Hussein out."[25] The personalization is obvious: in this locution, the U.S. armed forces are not destroying a nation, killing people; instead, they (or George) are giving Saddam a good pounding, or bodily removing him from where he does not belong. Our emotional response is to get fired up about a bully getting his comeuppance.

Yet this personalization, this conflation of Iraq and Iraqi forces with Saddam himself, also abstracts: it functions to substitute in the mind's eye the abstraction of an implacably, impeccably evil enemy for the particular human beings, the men, women, and children being pounded, burned, torn, and eviscerated. A cartoon image of Saddam being ejected from Kuwait preempts the image of the blackened, charred, decomposing bodies of nineteen-year-old boys tossed in ditches by the side of the road, and the other concrete images of the acts of violence that constitute "forcing Hussein [*sic*] out of Kuwait."[26] Paradoxical as it may seem, in personalizing the Iraqi army as Saddam, the individual human beings in Iraq were abstracted out of existence.[27]

In summary, I have been exploring the way in which defense intellectuals talk to each other—the comments they make to each other, the particular usages that appear in their informal conversations or their lectures. In addition, I have occasionally left the professional community to draw upon public talk about the Gulf War. My analysis does *not* lead me to conclude that "national security thinking is masculine"—that is, a separate, and different, discussion.[28] Instead, I have tried to show that national security discourse is gendered, and that it matters. Gender discourse is interwoven through national security discourse. It sets fixed boundaries, and in so doing, it skews what is discussed and how it is thought about. It shapes expectations of other nations' actions, and in so doing it affects both our interpretations of international events and conceptions of how the United States should respond.

In a world where professionals pride themselves on their ability to engage in cool, rational, objective calculation while others around them are letting their thinking be sullied by emotion, the unacknowledged interweaving of gender discourse in security discourse allows men to not acknowledge that their pristine rational thought is in fact riddled with emotional response. In an "objective" "universal" discourse that valorizes the "masculine" and deauthorizes the "feminine," it is only the "feminine" emotions that are noticed and labeled as emotions, and thus in need of banning from the analytic process. "Masculine" emotions—such as feelings of aggression, competition, macho pride and swagger, or the sense of identity resting on carefully defended borders—are not so easily noticed and identified as emotions, and are instead invisibly folded into "self-evident," so-called realist paradigms and analyses. It is both the interweaving of gender discourse in national security thinking *and* the blindness to its presence and impact that have deleterious effects. Finally, the impact is to distort, degrade, and deter roundly rational, fully complex thought within the community of defense intellectuals and national security elites and, by extension, to cripple democratic deliberation about crucial matters of war and peace.

NOTES

I am grateful to the John D. and Catherine T. MacArthur Foundation and the Ploughshares Fund for their generous support of my research, and for making the writing of this chapter possible. I wish to thank Sara Ruddick, Elaine Scarry, Sandra Harding, and Barry O'Neill for their careful readings; I regret only that I was not able to more fully incorporate their criticisms and suggestions. Grateful appreciation is due to several thoughtful informants within the defense intellectual community. This chapter was written while I was a fellow at the Bunting Institute, and I wish to thank my sister-fellows for their feedback and support.

1. A "counterforce attack" refers to an attack in which the targets are the opponent's weapons systems, command and control centers, and military leadership. It is in contrast to what is known as a "countervalue attack," which is the abstractly benign term for *targeting* and incinerating cities—what the United States did to Hiroshima, except that the bombs used today would be several hundred times more powerful. It is also known in the business, a bit more colorfully, as an "all-out city-busting exchange." Despite this careful targeting distinction, one need not be too astute to notice that many of the ports, airports, and command posts destroyed in a counter*force* attack are, in fact, in cities or metropolitan areas, which would be destroyed along with the "real targets," the weapons systems. But this does not appear to make the distinction any less meaningful to war planners, although it is, in all likelihood, less than meaningful to the victims.

2. The term is Helen Caldicott's, from her book *Missile Envy: The Arms Race and Nuclear War* (New York: William Morrow, 1984).

3. I have addressed some of these other factors in: "Sex and Death in the Rational World of Defense Intellectuals," *Signs: Journal of Women in Culture and Society* 12, no. 4 (Summer 1987): 687–718; "Emasculating America's Linguistic Deterrent," in *Rocking the Ship of State: Towards a Feminist Peace Politics*, ed. Adrienne Harris and Ynestra King (Boulder, Colo.: Westview Press, 1989); and *Deconstructing National Security Discourse and Reconstructing Security* (working title, book manuscript).

4. Some of the material I analyze in this paper comes from the public utterances of civilian defense intellectuals and military leaders. But overtly gendered war discourse appears even more frequently in informal settings, such as conversations defense intellectuals have among themselves, rather than in their formal written papers. Hence, much of my data comes from participant observation, and from interviews in which men have been willing to share with me interactions and responses that are usually not part of the public record. Most often, they shared this information on the condition that it not be attributed, and I have respected their requests. I also feel strongly that "naming names" would be misleading to the extent that it would tend to encourage the reader to locate the problem within individual men and their particular psyches; in this paper I am arguing that it is crucial to see this as a cultural phenomenon, rather than a psychological one.

5. For a revealing exploration of the ways in which gender shapes international politics more generally, see Cynthia Enloe, *Bananas, Beaches and Bases: Making Feminist Sense of International Politics* (Berkeley: University of California Press, 1989).

6. See Cynthia Enloe, *Does Khaki Become You? The Militarization of Women's Lives* (London and Winchester, Mass.: Pandora Press, 1988); and Jean Elshtain, "Reflections on War and Political Discourse: Realism, Just War and Feminism in a Nuclear Age," *Political Theory* 3, no. 1 (February 1985): 39–57.

7. While both the military and the news media presented the picture of a "surgically clean" war in which only military targets were destroyed, the reality was significantly bloodier; it involved the mass slaughter of Iraqi soldiers, as well as the death and suffering of large numbers of noncombatant men, women, and children. Although it is not possible to know the numbers of casualties with certainty, one analyst in the Census Bureau, Beth Osborne Daponte, has estimated that 40,000 Iraqi soldiers and 13,000 civilians were killed in direct military conflict, that 30,000 civilians died during Shiite and Kurdish rebellions, and that 70,000 civilians have died from health problems caused by the destruction of water and power plants (Edmund L. Andrews, "Census Bureau to Dismiss Analyst Who Estimated Iraqi Casualties," *New York Times*, March 7, 1992, A7). Other estimates are significantly higher. Greenpeace estimates that as many as 243,000 Iraqi civilians died due to war-related causes (Ray Wilkinson, "Back from the Living Dead," *Newsweek*, January 20, 1992, 28). Another estimate places Iraqi troop casualties at 70,000 and estimates that over 100,000 children have died from the delayed effects of the war (Peter Rothenberg, "The Invisible Dead," *Lies of Our Times* [March 1992]: 7). For recent, detailed reports on civilian casualties, see *Health and Welfare in Iraq after the Gulf Crisis* (International Study Team/ Commission on Civilian Casualties, Human Rights Program, Harvard Law School, October 1991), and *Needless Deaths in the Gulf War* (Middle East Watch, 1992). For a useful corrective to the myth of the Gulf War as a war of surgical strikes and precision-guided weaponry, see Paul F. Walker and Eric Stambler, "The Surgical Myth of the Gulf War," *Boston Globe*, April 16, 1991; and ". . . And the Dirty Little Weapons," *Bulletin of the Atomic Scientists* (May 1991): 21–24.

8. The RAND Corporation is a think tank that is a U.S. Air Force subcontractor. In the 1950s many of the most important nuclear strategists did their work under RAND auspices, including Bernard Brodie, Albert Wohlstetter, Herman Kahn, and Thomas Schelling.

9. In the context of the nuclear arms race and the cold war, even though a defense analyst might acknowledge that some American weapon systems served no useful strategic function (such as the Titan missiles during the 1980s), there was still consensus that they should not be unilaterally cut. Such a cut was seen to be bad because it was throwing away a potential bargaining chip in future arms control negotiations, or because making unilateral cuts was viewed as a sign of weakness and lack of resolve. It is only outside that context of hostile superpower competition, and, in fact, after the dissolution of the Soviet threat, that President Bush has responded to Gorbachev's unilateral cuts with some (minor) American unilateral cuts. For a

description and critical assessment of the arguments against unilateral cuts, see William Rose, *US Unilateral Arms Control Initiatives: When Do They Work?* (New York: Greenwood Press, 1988). For an analysis of the logic and utility of bargaining chips, see Robert J. Bresler and Robert C. Gray, "The Bargaining Chip and SALT," *Political Science Quarterly* 92, no. 1 (Spring 1977): 65–88.

10. For a discussion of how words and phrases can stop the thought process, see George Orwell, "Politics and the English Language," in *A Collection of Essays* (Garden City, N.Y.: Doubleday, 1954): 162–76.

11. Cohn, unattributed interview, Cambridge, Mass., July 15, 1991.

12. Ibid.

13. Ibid., July 20, 1991.

14. The Bush White House tried out a succession of revolving justifications in an attempt to find one that would garner popular support for U.S. military action, including: we must respond to the rape of Kuwait; we must not let Iraqi aggression be rewarded; we must defend Saudi Arabia; we cannot stand by while "vital U.S. interests" are threatened; we must establish a "new world order"; we must keep down the price of oil at U.S. gas pumps; we must protect American jobs; and finally, the winner, the only one that elicited any real support from the American public, we must destroy Iraq's incipient nuclear weapons capability. What was perhaps most surprising about this was the extent to which it was publicly discussed and accepted as George Bush's need to find a message that "worked" rather than to actually have a genuine, meaningful explanation. For an account of Bush's decision making about the Gulf War, see Bob Woodward, *The Commanders* (New York: Simon & Schuster, 1991).

15. Cohn, unattributed interview, Cambridge, Mass., July 20, 1991.

16. Within the context of our society's dominant gender discourse, this equation of masculinity and strength with the willingness to use armed force seems quite "natural" and not particularly noteworthy. Hannah Arendt is one political thinker who makes the arbitrariness of that connection visible: she reframes our thinking about "strength," and finds strength in *refraining* from using one's armed forces (Hannah Arendt, *On Violence* [New York: Harcourt, Brace, Jovanovich, 1969]).

17. My thinking about the importance of positions in discourses is indebted to Wendy Hollway, "Gender Difference and the Production of Subjectivity," in *Changing the Subject*, ed. J. Henriques, W. Holloway, C. Urwin, C. Venn, and V. Walkerdine (London and New York: Methuen, 1984): 227–63.

18. For a revealing exploration of the convention in strategic, military, and political writings of redescribing armies as a single "embodied combatant," see Elaine Scarry, *The Body in Pain: The Making and Unmaking of the World* (New York: Oxford University Press, 1984): 70–72.

19. Chris Hedges, "War Is Vivid in the Gun Sights of the Sniper," *New York Times*, February 3, 1991, A1.

20. General Norman Schwarzkopf, National Public Radio broadcast, February 8, 1991.

21. General Norman Schwarzkopf, CENTCOM News Briefing, Riyadh, Saudi Arabia, February 27, 1991, p. 2.

22. Transcript of a strategic studies specialist's lecture on NATO and the Warsaw Pact (summer institute on Regional Conflict and Global Security: The Nuclear Dimension, Madison, Wisconsin, June 29, 1987).

23. Several analysts of international relations have commented upon the way in which "the state is a person" in international relations theory and in war discourse. For example, Paul Chilton and George Lakoff, distinguished linguists who study war, offer very useful explorations of the impact of the state-as-a-person metaphor on the way in which we understand the Persian Gulf War. Yet neither of them find it noteworthy that the state is not simply any person, but a *male* person. See Paul Chilton, "Getting the Message Through: Metaphor and Legitimation of the Gulf War" (unpublished paper, 1991); George Lakoff, "The Metaphor System Used to Justify War in the Gulf" (unpublished paper, 1991).

24. For a lucid and compelling discussion of why it is an error to assume an isomorphism between the behavior and motivations of individuals and the behavior and motivations of states, see Marshall Sahlins, *The Use and Abuse of Biology* (Ann Arbor: University of Michigan Press, 1977), pp. ix–xv and 3–16.

25. Defense Secretary Dick Cheney, "Excerpts from Briefing at Pentagon by Cheney and Powell," *New York Times*, January 24, 1991, A 11.

26. Scarry explains that when an army is described as a single "embodied combatant," injury (as in Saddam's "pounding"), may be referred to but is "no longer recognizable or interpretable." It is not only that Americans might be happy to imagine Saddam being pounded; we also on some level know that it is not really happening, and thus need not feel the pain of the wounded. We "respond to the injury . . . as an imaginary wound in an imaginary body, despite the fact that that imaginary body is itself made up of thousands of real human bodies" (Scarry, *Body in Pain*, p. 72).

27. For a further exploration of the disappearance of human bodies from Gulf War discourse, see Hugh Gusterson, "Nuclear War, the Gulf War, and the Disappearing Body" (unpublished paper, 1991). I have addressed other aspects of Gulf War discourse in "The Language of the Gulf War," *Center Review* 5, no. 2 (Fall 1991); "Decoding Military Newspeak," *Ms.*, March/April 1991, p. 81; and "Language, Gender, and the Gulf War" (unpublished paper prepared for Harvard University Center for Literary and Cultural Studies, April 10, 1991).

28. For a fascinating treatment of that issue, see Sara Ruddick in M. Cooke and A. Woollacott, eds. *Gendering War Talk* (1993) Princeton: Princeton University Press.

Paintball as Combat Sport

James William Gibson

Big Navy had served aboard an aircraft carrier in the early 1980s, a member of a squadron that flew helicopters in search of enemy submarines. He was a good six-two, and he carried a lean, mean 220 pounds on his hardened frame. In his massive steel-like hands he carried a big gun to match, a real smooth piece equipped with extended 16″ barrel, a 12″ noise suppressor, state of the art "red dot" optic scope, and folding metal stock. The CO_2 tank powering this baby rode high on the back of his bulging shoulders in its own special olive-drab nylon harness, while the black neoprene high-pressure hose connecting the tank to the gun looped under his armpit. Black Cordura nylon and elastic bandoliers crisscrossed his chest, holding 100–150 rounds of ammo. The bandoliers perfectly matched the tiger stripes on his camouflage fatigues, Big Navy's third outfit of the day. An olive-drab bandanna, pulled tight against his forehead and wrapped over his hair with the corners tied in back, completed his fashion ensemble. He definitely knew what he was about, and what was going down. His assignment was to lead a group of men deep into enemy-held territory, capture their flag, and return to home base. Along the way they would face their opponents, each armed with heavy-duty guns

firing gelatin capsules filled with bright red, yellow, green, or blue paint. Big Navy and his men would have to "kill" as many of these bad guys as possible to win victory; they would also have to protect their own flag against enemy attacks.

All in all, the mission didn't look good. In front of him in the dusty parking lot stood his men, a motley assortment of ragtag pickup players. Cowboy's headgear, a genuine U.S. military Kevlar helmet, was an eye-catcher. He'd been badly hurt in a motorcycle accident not long before, and thought the $300 for the helmet well worth the price to protect himself. A complete set of U.S. military web gear—equipment belt, ammo pouches, canteen, and suspenders—wrapped around his waist and over his shoulders. He carried a big gun, too, and said that he liked full-scale firefights, no matter what the odds; they didn't call him Cowboy for nothing. Burnt-orange goggles obscured his eyes; a Darth Vader-type *Star Wars* mask hid the rest of his face.

Next to him was a former professional football player with seven years of experience on the Minnesota Vikings. It was his very first game, and he wore brand-new camouflage fatigues that fit skin tight (not exactly the military concept). Although he was the largest man on the field that day, far bigger than Big Navy, the ex-pro was nervous. He'd been forced to retire from football because of a leg injury. "There's still a lot of nerve damage down there," the big man said anxiously to his friend. His buddy nodded in sympathy. He, like Cowboy, had been the victim of a motorcycle accident.

Sometime before his accident, he had bought walkie-talkie radios with earplugs and mikes mounted on headsets, similar to the kind worn by police SWAT teams and counterterrorist units. He brought them along today for the fight ahead.

The youngest members of Big Navy's squad of ten were two high-school kids from a San Diego military academy. Although they normally were allowed to fire M14 rifles, Colt .45 automatics, and the new Beretta 9mm's at least twice a month at school, recently the academy had rented out its entire arsenal to a movie production company. They needed to keep their shooting reflexes honed if they were going to make it to Annapolis and then move on to F-14 fighter-pilot training. One said he was aiming for Top Gun, the Navy's elite air-to-air combat instruction school at Miramar Naval Air Station near San Diego. Of course they'd seen the movie. Big Navy tried to discourage them. There weren't enough port calls and "things happen out there the Navy doesn't tell you about," he warned, referring to murders and thefts and accidents aboard ship. But the kids didn't want to listen, and besides, it was time.

With his squad collected, Big Navy led his men across the parking lot, past the gun-metal-blue Jaguar V-12 sedan with the "Who-ever Dies with the Most Toys Wins" bumper sticker, on toward the gate. Overhead a Los Angeles County Sheriff's Department Bell Jetranger helicopter just cleared the tops of the Conquest playing field's palm trees as it approached the landing zone next door at the Malibu substation. As the thump-thump-thump of the rotors faded away, Big Navy fired his gun through the chronograph, checking to make sure it was shooting just under 300 feet per second, the field limit. He finally turned and faced his team, pulled his full-length plastic face mask down, and gave the battle cry, "Okay, boys, it's time to rock and roll."

When they passed beneath the old wooden beams that arched over the gateway, the men found themselves in what looked like a ghost town, something out of the American West. And sure enough, some thirty to thirty-five yards down the dusty street lined by Old West style buildings that made up this former movie set, the enemy stood, spread out and waiting. They were a Latino team from the San Fernando Valley, just north of Los Angeles. Their leader, owner of a machine shop that made parts for air-to-air missiles, had bought team shoulder patches for all his employees who wanted in on the game: the three corners of the inverted triangle were labeled Judge, Jury, Executioner, while in the middle in full caps stood the unit name—VIGILANTE.

Each player wore full camouflage, and each held an advanced "constant-air" gun with extended barrel and silencer like those used by their Anglo and black opponents. All of them carried a long 16″ brush (used to clear gun barrels) in camouflage sheaths that hung from their waists. It gave them a special Central American jungle-fighter look, as if they were packing machetes and had just hacked their way through the underbrush into town for a rendezvous with destiny.

David, the man who ran Conquest, ex-plained the rules for today's battle. He pointed to a line of banana trees that marked one of the boundaries; it wasn't legal to sneak past it. He described where each team's flag was, so that no one would be confused about where the key action was going to take place. He made sure every man was wearing a red or yellow strip of cloth on his arm and explained that a man who was hit was supposed to wave this cloth over his head as he marched off the field to keep from getting shot again. Any man seen with his eye goggles off would be instantly disqualified. Two referees were supervising the players to enforce these rules. Everybody looked bored; most had heard this story scores of times before, and even the new guys knew what to expect. Besides, it was a hot, dry August afternoon, a time when the Pacific breeze couldn't make it past the beach a half-mile away. At last David gave the countdown—3–2–1—and blew his whistle. An instant later twenty or more shots filled the air as players ran for cover, firing from the hip. The fight was on.

David couldn't afford to stay and watch. New players were driving up all the time. He got from 20 to 120 customers on each weekend day, and each paid $20 to get in, and another $20 to $35 to rent one of the modern guns with the big air tanks. Everybody needed extra tubes of paintballs, and that ran a couple of bucks for a tube of ten. He still kept a finger in his old office supply business, but he liked doing this a lot more. It was ironic, David chuckled. His mother had always been against his playing war as a kid. "Now I make my living playing war," he said to me. He was especially busy this Saturday because on Sunday he was playing with his own "expert" team. With so much to do, he couldn't talk much more. "You know," David added, "the *A-Team* used to film here all the time. Really."

By now the battle of the Vigilantes versus Big Navy's walk-on players had been going on nearly half an hour. Casualties had been taken on both sides. The first victims waited at the gate to minister to their more recently fallen teammates, using a garden hose to wash the bright yellow or red or blue or green water-color splotches off their uniforms. No one seemed to take getting hit personally; no angry words were spoken. In fact, no one said anything at all to the other side that afternoon.

Off the battlefield, each group partied by themselves. The men popped open cans of beer—Corona, Coors, and an occasional Bud. They lit up Marlboros and sucked in that first heavy drag of smoke. Girlfriends woke up from tanning naps taken on lounge chairs in the back of spotlessly clean four-wheel-drive pickups. Some listened dutifully to war stories, while others just wanted to know when they were leaving. But the men were all willing to hear another teammate's war story of a good shot or a shot missed, and of course how they came to get hit; in exchange they told their own. Some blamed their woes on their guns, first cursing them, then taking them apart for cleaning. After reassembling the guns, the men twisted knobs and valves, test fired the guns, and then cursed some more to start the cycle again.

As the last shots were being fired between Big Navy, his team's last holdout, and the surviving (and victorious) Latino machinists, two fresh groups got ready for their battle. One new guy had just stumbled upon paintball the day before, having found *Action Pursuit Games* on the newsstand next to his magazine of choice, the *Hollywood Reporter*. The Conquest advertisements showed a handful of male players being held prisoner at gunpoint by long-legged, big-bosomed women wearing shorts and tight-fitting camouflage tank tops. "Another typical day at Conquest" read the caption.[1] So he came looking for some action. When a teammate tied a red ribbon to his arm he quipped, "Does this mean we're Communists? Do we have to read Marx?"[2]

The development of mock-combat war games in the United States a few short years after the Vietnam War is not in itself surprising. One scholar of games and sports, Brian Sutton-Smith, argues that historically what he calls "games of strategy" are developed as "models of problems in adaptation. They exist to simulate some adaptive problem that the group is having . . . Players are not hunting real tigers, or taking a chance with angry gods or trying to outwit diabolical adversaries. The dangers that go with these excitements in real life are largely curtailed and can therefore be studied within manageable levels of anxiety."[3] As suggested by its original name, the National Survival Game, paintball in effect transformed the cultural and political crisis of defeat in Vietnam into a game that combined elements of both combat and play.

What is surprising, though, is how quickly the emphasis in paintball shifted from play to combat. This was not the intention of those who founded the National Survival Game in the New Hampshire woods in 1981. They were inspired by a more archaic vision of the lone hunter-woodsman sneaking through the forests, killing an opponent only when absolutely necessary to capture the flag. The game was to be a test of cunning and stealth. As Lionel Atwill writes in *The New, Official Survival Game Manual*, published in 1987: "There will be no machine guns on Game fields. No tanks. No helicopters. And the Game will always be played in the spirit in which it was conceived. In a spirit of fun and play. There will be no Viet Cong villages, no mock mutilations. No bogus wars."[4] But all these things would come to pass.

According to Mike Jasperson, publisher and editor of *Front Line*, the first paintball magazine, it was the coming of the New War movies in the mid-1980s that both helped the sport gain popularity and moved it in a paramilitary direction. In his words, "What they have done, more than saying war is good, they're saying that it is okay to wear camouflage, okay to play war." Paintball offered men the opportunity to participate in a film-fantasy world rather than just watch it. "You drive a forklift eight hours a day," says Jasperson. "You work a cash register eight hours a day or whatever; you watch television and here's *Magnum P.I.* and he's running around with his gun and here's Don Johnson running around with his gun on *Miami*

Vice."[5] Compared to the stultifying routines of work and family responsibilities, the lives of these warriors were exciting and glamorous. Paintball provided a way for average men—and the game was played mainly by men—to get in on the action. Some players even watched action-adventure films the night before a game as a way to get "psyched up" and shouted lines from movies as they played.

The popularity of these movies and television shows was in turn noticed by new entrepreneurs who were opening new playing fields. Denis Bulowski, the Los Angeles policeman who built the famous Sat Cong Village with its bamboo compound flying a Vietnamese National Liberation Front flag, and the Nicaragua playing field with its facsimile of a downed cargo plane used for resupplying the contras, said that before he constructed his mock battlefields the idea of playing war "was already in people's minds. People see it in the movies. They think 'I wish I was out there doing that kind of stuff.'"[6] Paintball offered "better toys" to play with, and attractive theme parks like the Vietnam and Nicaragua playing fields to enrich the fantasy. That movies such as *Platoon* were in part filmed at Sat Cong Village added to the magic aura of the place.

Similarly, the manager of War Zone in Fountain Valley, California, said that although the game first hit California in 1983–1984, playing areas did not change from plain old marked fields to full-scale warrior theme parks until the fall of 1985, after *Rambo: First Blood, Part 2* and some of the other New War movies appeared. War Zone was the first playing field to develop mock tanks, hire helicopters, and provide teams with walkie-talkies and special "Heavy Fire Machine Guns" with 800-shot capability.[7] Not surprisingly, the bases on War Zone's playing fields were named after recent movies—the Hanoi Hilton, for example, and the Temple of Doom, and the Rambo Hotel.

At the same time that the fields became transformed, blue jeans and old shirts stopped being acceptable clothing. Increasingly, full camouflage outfits were perceived by all players, even novices, as a fashion necessity, not just better for hiding in the brush. Mike Jasperson described the transition as one that "makes the fantasy a little more complete. You know, now it's gone from imaginary to visual."[8] Indeed, magazine articles such as Frank Hughes's "Picking Your Paintball Persona" began to appear regularly to help players interpret the outfits worn by others and thus choose the ensemble best for them. The foremost fashion rule, writes Hughes, is to "keep in mind that while everyone knows 'dressing up' is one of paintball's enduring charms, it is considered bad form to admit it. Your clothes must have a rough utilitarian look to them (like you stopped to play paintball on your way to Nicaragua), and must never seem to be a costume."[9] Said another way, the "good" player always stays in character; he does his best to help himself and others maintain their "joint engrossment," as sociologist Erving Goffman calls it, in a fantasy world.[10]

On the other hand, the new player should avoid purchasing the cheapest, most readily accessible kind of camouflage clothing, the standard-issue U.S. military BDUs [Battle Dress Utilities] in the common "woodland" camouflage pattern. Although such clothing can give newcomers a comfortable "anonymous look" for a while, they will be seen by others as "players who lack confidence." Instead the ideal fashion statement is that of the "Special Forces" soldier. According to Hughes, "this is more of a concept than a specific outfit. The basic idea is to look military, but not regular military. You're a specialist, a dangerous individual . . . With

the right patches and equipment, you'll leave them guessing as to whether or not you really were a SEAL."[11] As this paramilitary ideal spread, mixing and matching pieces of very expensive, exotic surplus outfits from Rhodesia, South Africa, and the Soviet Union became popular.

With the body now enclosed in full military camouflage, all that remained visible of the old self was the face. Although the advent of full-length plastic face masks was in some ways a "functional" improvement—paintballs sting painfully when they hit sensitive skin—more is at issue. In an effort to discourage aiming for the head, the overwhelming majority of field owners in the mid- and late-1980s declared that "head shots" did not count as legitimate hits. Still the masks became a regular accessory. As players hand painted fierce animal faces on them, and companies began marketing prepainted masks of wolves' heads or savage "wild men," the archaic elements of this ostensibly functional accessory became clear.

Anthropologist J.C. Crocker writes that the "ornamented body" is a mode of "communicating at once to society and to the self a specific identity." Ceremonial masks in particular have potentially transformative powers: "By donning a mask one becomes what otherwise one could never be. Men into women, old into young, human into animal, mortals into gods, dead into living (and vice versa)."[12] In paintball, masks facilitate a particular transformation: they help the civilian with no military experience "conjure up the spirit" and change into an imaginary warrior.[13]

Many players and paintball businessmen speak of the appeal of these costumes. One store manager alluded to the "military mystique" of "dressing up in cammies." His assistant manager put it plainly: "You dress bad to be bad."[14] But there are limits, as Mike Jasperson insists: "You know, the timid people are still timid on the field. The rest of the people—for example, salesmen—are aggressive. The underlying personality, well, I don't know if that changes. I don't think it does."[15]

Whether or not real personality changes occur through donning military fatigues, paintball certainly provides men the opportunity to gain the *appearance* of warrior power through playing dress-up. Ironically, then, an image of manhood is obtained by violating the social norms according to which playing with clothes is an exclusively feminine activity that real men disdain. As Brian Sutton-Smith says in his *Toys as Culture*, much of the appeal of games and sports comes from their openness and fluidity; games permit us "to express our desires and our contradictions in ways that are not possible within the conventional boundaries of society."[16]

.   .   .

The rise of paintball, however, cannot be explained merely by the invention of better toys or bigger and badder playgrounds. Its appeal was much more basic: some men, especially young men, wanted to get as close to combat as possible. Denis Bulowski, owner of Sat Cong Village, said, "There's such a thing as actual combat, and this is about as close as you can get to the real thing."[17] This, as one player put it, was "the dark side of the game."[18]

Perhaps it was this "dark side" that made paintball unattractive to most Vietnam veterans. Mike Jasperson thought that at most 10% of the California paintball players were military veterans, while in Illinois and Florida the percentage went up to perhaps 20%. Other estimates were much lower. Russell Maynard of *Action Pursuit Games* claimed that Vietnam veterans "wouldn't touch it with a ten-foot pole."[19] Out at Sat Cong Village one regular referee concluded that "maybe 5% of the players had seen action."[20] The owner of a large wholesale and retail store commented, "There's a lot of Vietnam veterans who come in here with their sons. They have no interest in putting on cammies and going out there."[21] Paintball businessmen thought that most combat veterans avoided the game because it threatened to bring back bad memories.

Indeed, most players of the game lacked any real combat experience; according to a Sat Cong employee, they were "people who wanted to be in a war; people who didn't get a chance."[22] Paintball was primarily played by men in their mid-twenties to their forties (playing fields do not allow players under sixteen). Most were white, except in California where Latinos and Asian-Americans also made very strong showings. Few black people ever played. No one knew why exactly, but one store salesman speculated that bad press coverage played a role, creating an impression among blacks that paintballers were "a bunch of Ku Klux Klan."[23] Nor was it a game for the very poor, as it required a significant outlay of cash. Beyond that, though, as one War Zone referee proudly explained, "all sorts of job types show up, blue collar and white collar. Everything from doctors, lawyers, down to the ditch digger. The field is an equalizer."[24]

Thus the two most commonly shared characteristics of players were that they were male, and that they had not fought in Vietnam. In the early 1980s, several books and magazine articles asserted that those American men who had missed the Vietnam War, either because of age or because they deliberately avoided the draft, were failures as men. Christopher Buckley published "Viet Guilt: Were the real prisoners of war the young Americans who never left home?" in *Esquire*'s September 1983 issue. Buckley (who did not go to Vietnam) stressed how the war had *confirmed* the veterans as men. They had the security of knowing "*I have been weighed on the scales and have not been found wanting,*" whereas, poor Buckley confessed, "my sense at this point is that I will always feel the lack of it and will try to compensate for it, sometimes in good, other times in ludicrous, ways."[25]

The following November, *Esquire* published a sequel, William Broyles, Jr.'s essay "Why Men Love War." Broyles, like Buckley, emphasized the serene self-confidence that comes from having faced the enemy; he waxed lyrical about the brotherhood of war. "The enduring emotion of war," Broyles gushed, "when everything else has faded, is comradeship. A comrade in war is a man you can trust with anything, because you trust him with your life."[26] Like the New War movies and novels, articles such as these helped resurrect the warrior ideal for men.

These lessons were not lost on paintball publicists. Lionel Atwill begins one chapter of his 1987 manual with an epigram from Dr. Samuel Johnson: "Every man thinks meanly of himself for not having been a soldier."[27] Curiously enough, Christopher Buckley had quoted the same line in his 1983 essay. For those who felt cheated out of a war, paintball could serve as a test of manhood. Atwill writes: "A player might extrapolate Game performance to other stressful situations. Thus how you react in a Game may be an excellent clue to your behavior in the rest of your life."[28] Indeed, one corporation sponsored games during a corporate retreat and hired a psychologist to rate players on their aggressiveness.[29]

Atwill also promoted paintball as a means of creating comradeship. The NSG founders, he says, are men who "enjoy camaraderie," and the game as a whole is "so infused with a sense of honor, camaraderie, and fun that few players can walk away from it without feeling uplifted."[30] The idea that paintball encourages close friendships showed up again and again in players' accounts of the experience. One player told of how during his regular team meetings the goal was "for everyone to be tight with each other, both on and off the field."[31] Grubbs "Gramps" went further, declaring that when he played at War Zone, he didn't worry about watching his grandchildren because "I've got 500 baby-sitters who will watch them."[32] Paintball, then, provided him a new, extended family.

Courage and comradeship are honorable values. But they cannot be separated from the essential truth of the game. At its core, paintball simulates killing. The fundamental sequence of play involves hunting other men, aiming a gun at them, pulling the trigger, and making the kill. That this sequence so closely resembles part of what is involved in real killing undoubtedly contributes to the high that many players experience. As the manager of Paint Pistol Express said: "I get an adrenaline rush out of this sport that I've never received from any other sport."[33] Military men speak of the "combat high." Time is experienced as moving very slowly—a few seconds can seem like minutes, minutes like hours. In focusing on the hunt and kill, sensory perceptions change. For example, peripheral vision usually disappears, leaving only a narrow "tunnel" straight down the barrel to the target. Players get so pumped up that oftentimes they don't even feel the sting when they themselves are hit—the pain and welts come later.

Moreover, despite its advertised good, clean fun, paintball in effect reproduces the notion that the only true men are those who have been tried in battle and become warriors, and that the highest form of friendship is the brotherhood of war. The simulated killings at the core of the game provide this magic touch of transcendence. A group of friends who play paintball are not just friends anymore, but "veterans." And at the end of a match, a player has not simply played a good game, but has proved his character under the stress of "combat."

At the same time, paintball puts men into contradictory relationships with basic social rules. On the one hand, the game allows men the fantasy of being soldiers legally and morally licensed to kill. On the other, since players are not really soldiers or police, the actions of aiming and firing a weapon at another person constitute a major *transgression* of law and morality. Only children can legitimately pretend to shoot other people during their play (legitimately, because children are not expected to know what real violence and death mean). Thus, paintball offers men the opportunity to act against the adult world in two ways: first, by approximating real violence, and second, by essentially playing a child's game.

Over and over the thrill of paintball is described by players in terms of returning to childhood. "Once you're on the field, you're five years old again," says paintball entrepreneur Russell Maynard.[34] One player exclaimed after his first game, "I can't remember having more fun. God! It's like being a kid again. The adrenaline rush alone—I mean, pretending I was in a war. When would I ever get a chance at that?"[35] Out at War Zone, Gramps said, "Cowboys and Indians have been popular for ages. This is being seven years old again and playing cowboys and Indians. I'm a toy maker. These are big kids' toys. That's what they are."[36]

Just like the New War movies and novels, then, paintball provides males a ritual transition to warrior adulthood through regression to childhood. All the posturing to create the aura of "badness"—the frightening face masks and elaborate military gear, the vicious sounding team names and the various battle cries, the casual references to body counts, and the "toy" guns with a rate of fire found in real military weapons—all these elements are shouts of defiance against an imaginary frowning adult.

On fields full of children in camouflage equipped with rapid-fire big kids' toys and lots of ammunition, the line between play and violence gets awfully thin. The role of adult is passed on to completely different people—the referees. A referee *freezes* the game when he calls out "Paint check. Nobody shoot. Nobody move." If a player has indeed been splattered, the referee cries, "Man's hit! Do not shoot him again!"[37] "We are the order out here," said a Sat Cong Village referee. "Without the referee this would not be a game."[38] In stopping paintball's violent momentum for everyone on the field, the referee temporarily breaks the "combat high" experienced by players.

After players are hit and officially declared out they walk off the field and wait for the rest of their teammates at a staging area. As they leave the war zone, new players confront paintball's fundamental lesson. Everyone told a similar story, but Gramps was the most eloquent:

> You find out very quickly that it's easy to die and as a result of that, you're just damn glad it isn't for real. They'd be putting you in a body bag. People realize that real fast. You ain't gonna get volunteers out of here for Nicaragua or anywhere else.
>
> This is one of the biggest anti-war movements in existence. To be against war in a parade is one thing, but it takes a change of thinking and heart. In this country most guys are raised with a semi-macho image, the John Wayne, the Rambo. We glorify war, all that. War, as any good general will tell you, is absolutely insanity at its most vulgar. Being raised with that macho, pro-war image in our mind is what must be overcome. This game destroys the image I'm invincible when the first paintball hits.[39]

The problem is not that Gramps and his fellow enthusiasts are lying or even that they are providing rationalizations for violence. On the contrary, it is undeniably true that being hit by a fast-moving gelatin capsule in two or three out of every four games played (common averages) offers a crucial insight into the perils of real combat. But their testimonies are only a partial truth. As in *Casca: The Eternal Mercenary,* the paintball player dies only to walk off the battleground and be reborn a warrior half an hour later. Surviving players in regular games never even see the "corpses" of their fallen comrades. Instead, just as in the old war movies when the camera quickly cuts away from the fallen soldier with the red dot on his chest, casualties simply disappear from view. When Colonel Wyle ordered the "dead" paintball soldiers to lie where they had fallen for five minutes so that he could see the casualty pattern, author and player Jason Rein sheepishly acknowledged, "I must admit that it was a highly unusual sight to see individual 'bodies' (and in some cases, clusters) as I made my way off the field."[40] Both the New War mythology and the game obscure the fundamental reality that war creates death.

Indeed, what paintball does best of all is to fragment experience and thus allow men to embrace contradictory thoughts and feelings. The rapid changes from battle to game to battle create unusual opportunities for the self to "float," suspended from ordinary identity. Men can play John Wayne or Sylvester Stallone when they posture with their guns and make successful kills, and simultaneously reject all fantasy warriors while nursing a stinging welt on the arm or leg. At one moment the game can be seen as a test of true grit. Minutes later a player can simply see himself as having become a kid again for an afternoon, with presumably no implications for his adult life.

In this shifting back and forth, the world blurs. Reality can be undone and reconfigured again and again. Even if the United States has problems winning military victories abroad, the Wolverines, Marauders, and Vigilantes can fight on indefinitely, with every man a hero and every hero a comrade for life. In this way good wars replace the bad one of the recent past. Yet it's all done, as Atwill says, tongue in cheek.[41] This is, after all, only a game.

NOTES

1. Advertisement for Conquest playing field, *Action Pursuit Games,* June 1988, 74.

2. All quotations from personal interviews at Conquest playing field, Malibu, Calif., August 12, 1988.

3. Brian Sutton-Smith, *Toys as Culture* (New York: Gardner, 1986), 64.

4. Lionel Atwill, *The New, Official Survival Game Manual* (New London, N. H.: The National Survival Game, Inc., 1987), 155.

5. Interview with Mike Jasperson, publisher and editor of *Front Line* magazine, Huntington Beach, Calif., May 16, 1987.

6. Interview with Denis Bulowski, Sat Cong Village paintball field, Corona, Calif., July 22, 1987.

7. Advertisement for War Zone playing field, *Front Line* magazine, February 1987, 31.

8. Interview with Mike Jasperson, publisher and editor of *Front Line* magazine, Huntington Beach, Calif., May 21, 1987.

9. Frank Hughes, "Picking Your Paintball Persona," *Action Pursuit Games,* April 1988, 27.

10. Gary Alan Fine, *Shared Fantasy* (Chicago: University of Chicago Press, 1983), 3, 182.

11. Hughes, "Picking Your Paintball Persona," 27, 72.

12. J.C. Crocker, "Ceremonial Masks," in *Celebration: Studies in Festivity and Ritual,* ed. Victor Turner (Washington, D.C.: Smithsonian Institution, 1982), 80.

13. The concept that individuals "conjure up the spirit" and so change their subjectivity comes from Jack Katz, *Seductions of Crime: Moral and Sensual Attractions of Doing Evil* (New York: Basic Books, 1988), 7.

14. Interviews with two managers working at Adventure Game Supply, Bellflower, Calif., August 10, 1988.

15. Interview with Mike Jasperson, publisher and editor of *Front Line* magazine, Huntington Beach, Calif., May 21, 1987.

16. Sutton-Smith, *Toys as Culture,* 252.

17. Interview with Denis Bulowski, Sat Cong Village, Corona, Calif., July 22, 1987.

18. Interview with one of the employees at Adventure Game Supply, Bellflower, Calif., August 17, 1988.

19. Interview with Russell Maynard, publisher and editor of *Action Pursuit Games*, Burbank, Calif., August 17, 1988.

20. Interview with Ken S., Sat Cong Village, Corona, Calif., July 22, 1987.

21. Interview with the owner of The Annihilator, a wholesale paintball company, Diamondbar, Calif., August 16, 1988.

22. Interviews with Denis Bulowski and one of his employees, Sat Cong Village, Corona, Calif., July 22, 1987.

23. Interview with an employee, Adventure Game Supply, Bellflower, Calif., August 10, 1988.

24. Interview with a paramedic and part-time referee, War Zone, Fountain Valley, Calif., August 1, 1987.

25. Christopher Buckley, "Viet Guilt: Were the Real Prisoners of War the Young Americans Who Never Left Home?" *Esquire*, September 1983, 72.

26. [William Broyles, Jr. "Why Men Love War." *Esquire*, November 1984, 55.]

27. Atwill, *Survival Game Manual*, 15.

28. Ibid., 153.

29. Ibid., 152.

30. Ibid., 23 and 153.

31. Interview with one of the Vigilantes, Malibu, Calif., August 12, 1988.

32. Interview with Lou Grubbs, War Zone, Fountain Valley, Calif., August 1, 1987.

33. Interview with the manager of Paint Pistol Express, Anaheim, Calif., August 15, 1988.

34. Ibid.

35. Rick Soll, "War Game: Adults Play Cowboys, Indians," *Los Angeles Times*, November 18, 1983, A1, 8.

36. Interview with Lou Grubbs, War Zone, Fountain Valley, Calif., August 1, 1987.

37. Referee, War Zone, Fountain Valley, Calif., August 1, 1987.

38. Interview with referee, Sat Cong Village, Corona, Calif., July 22, 1987.

39. Interview with Lou Grubbs, War Zone, Fountain Valley, Calif., August 1, 1987.

40. Jason Rein, "Tell It to the Marines," *Paintball Sports*, November 1990, 66.

41. Atwill, *Survival Game Manual*, 17.

Seville Statement on Violence

The document that follows, which has become known as the Seville Statement on Violence, was developed by a group of biologists and social scientists who were members or participants in a meeting of the International Society for Research on Aggression in May 1986. Since its formulation, it has been endorsed by many organizations: Psychologists for Social Responsibility; the American Psychological Association; the American Anthropological Association; the International Society for Research on Aggression; the Society for the Psychological Study of Social Issues; the American Association of Counseling and Development; and Movimiento por la Vida y la Paz (Argentina). It has served as a basis for course curricula, meetings and conferences, and peace research.

STATEMENT ON VIOLENCE

Believing that it is our responsibility to address from our particular disciplines the most dangerous and destructive activities of our species, violence and war; recognizing that science is a human cultural product which cannot be definitive or all encompassing; and gratefully acknowledging the support of the authorities of Seville and representatives of the Spanish UNESCO, we, the undersigned scholars from around the world and from relevant sciences, have met and arrived at the following Statement on Violence. In it, we challenge a number of alleged biological findings that have been used, even by some in our disciplines, to justify violence and war. Because the alleged findings have contributed to an atmosphere of pessimism in our time, we submit that the open, considered rejection of these misstatements can contribute significantly to the International Year of Peace.

Misuse of scientific theories and data to justify violence and war is not new but has been made since the advent of modern science. For example, the theory of evolution has been used to justify not only war, but also genocide, colonialism, and suppression of the weak.

We state our position in the form of five propositions. We are aware that there are many other issues about violence and war that could be fruitfully addressed from the standpoint of our disciplines, but we restrict ourselves here to what we consider a most important first step.

IT IS SCIENTIFICALLY INCORRECT to say that we have inherited a tendency to make war from our animal ancestors. Although fighting occurs widely throughout animal species, only a few cases of destructive intra-species fighting between organized groups have ever been reported among naturally living species, and none of these involve the use of tools designed to be weapons. Normal predatory feeding upon other species cannot be equated with intra-species violence. Warfare is a peculiarly human phenomenon and does not occur in other animals.

The fact that warfare has changed so radically over time indicates that it is a product of culture. Its biological connection is primarily through language which makes possible the coordination of groups, the transmission of technology, and the use of tools. War is biologically possible, but it is not inevitable, as evidenced by its variation in occurrence and nature over time and space. There are cultures which have not engaged in war for centuries, and there are cultures which have engaged in war frequently at some times and not at others.

IT IS SCIENTIFICALLY INCORRECT to say that war or any other violent behaviour is genetically programmed into our human nature. While genes are involved at all levels of nervous system function, they provide a developmental potential that can be actualized only in conjunction with the ecological and social environment. While individuals vary in their predispositions to be affected by their experience, it is the interaction between their genetic endowment and conditions of nurturance that determines their personalities. Except for rare pathologies, the genes do not produce individuals necessarily predisposed to violence. Neither do they determine the opposite. While genes are co-involved in establishing our behavioral capacities, they do not by themselves specify the outcome.

IT IS SCIENTIFICALLY INCORRECT to say that in the course of human evolution there has been a selection for aggressive behaviour more than for other kinds of behaviour. In all well-studied species, status within the group is achieved by the ability to cooperate and to fulfil social functions relevant to the structure of that group. "Dominance" involves social bondings and affiliations; it is not simply a matter of the possession and use of superior physical power, although it does involve aggressive behaviours. Where genetic selection for aggressive behaviour has been artificially instituted in animals, it has rapidly succeeded in producing hyper-aggressive individuals; this indicates that aggression was not maximally selected under natural conditions. When such experimentally created hyper-aggressive animals are present in a social group, they either disrupt its social structure or are driven out. Violence is neither in our evolutionary legacy nor in our genes.

IT IS SCIENTIFICALLY INCORRECT to say that humans have a "violent brain."

While we do have the neural apparatus to act violently, it is not automatically activated by internal or external stimuli. Like higher primates and unlike other animals, our higher neural processes filter such stimuli before they can be acted upon. How we act is shaped by how we have been conditioned and socialized. There is nothing in our neurophysiology that compels us to react violently.

IT IS SCIENTIFICALLY INCORRECT to say that war is caused by "instinct" or any single motivation. The emergence of modern warfare has been a journey from the primacy of emotional and motivational factors, sometimes called "instincts," to the primacy of cognitive factors. Modern war involves institutional use of personal characteristics such as obedience, suggestibility, and idealism, social skills such as language, and rational considerations such as cost-calculation, planning, and information processing. The technology of modern war has exaggerated traits associated with violence both in the training of actual combatants and in the preparation of support for war in the general population. As a result of this exaggeration, such traits are often mistaken to be the causes rather than the consequences of the process.

We conclude that biology does not condemn humanity to war, and that humanity can be freed from the bondage of biological pessimism and empowered with confidence to undertake the transformative tasks needed in this International Year of Peace and in the years to come. Although these tasks are mainly institutional and collective, they also rest upon the consciousness of individual participants for whom pessimism and optimism are crucial factors. Just as "wars begin in the minds of men," peace also begins in our minds. The same species who invented war is capable of inventing peace. The responsibility lies with each of us.

Seville, May 16, 1986

DAVID ADAMS, Psychology, Wesleyan University, Middletown, CT USA

S.A. BARNETT, Ethology, The Australian National University, Canberra, Australia

N.P. BECHTEREVA, Neurophysiology, Institute for Experimental Medicine of Academy of Medical Sciences of USSR, Leningrad, USSR

BONNIE FRANK CARTER, Psychology, Albert Einstein Medical Center, Philadelphia, PA, USA

JOSÉ M. RODRÍGUEZ DELGADO, Neurophysiology, Centro de Estudios Neurobiológicos, Madrid, Spain

JOSÉ LUIS DÍAZ, Ethology, Instituo Mexicano de Psiquiatria, Mexico D.F., Mexico

ANDRZEJ ELIASZ, Individual Differences Psychology, Polish Academy of Sciences, Warsaw, Poland

SANTIAGO GENOVÉS, Biological Anthropology, Instituto de Estudios Antropolóqicos, Mexico D.F., Mexico

BENSON E. GINSBURG, Behavior Genetics, University of Connecticut, Storrs, CT, USA

JO GROEBEL, Social Psychology, Erziehungswissenschaftliche Hochschule, Landau, Federal Republic of Germany

SAMIR-KUMAR GHOSH, Sociology, Indian Institute of Human Sciences, Calcutta, India

ROBERT HINDE, Animal Behaviour, Cambridge University, UK

RICHARD E. LEAKEY, Physical Anthropology, National Museums of Kenya, Nairobi, Kenya

TAHA H. MALASI, Psychiatry, Kuwait University, Kuwait

J. MARTIN RAMÍREZ, Psychobiology, Universidad de Sevilla, Spain

FEDERICO MAYOR ZARAGOZA, Biochemistry, Universidad Autonóma, Madrid, Spain

DIANA L. MENDOZA, Ethology, Universidad de Sevilla, Spain

ASHIS NANDY, Political Psychology, Center for the Study of Developing Societies, Delhi, India

JOHN PAUL SCOTT, Animal Behavior, Bowling Green State University, Bowling Green, OH, USA

RIITTA WAHLSTRÖM, Psychology, University of Jyväskylä, Finland

The Messenger of the Lost Battalion

Gregory Orfalea

Was it for this the clay grew tall?
—Wilfred Owen

I

In the dark period my father was out of work after he had closed his twenty-five-year-old garment manufacturing business, he gave in to the suggestion of a friend that he take his frustration to a shooting range. He was not a lover of guns and, unlike many in the San Fernando Valley who assure intruders of an "armed response," did not own a firearm. I wouldn't say he was without fear; but he was without that kind of fear.

Nevertheless, from boredom or loneliness, he accompanied his friend—whose dress firm was still puttering along—to shoot. It was a fateful decision. It's possible that Dad hadn't shot a gun since the Second World War and, aiming at the target with a pistol, the several explosions of an afternoon bent his eardrum. From that day forward he complained of a ringing in his ears—tinnitus, it's called. No doctor or friend could help.

As he struggled to get his work bearings, I would on occasion see him put his hand up to his ear. His own voice, and the voices of others, began to echo. I thought of him in those hard days as some kind of Beethoven trying to make music as the bustle of the world slowly ebbed out of him. Seven years after the factory closing he lay dead on the floor of his new photocopy

Used with permission of Gregory Orfalea.

store, a smile on his face. The ringing had stopped, the symphony begun.

In the many nights I have stayed awake thinking about him, I have wondered whether he heard that bullet coming for forty years without knowing it, and that the ringing from the shooting range was only the last warning. I mean forty years after a bad winter in Belgium in which he, like tens of thousands of men, had dropped.

My father repeated only two things about his life as a paratrooper in World War II: "I ate my K-rations on a silver platter at the Hotel Negresco in Nice," and "All my friends were killed around me." That last referred to the Battle of the Bulge. Though in retrospect I see him as the freest man I ever knew, for him the war was too painful an event to dwell on. And at sixty he was dead, the secrets of a most jarring event in his life, it would seem, buried with him.

Full of questions I had barely begun to formulate about my father, in August 1989 I was given a luminous chance to recover something of him. Members of his old battalion—a courageous and ill-fated unit—were returning to France and Belgium; my brother Mark and I didn't resist their invitation. Would we find someone who knew Aref Orfalea? What really had been his war experience and how had it shaped the unusual man he was? His driven life and tragic death? Would something in the men themselves recall him? At the last minute his seventy-nine-year-old eldest sister Jeannette, who at age five had sung "Over There!" for a World War I war bond drive, joined us, too.

Soon we were hustling down the Promenade d'Anglais in Nice, halted momentarily by a visionary sight of a man in parachute tugged out to sea by speedboat, para-sailing. The carmine dome of the whitewashed grand old Negresco loomed. We ducked in over the plush red carpet and under a giant chandelier. Our mission was belied by our attire—bathing suits.

The floor manager's mouth pursed cynically at our story of traveling with American veterans who had run the Nazis out of Nice long ago, "Oh yes, we were captured by Italy, then Germany, and we were lib-er-a-ted by you Americans." It was like the salad Niçoise—sour and cold.

But when I wondered aloud if the Negresco still served K-rations warm on silver plates, and mentioned my dead father had sure liked them that way, the man's face visibly changed.

"Go into the bar, please, and order whatever drink you would like—on the house."

Jean-Paul Marro later joined us, shaking his head at our gin-and-tonics. "What, no champagne?" He motioned for a mint drink himself and told us of his war experience in Algeria. His wife and he had toured the United States recently for their twentieth anniversary; Marro had found himself most moved by Arlington National Cemetery. "I realized there how many lives had been given by America for us," he bowed his head.

Seeing us off at the front of the Negresco, Marro took a green package from behind his back: "This is for your mother. Tell her France appreciates what her husband did for our freedom." It was a bottle of French perfume.

That was a moment of beauty and linkage across time, continents, and generations I will never forget, brought by joining our search with that of the few survivors of one of the most unusual units in U.S. military history—the 551st Parachute Infantry Battalion.

Why, exactly, was the 551st unique? One of only two independent U.S. parachute battalions which fought in the war, it evolved into a highly individualistic, cantankerous band of outsiders, some of whom comprised the original Test Platoon which first jumped out of planes at Fort Benning, Georgia, in 1940. On August 15, 1944 the 551st executed a near perfect jump into the foothills behind Nice as part of Operation Dragoon. It was the first daylight combat drop in U.S. history. Two months after D-Day in Normandy, General Eisenhower had overruled Churchill, who wanted an invasion of the Balkans, by opening up a second front in southern France.

The 551st had other distinctions. It was the first Allied unit to capture a Nazi general (in Draguignan), the first to reach Cannes and Nice. For a job that normally would have required a regiment (three times its size), the 551st patrolled a forty-mile stretch of the France-Italy border in harsh winter conditions under Nazi shelling in the Maritime Alps. Finally, on December 27, 1944, Gen. James Gavin of the 82nd Airborne gave the 551st the "signal honor," as he called it, of spearheading the Allied counterattack against the terrifying German "Bulge" in Belgium. Its heroic push came at great cost—on January 7, only 110 of its 793 men walked out of the decisive battle at Rochelinval. Other than the wipeout at Anzio, Italy, of the 509th—the other independent parachute battalion—the 551st had sustained the worst casualties of any U.S. battalion on the European front.

Strangely, shortly after Rochelinval, the 551st was disbanded, its records destroyed, its valor undecorated, and its existence forgotten—a fate more akin to Vietnam, it would seem, than the so-called good war.

It didn't take long to realize the re-union in Europe carried a great deal of emotional weight for all. There was familial weight, as well. With the twenty returning veterans were twelve spouses, thirteen children, and seven grandchildren. Phil Hand of Georgia, who had first begun to piece the few survivors of the 551st together in the late seventies, brought a son whose mind, he said, had been destroyed by glue-sniffing in the sixties. "He thinks he's a paratrooper," "Bubbles" Hand, a pink-faced man with sad, Irish setter eyes, said to me one afternoon on a veranda in Nice. Ralph Burns of Lake View Terrace, California—no youngster at sixty-nine with a Parkinson's shake—did not leave behind his crippled wife Ruth, but wheeled her everywhere we went, up and down war memorial steps, over the lawns of the graves at Henri Chapelle. A wealthy California developer with a taste for alcohol had brought his two feisty daughters—or they had brought him. (He took sick in Nice and would be confined much of the trip to his hotel room.) Jack Leaf was no deadbeat, though. Early on in the trip I asked if he had married a French girl. "Everytime I met one," he dropped.

Even Aunt Jeannette, to whom Dad had sent most of his war correspondence, would not let a black-and-blue knee bashed the week of our departure stop her. The flame of war is terrible and magnetic, especially for those whose youth was brought to a climax in it. For our journey Aunt Jeannette became the older sister many of the men had written to during the war.

I never asked my mother to accompany us. I knew what her answer would be—silence. Dad had promised her such a trip someday, too, to Europe. But the vagaries of raising three children, the crazy fashion industry, and his subsequent financial decline forestalled it. When she finally went to Europe it was with her brother and his wife on

their invitation. Dad minded the store. It was given to me to reach her that dim August night; she was in London. I instructed my uncle not to tell her husband had been shot, nor by whom. I had to get her home, after all, so I concocted a lie. "Car accident, bad shape" was all I said.

For her I am sure as she flew home the whole continent of Europe sank to a bottomless Sargasso Sea.

II

In addition to the about-face at the Negresco, three moments stood out in our twelve-day journey: the visit to the Dragoon drop-zone at La Motte, a troubled vet's hike to a machine-gun nest site at La Turbie, and Rochelinval itself, the site of the destruction of the 551st.

The men seemed in a trance as they moved out—now in their sixties and seventies—across the vineyards of the Valbourges estate at La Motte, trying to remember just which bush or plot of earth took their falling bodies forty-five years ago. Their maroon berets, navy blue blazers, white shirts and hair flickered among the grape vines, raspberries, apple and pear trees.

"There it is!" Will Marks of Pennsylvania pointed to a lone poplar in the distance fronting a pond. "All my life I dreamt of falling into a tree by itself. You guys have been telling me we fell in the woods. And there it is—my tree!"

Harry Renick, a retired machinist from Detroit who now makes, of all things, wishing wells, commented drily, "I made a three-point landing here: feet, butt, and helmet."

Others were seriously injured, impaled on stakes in the vineyard.

Approaching Valbourges to dedicate a plaque at the Stevens family chapel, Otto Schultz of West Virginia spied the tiled roof of a barn and remembered banging down on the tiles, riding his still-inflated chute to the ground. One of the Stevens family joked, "The broken tiles—they are still there. You may fix them!"

In the courtyard of the old, worn chateau like an apparition in a wheelchair sat ninety-one-year-old Mrs. Stevens, who had bound up the first wounds of the 551st. The men spoke to her in low, hoarse English; she followed their eyes, hugged them. As I approached someone said, "But you are too young to be one of the paratroopers, no?" I looked at Mrs. Stevens—she resembled my father's irascible Lebanese immigrant mother who had peddled on the streets of New York at the turn of the century. "I am here for my father, Madame," I said in basic French, tipping my beret. "He is dead now, but I give you his thanks." She clasped my hand in two of hers.

I wore that maroon beret the whole trip, some admission for an old Vietnam War protester. Col. (Ret.) Doug Dillard, then president of the 551st Association, had given the beret to me earlier in the day for a wreath-laying ceremony at the U.S. Rhone cemetery at Draguignan. It was cocked correctly for me by one of the *veilles suspentes* ("old attics," what the surviving French resistance paratroopers call themselves) who'd come all the way from Paris for the ceremony. When I heard the "Star Spangled Banner," the "Marseillaise," and "Taps," my hand instinctively moved from heart to forehead to join the men.

On our bus that night back to Nice I asked Harry Renick what the 551st motto—GOYA—meant. "Get Off Your Ass," Harry said mildly. That smacked of Dad's favorite "Go get 'em!" cried out whenever he was happy, challenged, or off on his beloved motorcycle into the Mojave Desert. My brother's Freebird restaurant in Santa Barbara, in fact, commemorates both the motto and the motorcycle, which hangs from the

ceiling above the diners. Listening to this, Otto ventured, "You know, we requisitioned a motorcycle from the Germans at Cannes. One guy was fond as hell of that thing. It could have been your father." Indeed, he and Otto shared the same company (Headquarters), and Dad had been a courier for the battalion.

Slowly the gray canvas of my father's life in the war gained an oval of color here, there, and the anger and gaiety we knew as he was raising us began to dovetail with the verve in darkness that got him through the war, or indeed, was caused by it. My father was a life-messenger. He always seemed to want to urge life along; left to its own means, life could atrophy or destroy or worst of all reveal itself meaningless. GOYA! "Go get 'em!" "Rise and shine!" "Up and at 'em!" "We're off and running!" "Zing 'em!" For Dad, reveille was a constant requirement in civilian life—at all hours, I might add.

How many childhood car trips to the Sierras began with his lusty version of "Blood on the Risers" (sung to the tune of "The Battle Hymn of the Republic" with all the irony toward Paul Fussell's "chickenshit" intact):

> "Is everybody happy?" cried the sergeant looking up,
> Our Hero feebly answered, "Yes," and then they stood him up,
> He leaped right out into the blast, his static line unhooked,
> AND HE AIN'T GONNA JUMP NO MORE!
> GORY, GORY, WHAT A HELLUVA WAY TO DIE!

I had a last curiosity about the La Motte drop. Dad once vaguely mentioned his most fearful moment in the service being a night jump. But the 551st had dropped in southern France on a late summer afternoon. Fear of the night was replaced by the fear of German guns which could sight them. When was the night jump? The men figured it wasn't in Europe but in training at Camp Mackall, North Carolina, where they participated in dangerous, innovative airborne tests, such as the first live parachute jumps from gliders. There on the foggy night of February 16, 1944, eight GIs were misdropped in lakes; they parachuted with eighty pounds of equipment straight to the bottom and drowned. The disaster jolted the bereaved relatives of drop victim Benjamin Preziotti of Brooklyn to contact columnist Drew Pearson. An angry piece by Pearson prompted the Army to adopt the British "quick release" harness.

The only quick release the horrific event engendered in the men was of jets of anxiety. Restless by nature (their first mission to drop on a Vichy-leaning Martinique was aborted), the 551st rebelled. At one point, two hundred of their men were in the guardhouse. I remember Dad once telling me, only half-jokingly, that he spent more time jumping in between two warring servicemen than in combat against the Nazis. When one is pumped up for war and the climax is withdrawn, or worse, one's own men are wasted in training, something in the muscles either goes limp or very taut. To blur training and combat, as Paul Fussell has noted in *Wartime*, is "so wrong as to be unmentionable."

Only the return of their charismatic, youthful commander, Col. Wood Joerg, calmed them somewhat. After a hearing, an older Col. Rupert Graves, who had overseen the tragic Mackall night jump, was transferred, but not before shouting at the 551st from his balcony, "You're not going to ruin my career! You're not soldiers! You're all rabble!"

In one of the ironies of war Colonel Graves ended up alongside the 551st at the Battle of the Bulge as commander of the 517th Parachute Infantry Regiment. And it

was the 551st which got the nod to enter the meat grinder. Colonel Dillard points out that the 551st was ordered to attack Rochelinval by the 504th Parachute Regiment, not the 517th, and that the survivors of the 517th have been avid to see the 551st receive a late justice. Still, not a few of the men of the 551st wonder if they were the victims of a clash of personalities at the top, if not outright vengefulness, that traced itself to their training days.

III

Maybe the rebellion was inbred.

What, in fact, makes a man want to jump out of a plane? And not just that—but be one of the first to do it in battle? It's a bit like running away to the circus, but worse— no one shoots at the acrobat on the high wire.

I can't imagine doing it myself. I am a born acrophobe. My wife, who thinks nothing of waterskiing in the ninth month of pregnancy, was ordered to grip my hand when, on our honeymoon, we ascended to the apex of the Eiffel Tower. I distracted myself by focusing on the stripes of her sweater. There is something about *terra firma* that is very dear to me, and I am being literal.

I queried the men about being "airborne." Otto Schultz, retired from Union Carbide (he had worked on the Bhopal project and shook his head about it) thought back to childhood, "I'd run along a wall to leap into sand as a kid—always the farthest one back." Charles Fairlamb, the oldest of our group at seventy-four and retired from Boeing in Seattle, joined the 551st in Panama where he was working with the phone company repairing lines. "I figured I liked to keep climbing poles!" he grinned. There seemed in the men an excess of energy, a critical mass of sorts, that had made them a chancy bunch. There was an almost cherished restlessness about them. "Most people who became paratroopers were dissatisfied where they were," Phil Hand put it bluntly.

Parachuting attracted the romantic, no doubt. Lt. Col. (Ret.) Dan Morgan, the unit's historian, joined the 551st after being disappointed to discover that there was no horse cavalry mounted to fight the Japanese: "They had replaced horses with halftracks." Perhaps more than most, they wanted to be unique. "If you could see it lightning and hear it thunder you could get into the Army," said Charles Austin of Texas. "Not everyone could be a paratrooper." It wasn't so much a question of being fearless. "After jumping thirteen times, I had never landed in a plane in my life, so the first time I landed it was like a screw propeller going into the ground—I was scared as hell," admitted a grizzled, trim Max Bryan from Yorktown, Virginia. "But you say to yourself—I was a man."

As for Dad, I can only guess the motive. He was the last of six children, after four sisters and a brother already stationed in Burma. He certainly had had plenty of babying and something to prove. As for heights it is known that he once fell out of a tree and broke his leg. The restlessness is harder to pinpoint, though I am sure it was there at an early age. It may have been that, unlike his siblings who had grown up in wealth, by the time Aref was coming of age in Cleveland, Ohio, his millionaire linen merchant father had lost it all in the Depression. He watched his father move from being a gent with a gold fob at the cash register to operating a lathe. There was plenty of rancor between my grandmother and grandfather at that time. Grandmother took up work in a cafeteria. In fact, in the mid-thirties the family had split apart—some going to Los Angeles and some holding the fort in Cleveland. A life of grandeur and wealth slipping into penury—what else to do but jump? A good war is a good place to jump.

Like all rebels, the men of the 551st seemed to be acutely skeptical of authority—not the best attitude for those involved in that hierarchical penultimate, the U.S. Army. (The murderous blunder at Camp Mackall only reinforced this.) Their very "551" was out of whack with the normal paratroop battalion sequence numbered 501 to 517 in order to dupe the Germans into thinking there were more U.S. paratroopers than actually existed. They savored their independent status, and relished it when their beloved commanding officer, Col. Wood Joerg, told them, "Each of you is worth five other men."

If one person appears to have epitomized the spirit of the 551st, it was Joerg himself. Ebullient, charming, [an] unreconstructed rebel "Jaw-Jaw" boy at West Point, he was not a great student. The 1937 Point yearbook lists him as 230th out of 298 in class ranking. But it also credits him as a "Rabble Rouser" who pumped up the stands during ball games and had "a heart a yard long and a smile a mile wide." By the time of the offensive at the Bulge, that smile and that heart would have to change places.

He liked to root, work his deep southern accent on the girls in a way that was both shy and confident, and dance. He was not, according to one classmate, "a hive (bookworm)" but a "hopoid." Joerg was hop manager for the Point. He was not a "make" (cadet officer) but a "clean sleeve" (no chevrons to denote rank or authority). He was also an "area bird"—someone who spent many hours walking punishment tours around the Point with a rifle because of his horsing around.

A classmate who outlived him enough to become a brigadier general said Joerg was "full of the milk of human kindness." He had a weakness for plebes who took a terrible beating as he had from upperclassmen, a sympathy he later felt—to reprimand—for men under his command.

The men of the 551st loved him, it seems, and he returned it; some remember him on the phone in a frenzy to get the suicidal mission at Rochelinval canceled. It appears the man from Jaw-Jaw saw death at an early age, and it made him dance. Joerg's first roommate at West Point died as a cadet, sending Joerg into great inner turmoil. The first Pointer killed in World War II was from Joerg's cadet company.

It fit the dark irony surrounding the 551st like a hard chute that one Maj. Gen. C.S. O'Malley would remember Wood Joerg's "heroic death at Bastogne," for when the hot shrapnel pierced his helmet and killed him, Joerg and the men who fell around him in the snow were twenty-five miles north of McAuliffe, his famous "Nuts!" and rescue by Patton, with no rescue at a snow-clamped, anonymous knoll called Rochelinval.

IV

My father was not a physical fitness nut. His generation as a whole found nothing particularly worshipful in the body—the generation that fought World War II worked like dogs to land on a circular drive or in a kidney-shaped pool, daily ate bacon and eggs, drank coffee before it was decaffeinated, smoked Lucky Strikes or Marlboros before the Surgeon General got tough, had affairs instead of relationships, and took up, if anything, bowling, or the somnolent game of golf. Dad vehemently was *not* a golfer.

As a teenager in Cleveland he played football and ice hockey. A split end for a rather accomplished neighborhood football team, the Cleveland Olympics, just before he entered the war he hit a peak when the Olympics copped a citywide championship during a warm-up game for the pro Cleveland Rams at Shaw Stadium.

His quarterback friend, Bud Lank, and he were the only two fellows who played on both first and second-string teams. They were never out of the Olympics lineup. Muscular in a lean way, about five foot ten, Aref was pound-for-pound the best tackler and blocker on the team, Lank thought. He recalled fondly, "Your father was a contact kind of guy."

That he was. He would hold your shoulder to make a point, touch a finger to knee to underscore it, bear hug with a grip that was not afraid to last. Lank said Aref was always slapping the players on the back in the huddle, spiriting them to a faster stop-and-go, a blunter block. He was, in short, a Wood Joerg type.

Los Angeles was not the best place for an excellent ice skater to bring up a family. As much as he loved Mother it was clearly a disappointment to him that she never learned to skate (and abhorred his motorcycle). I became his partner on ice as a boy, as did my sister, Leslie. But most of the time he skated alone with the slight crouch of a speed-skater, crossing over smoothly on turns, weaving gently, swiftly, in and out of the fumbling Angelenos, an anonymous messenger of grace. He loved skating music; if he heard "Frenesi" or anything by Glenn Miller, he immediately took off. An eve at the small Valley rink would end with him unlacing our boots, wistfully blowing over his hot chocolate as he confided that that ultimate female skating partner had eluded him.

If he had found her, earlier, would any of us children have existed? Perhaps a son would not have been afraid of heights.

I tried. I skated pretty well for a native Los Angeleno—I had a good teacher. But I never learned to stop on a dime as my father, who barreled toward the wall, pivoted at the last second, bit his blades sideways into the ice with a shuusssh, ice shavings sprayed on my sister and me. I suppose if you know how to stop you're not so afraid of speed. If I speed-skate anywhere it's on the page, or parachute to its bottom. It's not a bad substitute for innate, physical grace, which my father—unconscious of his own body—had in spades.

The jogging-and-health mania that began with my generation and Jane Fonda'd into a billion-dollar industry over the past decade seemed stupid and pointless to him even when he discovered, as did everyone, cholesterol. "I'm going puffing," he would announce to my mother's exhortations, exhaling smoke. He smoked seriously—inhales and exhales were dramatic billowing caesuras, smoke signals of dilemma or pain. Strangely enough, smoke for him was a life force. Toward the end he tried to quit for Mom, even adopted lower-tar cigarettes. But his heart wasn't in it.

I say all this to note the paradox of that generation of Americans which spent its childhood in the Depression, fought the Second World War as teenagers, and built as adults the country we are today, for better or worse, richer or polluted, in plutonium and in health. That paradox is one of excess and selflessness. It was a generation which acted first, thought later. Ours, on the other hand, thinks most everything into oblivion. Ours projects all, yet seems at a loss to do anything that will substantially alter what we so brilliantly project, most of which is payment for forty-five years of excess since the war— chemical water, dying forests, soaring deficits, clogged arteries, rockets and bombs like hardened foam from a million panting mouths.

I can't blame my father or his generation for the Age of Excess anymore than I blame my own for its Age of Informed Narcissism. History and time create us more than we fathom. I only note the ironies— Dad's excess was generous, selfless, and dealt the future some mortal blows. Our touted social consciousness seems drained to a pittance of the grand protest era that gave us "our" war crucible. We are late, curiously cranky parents. And we are not so hot with the future, either, sinking in the mire of the present, saving nothing but the bills from our credit cards.

Our sin is presbyopia; his generation's—myopia. Even then by the day we escape from the immediate, from *contact*. We are all learning to draw in our wagons quite well from the teeming hordes of the ghetto, crack wars, the homeless. We become kinder, gentler Republicans at a fair remove from what needs our kindness and gentleness less than our ability to act. To *act*? That might entail uncertainty, even heartache.

Perfectly healthy as I was in my twenties—a bicycler, basketball player, swimmer— I once prodded Dad that he needed exercise. He snapped, "I got my exercise hauling fifty dresses at a clip over my shoulders up and down Ninth and Los Angeles streets. I got my exercise lugging an eighty-pound radio over the Maritime Alps." It was the closest he ever came to bravado. It was as out of character as it was for him to be out of work.

I used to dream about the Maritime Alps, unable ever to find them on the map. They held a lofty, Tibetan image in my mind. After the 551st came down from the Provence foothills of their parachute drop, taking Cannes, Nice and other towns of the Cote d'Azur, it was ordered to go up into the high mountains separating France from Italy, where the retreating Germans fled. This was September 1944. These were the Maritime Alps. (Three months after serving the longest uninterrupted combat stint in Europe, the 551st was relieved in the Alps by the heralded Japanese-American unit, the 442nd.)

In 1989 on some bright August days we veterans and family ascended the Maritimes. I had my eye out for old Army radios. His had probably been an SCR-300 backpack version, good practice for hauling a garment bag stuffed with samples. German pillboxes still squatted in the crags of the mountain. Chuck Fairlamb remembered boulders the Germans had rolled into the dry riverbed of the Var River so that gliders couldn't land there. As the road narrowed and steepened, and the clear green Var flowed in lazy late summer falls past islets and cottonwoods, Harry Renick seemed dreamy.

"What a place to come at night with a girl!" he mused, his dull blue eyes brightening at the sight. "You lie down on a towel with the rocks and the water rushing by. And boy, the wind over you! After you're done, you go dip it in the cold water. Downstream it gets warmer!"

I asked Harry, a tall man who looked like he might hunt, if the 551st ever saw bears or other animals in the Alps.

"Animals?" he dropped. "We were too concerned with the two-legged animals."

At St. Martin-Vesubie, we embarked to a good-sized crowd which swarmed us in the town square where, *tilleuls* rippling in a mountain breeze, we had a wreath-laying ceremony with the mayor and town council and *vin d'honneur*. One gap-toothed woman, eyes sparkling in a leathery face, insisted I translate for her that she had done the men's laundry during the war. Another with eyeglasses had given them gum, she nodded shyly. Everywhere we went were townspeople clutching forty-year-old photos, trying to compare the burnished boyish GI faces with the men whose skin had turned to many dry rivers, but whose eyes were searching, too, for that one person who knew them then, who bound a bullet wound or even sold them *baguettes*.

Swerving up the steep, narrow mountain road to the next village of their Alpine duty—tiny Isola—I could just imagine Dad in his glory on the motorcycle bending to the precipice as he distributed messages to the battalion. A chapel from the Middle Ages jutted above the green valley.

"Helluva nice place to live—I wouldn't want to fight a war here," Max Bryan mused.

Phil Hand recalled that after the war his insomnia and bad nerves from the Bulge were relieved only by imagining the period the 551st had spent in the snow-covered Alps, "one of the most beautiful and peaceful things I'd ever known." It was arduous duty, as well. Many of the men had to learn cross-country skiing for their patrols; some were picked off in the snow by German snipers. Some did the picking.

In November 1944 Dad wrote his sister Jeannette that he helped "serve Mass," avoiding in the V-mail tradition saying where he was. It was the Alps period. Attending Mass in a little chapel in Isola, Mark and I lit a candle and thought of him pouring the cruets as [a] nineteen-year-old in fatigues. For all his passion, he had a deep well of humility and faith that began to ebb only with the onset of my sister's mental illness in the late 1970s. A rosary taken from a bombed shrine in 1944 by scout Joe Cicchinelli of Arizona—miraculously unhurt—was worn by a statue of the Blessed Mother at Isola chapel. Outside the chapel, Bob Van Horssen of Grand Haven, Michigan—father of ten—gave his wings to a crippled girl.

Before having lunch at the Hotel de France (which had been badly shelled during the war) we found ourselves made part of a procession for St. Roch, the local patron, through whose intercession the Black Plague of the Middle Ages bypassed Isola. Down the cobblestones we walked behind a wooden statue of St. Roch. Someone pointed up a wall. Bullet holes from the war still peppered it. St. Roch had not prevented that. And some mute collective protest bone in Isola had kept that evidence from being erased.

Higher we went, up to seven thousand feet and the last Alpine town patrolled by the 551st—St. Etienne de Tinée. We were mobbed. It seemed the entire town of one thousand turned out to greet us. There was another French Army band and a company of French troops for the ceremonies. A gaggle of French generals and an admiral stood pointing, nodding.

Chuck Miller of Rancho Cucamonga, California, remembered the long, arduous hikes up and down the mountain slope, playing a kind of hide-and-seek with the Germans above: "At St. Etienne we'd switch places with the Germans. We'd look up with our binoculars at them, and then they would go down and look up at us." I thought of a line from Melville on the American Civil War: "All wars are boyish, and are fought by boys."

By midnight we were beautifully beat and traveling down the mountain. In the dark Glenn Miller tunes bathed us in memory, like a warm tide. Doug Dillard had put on a tape. "Oh K-A-L-A-M-A-Z-O-Oh what a gal! In Kalamazoo! I'll make my bid for that freckle-faced kid I'm hurrying to. I'm going to Michigan to see the sweetest gal in Kalamazoo-zoo-zoo."

Wishing-well Harry, who really had taken to the willowy brunette waitress in St. Etienne ("Tell her she's got class. Tell her she's beautiful"), saw in the dimness Aunt Jeannette drink some spring water from a bottle.

"Don't drink that water, it'll rust your pipes," Harry said, having a last beer.

"I'm not going to worry about that now!" squawked almost-octogenarian Aunt Jen.

Harry leaned over and flicked on my reading light as I was taking out my note-book. "You gotta put a little life in this life," he made us laugh, garbling "life" for "light." Considering the 551st, perhaps that was not a garble.

At La Turbie, Joe Cicchinelli took me on a forced march up a hillside to a disturbing memory. In advance of the battalion and with the help of French civilian Charles Calori, Cicchinelli and two other GIs had lobbed grenades into the machine-gun nest in a shack, killing three young, blond Germans. Cicchinelli still has the ID photos taken off their bodies forty-five years ago.

But it was at the shadowy hutch out back—where two more Germans were surprised with bullets—that Cicchinelli jumped back and forth in the underbrush, squeezing his jaw. "One of them didn't die," he shook his head. It was that one, Joe said lowering his voice, that he shot in the head and watched, agog, the youth's brains spill in a stream on the floor.

"What could I do?" Joe raised his head up to the sky. There was no answer—not from the bracken he was breaking as he paced, not from the bleached wood of the shack, not from us.

A shorter version of our father with his weathered tan, mustache, taut strength, and share of ghosts—Cicchinelli had spent three years in psychotherapy working on that moment in La Turbie, a bayonet attack at the Bulge, and months as a German POW. Today Joe counsels Vietnam veterans.

That shack. That hutch. It was the first time he had faced it again since the war. And though Cicchinelli had returned three times to Europe and was staying with a maquis veteran rather than at our hotel, he admitted, "The reason I come back—I hope by coming I can forget it," looking at me with sincere, wood-colored eyes that were somehow burning.

On the dirt path back I came upon the incongruous rusted guts of a piano. It made me think about Dad, who had met Mother while playing his patented single piano tune at a party. Had he ever killed someone face-to-face in the war? Mark said he had asked him that question once, and that Dad had said, no, he hadn't.

He lied.

Some months after we returned from Europe, his old football-playing buddy Bud Lank sent me a revealing tape of his childhood memories of my father.

After the war, and after some months' stay at various Army hospitals for his frozen feet, my father came back to Cleveland. One night he, Lank, and two other ex-GIs (including Tommy Stampfl of the 551st) went out drinking. By midnight, they were fairly well loosened up in a bar and began to tell what many GIs would never tell again—their darkest moment in the war.

Danny Polomski's moment was his body, or what was left of it—he'd lost both legs and an arm to a mine. Lank had broken his leg in a jeep accident. Dad's dark moment was not his injury, however.

He said about forty German soldiers had holed up in a bakery. The 551st opened up with machine guns and rifles. As two Germans tried to escape out the side window, my father shot them both. Later, walking with a squad along a hedgerow some Germans jumped up, and at pointblank range he shot one of them.

At the Battle of the Bulge the 551st fought through farmland, for the most part. The towns they went through were barely a cluster of stone houses—Dairomont, Odrimont. It's probable that the hedgerow incident was in Belgium. But the bakery?

One day I took a close look at an old photo of Joe Cicchinelli crouching with townspeople in Draguignan just after he had helped capture the Nazi general there and torn down the Nazi flag from the mayor's office. I squinted at the store window behind him. There it said: *Patisserie.*

It is likely my father had to kill two men whose faces he could see all too well only a day into battle, a day after the jump into France. It must have stunned him. After 1945, he told no one about it.

In childhood games of cowboy and Indian, Aref was the only kid who always played the Indian, Lank said.

I think of Joe Cicchinelli now holding his jaw in anguish at La Turbie, and I think of my father holding his ear from the gunshot ringing at the range and at the bakery. What it must have cost one who had always been the Indian to have the upper, lethal hand, even for a few seconds.

Phil Hand spoke of "emptying into" a German soldier at La Motte. "Fifty others emptied into him," Hand thought—pure fear of first day in battle. The idea of killing being an emptying of self—a draining of one, violently, into another—there is something pathetically sexual about it, something utterly forlorn. You are emptying more than bullets. Your soul is switched in the kill. You become the dead one. In killing him, in "emptying into" him, his deadness, by implication, invades you. In death he is full of you; in life you are a vacuum.

The day before we left Nice for Belgium I sat with Cicchinelli on the roof of the Hotel Pullman. The sun glared off the mirror sunglasses of some women lounging topless by the rooftop pool. Around us the great bowl of Nice sparkled—its steeples, clay-tiled roofs, mottled, hazy hills. California by another name.

After a while we stopped talking. Joe fingered a napkin and looked up at me.

"How did your father die?"

"He was shot." I startled myself. Few who ask get the truth, and no one else in the 551st asked.

"Who shot him?"

"My sister."

He clamped my hand. His grip was hard, as if he were squeezing the handle of an elevator cut loose in a shaft. His head bent, ticking slightly.

"Oh, ooh."

There was less oxygen in Nice that afternoon, and much less sun, and no topless women. That languid roof shrank into a lonely hutch in back of a photocopy store—a place where people are put out of their misery.

V

"I know him."

Phil Hand held up a black-and-white photo of my father—the dashing GI home from the war, his Airborne patch captured on his shoulder, his thick black hair pleasantly awry at the widow's peak, "ears lowered." A slight mustache. He looks like Richard Gere. There's a gal tucked behind his ear, someone who didn't become my mother.

His feet are unfrozen, healed, and though they hurt in the cold, tonight is not cold, the liquor is flowing. He's at a club in Cleveland or some family shindig. He's manly, confident. But not too confident. He isn't smiling. His eyes are tree-bark in snow.

"I know him."

Phil Hand didn't nod, looking at the photo as we sat on the veranda of our Nice hotel. He was staring steadily through thick glasses. No histrionics here. He knows the man's soul, I think, but not the man. That may be better than the man, but that is not what I want. I want damn physical recognition.

I'd been showing the photo to the men of the 551st from the day we began the journey. No one knew him or recognized

him. Most wanted to, no doubt, for our sake. But recognition of buddies they knew then takes a while for the old vets, even with flesh-and-blood partners before them.

I began to realize that no one really remembered my father from the war. Perhaps my hopes were unrealistic. A battalion is 800 men; a company is 200 men; a platoon, 40. Of the four members of Dad's Headquarters Company on the trip (Hand, Fairlamb, Schultz, and Church Bernard of Cleveland, Ohio), Phil Hand was the only one in Demolitions platoon—in fact, he was its lieutenant (Hand was the only wartime officer on the trip). My father had trained in demolitions. Perhaps, I wanted to believe badly, Phil did know Aref Orfalea.

But in all Hand's wartime photo albums, Father is in not one picture. In only one of hundreds shown me is there a face so darkened, so inscrutable, I can pour my hope of recognition into it, one among fifteen grease-smeared men waiting to take off from Italy for the drop into southern France.

"It's yours. Take it." Phil gave the shade-man to me. I had thought the trip might lessen, not lengthen, the shadows I have come with live with.

Our Nice farewell speaker that night at dinner was Rear Adm. H. G. "Hank" Chiles, Jr., commander of a submarine group with the U.S. Sixth Fleet. Only about fifty people, we were hardly a big enough group to draw an admiral, not to mention one on active duty in the midst of another hostage-crisis (Colonel Higgins of the United Nations Truce Supervision Organization had just been hanged on videotape in south Lebanon). Chiles himself was substituting for the commander of the entire Sixth Fleet—Vice Adm. J. D. Williams.

"I and many of my generation stand in awe of you and the sacrifice of your generation during World War II," Chiles told the men. "You must know it's a humbling experience for a fifty-one-year-old rear admiral to stand here. I've asked myself over the past few days what I could possibly say that would be meaningful to people such as you. You see, you are *legends*."

The men looked stunned. They were, after all, mostly privates during the war. To be praised by an admiral in such an intimate setting for a feat long ago forgotten by the high brass—it was disorienting, to say the least. But very pleasing, too.

Chiles pointed with interest to "recent progress with the Soviets" and thought that *"glasnost/perestroika* give us hope for a more open, less militant Soviet stance." He cited the first cathedral opened in forty years in Lithuania (a year later Lithuania was a free country, and at the end of 1991 the great Soviet Union itself broke up into fifteen free-market states with hardly a shot fired). Chiles called recent fleet exchange visits to Norfolk and Sebastopol "very successful."

"There are signs of a more peaceful world, signs that perhaps future generations of Americans might know a world less disposed to violence than what you saw and fought for," he told the vets.

Who of us doesn't want to believe that? Yet I saw in my mind's eye the hot muzzle of my sister's gun—the hell it wreaked in a few seconds. That had nothing to do with Communism, foreign policy. If all the wars in the world suddenly stopped, the impossible time bomb of our waste would have to be dismantled; 200 million guns, 70 million of them handguns, would remain marking time in their American drawers, closets, beds, hands. And 2 million as sick as my sister was sick. No. There is another war. It is in front of us everyday. It stems from who we are, what we are—it is a war of being, of being fractured. Drugs, AIDS, the homeless, the insane—as they grow the war grows. As

do the guns. We are at war with ourselves. We very much need—in the midst of our tenuous plenty—an American *perestroika.*

A poet of Russia's Silver Age, Valerie Bruysov, noted that there are those who are freedom's "captives." Precisely.

Chiles ended with a surprisingly pacifistic reference to a soldier at Verdun, tipped his cap once again to the 551st for its "great contribution to freedom," and asked the men and their families to pray "for an America strong in peace so we don't have to be strong in war."

I couldn't have agreed more. Two hundred million guns on our streets is not strength.

VI

"I didn't want to live it—I didn't have to relive it. Maybe it's better to keep it cloudy. But I seem strong-willed enough not to be torn up by the past. I've been called cold-hearted. I knew we'd taken a horrible beating. But until I went to my first 551st reunion in 1988 in Chicago, I was under the impression we only had three people left."

It was Chuck Miller, an un-cold retired air conditioner repairman, looking out from a porch on the silent green hills of the Ardennes where, in a bitter two weeks at the turn of 1945, the 551st came to its end. Miller was talking about memory, the dread of it and its strange allure. There were few of the returning veterans who approached the killing field "with tranquil restoration," as Wordsworth would have it.

Memory. Drawn like moths to the flame of it, worried as to what it might contain, avid to share it with loved ones who might believe the otherwise unbelievable, or in Cicchinelli's case, to burn it so hot in the soul it would finally cool and come off like a scab. Something awe-full and awful to confront. What else but memory makes us human? As if preparing for the original battle, however difficult, the old men seemed to say: *We are what we remember.* Not the half of it we nurse or suppress, but the all of it we find, usually, with others.

The community of memory—the only community that lasts—quickened in the men when by train and bus following the route the 551st took in December 1944 as it rushed to the Ardennes to help stop Hitler's last onslaught, we arrived in Belgium.

Five facts: Ardennes horses, more nervous and quick than most, are exported to the United States. Belgians are the largest per capita drinkers of beer in the world. The towns of eastern Belgium in the Ardennes have been crushed three times this century by invading Germans. The world's largest mushroom industry based here uses the cool, damp, old Nazi bunkers for growth. And lastly, according to our host and former Belgian resistance leader Leo Carlier, Belgians are obstinately independent, each wanting "his house to be different." This sounded like 551st territory. It was also the scene of Hitler's last stand.

Over a million men in uniform fought in the month after December 16, 1944, the fiercest clash of the war in Europe—the Battle of the Bulge. Well over half those men were Americans, who took most of the 81,000 Allied casualties in that period. Begun with the Nazi SS massacre of eighty U.S. POWs near Malmedy, the Battle of the Bulge was Hitler's last desperate, and nearly successful, attempt to throw back the Allies who had been advancing steadily towards Germany since D-Day. No one thought he would attack in the dense Ardennes forest, or increase the attack in the midst of the worst European winter recorded in the century. He did both.

Pine shadows riddled the men on the bus while Carlier related, "You have been the Unknown Soldiers, the 551st. I met

Colonel Dillard in 1984 and heard for the first time about your story and your destruction. I promised him we would make a memorial and I vowed you would never be forgotten. Tomorrow you will be invaded."

He wasn't kidding. Hundreds of people, some from as far as Brussels, showed up for the dedication. Their fervor was moving, even for one as skeptical of American foreign policy as I am. A poster inside the town hall at Liernaux still warned children not to touch live bullets and shells in the fields—destructive relics of two world wars. (A united Germany is for eastern Belgians at least as nervous a condition as for Silesians and other Poles.)

Now in the village of Rochelinval a monument to the 551st exists. Not the Americans, not the U.S. Army, but the Belgians themselves built the stone memorial; it took them two years. A young architect, Claude Orban, did much of the spade work. We watched in hushed silence Heide and Bo Wilson, grandchildren of Col. Wood Joerg killed in an artillery treeburst nearby, unveil the memorial.

The next day, our last, the men roamed the fields and the woods. "Can you imagine the enormous sound then, and how quiet it is now?" mused Chuck Miller as he hiked, shaking off a question about his heart condition.

I stood with the man who fired the first mortar of that historic December 27 raid on Noirefontaine ordered by General Gavin that commenced the Allied rollback of the Bulge. He was Chuck Fairlamb, seventy-four, of Seattle. He remembered Colonel Joerg pointing out a sniper and ordering him to "Go get that apple!"

But the worst was the foggy, freezing, delirious stretch January 3–7, 1945, when over a snow-filled, forested area near Trois Ponts the 551st pushed the Germans back five miles in five days—very slow, agonized fighting, often hand-to-hand combat. "It's always easier to defend, as at Bastogne, than to attack, as we did toward Rochelinval," explained Phil Hand. "We had to swing over the area like a gate."

"By God, did we take that many casualties in that small area?" wondered Doug Dillard, who feels closer to the 551st than to battalions he himself commanded in Korea and Vietnam. Dillard pointed out a creek where the men soaked their boots, the beginning of their battle with frostbitten feet and trench foot in the subzero weather. Dad's feet froze up; he was evacuated to Liège. When I leapt over a barbed wire fence to photograph the creek, the men smiled. Airborne, if for a second.

Hard to conceive in the green, silent farmland, but many froze to death, too. No overshoes were issued. The men were given a merciless order not to wear overcoats so that they would be distinguishable from Germans. Cicchinelli remembered firing ("We were so pissed") at overcoat-clad 517th GIs. Hand recalled soldiers "circling a little sapling which they gripped," trying to stay both awake and warm. Sleep was death. After three days of no sleep or food, some slept.

On January 4, 1945, the only platoon-sized fixed bayonet attack in the European theater occurred—yes, it was Company A of the 551st.

They lurched forward together, the repressed and the haunted, remembering Lt. Dick Durkee of Maryland's order to fix bayonets so that they would not shoot their own people in the fog. It's an order given in a desperate situation to strike up a soldier's adrenalin. The Germans stood up in their gun depressions, stunned. Sixty-four of them were killed by gun butts and blades. "I could very well have blocked it all out because of this day," Miller admitted. "And you know I'm German. It's such a dirty shame

that someone like Hitler could change people's psyches the way he did."

"We were going a little mad, you know," Cicchinelli confessed. Company A stabbed and mutilated corpses until Durkee stopped them. They were breaking the stocks of their rifles off on the dead bodies. Durkee named it cruelty. But few of Company A survived, either. When Durkee ordered Pvt. Pat Casanova to get the rest of the men, Casanova of New Jersey shouted, "I can't, sir." "Why not?" Durkee yelled. "Because they're all dead, sir," was the reply.

Shortly after the bayonet attack Cicchinelli was taken prisoner by a Nazi patrol probably as lost in the snow as he was. Seventeen years later, working as a mail carrier he came to a wooded area near Flagstaff, Arizona, that resembled the Ardennes of Belgium. "I relived it all," he said, and had to rearrange his route before quitting altogether.

Finally we faced the mile-grade of hill below Rochelinval, now green, covered on January 7, 1945 with a foot and a half of snow. The day before, 1,262 rounds of artillery had been promised to the 551st for its attack on Rochelinval. But by dawn nothing had arrived, and nothing would arrive. Joerg tried to get the half-crazed unit relieved, to get the attack called off. He got neither. Only an order to take the hill, which was topped by dug-in Germans and their machine guns.

"He saved my life by giving me an order," Joe Thibault of Massachusetts said in choked voice, recalling Joerg's last moments. " 'Go get the self-propelled [gun]!' I saw it in his eyes. He knew." Charles Fairlamb also saw Joerg rise out of the protection of his foxhole and say, "Isn't the smell of mortars sweet, Chuck?" Fairlamb opined, "I think he knew he was doomed and we all were doomed. He just sort of stood up to take his fate."

Incredibly, their commander dead, down to less than a hundred men and a dozen officers, the 551st crested the hill and took Rochelinval, pushing the Germans behind the Salm River.

The 551st should have been one of the most decorated units in U.S. military history. Instead it became one of its most forgotten. In late January 1945, General Gavin told the 551st that they had been disbanded by the Department of the Army. Survivors filtered elsewhere. As Harry Renick put it, "I was disintegrated into the 82nd Airborne."

For all the "firsts" they notched, the 551st lost not only its existence, but its history. Dan Morgan of Washington (one of the first GIs to enter Dachau), in researching his self-published account of the unit, *The Left Corner of My Heart*, found twelve cubic feet of official records for the other independent parachute battalion—also disbanded—the heavily decorated 509th. For the 551st he found papers in a folder less than one-quarter of a inch thick. When Morgan visited Fort Benning in 1981, every parachute unit had a plaque on the wall—except for the 551st.

What explains this? The men chew on several theories: that Gavin was embarrassed enough by the losses as to wipe out all records and the remnant of the 551st; that the men were so heartbroken at their disbandment after Rochelinval they burned the records in the fields themselves; that the 551st was just snake-bitten from the beginning; that the death of their commander deprived them of their most credible pleading voice for honors; that their impossible objective at Rochelinval was punishment for being an oddball, maverick unit. But they have no answers.

Neither, apparently, does Gen. Matthew Ridgway, who commanded the XVIII Airborne Corps for the Bulge campaign and was Gavin's immediate superior.

Declassified in 1981, the Corps' March 1945 "Operation Report Ardennes" carries no mention either of the 551's historic attack on the Noirefontaine garrison, or of its capture in spite of terrible casualties of Rochelinval. Some of the men think the unit's final humiliation lies with Ridgway, who apparently disliked the independent paratroop units and was on the verge of disbanding them anyway before the Bulge hit. Yet Ridgway, now [ninety-four], wrote Colonel Dillard on July 29, 1989, that the blotting out of the 551st was "a grave error and injustice to as gallant a combat battalion as any in World War II in Europe." Declining an interview due to illness, Ridgway also wrote me on February 8, 1990, "I have an abiding admiration for the members of the 551st Parachute Battalion's record of gallantry in the Battle of the Bulge, but as far as I can remember, I had no personal contact with it. At one time I had a 65-mile front to cover with only a handful of troops, though there were no finer ones." Ridgway also noted that he was aware of "serious efforts" underway to bring the "full record" of the 551's heroism and tragic fate to public light.

After the few survivors were broken apart and stripped of their history together, thirty years went by. In 1977, Phil Hand determined "to find whatever buddies I had left before I died." He used telephone directories, ads in *Static Line*, the airborne newsletter, his wife's government WATS line. The first reunion in August 1977 brought eighteen members. Now there are about one hundred forty found, though many are in ill health.

How strange it is that these precious men could receive the French Croix de Guerre personally from General Charles De-Gaulle and many years after see a monument erected to their sacrifice in Belgium but be completely ignored by their own country. The men talk about the Presidential Unit citation received by the 509th, but they do not hold their diminishing breath.

Lt. Gen. (Ret.) William Yarborough, then commander of the 509th, their brother unit laden with honors denied the 551st, calls the independent units' disbandment "a crime of the first order." Speaking of the extraordinary intangibles that go into making an elite unit, he said, "For the Army as a whole to forget this, or to sublimate it to the degree that it is considered less important than bullets and bayonets, is to break faith with the real meaning of what it portends to be a soldier."

Or a man.

VII

One night in Liège, Fred Hilgardner of Missouri made me realize my brother Mark and I were not alone in our own search.

"I'm retracing my father's steps, just like you," he said, taking a good pull of his cigarette. The elder Hilgardner had lost a leg during the First World War at the nearby Meuse-Argonne, dying when his son was barely a year old. "Everybody loved him," Fred crushed his cigarette, and in the furl of smoke I saw emerge one last time in Belgium the phoenix-genie of our father. How a father can pull the wagon of a son's life, even from the grave!

The trip had shaken Fred Hilgardner: "I broke down at a lot of our ceremonies." He went on bitterly, "What is the Fourth of July? Firecrackers. We used to learn the history of the flag. The kids today don't even know the capitals of the states. They'll play the national anthem at a ballgame—ball players will scratch their nuts, chew gum. Men in the stands sucking their beer, not taking off their caps. Flags on the Fourth— some drag the ground. The flag means more to me than a piece of cloth. It represents men's lives."

Whether or not flag-burning should be unlawful, sentiments such as Fred Hilgardner's should never be taken lightly. There is no blind patriotism in the 551st— quite the contrary. Becoming "a shadow battalion," as Dan Morgan calls it, ensured that—discarded in the war by history, by the Army itself. Medals is not what the 551st is after or impressed with.

Truth is medal enough. "Setting the record straight" for a handful of children and grandchildren as to what their fathers did in history's near-suicide was really the purpose of going back, as Doug Dillard intimated one night. It uncovered the depths of the men's sadness and their sacrifice, not a small one.

Suddenly Hilgardner had a vision, and tapped me on the shoulder, "You get around these guys and you don't seem so damn old. You know, there were two guys that last night in Nice who'd swing a gal around so well. They topped everybody. They danced jitterbug. Maybe your Dad was one of 'em.'"

Did he love to dance! *That* my mother handled well, to the point that when they danced they seemed to fuse. They never looked at each other, but a quick touch at fingertip would trigger a whirl, a twist, a sidestep, a clinch. Different as they were, they were rhythm personified, *In the Mood*. And they taught us children to dance, plugging in the phonograph, scattering sand on the garage floor.

Maybe one of those hopoids was Dad, Fred. Maybe Wood Joerg was clapping. That last night before Belgium . . .

It became clear to me. From the first day of the trip when Joe Thibault, whose son died of a drug overdose at thirty-nine, came over with tears in his eyes, gripping me on the shoulder, to Otto's sequestered motorcycle, to Phil Hand's shadowy photo, to Hilgardner's last dancer, that the men of the 551st were looking for their messenger. He was unknown. That made him all the more sought after. He was their youth. He was the cipher of their strange, long-delayed coming together. He had something to say to them in the form of two sons. Just as we sought our father in them, they sought him in us.

Mark said it best with a spontaneous toast at our Liège farewell dinner, palpable in candlelight: "It's been painful to realize that none of you knew Dad personally. But I must tell you extraordinary men that in these short days I found a piece of my father in every one of you. Here's to the men of the 551st! May their memory live forever!"

From the troubled exuberance of Joe Cicchinelli to the stoic avoidance of Chuck Miller that spared others pain—these had our father stamped on them. Each was the kind of man in whose care you would place your life. And they evoked something of that in you— in their gracious, wry, self-abnegating way.

My sister placed her life in my father's hands. He did not drop it, though it killed him. During her sometimes frightening ten-year struggle with schizophrenia, my sister was not abandoned by Mother or Father.

In his old factory Dad gave employ to a Black with a cleft palate, a French dress designer with a hunchback, a Jewish book-keeper who, at seventy, supported an invalid brother. At home he brought in for help with housekeeping a magnificent human being named Margarita Cruz, whose son was killed by death squads in El Salvador. He was the Indian. He dropped from planes for others.

That inkling he had during the war intensified toward the end in his ear's ringing—of a war closer to home. He didn't see a way out of it. For one of his disposition, there wasn't any. Maybe this is why he clung so to life, with such abandon, knowing what a lucky gift a moment of joy was, knowing its duration, knowing how a landscape could be green with friends and too soon snow-covered with their bodies.

A few months before he died, he sat in front of me and said softly, looking up, "Life is hell."

I suppose I will think about that statement till I die. How out of character it was.

But maybe not. Maybe, for a GOYA, it was a compliment. I have come to see my father's fate as akin to the fate of the men with whom he served in battle so long ago. They became in their sacrifice what he became: anonymous, lost, but a messenger of life at all costs.

Remember that line of Hickey's from Eugene O'Neill's *The Iceman Cometh* about his doomed wife? "I could see disgust having a battle in her eyes with love. Love always won." Staring down the barrel of the past I think the 551st saw the same thing my father saw that terrible day in Belgium and in Los Angeles: ultimate love.

REFERENCES—AT WAR: THE SHADOW OF A SOLDIER

GARBARINO, J. (1999). *Lost boys: Why our sons turn violent and how we can save them.* New York: Free Press.

GORDON, M.R. (1990). For first time, a woman leads G.I.'s in combat. *New York Times.* January 4: A13.

GRIFFIN, S. (1992). *A chorus of stones: The private life of war.* New York: Doubleday.

JEFFORDS, S. (1989). *The remasculinization of America: Gender and the Vietnam war.* Bloomington: Indiana University Press.

MCBRIDE, J. (1995). *War, battering, and other sports: The gulf between American men and women.* Atlantic Highlands, NJ: Humanities Press.

STIEHM, J.H. (1989). *Arms and the enlisted woman.* Philadelphia: Temple University Press.

Men Changing: Visions of a Future

Although it would be incorrect to talk of "the" men's movement, despite the exclusive attention paid by mainstream media and publishing to a specific kind of organized group of men in the United States, there is no doubt that men are on the move. Dislodged from complacent hegemonic masculinity by the social and cultural changes effected by feminism and antiracist activism, many men have begun, singly and in groups, to question received notions of masculinity. Phenomena like Robert Bly's "Iron John" thesis, with its attendant gatherings of "wild men," and large-scale mobilizations such as Promise Keepers and the Million Man March have received lavish attention from the press (an indication, perhaps, of how little such movements affect the status quo), but there are many other ways in which men have been organizing for change in the past twenty years.

Groups such as the Oakland Men's Project, the National Organization for Men Against Sexism, and many smaller, local groups of men organized against rape and domestic violence receive little public attention but have been working for years to loosen the grip of an unhealthy and often dangerous masculinity on young men's lives (Johnson 261–264). A new campus movement for men has also begun transforming the lives of students (see "Sex, Love, and Power" section). The internet has enabled such groups to communicate their analyses to their peers across the globe, drawing confirmation and support for their activities (see mencanstoprape.org, for one significant example).

There has been backlash and outrage, soul-searching and struggle; undoubtedly, there is a new restlessness among men. Men have always gathered in groups, but in these times they are just as likely to gather to talk about their lives *as men* as to watch a ball game. A major part of this emerging new consciousness is centered on recasting the "traditional" family: "Men from Wall Street to homeless shelters speak with conviction about wanting to father their children more actively than they themselves were fathered" (Pruett, and see also Gross). In the academy, a shift has occurred from the focus on absent fathers to research on the effect of involved fathers on their children's lives. Men like Geoffrey Canada and Paul Kivel, John Stoltenberg and Michael Kimmel, travel widely to speak about a new consciousness among men and its hope for realizing a new vision of equality.

Just as there is no one women's movement, there is no monolithic men's movement. There are strains and stresses within organizations devoted to political activism around the issues of masculinity, and there are competing narratives about the direction that the "New Man" should take. In the following two pieces, Stoltenberg and Messner take different points of view on the issue of "masculinity" and "manhood," yet both are motivated by the sense of possibility that now exists for profound change in a long patriarchal history. Gloria Steinem has written that "Perhaps the psychic leap of twenty years ago, *Women can do what men can do*, must now be followed by, *Men can do what women can do*" (Hagan vii). Whether one follows a line of thinking like Stoltenberg's, which sees gender itself as a myth, or Messner's, which argues for new political coalitions to reform oppressive masculinities, there can be little doubt that masculinities are in flux.

Healing from Manhood: A Radical Meditation on the Movement from Gender Identity to Moral Identity

John Stoltenberg

As a human rights activist whose life and life-work have been enriched beyond measure by radical feminism, I have chosen to inquire, as searchingly as I know how, into the ethical meaning of manhood. Over the years I have observed, in myself and in other penised people, a vast discrepancy between two very different experiences and practices of personal identity. One of them I call moral identity (or "selfhood"), and the other I call gender identity (or "manhood"). I have come to realize that for anyone raised to be a man, at least in Western industrialized societies today, our selfhood—the fullest experience of our own and others' humanity—tends to get contradicted in practice by the behaviors and attitudes required for social maintenance of manhood. The personal identity we experience when we choose behavior in order to "be the man there"—when we choose acts that will make our "manhood" seem real—cannot possibly coexist with authentic, passionate, and integrated selfhood. Because I believe deeply that selfhood not only is a preferable mode of being but also promises a society premised on greater fairness and equality, I am committed to communicating to other penised people this revolutionary shift in how we can experience personal identity.

I understand manhood relationally, transactionally, as something one feels compelled to prove by *doing*. This is a crucial distinction, and it sets my views apart, philosophically and pragmatically, from many other formulations of the subject "feminism and men." I believe that everyone raised to be a man has to some extent been conditioned, by both bribe and trauma, into the same structural gender panic—the same fear of not seeming to be enough of a real man. So the approach I recommend is very different from those who believe that the manhood standard can somehow be revised and redeemed—"reconstructed," "reinvented," "redefined," "remythologized," "revisioned," or rewhatevered. That project is futile, I believe, for at least two reasons: (1) it is based on an inaccurate analysis of the way manhood operates ethically, and (2) it offers no meaningful hope to those at the bottom, many of whom are female, who are most subordinated and disenfranchised in the social construction of manhood.

Manhood is not static; it is not some nebulous array of qualities that one embodies merely by *being*. Nor is manhood some substance or *thing*, a metaphysical or ontological category. Manhood is instead an ethical category: it is experienced relationally and episodically according to a specific set of values in conduct.

There are many differences in the life experiences of penised people, including hierarchies based on class, race, sexuality, and physical stature, and some academics have attempted to describe these differences as varieties of "masculinities." But I believe we can understand and explain those differences more usefully by analyzing the ethics of manhood proving. Those ethics, I believe, are a constant, even as they impact variously on everyone. Viewing manhood as an ethical category makes plain— with tangible evidence from real life—the metastructure of social subordination. This transactional model of manhood takes accurate account of a given human male's experience of relative social powerlessness, *and* locates his gender identity in whatever acts of power he chooses over and against others, *and* explains the interconnection. The transactional model of manhood is thus a unified theory. Pointing toward interpersonal and social justice, the practical possibility of our healing from manhood is also a revolutionary vision.

Both selfhood and manhood are relational and ethical constructs, but experientially they are different identities because the ethics by which they are realized are profoundly different. The ethics of manhood proving—the values in the conduct by which manhood is made to seem socially and subjectively "real"—are in complete contrast to the ethics of affirming one's own and another's selfhood—the values in the conduct by which justice occurs interhumanly and socially. In order to discover the transcendent potential of selfhood, and in order to heal from manhood, we must understand exactly what the ethics of manhood proving are.

As a society we sort out kids who are born with penises and we raise them to have a lifelong panic about experiencing subjectively the feeling of being a real-enough man. But manhood as a personal identity belief—as a subjectivity—cannot occur except fleetingly through a relational act.

We construct the meaning of manhood socially and politically through our acts; it does not derive from our anatomy. The difference people perceive between "the sexes" derives mainly from social and political dominance, expressed interpersonally in an ethic that must put someone down so that someone else can be "the man there."

The problem of how to be "a real-enough man" has no solution compatible with justice. The more important problem, actually, is how to become one's own best self. And this cannot happen if one is striving to prove manhood. Whenever any human tries to act like a real-enough man, his action must have negating consequences for someone else or else the act doesn't work.

All of us have been treated or regarded as "less real" by *someone* who has been struggling to prove manhood. Now and then, of course, some of us have also treated or regarded others as less real in our struggle to be the man there.

To heal from manhood, we must learn to love justice.

Our humanity—our authentic selfhood—can be honored and understood only through loving justice. And I define loving justice this way: an act of intense desire for, and attraction toward, fairness, also: that quality of fairness which exhibits love as well.

The tricky thing is that one cannot love justice and love manhood at the same time. In my book *The End of Manhood*, I advocate amplifying ("turning up the volume on") one's sense of oneself as a moral choice maker, as someone who tries to find the most just thing to do circumstantially. A consequence of making that commitment, I believe, is that over time one pays less and less attention to whether what one is doing is the "man" thing to do. Because choosing selfhood means choosing an ethic of loving justice over an ethic of loving manhood, its expression is not so much a rejection (of the social gender into which one has been cast) as an affirmation (of a preferable mode of ethical relating, out of a preferable sense of self). For anyone raised to be a man, this is a profound and radical relocating of identity. I sum it up mnemonically in the epigraph to *The End of Manhood:* "The core of one's being must love justice more than manhood."

My heretical hope is that as more male human beings understand the fundamental dichotomy between manhood and selfhood, and learn in our everyday relationships to apply the practical lessons of that insight, there will be among us all more and more loving justice, and more and more of us will say "I" and "you" as if we each are equally real.

All humans who grow up to be a man are raised to pass tests of loyalty to manhood. These tests can be routine or episodically treacherous. Anyone who has been raised to be a man will recall this happening when you are confronted by another man who intimidates or scares you.

In the moment of the confrontation—when another man's threat rears up, when his opportunity to hurt or humiliate you becomes clear to you both—no amount of mental or physical preparedness seems to prevent your falling for the test. Naturally you wish to save your neck. But more important, you wish to pass the test of your loyalty to manhood, which another man may have impugned. At the flash point of confrontation, it is unlikely that your mind has time to reflect on the fact that this test of your loyalty to manhood also tests your *disloyalty* to selfhood.

There is a classic dramatic plot line that occurs every time two humans raised to be a man—flush with fight-or-flight fury—decide to lock horns in contest in order to pass the manhood test. This is how the drama goes when there is a duel at downstage center and you are a featured player in

it. When you and another man are in combat defending the manhood act, there are three (and only three) possible resolutions:

1. *You lose.* He manages to humiliate you or hurt you in such a way that he comes off more manly.
2. *He loses.* You manage to hurt or humiliate him so that he will learn not to mess with you.
3. *You both agree to pick on or put down someone else.* You end up in a truce, a tacit treaty that must have a third party—someone you both agree has a relatively inferior manhood act or someone who is simply female. With (and only with) that third party for contrast, you both become comfortable enough to concede that your mutual manhood acts pass muster.

The sellout of selfhood begins here, in this truce, in the gendering ethics of this endlessly recurring drama, in this pact between would-be men trying to experience their social gender by proving their manhood to each other. Once this agreement is struck—once someone offstage has been betrayed or disparaged in order that the curtain will ring down on two former combatants taking a bow arm in arm—something has drastically altered in the moral character of each human who played out the manhood act in order to convince another player. Once the duel becomes this particular deal, once this gender bond between "men" is forged at the expense of someone else who is "less manly"—someone queerer, younger, poorer, less abled; someone of an ethnicity despised; or someone simply female—each human's loyalty to selfhood has been abandoned for the sake of loyalty to manhood.

Note that whenever manhood is on the line, its zealous aspirants do not suddenly check in for a chromosome test or bang on a drum or curl up with an epic poem. Either they fight it out or else they gang up to derogate some third party. In this sense manhood is always an ethical, not a metaphysical, category.

In all transactions whereby male humans confer "manhood" on one another, specific others must be excluded and treated as inferior. For the ethics of this "manhood act" to work effectively, there must be a point of reference who is treated unjustly (be it disparagingly or violently—it's a continuum), and the mere fact of male genitalia does not exempt one from being this point of reference over and against which certain other male humans mark their "manhood" status.

Once you start observing the dynamic that happens whenever manhood is contested, you begin to see it happening over and over again everywhere. A given human raised to be a man might sometimes enact the transaction as contestant; that same human raised to be a man might be the butt of other men's manhood-proving pact. This structural theory of manhood helps explain a lot that is not explicable if one looks only at what happens between men and women. Manhood proving happens originally between would-be men, producing widespread inequalities and hierarchies of status, and the dynamics and the consequences are all interrelated.

One obvious and blatant expression of the manhood act happens whenever men do violence against women: they are proving manhood in other men's eyes. The same structural dynamic is happening whenever men do violence (including economic, racist, and homophobic violence) against other men: they are proving manhood relationally and transactionally according to the master plot I just described That which animates their social dominance over other male humans is the same compulsion to pass as sufficiently real exemplars of manhood. These systematic social ethics of manhood proving offer extremely low odds for escaping manhood's downside, as can be observed in the lifetime of any human male over and against whom other human males have allied on account of race, wealth, sexuality, and/or physique.

This is male bonding at its worst, of course. But if any two anatomical males are obsessed with manhood, when is their proof of it any more just, and when is their male bonding any better? The surviving fall guys may not require stitches, but the dominant ethics of manhood-proving behavior are a constant. This reiterated pattern of male bonding, writ large, also functions internationally, nation-state to nation-state. It not only conceptualizes how manhood proving fuels men's oppression of women; it also accurately theorizes how manhood proving drives groups of men's oppression of other men.

Violence proves and privileges manhood in a way that myths and sexual anatomy cannot. Derisive violence against third-party scapegoats is especially prized, because it keeps men safe from the violence of other men (at least some of the time). But disparagement that proves manhood has subtler forms as well, and the master plot's ethics are always operative: You lose. Or he loses. Or you jointly pick on or put down some other loser.

Millions of boys grow up with a life-threatening case of undiagnosed gender anxiety. If their "manhood" is ever in doubt, they must somehow rise to the challenge and *prove* it. Often the kid learns from traumatic experience: the way to prove manhood incontrovertibly is to commit some act of injustice or derogation against someone else. He knows how, because it happened to him. Every day this high-stakes gender drama is the stuff of countless schoolyard tiffs, sidewalk scuffles, and father-son feuds. Yet even when this drama is sublimated into games and team sports, coaches persist in a coarse pedagogy of humiliation. Poor performance is derided with antifemale taunts.[1] In locker rooms and practice sessions a fresh generation of young male athletes gets misogynistically shamed, rather than genuinely inspired, to excel. Little wonder so many penised humans grow up anxiously aspiring to manhood, a personal identity category that cannot withstand equality.

So long as our culture maintains its hallucination that there is such a thing as "manhood," male infants will continue to be coaxed into a lifetime of gender anxiety, trying to prove they qualify for this fiction, and injuring or humiliating someone else will remain a "defining moment" in the life of every would-be real man.

This recurring test of "manhood" has implications for the capacity of any penised human being to feel empathy. In order to stay on guard against another man's judgment on his manhood, he will have to cancel out, close down, his human capacity for empathy, since if he inadvertently feels any, feels *with* someone else, he will be disadvantaged in the next test of his loyalty to manhood: he may not be sufficiently able to distance himself from the selfhood of a third party so that he and another penised person can pass muster in each other's eyes as "real-enough men." It takes years to teach a male human infant the ethics of manhood proving—humiliations by bullies and bigger and older men, slings and arrows of derision by peers. We should not expect male humans to learn the ethics of selfhood affirming overnight, but the process will be completely different.

In my book *The End of Manhood* I explain that we teach social gender to penised kids with one culture-pervasive lesson. It can be summarized like this: "Not to be a man is to be less than nobody." I explain how fathers and other adult men, especially, pass that lesson on to sons. I chart many of the

rewards and punishments that make the lesson stick. I explain what sons tend to do in order to still their fears of what other men will think of their manhood, in order to feel real by treating someone else as less real. I explain how that splits the self.

I also explain that we pass on to some lucky children what I call the lesson of selfhood, which goes like this: "To be human is to be somebody."

If you were raised to be a man, you got some proportion of the lesson of manhood along the way, perhaps burned into your brain, perhaps bruised into your body, perhaps simply because you were bribed: "Not to be a man is to be less than nobody." You probably also got some proportion of the lesson of selfhood: "To be human is to be somebody." And you've been standing astride the chasm between those two lessons ever since, teeter-tottering, flip-flopping, because the lessons are contradictory. Manhood and selfhood are dichotomous.

Either you are trying to act like a real-enough man, in a moment of choice making (and the only way you can do that is by treating or regarding someone as less real than you, so that some other manhood contestant will not think you are faking), or else you are living the lesson of selfhood, in a moment of choice making, and you are temporarily oblivious to the judgment of other men on your manhood, and that is when you discover you are never more real than when someone else is real to you.

Manhood/selfhood. Flip-flop. You cannot experience them both at the same time. And empathy automatically tilts you toward selfhood, which can only be experienced reciprocally, horizontally, human self to human self. So if you feel you had better feel real as a real-enough man, then you are simply going to have to tune out empathy. You cannot feel empathy and act like "the man." Cannot be done.

Professional healers listen to people present the pain they have felt when someone tuned out empathy with them and treated them like less than nobody. Happens all the time. And professional healers' job is to somehow help the pain go away— the pain of being treated as less than nobody—through empathy, through *feeling with*. Then and only then can healing begin.

Empathy helps someone remember the lesson of selfhood: "To be human is to be somebody." Empathy helps heal, because empathy reminds someone they are real and they matter.

Our culture is in crisis because we do not teach the ethical difference between selfhood and manhood. We do not model how to love justice more than manhood. We still believe manhood is somehow, somewhere, metaphysical—some *thing* you can be. And it is not. Manhood does not exist. It is a cultural delusion. We simply keep teaching gender anxiety. We make each other *crazy* with gender anxiety. We keep teaching conformity to social gender expectations as if that is any kind of solution. It is not. It is the problem.

Humans are no more born with manhood than they are born with anxiety about whether they have it.

As human infants born penised, some of us started out prepared to experience manhood at times and selfhood at other times.

To whatever extent we were taught the lesson of manhood, we were left with a recurrent experience of gender-anxiety waves: a tension in the chest or throat, a palpitation in the heart, a spring tension in musculature, some episodic heebie-jeebies. In effect, these anatomical hot buttons are a remnant of our autonomic reflex system with the social gender schema branded on. For anyone to "get" the meaning of manhood so as never to forget it, the lesson had to boot to a body and brain in a physical,

palpable way. That is what those disconcerting gender-anxiety waves do now and then—they make you feel like attacking or ducking for cover when your abstract manhood seems in danger.

One of the reasons so many humans feel manhood like a fire in the belly is that when waves of gender anxiety strike, they seem emotionally and physically overwhelming. They play out involuntarily through your blood circulating, your breath inhaling, your nerve signaling, your muscle contracting. Just because manhood is makebelieve—it has no material basis whatsoever—does not mean your body and brain cannot be tricked into responding as if manhood is as vital to your survival as is keeping your body out of the way of speeding trucks. (Not surprisingly, gender anxiety in penised people also accounts for a common sort of erection—insistent yet disconnected from any empathic reality between the penised person and anyone else.)[2] So powerfully is the lesson of manhood imprinted onto our autonomic nervous system that you can sometimes feel as if you would be utterly numb, plowed down, limp, or dead without your manhood.

The good news: Just as there is a physical, resonating reminder in us of the lesson of manhood, there is also a physical, resonating reminder in us of the lesson of selfhood.

The body's memory of human selfhood is not always easy to detect, and it does not announce its presence with the persistent hullabaloo of gender-anxiety waves. The lesson of selfhood is nevertheless resident in us. It is in us and it is between us.

People sometimes call these feel-with feelings "empathy." To me that word seems a bit puny, so I coined a new term: *moral sonority.*

Moral sonority means "feelings that are resonant with interhuman affiliation." *Moral sonority* means "feelings that are therefore communicable from one human being to another."

Moral sonority means those feelings that seem like emotional mirroring or mimesis, except they are not imitation; they are as real as your own.

Moral sonority means those feelings that seem as though a viaduct has opened between you and another, a flooding passageway for fluent emotion exchange, or as though you and another have suddenly grown a common skin, a membrane for emotional osmosis, except that the feelings seem not so much to be *transferred* as to well up from within you, *in yourself, with* another self, *in joined witness* to your joint selfhood.

Moral sonority means those feelings that do not compute as feelings appropriate to social gender, and so they sometimes unnerve us; they were not the feelings we were expecting to have; they were not the feelings we always thought we needed in order to feel certain our manhood was real.

Moral sonority means those feelings that transparently tell us we are in the presence of another living human being, and we are the very being to whom that very life is present.

Moral sonority means those feelings that so rock us and astound us with our common humanity that we are speechless, agog.

Some of us feel these feelings more deeply than others do, more or less often, in some situations but never in others. There is an enormous range of people's experience of these feelings, just as there is an enormous range of people's experiential learning of selfhood.

Sometimes we penised folks feel our moral sonority right alongside our gender-anxiety waves. Even though we cannot experience the reality of our selfhood and the fiction of manhood in the same act, in the same ethical stance, in the same choice, we can sometimes experience moral sonority and gender-anxiety waves simultaneously.

It is our challenge as human beings to learn to tune in to moral sonority more and tune out gender anxiety. We shall all be more whole, and we shall all become better healers, to the extent that any individual one of us gives up trying to prove manhood.

Throughout history the jockeying for credibility between two or more manhood contestants has meant conquest, betrayal, and violence for billions of human beings, whether third parties to a temporary truce or ongoing losers in a permanent war. This insanity can cease only when one by one we each learn the commitment and the skills to empower one another's selfhood and to disempower the manhood act by laying to rest our subservience to it.

The way to experience this interpersonal potential of loving selfhood is practical, everyday attention to the matter of justice in interpersonl relating. Loving justice as human healing—what a concept.

Healing transpires when one's selfhood is witnessed and not betrayed. Healing transpires when one's selfhood feels safe and sustained, seen, and not alone.

Moral sonority is how anyone learns selfhood. Moral sonority is how anyone passes it on.

The measure of health and healing cannot be conformity to social gender, because no one gets to be "the man there" without someone underneath. Too many of us have been underneath. Underneath is a place where no one belongs. Choosing loyalty to manhood over selfhood leads inevitably to injustice. And to the extent that anyone you meet comes away from that encounter with the message that conforming to the lesson of manhood is a desired end, you have committed a kind of crime against human selfhood, theirs and yours.

But loving justice more than manhood relocates personal identity in selfhood—relationally, reciprocally, realistically. Loving justice more than manhood replenishes the selfhood of each one you encounter—and replenishes your own selfhood in each moment of relation.

The challenge is not to substitute some ostensibly lower-risk version of gender panic but instead to displace it altogether. The ethical courage that no longer feels compunction to accede to the manhood standard is not unknown to us. Episodically such choices can be, and have been, made in our lives. Such selfhood-affirming moral courage would become more familiar, and more constant in our personal relations and political outreach work, the less we insisted on giving it a gendered and genderizing name, which merely keeps us loyal, at some level, to other men's judgment on our conformity to social gender.

That's not necessarily rejecting gender identity. It's often more like just letting it go—and letting folks see that that's OK.

How do penised humans model and communicate the possibility of selfhood to other folks raised to be a man? That is partly what is at issue in the subject "feminism and men," because our fear of what "other men" might think about us "as men" so often keeps us from speaking (and living) feminism's liberating truth.

This is what I have learned about speaking from my selfhood to someone apparently committed to manhood: I believe it helps to think of one's own tiny expression of moral courage as a particular act of communication that has within it an empathic and justice-affirming ethical stance already—a medium that bears within it a selfhood-affirming message. All one can do, after all, is act in hope that someone else might witness, recognize, intuitively understand, and be emboldened—even if they are in lockstep with a power bloc of male bonding.

It is easy to forget that inside another "manhood mask" there resides a human being struggling to be free. I know well the feeling of peer-pressured panic: What will happen to me, what costly stigma will befall me, if I am found out, if my ungendered selfhood stands nakedly exposed to ridicule and reprisal in a manhood-proving contest? But over time I have learned to try to keep mindful that the ineluctable conflict between selfhood and manhood is not just within me; it's going on in just about everyone else raised to be a man as well. If I play out yet another manhood-proving number in my choice of how I address someone else raised to be a man, I am unlikely to elicit in the other any recollection of selfhood; and I am unlikely, in the event, to elicit even my own. But when I speak as if there is a gender-free selfhood with whom to communicate, that necessarily changes what I say, changes the "I" who is saying it, and (I act in hope) may help change the one who hears. Selfhood-to-selfhood communication is always based on the leap-of-faith hypothesis that I can bear witness to another's selfhood, just as another can behold mine.

Of course, the other person raised to be a man may not hear, may not get the message at all. It may not be the right time in that person's life. I may be the wrong message bearer. That person's gender panic may, at the moment, be unbreachable. Someone else, pandering to that panic, may have recently made a more persuasive case for reiterating manhood, and so the act of my words is tuned out.

And yet, it seems to me, the public and private act of choosing selfhood, of loving justice more than manhood, is not only a worthy pursuit, it is the future. We are none of us more real than when someone else is completely real to us.

I suggest that in our outreach communication with other penised people we frankly reassess how we depict and describe what really are the alleged benefits and downside costs of manhood as against self-hood. The lived benefits of selfhood, of re-garding other selves as being as fully human as oneself (without insistence on asserting oneself as being "the man there") are, I be-lieve, pragmatically experienceable. My catchphrase "You are never more real than when someone else is completely real to you" echoes, I believe, an experience that vast numbers of people have had in their lives, even if only fleetingly.

On the hierarchical vector of race, many people have had this transcendent ex-perience: they have been intimate compan-ions, loyal allies, across the social-political racial divide, and it has been as if, for a mo-ment suspended somewhere outside political strife and power plays, a human-to-human ethical interaction has occurred that is as close to an "I-Thou" encounter as people can possibly know. The fullness of such a mo-ment arises not from an "ought" so much as from a found and recoverable mode of being in the moment through the equality-based ethics of one's acts. And the fullness of such a moment happens temporally, sometimes transiently, because it arises solely from the particular ethics of a particular interaction at a particular time. Such a moment could not be possible, could not even be imagined, if the person who is, socially speaking, "white" brought to the encounter a headful of fears and panics (perhaps anticipating shaming from other "white" people for being a trai-tor) and therefore insisted on acting in ways that authenticated membership in the racial identity "white." Quite the contrary, such a transcendent and proximate moment de-pends utterly on declining to specify oneself as "white."

I urge that as we address people raised to be "a man," we find ways to recall—and reinforce by naming, by publicly recogniz-ing—the pragmatic possibility of meeting one another (including across the vector of

social gender) in a way that does not insist on being the man there; for to insist is to preclude the possibility of the moment of human-to-human revelation, just as to insist on being "white" would be, across the vector of race, to preclude the possibility of a mu-tual relationship grounded in the possibility of loving justice.

Our challenge is to make visible the tangible and pragmatic benefits that actually do occur selfhood-to-selfhood, in our lives of loving justice, in our moment-to-moment relating. We have to find the language. We have to find the way to express those tactile and interactional moments when choosing to recognize someone else's selfhood was the fullest choosing of our own at the same time.

We are too often at a loss for words in this regard. Too much of our language is stuck in the win/lose, cost/benefit-ratio vo-cabulary that is still reinforcing of manhood proving and gender anxiety.

The longing for a sense of sustainable safety for one's selfhood is only rarely ac-knowledged in communication with folks raised to be a man. How does one communi-cate with such people without becoming the butt of their (socially inculcated) propensity to ally against someone perceived as having less manhood than they, in order to (re)as-sure themselves that manhood can still be (and be *theirs*)? How in other words, does one choose the ethics of selfhood affirma-tion without prompting a bonding frenzy against oneself?

I want to hold up to view—at least for those of us who have made it our lifework to communicate a vision of justice meaning-fully with folks raised to be a man—a disqui-eting question: Are we indeed helping to create that needed sense of selfhood safety by furthering the illusion that there is a man-hood mask somewhere out there (one of a variety of "masculinities" perhaps?) that is not so discomfiting as all the rest, not so nec-essarily dependent on at least some episodic act of injustice? To do so—to promise safety for "selfhood" within terms still specified by "manhood"—are we not telling a lie to our-selves, to our own *selfhood* selves?

But if we let it be known, even under-statedly, that our deepest preference would be to speak selfhood-to-selfhood (without the mask, without having to prove or insist on our manhood credentials), might that be just the first step that someone hearing us has been dying inside to know it is possible to take?

Support for such courage is still in short supply. And it is a crucial part of the political healing work that we have yet to do.

The cutting-edge question for the next mil-lennium is this: Why must human experi-ence be "gendered" at all? Why must *any human* continue feeling the urgency to keep manhood feeling "real"? Why need we toler-ate any longer the injustice that is intrinsi-cally required in order to shore up the myth of manhood?

Answering this question privately and publicly will become the most radically liber-atory project in human history. How you choose to have a personal identity, how you choose to situate yourself in relation to hier-archical identity categories, ultimately has political consequences. One cannot possibly and positively be "the man there" without somebody underneath. Nor can one be "white" or "Aryan" without personally help-ing to keep the category "real" by helping to keep selected others outside it or put down. Any personal identity that is premised on

identification with a dominant social cate-gory is also premised on disidentification and inequality.

Manhood is a personal and social hoax that exists only through interpersonal and social injustice. Manhood is the *paradigm* of injustice. *Refusing to believe* in manhood is the personal and ethical stance of resistance to all injustice done in its name. And refus-ing to accept the manhood imperative—the lie that there *must* be a discrete and bound-aried gender identity to "belong" to—is a personal and political principle of revolu-tionary liberation beyond any amplitude we can now imagine.

You help liberate anyone whenever you say "I who am a human self like you" to "You who are a human self like me." Not in-cidentally, you also help liberate yourself.

Refusing to believe in manhood is the hot big bang of human freedom.

NOTES

A shorter version of this essay was delivered as a keynote address to "Changing Minds towards the Mil-lennium," an international conference for mental health practitioners and academics, September 26–27, 1996, at the Royal Geographical Society, London.

1. Some examples: "Take your skirt off and get aggressive," "You're playing like a bunch of sluts," "You're playing like a bunch of girls," "What are you, on the rag," "What's wrong, does your pussy hurt?" "You're acting like a bunch of wimps," "You don't de-serve to be called men." From Andrea Parrot, Nina Cummings, and Timothy Marchell, *Rape 101: Sexual As-sault Prevention for College Athletes* (Holmes, Florida: Learning Publications, 1994).

2. See *The End of Manhood: Parables on Sex and Selfhood* (rev. ed. London: UCL Press, 2000), chap. 12 ("What's Supposed to Turn a Real Man On?"), chap. 19 ("How Can I Have Better Sex?"), and chap. 20 ("Looking Really Turns Me On—So What's the Matter with That?").

Placing Multiracial Feminism at the Center of Political Discourse

Michael A. Messner

About 3 years ago, I received a call from a representative of the National Organization for Women (NOW) Legal Defense and Education Fund, who was searching for a male academic who would publicly take a stand against the controversial movement in Detroit to establish all-male public schools in predominantly African American districts. "Well," I waffled, "I'm not *for* it, but I do understand how the deteriorating conditions in urban communities and schools and the especially devastating impact on young African American males have led many African Americans to desperately search for solutions." "Yes," the NOW representative replied, "We know that too, but *our* position is that there is no evidence that separating boys from girls is going to solve those problems. In fact, we are worried that this approach ignores the problems faced by African American girls and will justify tipping more educational resources away from them. Would you be willing to testify on behalf of our position?" "Well," I sidestepped and backpedaled, "I really think it's more appropriate that you find African American scholars to talk about this."

In the end, I passed on the opportunity to take a public stand on this issue. My gut-level reason was that I felt it inappropriate for me, a white male academic, to take a public stand against a grassroots initiative in

Excerpted from Michael A. Messner, *Politics of Masculinities: Men in Movements*. Walnut Creek, CA: AltaMira Press 1997, pp. 103–10.

an African American community. But I also felt that in taking no public stand on this issue, I had failed in my commitment to support women's quest for equality. After having spent much of my time in the past few years researching, writing, and teaching about the ways that race, class, gender, and sexual systems of oppression often "intersect," this issue crystallized for me the fact that conceptualizing and theorizing are clearly not enough. Like many people, I have acknowledged that it is necessary to move beyond Marxist class reductionist or radical feminist gender reductionist theories that tend to oversimplify the world by falsely collapsing all forms of oppression into one supposedly "primary" cause. Instead, the current movement in progressive sociology is toward theories that conceptualize multiple, semiautonomous, crosscutting systems of inequality (Baca Zinn et al., 1986; Collins, 1990; Baca Zinn & Dill, 1996). Thus far, though, most attempts at grand theories of these interrelated systems of power, or even more modest conceptual efforts (e.g., Messner & Sabo, 1990), tend to fall short of the task. One reason is that these models tend to assume—altogether too optimistically—that different forms of oppression are part of the same social or cultural dynamic. As a result of this oversimplification, they also tend to assume an underlying congruence of interests, goals, and strategies among the various movements that struggle against these forms of oppression. But when progressive movements perceive their interests as conflicting—as happened in the Detroit case, in which an African American community attempting to take control of its schools came into conflict with feminists—our theories are revealed to be inadequate.

When facing these same complex realities, some postmodernists have argued that modernity has collapsed and with it has evaporated the hope for a transcendent "historical subject" (be it the working class, women, colonized people, etc.) that can attain a conscious grasp of the totality of social life, organize, and act to change it. Within the postmodern view (e.g., Lemert, 1994), a sociologist who asserts that her or his work is operating from the standpoint of a commitment to social justice is scoffed at as hopelessly mired in passé, modernist thought. Instead, postmodernists argue, we face an increasingly unstable and fragmented world in which knowledge can be, at best, only partial and groups can coalesce only temporarily around limited and short-term goals.

I agree that the world is complex. In fact, the idea of a single, transcendent revolutionary historical subject (such as the working class or women) that can understand and change the totality of social life was probably always an incorrect and naive assumption made by revolutionary intellectuals. "The working class" and "women" have always been internally differentiated and fragmented groups that, respectively, Marxists and some feminists have falsely universalized. However, I would argue that to abandon the project of human liberation now is to engage in an act of historical capitulation to the forces of greed, violence, and oppression, right at a time in history when new social movements have achieved partial (sometimes even dramatic) successes in decolonization, women's rights, gay and lesbian liberation, and antiracism. But as Todd Gitlin (1995) has recently pointed out, any movement for progressive institutional change will have to

transcend the destructive tendency of these new social movements to engage in narrow, single-issue identity politics that set them against each other. For this to happen, various groups must coalesce around a "common dream" of equality and social justice.

At this historical moment in the United States, I believe that the greatest potential force for serving as a nexus through which progressive discourses and practices can link up to broaden the push for such a "common dream" of social justice is what Baca Zinn and Dill (1996) have called "multiracial feminism." This approach attempts to take into account, simultaneously, a structural analysis of power and inequality with an appreciation of and respect for difference. Take, for example, some of the key issues that I discussed [elsewhere] that are being raised today about black masculinity within racial discourses in politics and popular culture. The current Afrocentric movement is surely not in the tradition of Martin Luther King's calls for racial integration. Instead, it echoes Malcolm X's calls for community autonomy. And just as was true of the Muslim and Black Power movements of the 1960s, central to Afrocentrism today is a militant assertion of "black manhood." This concern was depicted in the popular film *Boyz 'n the Hood.* The film suggests that the young males in the 'hood are faced with two major options. The first one is to follow the lead of the young hoodlum "new heads" and likely end up cycling in and out of prison and eventually getting killed at a young age. A second possibility is suggested in the case of the talented young football player who is being recruited by the University of Southern California. This option, too, is revealed as a dead end, as the youth's talents and dreams cannot safeguard him from the violence in his community. But *Boyz 'n the Hood* offers a ray of hope. Here, for one of the very few times in American cinema, a positive image of an African American father was presented. The son of this father, we see, eventually makes the right choices that allow him to escape the violent 'hood and attend college. This was undoubtedly a positive message in some ways, but in other ways this film raised the same troubling question that the Detroit all-male schools issue raised: What about the women? To make its point that a strong father is the answer to the problem of black male youth, the film went about depicting mothers as either irresponsible crack addicts, unfair bitches, or upwardly mobile professionals who neglect their children for their careers.

Twenty years ago, the masculinist gender politics of antiracism organizations were rarely questioned. The few black feminists such as Michelle Wallace (1978), who challenged assumptions of male superiority by leaders such as Eldridge Cleaver or Stokely Carmichael, were accused of undermining the cause of black liberation by dividing women from men. Today, with assertions of black manhood again taking center stage in Afrocentric discourse and political practice, there is a broader, more assertive and sophisticated response from black women. For example, a few years ago I attended a session on black males at the American Sociological Association meetings, where Elijah Anderson (1990) presented some of the findings of his ethnographic research that later became *Streetwise*. Anderson told the following story, based on the narrative of a black man, of a late-night street interaction between three black males and a white woman:

> A white lady walkin' down the street with a pocketbook. She start walkin' fast. She get so paranoid she break into a little stride. Me and my friends comin' from a party about 12:00. She stops and goes up on the porch of a house, but you could tell she didn't live there. I stop and say, "Miss, you didn't have to do that. I thought you might think we're

some wolf pack. I'm twenty-eight, he's twenty-six, he's twenty-nine. You ain't gotta run from us." She said, "Well, I'm sorry." I said, "You can come down. I know you don't live there. We just comin' from a party." We just walked down the street and she came back down, walked across the street where she really wanted to go. So she tried to act as though she lived there. And she didn't. After we said, "You ain't gotta run from us," she said, "No, I was really in a hurry." My boy said, "No you wasn't. You thought we was gon' snatch yo' pocketbook." We pulled money out. "See this, we work." I said, "We grown men, now. You gotta worry about them fifteen-, sixteen-, seventeen-year-old boys. That's what you worry about. But we're grown men." I told her all this. "They the ones ain't got no jobs; they're too young to really work. They're the ones you worry about, not us." She understood that. You could tell she was relieved and she gave a sigh. She came back down the steps, even went across the street. (pp. 167–168)

The point of Anderson's story—that in public places, black males are commonly unfairly suspected of being violent rapists—was well taken. But the woman in the story was a somewhat humorous prop for making this point about the indignities that black males face. Anderson did not appear to have much empathy for her. As he finished telling the story, a white woman sitting in front of me whispered to the white woman next to her, "He acts like she had no reason to be frightened of a pack of men. Of *course* she was scared! Women are attacked and raped every day!" It seemed clear to me that this woman identified and empathized with the white woman in the story but gave no indication that she understood Anderson's point about the impact of this omnipresent suspicion on the vast majority of black males who do not rape. After the talk, during the discussion session, an African American woman stood up and bridged this chasm by eloquently empathizing with the legitimate fears of the woman *and* with the cumulative public humiliation of the black males in the story. The woman *and* the men in this story, she asserted, were differentially victimized in public space. The solution lies in their learning to empathize with each other and then building from that common empathy a movement that fights against the oppressive system that dehumanizes them both.

This scene, it seemed to me, demonstrated both the limits of masculinist Afrocentrism and of white feminism and the role that multiracial feminism can play in creating new standpoints that bridge these two movements. As Patricia Hill Collins (1990) has so eloquently put it, black women are often "outsiders within"—as women, they are outsiders within the male dominated Afrocentric movement; as blacks, they are outsiders within white-dominated feminism. Their social positions "on the margins," to use bell hooks's (1984) terminology, give black women (and by implication, other women of color) unique standpoints through which the complex mechanisms and interweavings of power and oppression can be more clearly deconstructed and, possibly, resisted. From a multiracial feminist standpoint, African American males' unique experiences of oppression are acknowledged and struggled against. But multiracial feminists do not accept the analysis presented by some men of color (e.g., Peña, 1991; Staples, 1995b) that interprets public displays of misogyny, rape, and other forms of violence against women by men of color primarily as distorted or displaced responses to racism and to class constraints. Instead, gender must be viewed *not* as a "superstructural" manifestation of class and/or racial politics but as a semi-autonomous system of power relations between women and men (Baca Zinn et al., 1986; Collins, 1990).

In an essay on black masculinity, bell hooks (1992) charges that what she calls "conservative Afrocentric males" often draw on "phallocentric masculinity" as a resource to fight racial oppression. She observes that public figures such as Eddie Murphy and Spike Lee tend to exploit the commodification of phallocentric black masculinity. But, hooks argues, there exist also what she calls "progressive Afrocentric males," including many gay black men, who are, in her words, "not sitting around worried about castration and emasculation" (p. 102); instead they are exploring more egalitarian relationships with women and with other men.

BRIDGES TO THE TERRAIN OF PROGRESSIVE COALITION BUILDING

Some men and women are clearly already working within the terrain of progressive coalition building. . . . In fact, there are several groups of men and women who are currently constructing discourses and practices that might "bridge" otherwise more narrowly defined groups into the terrain of multiracial feminism and progressive coalition building. Clearly, we can expect very few men to move from the terrain of antifeminist backlash to multiracial feminism. On the other hand, the fact that some men are struggling to understand and overcome the "costs" of masculinity creates a potential opening for the development of a more fundamental critical analysis of hegemonic masculinity—including an understanding of how the costs of masculinity are linked to men's institutional power. The men who are most likely to serve as a bridge from the terrain of antifeminist backlash to the terrain of progressive coalition building are the fragments of the mythopoetic men's movement who are currently engaged in dialogues with profeminist men.

Radical profeminist men who are working within the terrain of antipatriarchal politics are often engaged in extremely important work. Their powerfully charged call for men to renounce masculinity clearly resonates with some men. And some of their educational and political actions to stop male violence support women who are working to make the world a safer place for women. The fact that they might convince even a few men to stop being violent against women is an invaluable contribution in and of itself. On the other hand, for reasons that I [have] discussed, radical feminist men are more likely to engage in a more insular and limited antipatriarchal politics than they are to engage in bridge building with other groups who do not necessarily share their analysis and assumptions about the centrality of male sexuality in the oppression of women and of other men.

By comparison, there is far greater potential for movement from the terrain of racial and sexual identity politics into the terrain of progressive coalition building. For instance, some African American men who have worked within a socialist framework, such as Manning Marable (1994) and Cornel West (1993), appear to be formulating a feminist-informed critique of hegemonic masculinity within their race and class political program. Similarly, profeminist gay men continue to provide bridges between feminist women, gay liberation, and profeminist men's organizations. And especially, gay men of color (e.g., Almaguer, 1991; Cochran & Mays, 1995; Leong, 1996; Mercer & Julien, 1988) are in the forefront of attempts to integrate a critical understanding of the interrelationships between race, class, gender, and sexual systems of oppression. I would speculate that this is because gay men of color are also likely to experience themselves as "outsiders within" in multiple ways. In their own racial and ethnic communities, they may be shunned (or worse) due to ingrained homophobia;

within gay communities, they may be marginalized (or worse) because of racism. As a result of this multiple marginality, gay men of color hold the potential to bridge gay and lesbian liberation, antiracism movements, and feminist organizations into powerful coalitions (Takagi, 1996).

I believe that it would be most fruitful for those who are engaged in progressive politics—both academics and movement activists—to listen to the public conversations taking place today between gay men of color, progressive men of color, and feminist women of color. An example of this conversation can be found in bell hooks's dialogue with Cornel West (hooks & West, 1991). Theory construction is under way in these conversations. One promise that these conversations hold is that even those of us who are not central players (and here I am thinking particularly but not exclusively of people such as myself who identify as "white," as "heterosexual," as "middle-class," and as "men") can listen in and learn to ask new, critical questions. Decentered theoretically, we can begin to turn commonly asked questions back on themselves: not, Why do black men so often misbehave? rather, Why are we so *obsessed* with this question and what, in fact, about the everyday misbehaviors of *white* men and *middle- and upper-class* men? The invisible presence in Elijah Anderson's street scene, discussed earlier, are the powerful upper-class white men, who, through their control of institutions, have removed jobs from the inner cities, cut aid to schools, and allowed police protection for citizens to deteriorate. Simultaneously, some police engaged in racist terror tactics and refused to take the measures that might make public life safe for women, thus imposing a *de facto* curfew on them. But privileged males are invisible in this story because the race, class, and gendered power of these males are attached to their positions in institutions, not to their personal behaviors in the street. In fact, their everyday actions in political, corporate, or educational institutions are commonly defined as "normal" male behavior.

The task of a sociology of masculinities, it seems to me, is to raise critical questions about the "normal" operation of hegemonic masculinity in such a way that these actions are redefined as "misbehaviors." I am convinced that today the conversations taking place within multiracial feminism offer us the best (though not a perfect, complete, or total) theoretical framework through which we might better begin to understand and confront the crucial issues of our day. Multiracial feminism invites us to shift our attention away from simplistic bickering between oppressed groups and, instead, to focus our energies on developing a critical understanding of the complex relations of power that structure our social realities. It is really beyond belief to imagine that a group made up primarily or exclusively of white, class-privileged, and heterosexual men could or

would ever develop such a radically progressive standpoint. In fact, I would argue that NOMAS [National Organization for Men Against Sexism], a group made up primarily of men, has been moving in these sorts of progressive directions in recent years precisely because its members have been listening to—and attempting to develop a practice in relation to—multiracial feminism. This organization starts with the assumption that men—even men from the most privileged class, racial, and sexual groups—can participate and contribute to movements for social justice. To make such a contribution will mean that men will have to work against our own narrowly defined economic and political interests. But men also have a stake in the movement for social justice. In rejecting hegemonic masculinity and its rewards, we also may become more fully human. For I am convinced that the humanization of men is intricately intertwined with the empowerment of women.

REFERENCES—MEN CHANGING: VISIONS OF A FUTURE

ALMAGUER, T. (1991). Chicano men: A cartography of homosexual identity and behavior. *Differences: A Journal of Feminist Cultural Studies*, (3): 75–100.

ANDERSON, E. (1990). *Streetwise: Race, class, and change in an urban community*. Chicago: University of Chicago Press.

BACA ZINN, M. et al. (1986). The costs of exclusionary practices in women's studies. *Signs* 11: 290–303.

BACA ZINN, M., and B.T. Dill. (1996). Theorizing difference from multiracial feminism. *Feminist Studies* 22: 321–331.

COCHRAN, S.D., and V.M. Mays. (1995). Sociocultural facets of the black gay male experience. In M.S. Kimmel and M.A. Messner, eds. *Men's lives*. 3rd ed., pp. 432–439. Boston: Allyn & Bacon.

COLLINS, P.H. (1990). *Black feminist thought: Knowledge, consciousness, and the politics of empowerment*. Boston: Unwin Hyman.

GITLIN, T. (1995). *The twilight of common dreams: Why America is wracked by culture wars*. New York: Metropolitan Books.

GROSS, J. (2001). These fallen fathers were heroes at home. *New York Times*. Oct. 1: F1 + 10.

HAGAN, K.L. (1992). *Women respond to the men's movement*. San Francisco: Pandora.

hooks, b. (1984). *Feminist theory: From margin to center*. Boston: South End.

hooks, b. (1992). Reconstructing black masculinity. In b. hooks, *Black looks: Race and representation*, pp. 87–114. Boston: South End.

hooks, b., and C. West. (1991). *Breaking bread: Insurgent black intellectual life*. Boston: South End.

JOHNSON, Allan G. (1997). *The gender knot: Unraveling our patriarchal legacy*. Philadelphia: Temple University Press.

LEMERT, C. (1994). Subjectivity's limit: The unsolved riddle of the standpoint. *Sociological Theory* 10: 63–72.

*LEONG, R. (1996). Introduction: Home bodies and the body politic. In R. Leong, Ed. *Asian American sexualities: Dimensions of the gay and lesbian experience*, pp. 1–18. New York: Routledge.

MARABLE, M. (1994). The black male: Searching beyond stereotypes. In R.G. Majors and J.U. Gordon, Eds. *The American black male*, pp. 245–260. Chicago: Nelson-Hall.

MERCER, K., and I. Julien. (1988). Race, sexual politics and black masculinity: A dossier. In R. Chapman and J. Rutherford, Eds. *Male order*, p. 112. London: Lawrence and Wishart.

MESSNER, M.A., and D.F. Sabo. (1990). Toward a critical feminist reappraisal of sport, men and the gender order. In M.A. Messner and D.F. Sabo, Eds. *Sport, men, and the gender order: Critical feminist perspectives*, pp. 1–16. Champaign, IL: Human Kinetics.

PENA, M. (1991). Class, gender, and machismo: The "treacherous woman" folklore of Mexican male workers. *Gender & Society* 5: 30–46.

PRUETT, K. (2000). *Fatherneed: Why father care is as essential as mother care for your child*. New York: The Free Press.

STAPLES, R. (1995b) Stereotypes of black masculinity: The facts behind the myths. In M.S. Kimmel and M.A. Messner, eds. *Men's lives*. 3rd ed., pp. 375–380. Boston: Allyn & Bacon.

TAKAGI, D.Y. (1996). Maiden voyage: Excursion into sexuality and identity politics in Asian America. In R. Leong, Ed. *Asian American sexualities: Dimensions of the gay and lesbian experience*, pp. 21–35. New York: Routledge.

WALLACE, M. (1978). *Black macho and the myth of the super-woman*. New York: Warner.

WEST, C. (1993). *Race matters*. Boston: Beacon.